1982

Listening to Music Creatively

Listening to

Edwin John Stringham

Former faculty member, Columbia University Teachers College, Juilliard School of Music, Union Theological Seminary, Queens College of the City of New York; Head of Music Department, U. S. Army University, Biarritz, France; guest professor, University of California, Los Angeles and The University of Texas

Music Creatively

SECOND EDITION

ENGLEWOOD CLIFFS, N. J.

Prentice-Hall, Inc. •

Library of Congress Catalogue Card No.: 59-6859

Frontispiece: Singing Gallery (upper panel) by Della Robbia. From the Cathedral Museum, Florence.

Current printing (last digit):
17 16 15 14 13 12 11 10 9

PRINTED IN THE UNITED STATES OF AMERICA
53714-C

This book

is gratefully dedicated

to my wife, Peggy ~

for her constant aid, inspiration, and encouragement

*The Art of Music must, by its very nature,
be considered supreme among the Fine Arts;
for it, more than any other of the Sister Arts,
ministers to human welfare.*

HERBERT SPENCER

Acknowledgements

It is not possible to mention here the names of all, or even many, of the individuals, publishers, and others who have contributed in one way or another to the realization of this new edition. I fully realize that no book is made solely by an individual. However, to all who have added their bit, whether mentioned here or not, I offer my gratitude, and assure them that I alone acknowledge the responsibility of what finally appears on the printed page.

Those to whom I am most indebted include Professor Robert U. Nelson, Musicologist at the University of California at Los Angeles, for a great number of helpful suggestions; Professor Jan Philip Schinhan, outstanding artist-musician and musicologist at the University of North Carolina, for his generous contribution of many constructive ideas for the new edition, and for the use of a reproduction of the original portrait of Johannes Brahms from his private collection; Professor Powell Middleton, State Teachers College, Chester, Pa., and Professor Cloe Thomas, Ohio State University, Columbus, for their valuable suggestions; and Professor Warren Allen, former professor at Stanford University, California, and later Florida State University, for many helpful discussions concerning aesthetics, music history, and appreciation over a number of years.

Also to Professor Victor Booth, F.R.A.M., Royal Academy of Music, London, for his personal aid in the British edition of this text (published by T. Werner Laurie, Ltd., London); to Houghton Mifflin Co., for permission to quote so freely from the works of the late Professor Addison Hibbard, Dean of the College of Liberal Arts, Northwestern University, Evanston, Illinois; to Professor Donald N. Ferguson, University of Minnesota and later of Macalester College, teacher of music history, music appreciation, and author of a number of superb books on music, for permission to quote from his writings; to Professor Curt J. Ducasse, formerly of the Department of Philosophy and Aesthetics at Brown University (Providence), and to his publisher, Oskar Piest (The Liberal Arts Press, Inc.) for permission to quote from his books; to my secretary, Virginia Gilmore Andrews of Chapel Hill, who faithfully typed this entire edition so efficiently and uncomplainingly from my cryptogrammic handwriting; and to Kemp Battle Nye of Chapel Hill, who generously permitted me to hear many recordings from his large collection as an aid in compiling the selected lists for Additional Listening Suggestions throughout this edition.

I wish also to express my thanks and appreciation to the many teachers in the field who have replied so faithfully to questionnaires, or who have reported on their own initiative, concerning the results of their use of the many early mimeograph or offset printings of my experimental lessons and of the first edition in their daily teaching. Their suggestions and personal as well as statistical findings have been of inestimable practical value in preparing this new edition, and they have further helped me to keep in close and constant contact with the working teacher and with the appreciation teaching methods being used all over the country and abroad, under all sorts of conditions.

It would be ungrateful of me to omit my sincere and appreciative thanks for the contributions that many thousands of students have made by their actual use of the text, both through their reactions during study, and the more lasting values that have been indicated in their resulting listening habits, tastes and discrimination since their classroom days. These are the highest rewards and indices of the ultimate value of any book—to the user as well as the author. I am especially grateful for an initial test by some ten thousand students who so agreeably and conscientiously served as subjects of experimentation during the very careful and critical "mimeograph stage" of "try, change, and try again" class lessons—for almost all of the text has been subjected to the severe and conclusive testing of actual classroom use in many cities of the country and in many different conditions and environments of study.

The many publishers of music, books, magazines, newspapers, reference works, etc., the public and private art museums, private art collectors, and others who have kindly permitted me to quote or to reproduce selected parts from their music, art, and prose works and other copyrighted possessions are properly acknowledged within the text.

E. J. S.

Chapel Hill, North Carolina

Contents

Courtesy The Metropolitan Museum of Art, Peter Juley, Photographer

MOTHER AND CHILD William Zorach

This contemporary work emphasizes the art of sculpture carved directly from a block of stone. It could not have been expressed so well in any other medium. Note the complex and concentrated uses of masses, angles, and planes, their interrelationships and, withal, the simple, understandable, and ingratiating emotional significance in which these matters are readily resolved by the observer. Its effectiveness is not unlike a great contrapuntal work of Bach in that, with all its complexities, it is readily apprehended by the appreciator,

1 The art of creative listening

All mankind seeks beauty in art as instinctively and as persistently as it searches for Truth, Happiness, Justice, Love, and Faith. These qualities have much in common and are indispensable facets of a good life. From one point of view, these attributes are among the greatest spiritual achievements of Man—the creations of his own imagination, the language of his innermost thoughts and emotions. From another angle, these may be considered among the major capacities and blessings with which Universal Man has been endowed by his Maker. Whichever way one views them, man has come to know these essences as essential to a rich and meaningful life. Yet these same attributes may be accepted or rejected as one chooses, for they are not inescapable forces. As every artist knows, however, the exercise of his gifts is almost as compelling as breathing itself; and, generally, self-compulsive creativeness is in a direct ratio to talent.

We are not all equally endowed in these capacities; and,

naturally, the perception and expression of them in artistic endeavors varies greatly among individuals. There are those, in music, for instance, who are especially attuned to the soul of Beauty, and are thus charged with the responsibilities of either creation or interpretation (performance), spreading broadcast these attributes of beauty for the enjoyment of others. At the other dynamic "pole," but equally indispensable and privileged, are most of us; we transform the "blueprint" guides of the art-creator and art-translator into what we shall later explain as the "complete consummation of a Work of Art." Thus the appreciator should not be a static, non-participative "consumer" of art. Rather, he should be a dynamic, distinctively *creative* entity in the artistic triumvirate without whom no "Work of Art" could be possible. In the world of the eight or so Fine Arts (Painting, Drawing, Architecture, Sculpture, Poetry, Music, the Dance, Drama, and some Prose Literature), these acquired and endowed human virtues coalesce and blossom forth as an outward expression of man's most intimate ideals, thoughts, feelings, and expressions of beauty. These can be expressed only through art, and they must be understood and interpreted in the same manner.

Throughout the ages, each art has established its own peculiar kind of "message" in its own individual medium of expression. This has been so well established that a creator in one art cannot transgress the artistic prerogatives or inherent limits of another, either in content or medium, with impunity. It is incumbent upon every creator, performer, or appreciator of art to develop to the utmost his inherent capacities and acquirable abilities in the arts that mean most to him and which are most essential for his happiness. It is fortunate that all can fulfill their "obligations and responsibilities" while at the same time experiencing the greatest degree of enjoyment and self-satisfaction.

The human values inherent in the "Ministry of Beauty through Music" have been very well understood throughout the ages—seemingly much better than in our own time. The Bible (adapted) says:

> Whatsoever things are true, pure, of good report, lovely and beautiful—think on these.

That enigmatical genius of American *belles-lettres*, Edgar Allan Poe, expounds the "Contemplation of Beauty" versus "Reason and Logic" in his critical work, *The Poetical Principle*, in this manner:

> ". . . That pleasure which is at once the most pure, the most elevating, and the most intense, is derived, I maintain, from the contemplation of the Beautiful. In the contemplation of Beauty, we alone find it possible to attain that pleasurable elevation, or excitement of the soul, which we recognize as the Poetic Sentiment. . . ."

Then Poe goes on to say, in essence, that through the "contemplation of beauty" one is enabled to distinguish between the "soulful satisfaction and elevation through Beauty" and mere facts or logical rationalization.

When a gifted and trained composer, sincerely intent upon expressing his emotional and artistic self, sets out to create a work of art, he works with musical ideas, the emotional feelings and the moods of which they are expressive, and all the technical "tools" and skills of his craft. But even before the composer can create a definite idea, he must be moved by an indefinite creative mood and inner urge. (We are omitting, for the present, those who deliberately "manufacture" music from a singular cerebrational process or by formulae.) No matter how great a genius the composer might be, neither he nor any one else knows precisely how and why and from whence comes the compelling creative mood or the emotional investiture of the basic ideas in the first place—whether the ideas be in fragments or flow forth full-blown. Primarily, the creator is concerned with freely expressing himself and communicating the expression to others.

The reader is cautioned not to be deceived by the apparent spontaneous flow of creation. This technique was not gained overnight. Rather, it was acquired and possible because, in the first place, the composer was naturally gifted; secondly, his discipline and special skills were gained through a lifetime of effort and intense self or guided tuition. Even the exemplar "composer's composer," Johann Sebastian Bach, of whom it has been said that "Music owes as much to him as a religion does to its founder," was moved to create by an *irresistible, intuitional, emotional process of self-expression* rather than the mere concern over a technical rule or academic problem of craftsmanship.[1] Musical, religious, and symbolic expressions were as one with Bach throughout his approximately fifty years of musical productivity.

It would be wonderful, indeed, if the listener's training were also a lifetime effort; unfortunately, formal training in listening skills is generally all too brief. "Creative listening" is perfected through wide experience, artistic contemplation, and careful maturation. It is also a matter of developing within one's self acute aesthetic susceptibility together with the greatest possible skills of listening and high standards of good taste.

Of course, any aural synthesis comparable to the composer's intuition and skills of craftsmanship should not be demanded of the average listener. Yet—and here is the nub of the thing—creation and appreciation are supplementary and necessarily interdependent, in a sense, for the ultimate realization of any musical work of art. No matter how perfect the skills, the architectonic structures, or the artistic ideas that embody

[1] See also *New York Times Book Review,* Nov. 30, 1952, page 6, par. 3, anent Bach's general apparent indifference concerning some technical aspects during the process of composition.

Courtesy The Galleria Nazionale D'Arte Moderna, Rome

HERCULES THE ARCHER Emile Antoine Bourdelle

Although few critics would call this one of the great works of sculpture, it is a significant and attractive work. Bourdelle was swept into prominence during the French Impressionistic movement, and is noted mainly for his architectural sculpture, as shown in his work in the Theatre des Champs-Elysees (Paris). HERCULES THE ARCHER, *a separate piece, was executed in 1909. It expresses great potential power, grace, and rhythmic movement; its outstanding sculptural virtues are immediately apparent. It reveals no great depth of feeling, meaning, or import.*

Here, in contrast to Zorach's carved stone sculpture, MOTHER AND CHILD, *is an example of a bronze statue made from a plaster of Paris matrix or mold; which, in turn, was formed from a clay model formed over iron armatures, wires, and screening. Thus certain decorative and ornamental effects, long unsupported lines, extended figures and forms, isolated masses, and so forth are easily obtained by techniques which cannot be used by the stone carver.*

them, they are for nought if the *effects* do not arouse due aesthetic contemplation and enjoyment in the listener, and thus bring to life what was, up to this point, a mere "blue-print" for music.

This sort of inter-play between creator (*via* the performer) and the listener is known among professional aestheticians as *aesthetic contemplation.* According to Professor Curt J. Ducasse, of Brown University, this means "the listening for the feeling impact—for the emotive reverberations—of the object attended to, . . . and is to artistic creation what impression is to expression." Further on, he continues, "Only through aesthetic contemplation of a work of art does the beholder have the chance to get out of the work the feeling the artist put in." [2]

Let us ponder over this composer-listener inter-play. In order that the listener might participate to the utmost in aesthetic contemplation, and appreciation, which includes discrimination and choice, it is essential that several fundamental listening conditions obtain. FIRST, *that the musical composition evokes, if possible, an immediate or proximate feeling of satisfaction in its beauty.* That is, it should not be necessary for the listener to subject the work to a theoretical or academic "microscopic examination" before it can be enjoyed. SECOND, *that in so far as possible, interferences to the full realization of this reaction should be reduced to the lowest possible minimum;* one should consider with disapproval any formidable rationalization, or the substitution of formal analysis for aesthetic feeling. Likewise, it is neither expected nor desirable that the appreciator should be in command of the highly specialized knowledges, techniques, and skills pertaining to poetry, painting, sculpture, or architecture *before* he may enjoy such works as Browning's poem, THE RING AND THE BOOK; Raphael's painting, the SISTINE MADONNA; Rodin's sculptured group, THE PROCESSION OF THE BURGHERS OF CALAIS (almost a painting in sculpture); and that immortal poem in marble, the TAJ MAHAL. Neither should similar knowledge be necessary before one can enjoy such musical masterpieces as Beethoven's FIFTH OR NINTH SYMPHONIES, Schumann's CONCERTO FOR PIANO, or the FOURTH SYMPHONIES of Sibelius and Brahms, to name but a few! However, the *integration* of the purely artistic aspects of, and reactions to, music with the other fine arts may be very effective. It is by enriching the general aesthetic and artistic background of the listener through such means that the masterworks of music become more meaningful and enjoyable. As a general result, the entire "artistic personality" of the listener widens its horizon of appreciation immeasurably.

One should be very careful to distinguish between genuine integration of the styles and tempers inherent in the examples of the arts being studied and meaningless and misleading coincidence of title, literary contents, or perfunctory chronological parallelism. Rightly planned and wisely ad-

[2] *Art, The Critics and You* (New York: Oskar Piest Pub., 1944, now the *Liberal Arts Press*). Used with permission.

ministered, integration in the arts can be a great blessing to student and mentor alike.

When the listener wishes to compare one work with another, or one part of a composition with another part, or to sense the balancing of section with section, then the faculties of tonal memory and interest-span become important considerations. This is especially true when the problems of choice, critical evaluation, and discrimination are at issue. Thoughtful, attentive, and increasingly meaningful repetition of a long work is one of the best solutions. This rightly posits the existence of two main types of music lovers dubbed by Vernon Lee (in MUSIC AND ITS LOVERS) as "listeners," those who really enjoy the music itself and its inherent beauty; and "hearers," those who use music to set off a kaleidoscopic series of dream-world fantasies. Those who seek to integrate simultaneous motion, painting, dancing, and so forth with music appreciation, when the latter is the real objective, should re-evaluate their methods frequently, lest these extraneous activities become the actual objectives and foci of attention, thus endangering the desired aesthetic appreciation of the *music.*[3]

In addition to the ever-present problem of mind-wandering and irrelevant fantasies, there is also the equally natural but ever more disturbing hazard created by the cycle of the *span of interest:* the "crest," and its alternate lapse into fancy, the "valley." This cannot be entirely eliminated. One can only try to lengthen the duration of interest and shorten the lapses. Even the best disciplined mind is capable of focusing attention on one idea for a relatively brief interval! Fortunately, pleasure, patience, interest, and habit can do wonders in extending the span of attention.

One of the most effective means of arousing desirable attention and thus guiding the lay listener more sympathetically and successfully, is to choose works with salient and satisfying primary and secondary themes, melodies preferred, recurring frequently throughout the composition. These become the "trail marks" in the course of a long work, or development section, in a real sense, and the listener will follow them in a rather involved work if these thematic "sign-posts" are not too distorted or disguised beyond recognition during the compositional intricacies; or if the work is not so lengthy as to produce excessive fatigue, and eventual loss of interest.

Ideally, the perception of the themes or melodies should be accom-

[3] See pertinent discussions in Max Schoen, *The Effects of Music* (New York: Harcourt Brace, 1927), pp. 104-120 and 199-243; Charles H. Farnsworth, *The Why And How of Music Study* (Boston: Oliver Ditson, 1927), Chap. V, pp. 34-50; Vernon Lee, pseu. of Violet Paget, *Music and its Lovers* (London: George Allen and Unwin Ltd., 1932), selected readings from Parts I, II, III; Chap. II of Part V; Chaps. I, II and IV of Part VI; James L. Mursell, *The Psychology of Music* (New York: W. W. Norton, 1937), Chap. VI, pp. 201-222; and from a different viewpoint, David Snedden, "The Waning Powers of Art," *Am. Journal of Sociology,* Vol. XXII, No. 6, May 1917.

panied by the general, rather than the specific or analytic, feeling for the harmonic or counterpuntal "aura"; the recognition of the instrumental or vocal timbre, or tone color, in which the melodies are couched; plus the salient emotion, rhythmic feeling, and tempo inherent in the themes—or underlying them—provided these factors are actually essential to the character of the melodies. Further, it is assumed that all these can be comfortably borne simultaneously in their proper places and values by the average listener without too much loss of interest, attention or enjoyment. *The theme is the lodestar in music!* The alternative is, especially at the onset, shorter excerpts, less complicated situations, careful guidance, and repeated hearing. Of course, in all this process of musical learning, the works to be studied should be of a high musical quality; otherwise the listener would be establishing low standards of taste. To summarize, some of the many benefits derived from this "natural" process are: (a) the listener's tonal memory and acuity of aural observation are almost unconsciously developed; (b) the music studied is easily added to the listener's repertory; (c) the listener develops skills in sustaining interest and perception in an extended or "difficult" work, while retaining some of the more salient musical impressions that have passed, and by anticipating, in feeling at least, what is to follow; and (d) the ability of discrimination, evaluation, and consequent effects upon one's musical taste and choice are developed along with enjoyment. *These are fundamental precepts out of which almost all other musical factors essential to intelligent listening enjoyment may be constructed, or are dependent for its realization.*

The listener can take consolation in the fact that some works defy understanding even by experienced professional musicians. Besides, the individual tastes of the well-trained listener should be considered. There will always be those composers who are "behind the times"; it is their indisputable right to revere the masters of the past. Others are of their own time, embracing the ephemeral fads, together with some of the worthy ideals of the time. Still others, unfortunately, are so far in advance of the times that they have slipped outside our orbit entirely. It is a truism that the present is built upon the past, and the future upon the present. A vigorous and ideally alert art must have a continuing transientness, with a reasonable infusion of new ideas, new blood, and new techniques, yet with a firm hold upon the precepts of the great masters of the past. The "progress" of art is a gradual metamorphosis rather than a violent change, especially in the sense of betterment. Most spurts of revolutionary novelty fizzle out in a short time.

Genius and novice alike must realize that great though the public's shortcomings may be, it actually is the final arbiter, the value of whose judgment is likely to be in direct ratio to the length of experience it has had with what are generally considered the best art "types." It is far more difficult for the average person to enjoy the music of the remote past and

From The Rodin Museum, Paris

THE PROCESSION OF THE BURGHERS OF CALAIS Auguste Rodin

The sculpture depicts an historical incident of a group of Burghers of Calais, obviously angry and disputing as they walk. One can readily observe the uses of the tempers of Realism, "refined" Naturalism, and romantic Impressionism. Especially evident is the effectiveness of the depiction of arrested motion, the play of lighting effects, and general aspects of the grouping and individual figures. It is a dramatic moment; one which forecasts, to a degree, the subjective expression that Rodin was also to depict in his sculpture of Balzac. Note the Greek influence in the graceful and artful working out of the falling folds of the figures' garments. This group has been aptly called "a painting in sculpture." It might also have been called "a work in prose."

the contemporary than, say, the music of several generations ago. Also, music embracing the Romantic tempers is more readily enjoyed, generally, than the music of the Classical or modern Expressionistic tempers. Proper musical (and allied arts) education seeks to effect a smooth transition from one epochal art-style to another; but it cannot be done completely, or immediately.

The essential listening assignments in the future chapters are carefully analyzed and annotated (when necessary) as to "architectural" design. The principal and secondary themes are shown in their initial sequence when possible, and the musical, poetical, and general spiritual character and temper of the composition are explained. The instrumentation of the themes is also indicated. There are brief biographical sketches of the composers and their historical, cultural, and social backgrounds, with adequate reference readings selected from widespread authoritative sources. In fact, such data as may enhance the interest in the music being studied are set forth.

Many users of this text have found it very helpful to follow the unfolding performance of the music at first hearing with the open text before them—the presentation of the material on the printed page accommodates such a procedure. Those who cannot read music notation may have the themes played on the piano, or better, "spot" the passages on a record. Incidentally, many have found this a powerful incentive to learn to read music.

After this factual and deductive step in the listening process, the inductive or emotional response is best achieved through hearing the composition again, *this time as an uninterrupted listening experience.* Insofar as this "completeness" of experience is not realized, just so much less will be the aesthetic reward for the listener. One may successfully summon all the artifices and techniques available in order to bring a listener and a great art work together, but such efforts can go only so far. The "second mile" can be made only by the eager appreciator himself—and thanks be that this is so! To these earnest listeners, we draw attention to the challenges provided in the Additional Listening Suggestions. They are intended to provide ample opportunities for individual initiative, exploration, and increased musical enjoyment; and they are sufficient in number and variety for most listeners.

The foregoing method of listening study assumes that the music used in the early stages will not be too involved and will have a fairly widespread appeal. However, when the listening skills, taste, and judgment are fairly well established, the listener should be free to choose, for his own pleasure, from unexplored works, providing he holds firmly to the best music he has already learned to love. Personal values and preferences will naturally undergo changes through the years, but such changes will then have been made intelligently.

These admonitions are especially pertinent when it comes to the "modern abstract" styles in art as well as music. In these, the emotionally creative contents, familiar or realistic representational organization, and the "square-cut" mechanical symmetry of compositional forms, are often reduced to a modicum. This is done for the sake of achieving certain objectives of purely cerebral composition or free fantasy of design. Even then, there are always the inevitable "reactions" that result from an observer's investiture. Therefore, in "abstract" art one should seek for other than the traditional artistic values, technical and craftsman skills, or architectonic designs. For instance, in some of the contemporary abstract paintings, one might look for such tehniques as: (a) the use of geometric or fancy free design, organization and manipulation of lines, balances in design and composition, perspective illusions, deliberate unrealities, masses, colors, brush techniques, and so forth, in and for themselves without any other representational significance; (b) the employment of one or two dimensions rather than the usual three, with several forms of perspective such as linear, conic, spherical, "bird's eye view" or circumambient (a composite view of 360°, put in a one dimensional picture, as in some Picasso paintings), or the orthographic projection seen in modern European as well as old Chinese prints; (c) the utter freedom of expression of emotion in painting and drawing even though the picture may not be immediately artistically communicative; (d) unlimited use of spectrum colors and the reverse—the "breakdown" analysis of colors; (e) representational realities in symbolical situations and meanings (as in surrealism); (f) geometric and design improvisation, isolated or integrated use of "biomorphological shapes, and fantastically interwoven calligraphic or ideographic tracing." *This "modern" art at its best may be of immense future influence, and a worthy small part of it may even become immortal.*[4]

The foregoing is a cursory listing of some salient technical means of creative craftsmanship in painting. A similar analytical "break-down" of artistic idioms and skills in their separate media may also be applied to the other fine arts, for all of them have much of a basic nature in common. The craftsmanship technics which pertain particularly to the art of music will receive detailed attention in subsequent chapters.

[4] Selected readings in the graphic and plastic arts may be made at this point from: Albert C. Barnes, *The Art in Painting*, 2nd ed. (New York: Harcourt, Brace & Co., 1928); Everard M. Upjohn, Paul S. Wingert, and Jane Mahler, *History of World Art* (New York: Oxford University Press, 1949); Helen Gardner, *Art Through the Ages* (New York: Harcourt Brace & Co., 1948); Morris Davidson, *Understanding Modern Art* (New York: Tudor Publishing Co., 1934); Thomas Craven, *Modern Art*, rev. ed. (New York: Simon & Schuster, 1950), for the average art-lover in language he can understand; Andrew Carnduff Ritchie, *Abstract Painting and Sculpture in America* (New York: Museum of Modern Art, 1951), an excellent survey and analysis--full of pictures; Sheldon Cheney, *Expressionism in Art* (New York: Tudor Publishing Co., 1948); and a good primer, A. C. Ward, *Enjoying Paintings* (London: Penguin, 1956).

Courtesy The Museum of Modern Art

STILL LIFE Gris

The still life objects in this picture, a bottle (left), two wine glasses (right), and a jar of some sort (middle), are evolved cubistically, though not completely so, into simple planes, angles, highlights and shadows, and masses. Cubism may be said to have originated with Cézanne, followed by Picasso and Braque, who were determined to simplify the complexities and, to them, the unessentialities of Impressionism. There were a number of differing manners of expressing Cubism; in fact, too many to reduce to a simple definition. However, we offer this brief explanation: (a), the reduction of natural forms (according to Cézanne) to "the cylinder, the sphere, the cube, and the cone"; (b), reducing three-dimensional objects to one- or two-dimensional masses, angles, planes, and other geometrical forms; (c), the simultaneous representation of views around and about an object; (d) the use of color assuming the functions of perspective, emotion, and even movement. Cubism is also used in sculpture and architecture.

AESTHETIC BEAUTY: BASIC TEMPERS: CONSUMMATION OF A WORK OF ART

In the analytical inquiry into artistic craftsmanship indicated in the first portion of this chapter, there are two fundamental questions which arise: first, concerning the concept of aesthetic beauty and what it is; and second, whether there are any other legitimate sources of beauty in a "consummated work of art" aside from those secured through the "feeling response" of aesthetic contemplation, plus empathy, catharsis, and what we have aggregated into "essences." These are vital questions, especially pertinent to the study of the inner character, tempers, and architectonic aspects of music and their effects upon the listener.[5]

The number of diverging views set forth in the books in footnote 4 indicate that the reader is inevitably forced to conclude either: (a) that a single, universally acceptable definition of either beauty or the beautiful does *not* exist; or, (b) that an indefinite number of concepts not only *do* exist, but that the differing conclusions may be valid because both concepts must involve to some degree intangible, subjective factors.

Not until beauty has been sympathetically and personally experienced does it become "consummated" and revealed in its fullest glory. Experienced beauty in a work of art is its own best definition and reason for being. It is a benign and human essential, as paradoxical and complex as love and truth; and beauty *is* truth to those who deeply love it. No amount of traffic with academic logic will replace in the slightest degree those values which are so readily intuited and enjoyed through the feelings and emotions. That is, for all save those few academicians who contend that "Beauty resides but in the object itself."

A fully consummated work of art (explained a few pages hence) is the final result of a co-operative, artistic, creative process between the creator, the performer, and the appreciator. (Thus a sunset, or a waterfall, or a flower are not "works of art" in the strict sense.) The term "A Work of Art" does not necessarily imply an estimation of merit, nor is it synonymous with the term, "A Consummated Work of Art."

When an object contains certain qualities which arouse in one who contemplates it the feelings and reactions of aesthetic pleasure, those intrinsic values, *plus* the reactions aroused by them in the observer, may be said to constitute *Beauty*. This aggregate of qualities is a dual one of intrinsic *and* extrinsic values.

Beautiful simply means that the object the observer contemplates is "the most delightfully pleasing and satisfying" of its sort that the observer can envisage. But we quickly add that ugliness is often justified in art.

[5] See Appendix I for list of reference readings on Aesthetics and allied subjects appropriate at this point. Valuable when this book is used in a course in the Humanities.

Beauty and *Art* are two different concepts, with "no essential connection between them." [6] *Art* is merely the application of taste and artistic skills towards creation according to aesthetic principles; or, it might also mean works that are produced through such means. As in the term "Work of Art," the single word "Art" implies no evaluation, or even the presence of inherent or comparative merit of artistic self-expression.

One of the great expressions of art throughout the ages has been architecture. In its form and mass and their extensions, its environment, design, style, ornamentation and use of color, it may be a manifestation of great beauty. However, there is a more or less general intent by contemporary architects to eliminate those embellishments and adornments not considered necessary to the structural design. Functionalism is the keynote of our time. This decorative austerity and restrictive form is an expected result of our basically steel and concrete age and limited urban space, but it is often productive of some strange examples in the application of glass, aluminum, steel, and other materials. (An architectural structure is not as ignorable as a poem, a bit of music, or a painting!) Perhaps architecture has not realized its fullest aesthetic expression in the recently developed engineering designs, techniques, and materials.

Ornamentation and sculpture have long been the glory of architecture through past centuries: [7] the graceful, repetitive designs to be found in the columns and entablatures from the Early Egyptian and Grecian types to our own day; the decorative mouldings, Gothic fan vaulting, ovoli, friezes, borders, and frets that have contributed to the beauty of famous edifices. Likewise, the tracery foliation of leaded stained-glass windows such as those of the Chartres Cathedral (1210 to 1245 A.D.), or the Rose Windows of Notre Dame (1257), of Amiens (1288), or New York's St. John the Divine in the light of the setting sun continue to be sources of wonder and beauty. The veritable fairyland of carved spires, lace-like openwork and statuettes of the unique marble Gothic Cathedral at Milan, and the jewels, carvings and mosaics of the Taj Mahal should also be included. All such ornamentations have intrinsic as well as enhancing beauty. One could not omit the Cathedral of Santa Maria del Fiore (Florence, Italy), more commonly called the "Duomo," 1296–1887, with its epochmaking dome, its Baptistry, a pagan temple remodelled in 1200, its beautiful bronze doors, and its Campanile or bell tower built by

[6] Curt J. Ducasse, op. cit. We also refer the reader to the same author's *Philosophy of Art* (New York: Lincoln MacVeagh, 1929).

[7] Similar uses of ornamentation in musical "graces" or "embellishments," as they are more properly called, may be heard in some of the works by J. S. Bach, François Couperin (*le Grand*), Mozart, Liszt, Chopin, Wagner, Beethoven, Richard Strauss and in a few contemporary works by Britten, Tansman, Scriabine, Delius, Copland, Gabriel, Fauré, here and there in Sibelius, Respighi and Stravinsky. The most conspicuous, and generally unrecognized examples of common embellishments, are to be heard in the improvisations of present-day jazz orchestras.

Courtesy The University Prints, Newton, Mass.

THE "DUOMO," CATHEDRAL OF SANTA MARIA DEL FIORE, FLORENCE, ITALY

The Campanile is to the right of the façade, and part of the roof of the Baptistry is seen on the lower right. The "Duomo" was begun by Arnolfo di Cambio in 1296, and the Campanile by Giotto in 1334. The Façade, by De Fabris, was completed in 1887. A number of architects and sculptors were eventually involved in the erection of the Cathedral, among them Brunelleschi, who completed the dome in about 1436. Michelangelo here found inspiration for the magnificent dome of St. Peter's, Rome, a century later. The Cathedral exterior in duotone, white and dark green marble, with red-tiled roofing—and its ornamentation and general design—indicate a meeting of Byzantine East and the West.

Giotto.[8] Of course, it would be a mistake to advocate a literal return to the styles of yesterday; but tasteful interpretations of non-functional

[8] A profusely illustrated booklet in English about Florence and, in particular, the Duomo is *Florence the City of Flowers* in the Medici Art Series (Florence: G. Fattorusso, 1928). The booklet also contains a brief bibliography of books in English about Florence and a chronological table from 1207–1865. Also consult A. D. F. Hamlin, *History of Architecture* (New York: Longmans, Green & Co., 1928).

beauty in architecture, especially in decorative elements, might well be advisable. As with some modern painting and music, much of our architectural heritage has been jettisoned in the quest for what is termed modern.

Few of us fully realize and appreciate the large number of common elements of Beauty there are in such typically divergent works of art as: the TAJ MAHAL, the DUOMO, Shakespeare's MACBETH, ENDYMION of Keats, Beethoven's FIFTH and NINTH SYMPHONIES, SYMPHONY NO. 6 IN E MINOR by Vaughan Williams, Mozart's SYMPHONY IN C MAJOR, the "Jupiter," the MARCELLUS MASS by Palestrina, Michelangelo's *frescoes* in the SISTINE CHAPEL, da Vinci's LAST SUPPER, Milton's PARADISE LOST, Wagner's RING OF THE NIBELUNGEN, Bach's B MINOR MASS, the PSALMS OF DAVID, Goethe's FAUST, Dante's DIVINE COMEDY, T. S. Eliot's FOUR QUARTETS, and Edwin Arlington Robinson's TRISTRAM, and so one might continue. All these masterpieces of art may be enjoyed by layman and professional alike, almost on *prima vista* if they really so desire, and "non-functional" graces are employed by many of them.

In the early section of this chapter we gave an abbreviated account of the composer's process in the creation of a musical work of art, with its realization from a vague creative mood, or urge, into an "aesthetical entity," and the effects of the whole upon the appreciator. More specifically: the composer first sought to express himself and his artistic ideas, through the medium of music, and to provide the "blue-print" score of his ideas and emotions so that others might share them. The score was thus an artistic *communication* of an intimate nature. Second, the performer (including the conductor) with his expressive skills, translated the composer's score into meaningful sound and time-rhythmic patterns and designs, necessarily adding a great deal of himself the while. Third, the listener, with his sensitive and delicate aural apparatus and the personal contributions of his imagination, his "mind," and his emotions translated what was heard into his own sensations and feelings, ideas, and physical reactions. Above all else, the listener added his own individual *creative aesthetic* contributions to the sensations he had perceived to the end that a complete work of art was finally consummated; and Beauty had revealed its secrets and potencies.

The listener tended to become intimately *sympathetic, en rapport,* with the art work itself, largely through his own experience, mood, taste, emotion, feelings, and imagination in the process of completion. This is known as *empathy.* It is not only a desirable state, but it is inescapable in the complete consummation of a work of art. The greatest enjoyment of any type of art is commensurate with the appreciator's own aesthetic sensitivity, empathic sympathy, receptivity and open-mindedness, and richness of general artistic background.

This book embodies the cardinal principle that self- or guided-tuition

The careful application of these tempers will greatly increase the listener's appreciation and understanding of the music being heard, as well as his discernment of stylistic characteristics and compositional pre-occupations, intents, and purposes of the composer. This skill in applying the tempers, as with all other skills, is successfully automatic only through earnest application and proper guidance. All these categories, established and identified through the use of tempers, are amply exemplified in the text, pictures, and music to be studied.

The lover of good art of all types usually enjoys most those works with which he is familiar, and which suit the mood of the moment. The listener is quite ready and eager to enjoy a new work—provided it has a reasonable degree of continuity with the music he already loves. Strange idioms should be introduced gradually, until the works of the *avant-garde* of contemporary composers are reached. The exact amount of "how much" and "how gradual" or "how long continued" the presentation of these unfamiliar works should be is very personal and individual, so much so that any mixed audience can only be approximately satisfied. Each audience is also an "individual problem" on a larger scale. Of course, the audience also has its proper share of responsibilities in listener response and co-operation. Apropos of audience response, enthusiastic applause tends to inspire a performer and affords a welcome aesthetic catharsis for the audience. Poorly written and poorly performed music does not elicit this same emotional reaction. *However, the prime purpose and justification of music is that it be enjoyed aesthetically, spiritually, sensually, and emotionally. Yes, even physically!* Marcel Proust has said that a work of art that contains theories is like a gift with the price-tag left on. Sir Jacob Epstein, the eminent American sculptor now living in England, is reported to have said that he was bored to death by the artist who, standing in front of his work when showing it, gives an extended explanation of what technical objectives he had attempted to achieve: "One look at the work is enough!" Few are as capable as Epstein in grasping the significance of a work at first glance, but with many glances and many hearings one might, perhaps, come close to his implication. It is certainly worth one's fullest effort!

NOTES FOR THE READER

We have not included the numbers and manufacturer's names of records of musical works mentioned because of the state of flux of commercial recording companies, the constant importations, addition of new issues, and the dropping of older and less profitable records.

We advise the reader to consider the use of such currently published and year-by-year bound revisions of record guides as: David Hall, *Records* (New York: Alfred Knopf); Irving Kolodin, *The New Guide to Recorded Music* (New York: Doubleday); Moses Smith, *Selected Record Guide* (New York:

Macmillan); Julian Morton Moses, *Collectors' Guide to American Recordings* (New York: American Record Collectors' Exchange), if you are looking for antiques; Robert H. Reid, *The Gramophone Shop Record Encyclopedia* (New York: Crown), one of the most popular; Compton Mackenzie, *Music on Record* (London: Robert Hale), for English recordings; and the most complete world-wide listing guide, F. F. Clough and G. J. Cuming, *The World's Encyclopedia of Recorded Music* (London: Sedgwick). We recommend as one of the best month-by-month catalogues the *Schwann Long Playing Record Catalog*, which may be obtained at your record dealer. The Sunday and yearly record section of the *New York Times* are also excellent.

Those who carry on the study of music appreciation along with integration of the other arts may secure prints, photographs, or half-tone cuts of paintings, sculptures, architectural structures, drawings and so forth from the following sources: *The University Prints Co.*, 15 Brattle St., Cambridge, Mass.; these New York City Art Museums—the Metropolitan, Frick, Museum of Modern Art (11 West 53rd St.), Whitney Museum of American Art, and the New York Historical Museum. In Washington, D. C., the National Museum of Art, Freer Museum, and the Corcoran Art Museum. Excellent Art Museums or Institutes located in the following cities have print facilities: Boston, Chicago, Charleston (S.C.), Grand Rapids Public Museum, Carnegie College of Fine Arts and The Art Institute (Pittsburgh), Pennsylvania Acad. of Fine Arts (Philadelphia), Philadelphia Museum of Art, Milwaukee Art Institute, Rochester (N.Y.) Museum of the Arts and Sciences, The City of Cleveland Art Institute, The Huntington Art Museum (Pasadena), and the North Carolina State Art Museum (Raleigh). The latter is unique in the U.S.A. in several respects, one of which is that it is state-owned!

Many art departments of leading colleges and Universities of the country have excellent print facilities, such as: Fogg Museum (Harvard Univ. at Cambridge, Mass.); University of Michigan Art Museum (Ann Arbor, Mich.); the library of Columbia University (New York City), to a limited degree; Yale University (New Haven, Conn.); University of California (Berkeley and Los Angeles); State Art Museum (Santa Fé, New Mexico, for American Indian Paintings).

To these, one should add a few of the larger art dealers who specialize in issuing art prints and art books, such as: The Seven Arts Book Society (215 Fourth Ave., New York 3, N.Y., especially for outstanding art books); Oestreicher's Art Co. (1208 Sixth Ave., New York City); the Phaidon Press, Ltd. (5 Cromwell Pl., London, SW 7, England), one of the best print makers; the New York Graphic Society, for its own art print series as well as the official UNESCO (United Nations Educational, Scientific and Cultural Organization) art catalogues and color prints, which are world wide in scope and source, and excellent in execution (95 East Putnam Ave., Greenwich, Conn.); Skiro, Inc. (381 Fourth Ave., New York 3, N.Y.), another of the best print makers; Harry N. Abrams, Inc., Art Publisher (421 Hudson St., New York City 14, N.Y.).

Courtesy The University Prints, Newton, Mass.

PRIMAVERA (*See p. 31.*)

Sandro Botticelli

2 Music and the social dances

It is no poetic fancy to say that the art of music has danced its way through history. Gay and carefree dance music—sad and often sentimental dance tunes too—has often served as the basis for serious secular vocal and instrumental "Art" music which is used apart from the social dances—arias, operas, suites, sonatas, symphonies, and others. Fortunately, music for the social dances did not cease with the creation of these more serious art forms. Quite the contrary, dance music has gone right alongside the "Art" music, changing with the times, the people, and the places of use, but always reflecting the spirit of those who dance for whatever occasion to which the music might lend its magic of sound, tempo, and rhythm. Music is a vital part of living, an indispensable means of arousing a desired emotional state, as well as a means of expressing or enhancing the emotions which are bursting for outward expression. The picture of the DANCING PEASANTS by Pieter Brueghel the Elder, a Flemish painter,

1525?–1569, portrays a happy and vigorous peasant festivity in the village square. Evidently "a good time is being had by all"—the music of the doodlesack (bagpipe) player to the left at the table is contributing to the occasion. (See also the Dürer picture in Chap. 12.)

The amusement values of social dance music are the most familiar. However, some sort of dance music has always been essential: in expressing religious feelings; as a primitive means of communication (as it was used by some of the slaves during the Civil War); as incantations against evil spirits; in preparation for war; in celebration of victory; in homage to heroes and sundry gods, or as a means of prophetic inspiration; as a means of expressing the pleasures of the hunt; as a lament for the dead; as an indispensable aid in love making; and in the many other ways that man has found dance music to be the *sine qua non* of living.

Social dancing and music have been referred to in the foregoing as a single entity. This is generally true. There are, however, modern dances that use only one or several simple percussion instruments, such as a drum, castanets, or tambourine; and there are many dances for which stamping feet and clapping hands are the only "orchestra." Music has always been important to the dance, however, for it serves to keep the dancers in step and, psychologically, creates and sustains the mood of joy and well-being that finds its natural expression in rhythmic bodily movement.

We begin our listening study by playing a recording of a currently popular ballad (a song-and-dance tune)—any of the better written "hits" of the moment will do.[1] Note how infectiously the restless, syncopated rhythms, the spicy harmonies, and oft-times imaginative instrumental effects of some popular music orchestrations, seem to reflect the feverish tempo of our everyday life! This is music of a sophisticated urban culture, breathing an air of gaiety and movement, awakening in the listener an almost irresistible physical response to its tempo. Listening to a marching band has somewhat similar effects.

One is almost immediately aware that in this modern equivalent of folk-dance music, rhythm is often more important than melody. The effects of the monotonously stressed beat in this music are as hypnotic and compelling to us as savage dances are to native tribes, although our responses are more controlled. When shifts of accent in the metrical pattern are

[1] Essential listening for this chapter to include one or several different types from the best of the current popular song-and-dance ballads; *Turkey in the Straw,* an early American dance arranged by David Guion, or *Irish Washerwoman,* arranged by Leo Sowerby; the *Beautiful Blue Danube* Waltz by Johann Strauss (contrast this with the probable progenitor of *all* Waltzes, the *Ländler,* and a country tune that everyone knows: *Ach, du lieber Augustin.* Note how the wooden shoes of the latter have been supplanted by the bejewelled dancing slippers of the formal ballroom); SLAVONIC DANCE IN E MINOR, Opus 72, No. 2, by Anton Dvořák; *Amaryllis* by Ghys; J. S. Bach's SUITE NO. 3, IN D MAJOR for orchestra. If time permits use *Golliwog's Cake-Walk* by Claude Debussy.

made to the normally unaccented beats, while free melodic improvisations of the various instruments are heard, one can readily recognize the fundamental characteristics of native American jazz.

There is not much originality or musical value in most current popular music; it is necessarily stereotyped in form, basic character, and musical make-up. It is inherently ephemeral and not apt to bring about a development of one's appreciation of the best in musical composition. Such a type of music generally contains its own destructive germs—it is non-poetical, monotonously repetitive, and banal in melody, harmony, and form, as musical scientists such as Drs. Schoen, Razran, Gilliland, and Moore have shown in objective tests. The average mortality rate is very high, according to the publishers of this kind of music.[2]

Our popular song-and-dance, ballad music is a type of native folk-music in the salient instances of long survival. In fact, *some* of the once popular tunes seem to have already fixed themselves in our cultural folk music literature. A random picking of such survivals might include such tunes as: *The Alice Blue Gown, Happy Birthday to You, Tea for Two, Ole Man River, The Easter Parade, White Christmas, St. Louis Blues, Dixie, Sweet Adeline, Home on the Range, Oh Susanna*—the reader can supply many more to the list. For convenience, rather than complete accuracy of terminology, these are called "composed folk songs"; that is, they were deliberately composed by a single, known person who was trained as a musician (see also Chapter 6). This kind of music may be sophisticated, musically involved, original in character, and as ornate and personal as some Art songs. The opposite may also be true; so much so that it is sometimes difficult to distinguish unpretentious composed folk-music from the traditional folk type.

Another broad classification of this art which is of interest at this point is "traditional folk dance music," so-called because, instead of having a single composer, it seems to have grown right out of the body and soul of a people. No one knows how, or why, or where this music evolved; who were the composers; or what happened to the music as it passed from performer to performer. Reflecting the character of the people from which it springs, traditional folk dance music is apt to be straightforward and naive, free from ornamental musical material, and making its appeal immediately to those who love it. Typical of these dance tunes, original and imported, are *Money Musk, Arkansas Traveler, Turkey in the Straw, Pop Goes the Weasel, Morris Dances,* square and round dances, reels, cake walks, and so forth.

Try listening to *Turkey in the Straw,* as arranged by David Guion. The

[2] Some idea of what can and has happened to those who are too much devoted to jazz music is shown in a scientific report of Howard S. Becke, of the University of Chicago, in the *American Journal of Sociology* (1951); see also *Scientific American,* Nov. 1951, p. 38.

melodies go along merrily, with clusters of rapid notes and clearly marked accents, in a manner dear to village fiddlers. This music, too, conjures up a definite way of life: the boisterous jollity of hard-working agricultural folk and the barn dance on Saturday night, with clapping hands and stamping feet. Before long you will find yourself beating time in the simplest of rhythmic patterns: ONE-two, ONE-two—an accented or strong beat alternating with an unaccented or weak beat (the musical equivalent of marching, LEFT-right, LEFT-right). This rhythmic grouping, two beats in a measure, is duple meter.

The lilting waltzes of Johann Strauss (1825–1899) sing of still another milieu, of a nineteenth-century dream city, Vienna, that has become the symbol of an era. Listen to his *Beautiful Blue Danube.* How well these flowing melodies combine urbanity and tenderness, gaiety and longing, the spirit of the dance with the nostalgic! Again you will find yourself beating time. But the rhythmic movement is broader here, more flowing. This is waltz time, to which we can count ONE-two-three, ONE-two-three: an accented beat followed by two unaccented beats, giving us three beats in a measure, or triple meter.

Since dancing and singing are such deep-rooted human impulses and so close to the life of the folk, it was natural that each nation should develop its own musical idiom. The great composers found inspiration in native folk song and attempted in their art to capture the spirit of their homelands. Their national dances vary in mood from gentle melancholy to joyous abandon, but all breathe the spirit of the folk, the vigorous peasant rhythms, the melodic richness and pungent flavor of the countryside. And all speak the simple language of the heart, which knows no barriers of nation, race, or time.

Fine examples of this folk-dance genre within the literature of "composed art music," to distinguish it from the traditional type, are the SLAVONIC DANCES of Anton Dvořák (DVOR-zhak), of which we should now hear the one in E minor. Dvořák (1841–1904), himself of peasant stock, was an ardent nationalist and stands in European music, together with his compatriot and guide, Bedřich Smetana (SMET-ah-nah) (1824–1884), as the musical voice of the Czech nation.

The SLAVONIC DANCE IN E MINOR, from Op. 72, No. 2 (Opus or Op. literally means "work." This designation is a universal system of showing sequence or order of composition or publication. Warning: Dvořák wrote two separate series of these dances, Opp. 46 and 72. Some publishers list the dance used here as No. 10. Op. 46 was for piano duet). This Slavonic Dance has become very popular in the orchestral version, as well as in Fritz Kreisler's arrangement for violin and piano (shown here). The opening section brings us a poignant melody in triple meter, with that undercurrent of melancholy so often found in the folk music of central and southeastern Europe, and with a strong gypsy coloring.

In the middle section the mood brightens, the pace becomes animated. A playful theme appears, followed by a broad lyrical melody, serene and folklike in character. Then we return to the somber mood of the opening theme.

Notice how clear-cut is the contrast in mood between the opening section and the two themes in the middle part. Having achieved a pleasant diversity of effect, the composer returns to his original melody, which balances and unifies the structural scheme of the composition.

A popular dance form of the eighteenth-century composers was the *Rondo, Rondeau,* or *Rondel,* based upon the old French singing round-dance (much like our ring-around-the-rosy or may-pole dance), in which the leader's tune (usually the verse) alternates with that of the dancing ring (usually the chorus). This form might be basically described as: A^1-B-A^2-C-A^3, and so on, although many variants are used. The distinguishing feature of this dance-music is the recurrence throughout of the main, or first, theme (A), separated by episodes, or contrasting material designated as B, C, D, E, etc., with the return of three or more "A" sections as a "must"—usually *more* than three returns of "A." An excellent example of a variant of this type of music, based upon the fundamental rondo structure, is the old French rondeau, *Amaryllis* by Ghys, the schematic design of which is as follows: A^1-A^2-B^1-A^3-A^4-C^1-C^2-B^2-C^3-A^5-A^6. (The superior numbers indicate repetitions.) Listen to this charming and graceful *Rondo,* and try to distinguish, first, the returning main theme, then, the contrasting episodes. If one listens carefully, the composer's fascinating methods of joining the three (A and B and C) sections together in order to unify the whole will become apparent. Haydn, Mozart, Beethoven, and countless other composers, including those of today, have used this type of dance form in their works.[3]

What Mozart and Haydn did for the common dance forms and their incorporation into serious types of music during the Classical period,

[3] Mozart and Haydn are generally referred to as the two outstanding masters of the so-called "Classical period." In this connection, it might not be amiss to clear up some misconceptions concerning the use of the word *classical.* In colloquial speech, the term is generally used to denote "artistic" or "serious" music as opposed to "popular," or "jazz" music. For the musician and other artists, "Classical" refers to an art style distinguished from "Romantic." The historian often applies the term "Classical period" to the second half (approximately) of eighteenth century Europe, when the spirit of Classicism was very much to the fore.

Johann Sebastian Bach (1685–1750) accomplished in the *early* part of the eighteenth century.[4]

THE CLASSICAL SUITES OF BACH'S TIME

In the so-called CLASSICAL SUITES of the time, one finds a sequence of characteristic dance rhythms of Western European nations, gathered into a fairly extended single opus, though the different dances are kept separate. They are all in the same key and selected with an eye for contrast, sustained interest, climax, and compositional compatibility. These classical dance suites probably began during the latter part of the Middle Ages, when musicians strung together a series of dances. In the seventeenth century, composers wrote original dance tunes, though in the general style and rhythmic character of the native dances, and they were called *partie* or *partita*, meaning, literally, "a portion or part of." The early suites contained four principal and basic divisions: (1), the *Allemande*, (2), the *Courante*, (3), the *Sarabande* and (4), the *Gigue* (jig). Between the last two, other dances were sometimes inserted. These interpolations were known as *intermezzi*, and such dances as the *Bourrée, Branle, Gavotte, Minuet, Musette, Passepied, Air, Rigaudon, Polonaise, Anglaise, Loure,* the *Pavane* and still other dances were often inserted by Bach and his contemporaries. Sometimes these "extra" dances supplanted one or more of the original four. The Classical Suite became almost extinct after 1800. Nowadays, a "Suite" can mean almost any arbitrary choice of separate numbers, arranged in different keys and in whatever sequence the composer desires. In fact, the separate numbers of a modern suite need not be dances at all! Of course, there should be some common, unifying idea in the suite.

Those who criticize the composers of today for using popular social dance rhythms should renew their acquaintance with J. S. Bach. Here is a composer who occupies the pinnacle among the greatest composers of all time. Yet he did not consider that he "lowered" himself as a composer by writing works that incorporated the rhythms, spirit, and even tunes of the popular social dances of his own day or before. Of course, he greatly idealized and dignified such dances.

Suite No. 3 in D Major for orchestra by J. S. Bach

The SUITE NO. 3, IN D MAJOR, for orchestra, has been selected for this chapter's essential listening study not only because it is an outstanding

[4] Bach shared this accomplishment with other composers in other lands, mainly Italy and some from France; but most significantly with another immortal who was born only a few miles from Bach's birthplace, in the same year, and who lived for almost the same life span—though the two never met. Tragically, both became blind. This was George Frideric Handel (1685-1759); see Chapter 9. For an extended account of Bach see Chapter 28.

example of the Classical Suite of the period but also because it is one of the most beautiful and melodic of the four Suites for orchestra that Bach composed during his stay at Cöthen and Leipzig. The SECOND and THIRD SUITES FOR ORCHESTRA were, according to Spitta, the great Bach authority, composed in Leipzig, probably around 1725. *The Third Suite* consists of five or six movements—depending upon the analysis of the so-called Gavotte I and II—entitled: *Overture, Air, Gavotte* I and II, *Bourrée* and *Gigue*—even in this choice of dances, Bach was not to be restricted to absolute conformities.

The *Overture* follows the general plan of older models (as do the other dance movements), and it is closely akin to the so-called *French Overture,* which consists of a slow-moving, well sustained, first section, usually repeated; then a fast moving (often fugal) section; finally, a slow dance of some kind, often the Minuet, or the dignified first section is recalled.[5]

The *Air* is a song of sublime beauty in two sections, each repeated. It is written in a wonderfully sustained mood, and represents a compositional conception and skill which seems to be a lost art today. The listener is probably more familiar with the transcription of this *Air* by the German violinist, August Wilhelmj (Vil-HEHL-mee), for violin solo to be played entirely on the lowest (G) string of the instrument. It is usually called *Air for the G string.*

The third dance is a moderately lively *Gavotte* of French origin. The Gavotte was originally a peasant dance which eventually found its way into the French courts; but in so doing, according to F. de Menil in his HISTORY OF THE DANCE, its once lively pace became much more restrained, more "proper"! The Gavotte in simple quadruple meter usually begins on the third beat of the measure and ends on the first half. In this particular Gavotte in Bach's SUITE NO. 3, the first dance is followed by a second and new Gavotte tune, after which the first one is repeated. In some suites, the so-called second dance of a Gavotte movement was called a *Musette,* the drone bass of which imitates a species of bagpipes popular in France, according to the late Dr. Felix Borowski, the composer-musicologist and critic.[6] (This bagpipe-like Musette instrument is not

[5] The traditional *French Overture* design may be briefly described as of three sections in the following speeds: slow: fast: slow. The traditional *Italian Overture* design may also be said to have been of three sections, the first of which was a lively (*allegro*) movement; the second, a slow, lyrical and sustained section (*largo* or *andante*); and the third, a lively and vivacious movement (*allegro* or *presto*). Thus, the *Italian Overture* divisions may be briefed as: fast: slow: fast. The latter probably served as the progenitor of the later complete *Sonata* form, for which the reader should consult the index.

[6] The French instrument called the "Musette" is similar to the old bagpipe, and an outgrowth from it, save that it has two "Chanters," one for the higher notes and the other for the lower; also, there are usually four or five drones. The playable scale of the Musette is more or less chromatic, instead of being tuned in a restricted scale as the more antique instruments are apt to be.

to be confused with a modern version of that instrument commonly heard in Shrine bands and also in certain fairs and circuses that still travel around the countryside.)

A *Bourrée* (boor-RAY), not unlike the Gavotte, is the next dance in this Suite. It begins on the fourth, or last, beat of the measure and ends, quite properly, on the third. This particular dance, as with most of the classical dances, is in two sections. The Bourrée, like the Gavotte, also was of French origin, in the provinces of Auvergne and Berri, and was introduced into the French courts by Catherine de'Medici in 1565. The dance is a "careless, skipping one" which, traditionally, had to be danced in short skirts. Nowadays, the Bourrée has fallen from grace and is an ordinary clog dance in the original provinces. There is usually a great deal of strongly accented singing during the dance itself.

The final dance is a very lively Gigue (Jig).[7] Thus the Suite ends, as all good Classical Suites should, with a gay, rousing, and bouncing tune —the kind that dance fiddlers like.

Here are the principal themes of the various dance movements, of Bach's SUITE NO. 3 IN D MAJOR, set forth in musical notation.

[7] The word "*jig*" is uncertain in origin. It may have come from Middle Dutch *ghighe*, Old French *gigue* or *giguer*, German *geige* or *gige*, Old Norse *gigja*, or Italian *giga*.

ADDITIONAL SUGGESTIONS FOR LISTENING

Inasmuch as present day popular social dance music changes from week to week, it would be impractical to list it here. There are, however, some unusual discs of folk and ethnological music recorded "on the spot" that deserve mention. These are long playing records issued by Folkways Records and Service Corp., New York, and Esoteric Records, Inc., New York. The catalogs of these firms will provide ample folk material. Also, there are the invaluable standard foreign and domestic sets of records, such as: the COLUMBIA RECORDED HISTORY OF MUSIC (Scholes ed.), MUSIK DES ORIENTS (ed. Hornbostl), 2000 YEARS OF MUSIC (ed. by Sachs), and the superb set, ANTHOLOGIE SONORE (Sachs *et al*).

As for listing important individual records, the task is almost an endless one, and we shall have to content ourselves with mere suggestions. Among such works, are: CREATION DU MONDE by Darius Milhaud, which uses "jazz" rhythms, themes, and effects, and which antedated George Gershwin's RHAPSODY IN BLUE. (Gershwin's work was first produced in New York, 1924, and Milhaud's in Paris, 1923.)

Along a parallel line of usage of native North American dance rhythms is the clever and frolicking dance and satire, Debussy's *Golliwog's Cake-walk,* one of the five pieces for piano solo embraced in THE CHILDREN'S CORNER. This piece makes delightful use of the characteristic rhythms of the *Cake-walk;* a dance which originated among the Negroes of the South. Its name derives from the custom of giving a prize of a cake for the winner of a "strutting" competition. The dance, done by successive pairs of male and female strutters dressed in fanciful costumes, soon made an appearance in the post-bellum days with the minstrel shows. Of course, the dance became elaborated and exaggerated, but the basic strutting dance rhythm and the general formations and style were preserved. A favorite tune of the black-face minstrels for this dance was *Georgia Camp Meeting,* which became popular as a novelty piece. Oscar Thompson, in his biography, DEBUSSY: MAN AND ARTIST, says that the composer probably heard the tune played either by his friend Gabriel Austruc who had witnessed the dance at the World's Columbian Exposition (Chicago, 1893), or that Debussy himself might have heard and seen the dance in some Parisian Music Hall. At any rate, Debussy was more than a little influenced by the rhythms and the tune of *The Georgia Camp Meeting.* The main theme of the middle section of the piece is fashioned as an obvious parody or burlesque of the "Confession of Love" *leitmotif* in Wagner's TRISTAN AND ISOLDE. Debussy abhorred Wagner's music and resented his popularity. *Golliwog's Cake-walk* is an interesting and amusing piece of well-executed music.

The masters often wrote in idealized dance forms—that is, they sought to capture the spirit of the dance in Art music rather than to create music for actual dancing. Thus, Frédéric Chopin (shō-PAN) (1810–1849), one of the most distinctive of the Romanticists, transformed the rhythms of the waltz into something altogether personal and subtle; what the critic James Huneker called "a dance of the spirit rather than of the body." Listen to his *Waltz in C-Sharp minor,* a poetic idealization of this dance form, tinged with gentle sadness.

Notice the clearly defined construction, each section introducing a melody and mood of its own. The hauntingly lovely opening theme is followed by a caressing melody in running notes. Then comes a broad, flowing theme of quiet lyricism and serenity. By introducing new melodic material, Chopin sustains our interest and achieves a pleasantly varied effect. By repeating the old at judicious intervals, he gives coherence and unity to his stuctural scheme.

Now listen to the *Rhumba* movement from Harl McDonald's SYMPHONY NO. 2, which is an American symphonic adaptation of an "Afro-Cuban" dance. Here, the Rhumba takes the place of the usual Scherzo movement, just as the Scherzo itself supplanted the Minuet or other classical dances. Note the complicated and syncopated rhythms, the reiterations of the same basic musical idea, and the over-all good humor and vivaciousness. You might also try out the same composer's SYMPHONY NO. 4 with its *Cake-Walk* movement. For further diversion, listen to the adaptations of social dance rhythms in such works as: DANSES SACRÉE ET PROFANE by Debussy; the *Polovtsian Dances* from the opera PRINCE IGOR by Borodin; the *German Dances* by Beethoven; the *Minuet in G* by Beethoven, and another by Paderewski; the *Syncopated Clock* by Leroy Anderson; selected South American dances by Villa-Lobos' BACHIANAS BRASILEIRAS Nos. 1, 2, and 5, and his CHÔROS Nos. 4, 7, and especially No. 10; the Ballet XOCHIPILI-MACUILIXOCHITL, LOS CUATROS SOLES by the Mexican composer Carlos Chávez; the Roumanian, Hungarian and many other dances by the late Hungarian genius, Béla Bartók; POLISH DANCES by Chabrier, and also Moszkowski; GOYESCAS by Grenados; *Incidental Music* from ROSAMUNDA Op. 26 by Schubert; Waltzes by J. Strauss, Brahms, Max Reger, and also by Waldteufel; *Dances* from WILLIAM TELL by Rossini; BOHEMIAN DANCES by Smetana; selected Hungarian Dances by Liszt or Brahms; *Sabre Dance* by Khachaturian; *Polka* from SCHWANDA by Weinberger; CAUCASIAN SKETCHES by Ippolitov-Ivanov.

RHYTHM: THE HEARTBEAT OF MUSIC

All compositions differ somewhat in individuality, form, style or content; but they all share certain basic artistic musical elements. These are, briefly: (1), the melody, or tune, which, with the rhythm, catches and holds our attention; (2), the time, or measure, of the piece, its tempo, its speed, and the time duration of the various tones of which it is made; (3), the harmony, or simultaneous grouping together of several tones, that accompany the melody; (4), the pulse pattern of strong and weak accents, as they group themselves into obvious rhythmic designs, (5) "germinal" patterns of greater and lesser stresses, which expand into the compositional unit known as the "measure," and sometimes overflow the bar lines marking off the measures, combining several of them and eventually aiding in the formation of the more extended phrases, periods, and so forth.

Further, each performing instrument has a distinctive tone color, which either blends with that of the other instruments sounding simultaneously, or stands out by itself. The various themes alternate, as we saw, in accordance with a definite structural pattern. In addition, the music varies in volume and pace. Of course, there are additional factors in music-making we have not mentioned, and much of this might have been felt "unconsciously" as the music unfolded. Let us begin with the element that plays so decisive a part in all dance music—the rhythm.

Rhythm itself remains one of those concepts that defy a succinct and over-all definition which will be generally acceptable. It has to be experienced through feeling to be understood and identified.

Rhythm is one of the basic elements in music, and one with universal appeal. One has only to watch people fall into step or nod their heads to the band to realize its power. In primitive society, the rhythmic beating of the drums often takes on a ritualistic or magical potency. When we hear a haphazard succession of sounds coming at irregular intervals, we remain indifferent. But as soon as these sounds are arranged in a regular sequence of beats, we become aware of a designed pattern. We begin to expect the accent in a definite place, and receive a pleasant sense of security from having our expectation fulfilled. Rhythm may be defined as the element of music that regulates its forward movement or flow through the regular recurrence of accented and unaccented beats arranged into patterns. Even the melody itself and the effective selection, sequence, and flow of the harmony are all dependent upon the presence and character of the rhythmic patterns.

Actually, rhythm is not restricted to music. It enters into painting and all the arts, where the subtle repetition of a compositional pattern reinforces the relationship of the parts to the whole, balancing, unifying and giving life to the composition. The great painters were masters of spatial rhythm. See in the PRIMAVERA of Sandro Botticelli (1447–1510), how subtle are the internal rhythms, uniting the individual figures and the groups to the total design. Within the rectangular framework, the sense of eye movement and the "flow" of action are shifted about in a vast oval from the allegorical figure of the wind on the right, along the curve of the trees, to the cherub on top and down again via the raised arm of the figure on the left; then back to the right along the curves of the lower part of the picture. Within this oval are three smaller patterns taking in the two groups of figures arranged symmetrically on either side, and the central figure of Spring, framed by the arching trees and the cherub overhead.

Rhythm and meter also play a prominent part in poetry, where the arrangement of the syllables and words into the versification unit of the "poetic foot" adds a strange power to the "music" of the words, which is increased as the compounded rhythmic and metric units become more

Courtesy The University Prints, Newton, Mass.

DANCING PEASANTS Brueghel

complex and conjoined, and eventually blend as one with the poetic beauty and meaning of the line, verse, and poem as a whole. While it is not correct to carry the analogy between poetic and musical rhythm too far, there are parallels. Through rhythmic patterns, poets have achieved a marvelous diversity of effect and have mastered the most subtle musical cadences of which language is capable. Rhythmic units and their combinations are no doubt familiar to the reader: *iambic,* ti-DUM, ti-DUM; *trochaic,* the reverse of *iambic,* DUM-ti, DUM-ti; *anapestic,* ti-ti-DUM, ti-ti-DUM; *dactylic,* DUM-ti-ti, DUM-ti-ti.

Here are a few illustrations of iambic, trochaic, dactylic and anapest measures. The first, in iambic pentameter, is from Shakespeare's *Sonnet* No. 18:

> So LONG as MEN can BREATHE or EYES can SEE,
> So LONG lives THIS, and THIS gives LIFE to THEE.

Henry W. Longfellow, in his "*Psalm of Life*," uses the trochaic foot in this familiar quotation:

> TELL me NOT in MOURN-ful NUM-bers,
> LIFE is BUT an EMP-ty DREAM.

The same poet's "*Evangeline*" (in dactylic measure), with its waltz-like rhythmic beats, goes this way:

> THIS is the FOR-est pri-ME-val,
> The MUR-mur-ing PINES and the HEM-locks.

Byron's "*Sennacherib*" discloses this anapest measure:

> The As-SYR-ian came DOWN like a WOLF in the FOLD;
> And his CO-horts were GLEAM-ing in PUR-ple and GOLD! [8]

In all ages man derives pleasure and satisfaction from the orderly arrangement of the accented and unaccented pulsations upon which rhythm depends. In the world that man has created for himself through art, these pulsations assume the importance of a vital force, a dynamic principle, a basic ingredient of the aural, visual, and poetic arts.

[8] In order that the reader might more fully savor the excitement of rhythmic patterns, we suggest the reading aloud of such poems as Carl Sandburg's *Chicago;* Vachel Lindsay's, *The Chinese Nightingale, General William Booth Enters into Heaven, The Congo,* and *The Sante Fé Trail;* Edgar Allen Poe's *Ulalume* and *The Bells;* and other poems of similar nature. Refer especially to *American Poetry Since 1900* by Louis Untermeyer (New York: Henry Holt Co., 1923); and selections from *The Limits of Art,* edited by Huntington Cairns (New York: Pantheon Books, 1948).

Courtesy University of Michigan Dept. of Fine Arts

THE TAJ MAHAL, AGRA, INDIA Mohammedan (Saracenic) Architecture

The outstanding and most perfect memorial of its kind that man has ever built. The Taj Mahal was built from about 1630 to 1653 by the Mogul Emperor, Shah Jahan, one of the rulers of India, as a memorial for his wife, Mumtaz-i-Mahall, and was later a place for his own entombment in 1666. The building is an exemplar of the finest craftsmanship and design in architecture—in the filigree carvings of stone and marble, the cutting, polishing, and setting of jewels, the exquisite mosaic designs, and the general landscape setting. All the exterior surfaces are of pure white marble, inlaid with precious and semi-precious jewels, decorative inscriptions and arabesques of all kinds, and perforated jig-sawed traceries of the most intricate designs.

3 Music, ceremony, and celebrations

What would a formal church wedding be without the magical effects of music? Appropriate music not only reflects the mood of the occasion but also creates and sustains the desired mood and spirit of the event itself. The same sort of action and reaction occurs in a coronation or similar investiture. Our own Presidential inauguration might be much enhanced with greater use of appropriate ceremonial music.[1]

No graduation exercise would be complete without dignified and stimulating music, including, of course, such ceremonial marches as Elgar's *Pomp and Circumstance, Wedding Day at Troldhaugen* by Grieg, *March of the Priests* from ATHALIA by Mendelssohn, the *Corona-*

[1] The essential listening for this chapter includes: *Marche Militaire* by Schubert, *Pomp and Circumstance* by Elgar, *Stars and Stripes Forever* by Sousa, *Polonaise Militaire* by Chopin, *Triumphal March* from AÏDA by Verdi, *Wedding March* by Wagner, and the *Funeral March* by Chopin. The other works mentioned may be considered optional.

tion March from LE PROPHÈTE by Meyerbeer, *March of Triumph* from Act II of AÏDA by Verdi, and *Marche Héroïque* by Saint-Saëns.

Public celebrations always have been indispensable activities in man's community life. They express and bring to renewed life the cherished occasions of the past, and also serve as wellsprings of inspiration for the future and wholesome encouragement for the present. They give renewed strength, hope, courage, and determination to our heritage. The present has also contributed something of lasting value to the ideals of the past. Considered in that light, public celebrations and ceremonies which reflect the highest principles, purposes, and achievements of the past and the present become the cornerstones of the future community.

During the Christmas season, the performance of Handel's MESSIAH has become a community social and religious ceremony throughout Christendom. What a potent inspiration this work has proved to be for more than two hundred years! The annual production of THE MESSIAH at Lindsburg, Kansas has been so wholeheartedly a community effort that almost every one in town can sing the work from beginning to end from memory. Consequently, the Biblical words and the music have become a living credo throughout the remaining days of the year!

On a more ornate level, the ceremonies at St. Peter's, Vatican City, are most impressive. All the arts combine to create a mood of awe and wonder —the colorful attire of the dignitaries and Swiss Guards; the soaring architecture of the church itself, brilliantly illuminated; the painting and sculpture; the sonorous phrases of the celebrants; and the chants, extended choral works, and other musical embellishments to the ceremonies. Many visitors maintain that the memory of the music remains with them even after the other impressions have faded.

Others are equally impressed with the civic celebration of the Bach Festival at Bethlehem, Pa., where men and women of all occupations spend about a week publicly singing the choral works of Johann Sebastian Bach. And they can, if necessary, do all this from memory, for such is the pride of the townspeople. The conducting by the late (John) Frederick Wolle, "father" of the festival and founder of the Choral Union (1882) and The Bethlehem Choir (1885), still remains a vivid memory.

These and similar occasions are public demonstrations-through-music of a genuinely religious folk, united in manifesting their feelings in the most beautiful form of unified public expression they know and love—Bach's choral music.

Only limited space precludes mention of many other large and traditional *community* celebrations wherein music is an essential part—such as the Cincinnati Biennial Festival, founded by Theodore Thomas in 1873, and the North Shore Festival at Evanston, Illinois, founded in 1909 by Dean Peter Christian Lutkin of Northwestern University.

There are other facets of musical ceremonies and celebrations. One of the most commonly used musical forms is the *march*. The military march, with its stirring trumpets, simple melodies, and regular beats that arouse and quicken the pulse, has always successfully served to arouse a festive and martial mood. A good example of what this type of music can become in the hands of a great composer is the *Marche Militaire* by Franz Schubert (1797–1828). The spirited opening theme, in very strongly accented duple meter (ONE-two, ONE-two; 2/4 time), is vibrant with energy and movement. Notice the contrast with the quieter middle section, where

the music takes on grace and lightness, after which it returns in simple, symmetrical, A—B—A′ formation to the opening theme.[2] Notice, too, that the music seems to be laid out in simple regular and symmetrical sections, a type of "architecture" highly appropriate to outdoor music.

The ceremonial march often creates an effect of dignity, pomp, and patriotic fervor. For an example of this type, play Edward Elgar's *Pomp and Circumstance.* The title for this series of marches came from Shakespeare's OTHELLO, Act III, Scene 3, line 354. Elgar had planned a set of six such marches under the same "generic name," as he himself put it, but he completed only five. The reference here is to the first and most popular of the set, in D Major, Op. 39. The themes are individual and contrastingly distinctive.

As you listen to a recording of this work, note the over-all character, the appropriately simple and stately themes, the instrumentation, the pulsating rhythmic beat, the prevailing mood. Consider how well the composer has achieved his intentions. Here, one should discover a festive, pompous, and gay, yet dignified ceremonial mood. This march should arouse a feeling of pride and dignity, a spine-tingling, foot-moving, and heart-quickening awareness that something important is in the air.

Then observe some of the larger and more salient thematic mile-posts that set off the several sections of the march. The minor or "in-between" musical activities will take on more significance in due time. Notice how arresting and gratifyingly brief the introduction is, and that it does, in fact, introduce the first theme, marked by the composer *Allegro con molto fuoco* (Italian for "Lively, with much fire"—Italian is the official inter-

[2] This A—B—A′ basic formation may be taken to mean, for the moment, first a statement of the principal theme, then an appearance of a contrasting section, and finally the restatement of the main theme after the contrast. Mutations and adaptations of this form will be noted in subsequent pages.

national language for musical usage). It is a bustling, "on-the-move" tune that still remains dignified.[3]

The composer then proceeds to "manipulate" or "develop" the theme in several ways. He sets forth the best tune to serve the immediate purpose and then proceeds to point out some of its more worthy aspects—just as the good preacher presents his text and then explains the different attributes of it. Then note the recurrences of the theme which tie the work together and eliminate a feeling of wandering. Observe how this section remains a part of the music already heard and attaches itself, by anticipation, to what is to come. This is one of the more subtle bits of craftsmanship of a good composer. Then comes the calmer, more lyric, though still dignified, section which is called the *Trio*. It is in contrast with the first section both in the smooth, singing quality of the theme, the difference in instrumentation—it is usually played by the wood-winds—and the key or tonality (either a fourth up or a fifth down from that of the first theme). The Trio is marked *Largaménte* (Italian for "in a broad and expansive manner"). Here is the theme of the Trio:

This trio theme is worked about a bit, and eventually one hears again the more agitated tune of the first section. Then the trio theme reappears and the whole musical picture seems even more aglow and vivid than ever. "Flash-backs" to the first part of the march join in the musical activity, which eventually reaches a fitting climax. Then follows the brilliant and appropriately reminiscent close, or *coda* (literally, coda means a "tail-piece," from the Latin *Cauda*). One can easily understand from this march alone what a really thrilling aesthetic and emotional experience a good piece of music can be.

It is interesting to note here, as in the case of FINLANDIA by Sibelius (see Chap. 15), that the trio of *Pomp and Circumstance* was made into a national patriotic song, *Land of Hope and Glory*. The march was composed for the coronation of Edward VII of Great Britain. Perhaps, someday, someone will do the same with the trio section of Sousa's march, *Stars and Stripes Forever.*

We have tried to indicate a general habit pattern of listening, the

[3] "Pomp and Circumstance" themes quoted by permission of the copyright owners, Boosey, Hawkes and Belwin (New York: 1902).

essence of which is this: listen to many repetitions of the work you wish to know, and in each rendition try to observe something new and different about the work—another facet of the gem. Then relegate these conscious, formal objectives to the back of the mind and simply enjoy the music and your reactions fully. You will find, as you go on with such a regimen, that fewer repetitions will be required in order to become acquainted with a really worthwhile musical work. The first hearing may be rather nebulous and chaotic, but with intelligent, sympathetic, and repeated listenings, the inherent beauties of the music will be fully revealed to those who persistently seek them.

Courtesy The University Prints, Newton, Mass.

CORONATION OF NAPOLEON AND JOSEPHINE Jacques David

Ceremonial marches are often used in a rather slowly paced quadruple meter (ONE-two-THREE—four, ONE-two-THREE—four). The primary accent on *one* and secondary accent on *three* imparts a broad span to the measure. The "quick-step" is a more rapidly paced type of march (120 or more steps a minute). Listen to *Stars and Stripes Forever* by our own "March King," John Philip Sousa. Such marches are very likely to be in a fast, two-four time (ONE-two, ONE-two), or in a fast six-eight measure, (ONE-two-three-FOUR-five-six, ONE-two-three-FOUR-five-six). To save exertion, however, the last is also counted ONE-two, ONE-two, using the primary and secondary accents and eliding the other unaccented portions of the measure. One often finds moderately slow marches in three-four—

or waltz—time (ONE-two-three) in such tunes as *America* and in the gay, brilliant, pompous *Polonaise.*

As we have already indicated, the march and the dance both depend upon rhythmic bodily movement, stimulated and determined by the music, which should be "catchy," comparatively simple, and must move along at an appropriate rate of speed (*tempo* is the Italian word that musicians use for this). Both the march and the dance come together in the broad triple meter (ONE-two-three) of the *Polonaise*—the happy and brilliant, though dignified and stately, processional dance in which the Polish nobles of a bygone day filed past the throne. Frédéric-François Chopin's stirring *Polonaise Militaire,* Op. 40, (1838) offers this march-dance in its proudest and most ceremonial mood. Notice the peculiar and moving rhythm of the accompaniment. The march is couched in simple melodies and symmetrical sections. Observe, also, the effective contrast

between the brusque *staccato* opening theme and the broad, lyrical second theme.[4]

For ceremonial music on the grand scale, we turn to the *Triumphal March* from Giuseppe Verdi's opera, AÏDA. Here is the perfect setting for pomp, pageantry, and general rejoicing, as the two bands of trumpets on the stage, the singers, and the orchestra in the pit roar a welcome to the victorious hero, Rhadames (RAH-dah-mays), general of the Egyptians, and his returning army at the gates of Thebes. Here is a building up of a climax, which has no equal in the entire operatic repertory. A supreme achievement for that great genius of Italian opera. See and hear the opera if you possibly can. In listening to the march, note particularly the rousing effect of the rich, massive chords at the beginning, the brilliant tone-color

[4] The smooth, connected style that we heard in the second theme, where every tone melted into the next, is known as *legato*—in contrast to *staccato*, a short, sharp, and disconnected manner of playing the notes.

of the brass instruments, especially in the second theme, and the imposing effect of the melody supported by a full, running accompaniment in the final section. See if you can hear where Verdi accomplishes a wonderful effect by suddenly lifting the whole march up to another key (from A-flat to B-natural). Compare this effect of Verdi's with a much later use of the same "trick" in Ravel's *Bolero.* There are also many similar examples to be found in the works of Beethoven. Perhaps Verdi sought to give musical expression in this particular situation to a familiar acoustical phenomenon of the rising pitch of an approaching source of sound or a listener approaching a fixed source—known as the *Döppler Effect*—though the original intent was more likely a purely aesthetic one.[5] Here is the familiar, flowing theme of the *Triumphal March* (A) as it is heard in the first part of the victory parade, marching across the stage with its "bands" of trumpets, and then (B) as it is heard with its transposed "lift" effect, played by the second "band" of trumpets as they usher in the remainder of the parade, including the victorious Rhadames.

Music plays no less a prominent part in ceremonies of a more personal and intimate character. The *Bridal Chorus Wedding March* from Richard Wagner's opera, LOHENGRIN, coupled with Mendelssohn's *Wedding March,* from incidental music for Shakespeare's A MIDSUMMER NIGHT'S DREAM, are indispensable parts of a formal wedding ceremony. Here is a portion of Wagner's *Bridal Chorus:*

Its steady duple meter has nobility and serious dignity. When played in the more correct tempo—faster than the usual pace—this music is an

[5] For supplementary processional music of similar character, listen to the majestic *War March of the Priests* from Mendelssohn's ATHALIE, the *Grand March* from Wagner's TANNHÄUSER, Entrance of the Knights, or the *Coronation March* from Meyerbeer's LE PROPHÈTE.

exalted, joyful, hopeful, but still dignified processional.[6] When one stops to consider the proper tempi of the Wagner and the Mendelssohn works and views them with their inherently different spirit and moods, it is not difficult to appreciate why the former, with its slower pace and dignified character, is used as the processional, and the latter, with its gay spirit and lively tempo, is used as the recessional.

Equally universal in scope is the somber march music that is an integral part of the ceremonial rites for the dead. Chopin's *Marche Funèbre*, from his SONATA FOR PIANO IN B-FLAT MINOR, Op. 35 (1839), is known and played throughout the occidental world. This and the *Marcia Funèbre* from the THIRD SYMPHONY, the "*Eroica*," IN E-FLAT MAJOR, Op. 55, by Ludwig van Beethoven seem to have established themselves as "official" ceremonial marches. Here is the main (the first) theme of Chopin's *Marche Funèbre:*

How eloquently the solemn tread of the supporting chords and the restrained melody and mood create the atmosphere of overwhelming grief! The music is surcharged with despair and sorrow. But soon, as if the emotions had won a surcease, there is heard an almost oversweet, sentimental melody. This is the second, or middle, section of the piece. To many listeners this is a song of hope, consolation, and tenderness. It soon ends, however, and the dark, ominously pulsating chordal background and the hypnotically monotonous melody of the first section return—a rather simple march adaptation of the "repetition after contrast," or A—B—A′, structure. It is interesting to note that Chopin's *Marche Funèbre* served for his own funeral in Paris, 1849. Here, indeed, music says the emotional and spiritual things that language cannot express.

ADDITIONAL SUGGESTIONS FOR LISTENING

As in the case of the dance, the diverse moods of ceremonial music found expression, on a more abstract plane, in the symphonies of the great composers. One of the noblest of all funeral marches, as we have just remarked, is the slow movement from Beethoven's THIRD SYMPHONY (the "*Eroica*"). The simple, march-like theme, announced by the violins, has that quality of intense feeling

[6] Different in mood are the *Norwegian Bridal Procession* of Grieg and the *Bridal Cortège* from Nicholas Rimsky-Korsakoff's fairy opera COQ D'OR. Try to discover others.

and sublimity of expression which is singularly Beethovenian. The movement sweeps on in lonely grandeur until we come to the second theme, which is rich in courage and vibrant humanity. The themes are worked out in rich symphonic style, steadily mounting in intensity. Then the sorrowful first theme re-enters. If the Chopin *Funeral March* is an outpouring of grief for an individual, the slow movement of the *"Eroica"* is a lamentation for all mankind. Here are the themes from the Beethoven *Funeral March:*

The mood of the "triumphal" march has been woven into the serious and dignified symphonic form of the third movement of Tchaikovsky's SIXTH SYMPHONY (the "Pathétique"). This movement, as we have declared elsewhere, is really the *finale* (fi-NAH-lay), compositionally speaking. The average audience detects the rightful ending at the close of the present third movement, *Allegro molto vivace,* and applauds as though it were a proper, satisfying close to the symphony.

Albeit, the third movement is a cleverly contrived "accumulative" march, as the violins and wood-winds bustle about in the mazes of an ever-increasing complex of orchestral tapestry and sonorities. There are definite traces of rather wild, dance-like gaiety, which seem to float across the scene and disappear. Presently, the first part of a fascinating march tune (in 4/4 meter) enters unobtrusively at the onset—in the ninth measure—played by the oboe; then this portion of the theme is tossed about the orchestra from instrument to instrument, and it is not revealed in its entirety until some time later—in the 71st measure, *leggieraménte*—in a light, nimble manner. Then it is played by two clarinets in unison. Here is the theme as the two clarinets play it completely for the first time. It is transposed to concert, or actual, pitch for the convenience of the reader.

Presently, the completed theme is heard in the full orchestra; it grows in strength from its modest beginning and eventually achieves an irresistible climax. Thus, it shines in full splendor, bursting forth from the brass, together with the entire orchestra, in a restless and overpowering movement. This movement sounds as though it were a mighty paean of victory, though no one knows exactly just what the victory was. At any rate, here is an outstanding adaptation of the march form and spirit into an exalted symphonic mold.

MELODY AND HARMONY

If rhythm is the heartbeat of music, melody is its soul. It is the melody that projects much of the emotional message of the music to the average listener; it is the melody that he will most likely perceive first and remember longest. True, in modern, sophisticated dance music, the rhythm seems at times to overshadow the melody. It is also true that in some contemporary music, lyrical melody no longer plays quite so important a part as it did in the music of the Classic and Romantic periods. Despite all this, as far as most music lovers are concerned, nothing quite equals the power of melody to captivate the human heart. Actually, it is not necessary to separate rhythm and melody, since the two more often coalesce. As we sing the melody, we are unconsciously responding to its rhythm. Melody must have a basis of rhythmic design. If we change the rhythm, the effect of the melody is changed as well. Of course, rhythm can exist without melody.

Melody might here be defined as a succession of musical tones arranged in a tuneful and meaningful pattern. We do not "get" the melody or tune until we have intuitively grasped the meaning and "feeling" of the pattern as a whole. We saw, in rhythm, that haphazard or isolated beats bear no special significance for us. It is only when these beats are arranged in definite, easily perceived patterns or "line" that they evoke in us an emotional response. So, too, with melody. A single tone tells us little. It is only when one tone leads to another, and still another, when each takes on a definite relation to the pattern as a whole, that a melody assumes fullest significance.

In this process, everything depends upon the ease with which the listener perceives the connection of the tones and the meaningfulness of the pattern. Folk songs and popular tunes usually present no problem. Their pattern is often so simple that everybody "gets it" after the first hearing. Other types of melodies may demand more expertness on the part of the listener. Still others are like the forbidding individuals whom one has to meet again and again before they reveal their true character. How often it happens that through repeated hearings we grasp the significance of a melodic pattern which in the beginning altogether eluded us! As we continue to listen to great music, we broaden our experience and increase our comprehension of tonal relationships: we become more and more sensitive to their implications until a melody of Brahms, Debussy, or Stravinsky may come to be as lucid and comprehensible as one by Stephen Foster.

We have called melody the soul of music. Harmony is said by many to be its body, its substance. The harmony supports the melody and serves as a background or foundation for it. Sometimes the two are felt as one.

Harmony, in its simplest form, consists of chords; these are clusters of tones, sounded simultaneously within the rhythmic pattern, which provide an accompaniment for the melody—the "UM-pah-pah" that the left hand sounds on the piano while the right hand plays the tune. Notice, in the following example, the first phrase of *Long, Long Ago,* how the cluster effect of the chords and the curvilinear quality of the melody are indicated in the two staves of "adapted" piano music:

Just as in a painting, the background harmonizes with and brings out the figures in the foreground, sometimes even revealing them in a new light; thus, harmony may color and enrich and even define the melody.

Various chords have distinctive "personalities" of their own. Composers often use harmonies as complete entities in themselves, as does Debussy. Some chordal combinations are sweetly harmonious, giving an effect of rest, fulfillment. Others are harshly dissonant, clangorous, restlessly seeking completion. There are chords softly sensuous and caressing—how well Wagner knew their secret! Others are grim with foreboding, or feverish and unstable. Suffice it to say that harmony not only adds support and a third dimension to melody, but also, through its chords, reinforces the rhythm. In our system of music, melody does not exist without rhythm. Nor does it often exist without harmony, either actual or implied. Even when we whistle or sing only the melodic line, we may "hear" the harmonic background in our imagination. Harmony is also produced by the incidence of several contrapuntal parts.

Like melody, rhythm, tone color, and form, harmony has a special contribution to make to the total musical effect. In a love song, where the melody holds the center of the stage, the harmony is likely to remain discreetly in the background. In the dance, where rhythm is important, the harmony often comes to the fore as percussive, thumping chords. In religious music, the swelling harmonies of organ and choir attain prime importance in creating the lofty, devotional mood.

Courtesy The University Prints, Newton, Mass.

MADONNA DELLA SEDIA

Raphael

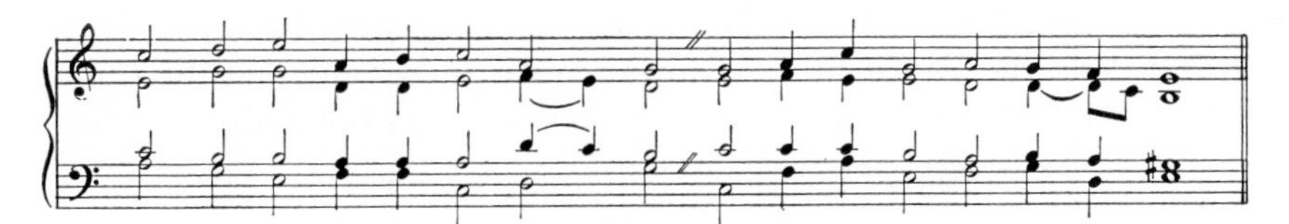

These are the original words of the *Pilgrim's Hymn:*

> He brings forth bread out of the ground,
> And joyes the heart of man with wine;
> Makes face with oil cheerful to shine,
> With bread man's heart upholdeth sound.

To sing the hymn is the only way to savor and experience its peculiar qualities. Henry Ward Beecher, the great Boston preacher (1813 to 1887), had this conviction:

> Singing is that natural method by which thoughts are reduced to feelings more easily, more surely and more universally than by any other (means) . . . In the singing (of Hymns) you come into sympathy with the truth as you perhaps never do under preaching of a discourse. There is a provision made in singing for the development of almost every phase of Christian experience . . .

We quote a modern viewpoint, with permission, from Dr. Norman Vincent Peale:

> The singing of a great hymn is one of the most potent medicines in the world. It fills one with the feelings of peace, gratitude, tranquility and hope; and it enables one or many to express these same sentiments at the same time, through the added beauty and benign qualities of inspired music and inspired poetry.

Since hymns were intended for performance by the entire congregation, they had to have tunes that could be readily remembered and easily sung; they had to function within a limited vocal range, to avoid rhythmic complexities and wide skips, to reflect faithfully the devotional spirit of the poetry, and to follow the metrical cadence of the words in so direct a fashion that the congregation would stay together in the singing. The words and music of a great hymn are reflective of their inherent qualities of spirituality and religiosity. One has only to recall *A Mighty Fortress Is Our God, Christ Lay in the Bonds of Death, Jesu, Joy of Man's Desiring, Lead Kindly Light,* and *Onward Christian Soldiers* to realize that these restrictions did not hamper the form but, on the contrary, aided it. It is suggested that you listen now to *A Mighty Fortress Is Our God,* which served as a battle hymn of the Reformation.[3]

The melody proceeds in short units and then pauses. We call these melodic units phrases, the stopping places, cadences. When words are set to music, the melody is molded, as it were, to the metrical patterns

[3] Or use the *Doxology.*

of the verse; thus both become indissoluble parts of a greater whole. Notice, too, that the rhythm moves in regular pulses and that the chords supporting the melody are simple but sonorous and full-bodied, as befits music of steadfastness and solemn purpose.

There is in the composition of a great hymn the same necessity for consummate musicianship and real inspiration, as there is in the creation of a great symphony. The difference in mere size is not of significant importance. Compare if you will, a small Vermeer painting with a large Veronese work.

There must have been some unknown and untutored "geniuses" scattered among the southern Negroes during the 19th century, for they blessed the world with a number of imperishable hymns, *Negro Spirituals.* These great hymns of the past are folk hymns in the truest sense. They simply "grow'd like Topsy," spontaneously and mysteriously. They express, through singularly original words and music, the deepest religious emotions and feelings of a transplanted and enslaved people, "seeking hope and redemption and final rest with their God." These hymns are free expressions of religious feelings. There are also spirituals of praise and exultation, as well as those used for Biblical "storytelling."

This free outburst of religious joy and happiness is not "funny," or "entertaining." True, the Negroes do have such songs, and they are often based upon some Biblical or religious reference; but they are not to be confused with the deeply religious spirituals, though the outward expressions of them may be misinterpreted. Then, too, some of the "modern" Negro spirituals, with their outright amusement value, are merely musical and religious travesties, as are jazzy gospel hymns that are manufactured on the tin-pan alley assembly line.

A few of the more outstanding and familiar among the Negro spirituals are: *Deep River; Were You There; Go Down Moses; Heav'n, Heav'n, It's-a-Me, O Lord; Roll, Jordon, Roll; Swing Low, Sweet Chariot; Steal Away; Follow the Drinking Gourd* (one of the secret "communication" songs of the slaves);[4] *The Old Ark A-Moverin' Along* (a Biblical narrative); and *Nobody Knows the Trouble I've Seen.* A portion of the latter appears below in a rather unusual version. Note its lovely melody, the characteristic use of syncopation, and the colorful chromatic "barbershop" harmony.

[4] See Carmer, *America Sings,* music by Edwin John Stringham (New York: Alfred Knopf, 1942).

Courtesy The Museum of Modern Art and the Architect

COONLEY HOUSE, RIVERSIDE, ILL. Frank Lloyd Wright

Frank Lloyd Wright is one of the great geniuses of architecture. The so-called "Prairie Houses" of his early period created an original and epoch-making stage of American architecture. His middle period, of which the Coonley House is an excellent example, is marked by the introduction of Romanticism and the beginnings of functionalism, in which decoration must contribute to, and fit into, the basic engineering structure as a complete entity. The building and its use must also blend into its natural surroundings. The word "home" thus assumes new and important significance.

Some Negro choirs are very ingenious in harmonic improvisation, once they have thoroughly learned the tune. It is significant that the southern Negroes have contributed two of the original and basic art forms our country has given to the artistic culture of the world—spirituals and jazz. Others are the skyscraper, the detective novel, and the so-called prairie-house architecture of Frank Lloyd Wright.

Of remote antiquity are the Hebrew chants, a living art in the synagogue handed down from one generation to the next for over 2,000 years. From its birthplace in the Near East, the Hebrew chant has retained some characteristics akin to those of the religious song of the Arabic world. At the same time, however, through the constant interchange between

Greek and Hebrew culture at the beginning of the Christian era, it assimilated many elements of Greek music. To these were added, centuries later, the influences stemming from close contact with Western European culture. Listen to the *Kaddish* (Chant for the Dead), a particularly impressive example of Hebrew religious song. Better known is *Kol Nidre,* the traditional melody that the Jews of Spain sang during the terrors of the Inquisition, and that has become part of the solemn service for the eve of Yom Kippur, the Day of Atonement. Note the exotic, almost oriental character of the melody of *Kol Nidre,* whether in the original violoncello solo, Op. 47, by Bruch, in subsequent violin or orchestral versions, or in the original traditional "hymn" or "song." Observe how the tones of the melody seem to "lean and press" upon the next to follow, and note the strange, underlying scale out of which the melody is formed and which seems to intensify this very feeling of "pressing insistence." In addition to the effect of the very nature of the oriental-like scale foundation, these emotions are further intensified by the frequently descending tendency of most of the musical figures in the piece. This is a common and successful form of musical expression used to secure a definite emotional response from the listener. This effective "falling" line may be found in paintings and etchings, such as the DESCENT FROM THE CROSS by Rembrandt and LAMENTATION by Rubens, and in a great number of memorial sculptures, such as Augustus St. Gauden's GRIEF, with its deep shadows and falling lines (Chap. 10), and also Michelangelo's PIETÀ (Chap. 23), to cite but a few. The motif of the "Weeping Willow Tree" was a favorite among the tombstone carvers following the Revolutionary War, and it is not difficult to know why.

Owing so much to ancient Hebrew and Greek cultures, the Christian service naturally included the heritage of both in its early liturgical chants. These religious, songlike expressions evidenced themselves in many styles and directions until codified in the latter part of the sixth century, when they became known as Gregorian and Roman chants. They remained the predominant form of European sacred music throughout the Middle Ages. Actually, they have continued quite unchanged right into our own day, and are still a regular part of some church services.

In many Protestant services, where these very old chants are adapted or put into new versions, they are called Plainsong or Plainchants rather than Gregorian Chants.[5] In the Protestant Episcopal Church, a distinctive type of chant having a fixed, non-symmetrical design, rhythmically metri-

[5] For instance, in the *Official Choir Service Book of Choral Responses of Morning and Evening Prayer* (London: Novello & Co., Ltd., 1902) and in the Official *Hymnal of the Protestant Episcopal Church of America* (New York: Church Pension Fund Pub., 1943) there is not a single mention of Gregorian chants. They are called "Plainsongs." So there is here an authoritative distinction made between Plainsongs or Plainchants and Gregorian chants.

cal, with four-voiced harmony, single or double form, and usually tonal rather than modal is used in the singing of canticles. These are called Anglican chants. The single form of the chant is shown below; the double form would be merely two such similar structures, naturally permitting more extended melodic and harmonic opportunities, though never departing from the fixed form. Note the asymmetrical "three measures succeeded by four measures" design. The following is an excellent example of the single Anglican chant, composed by Joseph Barnby, an English composer-organist (1838–1896). The liturgical words and music are especially emphasized by a system of stress accents or "pointing," by temporal elongation, or by both.

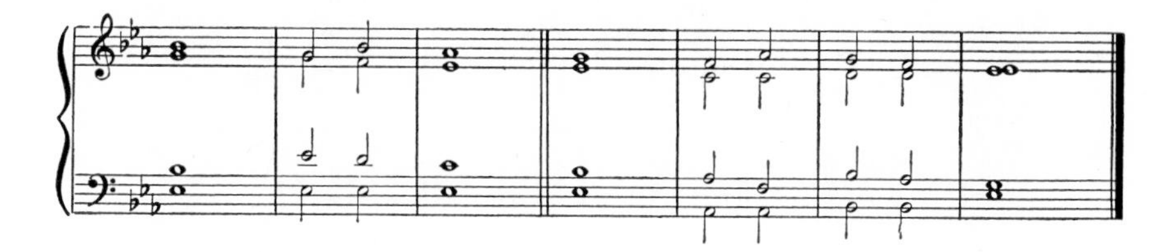

The Gregorian chant, so named after its sponsor, Pope Gregory the Great (540?–604), is quite different in character from the Anglican chant, though the Gregorian chant is likewise often called Plainsong or Plainchant. The general character of the melodic line (traditionally unisonal, though often heard in four or more voiced harmony) is set by a combination of tradition and Papal fiat. But the immediate nature and behavior of the vocal line of the chant is determined by the sacred words to which the music is set, and the chant is never mensurated or barred. This combining of words with music is wonderfully wrought in the traditional Gregorian chants, so that there is no feeling of apparent strife of "transient primacy" of either. Emphasis is secured by raising or lowering the pitch, by stress or accent, or by a typically oriental and ancient Hebrew trait of temporal elongation—stretching out the duration of time—by means of the interpolation of florid passages on a single word or syllable; traditional Gregorian chants never use two or more syllables or words on the same note or melody tone. Many of these embellished passages—*fioituri*—are very beautiful. (See the reproduction of an old medieval church manuscript in this Chapter.) The vocal line of a chant, instead of being built upon our major or minor keys, is founded upon one of the eight scale-like medieval church modes. Based upon, or greatly influenced by, the ancient Greek modes, these were largely determined by the character of the music of the Byzantines and ancient Hebrews. There was some passing secular influence, too, such as the use of the pentatonic scale, chromatics, etc. The internal rhythms of Gregorian chants are very intricate and subtle, requiring the services of specialized experts to explain them. The

Courtesy The Metropolitan Museum, New York

A MEDIEVAL MANUSCRIPT

time values of the tones are relative, not absolute or fixed. Listen to some of the characteristic Gregorian chants, such as those sung by the Monks of Solesmes: the *Kyrie* and *Gloria* from the *Ordinary* of the Mass, or the *Tenebrae Factae Sunt*, which describes the death of Christ on the Cross.[6]

From about 800 A.D. to about 1750, composers of Western Europe experimented with combining two or more (some up to 30!) voices or distinct melodic lines to be sung simultaneously. From these early beginnings, an art style of polyphony, especially in religious music, grew and reigned supreme in Europe for centuries, though the harmonic secular music continued the while. This last was especially true for instrumental social dance music, music for the lute solo, or lute with the voice. The history of this colorful instrument, which still continues in derived and adapted forms, is hidden in the unknown thousands of years B.C. This instrument provided either melodic or harmonic music, or sometimes both. The "Golden Age of Choral Music" of this European contrapuntal art came largely, but not exclusively, through the Netherlands and Italian schools of composers, Willaert, Orlando Lassus, Vittoria, Leo, Arcadelt, Okeghem, Palestrina, the greatest Roman master of sacred music (1524–1594), and many others. This polyphonic movement came to its later fruition in the sacred and secular forms of music of the immortal Bach, with Handel close by.

Of late years, there has been a sort of renascence of this contrapuntal art in a period marked, in one direction, by extreme uses and experiments in harmonic systems, of cacophonous music, and, in the other direction, by renewed emphasis upon the application of the classical tempers and the revival of the contrapuntal arts. In this sense, it is difficult to know whether the late Arnold Schönberg was the culmination of the contrapuntal schools of the sixteenth and seventeenth centuries or the forerunner of a new era.

Polyphony comes from the Greek *poly* (many) and *phone* (sound). Polyphonic music or, as it is more often called, *contrapuntal* music, is distinguished from the prevailing style of more recent times called *homophonic music*, where only one or several voices carry the principal melodic line or lines, while the rest of the voices combine together into a harmonic or chordal background.[7]

[6] It is suggested that the listener hear the records of the Gregorian chants prepared by the Monks of the Abbey of Saint-Pierre de Solesmes which were approved by Papal assent. They are issued by the Victor Company as *Masterpiece Album M-87* (78 R.P.M.). The qualifying terms often applied to chants, such as *Gregorian, Anglican, Ambrosian, Gallican, Byzantine, Parisian, Roman, Cologne,* etc. allude to the derivation or historical origin or prototypes of the chant. Dr. Willi Apel, the musicologist, observes that what is generally meant by the present-day use of the term "Gregorian Chant" is a *Cantilena Romana,* or *Roman chant.*

[7] For those who are interested in pursuing the subject of the various types of religious music in greater detail, we suggest the following references: See the topics "Gregorian Chants," "Anglican Chants," "Modes," "Plainsong," etc. in *Harvard Dict.*

Now listen to the *Sanctus* and *Gloria* from the MASS FOR POPE MARCELLUS, by Palestrina. Note how smoothly the vocal texture flows along, how beautifully the different voices are blended and contrasted. There is, in the music of Palestrina, the note of true religious fervor, of contemplation and purity of true vocal character, that marks it as one of the high points in the history of religious music.

In the early sixteenth century, Luther, in carrying through his religious reforms, substituted for the intricate polyphonic church music that could be performed only by a choir of highly trained singers simple hymn tunes with texts in the vernacular that the whole congregation could sing —the *chorales*. In the course of nearly two centuries, a rich chorale literature sprang from the very roots of the Lutheran faith and music. This was Bach's heritage, and upon it he developed the structure of his unsurpassed art. The spirit of the chorale permeates his church cantatas, chorale preludes, hymns, and sacred songs, and receives its ultimate expression in the ST. JOHN and ST. MATTHEW PASSIONS.

A cantata is a choral work of comparatively modest dimensions, either sacred or secular. Bach, as Cantor of St. Thomas' Church, wrote cantatas for each Sunday of the church year, in addition to works for festivals and special occasions. The cantata was generally named after the principal chorale upon which it was based, and consisted of several sections for solo voices, with ensemble numbers, choruses, and chorales interspersed, accompanied by organ and groups of instruments. The form was extremely flexible, and varied with the particular resources at the disposal of the composer. Bach's bold harmonies, rich counterpoint, and melodic invention reveal the inherent beauties of such a famous chorale as *Jesu, Joy of Man's Desiring*, from CANTATA NO. 147, with its quality of naive joy and faith. Note that the theme in the following excerpt of this

---

of Music and *Oxford Companion to Music;* Ch. II and VI of *Oxford History of Music;* Grove's *Dictionary of Music and Musicians,* Vol. II, p. 234; Donald N. Ferguson, *A History of Musical Thought,* Ch. 3 and 4 (New York: F. S. Crofts & Co., 1935); Paul Henry Lang, *Music in Western Civilization,* Ch. V (New York: W. W. Norton & Co., 1941).

The following books might afford still greater detailed and extended information as indicated by their titles: A. Z. Idelsohn, *Jewish Music: Its Historical Development* (New York: Tudor Press, 1948); Peter Gradenwitz, *The Music of Israel* (New York: Norton, 1949); Leonard Ellinwood, *The Hymnal* 1940 *Companion,* (Protestant Hymns) (New York: Church Hymns Corp., 1949); Wallace Goodrich, *The Accompaniment of Gregorian Chants* (Boston) a translation of *Methode d'accompagnement du plainchant* by Niedermeyer and d'Ortigue (Paris: Novello Ewer and Co., 1905); and a book of very unusual mixtures of Gregorian and Anglican chants with secular and ethical as well as sacred words, *Social Worship,* edited by Stanton Coit and Charles Kennedy Scott, Vol. II (New York: Macmillan Co., 1914); Robert M. Stevenson, *Patterns of Protestant Church Music in America* (Durham: Duke Univ. Press, 1953); James Moffatt, *Handbook to the Church Hymnary* (London: Oxford Univ. Press, 1935); R. G. McCutchan, *Our Hymnody* (New York: Methodist Book Co., 1937); Paul Nettl, *Luther and Music* (Philadelphia: Muhlenberg Press, 1948).

chorale, in the form of a *Chorale Prelude*—an instrumental transcription and development of the choral work—is in the tenor part, immediately above the bass part.[8]

From the preluding (extemporization) of the organist, when he announced to the congregation the chorale to be sung, arose the art of the instrumental *Chorale Prelude,* in which the tune of the hymn to be sung served as the basis for the improvisation.[9]

Most imposing of Bach's religious works are the PASSION ACCORDING TO ST. MATTHEW, and above all others, the B MINOR MASS. Although the MASS was written to the Latin text of the Catholic service—Bach sent the *Kyrie* and the *Gloria* to the Catholic Elector of Saxony, whom he hoped to make his patron—the music is quite Lutheran in outlook and spirit. Indeed, some of the material was borrowed by Bach from his earlier Protestant masses and cantatas. In addition, the use of an orchestral accompaniment makes the MASS impractical to perform during the regular church service. It is a festival piece.

The B MINOR MASS represents the apex of the polyphonic tradition which had nurtured generations of church composers. Yet, beside the "seraphic harmonies" of Palestrina, so close in spirit to the placid or smiling Madonnas of Raphael, the B MINOR MASS appears, like Michelangelo's Sistine Chapel frescoes, stern and rugged, a song of strength attained through suffering and grief. The sorrow of Christ, the soul tormented and longing for union with God, salvation, and life eternal—those were the issues that fired the imagination of Bach. Listen to the soaring phrases of the *Credo;* the mournful *Crucifixus,* in which the reiterated descent of the bass and the motive of grief in the strings give a vivid tone painting of Christ's suffering on the cross; the joyous and hopeful

[8] It is earnestly suggested that the listener hear both the original choral form of the chorale and the instrumental versions for organ, piano, or orchestra.

[9] See Chapter 28 for fuller exposition of the chorale prelude.

Et Resurrexit; and the massive polyphonic architecture and deeply religious expression of the *Sanctus.*

ADDITIONAL SUGGESTIONS FOR LISTENING[10]

So profound an impulse as the religious naturally made itself felt in many works of the great composers that were not intended for use with any actual church service. Although Richard Wagner (1813–1883) wrote for the opera house, certainly the *Prelude* to LOHENGRIN, depicting the descent of the Holy Grail from Heaven, breathes a spirit of devotion and faith. Celestial harmonies steal upon the air from out the highest register of the strings. Gradually the music descends, growing ever richer in color; the crescendo builds unerringly toward an overpowering climax; now the "Grail" theme is intoned in all the sonorities of the brass, as though to envelop the worshipper in its splendor. Then the music fades away.

Religious legend receives an even more mystical expression in Wagner's *Prelude* to his last work, the festival drama, PARSIFAL. Here the motives symbolize the Last Supper of Christ with his Apostles, the lance that pierced the side of the Saviour, the "Good Friday Spell," the "Grail" theme based upon the *Dresden Amen,* and the powerful "Faith" theme. Wagner believed that art could have as purifying an influence on the souls of men as religion, and that the music drama could achieve the same spirituality as the rites of a church. (Traditionally, there is no applause during the performance of PARSIFAL.)

Among symphonic movements, the *Finale* of Mendelssohn's "REFORMATION" SYMPHONY builds up to a stirring climax on the Lutheran hymn *A Mighty Fortress Is Our God.* Mendelssohn was the composer who rescued Bach from the neglect into which the old master had fallen in the half-century after his death. It was fitting that in this "REFORMATION" SYMPHONY, Mendelssohn should have returned to the chorale, which had been so vital an inspiration to the great master Bach, the composer whom Mendelssohn admired above all the others.

One of the most eloquent expressions of the religious spirit in all music is to be found in the exalted setting of Schiller's ODE TO JOY in the *Finale* of Beethoven's last symphony, the NINTH:

> Praise to Joy, the God-descended Daughter of Elysium!
> Ray of mirth and rapture blended, Goddess, to thy shrine we come . . .
> O ye millions, I embrace ye, with a kiss for all the world.
> Brothers, o'er yon starry sphere surely dwells a loving Father.
> O ye millions, kneel before Him; World, dost feel thy Maker near?
> See Him o'er yon starry sphere, o'er the stars enthroned, adore Him! [11]

[10] Further discussion of religious music may be found in Chapters 9 and 28.

[11] The English translation generally used in performances in this country is by Natalia Macfarren (London: Novello and Company, Ltd.; the H. W. Gray Company, New York, agents). Printed by permission of the publishers.

DYNAMICS AND TEMPO[12]

We have seen how the composer uses rhythm, melody, and harmony to achieve his musical effects. Closely associated with these elements is *dynamics* (from the Greek *dynamis*, "power" or "strength"), the element of power and volume in music. From the whisper of the muted violins to the thunderous jubilation of the *Et Resurrexit* chorus of the B MINOR MASS, music is capable of innumerable gradations, each producing a different emotional effect. Every emotion expressed in music calls for its appropriate dynamic scheme. Needless to say, the effect of the other musical elements is interwoven with the dynamics in closest degree. If we were to play the *Triumphal March* from AÏDA in a subdued tone, the entire effect would be changed, even if melody, harmony, and rhythm remained the same.

The broader emotional implications of loudness and softness are fairly obvious. A mood of triumph calls for brilliant sonority and volume. Sadness needs subtle shadings within a more subdued range of volume. The emotional meaning of the music imposes the proper dynamic scheme.

In ordinary speech, the word "dynamic" pertains to energy, accent, and action. It is evident that in an art such as music, which moves forward steadily through time, the driving force behind that forward movement is of paramount importance. It is for this reason that rhythm, which regulates the forward flow of the music, is so basic a factor. But rhythm depends upon the recurrence of accent, and accent usually depends upon playing certain beats louder than others. Thus, rhythm is the most potent application of the principle of dynamics in music. Pitch, harmony, tone-color, time extension or anticipation, and even rests may also affect or determine rhythm.

Dynamics enters into the general emotional projection of the mood in a larger sense. Music, like motion pictures, exists as a series of impressions following each other in rapid sequence. Music impinges upon the listener a ceaseless alternation between movement and rest. Between the points of rest, the movement must be inexorable. We shall see in subsequent chapters how melody, harmony, rhythm, and form all contribute to this supremely important forward drive. Dynamics plays an exceedingly important part. The music undulates forward between a succession of high points or climaxes. Graphically, this movement resembles the rising and falling line of a series of mountain peaks. The dynamics helps to regulate this steady undulation. The music accumulates force in a gradual *crescendo* (kree-SHEN-doh). It often reaches a peak or climax. Then there is a gradual decrescendo (DEE-kree-SHEN-doh), or lessening of volume; until we begin to approach the next climax.

[12] See also similar essays on topics of technical matters in several standard musical dictionaries and encyclopedias.

In subtler fashion, dynamics enters into the composition as a means of highlighting the musical line. By varying the volume of sound, the composer achieves an effect analogous to what the painter achieves with the brush. The musical canvas at times is painted in broad vigorous strokes; at others in vague outlines and subtle shadings. Through changes in dynamics, the composer is able to achieve a tonal equivalent of perspective and depth.

It is plain that dynamics exists in two aspects: first, as a number of distinct levels of tonal volume; and second, as a series of nuances from one volume to another. These are part of the very life stream of the music. The principal dynamic indications, going from very soft to very loud—arranged in a *crescendo*—are:

pianissimo (*pp*): (pee-ahn-ISS-ee-moh) very soft
piano (*p*): (pee-AHN-o) soft
mezzo piano (*mp*): (MAY-tso pee-AHN-o) medium soft
mezzo forte (*mf*): (MAY-tso FOR-tay) medium loud
forte (*f*): (FOR-tay) loud
fortissimo (*ff*): (for-TISS-ee-moh) very loud

Closely associated with dynamics is the element of *tempo*, or speed, in music. This, too, has a large part to play in the total effect. A light-hearted dance requires a brisk tempo. A stately march goes at a moderate rate of speed. A song of sorrow is slow. Changes in mood require corresponding changes in tempo. The principal nuances are *accelerando* (ah-chell-er-AHN-doh), a gradually increased tempo resembling a quickened pulse which produces an effect of emotional intensification upon the listener; and *ritardando* (ree-tahr-DAHN-doh), a retarding or slowing up that suggests a slackening of emotion.

The reader should distinguish between *meter* and *tempo*. *Meter* broadly refers to the time unit measurement; specifically to the number of beats in the measure—duple, triple, quadruple, sextuple, and so forth. *Tempo* refers to the speed at which the meter is counted. Thus, a fast waltz and a stately minuet are both in triple meter; Chopin's *Funeral March* and the *Battle Hymn of the Republic* are both in quadruple meter.

Tempo is subtly connected with dynamics in building up to the climax. If the music, as it grows louder, also increases in speed, there will be marked accumulation of forward driving power. We shall frequently meet the two associated in the brilliant climax at the end of a piece, as in the *Finale* of Mendelssohn's "ITALIAN" SYMPHONY. Conversely, the *ritardando* is frequently used in conjunction with the *descrescendo* to produce the fadeout or dying-away effect so often met at the end of a composition, as in the *Prelude* to LOHENGRIN.

A climactic effect of another kind is achieved by having the *crescendo* accompanied by a marked increase of intensity, giving an effect of great dignity and strength. The climactic entrance of the final theme in the *Triumphal March* from AÏDA illustrates this. Also, the final climax in Franz Liszt's LES PRÉLUDES shows how effective a *crescendo-ritardando* can be.

The principal tempo indications, going from very slow to very fast—arranged in an *accelerando*—are:

largo: (LAHR-go) broad and stately
adagio or *lento:* (ah-DAHJ-eeoh) or (LEN-to) slow
andante: (ahn-DAHN-tay) fairly slow
andantino: (ahn-dahn-TEE-no) a little faster than *andante*
moderato: (mah-der-AH-toh) moderately fast
allegretto: (al-lay-GREHT-toh) fairly fast
allegro: (ah-LAY-gro) fast
vivace: (vee-VAH-chay) lively
presto: (PRESS-toh) very fast [13]

[13] One of the most scholarly expositions in the English language on the functions of the elements of expression in the art of music is Donald N. Ferguson, *On the Elements of Expression in Music* (Minneapolis: University of Minnesota Press, 1944). For a clear and understandable text on the use of Italian terms in music, consult Karl W. Gehrkens, *Music Notation and Terminology* (New York: Laidlaw Bros., Inc., 1914); Louis C. Elson, *Elson's Music Dictionary* (New York: Oliver Ditson Co., 1905); W. L. Hubbard, ed., "Musical Dictionary," in *The American History and Encyclopedia of Music* (New York: Irving Squire, 1910); Percy A. Scholes, *et al.*, *The Oxford Companion to Music* (New York: Oxford University Press, 1950).

THE FORGE Goya

5 The traditional folk song: music in work and play

The two previous chapters have shown the solemn occasions of our daily living, and how music plays an important part in them. Since the daily living of the average person is not devoted to formal ceremonies, music and the other fine arts are not so restricted. All persons are free to express personal and mundane feelings through art.

Long before music was practiced by trained composers and performers, songs and dances flourished among people as a vital, expressive folk art. From these humble sources grew a magnificent literature that together with folk tales, myths, and sagas constitutes an enduring monument to the inexhaustible creativeness of the human race.

Folk song is, in the truest sense, a product of the national group from which it springs. A singer or fiddler in some hamlet makes up a song. His neighbors like it and sing it over and over, changing a phrase here, adding a verse there. In the course of time, the song spreads to the neighboring village, then through the entire countryside. It is polished by many talents and passed down from one generation to the next until it becomes the essential spirit of the over-all national song and speech.

In a broader sense, however, folk song transcends national boundaries. It is the musical equivalent of the folk tale; it has that quality of simplicity and universality which sums up human experience in a few strokes, as do the myth and legend. The folk song springs out of man's primal need to give personal expression to his feelings—devotion to home and fatherland, rapture in love, sadness at parting, and awe of death. It addresses itself straight to the heart in a language that all mankind understands.

We may well begin our listening with a romantic folk ballad which exists in hundreds of versions in our own country and in the north country of England, where the song was probably born—*Barbara Allen.*[1] The poem, as taken from an ancient ballad in PERCY'S RELIQUES, relates how William Green lay dying for love of Barbara Allen, and how she, hard-hearted, repulsed him until it was too late. The song—words or music—is known in some 200 versions, 150 in our northeastern and southeastern states alone. The ballad is considered by many musical authorities to be among the most beautiful of English airs. In his STUDIES IN MODERN MUSIC the eminent author and critic, Sir William H. Hadow, calls it a perfect example of the power of simplicity, "with each strain more beautiful than the one before, till it culminates in the perfect sweetness and pathos of its final cadence." The same melody is repeated with each different stanza, a type of narrative or ballad song that is called *strophic*. The melodic symmetry of *Barbara Allen* is emphasized at the end of every other line of poetry by a distinctive rhythmic and melodic device used on the rhymed words "swel-in'," "Allen," "dwell-in'," and again on the word "Allen." A note of small value on the accented first beat of the measure—in this instance, a sixteenth note, as the two flags on the note stems indicate—is followed by, and slurred to, a note of longer value, off the beat.

[1] Essential listening for this chapter includes *Barbara Allen, Marlborough, Home on the Range, John Henry, Drink to Me Only with Thine Eyes, Comin' through the Rye.* The other songs mentioned, plus additional favorites, may be used as time permits.

The following collections of folk songs have proved to be of value: *Twice 55 Songs, The New Brown Book* (Boston: C. C. Birchard & Co., 1930), four-part songs; *The Golden Book of Favorite Songs* (Chicago: Hall and McCreary Co.), four-part songs; *America Sings* (New York: Knopf, 1942); Carl Sandburg, *The American Songbag* (New York: Harcourt, Brace) lyrics, legends, and some melodies; B. A. Botkin, *A Treasury of American Folklore* (New York: Crown Publishers), tunes only; Downes and Siegmeister, *A Treasury of American Song* (New York: Knopf, 1943), voice and piano; Charles and Ruth Seeger, *Folk Songs U.S.A.* (New York: Duell, Sloan & Pierce, 1947), voice and piano; Florence H. Botsford, *Botsford Collection of Folk Songs* (New York: G. Schirmer, 1930-33), Vol. I—N. and S. America, Asia, and Africa, Vol. II—N. Europe, Vol. III—S. Europe, words and music. Other folk-song collections will be named later.

Although this rhythmic figure is rather universally used, it was probably associated in this particular instance with a little hopping step "off-the-beat" dance found in the country dances of North England. In Scotland, this "off-the-beat," or syncopated, figure is so commonly used that the device is usually known as the "Scotch Snap." This "Scotch Snap," along with the equally universal pentatonic scale, is found in primitive and cultivated music all over the world. The music of the American Indian abounds with the use of this rhythmic figure, where the device is associated with a peculiar "shifting" movement, and a sudden rise or fall of the voice. Swiss yodelling employs the "snap" in the sudden change of the voice into the falsetto, and vice versa. Our own popular ragtime jazz music abounds with this syncopated "Scotch Snap" figure adapted a bit. The music of our own great composer of Celtic descent, Edward MacDowell, is replete with this "Snap," as is *Comin' through the Rye.*

A rather unusual Scottish version of *Barbara Allen* has been chosen to illustrate the point of discussion. It is based upon a five-toned, pentatonic scale, similar to an ancient Javanese scale.[2] Sing this beautiful folk song of *Barbara Allen* so as to savor its peculiar flavor and quaint beauty. Note, also, that the tune consists basically of the repetition, with word accommodations, of an eight measure (four lines of poetry) period, each period in turn being divided into two phrases of two lines of poetry for each, marked off by the words we have already indicated. Further, the internal design may be seen in the simple analysis shown on the music engraving itself. This song is an excellent illustration of how a simple folk song is able to communicate the maximum amount of beauty with the minimum amount of musical means.

Here are two of the many verses, and the music of *Barbara Allen:*

All in the merry month of May,
When green buds were a-swellin',
William Green on his death bed lay,
For love of Barb'ra Allen.

He sent his servant to the town,
To the place where she was dwellin',
Saying, "Love, there is a call for you,
If your name is Barb'ra Allen."

[2] If interested in the acoustical bases of non-harmonic scales, of which the pentatonic is one, consult Herman Helmholtz, *Sensations of Tone,* translated and edited by Alexander Ellis (New York: Longmans, Green & Co., 1930), pp. 514 to 519, and more especially pp. 518 and 519 on pentatonic scales—for advanced students. For others, read topic "Pentatonic Scales" in Grove's *Dictionary of Music* (Philadelphia: Theodore Presser Co., 1918). The pentatonic scale basis of this particular version of *Barbara Allen* may be simplified by saying it consists of the tones d—e—(no f)—g—a—(no b)—c—and the duplication of the octave d. Observe that the scale is minus the third and sixth steps. It is not known just how old this music is or just what changes, if any, have been wrought upon the original version down through the centuries.

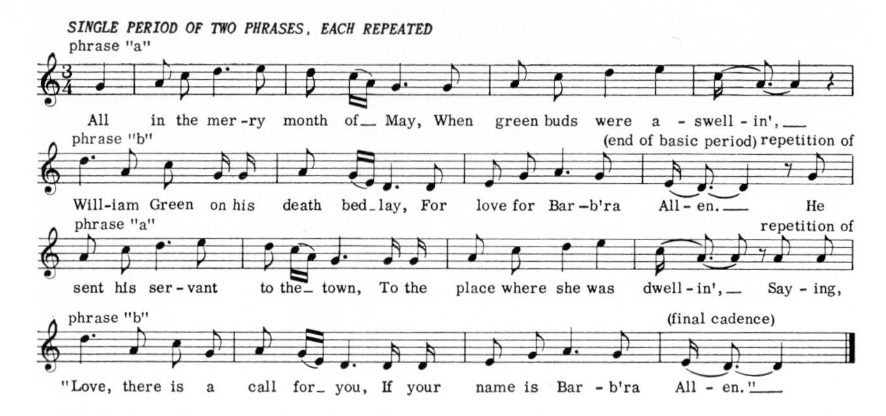

The following jolly drinking song exemplifies the changes in fortune that a song may undergo through the centuries, and how easily a melody may transcend the barriers of language and race. The melody appeared first in the Holy Land during the period of the Crusades as the *Chanson de Mambron,* in praise of a French knight who lost his life near Jerusalem. It is sung today in Egypt and Arabia and is mistakenly considered to be an old Egyptian folk tune. The "Mambron" in the title changed to "Malbrooke," and the song ultimately became the popular French *Malbrooke s'en va-t-en Guerre,* sung in England as *Marlborough Is Going to the War;* for a time, it was supposed to have referred to the famous English general, the Duke of Marlborough (John Churchill). Then, for some time, the song apparently disappeared—until Marie Antoinette of France heard a nursemaid sing it to the Dauphin. She liked the tune and soon the melody became enormously popular in Paris. It was also a favorite tune of Napoleon, and even Beethoven used it in his potboiler, the "BATTLE SYMPHONY," written to commemorate Wellington's victory at Vittoria. Eventually, after all these transformations, the onetime pious lay of the medieval Crusader ended as *We Won't go Home Until Morning:*

A glance at the varied and almost inexhaustible treasury of American folk songs reveals an untold number that disclose varied and widespread foreign influences.

A great number of our folk songs and dances naturally show British influence. Some of these have preserved their original states more perfectly than the same songs extant in Britain, according to the English musicologist, Cecil Sharp.[3] French, Negro, and Creole influences are most strongly shown in the folk songs of the Louisiana region, and French in the states bordering central and eastern Canada. Spanish influences are shown in the songs of the southwestern states from southern Texas to California. The German and Moravian influences have been felt in Pennsylvania, North Carolina, and later in Wisconsin. Scandinavian evidences are centered mostly in Minnesota, northern Wisconsin, and Michigan. Jewish songs are heard in and around New York City. In addition to scattered groups in the East, there are rather large settlements of Bohemian and other Slavic peoples in the central states, especially parts of Iowa, where Dvořák wrote some of his greatest works. American Indian songs may be found almost everywhere.

Throughout the country, we have our own folk songs. These are songs that could not have originated anywhere else, among any other people, or at any other time.

One of the best of the Negro slave "communication" songs—songs that conveyed secret messages to other slave groups—is *Follow the Drinking Gourd.* The "drinking gourd" is the constellation of the "Great Dipper," which indicates the direction of travel or escape; the time signal is shown by the "first quail calls" and "when the sun comes back"; then follow, in subsequent verses, detailed instructions of travel—"where the river ends," "between two hills," "the great big lake," where it "flows into the stream," and so forth. These instructions are given in symbolical terms so that only those "in the know" could translate the song. The slaves used many such communication songs, which have since been largely accepted on their literal rather than figurative meanings, the latter being rapidly on the way to oblivion.

There are many songs and folk tales relating the fabulous exploits of Paul Bunyan, David Crockett, Daniel Boone, Pecos Bill, Rip Van Winkle, Casey Jones, and others.

Another folk song, with a strongly mixed background, became the outstanding song of the Spanish–American War, and has since taken its proper and permanent place among our native folk songs: *There'll Be a Hot Time in the Old Town Tonight.* This song has an interesting, frontier-days origin. According to one story, snatches of it were sung, in simple form, by miners in Cripple Creek, Colorado, in the late 1800's. The "musical director" of the local Palace Theatre, Theodore Metz, heard the tune and fashioned out of it a song for one of his many shows. The song made an especial hit, and when the Cripple Creek company of the Colorado National Guard went off to the Spanish–American War, they took it with them. Other men in other outfits soon picked up the tune, and "Hot Town" became an important part of our native folk song litera-

[3] Consult Cecil Sharp, *English Folk Songs from the Southern Appalachians* (New York: Oxford University Press, 1932).

ture. Although some claim for Metz the original composition, the folk-like genesis is more typical of the times.

A folk ballad of a frontier tragedy is *Frankie and Johnnie,* of which there are now some 300 known versions. As with many ballads, it is partly factual history and partly pure fiction. The story concerns Frankie Baker and her "two-timing" lover. The scene is St. Louis around 1890. When Frankie discovered Johnnie's faithlessness, she "shot him dead." She was tried for murder and acquitted. The ballad was picked up by the local people in the streets and then followed Frankie across the country, as she travelled to Oregon, where she died at the age of 75.[4]

For the so-called "work songs" we have devised three basic categories that might well be borne in mind while studying the confusing and almost endless number of such songs that may be heard everywhere.

The first category is the largest. The songs in this category are composed by "tin pan alley," the professional "songsmiths." Though these creators may have had little or no personal experience in manual labor, they do bring a great deal of amusement and enjoyment to a large number of listeners, just as the traveling minstrels, trouvères, and troubadours did about eight hundred years ago. It has been said that a few of these "vaudevillian" songs might be adopted in the future as folk songs. *Dixie* was once a minstrel-vaudeville song, and *The Star Spangled Banner* was a "hard-working" German drinking song before the English made it first into a music hall type of song, then into *To Anacreon in Heaven,* to which tune Francis Scott Key set his immortal patriotic poem.[5]

The second category includes the next largest number of songs. These are hybrid songs conceived by capable—often professional—individual poet-musicians, which might be adopted for actual use by those who do the manual labor. Some of these songs apparently missed the boat as far as original intent and ultimate uses are concerned—for example, *I've Been Working on the Railroad.* Track maintenance gangs are not known to sing this song. On the other hand, the song *has* become popular. Cowpunchers on the range sing such professionally composed songs as *Old Man River, Sweet Adeline, Down by the Old Mill Stream,* and *Home, Home on the Range.* This last-mentioned "composed folk song" is discussed in the next chapter. We are still a young country and it may be that a few of these professional- or amateur-composed songs will some day be considered just as "anonymous" and "traditional" as *Barbara Allen* or *The Star Spangled Banner.*

It is the third category of folk songs with which we are most concerned

[4] For details on *Frankie and Johnnie,* see *Time,* Jan. 21, 1952; and for the story of *A Hot Time in the Old Town,* see Malcolm Wyer and Edwin J. Stringham, *The Lookout* (Denver Public Library, Jan. 1927), Vol. 1, No. 1.

[5] See Oscar G. Sonneck, *The Star Spangled Banner* (Washington, D. C.: Government Printing Office).

in this chapter, although these songs are least in number. These songs originated among actual laborers, and were created to use during periods in which they sought relief from fatigue and boredom. Often, these songs are "borrowed" from other types of labor. Such songs as these are real, typical work songs, for example, *Low Bridge, Everybody Down* (*On the Erie Canal*). Compare this with a foreign song of the same type, *The Volga Boatman.* How different in spirit they are!

A group exerting physical force can work more efficiently with the aid of some medium which provides a rhythmic time signal.[6] These signals may be inherent in the melodic figure, tempo, or rhythmic elements of music, or in the grunts or stresses of syllable, during a chant-like fluctuation of a tone. Anyone who has travelled on the Mississippi River or frequented seaports has very likely heard such use of "sound," ranging from a primitive "a-UP," "a-UP" to the employment of a regularly repeated rhythmic (musical) figure or a real song itself. A song, any other piece of music, or any art work, does not come into being automatically. Some single individual has to conceive and create an art work. The initial conception of a song may continue as is, or it may be altered by an indefinite number of subsequent musicians or poets, who, in turn, remain as completely unknown as the original creator. This is what is meant by the term "genuine traditional folk song."

Then, too, one might hear groups of laborers sing almost anything that one of their number might lead off with, and such songs include popular ditties, old folk songs, patriotic songs, and even gospel hymns—anything to sing that will relieve their tired muscles or bored spirits. It is not at all unusual to hear groups of road builders in the South spring full-voiced into folk or gospel songs, with "barber-shop" harmonies, jazzed-up rhythms, or a gay, antiphonal, responsive or "Hallelujah" type of singing. Northern counterparts might well be the *Sweet Adeline* or *Down By the Old Mill Stream* kind of song, with extemporized responses and harmony.

Since there are not a great many genuine work songs in the United States, it might be well to inquire into some of the reasons for this condition. Especially when one recalls that almost every European country can boast of many occupational work songs. It is true that our country is less than 200 years old, and the culture is largely inherited or directly transported here with few changes from other shores. There has been, consequently, insufficient elapsed time, real inspiration, or proper "soil" and sustenance for indigenous folk songs to be created, nurtured, and adopted by our people as their own. Second, our country has whizzed

[6] The Stevens Institute of Technology, Hoboken, New Jersey, has made important discoveries concerning the use of music during work and rest periods. The results of some of these experiments are available in monograph form or in professional periodicals. See also Charles Diserens, *The Influence of Music on Behavior* (Princeton Univ. Press, 1926), Max Schoen, *The Effects of Music* (New York: Harcourt, Brace, 1927). Consult Mursell, *The Psychology of Music* (New York: Norton, 1937).

through the transitional stages of pioneer, agrarian, and rural life, into the present-day phase of urban settlements and industrialized environment. We have taken our adopted, and not yet amalgamated, citizens with us on the same wild roller coaster ride! Thus, genuine songs of the various sociological stages are not very plentiful. Also, our "laboring population" has not remained intact or in sizeable concentrated groups working and living in comparative "isolation"—as obtains in Europe and elsewhere—for a sufficient length of time to produce different art types peculiar to each basic kind of labor. In America, the various crafts are rarely maintained in definite groups or passed on from one generation to the next. In securing certain desirable individual advantages, *some* of the more traditional and national art expressions have been temporarily sacrificed.

There has been also little of the essential *contemplative, creative* leisure time, social and aesthetic maturation, or gradual social development in which a great national art can be born. Great art needs the proper creative "soil," a few highly trained geniuses, many talented creators, and a large number of intelligent appreciators.

There has been little genuine musical idealization of industrialized and mechanized labor. It might be remarked, that, from an artist's vantage point, one does not discover such song expressions as: "My Versatile Turret Lathe Is So Like a Spouting Spring," "The Song of the Universal Milling Machine," "The Happy Hum of the Spindles," or "Oh, Ride With Me in My Overhead Crane"—or something equally "aesthetic." Somehow, man does not love a machine, at least not enough to sing sentimental songs about it!

Now to cite a few native folk songs that are identified with certain types of labor. From the northern and northwest states come the lumberjack and shantyboy tunes, such as *The Logger's Boast, The Shantyman's Life, Driving Saw-logs on the Plover,* and, of course the folk songs inspired by Paul Bunyan. From the southern Appalachians come mining and hillbilly tunes, such famous songs as *Down in a Coal Mine, The Ground Hog, High Up on Old Smoky, Cumberland Gap,* and the very beautiful and soulful *Shenandoah.*[7] Concerning transportation and the early railroads, there is the saga of *Casey Jones, The Train That Never Pulled In, Mama Have You Heard the News.* Cowboy songs of the traditional kind, rather than the made-to-order radio types often heard today, are distinctive: the day-herding songs with loud refrains, sometimes based on cattle calls, used to keep the herds moving; and the night-herding songs with soft and soothing "dogie" refrains to quiet the herd: *The Old Chisholm Trail, Git Along Little Dogie, Goodbye, Old Paint, Bury Me Not on the Lone*

[7] The Duke University Press is publishing a set of seven volumes entitled *The Frank C. Brown Collection of North Carolina Folklore.* Volume IV, Music of the Ballads, and Vol. V, Music of the Folksongs, were prepared by Prof. Jan Philip Schinhan, formerly of the University of North Carolina.

Prairie, and, of course, *Home, Home on the Range* and *Get Along Cayuse, Get Along.*[8] At round-up time on the western ranges, there is a constant shift of cowpunchers from one outfit to another. Sometimes the trekking is hot and monotonous. To while away the time and banish lonesomeness, the cowpoke sings songs of the range and bits of popular ditties learned during evening "sings" around the campfire. Sometimes, as in *Get Along Cayuse, Get Along,* he sings about his pony, mixing in other memories, as the words indicate:

> We're leaving here, and we're going there,
> Get along cayuse, get along;
> We're leaving here, and we're going there,
> Get along cayuse, get along.
> There ain't no water and there ain't no shade,
> There ain't no beer and no lemonade;
> But I reckon somehow we'll make that grade;
> Get along cayuse, get along,
> Get along cayuse, get along.

The music is descriptive of the lazy, loping motion of the horse and the spirit of the rider.

Home, Home on the Range is very much loved among cowpunchers, though there has been quite a controversy concerning the song's origin. It had long been considered a genuine traditional folksong, until some time after 1905 when the origin was established—at least to the satisfaction of the Music Publishers' Protective Association. The words were written by a Dr. Brewster Higley of Beaver Creek, Smith County, Kansas, in 1872; the music by Dan Kelly of Gaylord, Kansas. The original words were published in the *Smith County Pioneer* in 1873 and entitled "My Western Home."[9] Nevertheless, the song will be generally considered a traditional folk song, and, of course, "in the public domain."

Here are melody, verse, and refrain of *Home, Home on the Range:*

[8] For words and music of the *Cayuse* song, along with other North American folk songs and folk legends, including *John Henry,* see Carmer, *America Sings,* with music by Edwin John Stringham (New York: Knopf, 1942).

[9] See *Saturday Evening Post,* May 7, 1949.

Notice the simple design of the song: the first two lines of music (Part One) are for the Verse, the third and fourth lines (Part Two) for the Refrain. The first line of music may be dubbed phrase "A," the "assertion"; the second, phrase "A" repeated; the third, contrasting phrase "B"; and the fourth line of the music, phrase "A" restated. Note also the unifying character of the repetition of the musical figures for the words: "Oh give me a home," "Where seldom is heard," and (fourth line), "Where seldom is heard." Observe the refreshing touch given by the contrasting change of melody for the first part (line three) of the Refrain, and, finally how the restatement of the very first phrase (line one), together with its final and closing cadence (end of line four), ties the song firmly together.

Among real work songs, *John Henry* is of the very essence of American folklore. Its legend concerns the protest of the pioneer railroad track-layers against the encroaching steam hammer. John Henry protested so much that he was drawn into a contest to see whether he or the machine could drive more spikes in a given time. Through determined and valiant effort, our hero won; but the great effort cost him his life. John Henry's fighting spirit lives through the song. How descriptive of the spike-driving action the song is! Note the emphasis upon a descending musical figure which recurs about five times and which eloquently shows how well John Henry is wielding his heavy sledge hammer, driving in the large iron rail-spikes. Observe the emphatic last three notes. Discerning listeners will note that the strange scale foundation of the melody and harmony consists of only four different tones, not counting the repetition of the octave: D–F-sharp–A–B–(D) or downwise, as it is in most of the song, D–B–A–F-sharp–(D). This tune of "John Henry" is worth much further inquiry and discussion on the part of the reader. Here is the song *John Henry;* sing it!

Close in spirit to folk songs are folk dances, practically all of which display the same general characteristics noted in Chapter 2—simple, catchy tunes, symmetrical and uninvolved phrase structures, and vigorous rhythms. The boundary line between the music of the song and the dance is indeed a tenuous one, and many folk dances were sung long before they were played for dancing.

Of the various idioms we have absorbed as is or adapted for our use, those coming from the British Isles seem closest to our own, and that is naturally to be expected. The melodies are usually forthright, simple, without superfluous accents, and in conformity with the simple patterns of the everyday idioms of our common language. Many of them make use of the old medieval church modes—or pentatonic scales.[10] Thus, many of these tunes are centuries old. Some of the virtues just pointed out may be clearly and easily observed in the well-balanced and symmetrical structure of the tune, which many authoritative musicians have proclaimed to be one of the most beautiful in English folksong literature, the traditional tune to which Ben Jonson wrote his lovely lyric, *Drink to Me Only With Thine Eyes.* Here it is; sing it![11]

Notice that each musical unit, or line of four measures of music, involves two lines of the lyrics and that the melody has a halt, or cadence, at the

[10] See articles on "Modes," "Scales," and the like in Grove's *Dictionary of Music and Musicians.*

[11] From the songbook, *Twice 55 Brown Book* (Boston: C. C. Birchard and Co.). Used with the permission of the publishers.

end of each unit. A *musical cadence* is a melodic and harmonic formula imparting the feeling of a lingering, avoided, partial, or complete close. For instance, compare the feeling that the cadences impart to the four-measured phrase at the word "di-vine" at the end of line three, with that at the end of line four with the words "change for thine." The former leaves one with the feeling of incompleteness, of a partial halt, of a half close quite like the effect of a comma. The latter gives one a feeling of completeness and finality, as though the song had—as it does in fact—come to its final cadence. Now note that the music of the first "A" line or phrase is exactly repeated in the second. At the last chord of line two—called the "up take" or, more exactly, the *anacrusis*—on the word "The" under the capital letter "B" there appears a contrasting phrase. Then follows phrase "A" restated after the contrast, which serves to unify and tie the work closely together. This is a *ternary form*. This A–B–A structure is a basic one in all the fine arts, for it best satisfies our aesthetic desire for balanced variety within unity—a result of securing a symmetrical disposition of the internal elements of compositional design, whether it be painting, sculpture, poetry, dance, prose, or music. With these ideas in mind, study the picture, THE TOMB OF GIULIANO DE' MEDICI by Michelangelo.

We have already pointed out the rhythmic figure peculiarly known as the "Scotch Snap." According to some authorities, this was originally characteristic of an old national dance, the *Strathspey*, but later found its way into all kinds of tunes with astounding frequency. Notice, for example, how often the figure of the "snap" occurs in the next song we shall study, *Comin' through the Rye*. (The words are by Robert Burns). We have indicated these figures with a star. There is still some dispute as to whether the word "rye" refers to a geographical location, a brook, or the cereal grass—the last being most likely. The poem by Burns was "dished up" from an older, less traditional lyric. Here is *Comin' through the Rye*. Sing it!

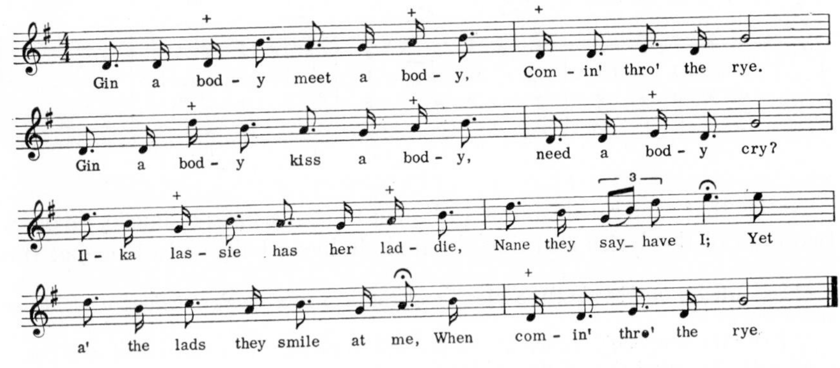

Gin a bod - y meet a bod - y, Com - in' thro' the rye.
Gin a bod - y kiss a bod - y, need a bod - y cry?
Il - ka las - sie has her lad - die, Nane they say_ have I; Yet
a' the lads they smile at me, When com - in' thro' the rye

Courtesy The Metropolitan Museum of Art

THE TOMB OF GIULIANO DE' MEDICI Michelangelo

ADDITIONAL SUGGESTIONS FOR LISTENING[12]

The poet Thomas Moore played an important part in creating the folk songs of Ireland, most familiar of which are: *The Harp that Once through Tara's Halls, Believe Me if All Those Endearing Young Charms,* and *The Last Rose of Summer.* Other Irish folk songs are popular in this country, especially *The Wearing of the Green* and *Londonderry Air. Greensleeves* is a lovely English ballad, mentioned by Shakespeare in his play, THE MERRY WIVES OF WINDSOR. Vaughan Williams has made a very beautiful set of symphonic variations on this tune.

The German folk song has much in common with its English counterpart: regular formations, forthright melodies, simple lyricism, homely sentiment, and not much superfluous ornamentation. The songs are often sentimental and of much emotional fervor, yet there is something solid and foursquare about them. German folk tunes are usually in simple rhythmic patterns, in which vigorous duple and triple meters predominate. A favorite type is the Ländler, the peasant song and dance in three-four time that was the ancestor of our waltz. *Ach du lieber Augustin* is an example.

The folk songs and folk dances of the German people have had a great influence on the composers of that nation. We saw in Chapter 4 how Bach was indebted to the chorale and what effect that form and style had on his music. In a similar way, the national heritage echoes through the works of Haydn, Mozart, Beethoven, Schubert, Schumann, Mendelssohn, and Brahms, to name only a few, all of whom either used folk songs outright in their works or translated the spirit and idiom of them into their compositions. Some German traditional airs are almost as well known in this country as in Germany, for example: *Der Tannenbaum,* the melody of *Maryland, My Maryland; Die Lorelei;* and the student song, *Gaudeamus Igitur.* Brahms used this last song in his ACADEMIC OVERTURE.

French folk songs have the cool, limpid quality generally associated with the Gallic spirit. Many of the songs are of great antiquity and bear marks of the influence of the troubadours and trouvères and early church music of the twelfth and thirteenth centuries. Many of the children's songs are well known in this country: *Sur le pont d'Avignon; Il Etait un Bergère; Ah! que Vous Dirai-je, Maman;* and the two most popular songs of the Revolution, the *Carmagnole* and *Ça Ira.*

Italian songs, so often gay and impetuous, reflect the mercurial temperament of the South European—the passionate abandon to the mood of the moment. Neapolitan street songs, Venetian boat songs, Sicilian serenades—these stem from an intensely musical people to whom song is almost as natural as speech. *Santa Lucia,* a good example of the Neapolitan folk style, has attained much popularity in America.

Spanish folk songs reflect the dance rhythms of the various provinces—*seguidillas, jotas, boleros, sevillanas,* and the like. Outstanding are the passionate *flamenco* songs, the idiom of the Spanish gypsy, a rhapsodical, ornate vocal melody which bears the character of an improvisation. Such a song is

[12] Consult a good record catalog for additional folk songs of all nations.

Saetas, one of the flamenco songs used in Holy Week festivals. The rapturous incantation of the voice over the steady beating of the drums and the blare of cornets releases a flood of emotion as only the greatest of music is able to do.

Russian folk music is variegated, including idioms from Greek, Slav, Tartar, Norse, Gypsy, German, Finnish, Mongolian, Middle Eastern, and Oriental sources, as well as tribal songs of the Caucasus and melancholy tunes of the Siberian Steppes. Cossack dance songs are extremely rhythmic and vigorous, as are the Ukrainian peasant tunes. Many currents meet in the richly imaginative folk music of central, northern, and southeastern Europe—Scandinavian, Slavonic, Gypsy, Magyar, Czech, Teutonic, Croat, Bulgar, and Turkish. In particular, the gypsy's rhapsodical improvisations have become a real part of western music. The highly ornate melodies of the gypsy fiddlers and singers, passing abruptly from one mood to the next, with capricious rhythms and emotional fervor, are outstanding.

Courtesy Brown Brothers

STEPHEN FOSTER

6 The composed folk song

When one is enjoying the singing of such old favorites as *My Old Kentucky Home, Funiculi, Funicula, La Paloma, Sweet Adeline, Home, Sweet Home, Old Folks at Home* and many others, it is seldom realized that these songs did not spring spontaneously from the simple folk. These songs were, in fact, composed by professional or semi-professional song writers.[1]

Between the traditional folk song of the previous chapter and the so-called "art song" of the succeeding chapter stands what is known, somewhat paradoxically, as the composed folk song. Certain composers are so thoroughly imbued with the spirit of their people and their native

[1] Essential listening for parts one and two of this chapter includes: *America the Beautiful, Old Folks at Home, Lullaby* by Brahms, *The Birch Tree* (Russian folk song used in *Finale* of Tchaikovsky's FOURTH SYMPHONY), part of a *Fiji Island Ritual Song, The Girl I Left Behind Me, Vicar of Bray, Galician Folk Song,* and *Rondino* by Beethoven (arr. by Kreisler). Other works mentioned may be considered optional.

musical idioms that their original creations become beloved and generally used among the people to such an extent that they become traditional folk songs. Dvořák, Sibelius, and Grieg, to name but a few, have often been charged with using actual traditional folk-song material, when, in fact, these melodies were their own.

The composed folk song, being the product of a single creative personality, allows for wider ranges of subject and technical perfection than does the traditional folk song. Although well within the universality and simplicity of the folk style, it will nonetheless bear the marks of more personal expression. Then, too, when the composer is a musician of background and training there is a smoothness of style, a subtlety of effect, and an objective design in his compositions which would normally not be present in true folk art.

The composed folk song crystallizes within the span of a single career and through the medium of a single personality what it might take generations of spontaneous growth to achieve. In any case, the composed folk songs of a nation are as much a part of its national lore as the pure folk songs. Indeed, it is entirely possible that had the composers of such songs as *O Sole Mio, La Paloma, My Old Kentucky Home,* and *America the Beautiful* lived some ages ago, they might have been gifted village singers and players who had some part, however small, in the creation of true traditional folk music, just as we now do not know the architects of most of the great Gothic cathedrals of Europe.

One of the great names in composed folk songs of our own country is Stephen Foster (1826–1864), whose songs have become part of our heritage. Foster's songs actually represent the essence of the American folk idiom in music. His was a fresh, self-tutored genius which has touched the hearts of his countrymen as no other. Some of his songs, *Old Black Joe, Swanee River, My Old Kentucky Home, Massa's in de Cold, Cold Ground, Jeanie with the Light Brown Hair,* to name but a few, are deeply loved and sung throughout our country and beyond.

Similarly, how much poorer the English-speaking peoples, especially those of America, would be without the immortal song by Sir Henry Bishop, *Home Sweet Home,* the words of which were penned by John Howard Payne. There are also anthems which, through long association, have become symbols of patriotic emotion. Here the intimate folk style is superseded by a vigorous martial tune. Typical of these are *America,* or *God Save the King,* an old English song attributed to one of a number of composers; the *Battle Hymn of the Republic,* a hymn tune for which Julia Ward Howe wrote the words we now use; Rouget de Lisle's *Marseillaise,* written overnight in the heated atmosphere of the French Revolution; *Rule Britannia* by Thomas Arne; and the hymn of the old Austrian Empire, *God Preserve Our Gracious Emperor,* by Joseph Haydn, one of the very few national anthems composed by a great music master. *America the Beautiful,* follows. Sing it! [2]

The words of *America the Beautiful* were written in the summer of 1893 by Katherine Lee Bates (1859–1929), a professor of English at Wellesley College in Massachusetts. The poem was inspired by her first trip to the top of Pike's Peak in Colorado and first appeared in print on July 4, 1895. Several different tunes were tried with the words; finally the people of the country made their own choice of the beloved hymn tune "Materna" by an American composer, Samuel A. Ward (composed in 1882). This was a musical setting for a sixteenth-century Latin verse with the familiar opening, "O Mother dear, Jerusalem, when shall I come to Thee?"

Now that the listener has "experienced" the song aesthetically, let us note some of the architectural and musical features. Note that this song divides itself into two distinct principal parts or musical "periods," thus the designation as a two-part, or binary, form (we have marked the two periods as Part I and Part II on the musical score). The first part begins at the onset and ends with the word "plain"; the second part, beginning

[2] From the *Twice 55 Brown Book* (Boston: C. C. Birchard and Co.). Used with the permission of the publisher.

with the word, "America!" ends with the final measure on the word "sea." Notice further, that each of these parts is also divided into two still smaller sections, styled "phrases A, B, C, and D," in order to accommodate the lines of the poem and at the same time lend character and balance to the music. Of course, the listener must be interested to discover some of the melodic and rhythmic figures that recur many times and which add to the feeling of unity and coherence in the melody. Note the melodic and rhythmic figures accompanying the words "O beautiful," "spacious skies," "purple mountain," "majesties," "America!" "crown thy good," and finally "with brotherhood." Observe the symbolic as well as climactic functions of the unisonal passage in the final line, "From sea to shining sea." Have you also noted the march-like character imparted to the song by the rhythmic figure which is repeated so often, such as accompanies the words "O beautiful," "for spacious skies," and so forth?

As one might expect, the nineteenth-century composer's approach to folk music was more romantic than that of contemporary musicians. Often the simple folk idiom was dressed up with all the tricks of the composer's craft. Characteristic among such are the HUNGARIAN RHAPSODIES of Franz Liszt in which the native tunes were treated in a dramatic and brilliantly technical manner. Some of these virtuoso piano piecs have received a new lease of life in brilliant orchestral arrangements. Listen to his Second, Sixth, or Twelfth *Hungarian Rhapsody*, and note how a highly charged romantic composer can treat his folk material.

Many great composers betray a startling closeness to their native soil. Many melodies of Schubert and Brahms, for example, evince the characteristics of true German folk song. Brahms carried the folk spirit into some of his original songs so successfully that at least two of them have become virtual folk songs—the universally loved *Lullaby* and the delightful *Vergebliches Ständchen* (Futile Serenade) with its lilting tune.

The *Lullaby* by Brahms possesses a number of characteristics that are associated with the folk-song genre. Its simple and straightforward internal structure consists of four phrases, each four measures in length with a salient cadence at the close of each. Sincere and deep feeling is presented with simplicity, and the elements of unity, contrast, and symmetry are unpretentious. Sing it first, then study it. Here is the music for the *Lullaby* by Brahms and the words of a recent translation:

Sleep my darling, good night!
Sweet dreams come to thee;
Flowers red and white
Will thy soft pillow be.

So when morning shall break,
With the lark's song on wing;
Our good Lord will thee wake,
His kind blessings to bring.

It will be noted that this simple song by Brahms, which already functions as an international, composed folk song, has the same sort of basic binary internal architecture as was noted in *America the Beautiful.* There are two periods or parts—marked I and II on the music—having two phrases each: a and b, and c and d. Note here also that certain melodic and rhythmic figures recur more or less identically, and serve to unify and balance the song.

As a further challenge, listen to the *Finale* of Peter Ilyich Tchaikovsky's FOURTH SYMPHONY. In this work, the composer uses the following Russian folk song, *The Birch Tree,* with its curious phrase structure of three (not four) measures each, with a cadence at the end of each phrase and a repetitious design that is almost primitive. Here is the music of this *traditional* folk song:

Compare the original *Birch Tree* song with the more sophisticated *arranged version* of it that Tchaikovsky uses in his symphony. Note the regular two-measure phrase, as compared with the three-measure phrase in the folk song; also observe that the repetitions of the Tchaikovsky version are even more exact than in the original. Here follows the folk

Courtesy National Gallery of Art, Kress Collection, Washington, D. C.

THE VISITATION WITH TWO SAINTS Piero di Cosimo

This picture is vertically divided into two symmetrical parts corresponding to the two balanced periods of the musical form known as two-part or binary. Note the over-all pyramidal form and the flowing, wavelike contour described by the heads of the four figures.

song as used in the *Finale* of the FOURTH SYMPHONY, as it first appears in the tenth measure played by the wood-winds:

Upon this tune and a contrasting theme is built a mighty symphonic development. The movement advances precipitously. Powerful fanfares in the brasses pronounce the ominous "fate" motive, heard at the onset of the first movement. The work builds up, the gay opening theme returns, and the mood of triumph is powerfully reaffirmed. The movement closes in a blaze of color and animation.

THE ARCHITECTURE OF MUSIC: EXPRESSIVENESS OF FORM AND DESIGN

There are several hypotheses apropos of the metamorphosis of music. Although these have not yet reached the force and dignity of theories, they purport to explain the genesis of the art of music.[3] These explanations are intended to include all types, from the simplest aboriginal music or germinal idea up to and including the very complex structures, internal organization, and designs of contemporary compositions such as those by Sessions, Sibelius, Berg, Schönberg, Křenek, etc.

In spite of our doubt in some of these theories, one must remember that there is a body of knowledge pertaining to each one of the fine arts, part of which is common to all the arts. Some of this information which arouses interest and gives the listener certain clues to follow, such as historical background, principal themes and general structural designs, instrumentation, literary programs and poetic content, and so forth, should be given *prior* to the initial hearing; and some of these, such as the principal themes, instrumentation, and structural outlines, may also be unostentatiously indicated again *during* the first hearing. Almost all other technical matters may best be considered *after* the listening experience. Many mentors, however, prefer to have some first hearings of a new work free and uninterrupted after the factual matters are given. After this sort of listening experience, the ideal would be to listen to the music once again in aesthetic contemplation, with all technical matters relegated to the subconscious.

Obviously, much care is to be exercised in the proper learning of technical matters; they should be used only when positively indicated for the enhancement of listening enjoyment and intelligent appreciation. The author has endeavored to include academic matters only in appropriate dosages, at the proper moments, and in the necessary places. Neither the acquisition of specialized skills nor the possession of technical knowledge can substitute for creative listening. Lack of academic knowledge or of musical background should never deter a prospective student from a formal appreciation class, though homogeneous grouping is to be desired, where possible. By the same token, the possession of a great deal of such technical knowledge should excuse no one! A first-rate course in music appreciation is as highly specialized and as important as any other course in the music curriculum. As a matter of fact, for most students the course in appreciation should be the *synthesis, realization, and artistic projection of all the formalized courses!*

While most of the emphasis so far has been upon the listening process, it is fully realized that there are other legitimate purposes in listening. Thus, listening to a composition for reasons of detailed study of its craftsmanship and other technical factors sometimes presents different problems, with different

[3] C. Hubert H. Parry, *The Evolution of the Art of Music,* first published by Kegan Paul, London, in 1893. Latest edition is 1930, published by D. Appleton & Co., New York.

approaches. Usually separate hearings are made for such different purposes, for it is only in aesthetic contemplation that the musical composition stands out as a finally consummated work of art.

We believe that we can best convey initial ideas on the expressiveness of architectonic designs and forms by first relating experiences derived from witnessing some non-public performances of the Navajo Indian *Corn Dance.*

The dancers and the "orchestra"—four or five players of native flutes and percussion instruments, and chanting "leaders"—formed themselves and, at an unseen signal, began the dancing and chanting. The latter consisted almost entirely of nonsense syllables, explosive yells, grunts, and chanting, simultaneously pitched in the low bass line of the "braves" and in the high, shrill sound of the squaws and children. The dancers conformed to definite designs, determined almost entirely, it seemed, by the nature of the changing steps and character and plan of the dancing. At times the women and the children danced quite differently from the braves, and in distinctively separate formations. When the dance steps changed in pattern, the instrumental music and the singing also varied. All these activities were well-established tradition which everyone in the pueblo learned from early childhood.

A chanting section or figure may be shown phonetically and simulatively as follows: The capital letters or syllables indicate strong or explosive accents; repeated letters or syllables represent a drawn out sound, usually descending in pitch like a deflating bag-pipe and becoming softer, ending in a sort of mumbling sound.[4] Sometimes the "falling slide" ends in off beat, explosive yells, not unlike the first few measures of Stravinsky's *Le Sacre du Printemps* ballet:

HI–ya–ya–ya–ya–ya–HO, etc.

This would be repeated, over and over again, until the dancing steps changed; then something like this might follow:

HO–ya–ya, HO–ya–ya, HO–ya, HO–ya, HO, etc.

Again the steps and dance change, and with them the chant (a descending *glissando* on "YOW"):

e–YOW–ki–ya–YOW–ki–ya–ho–ya, YOW–YOW–YOW, etc.

Thus, the ritual and the dance find a salient and conspicuous form of emotional and religious expression in vocal designs or patterns. Very

[4] Apropos of the descending or "falling" tendency of the melody, compare this American Indian example with the Russian folk song used by Tchaikovsky in the *Finale* of his FOURTH SYMPHONY (in Part One of this chapter); and the *Gambling Song* of the Rogue River (Oregon) Indians, quoted in an article on *American Indian Music* by Charles Sanford Skilton in the *International Cyclopedia of Music,* Oscar Thompson, ed. (New York: Dodd, Mead & Co.).

often in our "civilized" dance music—the reverse process holds true, the dance is derived directly from the music. This may also be noted in our American "barn dances" (square, round, reels, and a number of other allied types); in such works as the brilliant orchestral "stunt," Ravel's *Bolero;* and in especially composed ballet music where the basic starting point and inspiration for the choreography is derived from the previously composed music.

Perhaps the American Indian has come pretty close to the ideas of the "modernists," as we have just observed in the description of the *Corn Dance.* In it the chanting consisted of many repetitions of a phrase or figure; then another new idea was used, and so on to the end of the dance. The succeeding illustration is one consisting of repetition plus an alternating figure, which also might undergo repetition. This is a Fiji Island ritual song and dance.[5]

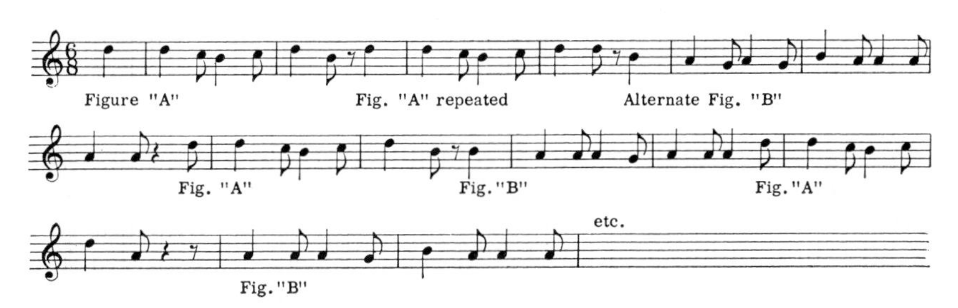

Note how the feeling of variety is expressed through the two musical figures, marked "A" and "B" and their alternation; observe also how the feeling of unity with variety is achieved through the repetitions and contrasts of "A" and "B." Later in the dance, other alternations are introduced. These alternating responses are also used in the Maypole dances of the twelfth century *Kalendas Mayas,* the spring celebrations and festivals of the troubadours in Provence, France, and almost identical dances of our own times. Here, too, the leader in the ring sings the changing verses and the ring-around-the-Maypole dancers repeat the constant chorus. One may see a likeness of expressive design between the dances of the *Kalendas Mayas,* the rondeaux of the French lyric poet François Villon, and the instrumental and vocal rondos, rondels, or roundelays of a later day. (See Shakespeare's MIDSUMMER NIGHT'S DREAM, Act II, Scene 2, for such a circular, or round-dance.) Ever since the time of Karl Phillip Emanuel Bach, the third son of Johann Sebastian Bach, the *rondo,* consisting of a reappearing theme with contrasting musical material between recurrences of the principal theme, has long been a favorite and expressive design for the last movement of various forms. The design lends itself admirably to the expression of spirited moods. Doubtless, this is brought

[5] C. Hubert H. Parry, *op. cit.*

about by the traditionally lively spirit of the principal (recurring) theme, plus the pleasure gained by recognition of the familiar principal theme against the contrasting sections.

Similarly, tragedy in a play is greatly intensified when properly and artfully contrasted with moments or scenes of wit, humor, or farce. After all, the dramatist, the dramatic and narrative poet, and the composer have much in common in their art. All three seek to arouse desired feelings, moods, emotions, and empathy, and to manipulate and play upon them at will.

The reader may recognize a few of these old expressive musical designs based upon "dressing up" a single theme to result in a satisfactory, extended work. Ravel's *Bolero* has already been mentioned. Perhaps some listeners are more familiar with *Liebestraum* by Franz Liszt; the SYMPHONIC ETUDES for piano, by Robert Schumann; VARIATIONS ON A THEME BY PAGANINI for piano, by Brahms (Rachmaninoff wrote a RHAPSODY on the same theme); the *Finale* to the FOURTH SYMPHONY by Brahms; and Vaughan Williams' FANTASIA ON A THEME BY TALLIS.

We have already met with a binary musical pattern in the *Lullaby* by Brahms; in some of the movements in the Bach SUITE IN D MAJOR; the songs *Get Along Cayuse, Get Along* and, less obviously, *America the Beautiful.* Here is another which should cinch the point, an old Irish tune that became popular during the early American Colonial days. It lay fallow until the Civil War, when it became known as "*The Girl I Left Behind.*" [6] Sing it and note the catchy liveliness and march-like spirit of the music. Then see if you can discover, through listening alone, the two main parts. Observe the recurring melodic and rhythmic figures that impart unity, coherence, and character to the tune as a whole, and note the similarities and differences in the smaller phrases:

The most widely used of all basic musical designs is the one fashioned in three distinct parts, the *ternary form.* This ternary design has already been pointed out in connection with the English folk song, *Drink to Me Only with Thine Eyes* and the cowboy song, *Home on the Range.* Follow-

[6] Refer to *The New Blue Book of Favorite Songs* (Chicago: Hall and McCreary), p. 221.

ing are another English tune, *The Vicar of Bray,*[7] and one from the mountains of old Galicia in the northwestern part of Spain.[8] Note what a satisfactory feeling of variety, contrast, and balance this ternary "Assertion-Contrast-Reassertion" scheme imparts. Observe the climax in the next-to-the-last measure of the second (contrasting) line of music. The musical illustrations shown are elementary because of their naive, folk-song character. However, the underlying structural elements in the greatly enlarged and cleverly contrived compositions of later days are essentially similar to these and other expressive and unpretentious folk tunes of long ago. Here is *The Vicar of Bray:*

The second example, the *Galician Song*, is also an elementary ternary form. Yet, it is crystal clear and communicative in its expressive design, even to the use of unifying musical figures. Observe the alterations and adornments of the melody, especially the telltale grace notes and triplets in the closing measures of the lines of assertion and contrast in the music engraving. All these combine to point to the national musical idioms more eloquently than words. Note also the effective climax in the third measure of the last (reassertion) line of music. The *Gallician Song* follows:

Some readers may want to pursue applications of the basic ternary form. The following compositions may lead to still larger and fresher fields of exploration: *To a Wild Rose* and *To a Water Lily* by Edward MacDowell; *Lullaby* and *The Butterfly* by Edvard Grieg; *Moment Musi-*

[7] From Sir William Henry Hadow, *Sonata Form* (London: Novello & Co., 1896), page 4.
[8] From C. Hubert H. Parry, *op. cit.*

cal, No. 2 by Schubert; selections from Mendelssohn's *Songs Without Words,* especially the *Spring Song* and *On Wings of Song;* selections from Chopin's *Nocturnes,* the one in E-flat, Op. 9, No. 2 and *Mazurkas,* and *Prelude in C-Sharp Minor* by Rachmaninoff.[9]

The musical examples given so far show very clearly the expressiveness of the basic elements in music as well as something of the artistic idioms of the peoples from which the music sprang, the effectiveness of a climax, and the feeling for the phrase or period endings (or cadences). But even more than all these, they show how the deepest, universally-endowed human feelings of a spiritual and aesthetic nature find eloquent expression through the art of music—simple or sophisticated. These illustrations also show that form is not of primary significance in itself; rather, it is secondary and is the result of these other factors. This is from the standpoint of the listener. As for the composer, if he has something really worthwhile to say, is irresistibly urged to say it, and has the necessary skills to say it effectively, then the proper form for his composition will come directly from the artistic ideas themselves. Apropos of the feelings aroused by the music, here is a sympathetic passage by an eminent American poet–musician–philosopher–teacher, Donald N. Ferguson.[10]

Of late years the notion has been much bruited about that music has nothing to do with these things (emotional, spiritual, and human feelings), that its excellence lies wholly in its perfection of design, and that the ideal of perfect form in art is higher and nobler than that profound expressiveness which has always been supposed to be the glory of music. That is a notion which not only Beethoven but every great artist of the past would have laughed to scorn. Great art speaks of human things, not of abstractions. The form of great art must indeed be perfect, but that perfection reveals only a part of the artist's effort. He is moved to utterance by spiritual realities, and his forms are not the forms of idle dreams but are designs which embody the meaning of realities.

We have concerned ourselves almost exclusively with the art of music. Do these same principles mentioned here hold true for other arts? Every one of the separate fine arts naturally develops its own principles, largely because of what the creator seeks to express and the separate media and techniques employed. Nevertheless, certain underlying principles seem to be common to all. First and foremost is that of *unity:* the desire to organize all the components of the art work into one cohesive design, so that each part of the cathedral, the novel, the painting, or the symphony

[9] Advanced music students may gain some academic and theoretical information from Percy Goetschius, *The Homophonic Forms of Musical Composition* (New York: G. Schirmer, 1898); Goetschius, *Larger Forms of Musical Composition* (New York: G. Schirmer, 1943); Karl Eschman, *Changing Forms in Modern Music* (Boston: E. C. Schirmer Music Co., 1945).

[10] From his book *Piano Music of Six Great Composers* (Englewood Cliffs, N. J.: Prentice-Hall, 1947). Used with permission.

will function organically within the total framework. In this connection, Poe's dictum on the short story, "In the whole composition there should be no word written of which the tendency, direct or indirect, is not to the established design," is pertinent.

Closely allied to unity is the need for *symmetry* and *balance,* which make more readily perceptible the fundamental unity of the pattern. Man seems to take great pleasure in orderly arrangement, in the repetition of familiar quantities, in balancing one side against another. As in the case of rhythm, he expects certain things to happen in a certain order, and he achieves a pleasant sense of fulfillment when his expectation is realized.

But this "security" alone would soon grow wearisome, were it not enlivened by novelty and surprise within the pattern; the unity of the art form must be adroitly balanced with *variety* and *contrast.* From man's paradoxical need for both safety and adventure springs the basic aesthetic problem of the artist. If he were continually to introduce new material into his work, the result would be chaos. If, on the other hand, he were to continue to repeat the same motif again and again he would become insufferably boring. Satisfaction results from the artist's attempt to achieve balance between the two factors, from repeating enough of the old to give a sense of pattern, while introducing enough of the new to achieve variety and sustain our interest.

In addition, the artist introduces into the material elements of *suspense, surprise, movement,* and *growth* toward a *climax.* Whether it be the soaring dome in architecture, the denouement in drama, or the *crescendo* in melody, the climax carries the spectator aloft to the high point of emotional and aesthetic satisfaction and then a balancing termination. Thus the art work takes on shape and form—a *beginning,* a *middle,* and a *close.*

The arrangement of the material is of crucial importance in spatial arts. Painting, sculpture, architecture, and interior decoration all place emphasis upon the problems of organizing space into a contrasting, unified whole. One has only to look at Raphael's celebrated SCHOOL OF ATHENS to see how masterfully the painter has arranged his material with an eye to a formal unity and variety of structure. The rectangular space of the whole is bound together and contrasted by the curve of the arch, reinforced by the three successive, concentric arches. These, like a reiterated figure working to a climax in music, frame the central figures of Socrates and Plato and the other figures. Notice how effectively the figures on either side of the two philosophers focus the movement upon the two philosophers. Although analogies between different arts must be made only in a broad, general way, the reader will have no difficulty in recognizing in this design an equivalent of the A–B–A′ structure in music. The larger rhythms of the three areas are subtly varied with all kinds of cross rhythms within the groups and by the gentle elliptical

Courtesy The University Prints, Newton, Mass.

SCHOOL OF ATHENS Raphael

movement between the figures in the middle distance and those in the foreground. The canvas of this Renaissance master presents an extraordinary example of great diversity within a unified pattern, with symmetry, balance, climax, and richly variegated rhythms all contributing to the monumental effect.

Even more important is the problem of form in architecture, where the artist is faced with the task of organizing great expanses of mass and space into a coherent pattern. He does not begin with a definite form into which he pours his conception. Rather, he considers the use to which the building will be put, the environment, the materials, the engineering prob-

Courtesy The University Prints, Newton, Mass.

THE CAPITOL BUILDING IN WASHINGTON

lems, and the costs. Out of these considerations grows the particular form that he will use. Notice, for example, in the Capitol at Washington, how appropriate the serene, majestic form is for a building intended as a seat of government. The magnificently climactic dome towering over the two symmetrical and angular wings at either side, with connecting sections, is an architectural equivalent to the A–B–A′ structure in music. Considered in detail without the dome, the building presents three similar façades—the repetition of an idea—which are brought out dramatically by means of the steps, the pillars, and the cornices, alternating with two sections—the contrast—which are fairly well in the background. Here is a kind of A–B–A′–C–A″ structure, with the dome as the contrasting climax, which is precisely what we shall discover the classical musical rondo form to be. As in the painting of Raphael, we have here unity, variety, symmetry, balance, contrast, climax, and diversified rhythms expressed in appropriate architectural values.

These values, which depend on space and rhythmic measurements in the plastic arts, are translated into time measurements in the time arts. In poetry, the stanzas are often symmetrical in substance and time-length, and the lines are often symmetrical in the number and arrangement of metrical pulses, rhyming, and internal design elements. The *rondo, rondeau,* or *rondel,* with its subtle reiteration of a unifying element separated by contrasting sections, is one of the most flexible lyric forms in poetry. Notice in the following *Rondel* by Jean Froissart how the reiterated phrase takes on new meaning with each repetition. We have here an A–B–A′–C′–A″ pattern, with the repetition of the first two lines in the middle of the poem and at the end, separated by two contrasting lines:

RONDEL [11]

A′ Love, love, what wilt thou with this heart of mine?
Naught see I fixed or sure in thee!
B I do not know thee,—nor what deeds are thine:
A″ Love, love, what wilt thou with this heart of mine?
Naught see I fixed or sure in thee!

C Shall I be mute, or vows with prayers combine?
Ye who are blessed in loving, tell it me:
A‴ Love, love, what wilt thou with this heart of mine?
Naught see I fixed or sure in thee!

At this point, we should listen to Beethoven's *Rondino* as arranged by Fritz Kreisler for violin and piano. The discovery of the detailed internal structure is left to the listener, with one admonition: watch for the recurrent theme and the episodes that alternate with that theme; then compare the form you have discovered with the general design of Froissart's *Rondel.* Bear in mind that the composer may have as many alternations of the theme and contrasting sections as he desires.

So, too, the other literary arts all have their individual problems of organization and structure, of tempo and transition, of climax and denouement. One need only watch a well-written and well-directed play as it unfolds from its leisurely beginning, gradually accelerating its pace, piling up suspense in a steady crescendo, yet adhering to the firmest kind of unity up to the inexorable climax, then to the close, to realize how

[11] Translated by H. W. Longfellow. The old traditional French rondeau proper generally contains 15 lines, divided into three stanzas. There are several variants, however, such as the "Villon" rondeau containing only 10 lines. Swinburne is said to have invented a variant, a rondel of 11 lines. The Rondel is also to be found in 13 lines. Leigh Hunt used a Rondeau of 8 lines, and a more distant one much used by another English poet, Austin Dobson, favored a form called the "triolet." There are still other varieties, but they all have recurrent lines. For further details, read Walter Blair and W. K. Chandler, *Approaches to Poetry* (New York: Appleton-Century, 1935), Chap. VIII, pp. 394-407. *Rondel* by Jean Froissart (shown above) is of 9 lines divided into two stanzas of 5 and 4 lines respectively.

all-pervading are the basic expressive elements of design and structure, tempo and dynamics.

If these compositional values are of such importance in the static arts, where the spectator may linger at will over every detail, how much more important they are in an art where all is flow and movement, where the "landscape" rushes past before the listener has had a chance to grasp details, where the tone lives but for an instant before dissolving into mere memory, where unity and coherence of form are perceived mainly in retrospect or imagined in anticipation. It took composers centuries of groping, of trial and error, to develop the techniques of form as we now know them. They gradually learned how to achieve the orderly and architectonic arrangement of structures in space. The great masterpieces of music may be considered veritable cathedrals in tone and time.

Courtesy Theodore Presser Co.

FRANZ SCHUBERT

7 Personalized vocal expression: the lied and the art song

The *art song,* or *lied,* depends for its success upon the performance itself, the fusion of the text with the music, and intensification of the emotions in the poetry or prose which inspires the composer's musical setting for voice and piano.[1] There may be a tendency for one of these

[1] Essential listening and alternates for this chapter include: *My Mother Bids Me Bind My Hair,* Haydn; *Das Veilchen* (The Violet), Mozart; *Who is Sylvia, Serenade* and *Der Erlkönig* (The Erlking), Schubert; *Ich Grolle Nicht* (I'll Not Complain) and *Im Wunderschönen Monat Mai* (from the DICHTERLIEBE Cycle) or *Widmung* (Dedication), Schumann; *Wiegenlied* (Lullaby) and *Minnelied* (Love Song), Brahms; *Ich Liebe Dich* (I Love You), Grieg; *Nur wer die Sehnsucht kennt* (None but the Lonely Heart), Tchaikovsky; *The Flea,* Mussorgsky; *Im Herbst* (In Autumn) or *Für Musik,* or *Der Sommer ist schön,* Franz; *The Sea* (from Op. 47), *To the Golden-Rod* (from Op. 60) or *The Robin Sings in the Apple Tree* (Op. 47), *Thy Beaming Eyes* Op. 40, or *Sunrise* Op. 58, MacDowell; *I Bring The Colored Toys,* from the set GITANJALI, Carpenter; *Lilacs* Op. 21 and *Vocalise* (Op. 34), Rachmaninoff; *Verborgenheit* (Secrecy), and *Er Ist's* ('Tis Spring), Wolf; *Mandoline,* and one from the *Chansons de Bilitis,* or one from the set

three arts, singing, poetry, or piano, to assume primacy, above the normal "give and take." The composer must control and balance these tendencies so that the artistic values of the three arts are given their respective merits without sacrificing anything essential. This union results in a new and distinctive form which we here call the *Art Song* or the *Lied*. The "Great Five" figures in the history of the German Lied are, Schubert, Schumann, Brahms, Franz, and Wolf.

The diversity of mood and immediate emotional appeal that we notice in the folk song animates its "city cousin," the art song, to a far greater extent. Here we meet with every shade of human feeling. For the simple universality of the folk song, the art song substitutes a more individualized idiom, the expression of a highly skilled creative personality, subtly evocative in mood and atmosphere—an art form that has enlisted the talents of the most distinguished composers and performers.

Although art songs and folk songs have flourished side by side since the days of the troubadours of the eleventh century, important points of difference do exist. The art song is generally set by a professional composer to a high order of lyric poetry, whereas the folk song is usually couched in unsophisticated strophic or ballad type of construction—that is, the tune is not a complicated one and is apt to be repeated over successive stanzas. The art song, known as "*durchkomponiert*," "thoroughly composed" or "composed throughout," captures the changing moods of the various stanzas more intimately than the strophic-type of song. There are a number of variants of the strophic form of song but, by and large, the "thoroughly composed," and later the highly dramatic and "declamatory" types of art song, have predominated since Schubert, Schumann, Brahms, Wolf, *et al.*[2]

In some of the best art songs, the interplay between the arts is so complete that it is difficult to think of one without the other. Having selected a singable text that evokes his imagination, the composer uses all the resources of his art to bring out every hidden poetic implication of the words. The music must bear the text along and arouse in the listener a "fitting" response. The art song or lied must be inherently superior as vocal music—unlike the *usual* operatic aria, it is complete and self-sufficient.

Trois Ballades de Mallarmé, Debussy; *Extase* (Ecstasy), Duparc; *From the Land of the Sky-Blue Water* (based upon American Indian idioms), Cadman.

(Note: As most of these songs are brief, the foregoing should provide the listener an enjoyable and excellent orientation recital to the literature of the Art Song—of an hour, if properly managed.)

[2] Compare Schubert's *Heidenröslein,* with *Du bist die Ruh* or selections from his *Winterreise* set. For more extensive discussions of the various types and forms of songs, see: Conway Walker, *The Art Song and its Composers* (New York: Caxton Institute, 1926), esp. article on "Franz Schubert" by Herbert F. Peyser, p. 1648 *et. seq.;* Ernest Newton, *How to Compose a Song* (New York: E. P. Dutton, 1925).

All the pertinent elements of music must play their separate parts. The musical rhythm not only enhances the general meter and phrases of the poetry, but should provide a complement and support for the words. The contour and flow of the melody rises and falls with the implication of the text; yet, the pitch and character of the melody must carefully allow for the word, syllable, or vowel falling on individual tones. Some vowels are more "at home" (or naturally resonant) on certain pitch levels than others; for instance, *ah* is better suited to an over-all range or high pitch level than an *ē* or an *ōō*, and *ōō* is more naturally singable on a low pitch than *ē*. "*The voice should always sing on the vowel,*" says the best singing tradition. Nevertheless, consonants demand great care. The letters of Verdi, Debussy, Puccini, Cadman, *et al.*, are replete with demands upon the librettists for proper word and vowel consideration and treatment in specific instances of melodic flow, pitches, tempo, time, and contours. Important words and syllables should be brought out and emphasized by the rightful musical pitches, rhythm, and accents. The harmonic background in the musical setting, dispersed as chordal structures and their infinite number of figurations, provides an emotional complement to the words, ranging from lightness and gaiety to somber drama. *Timbre* (tone-color) is also brought into play: the bright, lithesome melody given to the *coloratura* soprano voice differs from the low heroic ballad assigned to the contralto, baritone, or bass; and the higher timbre of the *lyric* soprano and *robusto* or *lyric* tenor provides still further individual differentiation.

The *tessitura*, or general "lie" of the melodic pitches, plays an important part, also. The themes in the voice and supporting parts alternately coincide, interplay, and contrast with each other in a design that, in the taste of the composer, best suits the meaning and spirit of the text. The composers of the more recent German art songs, beginning especially with Schumann, Brahms, and Hugo Wolf, sought not only to make the supporting instrumental melody part-and-parcel of this overall compositional warp-and-woof, but they also endeavored to make its companion melody as distinctive in character as a sort of *descant*, or *discant*, with the voice. Yet this counterpoint should not be too conspicuous.[3] It is a real test of the song composer to be original in both melody and the accompanimental figuration and yet secure balance between the two. The many variants of tempo, nuance, and dynamics underscore the mood of the

[3] Apropos of *Descant, Discant* or *Discantus*, an old versification of more than three centuries ago has put it this way:

> Ye little youths and maidens neat,
> We want your voices high and sweet.
> Your study to the Discant bring,
> The only part that you should sing.

(See also, Dowland's version of "Old Hundred" with descant in Elson's *Dictionary of Music*, p. 243.)

text. Of course, words can change mood more abruptly and with more aesthetic continuity than is possible with music—a formidable problem.

The process of composing a first-rate art song is involved and complex —differing, naturally, from the manufacturing process which produces most of tin pan alley "hits." Yet in spite of these tremendous demands, Schubert, Schumann, and Wolf often wrote three or more songs a day when they were seized by the "white heat of creation," as William James has put it. What emerges from this inspiration is, in fact, a sort of miniature "tone poem."

The art song is not a comparatively recent art form. As used in its more general sense, it goes back in *recorded* evidence about eight hundred years. As an individual and distinct form of personal expression, it was commonly used by the French troubadours and trouvères with their *Chansons* and *Roundelays,* especially Adam de la Halle (c. 1240–c. 1287); their German counterparts, the minnesingers (love singers) with their *Liebeslieds* and *Minnelieds,* especially Walter von der Vogelweide, (c. 1230), whom Wagner has used in TANNHÄUSER as one of the rival singers at the Wartburg Thuringian festivals; and later the *Master Singers,* with the renowned cobbler-poet-musician-cupid, Hans Sachs (1494–1576), whom Wagner depicts most endearingly in his music-drama DIE MEISTERSINGER VON NÜRNBERG.[4]

The masters of the Baroque and Classical periods left a number of art songs that are still part of the repertory. *If Music Be the Food of Love,* by Henry Purcell (1658–1695), Haydn's *My Mother Bids Me Bind My Hair,* Mozart's *The Violet,* as well as a number of art songs by the Italian masters, such as *Come Raggio di Sol* (As a Ray of Sunlight) by Antonio Caldara (1670–1736), and *Vittoria, Mio Core* (Victoria, My Love) by Giacomo Carissimi (1605–1674).

THE GERMAN LIED

Actually, even before the German lied was completely realized, the traditional German solo song with accompaniment, to make a fine distinction, was rooted deep in the character of the German folk song. It is difficult to tell where one left off and the other began.

[4] The *Madrigal,* (a rather "conversational," and contrapuntal part-song, a counterpart of the art song and generally of an animated, idyllic, and secular nature), was cultivated in Italy in two different periods, the fourteenth and the sixteenth centuries. Carlo Gesualdo (Naples, c. 1560–1613), Cristobal Morales (c. 1500–1553) and Tomás Victoria, or Vittoria (c. 1535–1611), composed madrigals in Spain. The next most important development of the part-song was in England at the time of Shakespeare, with William Byrd (c. 1542–c. 1623), John Wilbye (1574–1638), Thomas Morley (c. 1557–c. 1603), Orlando Gibbons (c. 1583–1625), Thomas Weelkes (c. 1575–1623), and others as the outstanding composers. The English madrigal assumed a very distinctively rhythmic and informal air. Almost simultaneously, France, Germany, and the Netherlands cultivated this part-song form and a rich and varied literature accumulated during the seventeenth and eighteenth centuries.

Yet, despite the excellence of these songs, when we say "art song" to a music lover he immediately thinks of the early nineteenth century and of the lyricism that welled out of the early German Romantic period through the transcendent genius of the greatest of song composers, Franz Schubert, who wrote over six hundred! He was the most eminent of a line of great composers who firmly established the art song in music, capturing the essence of the poem and translating it into song with an almost clairvoyant insight. Although Schubert left a legacy of first importance in almost every branch of music except opera, the composer of the *Erlking, Serenade, Hark Hark the Lark, The Linden Tree, Death and the Maiden,* remains the master of the art song.

In Schubert, the time, the place, and the man came together in fortuitous fashion. To begin with, a group of German lyric poets, headed by Goethe, had raised aloft the banner of Romanticism and created a new literary form, the intimate lyricism of mood in which language was so surcharged with feeling as to cry out for fulfillment in music. *Great songs usually follow a period of great poetry.* Then, too, the art of music, as a whole, was beginning to move closer to literature, a development that can be noticed throughout the nineteenth century. The short piece, lyrical and emotional, was ready to take its place beside the large structural forms of the German Classical period. The piano had become a flexible, highly imaginative, instrumental assistant to the voice. When all these influences had blossomed, there appeared the master who was able to bring them all to fruition.

Although the moods reflected in the art song are as diversified as those of the folk song, that of romantic love holds first place. We begin our listening study with Schubert's beloved *Serenade.* Over an accompaniment of simple chords, there unfolds a melody so expressive, so attuned to the most intimate inflections of the human voice, that it conveys its message even if one does not understand the German in which it is usually sung. Here, the mood of tender longing, so characteristic of the early Romantic movement in Germany, finds expression:

Softly goes my song's entreaty
Thro' the night to thee, (repeat)
In the silent woods I wait thee,
Come, my love, to me. (repeat)

Whisp'ring slender treetops rustle
In the moonlight clear,
Do not fear the hostile watching,
Fear it not, my dear.

Hark! the nightingales are singing,
Ah, they plead with thee!
With their notes so sweet, so ringing,
They would plead with me.

Well they know a lover's longing,
Know the pain of love,
With their silver-toned voices
Tender hearts they move.

Ah, let thine, as well, grow tender,
Sweetheart, why so coy?
Anxious, fevered, I await thee,
Come and bring me joy! [5]

The folk song's regular construction is of four measures in a phrase and four phrases (or two periods) in the melody. You will find an analogous construction in these verses—four lines in a stanza, four feet in a line (alternating with lines of three feet. When set to music, these shorter lines are filled out, so that they become equal in rhythmic-time length to the others). Schubert has skillfully avoided an excessively four-square construction, first, by introducing short interludes in the accompaniment; then by repeating certain lines of poetry.

Notice the characteristic introduction of the piano accompaniment; the interplay between the regular phrases of the voice part and the piano interludes; the effective repetition of the melody to other words, in *strophic* style; the intensification of mood, building up to the wonderful climax in the last stanza, with the accompaniment subtly imitating the vocal line; and the rounding off of the design in a gentle subsiding of emotion, dying away in the tender piano postlude.

If the *Serenade*, written to verses by Rellstab, represents the lyric genius of Schubert, his setting of Goethe's narrative poem *"Der Erlkönig"* (The Erlking) reveals his dramatic powers. The song was composed in 1815, when he was but eighteen, and is considered by many to be the greatest lied ever written. Schubert's friend Spaun told how he and another companion went one afternoon to call on Schubert. They found him enthusiastically reading Goethe's dramatic ballad aloud. He walked up and down the room, book in hand, then sat down and, as fast as he could write, put the song on paper, practically in its finished form.

Nothing is more characteristic of the first period of German Romanticism than the somber mood of this ballad, with its commingling of the supernatural and the strangely picturesque. It is an outstanding example of the successful integration of such tempers as poetic Romanticism, emotional dramatic personification and narration, Realism, and Symbolism. Here is the Goethe poem:

[5] English version (except the second verses of these songs, for reasons of copyright permission) by Henry G. Chapman, copyright 1911 by G. Schirmer, Inc. Copyright renewed 1939 by G. Schirmer, Inc. Quoted by permission of the publisher. Free and literal translation of second verse by Jan Philip Schinhan.

Who rides so late through night and wind?
It is the father and his child.
He holds the boy in his arms,
He clasps him firmly, he keeps him warm.

"My son, why do you hide your face in fear?"
"See you not, father, the Erlking?
The Erlking with his crown and train."
"My son, that is but the mist trailing down."

"Thou lovely child, come with me!
And I'll play lovely games with thee,
Where many gay flowers lie in the field,
And my mother has many garments of gold."

"Father! Father! don't you hear
What the Erlking is softly promising me?"
"Be calm, my child, have no fear,
That is but the wind moaning through the leaves."

"Won't you go with me?
My daughters will wait upon you,
They will play in the evening
And they will sing and dance."

"Father! Father! don't you see
The Erlking's daughters in that dark place?"
"My child, I see it quite clearly—
Those are but the hoary willows so gray."

"I love thee, thy beautiful face arouses me,
And comest thou not freely, I shall use force!"
"My father, my father, he clasps me now,
His icy grasp hurts me!"

The father shudders, he rides on faster,
Clasping in his arms the ailing child.
He reaches home in dread and anguish—
In his arms the child lay dead! [6]

The octaves in galloping triplets with which the accompaniment opens, the ominous figure in the bass, at once set the mood of the drama. The three protagonists—father, son, and seductive Erlking—are clearly differentiated through changes in tempo, in vocal line, and in tonal register. (*Register* is the general location in regard to high or low; the "lie" of the music.) Thus, the father's tones are conspicuously lower than those of the child, while the Erlking sings a soft alluring strain, as if from another world. The cries of the child are high, abrupt, and harrowing; the father's reassurance is sonorous, giving an impression of strength; the Erlking sings sirenlike in a broad, suave melody. As the father rides on in terror, we hear the galloping figure of the opening, leading to the dread

[6] English version (except the literal fifth verse), by Arthur Westbrook. Copyright by Oliver Ditson Company, 1931. Quoted by permission of the publishers.

climax. The final line is declaimed, with a dramatic pause (a *cæsura*) before the two *parlante* words at the end, "lay dead," followed by two simple chords.

To get an inkling of Schubert's achievement in song, one should hear several of the masterpieces that music lovers the world over have come to treasure almost as a personal possession. *Hark Hark the Lark,* said to have been written at one sitting after he had glanced through a volume of Shakespeare; *Ave Maria,* to the words from Walter Scott's *Lady of the Lake;* the dramatic masterpieces *Death and the Maiden, The Wanderer, The Phantom Double;* the folk-songlike *Heidenröslein* (Hedge-Rose); *Who Is Sylvia?; My Peace Thou Art; The Post; The Linden Tree*—each has become an integral part of our song inheritance.[7]

Schubert's successor in the art song was Robert Schumann, one of the most original and striking figures among the Romantics. Schumann possessed unusual dramatic power and a deep sensitivity to poetry, which he projected into his songs by a melodic line, harmonies, and accompaniments which were much more complicated, as a rule, than those of Schubert. He was not nearly so fertile, nor so great a melodist, but his choicest works must be counted among the glories of the lied.

For Schumann, the lyrics of Heinrich Heine provided the same inspiration that those of Goethe, Schiller, and the earlier Romantic poets of Germany had for Schubert. Unlike his predecessor, who set to music all kinds of poetry—it was said that he could set even a placard to music—Schumann needed a really beautiful poem to be inspired to musical creation. As a result, the poetry in Schumann's songs is far more worthy of the music than is the case in some of Schubert's songs.

Among the popular favorites of Schumann's songs are: *The Lotus Flower, Moonlight, Dedication, The Almond* (Nussbaum) *Tree,* and *I'll Not Complain* (which is used presently); and the song cycles, *Aus Wilhelm Meister,* Op. 98A; the *Myrthen,* Op. 25 (The Myrtles); *Frauenliebe und Leben,* Op. 42; and one of the favorites among the song-cycles, the *Dichterliebe* (Poet's Love), Op. 48. From the last cycle is the very beautiful song *Im Wunderschönen Monat Mai* (The Wonderful Month of May), which is generally considered one of Schumann's best songs. We have selected *Ich Grolle Nicht* (I'll Not Complain), set to an exceedingly intense lyric of Heine, which employs the most characteristic of Schumann's traits and idioms:

> I'll not complain, even though my heart be breaking.
> O love for ever lost! O love for ever lost!
> I'll not complain, I'll not complain.

[7] Besides the single songs mentioned, the listener is urged to hear the song-cycles *Die schöne Müllerin* (1823, a cycle of 20 songs), the *Winterreise* (1827, a cycle of 24 songs), and *Schwanengesang* (1828, of 14 songs). (See reproduction of the original manuscript of Schubert's *Hedge-Rose* ("Heidenröslein") on another page.)

Courtesy The Juilliard School of Music, New York

FROM THE ORIGINAL MS. OF THE SONG "HEIDENRÖSLEIN"

Franz Schubert

Even though you shine as a diamond rare,
No rays of it brighten your dark heart.
But I know full well I'll not complain,
Even if my heart is breaking apart.

I saw thee in my dream,
And saw the night within thy heart's abyss,
And saw the snake that on thy heart doth gnaw,
How all forlorn thou art, my love, I saw.
I'll not complain, I'll not complain.[8]

The brooding chords under the vocal line, with their acrid dissonances, communicate the emotion of the rejected lover. Gradually the music builds up to a climax on the line, "And saw the snake that on thy heart doth gnaw." For emotional projection, this song composed in 1840 remains one of the best of its type in the full-blown German Romanticism.

Next in the dynasty of the masters of the German lied was Johannes Brahms, who united with the utmost lyricism a quality of inner fervor, perfection of technic, and introspection that has given his songs a high place in the literature. Brahms' songs have restrained passion and marked intensity, a distinctive coloring in the vocal line and in the intricate piano background, which stamp them as unmistakably his.[9]

There is brooding melancholy in such songs as *May Night* and *Death Is Like a Cool Still Night,* contemplation and gentleness in *In Summer Fields;* and the lyricism pervading the slow movements of his symphonies is matched in such a song as *Minnelied* (Love Song). The flowing accompaniment that serves as the introduction in the *Minnelied*—Brahms directed it to be played "with much tenderness, but not too slowly"—leads into a vocal melody of deep feeling and the "inwardness" that is so peculiarly his own. Note the despondent effect of the low pedal point (a sustained or reiterated tone) in the bass of the piano throughout the verse beginning with "But for thee all joy were dead." The eminent authority on the lied, H. T. Finck, has said that the *Minnelied* is the most inspired, spontaneous, and delightful of Brahms' art-songs. The words follow:

Sweeter sounds the song of birds
When she roams the meadows,
When she comes with step so light
'Mid the woodland shadows.

[8] English version (except the literal second verse) by Arthur Westbrook. Copyright by Oliver Ditson Company, 1931. Quoted by permission of the publishers.

[9] The interested listener will want to become acquainted with such songs of Brahms as the following: *Sapphic Ode* ("Sapphische Ode," Op. 94, No. 4—a very superior song) *My Little Queen* ("Wie bist du meine Königin," Op. 32, No. 9), *My Love is Fair* ("Meine Liebe ist Grün," Op. 63, No. 5). *A Strain of Song Seems Drifting* ("Wie Melodien Zieht es mir," Op. 105, No. 1).

Brighter is the blooming Spring,
Greener are its bowers,
When her tender fingers touch
Their countless flowers.

But for thee all joy were dead,
All earth's brightness faded.
E'en the glow of evening sky
Were for me o'ershaded.

Dearest sov'reign of my heart,
Never leave me, never,
Bloom sweet blossoms of thy love,
In my soul forever.[10]

Notice the richness of the chords in the piano and the symmetrical lyric structure of the voice, and how both the melody and the piano accompaniment interpret and intensify the spirit of the poem—a perfect wedding of the arts! Each of the four stanzas is given to two four-measure phrases. Each stanza is separated from the next by a brief piano interlude. The first, second, and fourth phrases are similar in contour, the third is contrasting, outlining the phrase-period pattern we met so frequently in the folk song—A–A′–B–A″. The last line of the poem is repeated, bringing us to the peak of the melody and the climax of the emotion. It has often been pointed out that in Brahms, profundity of emotion and intricacy of texture go hand in hand with the simplest structural formations. In the *Minnelied* we have a good example of this.

German Romanticism, in the second half of the nineteenth century, strongly influenced composers throughout the entire musical world; even such ardent nationalists as Grieg, Tchaikovsky, and our own Edward MacDowell came under its spell. In their songs they combined the lyricism of the lied with their own individual and national idioms. A number of Edvard Grieg's songs (about 165 in all) are completely nationalistic, such as *Solvejg's Song* from the incidental music for Ibsen's play PEER GYNT. However, one of the most famous, *Ich Liebe Dich* (I Love You) was written when he was twenty-one and under the influence of Schumann. Like Schumann, who turned to song in the year of his marriage to Clara Wieck, Grieg wrote *Ich Liebe Dich* as an outpouring of his love for his cousin, Nina Hagerup, whom he later married. In a letter to the American critic, Henry Finck, Grieg said, "My best songs were composed for her, they embody my personal feelings, and I could no more have stopped expressing them in songs than I could have stopped breathing." The sincerity of the songs, and the gentle lyricism which is so much a part

[10] Translation (except the second verse) by Arthur Westbrook. Copyright, 1931, by Oliver Ditson Company. Quoted by permission of the publishers. The second verse is a literal translation by the present author.

of Grieg's musical personality, have established him as one of the most popular composers of song. While Grieg was a Norwegian and expressed himself in national idioms, the songs he wrote, considered as a distinct art form, were of the German lied genre and influenced by Schubert, Franz, Schumann *et al.* The same sort of reasoning, bearing in mind certain reservations, may also apply to the accompanied-solo art songs of Russia, Italy, England, America and many other countries of western culture, allowing for national differences and the personal styles of individual composers. It is the vital essence of the "taproot" of the artistic form of the lied that concerns us most.

Grieg wrote the music of *Ich Liebe Dich* to the lyrics of Hans Christian Andersen; but the German words are almost always used. The lyrics follow:

My thought of thoughts, my very inmost being,
Thou only art my heart's felicity!
I love thee more than all else under heaven,
I love but thee, I love but thee,
I love but thee thro' all eternity!

For thee alone my thoughts are turning.
My heart is happy only for thee!
Where ever God wills that I go,
I love but thee, I love but thee,
I love thee only thro' all eternity! [11]

This song has become one of the most popular of love songs, for it fairly "sings by itself." It is a passionately expressive outburst of amorous emotion, tuneful and ingratiatingly vocal throughout, and as spontaneous as the universal declaration of love itself. It is concise and strophic in style, and contains an excellently contrived climax.

It is a pity that great geniuses like Mozart and Beethoven did not write more lieder. True, Mozart has left the beautiful *Das Veilchen;* and Beethoven, though he once declared, "Songs, I do not like to write!" did compose the sacred song *Die Ehre Gottes aus der Natur,* and the love song masterpiece *Adelaïde,* as well as *Sehnsucht* and the less frequently heard song-cycle, *An Die ferne Geliebte* and some seventy-five other songs with piano accompaniment. In spite of possible accusations of artistic heresy, we say that most of Beethoven's art songs are far from being masterpieces.[12]

[11] Translation (except the second verse) by Auber Forestier. Copyright, 1936, by Oliver Ditson Company. Quoted by permission of the publishers. The second verse is a literal translation by the present author.

[12] Inasmuch as this chapter is largely concerned with the German lied as a distinctive art form, some readers may desire further information concerning the early beginnings of the German lieder (solo-voice) with accompaniment—to distinguish it from the polyphonic part-songs, either accompanied or *a cappella.* The following composers' vocal works and biographies may be studied from musical encyclopedia

After the heights achieved during the "Golden Age" of the German lied, mainly through the genius of Schubert, Schumann, Franz and Brahms, there seemed to come a calm or artistic leveling among the German composers. This "plateau" of lieder becomes more understandable when one considers that these composers were either attracted to other types of composition or were so overawed by the masters who preceded them that they followed the tradition of the classical lied rather than explore deviations of the form. However, these other German lied composers are not "also rans," for among them were men of great gifts and even genius: Richard Strauss (1864–1949), Adolph Jensen (1837–1879), Gustav Mahler (1860–1911), and Ferdinand Löwe or Loewe (1865–1925). (See "Additional Listening" for listing of songs.)

A veritable renascence of the German lied was awakened by the songs of the Austrian, Hugo Wolf (1860–1903). His personal life was filled with strife, turmoil, and grief—largely of his own making. The end of his life (through insanity) marked another tragic sacrifice of genius. His formal training was secured at the Vienna Conservatory, but he was discharged after two years of study "as an unruly student," so historical rumor has it. From then on he gleaned his craftsmanship through "trial and error" and study of the masters. He became second conductor to Karl Muck at Salzburg in 1882, but that lasted only a few months. From 1884 to 1887, he was the music critic for a local publication, where he created a large number of enemies with his unbridled attacks upon Brahms, the idol of Vienna at the time, and by proclaiming his fanatical adoration of Wagner.

In spite of Wolf's difficult personality, his songs won him friends, homage and eventual placement among the great composers. He composed in many other forms, including choral works, operas, symphonic works, string quartets and so forth, but they were not very successful.

The song was his real metier, and the form of expression which gave him the greatest joy and outlet for his genius. This was evident from his earliest songs *Die Spinnerin,* which he composed at 18, and *Zur Ruh, zur Ruh,* at 23! From then on, his best songs were destined for immortality alongside the great songs of Schubert, Schumann, Franz, and Brahms. Wolf himself realized that he had struck "pay dirt" in his lieder; so much so that he composed songs with a feverish fervor, as though he were afraid that time would run out before he had finished with the music that was singing in his creative soul, waiting to be expressed.

The bulk of Wolf's lieder is included in a number of sets, or groups,

---

and other references: Heinrich Schütz (1585–1672), Heinrich Albert of Königsberg (1604–1651) and Johannes Eccard of the same city (1553–1611), Johann Stader (1581–1634), Andreas Hammerschmidt (1611–1675), Georg Phillip Telemann (1681–1767).

now known by the name of the poet, or source, of the lyrics: i.e. *Gedichte von Mörike,* 53 songs; *Goethe,* 51 songs; *Eichendorff,* 20 songs; *Spanisches Liederbuch,* 44 songs; *Italienisches Liederbuch,* 46 songs; and lesser musical settings of such poets as Shakespeare, Heine, Byron, Keller, Ibsen (as incidental music for *Das Fest auf Solhaug*), Michelangelo, etc.

Wolf's songs are to be considered for solo voice *and* piano, rather than solo voice *with* piano accompaniment. The melodic character, ideas, and lyrical lines of the voice and that in the piano part are thoroughly combined and equally important. The voice part endeavors to reflect the essence of the words. In dramatic manner, the voice is an integral part of the marvelous tapestry of sound woven by the piano. The declamatory style is not to be considered unmelodic in the same sense which one applies the term to many of the typical solo songs by such composers as Debussy, Ravel, Duparc, Gabriel Fauré, Berg, or Schönberg. Neither is this style to be confused with the operatic *recitativo.* (See chapter on opera.) Quite the contrary, Wolf's vocal line preserves the beauty of the lyrical melody, combines it with dramatic emotionalism, gives the voice great freedom of interpretive flight and expressiveness, and enhances those peculiar beauties that only poetry and the untrammeled singing voice can produce.

The piano parts of his songs are often works of art in themselves—even more so than those of Schumann and Brahms and sometimes Schubert—and, more often than not, are organically spun out of some salient melodic or rhythmic figure. The harmonies are refreshing and vital, often almost as chromatic as those employed by Wagner! Even though the piano part seems to be complete in itself, when the vocal part is sung *with* the piano one is fully convinced that the wedding of the two parts is essential.

Wolf, like Schubert before him, was not confined to any one design within the proper stylistic framework of the lied. Wolf could be simple and folk-like in using the elementary "strophic" form, as in *Der Musikant, Morgenthau,* or *Die Kleine.* He could break the bonds of regular formalism of phrases as in *An die Geliebte.* He could be as free as fancy indicated in a ballad or narrative form in such a happy-go-lucky song as *Der Rattenfänger.* He was very adept in using the simple period form, the binary form (two-part) or the ternary form (three-part) for the traditionally sedate classical German lied style, as in *Anakreon's Grab.* In Wolf's compositions, form was ever "an obedient conformer to his creative imagination rather than a troublesome concern" during the process of composing, as Edwin Evans, the English musicologist, once wrote about Beethoven.

Now for the listening study of two from the best of Wolf's lieder, *Verborgenheit* ("Secrecy") and *Er Ist's* ("'Tis Spring"). Here is a free, interpretive translation of the romantically forlorn and highly introspective poem of *Verborgenheit* (this version is obviously not intended for

talism, Muscovitism, eclecticism and something that is absolutely his own," according to the English Critic, Ernest Newman, paved the way for "The Five," with their intense Russianism. But before we discuss this group, consider a composer who, especially in his earlier works, carried on the Germanic influences of the lied—Peter Ilyich Tchaikovsky (1840–1893), who was *not* considered one of *"The Five."*

Of Tchaikovsky's 107 or so songs, the most popular is his setting of Goethe's *Nur Wer die Sehnsucht Kennt* ("None but the Lonely Heart") from SIX SONGS, Op. 6, which he wrote in his twenty-ninth year, the same year that produced his "ROMEO AND JULIET" OVERTURE. He not only succeeded in capturing the essence of Goethe's poem, but he also intensified it with a lyricism and dramatically tragic fore-feeling which greatly enhance the effects of the poem. This song was characteristic of the melancholy that pervades so many of Tchaikovsky's works, and which reaches its apex in his SIXTH SYMPHONY, Op. 74, the *"Pathetique."* Here are the English words of *None but the Lonely Heart:*

None but the lonely heart
Can know my sadness;
Alone and parted far
From joy and gladness.

Heav'n's boundless arch I see
Spread out above me.
Ah! what a distance drear
To one who loves me!

[The first stanza is repeated here.]

My senses fail,
A burning fire devours me.
None but the lonely heart
Can know my sadness.[14]

Both the choice of Goethe's lyrics and the manner in which they are handled stamp this song in the tradition of the lied, shot through with the same quality of *sehnsucht* that permeated German romantic poetry of the early nineteenth century. The highly emotional vocal line, with the downward leap in the first two measures, projects a mood of lassitude and despair. The melody undulates in a broad curve, a true outpouring of feeling, which works up to a climax. Notice how masterfully the emotion is carried to its peak in the accompaniment, after the voice has stopped, on the last line of the third stanza (that is to say, the first stanza repeated as the third). After a dramatic pause, the voice droops in despair, while the piano mournfully intones the original melody. The intertwining of both parts is achieved with rare eloquence and skill.

[14] Translation by Arthur Westbrook. Copyright by Oliver Ditson Company. Used with permission.

In several respects, the songs of Modeste Mussorgsky (Moss-AWRRG-skee, 1839–1881) are even more indigenous to the folklore of Western Russia than were those of Tchaikovsky. Mussorgsky, one of the most tragic of comparatively modern composers, was one of the original, imaginative, and creative spirits of the famous Russian *"five"*—Balakireff (Bah-lah-KEE-reff), Cui, Borodin (Boor-oh-DEEN), Rimsky-Korsakoff (REEM-skee-KORRSS-ak-off),Mussorgsky. Mussorgsky wrote about 65 separate art songs and ballads, some of which were grouped into sets or song-cycles. Many of these works disclose a highly personal idiom, colorful and with intensely realistic dramatic expression; yet his lyrical songs were often filled with melodic beauty and charm, though not altogether free from the influences of the German lieder, especially those of Schubert. One can believe the composer when he wrote his *credo:* "Life wherever it shows itself, truth no matter how bitter, courage and frankness above hope to achieve."

The musical world knows Mussorgsky mainly through his operas, the comic opera THE FAIR AT SOROTCHINTSI (or *Sorochinsk*); the grand opera, KHOVANTCHINA (Hoh-VANTS-chee-nah), and his masterpiece, BORIS GODUNOFF (Borr-EESS God-oo-NOFF).

Yet this same enigmatic creator could compose such lovely lyrical songs as: *The Peasant Cradle Song, The Goat, Trepak, Hopak* and *Nursery Songs,* the set *Sunless* (consisting of six songs), *The Little Star;* songs of free fancy like: *The Magpie* or *The Garden of the Don;* or the romantic and dramatic *Songs and Dances of Death.*

The *Ballads* have proved to be his best songs, most famous of which is *The Song of the Flea* (1879), which comes from the mouth of Mephistopheles in Goethe's poem of FAUST.[15] In this, the cold, scoffing, and fiendish Devil vents his satirical spleen upon the Russian Court of the time. Here are the words of Mussorgsky's allegoric and symbolic song, which vividly recalls the poem, *To A Louse,* that Robert Burns wrote in 1786:

Once upon a time there was a king
Who had a big flea;
A flea? A flea!
Whom he loved
As if't were his own son.
The flea? Ha, ha, ha, ha, ha!
The flea! Ha, ha, ha, ha, ha!
The flea!

The king called his tailor,
The tailor came
"Make clothes for my pet,
And trousers too!"
Trousers? Ha, ha, ha, ha, ha!
The flea? Ha, ha, ha, ha, ha!
The flea? Ha, ha, ha, ha, ha!
Yes, trousers!

[15] See FAUST, Part I, Scene in Auerbach's cellar.

In silks and satins
He was now arrayed,
With ribbons across his chest,
And a star.
The flea? Ha, ha, ha, ha, ha!
The flea!

He became Minister of State,
And received many decorations;
And all his relatives
Were most important at court.
Ha, ha!

And the courtiers and their ladies
Were plagued by fleas,
The queen and maids of honor
Had quite a time of it!

Not one of them dared scratch
Or kill the pests.
Yet we ordinary folks are free
To scratch whene'er we like, and kill
As soon as one bites us!
Ha, ha, ha, ha, ha, ha, ha,
Ha, ha, ha, ha, ha, ha, ha!

It is impossible to cover all the Russian composers of the lieder genre, but we cannot omit one of the foremost contemporary Russian masters, who, in 1917, became a voluntary exile and lived his last years in the United States, Sergei Vassilievitch Rachmaninoff (1873–1943). Besides being one of the outstanding concert pianists of Russia, he was certainly one of its greatest composers, with such works as piano solos, songs, choral works, operas, symphonic works, concertos, and the many forms of solo or ensemble works. For a start, we suggest *In the Silent Night* and *The Harvest of Sorrow* from SIX SONGS, Op. 4, *The Lilacs* and *Vocalize.* Other lieder by Rachmaninoff to choose from are *O, do not Sing Again; So Many Hours, So Many Fancies,* from Op. 14; *Floods of Spring; Before My Window,* Op. 21; *Loneliness;* and *By A New-Made Grave,* Op. 34.

THE LIED OR SOLO ART SONG IN FRANCE

The origins of the French Art Song and the German Lied, considered as solo songs with accompaniment, were similar in that both were mostly outgrowths of native folklore and native folk songs. The general observation might well apply to the art songs of most other European countries. Also, because of intersectional and inter-nationalistic artistic influences, there are certain similarities among folk art expressions. Some influences are quite obvious to the layman as well as to the musicologist. Others, subtle and minute, crept into the art songs of various countries, such as:

Mussorgsky's influence upon Debussy, then, in turn, the Debussy influence upon some of Stravinsky's songs, as well as those of the Englishman Cyril Scott; or the Grieg influence upon our own composer, Edward MacDowell; or the influences of the French Impressionists in general upon the American art songs of such composers as Charles Loeffler, John Alden Carpenter, Bainbridge Crist, the last songs of Charles Tomlinson Griffes, and others. Of later years, the influences of the Viennese composer, Arnold Schönberg and those of his immediate "school" have been felt throughout Europe and America. And so goes the story of artistic influences everywhere.[16]

The forerunners of the "modern" art song of France were the folk songs, such as the old *polyphonic chanson;* then followed the popular monodic *romance,* the prevalent monodic *chanson d'amour,* the *ballades,* and, still later, the *chanson musicale,* which last were artfully composed by capable, trained musicians, set to words equally artistic. These were for a single solo voice, accompanied by the simple lute, the elaborated seventeenth century lute, *theorbe, theorbo* or the *archlute,* a wood-wind instrument such as the *recorder, flageolet,* or early oboe types, or whatever instrument was handy. These songs for solo-voices, or accompanied romances, ballades and chansons, were very often rooted in, and colored by, the old *medieval ecclesiastical modes* or adapted from bits of *Gregorian Chants.*

Then came a long period when the genuinely indigenous French art songs were quiescent, probably overshadowed by much Italian and some German influence. However, research has uncovered some creative activity in the seventeenth century: the *brunette,* a simple love song; the *bergerette,* a pastoral lyric; the *vaudeville,* adapted street songs, often bawdy; the *aubade,* at best a morning serenade and at worst a derisive and noisy *charivari;* the inevitable *chanson bachique,* drinking songs, ballades, rondeaux and the like; and the satirical *mazarinade.* There then followed the many diverse forms of the *chanson amoureuse.* It was out of these unseemly chrysalises that the *chanson musicale* and eventually the modern art song emerged.

The French revolution and later the rebellion against Charles X in 1830 stirred up the patriotic fervor of France, and with that awakening

[16] We refer the reader interested in art songs of Europe and North and South America to articles on *Song* in the following books—consult their indices: Donald Ferguson, *A History of Musical Thought* (New York: F. Crofts & Co., 1935); Paul Lang, *Music in Western Civilization* (New York: W. W. Norton & Co., 1941); *Oxford History of Music* (1931 Ed.) Vol. V, p. 324 on; Vol. VI, p. 271 on; Vol. VII, p. 354—note the remarkable comparison between Brahms' and Wolf's settings of the poem *Phänomen* by Goethe on pp. 386-396; *Encyclopædia Britannica* (Cambridge, England: eleventh edition, 1911), Vol. XXV, an excellent survey of the art song; Grove's *Dictionary of Music and Musicians,* Vol. IV, pp. 536-617; *The Encyclopedia of Music and Musicians; Oxford Companion to Music,* p. 881 on—a very extensive list of composers of song by countries and dates. Also consult Gilbert Chase, *A Guide to Latin American Music* (Pan American Union: Washington, D.C., 1945).

were born such national songs as *Ca ira!* ("It will succeed," adapted from a popular *contra-dance,* Cavillon National), and the famous *Marseillaise,* both words and music by Rouget de l'Isle (or Lisle), 1792. It was in this milieu that poets like Victor Hugo, Lamartine, Delavigne, Alfred de Musset, Béranger, and others poured forth beautiful lyrical poetry that was inspiration and sustenance for song. Such favorable "creative soil" seems to have been present at the onset of the so-called Romantic period in France around 1800. In 1828, there came an untrained musician, Francois Monpou (1804–41), whose song based upon Beranger's *Si j'etais petit oiseau,* served to awaken de Musset and Hugo to write many ballads and romances; and their influence, in turn, spread throughout France.

The modern art song in France begins with Berlioz (1803–69)—one could extend that boundary to include most of Europe.[17] He composed only twenty-seven art songs, which disclose both his highly imaginative genius and his shortcomings and excesses. Among the best of his songs are *Nuits d'été,* Op. 7, *Sur les Lagunes, L'Absence, La Captive,* Op. 12, *Le Spectre de la Rose,* Op. 7, and *Élégie,* Op. 2.

The art song which the world has come to recognize as distinctively French in character and style became firmly established with the appearance of César Franck (frahnk), Fauré (foh-RAY), Debussy, Duparc, and was later sustained by d'Indy (dahn-DAY), Chabrier (shah-BR'YAY), Dukas (dee-KAHS), Pierné (peyr-NAY), Chausson (shoh-SOHNN), Ravel, Milhaud mee-LOH), Poulenc (poo-LAHNK), Koechlin (KEK-lah-ng), Lekeu (lu-KO), and others. The treatment of the art song and individuality of style was typical of French composers of that time. César Franck (1822–1890) may be thought of as a bridge to the modern school of French Impressionism. He wrote only a few art songs, but they command a high place in a singer's repertory because of their mystical beauty, expressiveness, and their harmonically colorful piano parts. We mention especially the songs, *La Procession* and *Le Mariage des Roses.* Franck inspired a productive school of composers who were more prolific.

In spite of the fact that Henry Duparc (1848–1933) wrote only sixteen art songs, and those before he was thirty, they are among the most beautiful and original to be found in the literature. The song *Extase* ("Ecstasy") is a setting of a poem by Jean Lahor. It is subtle, strange, and subdued, a perfect reflection of the mood of the poem. The dynamics of the entire song, both voice and piano, are marked very soft (*pp*) throughout—save for *one* measure in a piano solo passage after the first verse. Note how the piano rounds out the song in the *coda,* as it did in

[17] But this form does not exhaust the many contributions of Berlioz. The best works of Berlioz are among the finest of nineteenth century Romantic composers of all Europe, and some of these (mainly orchestral and choral works) still retain their high position in the world of music. Consult Jacques Barzun, *Berlioz and the Romantic Century,* 2 Vol. (Boston: Little Brown & Co., 1950).

Wolf's "*'Tis Spring,*" though in "Ecstasy" it is much less extended. The piano part as a whole is composed of a very effective counter-melody, or descant, to the voice, which is so deceptively simple, as it flows along in the semi-declamatory manner so commonly heard in the art songs since Franck. The harmonic structure is fresh and unstilted, and is figurated between the descant in the upper piano tones and the bass. The poem is redolent with the idea of "love-death"—one of the characteristics of nineteenth century Romanticism. The following is a free translation, not intended for singing:

> On a pale lily, my heart sleeps;
> And in its dreams, comes death's strange sweetness.
> Death is as delicately scented,
> As the breath of love.
> On thy pale bosom, my heart sleeps,
> And in its dreams, comes death's strange sweetness.

The most distinctive and generally esteemed song composer of modern France is Claude Debussy (day-BU-see) (1862–1918), a master of Impressionism, or "Symbolism" as he preferred to term it. The crystal clear, fluid style in Debussy's music reflects his reactions to the over-emotionalism of the Romantic era and the Wagnerian school. Debussy was, along with the best of the French Impressionistic school, less affected by the German classical lieder than were other composers.[18]

The songs of Debussy may be generally considered coolly intellectual, of an unreal world to the point of vagueness, and of apparent fragmentary character. They are fastidious, even "precious" and fragile at times; of varied moods and emotional content, according to the composer's own peculiar ways; and suggestive rather than realistic, although some songs come close to naturalistic representation. Instead of "sounding the depths of feeling" as many German lieder do, Debussy's songs explore the heights of the imagination. They are products of directed, highly reasoned sensibility rather than mere emotional outbursts.

The vocal line of Debussy's songs is subordinated to the poetic or symbolic import and aesthetic "aura" of the words. This results in a subtle manner of compositional technique which has became generally recognized as "modern French." The sublime lyrical and dramatic melodies of Schubert, Schumann, Brahms, *et al.*, were developed by Debussy into a declamatory vocal line of exquisite subtlety, demanding from the performer sensitivity to nuances of timbre. This declamation is quite different from that of Wolf. The piano parts of Debussy's songs are "atmospheric" and essentially a background while being, at the same time, an integral part of the whole. The harmonies are very original, replete with

[18] Save for Mélisande's single tower song in the opera PÉLLEAS ET MÉLISANDE, there is little "music drama" in Debussy's songs, the late Oscar Thompson has intimated in *Debussy: Man and Artist* (New York: Dodd, Mead & Co., 1937).

tonal colors and effects, and marked with ingenious pianistic dispersions, or figurations, and rhythmic patterns of the harmonic content. What has been previously remarked concerning the oneness of the voice and piano parts in the songs of Wolf applies with greater emphasis to the songs of Claude Debussy, though achieved in a different style. Debussy was especially at home in setting to music the poems of François Villon, Charles Baudelaire, Stéphane Mallarmé, Paul Bourget, Paul Verlaine, and Pierre Louÿs.

A pleasant introduction to his very early style of song composition is afforded by the setting of Verlaine's *Mandoline,* from his FÊTES GALANTES. In this song the tinkling piano chords give a suggestive atmosphere of the "gallants who go a-serenading, and fair damsels who to them do listen." Their shadowy forms

> "Whirl ecstatic where the moonlight
> Falls in rose and silver splendor;
> A mandolin softly tinkling
> Answers the wind, gay and tender." [19]

This song *Mandoline* can hardly be set forth as a typical example of the mature style of Debussy. It was written when the composer was twenty-one, and it still bears the strong early influence of Massenet. Yet it does foreshadow the later master, for the song is plainly distinctive, and shows Debussy's inherent gift for creating mood.

To illustrate the mature Debussy in full command of the techniques of his art, we have selected one of three CHANSONS DE BILITIS, settings of prose-poems of Pierre Louÿs, composed in 1897, some seventeen years later than *Mandoline,* and during the same productive period as the orchestra masterpieces, L'APRÈS MIDI D'UN FAUNE, THE NOCTURNES, and the unique opera," PÉLLEAS ET MÉLISANDE. The CHANSONS DE BILITIS are three in number, *La Flute de Pan, Le Chevelure* and *Le Tombeau des Naïades.* Bilitis, wholly a product of the imaginative Louÿs, was depicted as a Greek goddess, symbolizing sensualism, voluptuousness, and hedonism.

The first song of the set, *La flute de Pan,* is concerned with the hedonistic Pan, ruminating as he plays upon his *Syrinx*—a series of whistle-like graduated lengths of hollow reeds bound together, and blown by sliding back and forth under the upper lip. Pan plays a song of love for Bilitis. The musical atmosphere is focused by being modal, the modal feeling "of pagan Greece rather than the church"; and, following a typically syrinx-like melody, the music becomes more complex when Pan tells of "the chant of the green frogs." A passage of declamatory nature in the voice, accompanied by a play of parallel fifths, leads to the conclusion, where a repetition of the opening syrinx melody is heard. The voice part then vanishes. The second song of the set, *Le Chevelure,* is one in which Pan tells Bilitis about her beautiful, long, flowing hair which en-

[19] Translation by Bliss Carmen. Copyright by the Boston Music Co. Used here with permission.

twined him, and bound him to her. This song is the most passionate and warm-blooded of the three. However, there is still the feeling and atmosphere of the archaic in the voice part as well as the piano. The harmonies are rich, thickly clustered, and colorful, flowing with subtle rhythms and leading to a tender and eloquent ending. (If there is time for but one song from this set, this one will serve very well.) The third song, *Le Tombeau des Naïades,* is a solemn, ceremonial march, as though it were a procession on the way to a tomb of the Naïades (a nymph presiding over fountains, lakes, brooks, and wells). The voice is chant-like, as Pan tells Bilitis that she has been following the trail of a goat! The winter is cold and inhospitable; the satyr and nymphs are now dead and gone . . . Such is the combination of the general mood, symbolism, and atmosphere of the final song of the set—as only Debussy could evoke it.

The alternate listening study for the BILITIS set is one song chosen from TROIS BALLADES DE MALLARMÉ, the last group of songs that Debussy wrote—some three years before his death. This set consists of *Soupir* (Sigh), a personification of Autumn as in a vague dream, with such symbolic phrases of almost intangible metaphors as "the tawny agony of leaves," an Autumn "freckled with russet spots," "dead water on which the wind plows a cold furrow," and the like; *Placet Futile* (Futile Petition), with its words of ironic humor, free imagery, and capricious fantasy that elude satisfactory translation into English, concerns a hopeless petition to a lady. The music is realistically humorous, even sardonically and mockingly so. There is sketchy use of the piano in this song, for Debussy purposely left the burden of communication to the words and the voice. The rhythmic suggestion in the piano part is that of a slow, stately *minuet*—or perhaps a *sarabande. Eventail* (The Fan), is even more vague and symbolic than the other songs. Roger Elliot Fry, the late English authority on Mallarmé said, in essence, that *the real meaning of this poem is its lack of meaning!* The narrator of this last song is the Fan itself, which, by its movements of opening and closing, choses what is to be disclosed or concealed. Thus it may be said to symbolize futility, vanity, or unfulfilled enticement. The piano part is in the character of a *Scherzando* which serves to enhance the spirit of the poem and gives substance and background for the voice part. This set of songs which, at first, seem to be "caviar" to many listeners will, with repeated sympathetic hearings, find a place in the listener's repertory.

THE ART SONG IN THE UNITED STATES[20]

Our own early art songs did not spring from our folk songs and ballads, or their composed counterparts, save for a few, like *Seven Songs* (dedicated to his friend, George Washington), and the song "*My days have been so wondrous free,*" by the amateur colonial poet, musician, and signer of the Declaration of Independence, Francis Hopkinson (1737–1791). One might also consider some of the "lost" songs from the early Colonial *pasticcio* (medley) musical plays produced in Charleston, S. C., New York City, or Philadelphia, which were patterned after the popular,

[20] We refer the reader to William Treat Upton, *Art Song in America* and *A Supplement to Art Song in America,* 1930–38 (Bryn Mawr: Oliver Ditson Co., 1930–38). Serious students of the subject should also read *Styles and Schools of the Art Song in America, 1720–1850,* a Ph.D. thesis, Indiana University, 1954, by Grace Helen Yerbury, Dissertation Abstracts, Vol. XIII, No. 6, pp. 1219-1220; Indiana Univ. microfilm No. 6459.

risqué, English satire, the BEGGAR'S OPERA by the poet Gay and the "borrowing" musician, Papusch—produced in London, 1728.[21]

Our earliest art songs came directly from Europe, or were later composed here by transient foreigners (or their American pupils), and were written in the current European style.

Among these was James Bremner, the teacher of Francis Hopkinson. After the Revolutionary War, many English and German composers resumed their visits; notable among these were Victor Pelissier, a French virtuoso on the horn who composed an "American Opera," EDWIN AND ANGELINA, first produced in New York, Dec. 19, 1796. A song from that work, *The Bird When Summer Charms No More,* is sometimes heard today; Charles E. Horn (1786–1849), a musician of German lineage who wrote popular songs about the American scene—especially of New York City, but who is remembered most for his more serious songs *Cherry Ripe, I Know a Bank whereon the Wild Thyme Grows,* and *I've Been Roaming*—songs that are occasionally heard in some recitals today. An English concert 'cellist, as a contrast to the many English organists, F. N. Crouch (1808–1896), left us the lovely song, *Kathleen Mavourneen* with words by Julia Crawford. Another Englishman, Joseph Philip Knight (1812–1887) wrote over two hundred songs, the most famous of these being the part-song pet of extrovert bassos—*Rocked in the Cradle of the Deep* (1840)!

This period witnessed the rise of a group of native born song composers, "bona fide American musicians" as William Treat Upton calls them. This "crop" contributed some works of value to the development of our native musical literature and artistic traditions, and included George F. Bristow, (1825–1898) —his *Spring Time Is Coming* (1852) is typical—the immortal Stephen Foster (1826–1864)—more about him elsewhere—and Francis Boott (pseu. "Telford," 1813–1904), who composed a large number of songs and choral works. (Incidentally, he left $10,000 to Harvard, his Alma Mater, "the interest of which was to go yearly to the best four-part vocal composition by a Harvard man.") There was also a Vermont composer, Lucien H. Southard (1827–1881), who wrote two complete operas! A Philadelphian, William Henry Fry (1813–1864) composed many songs, and operas—especially LEONORA. Fry was gifted and erudite, and one of the first "to take to the stump" in order to awaken the

[21] Data concerning the authentic *first* American opera and the *first* American "art song" are quite "at sixes-and-sevens." Charleston, South Carolina, claims *both* the first and the second operas in FLORA: OR HOB IN THE WELL (1735), and CLEOPATRA (1773). Authentic, detailed data is missing concerning both these song-ballad-pasticcio "operas." See Donald J. Grout, *Short History of the Opera* (New York: Columbia Press, 1947), Vol. II, pp. 500-501; John Tasker Howard, *Our American Music* (New York: Crowell, 1946), pp. 19-114; and Oscar G. Sonneck, *Early Operas in America,* consult the index. New York City claims the production of "the first serious American opera," TAMMANY: OF THE INDIAN CHIEF by James Hewitt, on March 3, 1794. This is, supposedly, the first performance of an American opera upon on indigenous American theme. The libretto, by Mrs. Anne Julia Hatton, was based upon on Indian story, and much of the music was adapted from real Indian themes. See Edward Hipsher, *American Opera and Its Composers,* pp. 20-27 (Philadelphia: Theodore Presser, 1927). There was an even prior claim by a native American, James Ralph (Phila. c. 1698), THE FASHIONABLE LADY, first produced in London, April 2, 1730. These operatic references are made in this chapter on the art song because the early American operas consisted of sequences, medleys, or *pasticcios,* of separate songs or ballads.

public to appreciate and encourage its native composers. During this period the first American publication of Schubert's songs was made in Philadelphia in 1847. Richard Storrs Willis (Boston 1819–Detroit 1900) established the *Musical World and Times Magazine* in New York, 1854, and issued a number of his art songs in that magazine—*Sleep, the Kind Angel is near Me,* and a song cycle, *March, April,* and *May.*

With the appearance of J. C. D. Parker (1828–1916), not to be confused with Horatio Parker, and his solo song, *Come into the Garden Maud* (1855), there is evident a strongly felt German rather than English influence. Alfred H. Pease (1838–1882), is one of the most prolific art song composers in this group. Among his songs, *Blow, Bugle, Blow* (Tennyson), *Stars of the Summer Night,* and *O, if my Love Would Come to Me* are typical works that indicate he was a composer with a real talent for the medium, and that he possessed much skill (especially in the invention and use of harmonic color) in fashioning art songs which were beyond their time—and, we might add, songs that are worthy of revival today. Following Otto Dresel (1826–1890), who published in Leipzig a large volume of his songs, a veritable swarm of excellent German musicians sought a new home in America. Among them were such artists as Wulf Fries, Frederic Brandeis, Fred Ritter, and Robert Goldbeck—in fact, the typical "musical professor" became generally characterized as the portly, gruff, German musician!

With the appearance of John Knowles Paine (Portland, Me. 1839–1906), Dudley Buck (Hartford, Conn. 1839–1909), and Homer N. Bartlett (Olive, N.Y. 1845–1920), there came into being a significant group of American born composers, well trained, first in their own land and then in Germany—except Bartlett, an infant prodigy, who received his training in New York City, and who is also noteworthy as one of the founders of the American Guild of Organists. Furthermore, Paine, Buck, Bartlett and their pupils were to be the vanguard of several successive "Bostonian schools of music" that made Boston the unquestioned musical center of the entire country—a position gained by New York around 1900. John Knowles Paine is far more noted today for his opera AZARA, the large choral works, instrumental soli, chamber music, and symphonic compositions, than he is for his art songs, four songs each in Op. 29 (1878–1889) and Op. 40 (1885). But this small output was of high quality: the ingratiating melody and flowing piano accompaniment of *I Wore Your Roses Yesterday* (1879, Celia Thaxter); *Early Spring-Time* (1879, Thomas Hill), an original prose-song with a number of daring compositional surprises for the time; and *Martin Song* (1879, Baynard Taylor) with its extraordinary rhythmic and metric patterns. There are but eighteen measures in the voice part, twelve of which are each in a different rhythmic pattern! Paine was the first Professor of Music at Harvard and, in 1875, the holder of the first chair of music in any American university. He left a legacy of distinguished pupils who, in turn, left their permanent influence upon American music: John Alden Carpenter, Arthur Foote, Edward Burlingame Hill, Frederick Converse, the critic Henry T. Finck, and Daniel Gregory Mason who followed Edward MacDowell as head of the music department of Columbia University, New York. A wonderful heritage from a single musician!

Dudley Buck was facile and versatile and wrote many sacred choral works, several operas, a large number of organ compositions, and numerous art songs. Many of his early songs are gaudy, tinsel-like "pot-boilers." After about 1900, however, Buck became more self-critical and wrote a number of worthy works, such as *Hamlet's Soliloquy: To be or not to be* (1903), and the choral works, *The Coming of the King, The Story of the Cross* and *Christ the Victor.* Previously, his symphonic cantata, THE GOLDEN LEGEND, had won a $1,000 prize at the Cincinnati Festival in 1880. In his day, Dudley Buck was, as John Tasker Howard maintains in his OUR AMERICAN MUSIC, a musical missionary with his organ recitals fully as much as Theodore Thomas was with his symphonic organization. In fact, Buck was once an assistant conductor to Thomas. He wrote many art songs, such as: *Sunset, Thou Art Mine, The Bedouin Love Song, Blessed are They, Love's Remorse, Spring's Awakening, Crossing the Bar,* and *It was a Lover and his Lass.* Dudley Buck left a legion of prominent organ and composition pupils, among whom were John Brewer, Harry Rowe Shelley, Raymond Huntington Woodman (whose art song, *The Birthday,* words by Rosetti, has been a popular encore song), Frederick Grant Gleason, Charles Beach Hawley, Charles Ives, William Neidlinger, etc. Another of this group was Homer N. Bartlett, who wrote a great number of solo songs.

Following closely after Paine, Buck, and Bartlett, there appeared another group of native born composers of art songs of the Bostonian school. Among these were Samuel P. Warren (1841–1915), who wrote a number of songs patterned after the styles of Schumann and Brahms, such as: *Sea Foam* with its suggestive figuration in the piano part, and *Love That Hath Us in the Net* (Tennyson). There are two "one-song-composers" whose general popularity has been in inverse ratio to their creative output and musical value; Hart Pease Danks (New Haven 1834–1903), *Silver Threads Among the Gold,* and James Carroll Bartlett (1850–1929), who is known principally for his song, *Dream,* more familiarly called "*Bartlett's Dream.*" There was also the English born composer of skillfully written songs, Clara Kathleen Rogers (1844–1930). Of her songs, *Sudden Light,* Op. 33 (1900, Rosetti) and *Overhead the Tree-tops Meet,* Op. 36 (Browning, 1903), are representative.

The succeeding period up to 1900 disclosed a number of excellent composers who were, aside from Paine, the most distinguished of the Bostonian school so far. These composers and performing artists, through their number and wealth of creative gifts, spilled over into other parts of New England, and then into New York City to form the foundation for the present national musical center. They traveled also to the remote cities of the midwest, even to the West coast. This particular group may be very fairly represented by Arthur Foote, George W. Chadwick, Edward MacDowell, Horatio Parker, Sidney Homer, Harvey Worthington Loomis, Mrs. H. H. A. Beach, Henry F. Gilbert, and Frederick Shepherd Converse. One might also include a contemporary, Charles Wakefield Cadman, for though he was born in Johnstown, Penn., studied in Austria and Germany, and was identified with California in his later years, he spent most of his summers composing at the MacDowell Colony, Peterborough, N.H. Also one might add Ethelbert Nevin (1862–1901), and his popular, sentimental songs, *Oh! That We Two Were Maying* (Kingsley) and *The Rosary;* and Reginald De Koven (1859–1920) for his *O Promise Me,* generally identified with weddings.

Songs by Edward MacDowell, John Alden Carpenter, and Charles Wakefield Cadman are in this chapter's "Essential Listening Study." Lawrence Gilman, music critic of the New York Tribune until his death in 1939, and the leading biographer of MacDowell, said that the best of MacDowell's songs "are not excelled in any body of modern song-writing." [22] Among the best of his songs are: *The Sea, Midsummer Lullaby,* and *The Robin Sings in the Apple Tree,* from EIGHT SONGS, Op. 47; *The Sunrise* from THREE SONGS, Op. 58; *The Swan Bent Low to the Lily* (one of the best), *Long Ago,* and the lilting *A Maid Sings Light* from FOUR SONGS, Op. 56; *To the Golden-Rod* from THREE SONGS, Op. 60—MacDowell's last song group; and the "runners-up," *Constancy,* from Op. 58, *As the Gloaming Shadows Creep,* from Op. 56, and *Fair Springtide,* from THREE SONGS, Op. 60.

Here are the words of *The Sea,* written by William Dean Howells. Observe how the iambic meter (ti-DUM, ti-DUM, etc.) of the poem and the six-eight meter and rhythmic pattern of the music impart a gently swaying effect. MacDowell marked the tempo of the song, "Broadly, with rhythmic swing." The rich chords in the piano part dim the tragic import of the poem:

One sails away to sea, to sea,
One stands on the shore and cries;
The ship goes down the world, and the light,
And the light on the sullen water dies.

The whispering shell is mute,
And after is evil cheer;
She will stand on the shore and cry in vain,
Many and many a year.

But the stately wide-winged ship lies wrecked,
Lies wrecked on the unknown deep;
Far under, dead in his coral bed,
The lover lies asleep.

(It should be noted that MacDowell wrote the lyrics for many of his songs as well as those prefacing his piano pieces.) As with all the other compositions of MacDowell, save for some of the earlier ones written in Germany, there is in his style an originality of harmonic and melodic

[22] See Lawrence Gilman, *Edward MacDowell: A Study* (New York: John Lane, 1908); John F. Porte, *Edward MacDowell: A Great American Tone Poet: His Life and Music* (New York: E. P. Dutton, 1922); and a Ph.D. thesis, John Miller, *Edward MacDowell: A Critical Study* (University of Rochester: Eastman School of Music).

invention and treatment, an ever present lyrical and poetic charm, a lively, buoyant spirit, and an unabashed expression of deep romantic feeling, with a pervading nostalgia; and here and there in his compositions, especially those for piano, there are also signs of the tempers of Impressionism. (See Additional Suggestions for Listening, Chap. 29.)

MacDowell's voice parts are melodic, flowing, and ingratiating to the listener as well as the singer, and they seem to grow right out of the poetry itself. The piano parts are harmonically colorful and unmistakably MacDowell; but the composer did not make the most out of the possibilities of the accompaniments—a shortcoming which detracts from the effectiveness of his songs.

From the 450 to 500 songs by Charles Wakefield Cadman (1881–1946), we have selected two art songs that are typical of him and the native American traits he personified, i.e., the use of American Indian themes or characteristics, idealized and incorporated into Western musical styles —a national idiom which MacDowell had pioneered years before him. The song, *From the Land of the Sky Blue Water,* from FOUR INDIAN SONGS, Op. 45 (1909), is an expert idealization of Indian themes. The piano part is original in harmonic and melodic treatment simulating an Indian flute here and there, and serves admirably as support and background. (Cadman sent the FOUR INDIAN SONGS to twenty-eight publishers before they were accepted for publication—and they are still being issued!) Another Cadman art song is *The Song of the Robin Woman,* originally from his American Indian Opera SHANEWIS. It is sung by the Robin Woman, as she paddles her canoe, and contains some interesting poly-rhythms, including the motions of the paddling, such as are in some native Indian dances and songs. As with many prolific professional composers, there are many inferior "pot-boilers" in Cadman's output; but even those exhibit an innate feeling for the voice and lyrical melody. Among his other worthy art songs are *I Hear a Thrush at Eve* (the actual thrush "song" is used in the first measures of the melody), *At Dawning,* which is considered among his best songs, and *The Heart of Her.*

John Alden Carpenter (1876–1951), unlike MacDowell and Cadman, was an amateur in the strictest sense, for he made his living in business. He was a superb musician and creative artist, however, thoroughly schooled in musical craftsmanship, and abundantly endowed by nature in those rare poetic and imaginative gifts that cannot be acquired. Carpenter wrote some of the finest works of their kind to be found in American music literature—instrumental compositions of various sorts, ballets, works for symphony orchestra, concerti, chamber music, choral writings, and art songs. Of his art songs, we have chosen for listening study the lovely *When I Bring You Colored Toys* from GITANJALI (1915), a setting of six poems by Sir Rabindranath Tagore, East Indian poet and Nobel Prize winner (1913), consisting of the song just mentioned, plus *On the*

Day When Death Will Knock at Thy Door, The Sleep that Flits on Baby's Eyes, I am Like a Remnant of a Cloud of Autumn, On the Seashore of Endless Worlds, and *Light, my Light.* The piano parts with their contra-melodies, unusual invention of figuration, the use of original, colorful, chromatic harmonic writing, and the inherent unity of the accompaniment with the voice and poetry fuse the whole into an art song of distinctive beauty.

Besides the GITANJALI CYCLE, we also suggest the following songs: *Water Colors* (1916, from the Chinese), *Two Night Songs* (1927), *The Green River* from EIGHT SONGS (1912), *Worlds* (1935), *The Pools of Peace* (1936), *Go, Lovely Rose* (1912) and *Looking-Glass River* (1912, Stevenson), *Chanson d'Automne* from FOUR VERLAINE SONGS (1912). The listener will enjoy the jazz rhythms in FOUR NEGRO SONGS consisting of *Shake your Brown Feet, Honey; The Cryin' Blues; Jazz-Boys;* and *That Soothin' Song.*

One of the most promising and original American geniuses was Charles Tomlinson Griffes (1884–1920), whose untimely death cut short a career with a legacy of comparatively few eloquent and skillfully written works. His earlier compositions reflected his rigid Germanic training, and show strong leanings toward Brahms and Richard Strauss. Many of Griffes' art songs, and his instrumental and orchestral works too, were tinged with orientalism and mysticism as shown in the chromatic melodic line, oriental scales and effects, and colorful impressionistic harmonies, instrumentation, and exotic rhythms. Of his art songs, *Lament of Ian the Proud, Thy Dark Eyes to Mine, The Rose of the Night* (1918, to poems by Fiona MacLeod) are among the best. *In a Myrtle Shade* (1918, William Blake), *Wai Kiki* (1918, Rupert Brooke), a pair, *An Old Song Resung* and *Sorrows of Mydath* (posthumous, 1920), with common themes interwoven in both songs, and *Five Poems of Ancient China and Japan,* Op. 10 (1917), are interesting and varied early efforts. Griffes showed in the first five songs that he was already capable of expressing deep emotions with grace and natural flow of melodic line, poetic sensitiveness, and sureness of compositional technique. The piano parts of his songs glow with vivid and, for their time, daring harmonic colors. (For his orchestral and other instrumental compositions see Additional Suggestions for Listening, Chap. 29.)

ADDITIONAL SUGGESTIONS FOR LISTENING

GERMANY: Schubert: *Liederalbum für die Jugend,* Op. 79 (1849), 28 songs. Schumann: *Lieder und Gesänge* (5 sets, Opp. 27, 51, 77, 96, 127); *Zwölf Gedichte,* Op. 35 (1840), 12 songs; *Liederkreis,* Op. 39 (1840), 12 songs; *Frauenliebe und Leben,* Op. 42 (cycle of 8 songs); *Vergebliches Staendchen; O versenk' dein Leid, mein Kind.* Brahms: 15 Romances, Op. 33, from Tiecks ("Magelone"); *Songs Book I,* Op. 32; *Vier ernste Gesänge* (very important); *Vier Gesänge,* Op. 43 (1857–68), composed of such great songs as: *Von ewiger*

Lieber, Die Mainacht, Ich schell' mein Horn, and *Das Lied vom Herrn von Falkenstein; Fünf Gesänge,* Op. 49 (1864–68), composed of *Am Sonntag Morgen, An ein Veilchen, Sehnsucht, Wiegenlied, Abenddämmerung;* and from here it will not be difficult for the listener to find his own way.

Wolf: *Anakreon's Grab, Wiegenlied im Sommer, In dem Schatten, Meiner Locken, Zur Ruh, Komm' O Jod, Dereinst, An eine Aeolsharfe, Gesäng Weyla's* (in Aria form), *Abschied* (with its nostalgic and quasi-atonal melody), and *Der Rattenfänger* (the happy-go-lucky, humorous ballad about the Rat-catcher, or Pied Piper).

Richard Strauss (1864–1949) was a man of stature, and his lieder, with their distinctive chromaticism, in some instances came very close in artistic merit to the songs of Schubert and Schumann. We suggest his *Zeignung, Die Nacht,* and *Allerseelen* from Op. 10, the ever-popular *Ständchen,* and the *Barcarole,* both from Op. 17, *Breitüber mein Haupt,* Op. 19, *Cäcilie* and *Morgan,* from Op. 27, *Traum durch die Dämmerung* which Strauss quotes in his tone poem, *Ein Helden leben,* from Op. 29, *Ich trage mein Minne* from Op. 32.

Robert Franz (1815–1892), family name Knauth, was one of the "five great" German lied composers. He published 350 songs, some of which have been universally admired for their "perfect fitness and exquisite finish of the musical setting" The songs are marked by short strophic treatment in a formal sense—dignified and reticent rather than dramatically bold. These are among his better known songs: *Die Lotos Blume,* Op. 1, No. 3, *Mutter, O Sing mich zur Ruh,* Op. 10, No. 3, *Widmung,* Op. 14, No. 1, *Es hat die Rose sich Beklagt,* Op. 42, No. 5—a favorite along with *Widmung* and *Aus meinen grossen Schmerzen,* Op. 5, No. 1, *Wonne der Wehmuth,* Op. 23, No. 1, *Madchen mit dem Rothen Mündchen* ("Little Maid with Lips so Rosy," Op. 5, No. 5—a great favorite), and *Mein Schatz ist auf der Wanderschaft,* Op. 40, No. 1. The songs of Adolf Jensen (1837–1879) are about 160 in number, and are much influenced by Schumann. These are among his best: *An den Linden, Im Walde, O lass dich halten, Gold'ne Stunde, Lehn' deine Wang,* and *Alt Heidelberg.*

The best songs of Gustav Mahler (1860–1911) are his dramatic narratives for voice and orchestra, such as *Das Lied von der Erde.* The songs of Ferdinand Löwe or Loewe (1865–1925) are of a different style from those of the composers we have just mentioned; for, in addition to his 250 art songs, he wrote about 150 ballads for voice and accompaniment. The better known of these dramatic ballads are: *Edward,* Op. 1, No. 1 (which same old Scottish tale also served Brahms for his very dramatic *Ballad No. 1,* the first of four *Ballads and Romances,* Op. 75, for alto, tenor and piano), *Erlkönig* (see also Schubert's song of same title), *Der Nöck, Heinrich der Vogler, Die verfallene Mühle* (The Broken Down Mill), etc.

SCANDINAVIA: (Danish), Weyse, F. Kuhlan, Hartmann (father and son), Gade, Woldemar Bargiel, and the more recent Carl Nielsen and Gosta Nystroem; (Norwegian) Sinding, Lie, and Kjerulf; (Swedish) Geijer, Lindblad, J. Josephson, Södermann, Kurt Atterberg, Stenhammer, and especially Emil Sjögren. (Finnish) Jean Sibelius, who wrote some 90 songs with piano. These are recommended: the popular, sentimental *Black Roses,* the elegiac *Ingallil,* the biting satire of *Tennis at Trianon,* from Op. 36, *On a Balcony by the Sea,*

Op. 38, *Echo Nymph,* the effective setting of Runeberg's *A Hundred Ways* from Op. 72, or the excellent songs from Opp. 86, 88 or 90.

RUSSIA: Alexander Borodin (1833–1887), a musical amateur and world renowned chemist, is best known for his symphonies, string quartets, symphonic poems, ballets, especially the one from his opera, PRINCE IGOR, and other instrumental works. He also wrote some beautiful art songs, such as: *Sleeping Princess, The Song of the Dark Forest, Dissonance, My Song is Fierce and Bitter, The Princess of the Sea, The Sea, The Wondrous Garden,* that show marked oriental and exotic influences. Alexander Dargomijsky (Dahrr-gom-ISH-key, 1813–1869) wrote a number of atmospheric, oriental, and lyrical songs, such as *O Thou Rose Maiden.* Alexander Gretchaninoff (Gretch-an-EEN-off, (1864–1956) lived in America from 1941. He wrote some 258 songs for solo voice with piano, and some with orchestral accompaniment. He is one of the best of the Russian composers with such songs as: *Snowflakes, The Captive, Slumber Reigns, The Siren On the Steppe* ("Triste est le Steppe"), *Palm Branches, Another Little Hour I Begged,* etc.

The earlier songs of Igor Stravinsky (1882—a U.S. citizen in 1945), show acquaintance with the German lied, Schubert and Schumann in particular; but a short time later, one may observe the strong influences of the French Impressionistic school, especially Debussy. These traits may be observed in *The Cloister,* Op. 6, No. 1, and *Le Faune et la bergère, Un grand sommeil noir,* Op. 9, No. 1, and *La lune blanche,* Op. 9, No. 2—both set to Verlaine's poems, *Trois Petites Chansons* (1913) and, similarly, *Four Russian Songs* (1918–1919). His much later works which involve the voice are very individual, neo-classical, and even pan-tonal in style and are far removed from the type of song we have been discussing in this chapter. Serge Prokofieff (1891–1953) wrote more than twenty-five art songs among which are: *The Ugly Duckling,* Op. 18 (1914) and *Songs on Pushkin's Poems,* Op. 73 (1936). Dmitri Shostakovich (1906–) though he has written *Songs on Poems by Robert Burns,* for bass voice, is not renowned as a song writer.

THE UNITED STATES: Mrs. H. H. A. Beach (1867–1944) who wrote some 150 art songs, of which *The Year's at the Spring, Ah, Love, but a Day, Ecstasy,* and *Fire and Flame* are well-known; Louis Campbell-Tipton (1877–1921), best known for his popular *The Spirit Flower,* though it hardly equals *After Sunset, Darkness, The Crying of Water and Requiem* from FOUR SEA LYRICS (1907); George W. Chadwick (1854–1931), *Bedouin Love Song, Told in the Gate* (eleven songs to poems by Arlo Bates), *When I am Dead* (Rossetti) and *Three Nautical Songs* to words by Conan Doyle of "Sherlock Holmes"; Israel Citkowitz (1909–), *Five Songs* (1930), settings of "CHAMBER MUSIC" by James Joyce. Note the prevalence of modern counterpoint, dissonant harmony, and quasi-atonality (also *Gentle Lady* (James Joyce) in which Citkowitz ventures further into Schönbergian techniques and style); Bainbridge Crist (1883–) *Four Songs* (Conrad Aiken), *O, Come Hither* (for coloratura), *If there were Dreams to Sell, Mistletoe* and especially the following from a cycle of four songs, *Into A Ship Dreaming, April Rain* and *Colored Stars,* for in these Crist is at his best. Walter Damrosch (1862–1950), the late conductor, composed a number of narrative ballads the best known of which are *Mandalay, Death and General Putnam,* and *Danny Deever.*

Arthur Farwell (1872–1952) wrote *The Wild Flower's Song, On a Faded Violet,* and many American Indian adaptations; Vivian Fine (1913–), *Comfort to a Youth that had Lost his Love* (1933–) (note the constantly changing meter and rhythm and the use of Schönbergian atonality); Arthur Foote (1853–1937) wrote more than one hundred art songs including: *Tranquility,* Op. 39, *Ships that Pass in the Night, How Many Times do I Love Thee, Dear; Persian Song,* Op. 40, *In Flanders Fields; Oh, Red is the English Rose,* Op. 79; Vittorio Giannini (1903–), a very gifted and capable composer has written many beautiful art songs among which are: *Waiting, Song of the Albatross, the Poets Prayer* and *Moonlight.* Walter Golde (1887–), *O Beauty, Passing Beauty* (sonnet by Tennyson). G. A. Grant-Schaefer (1872–1939), *The Eagle, The Sea* and the popular encore song, *Cuckoo Clock.* Henry Kimball Hadley (1871–1937) composed about two hundred art songs of which our limited choices are *The Time of Parting* (Tagore) and *Colloque Sentimentale* (Verlaine). Richard Hageman (1882–) *Song Without Words* (for coloratura voice), *Christmas, Charity,* and *Do Not Go My Love,* which is undoubtedly his best known and rightly favored song.

Sidney Homer (1864–1953), *Banjo Song* (a great favorite), *The Song of the Shirt, Sing Me a Song of a Lad that is Gone* (Stevenson) one of his most representative songs. Charles E. Ives (1875–1954) privately published a volume of 114 songs—an uneven "rag-bag" accumulation composed between 1888 and 1922. Our pick of the songs, No. 17, entitled *Grantchester.* Horace Johnson (1893–) a gifted composer of songs, wrote *Thy Dark Hair, The Pirate, When Pierrot Sings* and *The Cherry Trees.* A. Walter Kramer (1890–), *The Great Awakening, Invocation, Beauty of Earth* (a cycle of Sonnets by Towne) and *The Last Hour* are typical of Kramer's songs. Frank La Forge (1879–), *I Came with a Song, When Your Dear Hands, A Song of the Open* and *Longing.* Roger Sessions (1896–), *On the Beach at Fontana* (James Joyce). Arthur Shepherd (1880–1954), *There is a Light in Thy Blue Eyes* and *The Lost Child,* from FIVE SONGS, Op. 7—very colorful songs. Leo Sowerby (1895–), *O God of Light, O Jesus, Lord of Mercy Great,* and *Thou Art My Strength* (for soprano with organ). These are among the best religious art songs in American song literature.

Oley Speaks (1876–1948), one of the best composers of the lighter vein, has written more than 300 songs. Among the best known are, *On the Road to Mandalay, Life's Twilight, To You* and the tender, ever-popular love song, *Sylvia.* Randall Thompson (1899–), *Velvet Shoes* and *My Master Hath a Garden.* Bernard Wagenar (1894–), *Song of Agamedes* (an excellent song) and *From a very Little Sphinx,* a song cycle (1925). Wintter Watts (1884–) *Alone, The Poet Sings; Joy* (one of his best) and *Vignettes of Italy,* a cycle of nine songs. We might readily mention many more American composers had we the space.

BRITAIN: [23] John Dowland (c. 1562–1626) whose first book of "songs and

[23] Only a limited list of composers and their works can be mentioned. Those who desire to delve still further into British art songs, we refer to: *British Music of our Time,* edited by H. L. Bacharach (Penguin Books No. A-156), which lists composers, pertinent works, and recordings on pp. 228 to 256; *Music in England* by Eric Blom (Penguin Books No. A-107); *Music and Society: England and the European*

ayres" appeared in 1595; Thomas Arne (1710–1778) who is more generally known today for his patriotic song, *Rule Britannia* (*The Lass with the Delicate Air,* was composed by Thomas Arne's son, Michael); John Dunstable (c. 1390–1453), the "Father of English Composers" composed many art songs with accompaniment. Henry Purcell (c. 1658–1695), one of the greatest English composers, composed many solo songs accompanied by viols or virginal.[24] William Byrd (c. 1542–1623), Orlando Gibbons (1583–1625), John Bull (c. 1562–1628), Thomas Tallis (c. 1505, or 1510–1585), Thomas Weelkes (c. 1575–1623), and Thomas Morley (1557–1603) are among the foremost English composers of all time though their extant works are largely contrapuntal *a cappella* part-songs. Morley is well known for his art song, *It Was a Lover and His Lass,* to words from Shakespeare's AS YOU LIKE IT. The introduction of Italian opera into England (c. 1600) stimulated the composition of art songs, though part songs went on their separate ways.

George Frideric Handel visited England in 1710 and in 1712, and came to stay permanently in 1714. Thereupon he introduced his versions of Italian opera, and they soon became the accepted fashion for sometime to come. Not until the time of Sir Edward Elgar's ascendancy, around 1890, did England make any progress in shaking off the over-powering influences of Handel, Haydn, Mendelssohn, Wolf, and the German Classical and Romantic schools in general. (Later British music was also to feel the strong impact of Debussy and the school of French Impressionism.) This newly found freedom of a distinctively British verve of self-expression, "a hearty, bluff Englishry," has been the most marked period of its kind since Henry Purcell. The "come back" has been so productive of outstanding works that the contemporary movement has already placed Britain to the fore among musical nations.

In addition to his preoccupation with comic operas in collaboration with William S. Gilbert (1836–1911), Sir Arthur Sullivan (1842–1900) composed some excellent religious music and a number of art songs. Among these last are his settings of Shakespearian Songs, *Song of the Wrens* (Tennyson), and the popular *I'll Sing Thee Songs of Araby.*

Sir Charles Hubert H. Parry (1848–1918), one of the outstanding composers in English musical history, wrote over one hundred art songs. Of especial merit are *Gone Were but the Winter,* and the *Tenth Set of English Lyrics.* Sir Charles Villiers Stanford (1852–1924), who has been called by the English writer A. L. Bacharach "the most distinguished and capable British composer at the end of the nineteenth century," wrote a large number of art songs, in-

---

Tradition by W. H. Mellers (New York: Roy Pub., 1951); *A History of Music in England* by Ernest Walker (New York-London: Oxford Press, 1931); *Oxford Companion of Music* (London: Oxford Press, 1956)—articles "Song" and "England," but distinguish between polyphonic songs, harmonic part songs and solo art songs, with or without accompaniment. See also *Music in the Renaissance* by Gustave Reese (New York: W. W. Norton, 1954), Chap. XV, pp. 763-814 and Chap. XVI, pp. 815-883 and references to the individual composers in *The International Cyclopedia of Music and Musicians* (New York: Dodd, Mead & Co., Ed. 1938), one of the very few such references to list art songs!

[24] The popular art song *Passing By* was composed by Edward C. Purcell—pseudonym for E. Purcell Cockram (d. 1932)—and not by *the* Henry Purcell as is usually supposed.

fluenced by German lieder, among which are: *Settings of Poems* by Heine, Opp. 4 and 7, *Clown's Songs* from TWELFTH NIGHT, Op. 65, *Die Wallfahrt nach Kevelaar* by Heine, Op. 72, *Sonnet After Holmes,* Op. 82, *My Love's an Arbutus,* and others. Sir Edward Elgar (1857–1934) wrote more than fifty-seven art songs, some of the best of which are: *Where Corals Lie* from SEA PICTURES, Op. 37, *Millwheel Songs I* and *II, A Song of Autumn, Under Thy Window, Rondel* from Op. 16, *In the Dawn,* Op. 41, *Twilight* and *Oh! Soft was the Song,* Op. 59, and *The Torch* and the *River,* Op. 60. Sir Granville Bantock (1868–1946) composed a large number of art songs, many with an oriental "flavor": PERSIAN SONGS, from which we select the *Drinking Song.* Goring Thomas (1851–1892) is most noted abroad for his beautiful art song for tenor, *Summer! Summer! I depart,* from THE SWAN AND THE SKYLARK.

Here are a few songs representative of the modern British renaissance composers: Sir Arnold Bax (1883–1953), *I Heard a Piper Piping* and *The White Peace* from SEVEN SELECTED SONGS. Frank Bridge (1879–1941), the popular *Love Went A-Riding* and *Come to me in My Dreams.* Benjamin Britten (1913–), the set of nine songs, THE HOLY SONNETS of John Donne Op. 35, and the SEVEN SONNETS OF MICHELANGELO, Op. 22. Frederick Delius (1863–1934), "the British Impressionist" was a musical "maverick," for his works show the influence of Wagner, Debussy, Thomas E. Ward, his American teacher in Florida (1834–36), Richard Strauss and Grieg. Witness the melodramatic *Paa Vidderne* after Ibsen and his orchestral suite, EVENTYR (1917) after Norwegian folk stories by Asbjorensen and Moë. He composed about fifty art songs among which are: *Black Roses* (1901), *Indian Love Song, To the Queen of My Heart* and *Love's Philosophy* from THREE ENGLISH SONGS (Shelley, 1891), *Autumn* (1900) and *Irmelin Rose* from SEVEN SONGS FROM THE DANISH (1897).

Ivor Gurney (1890–1937) wrote some beautiful songs such as: *Seven Meadows* (Gurney); *The Folly of Being Comforted,* LUDLOW AND TEME and THE WESTERN PLAYLAND (two song cycles based upon poems by Housman) and *Desire in Spring* (Ledwidge). Gustav Holst (1874–1934), NINE HYMNS FROM THE RIG-VEDA, Op. 24, FOUR SONGS FOR VOICE AND VIOLIN, Op. 35 and TWELVE SONGS, Op. 48, to words by Humbert Wolfe. John Ireland (1879–), wrote over one hundred beautiful art songs. Representative among these are: FIVE SONGS TO POEMS BY THOMAS HARDY, WE'LL TO THE WOODS NO MORE (a cycle of songs on poems by Housman), *Spring Sorrow, I have Twelve Oxen,* and *Sea Fever.* Ernest John Moeran (1894–1950) whose music smacks of an Irish character, wrote a number of art songs. Among these are SEVEN POEMS OF JAMES JOYCE and some early settings of Housman's poems. Roger Quilter (1877–1946) was a composer of lighter art songs, and is well known for the concert songs, *Now Sleeps the Crimson Petal,* from SEVEN ELIZABETHAN LYRICS, *To Sylvia* and *Three French Nursery Songs.* Cyril Scott (1879–) wrote some eighty Impressionistic art songs such as: *My Lady Sleeps, An Old Song Ended, Lilac Time, Waiting* and *A Picnic* (from TWO CHINESE SONGS).

Ralph Vaughan Williams (1872–1958) has composed comparatively few art songs, in the strict sense, but they are superb. The FIVE MYSTICAL SONGS (Hubert) for baritone solo with chorus are generally considered among his finest. His other art songs include: *Silent Noon* from THE HOUSE OF LIFE (six sonnets by Rosetti), *The Water Mill,* the popular *Linden Lea, Whither Shall*

I Wander, and THE PILGRIM'S PROGRESS consisting of seven songs. Peter Warlock (1894–1930) published his musical compositions under the name of Warlock and his musical prose writings under his real name, Philip Haseltine. From his many songs, we have chosen: SAUDADES of 1916–17, nostalgic and atonal, especially *As Ever I Saw* and *My Ghostly Fader, Romance* (a gem), LILLYGAY (a set of five songs), *Captain Stratton's Fancy, Sleep* (from the set, THE WOMAN HATER, poems by Beaumont and Fletcher). These last mentioned songs remind one of the early sixteenth century English lutenist, Dowland. Last, and outstanding is THE CURLEW (a song cycle on poems by Yeats) for tenor, English horn and string quartet. It won the Carnegie Award in 1923!

ITALY: [25] Unlike the extended history of the transformations and development of the art song in Germany, France, and Britain, this type of concert art song seems to have been a rather modern development in Italy—the cradle of song! Of course there existed, as elsewhere in Europe, the traditional, minstrel-like songs and a few composed folk songs of love and adventure, ballad and narrative; but not many of these reached the stage of transformation to the real art song.

Throughout the late seventeenth and most of the eighteenth centuries, there appeared small collections of *arie, ariette, canzonette* and other types of lyric songs, generally in the A–B–A′, or *da capo* forms common to operatic arias. Following are some typical examples of the styles and forms of songs that have survived: ITALIAN ANTHOLOGIES OF SONG, includes such songs (*arias*) as: *Vittoria mio core* by Giacomo Carissimi (1605–1674), *Spesso vibra per suo gioco* (a jolly "patter" song) by the Italian Master Alessandro Scarlatti (1659–1725), father of the composer and harpsichordist, Domenico Scarlatti (1685–1757). Other excellent examples of that period are *Piu bella aurora* and *Chi sente interno al core* by Bonifazio Asioli (1769–1832); the still popular *Caro mio ben* by Giuseppe Giordani (1744–1798), often called "The Italian Schubert"; *La foletta,* a brilliant song in operatic style, by Salvatore (*recte* Cavaliere) Marchesi who was a great singer and teacher of "bel canto." *Nina* by Giovanni Pergolesi (1710–1736) is one of the finest songs from this golden period. He is noted for his opera, *La Serva Padrona,* which served as a model for Italian Opera for a long time and is sometimes performed in our time. An excellent example of classical Italian-type song is *Per questa bella mano* (for basso) by an Austrian, Mozart. One can hardly omit mention of Sir Francesco Tosti (1846–1916), a voice teacher and composer born in Italy who lived many years in England where he was knighted. He is well known for his popular songs *A Vucchello* (a little posy) and *Forever, Goodbye,* and *Mattinata.*

Among the contemporary Italian composers of proved eminence and a few of their representative art songs are the following: Ottorino Respighi (1879–1936), whose most popular individual songs are *Nebbie* (the most famous), *Nevicato Contrasto, Invito alla Danza, Scherzo, Stornellatrice, Stornello dell Opera Re Enzo* (1906). These songs have original accompaniments, excellent vocal parts, filled with emotion, dramatic feeling and Impressionistic tempers. Respighi's prolific gifts poured forth art songs in groups, or sets, such as: FIVE

[25] For lists of art songs of Italy, Spain, and South American countries, consult biographical sketches of individual composers in the *International Cyclopedia of Music and Musicians* (New York: Dodd, Mead and Co., Ed. 1939 or 1949).

SONGS IN THE OLD STYLE (1906); SIX LYRICS (first series, 1909); SIX LYRICS (second series, 1912); FIVE LYRICS (1917); FOUR LYRICS (1920); FOUR ARMENIAN LYRICS (1921) and THREE VOCALISES (1933). Alfredo Casella (1883–1947) composed *Sonnet* (1910), *Two Songs* (1913), *Two chansons anciennes* (1914), *L'Adieu a la vie,* a cycle of four Hindu songs based upon Tagore's GITANJALI (1915. Compare these with the songs by John Alden Carpenter based upon the same poems mentioned elsewhere in this chapter), *Four Favole romanesche* (1923), *Ninna Nanna popolare genovese* (1934); and *Cinque liriche* (1903). These are marked by his neo-classical and modern polytonal style.

Mario Castelnuovo-Tedesco (1895–) a modern romanticist, who writes in a distinctive contemporary harmonic style, uses themes closely modeled after Italian folksongs. Castelnuovo-Tedesco has lived in the United States for many years, but he has, like many other worthy composers, been swallowed up artistically by the movie industry. Among his representative songs written before 1927 are: *Ninna Nanna* (1914), *Briciole* (1916), *Girotondo dei golosi* (1917), *L'Infinito* (1921), *Four Scherzi* (1924–25), *Thirty-three Shakespeare Songs* (1921–25), *Three Sonnets from the Portuguese* (1926), *Six Heine Songs* and *Six Odes di Orazio.* G. Francesco Malipiero (1882–), a modern eclectic, is a master craftsman. Among his songs are: I SONETTI DELLE FATE (a set of six songs based upon poems by d'Annunzio, 1914), CINQ MELODIES (a set of five French songs, 1918), LE STAGIONI ITALICHE ("The Italian Seasons," a song cycle, 1924) and many more. Certainly one of Malipiero's finest songs and considered among the best of Italian songs of our time is *Inno a Maria Nostra Donna* ("Hymn to Mary, Our Lady").

Courtesy The Metropolitan Opera Co., Louis Melancon, Photographer

Giuseppe Verdi

8 The opera

Looking back upon the study we have made so far of vocal music, it becomes apparent that a song is an independent, self-contained work of art. Whatever the song, the words and the music contain all there is to say for the moment, and only a singer is necessary to reveal the content, save when a series of songs constitute a more-or-less continued story or mood—such as one may find in the *song-cycles* of Schubert, *Die Schöne Müllerin,* Op. 25, or *Die Winterreise,* Op. 89; Schumann's *Dichterliebe,* Op. 48, or *Lieder Kreis,* Op. 24; or the more popularly known song-cycle *In a Persian Garden* (from the "Rubaiyat") by Liza Lehmann.[1]

It is a logical step, now, to consider songs that require the addition of something outside themselves, and which are an integral part of a more extended story or environment. There is a type of song that involves participation

[1] Essential listening for this chapter is in Part Two: the opera CARMEN. Other listening selected from Part One is optional.

of others that is incomplete without the cooperation of one or more of the other arts. Such a song is only a small portion of the whole, and thus a number of songs are required in succession, together with connecting singing, spoken dialogue, musical declamation or *recitative* (reh-sih-tah-TEEV), acting, or orchestral music, for the unfolding of the drama. As the moods and situations of the scenes change, so must the songs also change.

Such a type might well be considered an operatic song; and so a number of them in sequence and involving a number of persons might well be a kind of opera. If the tale were a tragic one and much of it sung and acted, it might be called a "grand" opera; if, on the other hand, there were spoken dialogue and action between the songs, and the plot of a cheerful, romantic, and even humorous nature, it might well be an operetta or a "light" opera. Thus the song, or *aria* (AH-ree-ah) as we should now call it, is to be considered as helping to tell a story.

The combination of these different elements into one unified art form seems to answer some deep human need, for we find it throughout history. The Greeks and the Romans had elaborate dramatic performances with song and dance; the Middle Ages and Renaissance saw the emergence of various types of musical plays. We find dramatic spectacles with song and dance, some of great antiquity, in India, China, Japan, Java, and Persia, some inspired by the religious ritual, others quite secular, romantic, or humorous, and of high artistic order. Even primitive cultures have song-and-dance cycles, highly symbolic in character, that display in rudimentary form the elements of the musical-dramatic genre.

In the eighteenth century, especially in Italy, short comic skits, and even sequenced portions of comic operas, were often introduced as *interludes, intermezzi,* or *divertimenti* between the acts of the performance of a grand opera. This afforded an opportunity to pass the time away pleasantly while the scenery and costumes were being changed. The "popular" operas, constructed by the assembling and revamping of these divertimenti, came to adapt some of the techniques and characteristics which grand opera itself had evolved. In return, grand opera seized upon some of the adaptable ideas of comic opera, and thus the two flourished side by side and interacted upon each other—as they still do today! In the early 1950's, the Metropolitan Opera was influenced more by Broadway than the reverse, perhaps to the detriment of grand opera.

Grand opera production in the United States has had an "up-and-down" career. In the 1950's there were hardly more than six, local, full-season, first class opera companies in the land. The *New York Times* music critic (Nov. 15, 1953) insisted that the Metropolitan Opera Association of New York City and the San Francisco companies were the only ones in the country "to produce and support a major operatic season." New York musicians have long insisted that the "Met" was "the only company that compared favorably with the best abroad." Naturally, cities like

the listeners or to opera companies, save in France. The German singspiel (literally "sing-talk") is similar to the French opéra comique, or, at times, like the operetta or even musical comedy. Mozart's DIE ENTFÜHRUNG AUS DEM SERAIL (The Abduction from the Harem, or "Seraglio"), is a good example of the singspiel, and also indicative of the oriental influences which were felt in Europe at the time.

MUSIC DRAMAS. A designation restricted pretty much to the later Wagnerian forms of grand opera, particularly to THE RING OF THE NIBELUNGEN (consisting of the separate works, *The Rhinegold, The Valkyrie, Siegfried* and *The Twilight of the Gods*), PARSIFAL, and TRISTAN AND ISOLDE. These "operas" differ from the typical Italian and French operas of that time mainly in internal compositional and dramatic elements as follows: (a), in the adoption of the leit-motif technique (see Chapter 18) and the cyclic-organic development of the motifs into a continuous flow of melody from the singers *and* the orchestra instead of interposing solos, ensembles, or choral pieces; (b), by greater emphasis upon the plot, the composer's own libretto, and philosophical content, and upon the dramatic elements and actual stage mechanisms; (c), in the greater importance of the narrative value and actual integration of the orchestral part of the score into the fullest meaning of the opera. The orchestra, with Wagner, is no longer mere accompaniment or support.

VOICE CLASSIFICATIONS. The *dramatis personae* of a musical play of any kind are distinguished by their vocal characteristics as well as their dramatic roles. The usual vocal designations are simply: soprano, alto, tenor and bass, but the seasoned opera-lover will encounter some of the following finer shades and distinctions of vocal range, quality, and performing characteristics. Listed are four categories arranged largely in order of range, the highest first: coloratura (high and florid) soprano, lyric soprano, dramatic soprano, mezzo-soprano, mezzo-contralto, contralto and real alto (rare—alto-tenor and alto-baritone). The men's voices are: tenor, high or low, dramatic or heroic tenor, lyric tenor, mezzo-tenor or low second-tenor, almost a baritone, high baritone (sometimes called "Rossini" baritones because of the demands of that composer for very high and extremely agile voices), bass-baritone, basso-cantante, and basso-profundo. The range, *tessiture* (general "lie" of the voice), timbre, and peculiar performing characteristics determine the classifications.

ADDITIONAL SUGGESTIONS FOR LISTENING

For excerpts from the MARRIAGE OF FIGARO, listen to the *Overture*, a tidbit of musical merriment which, although it does not use any of the themes of the opera itself, fully captures the spirit of what is to follow; the aria of Cherubino in the first act, *Non so più cosa son* (I Know Not What I am Doing), in which he pours out his love for the Countess; the Countess' aria in the second act,

Porgi amor (Love, Thou Pure Impulse), in which she begs the God of Love either to bring her husband back or to let her find release from grief in death; the wonderful *Voi che sapete* (You Who Know, Tell Me), in which Cherubino expresses all his youthful ardor; the song of the Countess in Act III, *Dovo Sono* (They Are Over), in which she looks back with longing to her former days of happiness; and Susanna's beautiful *Deb vieni, non tardar* (Oh Come, Do Not Delay), in the final act. Here is sparkling vocal melody, spontaneous and flowing, pure in form and luminous of texture. The listener might wish to include in his supplementary listening the vivacious and humorous aria from Rossini's THE BARBER OF SEVILLE, *Largo al factotum* (Room for the Factotum), sung by the leading male character, Figaro—a possible prototype of all modern comic "patter-songs."

GRAND OPERA

In the operetta, we found, the plot is carried on through spoken dialogue which, at lyrical moments, reverts to song. In the opera, the dialogue is also sung, in the flexible musical declamation or song-speech known as *recitative,* which gives way, at the lyrical high points, to the arias, the songs, or the airs. This procedure gives us a dramatic work set to music from beginning to end.

Since the theater is a world of fantasy, and the function of music or poetry is to heighten the emotional intensity of the dramatic situation, it is no surprise that theater-goers have accepted the conventions of the play that is sung instead of spoken. Indeed, for over three hundred years the opera has been one of the most popular forms of entertainment.

This acceptance of musico-dramatic art goes back much farther than is commonly supposed. We have already pointed out (in Chapter 4) the role of music in religious ritual. The formal theater, whether in ancient Greek or medieval European civilization, probably sprung out of the religious ceremonial. From the beginning of the Church, the supreme drama of Christendom—the life and death of Christ—has been presented within a framework of words and music. The ceremonial mass became the supreme music drama of Europe. In the later Middle Ages there sprang up the *mystery* and *miracle* plays, containing basic elements of both opera and poetic drama. Based on incidents in Scripture or on the lives of the saints, these plays were originally given either inside the church or in the open space before it, with such realistic props as calves, donkeys, and other Biblical animals. Such episodes as "the lament of the mothers over the slaying of the Innocents" or "the repentance of Magdalene" lent themselves to effective musical treatment. Thus, for centuries before the actual development of the opera, music had become an integral part of the most engrossing symbolic drama known to European man.

On the other hand, no less important elements of the opera came from secular sources. Dance, pantomime, scenic splendor, and certain musical characteristics were derived from the *masques* and *spectacles* which, throughout the feudal period, predominated at the entertainments of the princely courts. The musical-religious play, however, continued its own way.

Musical *declamation* as such stemmed out of the experiments of a group of Florentine noblemen who, spurred on by the spirit of the Italian Renaissance, sought to revive the then lost musical-dramatic art of ancient Greek tragedy, as performed in the works of Aeschylus, Sophocles and Euripides. Among this aristocratic Florentine group were the poets and enthusiasts, Rinuccini, Bardi, and Galilei (the father of the great astronomer-inventor, Galileo), and two composers, Jacopo Peri (1561–1633) and Giulio Caccini (1546–1618). These two, working separately, produced the first real operas. Both were based on the poem EURYDICE and commissioned for the wedding of Henry IV of France to Marie de Medici of Florence, Italy. Peri's version received the first performance in the year 1600, and the score is still preserved. The published work also shows the incorporation of several selections from Caccini's version.

In about 1607, Monteverdi developed the harmonic inventions and increased the effectiveness of the orchestration and the dramatic function of the *recitative,* as shown in his operas ORFEO and ARIANNA. From then on, opera continued to reflect the traditions of the past, the immediate milieu, and the personal idioms of the individual composers, as the drama has done in its own way.[3]

The opera today consists of a number of artistic elements—poetic mood, dramatic action, vocal and orchestral music, painting and stage craft, and, of course, the timing. Even the social atmosphere of the audience and the very occasion itself are "part and parcel" of the total performance. The basic problem in operatic aesthetics is the need to fuse all these separate elements and their many concomitants into an artistically satisfactory, unified production. The fundamental differences between the various operatic styles, in all the periods of operatic history, have sprung largely from the various ways in which the synthesis of all the component parts is accomplished, and from different emphases. The omission of any characteristic components may affect the distinguishing style. Even the styles of individual composers may be differentiated by this mode of analytical thinking. The appreciative listener should bear these principles

[3] For more detailed accounts of the early Italian opera and Florentine Monodists, especially Peri, Caccini, Monteverdi and the poet-librettist of their works, Ottavio Rinuccini (1562–1621), consult *Baker's Biographical Dictionary of Musicians* (New York: Schirmer, 1940); Edward J. Dent, *Opera* (London: Penguin Books, 1940), p. 27 on; Donald J. Grout, *A Short History of Opera* (New York: Columbia University Press, 1947), Chap. 4, p. 27, Chap. 5, p. 51 and Chap. 6, p. 60; W. J. Henderson, *Some Forerunners of Italian Opera* (New York: Henry Holt & Co., 1911), Chaps. 1, 2 and 3.

of stylistic determinants well in mind, but *never* at the expense of listening enjoyment.

The Italians, throughout operatic history, have been enamored of the voice, and developed in their lyric theater a style of *bel canto,* or beautiful singing, that has, in the opinion of many musicians, never been surpassed. Italian opera, consequently, is primarily vocal opera, depending for its appeal on the power and beauty of the human voice. This preoccupation led, on the one hand, to showy exhibition pieces calling for prodigious technique on the part of the singer and, as often as not, having little to do with the mood of the drama, and, on the other, to the development of a style of flowing, sensuous vocal melody that is the glory of the Italian school. The tendency to subordinate drama to voice was pushed so far that in the classical opera of the eighteenth century, the plot became little more than a meaningless, artificial framework for brilliant arias and ensemble numbers. This was the "prima donna opera"—little more than a vocal concert in costume.

By the beginning of the nineteenth century, the Italian opera had already begun to return to the dramatic principles with which it had started. The change was made by three great masters of vocal melody who flourished in the first half of the century, the earliest composers of Italian opera whose works are still performed today: Rossini, whose masterpiece, THE BARBER OF SEVILLE was mentioned earlier in the chapter; Gaetano Donizetti (1797-1848), known for his setting of Walter Scott's tragic story of "Lucy of Lammermoor" (LUCIA DI LAMMERMOOR), as well as the delightful comic operas DAUGHTER OF THE REGIMENT, DON PASQUALE, and ELIXIR OF LOVE; and Vincenzo Bellini (1801–1835), composer of NORMA. Their successor was Giuseppe Verdi (1813–1901), a great dramatic composer, who brought the Italian operatic style to its peak. He perfected a type of melody that was not only attractive to the ear and admirably shaped to the contours of the singer's voice, but essentially dramatic melody: that is, it sprang logically out of the situation on the stage. The famous works of his middle period, RIGOLETTO, LA TRAVIATA and LA FORZA DEL DESTINO (The Force of Destiny), and the three masterpieces of his maturity—AÏDA, OTELLO and FALSTAFF—represent a superb fusion of the great *bel canto* tradition with dramatic truth and musical expressiveness.[4]

The French, on the other hand, loved not only the voice but also logic, literature, elegant diction—and the ballet. They insisted on understanding

[4] His successors followed in his footsteps, adapting the Italian vocal style to the exigencies of modern dramatic realism. Chief among them were Giacomo Puccini (1858–1924), composer of LA BOHÈME, TOSCA, and MADAME BUTTERFLY; Ruggiero Leoncavallo (1858–1919), known chiefly for the ever-popular I PAGLIACCI (The Clowns); and Pietro Mascagni (1863–1945), who wrote CAVALLERIA RUSTICANA (Rustic Chivalry). Although less gifted than the master, they and their confrères all had a flair for vocal-dramatic music that was the essence of their Italian heritage.

what the singers were singing. Consequently, pure vocal line could not gain complete ascendancy over dramatic coherence. Since the composers stood in close contact with the literary men, the principles of French classical drama had some influence on operatic procedure. At the court of the Bourbons, poetic drama, music, and the dance attained a greater homogeneity of style than anywhere else in Europe.

Opera in France had its roots in the elaborate ballet spectacles and masques performed at entertainments for the nobility. It was an Italian, Jean Baptiste Lully (1632–1687), who introduced the new Florentine music drama to the court of Louis XIV and who, by adapting it to the tastes of the French genius, became known as the "father of French opera." His successor in the period of Louis XV was Jean Philippe Rameau (1683–1764), a friend of Voltaire, several of whose librettos he set to music. Rameau was a theorist as well as a composer, and wrote several important treatises on harmony. He was, besides, a trenchant critic who carried on extensive polemics with Diderot, Rousseau, and d'Alembert on the aesthetics of the opera.

In the reign of Louis XVI, it was a foreigner again who guided the destinies of French opera—the German, Christophe Willibald Gluck (1714–1787). Gluck, who achieved his greatest triumphs in Paris under the patronage of his one-time pupil, Marie Antoinette, attempted to lead eighteenth-century opera back to the principles of sound dramaturgy which had been espoused by Monteverde and the Florentine founders of the music drama. For this he is remembered as one of the reformers of the opera. His famous preface to his opera ALCESTE formulates his artistic creed and gives a clue to the significance of his reforms:

> When I undertook to set this poem it was my intention to avoid all those abuses which had crept into Italian opera through the mistaken vanity of singers and the unwise compliance of composers, and which had rendered it wearisome and ridiculous instead of being, as it once was, the most beautiful and imposing spectacle of modern times. I endeavored to reduce music to its proper function, that of seconding poetry by enforcing the expression of the sentiment and the interest of the situations without interrupting the action or weakening it by superfluous ornament. . . . I also thought that my first and chief care as a composer was to aim at a noble simplicity; and there is no rule of composition which I have not thought it my duty to sacrifice in order to favor truthfulness of emotion and produce the proper effect.

The first half of the nineteenth century saw the triumph in Paris of grand opera, a type of heroic drama set in a background of orchestral and scenic splendor. Despite the intensity of its tragic moments and the lofty plane of the action, this genre strikes us today as being somewhat bombastic and pompous. In this period French grand opera reached its peak in the works of the German, Giacomo Meyerbeer (1791–1864), and the Italian, Gasparo Spontini (1774–1851), composer of LA VESTALE.

Meyerbeer's works, enormously popular throughout the nineteenth century, are gradually disappearing from the repertory, although we still hear the *Coronation March* from LE PROPHÈTE, the aria *O Paradiso* from L'AFRICAINE, and that wonderful show piece for the coloratura soprano, the *Shadow Song* from DINORAH.

Until this point, French grand opera was largely the work of Italians or Germans who adapted the international Italian opera style to Parisian tastes. Yet, side by side with this type of opera, there flourished the truly native *opéra comique.* Out of the combination of the two there came into being, about the middle of the nineteenth century, what we consider today the distinctive French contribution to opera, the *drame lyrique* or lyric drama, as typically French in its conception and execution as the opera of Verdi and Puccini is Italian. In the French lyric drama, we have convincing dramatic situations; a type of musical declamation that grows out of the French language; a certain literary quality in the libretto; and a sweet lyricism that is distinct from the dramatic melody of the Italians. The most popular of these French works are Charles Gounod's FAUST (1859), based on an episode from Goethe's drama; Jules Massenet's MANON (1884), a setting of the appealing novel of Abbé Prevost; Camille Saint-Saëns' Biblical opera, SAMSON ET DELILAH (1877); and the finest of French operas, Georges Bizet's CARMEN (1875), a masterful setting of Prosper Mérimée's exciting story. To these may be added two more recent works, Gustave Charpentier's LOUISE (1900), an opera of modern working-class life in Paris; and Debussy's memorable setting of Maeterlinck's symbolist drama PELLÉAS AND MÉLISANDE, the quintessence of the French spirit in modern music drama.

Just as the Italians emphasized vocal melody, and the French, musical declamation, the Germans tended to use the orchestra as the foundation of their music drama. With Richard Wagner this tendency became so pronounced that we may with justice speak of his works as symphonic operas, although the first great composer of German opera, Mozart, had used his orchestra for dramatic characterization and theatrical effect as it had never been used before. When Napoleon asked Grétry the difference between the style of Mozart and that of Cimarosa, he replied: "Sire, Cimarosa puts his statue on the stage and the pedestal in the orchestra; Mozart puts his statue in the orchestra and the pedestal on the stage." We believe today that in Mozart statue and pedestal are one; but the remark provides some insight into the reactions of his contemporaries.

Mozart was one of the outstanding symphonic composers of all time. He was heir alike to the Italian tradition of *bel canto* and the German instrumental style. The combination of the two, plus Mozart's new ideas, produced, in DON GIOVANNI, one of the greatest of operas. In it the orchestra and voice fuse in a perfect unity, and the symphonic background, some of which is epoch making in invention, interprets every significant nuance of the drama with the utmost psychological penetration and power. In the Italian opera buffa tradition, he produced the MARRIAGE OF FIGARO; and in the style of the native comic opera, the *Singspiel,* he wrote, three months before his death, THE MAGIC FLUTE, a fairy opera. With these works, as far as present-day audiences are concerned, German opera begins.

Carl Maria von Weber (1786–1826), generally called "the father of German Romantic opera," is today chiefly remembered for the overtures to his three operas, FREISCHÜTZ, OBERON, and EURYANTHE. In him we find the beginnings of that ardent nationalism, the glorification of German folklore and myth, which reached its culmination in the music drama of Richard Wagner (1813–1883). Outside of Germany, where his operas still hold the stage, Weber is considered of importance in operatic history mainly as having prepared the way for his illustrious successor. Weber is also important because of his general contributions to the establishment and character of German Romanticism of the period and, more specifically, for his colorful, imaginative effects and the furtherance of the techniques of the art of orchestration. Romantic composers like Marschner, Schumann, Berlioz, Wagner, and many others owed a great deal to Weber.

Richard Wagner, particularly in the music dramas of his mature period —TRISTAN AND ISOLDE, the cycle of THE RING OF THE NIBELUNG, and his comic masterpiece DIE MEISTERSINGER (The Master Singers)—represents the peak of German operatic style in the same way Verdi represents the Italian, Bizet and Debussy the French. In Wagner's works the chief protagonist and mainspring of the action is the orchestra. The orchestra reminisces and warns of things to come; it comments on the action like the chorus in Greek tragedy; it weaves a symphonic web that encases actors and audience alike. Out of this seething harmony rises the vocal line, which is declaimed by the singers, geared to the German tongue as intimately as is Debussy's declamation to the French.

Wagner believed that the poetic drama was worthy of the same reverence as a religious ceremonial. His life work represents an attempt, carried through with singular devotion, to purge the lyric theater of the triviality into which it had fallen, and to restore it to the place of honor it had occupied among the Greeks. One of the most original figures in the history of art, he inaugurated a revolution in musical thinking comparable to that effected by his contemporary Darwin in scientific thought. (He has been called by so trenchant a critic as H. L. Mencken "one of the greatest geniuses in the history of man.") Yet, despite the elaborate aesthetic theory that he built up in his philosophical works (his prose writings fill twelve volumes), by making the orchestra more important than the voice in his dramas, he laid himself open to the charge of having misunderstood the fundamental nature of opera. (In any case, his theoretical writings do not always offer a trustworthy guide to what he actually achieved in his operas, for his practice often differed widely from his theory.) Excerpts from his music dramas are played continually at symphony concerts, where they sound effective without the voices—in the opinion of some, even more so. This means, in effect, that Wagner's voices are not indispensable, a condition that would be almost unthinkable in Italian or French opera. Whatever the merits of the controversy, the Wagnerian dramas remain with us, despite their faults, as extended vocal-symphonic tone poems with passages of sweeping power and beauty; and the great moments in them rank unquestionably with the enduring achievements of musical-dramatic art.

As might be expected, German opera is somewhat slower in pace than either Italian or French. The action is less externalized, and the music is less likely (especially in the later Wagner) to be a series of set pieces, or arias. Rather, there is likely to be a continuous flow of song—either one song going imperceptibly into another, or assuming the half-lyric and half-declamatory style that Wagner used in his late music dramas. In the early Wagnerian operas, and those of his contemporaries, one finds the Italian traditions well established.

We have already referred to the *Prelude to Act I* of LOHENGRIN as an example of religious sentiment in music. (The function of the prelude is to create in the audience the proper receptivity for the unfolding of the drama.) The motive reappears in the first act, in Elsa's great aria known as *Elsa's Dream,* in which the falsely accused Princess describes a vision that appeared to her of a knight in shining armor come to do battle in her behalf. The shimmering theme originally heard in the *Prelude* accompanies her recital in the aria, indicating that the deliverer of whom she dreamed is a knight of the Holy Grail. Then, softly, in the brass, we hear a chivalric motive that well describes the brave knight who is on his way to help her—the orchestra assuming the function of a commentator.

The *Prelude to the Third Act* of LOHENGRIN is an outburst of jubilation to celebrate the marriage of the "Swan Knight" of the Grail and Elsa. The tumultuous theme in the trombones sets a mood of festivity, which gives way, in the middle section, to tender lyricism and meditation; then the exuberance returns. At the very end, in the concert version, we hear the ominous theme of doubt, which is to prove Elsa's undoing—she had promised Lohengrin that she would never inquire into his identity. Then, softly, in the brass, we hear repeated the chivalric motive describing the brave knight.

If LOHENGRIN represents the German Romantic opera of Wagner's first period, TRISTAN AND ISOLDE belongs to the fully developed music drama of his maturity. Here is a great paean of love as seen by nineteenth-century Romanticism—love as escape, ecstasy, oblivion. The essence of this mood is captured in the magnificent duet in the second act, *Hymn to the Night* (O Descend Upon Us, Night of Love), sung by the two lovers in the garden of Isolde's palace. Never did dramatic music so eloquently capture the mood of rapture, of sheer sensuous beauty, the power of romantic passion, of wonder and ecstasy—and sustain it to such length!

We shall return to Wagner as a symphonic composer in a later chapter. Suffice it now to point out several other favorite excerpts from his operas that should be heard when time permits—and inclination directs. Among those selections are: *Song to the Evening Star*, the *Pilgrims' Chorus*, and Elisabeth's aria, *Dich teure Halle* (Oh! Hall of Song), from TANNHÄUSER; the *Prize Song* from DIE MEISTERSINGER; Siegmund's *Love Song* from DIE WALKÜRE; Senta's *Ballad* and the *Spinning Chorus* from THE FLYING DUTCHMAN; and Isolde's hymn to love and death, the *Liebestod*, from the final scene of TRISTAN. Acquaintance with these will lead the listener to the complete operas.

The Opera, Carmen, by Georges Bizet (1838–1875)

CARMEN, the essential listening project for this chapter, is generally conceded to be one of the two or three most popular operas of the standard repertory, though its première in Paris in 1875 was a failure.[5] Thus, there is a good chance of hearing it either on the stage or over the radio. CARMEN is filled with beautiful *recitatives*,[6] arias, and ballet tunes that are captivating on the first hearing.[7]

The underlying drama, based on the novel by Prosper Mérimée, adapted for opera by Henry Meilhac and Ludovic Halévy, is more real than that met in most operas. The general tempo of the opera is moving, vivacious, and tragically gripping from the brief overture, or prelude, to the fall of the final curtain. It is a brilliant piece of operatic writing, with vocal parts so well conceived that they almost sing themselves; and the orchestra-

[5] In a series of polls made by the Metropolitan Opera Company several years ago, some 125,000 persons replied and chose as their favorite operas, in the order of preference: 1. AÏDA, 2. CARMEN, 3. LA TRAVIATA! Only a very narrow margin separated the first and second choices. AÏDA, CARMEN, and FAUST as well as LA TRAVIATA, and BOHÈME usually rank among the topmost favorites of opera fans.

[6] A *recitative* is a kind of vocal declamation, free of the restrictions of regular rhythm, form, meter, or regularity of lyrical song, so as to follow more faithfully the accents and inflections of emotionalized speech, or rapidly changing moods in action. It usually parallels the function of the monologue, dialogue, and speech accompanying action in the ordinary drama. The recitative usually precedes the lyrical and necessarily more static set-piece, the aria, throughout the opera; the arias being, more often than not, in the familiar three-part, or ternary, form. The *recitative* permits freedom of action and emotional changes, for one or several parts.

[7] It should be noted here that Micaela's aria in Act III was "lifted" from GRISÉLIDIS, and the ballet scenes in Act III and IV were from ARLÉSIENNE and THE PEARLFISHER—a practice common enough among operatic composers. Also, when Bizet composed CARMEN he wrote it in *opera comique* style with the dialogue spoken; these dialogues were replaced with recitatives, singing parts, composed by Ernest Guiraud (Paris, 1837–1892), thus transforming the work into a more traditional "grand opera" type.

Courtesy The Metropolitan Opera Co., Louis Melancon, Photographer

CARMEN Georges Bizet

tion is so expertly executed that it stamps Bizet a master of that craft. There is in CARMEN musical characterization of a very high order, and a dramatic insight into the persons of the cast as people of real life and not merely stage appurtenances.

If the story of the opera is gone over beforehand and held in mind, the selections indicated for listening will give a good idea of the continuity of the whole, and we hope will create a desire to attend a stage presentation—for nothing can take the place of that. A large number of good recordings are available, from separate pieces to a well-executed condensation. Only the listener's interest and available time can determine the limitations. No other opera adapts itself more naturally to a "record" performance than does CARMEN.

The characters of the opera are, in order of appearance:

Morales, an officer: *baritone*
Micaela, a peasant girl: *soprano*
Don José, a corporal of dragoons: *tenor*

Zuniga, captain of dragoons: *bass*
Carmen, a cigarette girl and Gypsy: *mezzo-soprano*

Gypsies, friends of Carmen, Frasquita, *soprano;* Mercédès, *contralto*
Escamillo, a toreador: *baritone*
Smugglers, El Remendado: *tenor;* El Dancairo, *baritone*
Innkeeper, guide, officers, dragoons, Gypsies, boys, cigarette girls, smugglers, etc.
Time: About 1820
Place: Seville and near-by mountains

Prelude to Act I

The short, potpourri-type *Prelude* to Act I introduces several principal tunes of the opera, especially the *Aragonaise* from the final scene, Act IV, the *Toréador Song* from Act II, and closes with the ominous fate motif which will appear again and again in various guises. This motif is Bizet's adoption of Wagner's leit-motif. The remainder of the opera generally follows the traditional Italian styles, peppered here and there with French idioms. Here is one of the more obvious appearances of the fate motif played at first by the French horns some twenty-five measures from the close of the *Prelude*—these final measures are devoted to elaboration and repetition of this motif.

"Fate Motif."

Act I

The curtain rises, disclosing a guardhouse to the left, a cigarette factory to the right, an overhead bridge in the rear, and an open square to the fore. As center-stage fills with folks waiting to witness the changing of the guards, one hears the lively choruses of the dragoons (soldier-police) and the street boys imitating them, a jolly bit of foolery—note the orchestration here. The chorus of cigarette girls enters from the factory for the noon recess, the principals enter at appropriate moments, and presently the lively stage is ripe for the appearance of Carmen. She emerges from the factory, takes the center of the stage, and sings her saucily fascinating *Habañera.* This particular Habañera owes its origin to Sebastian Yradier (more generally known as the composer of *La Paloma*). It was a popular tune at the time that Bizet composed the opera, so he simply "appropriated" it—and, as the listener will observe, made a great deal out of it.

Here is Carmen's *Habañera* as she sings a song beginning with:

"Love is like any wood-bird wild,
That none can ever hope to tame;" [8]

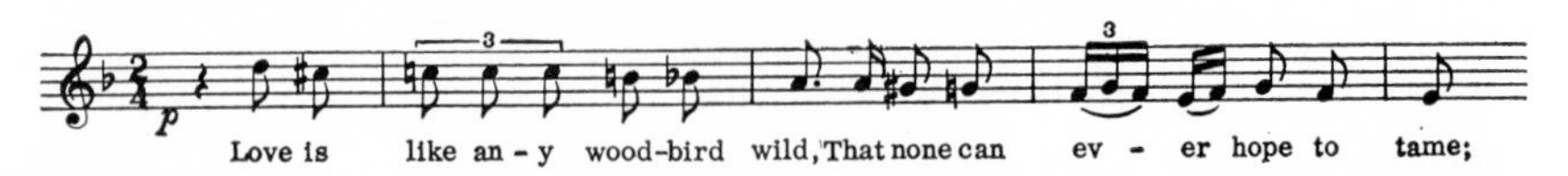

Note how cleverly Bizet has fashioned this song so that it reveals the very essence of the character of Carmen and the situation of the moment. The gypsy girl sways, circling about the quiet soldier, Don José, who has caught her eye, but he remains uninterested and apparently displeased. Carmen continues to work her wiles and Don José seems to succumb somewhat. The factory bell calls the girls back to work, Carmen with them; but before she departs, she takes a flower from her bodice and throws it at Don José. The stage soon empties and Don José is left alone. Slowly, he picks up the flower.

Micaela, a family friend of José and a sort of courier between him and his ailing mother, makes her entry with a message for José. Micaela is not a character in the original Mérimée story (nor was there an Escamillo —only a minor picador, Lucas. She was added by the librettists, not only for her dramatic function but, we believe, to provide a higher soprano role, for the part of Carmen is for a lower, mezzo-soprano voice.) She tells him about a letter from his mother, in the following air:

The two join in a duet, recalling fond memories of home. Micaela exits, and José, after reading the letter in silence, bursts into an avowal of love for Micaela. Presently, a commotion is heard coming from the cigarette factory. The girls rush noisily upon the stage and report that Carmen has stabbed another girl in a fight. José is sent by his superior, Captain Zuniga, to arrest her. When apprehended, Carmen is tied to a chair for

[8] The listener should exercise tolerance when considering opera libretti, especially when they are translated into English. Some libretti do not make the best poetry or the best drama, but they are enjoyed, nonetheless. Besides, directors and singers ofttimes change the words here and there to suit themselves and their voices, and more often than the keen listener suspects, the singers indulge in simple, nonsense syllables instead of words, especially on extreme high or low pitches, awkward passages and long, sustained tones. These are legitimate tricks of the art of singing! The translations in this chapter are from a "working copy" once used at the Metropolitan Opera Company.

temporary safekeeping. Even in this turmoil Carmen continues to flirt with the Captain as well as José, and she sings the captivating *seguidilla*, "Near the Walls of Seville." Here is the beginning of Carmen's *seguidilla:* [9]

By this time, José seems much affected by Carmen's bewitching wiles. The guards return to lead Carmen away, but in the shuffling ruse that ensues, she makes her escape. José is held responsible and he is arrested.

Act II

The first scene is of the inn of Lillas Pastia outside Seville, where Carmen has gone for a rendezvous with José, and also where the two were to join the band of smugglers.

The vivid and atmospheric *Smuggler's Dance* introduces the scene. The delightful rhythmic music of running thirds and "tra-la-la" refrain ushers in the ballet of the gypsy girls. As Carmen watches the dancers, she sings the gay *Gypsy Song* in praise of the wild, carefree gypsy life: [10]

When the sound of gay guitars floats on the air,
The Gypsies spring forth in a merry dance,
Tambourines beat in time with the music
And every voice repeats a merry song . . .

[9] The *seguidilla* is an ancient Spanish dance, probably of Moorish origin, which is in a lively triple measure—in this instance 3/8, M.M. the equivalent to 180 eighth notes per minute. The castanets are usually prominent in this dance. (The M.M. is an abbreviation for *Maelzel's Metronome*, so named after the alleged inventor, J. N. Maelzel, about 1816. Priority claimed and legally accredited it to a Dutch mechanic, one Winkel. The *metronome* is a clock-like mechanism with a swinging pendulum which can be adjusted by a movable weight so as to tick-off loudly at any desired number of times a minute, between 40 and about 208, providing the musician with a fixed standard of playing speed. Beethoven indulges in a bit of burlesquing on the metronome in the *Allegretto* Movement of his EIGHTH SYMPHONY.)

[10] The first phrase of the musical illustration mentions "The tingling of the *sistrum bars,*" a very ancient instrument whose history goes back more than 3000 years to Egyptian and Sumerian times. The Old Testament also mentions it, and it is often evidenced in ancient Egyptian ceremonies to Isis and in various oriental functions. It is not known just where the gypsy tribes picked it up, or if the actual use of the instrument in this song is not wholly a fiction of the librettists, as we suspect it is. The instrument consists, usually, of a hoop with a handle on the bottom of it, and cross bars of metal or strings of small metal discs which give a tingling, metallic sound when shaken like a rattle, which it really resembles.

The rhythm, the melody which grows out of the gypsy smuggler's motive, and the accompaniment of the plucked strings in the orchestra to simulate a guitar, produce a definite Spanish flavor. Oftentimes a cembalo, a type of gypsy zither, joins in with the singing which, together with the familiar clicking of the castanets, the stamping of the feet by the singers, and the ballet that has appeared as if by magic, unite to produce a very colorful scene. The music grows faster and increasingly louder and more abandoned to the close—so typical of this type of Spanish music. It is rare indeed when this scene fails to evoke enthusiastic applause: it is good opera as well as good theatre.

The shouting of the crowd announces the arrival of Escamillo, the popular toréador, at the inn. From the famous, vigorous *Toréador Song,* we now quote part of the beginning and the refrain:

The toréador glowingly describes the exciting life in the bull-ring as one of swift action, reckless courage, applause—and, of course, love. Here we have another melody which is beautiful, fascinating, and adorned with a rainbow coloring of sound effects; it is a faithful portrait of the personality of Escamillo. The entire ensemble joins with Escamillo to build up the peak of the scene, after which the toreador readies to exit amidst noisy plaudits—but before he disappears, he declares his love for Carmen, to which she responds with a sort of "no-but" spirit, for her fascination for José has not quite ceased—so the inevitable triangle is firmly cast with destiny!

After several quintets of differing emotions, sung by Carmen, two companions, and two gypsy smugglers—Frasquita, Mercédès (both mezzo-sopranos), El Remendado (tenor) and El Dancairo (baritone), Don José arrives from the guardhouse, searching for Carmen. Fascinated by the amorous Carmen, he overstays his leave. When she chides him for whatever eagerness he may have had to return to duty, he takes from underneath his coat the remains of the flower she had tossed to him earlier. As José shows the flower to Carmen, he sings one of the most lovely and lyrical airs in the entire work, the *Flower Song.* Here is the beginning of it:

> This is the flow'r you threw to me,
> E'en in the prison, I kept it close.
> Although faded, for me it still retains
> Its sweet perfume.
> Night and day I inhaled its lovely odor,
> And wildly called to you—in vain—
> Hoping only, beloved, to see you once again!

José is torn between love for Carmen and desire to return to duty, but the issue is decided by fate. His superior officer, Zuniga, who has flirted with Carmen at the beginning of the act, returns to the inn. A fight breaks out between Zuniga and José, but they are separated by the gypsies. José then realizes that his life as a soldier and law-abiding citizen is over. He has no choice now but to join Carmen and the smugglers. A forceful and accumulative finale to the act is built up by the entire ensemble and chorus, upon the themes of freedom and love.

Between Acts II and III is an *Intermezzo* of great simplicity and charm. It always seems, to one listener at least, to be a bit out of place in this red-blooded, dynamic opera, and especially inept as a proper and fitting introduction or preparation for Act III.

Act III

The opening scene discloses the gathering place of the smugglers in the mountains. A few left on guard may be seen, lying here and there, wrapped in their long black capes. The *March of the Smugglers* is played by the orchestra as the gypsies enter:

At the termination of the march, a rousing chorus recounts the fearlessness of the gypsies and the rewards of fortunes soon to be had, but it ends with a stout warning, "Be on guard. Be wary."

Don José, tormented by remorse over leaving his dying mother behind and dogged with feelings of jealousy and the consequent quarrels with Carmen, takes no interest in the activities of the smugglers. Carmen walks away from him and joins the gypsy girls, who are telling their fortunes with cards. She shuffles the deck and draws the ace of spades! Again she tries; but the same card turns up—always the ace of spades. *Death—Always death!* she sings desperately, and the orchestra sounds out the Fate motif a half-dozen times—a dramatic stroke!

After a long ensemble and chorus number, the smugglers depart on an expedition, leaving José on guard. All is quiet. The mountain pass seems deserted. Suddenly, Micaela appears. She sings of her love and determination to win José back, asking heaven's aid and protection. This is an excellent example of the French equivalent of Italian dramatic melody. We also note Bizet's genius at delineating character and dramatic situations through the aria:

Micaela spies José high above her on a cliff. She hails him, but he does not hear. A shot is heard, fired by José at Escamillo, who has come to get Carmen. A duel takes place between the two rivals, but it is stopped by Carmen herself when she appears on the scene. Micaela is discovered hiding nearby and is brought to José by the guards. She tells him that his mother is dying, and pleads with him to return to the city with her. Carmen urges him to go for she is now in love with the toréador. José finally leaves but threatens Carmen, "We shall meet again!" She shrugs her shoulder and is soon engrossed in listening to Escamillo's singing of the "Toréador Song" which she hears as though coming from a distance. The cards are flung to the winds, and as the curtain falls, Carmen, defiantly laughing at fate, is heard above the hurried and bustling music of the orchestra.

Act IV

The gay and impassioned *entr'acte* to the fourth act is an appropriate introduction to the spirit and character of the ensuing drama. This orchestral prelude opens with an *Aragonaise* [11] which was first heard in the Prelude to the first act, thus lending unity and coherence. It subsequently provides a lively accompaniment for the opening ballet and chorus, and for the colorful procession led by the children in the square before the bull ring. The Toréador theme follows in the Prelude just as the *cuadrilla* announces the entry of the toréadors in the procession. As we have intimated, the Prelude leads directly to the opening choral and dancing scene. This is Seville on a festive occasion, which, in the larger opera company productions, is one of the most elaborate of stage spectacles. The bullfighters march by in a jolly procession. A shout goes up from the crowd as their favorite, Escamillo, appears in a gaily decorated open carriage with the proud Carmen at his side. Amid the cheering throng, he takes affectionate leave of her, and Carmen reciprocates in song. Carmen remains for a moment, and espies José milling about the crowd. The Fate motif is heard in the orchestra, and a sinister mood fills the scene. Now observe how wonderfully this scene is juxtaposed with the

[11] Aragonesa (Spanish) and Aragonaise (French) is a lively polo Moorish dance in duple meter from Aragon, an old medieval kingdom in NE Spain, now the provinces of Huesca, Zaragoza, and Teruel.

gaiety of the opening scene. The shouts of excitement and praise for Escamillo that come from the crowd in the arena off stage are contrasted with the tragedy that is rapidly unfolding before one's eyes. By this simple means, the tragedy is greatly emphasized and made more poignant.

In the final moments of the scene, we see Carmen confess that she loves only Escamillo, and that she is finished with José. The drama mounts to the climax where José draws his dagger and plunges it into Carmen's heart! The Fate motif thunders and screams forth from the orchestra. The crowd reappears from the entrance to the arena, shouting the praises of the brave and victorious Escamillo. But the gruesome scene changes all that in a flash. The themes of the Argonaise and the Toreador song mingle with the sinister Fate motive. Gendarmes appear to arrest José. He does not resist; instead he weeps bitterly and falls beside the lifeless form of the once gay and carefree Carmen. "Do what you will with me," he sobs, " 'Twas I who struck her down. Ah Carmen! My Carmen! My beloved!" José collapses, heartbroken and remorseful.

And so the final curtain falls upon this stirring tragedy.

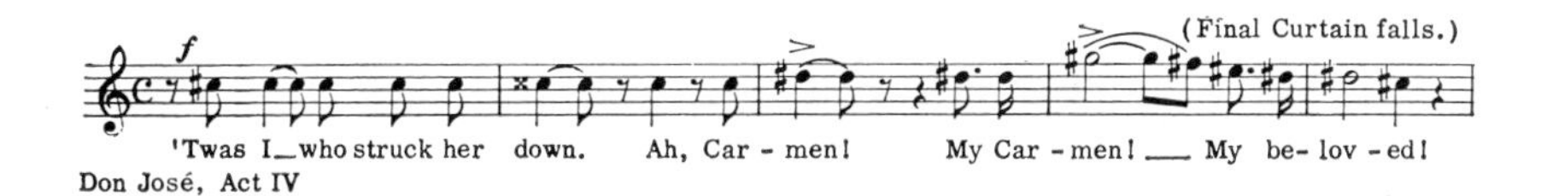

Don José, Act IV

ADDITIONAL SUGGESTIONS FOR LISTENING

Another of the three or four most popular operas in the standard repertory is Verdi's spectacular AÏDA, and we suggest the following numbers, which are readily obtainable in good recordings:

ACT I: *Celeste Aïda* (Heavenly Aïda), sung by Rhadames, tenor; *Ritorna Vincitor* (Return Victorious), sung by Aïda, soprano. ACT II: the opening *Balabili Dance* ballet music, the ballet from Scene 2, and the March of Victory. ACT III: *O cieli azzurri* (O Sky of Azure Hue), sung by Aïda; *Pur ti riveggo mia dolce Aïda* (Again I See Thee, My Own Aïda), sung by Rhadames. ACT IV: *O terra addio* (Farewell, Oh Earth), duet sung by Rhadames and Aïda as the final curtain falls upon their impending death together in the sealed tomb. AÏDA is often chosen to open an operatic season because of its spectacular and colorful pageantry and the many opportunities for impressive scenes on the stage—to say nothing of the countless beautiful arias, the superb choral writing throughout, and the timely and graceful ballets. As for potential scenic effects, AÏDA has few equals. It is an excellent "first" for anyone who has never heard or seen an opera. This is Italian opera at its peak, composed by a master of the stage and traditional vocal styles, one who defies equality of comparison—even with Wagner, in many respects.

It is fitting to follow Verdi by another of his countrymen who has, in many ways, departed from the older traditions and has taken up the more realistic type of thought and expression: Giacomo Puccini (1858–1924), who wrote a popular setting of Henri Murger's sketches of the life of young artists in Paris, LA BOHÉME (Première, Turin, 1896). Characteristic of Puccini's rich vocal line and appealing lyricism is the music of the love scene between Rudolph and Mimi in the first act: Rudolph's vibrant aria, *Che gelida manina* (Your Tiny Hand Is Frozen); Mimi's reply, *Mi chiamano Mimi* (My Name Is Mimi); and the love duet *O soave fanciulla* (Oh Lovely Maiden). From Puccini's other works, the stirring aria from the second act of MADAME BUTTERFLY, *Un bel di vedremo* (Some Day He'll Come), in which the little geisha affirms her belief that her American lover will return to her; Tosca's impassioned plea to Scarpia in the second act of LA TOSCA, *Vissi d'arte* (I've Lived for Art and Love), and Mario's song before his execution, in the third act, *E lucevan le stelle* (The Stars Were Shining) are favorites.

From the two outstanding examples of *verismo,* or dramatic realism, in Italian operas, Leoncavallo's PAGLIACCI and Mascagni's CAVALLERIA RUSTICANA, a number of excerpts have achieved great fame. From the first comes one of the most intense of operatic arias, Canio's anguished outcry that he must go on with his clowning before the audience while his heart is breaking with grief, *Vesti la giubba* (On With the Play):

> Put on your smock, smear your face with powder—
> The people pay you; they must have their fun.
> Even though Harlequin take your Colombine from you,
> Laugh loud, Pagliaccio,
> Hide your grief and play your part.
> Laugh, Pagliaccio, for your love that is destroyed,
> Laugh for the pain that is breaking your heart!

From CAVALLERIA RUSTICANA, the *Intermezzo;* the *Brindisi* or Drinking Song; and the *Siciliana,* the serenade of Turiddu in which he expresses his love for Lola (Thy Lips Like Crimson Berries), are most popular.

From the French opera, a group of representative excerpts would include Delilah's seductive song, *Mon coeur s'ouvre a ta voix* (My Heart at Thy Sweet Voice), from the second act of Saint-Saëns' SAMSON AND DELILAH; the *Jewel Song* (*Air des Bijoux*) in which Marguerite expresses her delight at Faust's gift, from the third act of Gounod's classic, as well as the *Soldiers' Chorus* and the *Serenade of Mephistopheles* from Act IV, and the celebrated waltz, *Ainsi que la brise legère,* from the scene of the Fair in Act II; Juliet's *Waltz Song* from Gounod's ROMEO AND JULIET; Manon's farewell to the little table at which she and Des Grieux have been so happy, *Adieu, notre petite table,* from the second act of Massenet's MANON, as well as Des Grieux' aria later in the act, *Le Rêve* (The Dream), in which he describes the home he plans to share with her; from Massenet's THAÏS, the courtesan's passionate invocation to her mirror, *Dis-moi que je serais belle eternellement* (Tell Me That I Shall Always Be Beautiful!), and the *Meditation,* symbolical of Thaïs' conversion, as famous an instrumental interlude as the *Intermezzo* from CAVALLERIA RUSTICANA; and the rapturous aria of Louise, *Depuis le jour* (Ever Since the Day), in which she expresses her happiness at being with her lover Julien, from the third act of Charpentier's opera, LOUISE.

The finest example of Russian operatic style unquestionably is Mussorgsky's

BORIS GODUNOFF, one of the few Russian operas that has attained a permanent place in our repertory. Listen to the two excerpts from the magnificent final scene, the Farewell of Boris, *Farewell, My Son, I Am Dying*, and the Death of Boris, *Hark 'Tis the Passing Bell!* Boris, who had gained the throne by causing the rightful heir, Dmitri, to be assassinated, realizes that he has reached his end. He asks his nobles to withdraw, and remains alone with his son. With great feeling he bids the child rule justly, and protect his sister Xenia; he hopes the boy will never learn how his father came to the throne. Laying his hands on his son's head, he calls down heaven's blessing upon him. Bells toll mournfully while the voices of the people outside the Kremlin rise in prayer for their Czar. The choral writing here, as in the Coronation Scene, is of surpassing beauty: with Mussorgsky, the emotional base of national opera lay in the chorus. The music, which depicts the anguish of the tormented Czar, rises to a climax of great power, with something of the grim realism that we found in Mussorgsky's songs. A procession of priests files into the royal apartment, followed by the nobles. Boris, in his final struggle with death, points to his son: "Behold your Czar!" and falls back dead, the word "Mercy!" upon his lips.[12]

Throughout the later nineteenth century, German opera was wholly dominated by the Wagnerian "music drama." A new note was introduced by Richard Strauss who, with the orchestral wizardry that was his heritage from the master, Wagner, combined the lyricism and freshness of the lied with the sophistication and sensuous charm of French influences. The result was an idiom creating three works that made operatic history in the first decade of the twentieth century—the brilliant setting of Oscar Wilde's SALOMÉ; the stark and terrifying ELEKTRA, to the libretto of Hugo von Hoffmansthal; and the captivating comedy of eighteenth-century Vienna, DER ROSENKAVALIER (The Cavalier of the Rose). For the full flavor of Strauss' style, listen to the *Dance of the Seven Veils* from SALOMÉ, and the Princess' delirious exultation as she receives the head of the Prophet on a silver charger, *I Have Kissed Thy Lips, O Jokaanan.* The more wholesome side of Strauss' genius animates his immortal DER ROSENKAVALIER. Listen to the enchanting waltzes; the resigned *Soliloquy* of the Marschallin in the first act, as she realizes that soon her charms will fade, and she will no longer hold her youthful lover; the ecstatic *Presentation of the Rose* in the second act, when Octavian meets Sophie and forgets the Marschallin; the great trio in Act III, when the Marschallin unites the youthful lovers and graciously accepts her inevitable defeat; and the final duet of Sophie and Octavian, Mozartian in its limpid beauty and simplicity.

We recommend that the listener hear and see one of the most charming of operas—PÉLLEAS ET MÉLISANDE by Claude Debussy. It will require and amply repay repeated hearings. It is filled with magical fantasy and imagination, originality, unique atmosphere, superb orchestration and a *tout ensemble* that beggars description.

[12] The version of BORIS GODUNOFF one usually hears is that which was completed, orchestrated, and edited by Rimsky-Korsakoff. Prior to that "edition," Mussorgsky himself had prepared a new (or second) version in addition to the so-called original, and many incapable synthesizers have subsequently tried their hands at editing the opera. Naturally, there are arguments of choice. However, we still prefer the Rimsky-Korsakoff version as a whole, with re-arrangements of certain scenes in the last act, for increased dramatic effect.

We have refrained from mentioning many of the larger ensembles to be found in opera, for they are likely to be quite unsatisfactory in records—they must be actually heard and seen on the stage to be fully effective, for dramatic action, the setting, and the function of the ensemble are likely to be of prime importance. However, two very popular ensembles (not choruses) are pointed out here, as illustrating how the composer, by weaving together several threads of song, is able to pour out the emotions of several of his characters simultaneously, the voices joining in a single tonal web of power and effectiveness, though the individual emotions of the participating characters might differ widely.

Perhaps the most famous of ensemble numbers is the *Sextette* from Donizetti's LUCIA DI LAMMERMOOR. Although the broadly flowing melody is known to all the world, it requires some knowledge of the opera to realize how well the music expresses the dramatic situation in the play, and how adroitly each of the six voices reveals the conflicting emotions of each individual character. The *Sextette* is sung in the second act, when Edgar returns to the castle of his enemy, Lord Henry, to find that his beloved Lucy—sister of Lord Henry—has just married another. Edgar is swept by rage and hatred of Henry, yet realizes that he still loves Lucy; Henry, who has engineered the marriage for his own ends, fears for the success of his project; Lucy, who was led to believe by her brother that Edgar was faithless, is overcome with grief and shame when she realizes that she has wronged her lover; Raymond, the kindly chaplain, prays that Heaven will protect Lucy; Lord Arthur, the man whom Lucy has just married, is utterly bewildered; and Alice, Lucy's companion, shares her mistress' sorrow. The individual voices soar and intermingle in a rich harmonic pattern that constitutes one of the great moments in opera.

Equally effective is the *Quartet* from RIGOLETTO, one of the finest of Verdi's many ensemble pieces. Rigoletto, the hunchbacked court jester, attempts to cure his daughter of her love for the profligate Duke, who wooed her, won her, and has now forgotten her. He takes her to the inn where, peering through the door, she may watch the Duke making love to the barmaid Maddalena. The Duke sings a smooth amorous melody to Maddelena; the coquettish barmaid, wise in the ways of the world, retorts that she knows full well he is only trying to flatter her; Gilda, concealed in the darkness outside, pours forth the grief of her broken heart, while Rigoletto sternly vows to avenge his betrayed daughter.

Opera in this country has had a difficult time in overcoming the readiness of American audiences to bask in the Italian, French, and German heritage. Also, it has had to shake off the Old-World operatic traditions in trying to work out native idioms and new means of expression. Then, too, the opportunities for hearing operas written by native composers are not many, and, consequently, the inspiration, encouragement, and tuition that would normally be derived from such performances are absent. A relatively small number of American composers have devoted their efforts to native opera. Among the outstanding composers and their works, some of which are obtainable, in part, on records are: Charles Wakefield Cadman's SHANEWIS (it is interesting to note that Cadman's Indian opera was the first American work to be performed for two consecutive seasons by the Metropolitan Opera Company), and his

WITCH OF SALEM which has not been as successful; Louis Gruenberg's THE EMPEROR JONES; Howard Hanson's MERRY MOUNT; Deems Taylor's THE KING'S HENCHMEN and PETER IBBETSON; Richard Hageman's CAPONSACCHI; Victor Herbert's NATOMA; Gian-Carlo Menotti's full scale opera, AMELIA GOES TO THE BALL and the short radio operas THE TELEPHONE, THE MEDIUM, and his beautiful Christmas one-act opera AMAHL AND THE NIGHT VISITORS, based upon the picture, *"The Adoration of the Magi"* by Hieronymous Bosch (c. 1488–1516, Flemish); and Samuel Barber's VANESSA, libretto by Carlo Menotti, which was successfully premièred by the Metropolitan Opera Co. in New York, Jan. 15, 1958. Here are some American operas that seem worthy of recording, at least in part: Vittorio Giannini's SCARLET LETTER and THE TAMING OF THE SHREW; Walter Damrosch's THE SCARLET LETTER, CYRANO DE BERGERAC, and THE MAN WITHOUT A COUNTRY; Henry Hadley's CLEOPATRA'S NIGHT and AZORA: Horatio Parker's MONA and FAIRYLAND; CASTLE ARGAZANT by Ralph Lyford; John Knowles Paine's AZARA; and many others.

Our suggestions of selected reading references concerning the history of opera, light opera and musical comedy, stories of their libretti and plots, and some musical excerpts may be had from certain of the following books: Edward Hipsher, *American Opera and Its Composers* (Philadelphia: Theodore Presser Co., 1927); Cecil Smith, *Musical Comedy in America* (New York: The Theatre Arts, 1950); R. A. Streatfield, *The Opera* (New York: E. P. Dutton Co., 1948); Donald Grout, *A Short History of Opera* (New York: Columbia University Press, 1947), the latest and most extensive study of Opera in the English language; *The Opera Libretto Library*, 3 vols. (New York: Crown, 1938 and 39), includes Italian, French, Wagnerian and other German Operas with English translations; Ernest Newman, *The Wagner Operas* (New York: Alfred Knopf, 1949), the best single book on the subject; Albert Lavignac, *The Music Dramas of Richard Wagner* (New York: Dodd, Mead, 1940); Ernest Newman, *Stories of Great Operas* and *More Stories of Great Operas* (Philadelphia: The Blakiston Co., 1945 and 1946); Gustav Kobbé, *The Complete Opera Book* (New York: G. P. Putnam, new ed. by the Earl of Harewood, 1954); Milton Cross, *Complete Stories of the Great Operas* (New York: Doubleday, 1948); Henry E. Krehbiel, *A Book of Operas* (New York: Macmillan, 1936), contains histories, plots, and musical excerpts; Mary Peltz and Robert Lawrence, *The Metropolitan Opera Guide* (New York: Modern Library, 1947), a synopsis of plots; and articles on opera and related subjects as found in standard reference books such as *Grove's Dictionary of Music, International Cyclopedia of Music and Musicians,* and *Encyclopedia of the Arts.* Appropriate selections from this list should give an excellent background of knowledge about opera, including history, music, composers and plot stories. Consult the latest record catalogues for listening and study possibilities.

Courtesy Italian State Tourist Office

MILAN CATHEDRAL

9 The oratorio

In the introductory paragraph of the preceding chapter, we suggested that a simple opera might be constructed through the use of a series of songs having a common theme, or story, for acting on a stage with the usual trappings. To carry the idea further, if those solo songs, ensembles, and choruses were built around a religious subject and the whole were sung without actions in a concert hall or a church instead of the theater, we might have a fair representation of the basic idea of an oratorio. So the humble song of our early chapters assumes still greater importance. Keeping in mind that much of what has been said in the preceding chapter applies equally well in this, let us discuss the immediate subject more precisely.[1]

We think of the oratorio as a dramatic poem, generally of a sacred or spiritual character, which is sung through-

[1] For essential listening, see section on THE MESSIAH.

out by soloists and chorus to the accompaniment of an orchestra. It is distinguished from the mass and church cantata in that it is intended for concert or festival performance rather than as part of a regular religious service, and from the opera in that—at any rate in modern times—it is presented without scenery, costumes, or action.

Today the oratorio is considered as a type altogether distinct from the opera, although, from what we said in the preceding section about the origins of the music drama, it should be apparent that the two were derived from common sources. From the twelfth to the sixteenth centuries —a period that saw the brilliant flourishing all over Europe of the miracle and mystery plays—there developed in Italy, France, Germany, and England a species of musical drama based on incidents in the Old and New Testaments and on the lives of saints. These were intended to reinforce, on a popular basis and with strong emotional appeal, the teachings of the church, and were generally performed under the supervision of the clergy. Often performers traveled from town to town in wagons, giving performances in public squares, palace courtyards, or the market place—a practice that may be seen in the episode of the strolling players in HAMLET, or in the "play within a play" in Leoncavallo's PAGLIACCI.

Toward the end of the sixteenth century, at about the same time that the poets and musicians at the court of Florence were experimenting with the type of musical dramatic declamation that ultimately led to the opera, St. Philip Neri, founder of the congregation of the Oratorians at Rome, encouraged the performance of sacred musical dramatic allegories as a means of religious instruction. Since these performances were given in the oratory of his church, the sacred drama with music soon became known as *oratorio*, while the secular drama with music took the title of *opera*. At this point, opera and oratorio differed from each other mainly in the choice of subject, for both used all the resources of the musical dramatic theater. In 1600 Emilio del Cavalieri (*c.* 1550–1602) presented in Rome an elaborate allegory of the struggle between body and mind, LA RAPPRESENTAZIONE DI ANIMA E DI CORPO, a spiritual opera in the tradition of the mystery and miracle plays that is often erroneously set forth in histories of music as the first oratorio. Since secular and sacred music drama were arising simultaneously from a common ancestry, it is difficult to mark clearly the first separation of their paths. For additional matter on the historical background, the reader is referred to the plentiful number of texts on music history available in most libraries.

Opera and oratorio thenceforth developed side by side, borrowing from each other, and often crossing over into each other's territory. Thus, in our own time Saint-Saëns' Biblical opera SAMSON ET DELILAH has been performed in concert, without the trappings of the opera house, as an oratorio. Similarly, Mendelssohn's oratorio ELIJAH received a memorable performance in America with scenery, costumes, and acting. The two genres have, however, steadily gone farther and farther apart in character, style, and outlook. With opera we associate swift dramatic action, tense emotional climaxes, ardent romanticism, sensuous melody, and brilliant effect. With oratorio we connect vast harmonies, sublime choruses, lyricism of an introspective nature, and spiritual exaltation. Where opera remained a dynamic form, the oratorio became increasingly static and contemplative. The last trace of dramatic action disappeared from the oratorio with the introduction of a narrator, whose function it was to relate the connecting incidents in the sacred play, instead of having them acted out. Above all, while the opera continued to rely for its emotional effect on the inner conflicts of individuals, the oratorio depended increasingly for its majestic effects on the chorus.

GEORGE FRIDERIC HANDEL (1685–1759)

Interestingly enough, the composer who is considered to have played the decisive role in the oratorio as we know it today, George Frideric Handel, spent the greater part of his career in writing operas. For well on to twenty-five years, the great Saxon guided the destinies of opera in London. It was only when his audience began to tire of the conventional, artificial Italian opera of the period and turned with avidity to the freshness and charm of Gay's BEGGAR'S OPERA that Handel, sensing a competition he could no longer meet, turned his inexhaustible energies to the oratorio. With Handel the oratorio took on new life and color, and the chorus became the chief protagonist of the drama, much as the orchestra did a century later in the Wagnerian music drama. His great oratorios—THE MESSIAH, SAUL, ISRAEL IN EGYPT, JUDAS MACCABAEUS, JEPHTHA—are, in effect, choral tragedies in which the lives and destinies of the individual heroes take on meaning and direction from the dynamic force embodied in the chorus. Master of a spacious architecture, of bold dramatic effect, of vivid musical characterization, and of a variegated style of writing, Handel poured all the riches of his imagination into these works, which so perfectly hit off the taste of English Protestantism. For a century after his death, they completely dominated the musical life of his adopted land.

Handel and his great contemporary, Bach, represent the peak of that era in music which is known as the *Baroque*.[2] We shall have more to say of the Baroque in a later chapter. Suffice it for the present to point out that this term is used in painting, sculpture, architecture, and music to indicate the spirit of bold design and vigorous execution of sweeping lines, richly imaginative ornamentation, imposing dimensions, and dra-

[2] For extended discussion on the *Baroque*, see Chap. 28.

Courtesy New York Public Library

GEORGE FRIDERIC HANDEL

matic effects that characterized European art in the seventeenth and early eighteenth centuries. The Baroque was the counterpart, in the realm of art, of the spirit that pervaded the age: a spirit of bold questing for new horizons, of restless questioning of accepted norms, of exuberant self-confidence and achievement, and of intellectual inquiry. It symbolized the far-flung religious and dynastic struggles, the vigorous colonization of the New World, and the steady forward movement of the *bourgeoisie*—the "burgesses," the merchants, and industrialists—as they consolidated their power in their five-hundred-year-old struggle against the feudal agricultural aristocracy. This was a dynamic, rapidly changing world demanding pomp and external splendor, opulent façades riotous with ornament, magnificent curves and stairways and candelabra—a style that found its perfect expression in the palaces of the absolute monarchs of the seventeenth century, in the bold and teeming canvases of a Rubens or a Caravaggio. It is the spirit of this world that is immortalized in music by the sweeping recitatives, arias, and ensembles, above all by the grandiose, stirring choruses of the Handelian oratorio.

The Messiah

We know of no better introduction to the oratorio style at its best than the study of Handel's immortal work in that form, THE MESSIAH, which he wrote in twenty-four days in the late summer of 1741. It was first produced in Dublin, Ireland, April 13, 1742, with Handel conducting. The work consists of a series of recitatives, arias, choruses, and orchestral numbers arranged in three parts—analogous to the acts of an opera. There is an overture and an instrumental interlude in the first part, the latter known as the *Pastoral Symphony.* The text is made up of appropriate verses from the Bible, some direct quotations, and others adapted to Handel's needs by the librettist, Charles Jennens. The first part prophesies and anticipates the coming of Christ; the second speaks of His sufferings and death; and the third tells of His resurrection. In order to make the work more acceptable for use during the Christmas season, a large part of sections two and three are omitted.

To enable the listener to follow the vagaries of concert as well as recorded performances of THE MESSIAH, we present here the complete outline of the arias and choruses.[3] For practical reasons, we have indicated with one star (*) those numbers we should like to use as minimum essential listening for this chapter. A further abridged series is reluctantly proposed for still greater limitations of time. These are indicated with two stars (**) before the title. (Other choices than these are possible.)

Part the First:

1. Overture.
* ** 2. Recitative (Tenor), "Comfort ye my people."
* ** 3. Aria (Tenor), "Every valley shall be exalted."
* 4. Chorus, "And the glory of the Lord."
5. Recit. (Bass), "Thus saith the Lord."
6. Aria (Bass), "But who may abide the day of His coming?"
7. Chorus, "And He shall purify."
8. Recit. (Alto), "Behold, a virgin shall conceive."

[3] As shown in the Schirmer Edition, (New York: 1912), edited and revised according to Handel's original score by T. Tertius Noble. Even more recent and accurate is the edition edited by Dr. J. M. Coopersmith (New York: Carl Fischer, 1947).

9. Aria (Alto) and Chorus, "O Thou that tellest good tidings."
*10. Recit. (Bass), "For, behold, darkness shall cover the earth."
*11. Aria (Bass), "The people that walked in darkness."
* **12. Chorus, "For unto us a child is born."
*13. Pastoral Symphony.
* **14. Recit. (Soprano), "There were shepherds abiding in the field."
Recit. (Soprano), "And lo! the angel of the Lord."
15. Recit. (Soprano), "And the angel said unto them."
16. Recit. (Soprano), "And suddenly there was with the angel."
*17. Chorus, "Glory to God."
*18. Aria (Soprano), "Rejoice greatly, O daughter of Zion."
19. Recit. (Alto), "Then shall the eyes of the blind be opened."
* **20. Aria (Alto), "He shall feed His flock like a shepherd."
* Aria (Soprano), "Come unto Him."
*21. Chorus, "His yoke is easy, and His burden is light."

Part the Second:

*22. Chorus, "Behold the Lamb of God."
* **23. Aria (Alto), "He was despised."
* **24. Chorus, "Surely He hath borne our griefs."
25. Chorus, "And with His stripes we are healed."
26. Chorus, "All we like sheep have gone astray."
27. Recit. (Tenor), "All they that see Him, laugh Him to scorn."
28. Chorus, "He trusted in God that He would deliver Him."
*29. Recit. (Tenor), "Thy rebuke hath broken His heart."
*30. Aria (Tenor), "Behold, and see if there be any sorrow."
31. Recit. (Tenor), "He was cut off out of the land of the living."
32. Aria (Tenor), "But Thou didst not leave His soul in hell."
33. Chorus, "Lift up your heads, O ye gates."
34. Recit. (Tenor), "Unto which of the angels said He."
35. Chorus, "Let all the angels of God worship Him."
36. Aria (Bass), "Thou art gone up on high."
37. Chorus, "The Lord gave the word."
38. Aria (Soprano), "How beautiful are the feet of them."
39. Chorus, "Their sound is gone out into all lands."
* **40. Aria (Bass), "Why do the nations so furiously rage together?"
41. Chorus, "Let us break their bonds asunder."
42. Recit. (Tenor), "He that dwelleth in heaven."
43. Aria (Tenor), "Thou shalt break them."
* **44. Chorus, "Hallelujah!"

Part the Third:

* **45. Aria (Soprano), "I know that my Redeemer liveth."
46. Chorus, "Since by man came death."
47. Recit. (Bass), "Behold, I tell you a mystery."
48. Aria (Bass), "The trumpet shall sound."
49. Recit. (Alto), "Then shall be brought to pass."
50. Duet (Alto and Tenor), "O death, where is thy sting?"
*51. Chorus, "But thanks be to God."
52. Aria (Soprano), "If God be for us, who can be against us?"
*53. Chorus, "Worthy is the Lamb," "Amen."

THE MESSIAH took England by storm and it was during the first London performance that the audience, carried away by the lofty sentiments, the impressive power, and the noble character of the *Hallelujah chorus* (number 44 in the listing) arose in concert as though by prearranged signal. Ever since, audiences the world over have expressed a similar respect by rising at the onset of this chorus and remaining standing until its conclusion. More often than not, a performance of THE MESSIAH appropriately closes with this great choral number. Of course, there is usually no applause throughout the entire Oratorio. The listener is cautioned to be on guard for omissions, especially in Parts II and III, and for transpositions of certain numbers from Part II to Part III in order to affect a climax at the close. The comprehensive outline provided above should be a helpful guide.

ADDITIONAL SUGGESTIONS FOR LISTENING[4]

If Handel represents the pomp and splendor of the Baroque, Bach, as the reader will remember from our discussion of his religious music, stands for its other side—mysticism, introspection, passionate religiosity, and otherworldliness. Where Handel was at home in the glare of public life, in the atmosphere of royal courts and theaters, as artist, producer, and businessman all in one, Bach lived his life within the circle of his family, circumscribed by his duties as Cantor of St. Thomas', completely devoted to his religion and his art. By native temperament and mode of life he was eminently suited for the most eloquent projection, through his music, of the intense pietism which pervaded his native Thuringia. Where Handel was fired by the dramatic conflicts in the Old Testament, Bach addressed himself almost exclusively to what was for him the supreme religious tragedy—the Passion of Christ. In Bach's three PASSION oratorios according to the Gospels of St. Luke, St. Matthew, and St. John, and in the CHRISTMAS ORATORIO, it is the reflective lyrical note that predominates—a brooding tenderness, a grandeur of resignation and peace—rather than one of action, the spirit of evangelical mysticism rather than the spectacular dramatics of Handel. Throughout, there is that mingling of profound lyricism and pathos which makes Bach, for many listeners, the *sine qua non* among composers.

Of the two masters of the Classical Period in the late eighteenth century, Mozart devoted his best efforts to actual church music rather than to festive religious drama. On the other hand, Haydn, who achieved a triumphal success in England toward the end of his career, continued in the tradition of Handel with two works well calculated to please English taste—THE CREATION, after the first part of Milton's *Paradise Lost;* and THE SEASONS, after the famous poem of James Thomson. Haydn was a devout Catholic writing for a Protestant audience

[4] In this chapter, we have had to relax the policy of restricting the references to recorded works because of the scarcity of phonograph records. Here, even more earnestly than elsewhere, we advise hearing actual performances, and better still, that the reader participate as a singer in the chorus.

on the heels of the Enlightenment; the result was a beautiful hymn to the Creator couched in language that men of all creeds and loyalties could understand. Haydn applied well to his own idiom the lessons he learned from his great predecessor. THE CREATION has remained second only to THE MESSIAH in popularity. The reader should also be acquainted with characteristic examples from THE CREATION, the exciting choruses *Achieved Is the Glorious Work* and *Rolling in Foaming Billows*; also, the touching *Dove Aria* for soprano.

The nineteenth century saw intense cultivation of the oratorio, even though the spirit out of which it had come into being no longer held undisputed sway over the souls of men. Neither Beethoven's MOUNT OF OLIVES nor Schubert's VICTORY SONG OF MIRIAM have retained their hold on the musical world; the genius of these composers flowed in other channels. It is in Mendelssohn who, like Handel and Haydn, met his greatest success in England, that we have a continuation of the "great choral tradition." His ELIJAH and ST. PAUL have taken their places in the literature along with THE MESSIAH and THE CREATION. The cycle of German oratorio closes with Brahms' GERMAN REQUIEM. Brahms was perhaps the last of the great masters to express the religious emotion of the late nineteenth century with something of the profundity and passion of the masters of the Baroque.

In France, the Catholic revival, which was part of the Romantic movement, created an atmosphere most favorable for the oratorio. The finest examples are Liszt's CHRISTUS and ST. ELISABETH, Berlioz's sacred trilogy THE CHILDHOOD OF CHRIST, and César Franck's THE BEATITUDES. The oratorio has always been most popular in England, where outstanding works are presented in all forms. Among the better known examples of English oratorio are Charles Hubert H. Parry's JUDITH and SAUL; Charles Villiers Stanford's THE HOLY CHILDREN and EDEN; John Stainer's GIDEON and Edward Elgar's DREAM OF GERONTIUS, LIGHT OF LIFE, THE APOSTLES, and THE KINGDOM. Among contemporary English composers, William Walton has written BALSHAZZAR'S FEAST; Frederick Delius THE MASS OF LIFE; Gustav Holst a HYMN TO JESUS; and OMAR KHAYYÁM by Granville Bantock.

American composers have contributed a number of notable oratorios to the repertory. Among the best known are John Knowles Paine's ST. PETER; Horatio Parker's HORA NOVISSIMA and LEGEND OF ST. CHRISTOPHER; Edgar Stillman Kelley's PILGRIM'S PROGRESS; Charles Martin Loeffler's CANTICLE TO ST. FRANCIS; Harry Rowe Shelley's DEATH AND LIFE, and David Stanley Smith's RHAPSODY OF ST. BERNARD.

Twentieth-century composers continued the established traditions with such oratorios as Vincent d'Indy's LEGEND OF ST. CHRISTOPHER; Ermanno Wolf-Ferrari's LA VITA NUOVA, based on Dante's poem; Pierné's CHILDREN'S CRUSADE; and Igor Stravinsky's great works, SYMPHONY OF PSALMS, OEDIPUS REX, and CANTICUM SACRUM.

Not many contemporary oratorios have as yet been made available on records. Consequently, to gain an idea of what the modern idiom in this form is like, one has, in most cases, to hear an actual performance. For a contrast between the old and the new, listen to the recorded excerpts from Honegger's oratorios: KING DAVID, *De mon coeur jaillit un cantique* (From My Heart There

Sprang a Hymn); the *Penitential Psalm;* the Psalm, *I Was Conceived in Sin;* and the *Death of David.* This is powerful choral music, with a quality of primitivism, if you will, and an abundance of dissonances. One should also add Kodály's PSALMUS HUNGARICUS; DAS UNAUFHORLICHE by Paul Hindemith; OEDIPUS REX by Szymanowski; MESSE DE REQUEIM by Gabriel Fauré, Op. 48; CANTICLE TO THE SUN, which won a Pulitzer Prize in 1945, by Leo Sowerby; MASS IN G MINOR by Ralph Vaughan Williams; and others.

Courtesy New York City Ballet, Roger Wood, Photographer

THE PRODIGAL SON Serge Prokofieff

This Biblical story, in a new guise, may appear strange to those unfamiliar with the modern dance. These new dances are deceptively Romantic in temper, often emotionally depressing, angular, and somwhat stiff in action, and expressive of, though not necessarily describing, an underlying story. Often the modern dance may exhibit the use of Classical tempers in working out predetermined gestures, foot, body, and arm movements, ensemble actions, all having no other significance. However, the modern dance derives more from the Russian than from the traditional classical dance. Many orchestral suites heard in concerts are compiled from sections or movements of ballets.

10 Music in the theatre: incidental music: the suite

As we saw in our chapter on the opera, music has been used in connection with dramatic performances since ancient times. The theater of the Greeks, of the Middle Ages, of Shakespeare and Molière and Calderon, all made extensive use of music. When the songs and dances become so important as to change the character of the play, we have the several varieties of operetta and comic opera. When the music remains in the background, we have one of the most delightful genres of the art—incidental music.[1]

[1] Essential listening for this chapter includes: PEER GYNT SUITE by Grieg, MIDSUMMER NIGHT'S DREAM SUITE (Overture, Nocturne, Scherzo, and Wedding March) by Mendelssohn, and MacDowell's INDIAN SUITE. Others, including Taylor's THROUGH THE LOOKING GLASS SUITE, are supplementary and optional. In all the thematic descriptions of musical compositions here and in succeeding chapters, it is suggested that the listener follow the musical work with the open text showing the themes in musical notation with narrative descriptions, at least for the first few auditions.

Incidental music may be played before the curtain goes up (*overture*); between the acts (*entr'acte* music); between two scenes (*interlude* or *intermezzo*); or during the course of a scene. It must rise out of the salient incidents in the play; it must capture and project the mood. If it is used as an integral part of a dramatic scene; it must either heighten its emotion or underscore the feelings and actions of the characters. Just as the high points of the poetry and of the music must coincide in a song, so here the music becomes part of the forward-driving momentum of the scene and helps to carry it to its climax. Because it can be so effective, incidental music as a rule is used rather sparingly and is reserved, in most cases, for high points of the play.

Often the incidental music for a play is arranged by the composer as a *suite* for concert performance, and in this form becomes far more popular than the play for which it was written. Thus, thousands of people who have never seen Ibsen's poetic drama, PEER GYNT, are familiar with Grieg's PEER GYNT SUITE. In this sense, the word *suite* is used to indicate a group of movements of instrumental music, often concert versions of theater or ballet music, and therefore bound together by some literary thread. In the eighteenth century, as the reader may recall from the Bach suite that we heard in the chapter on music and dance, the word denoted a group of dances in contrasting moods and meters often in the same key, or in closely related keys.

"Peer Gynt Suite" by Edvard Hagerup Grieg (1843–1907)

Grieg's incidental music for PEER GYNT, which he arranged in two concert suites, each containing four numbers, is imaginative mood-painting. The SUITE NO. I has become quite popular. It opens with *Morning*, a serene picture of day settling over the Norwegian forest, done in Grieg's best lyrical manner. There is something cool and transparent about the music, with its broadly flowing melody in six-eight time.

The second number, *Ase's Death,* is the dirge for the mother in the play. The solemn chords and the heartfelt melody, first ascending, then midway in the piece falling gradually in accents of grief, communicate with proper simplicity the tone of elegiac music. The repetition of the repeated descending melodic figure grips one thoroughly, arousing in the listener a feeling of depression and resignation.

Next comes the seductive *Anitra's Dance* (performed in the play by the exotic beauty whom Peer encounters during his travels). This music is, strictly speaking, not incidental, since it actually enters into the action of the play. The dance is in graceful three-four time. The use of muted strings, the *staccato* figure in the accompaniment, and the *pizzicato* (plucked strings) effect create an atmosphere of subtle oriental allure. Note particularly that when the original dance theme returns,

Courtesy C. O. Buckingham, Photographer, Washington, D. C.

GRIEF Augustus Saint-Gaudens

This vivid depiction of poignant grief is remarkable for its conveyance of mood, its simple composition of contrasting highlights, and the deep shadows that create a feeling of intense brooding. Note the face of the figure deeply recessed in the shadow as though enshrouded in mystery, the pyramidal mass singularly free of adornment, and the continual—almost unbroken—lines of falling folds. This work, in bronze, is known as the Adams Memorial, and is located in the Rock Creek Cemetery, Washington, D. C.

Grieg varies the effect by having the 'cellos sing a new, full-throated melody against it—in other words, a *countermelody*. The addition of a countermelody to a repeated theme is obviously a subtle and effective means by which a composer may vary his material.

The final number, *In the Hall of the Mountain King*, depicts the exciting scene when Peer, lost in the mountains, is surrounded by mischievous trolls and sprites who perform a grotesque dance around him. The piece presents an extraordinary combination of the three most striking devices for building a climax—*crescendo, accelerando,* and a steady rise in pitch. The dance opens at a fairly slow pace, softly, in the lowest register, with a bizarre *staccato* effect on the bassoons. From then on the simple motive is repeated again and again—somewhat in the manner of the ascending half of the *Ase's Death* pattern—each time louder, faster, and higher, building up steadily until all the sonorities of the orchestra are engaged in an overpowering climax at breakneck speed punctuated by the shattering exclamations of cymbals and drums. Here, too, the music is not incidental in any sense of the term, but captures the very essence of the scene as envisaged in the imagination of the poet-dramatist.

Suite from "Midsummer Night's Dream" by Felix Mendelssohn (1809–1847)

For a full century, Mendelssohn's incidental music to Shakespeare's MIDSUMMER NIGHT'S DREAM has been a universal favorite. The Suite as finally completed by the composer consists of: (1) *Overture,* (2) *Scherzo,* (3) *Melodrama No. 1* and *March of the Elves,* (4) *Songs for Soli* and *Women's Chorus,* (5) *Melodrama No. 2,* (6) *Intermezzo,* (7) *Melodrama No. 3,* (8) *Nocturne,* (9) *Melodrama No. 4,* (10) *Wedding March,* (11) *Melodrama No. 5* and *Funeral March,* (12) *Bergomasque Dance,* (13) *Melodrama No. 6* and *Finale.* Of these, the *Overture, Nocturne, Scherzo,* and *Wedding March* are the ones most often heard in concert performance. Sometimes the *Intermezzo* is inserted between the *Nocturne* and *Scherzo.*

Mendelssohn's genius actually brings into audible reality the grace, naive charm, sprightly elfin lightness, and caprice inherent in the spirit of Shakespeare's poetry and play. Shakespeare and Mendelssohn become as one. It will be very helpful and enjoyable to read Shakespeare's play at this point.

The *Overture* (1826) ranks as one of Mendelssohn's best works and it is an amazing production, particularly for a boy of seventeen. It is a very fitting prelude and complement to the play. In a way, it is really a symphonic poem, and a most romantic one, previewing the story of the drama to follow, much as Wagner, years later, employed the overture or the prelude. This early conception of its poetic form and literary function is an added glory. Its structural form follows rather loosely the classical sonata-allegro design. First one hears four sustained, mysterious chords in the wood-winds alone, as a sort of introduction to the magic world of Oberon and Titania. They sound like calls blown on elfin horns to announce the opening of the curtain to Fairyland. Note the striking effect, as though solemnly quieting the audience, of the simple minor chord (E^2–G^2natural–B^2) in the sixth measure, immediately following the full-toned, magical wood-wind chords; see the first musical example following. It is interesting to observe that the French composer, Dukas, also employs a similar idea of a "magic spell" motto at the onset of his tone poem, THE SORCERER'S APPRENTICE (see Chap. 14). Here are the opening measures of the *Overture* to A MIDSUMMER NIGHT'S DREAM:

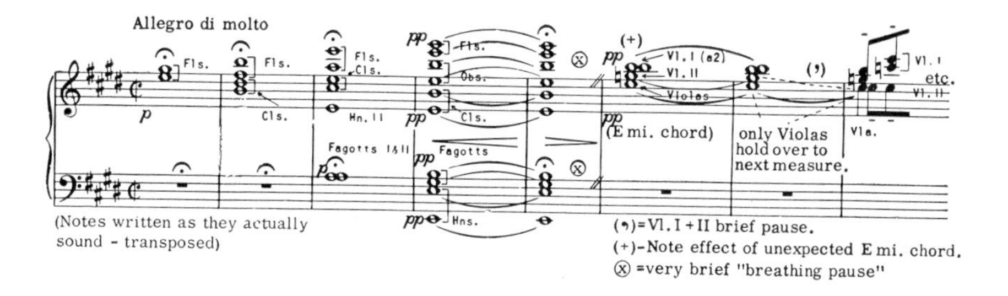

The violins, divided, then enter with the first theme proper. It depicts the playful antics of the elves and fairies and sets the spirit and mood of the overture as a whole, besides revealing more of the story itself. This theme of gossamer lightness and playful spirit recalls the attempts of Weber and Berlioz to depict the effervescent, delicate fancies of Fairyland. Mendelssohn, however, seems to come closer to the peculiar imagination of childhood. Weber and Berlioz always seem to us to show the world of childlike make-believe as an adult looks at it, with his grown-up sophistication. Here is the first theme proper (condensed):

Now and then the lightly bustling first theme is interrupted by a mysterious, mildly dissonant chord played by the wood-winds that seems to say "Hush!" It is interesting to learn that the dissonance of this chord, made more salient by its instrumentation, disturbed the academic musicians when first heard. Here is the "Hush!" motif.

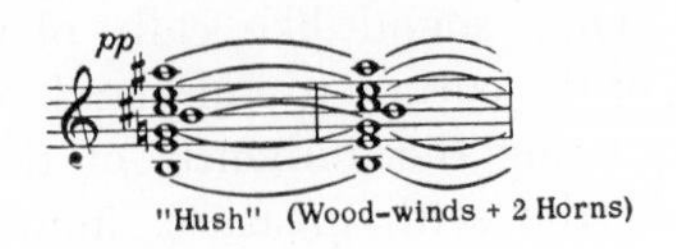

The buoyantly tripping *staccato* theme just heard soon grows into a joyous outburst from the entire orchestra which signifies the March of Duke Theseus and his court. Note the interruptions by the "Hush" chord! This march theme is contrasted with a theme which denotes the Duke's hunting horn on the chase. See if you can hear the themes on top and bottom. Here are the two themes:

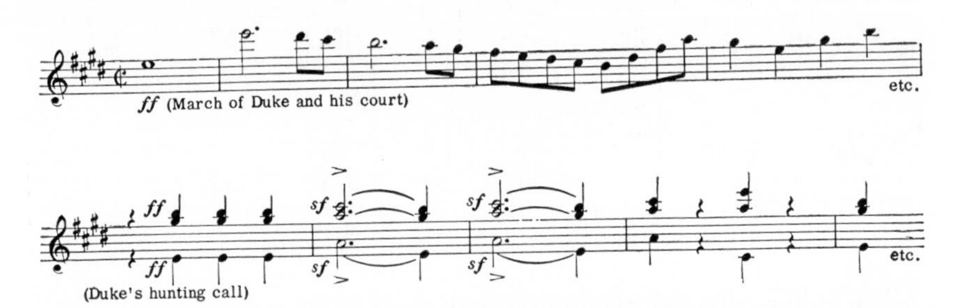

Soon a more sustained, chromatic theme is heard, faintly suggesting the lovers in the play:

This suave second theme proper offers a perfect contrast to the high-pitched, *staccato* first theme.

Then comes the jolly and not a little bumptious *Bergomasque Dance*, Pageantry and "Horse-play" from Acts IV and V of the drama. Mendelssohn has sought to express the dancing of the peasants and their players, and especially the character of the immortal clown, Bottom, with his head in the mask of a donkey. We hear a realistic braying-like "Hee-haw" figure, first in the strings and eventually in the appropriate low tones of the tuba. Mendelssohn wrote this part for the obsolete instrument, the *Ophicleide,* a tuba with saxophone-like keys, the tone of which is more raucous than that of the refined modern tuba. Through a magic spell, Bottom has received the head of a donkey and, as a ridiculous contrast, the constant and fervent adoration of Titania! Here we present first, the "Bottom" theme (note the "Hee-Haw" at the end) and, second, the happy, carefree, swaggering march theme which comes hard after the "Hee-Haw" theme:

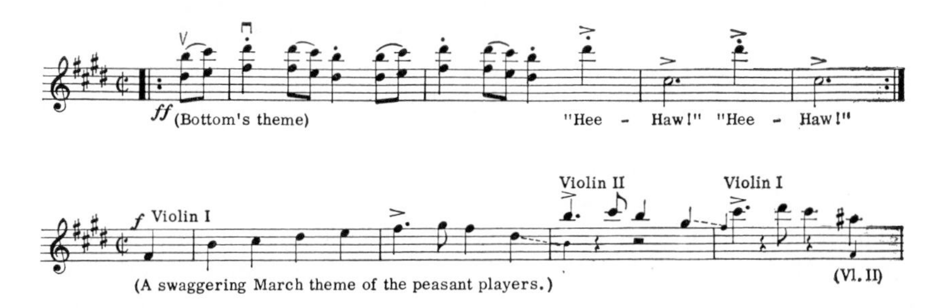

These themes are developed at some length with imagination, free fantasy, and zest; finally the themes return to their original statements. The mysterious opening wood-wind chords are heard again. The music floats away, higher and higher into the dream world of Fairyland, reflecting the essence of the lines of Robin Goodfellow, King Oberon and Titania, the Queen of the Fairies, at the close of Act V, Scene I, especially when Oberon says:

> With this field-dew consecrate,
> Every fairy take his gait,
> And each several chamber bless
> Through this palace, with sweet peace;
> And the owner of it blest
> Ever shall in safety rest.
> Trip away; make no stay;
> Meet me all by break of day.

The lovely *Nocturne* (written in 1843) comes at the end of Act III, when sleep has descended upon the bewitched Titania and her doltish lover, Bottom. The serene melody for the French horn is one of the most famous passages written for that instrument. (See also chapter on orchestral instruments.) Here is the horn solo from the *Nocturne:*

All the mystery and beauty of its tone are used by Mendelssohn to paint the dream-filled loveliness and magic quiet of the summer night. Often, after years of success and fame, Mendelssohn, rather unconsciously we believe, substituted the classical tempers pertaining to perfection of form and exhibition of adroit craftsmanship in developing thematic material, rather than continuing the expression of the romantic temper, of emotion, spontaneity, originality, and infectious buoyancy of his youth. This nocturne, however, seems to belie the statement just made. Mendelssohn recaptures the romantic fervor of his youthful feeling, in accents of unmistakable sincerity, but together with a perfection of craftsmanship and expression that mark the adroit use of the classical tempers. (A *nocturne* is either a composition that describes the romantic beauty of the night, or a pensively lyrical outpouring of romantic feeling, such as a night song or serenade that a lover might address to the object of his affection. The word comes from the Old French.)

The next movement we are to hear is the happy and animated *Scherzo,* always a favorite with listeners. (The word *scherzo* comes directly from Italian, where it denotes a joke or sportive humor. It may be applied to a single, separate piece as Chopin, Brahms, and others used the term; or it may mean a movement in a larger work. It was Beethoven who was largely responsible for transforming the traditional, dignified minuet into the vivacious and usually humorous scherzo. Schubert, Schumann, Bruckner, Berlioz, and many other composers use this fast-moving, jolly triple-meter movement. The term also signifies a vocal piece of lighter vein in the Baroque Period.) This movement is a bit of delicate playfulness in triple, three-eight time that serves as a sort of prelude to Act II of the play. The opening theme, in the wood-winds, vaguely resembles the first theme of the *Overture* in its use of the high staccato notes of the violins; this is in "A" following. Example "B" is a later evolvement of the "A" theme of the *Scherzo,* and it, too, is in the strings. Observe, however, that the tones are pitched in the lowest strings of the violin—a lusty dance tune of peasant type.

After these two themes, the music returns to the first theme; little wisps of sound dart through the air and finally dissolve in a silvery mist.

This Concert Suite, culled from the thirteen separate numbers, comes to a fitting close with the famous *Wedding March.* The opening measures of the march succeed in establishing a unified expression of stateliness, solemnity, and happiness, so much so that it has become the symbol of the wedding ceremony itself.

Following, in themes marked "A" and "B," are the thematic essences of this gay march, which is used for Act V, Scene I, and serves to introduce the two marriages between Lysander and Hermia and Demetrius and Helena. It is a happy ending after the removal of the rather mixed-up spell put upon them by Robin Goodfellow. The ceremony is presided over by Theseus and Hippolyta, and blessed by the royal couple of Fairyland, Oberon and Titania.

EDWARD ALEXANDER MACDOWELL (1861–1908)

We have previously seen that suites may be made up of contrasting dance tunes, and in this chapter we have learned that suites may be an assembly of incidental music written for plays. Now we direct attention to suites that have no connection with the ballet or dramatic performance; instead, they were composed directly for the concert program and have as their underlying element of unification a poem, a story, or a series of related or parallel moods. A good example of the so-called concert suite is MacDowell's INDIAN SUITE, where the unification is secured through the use of American Indian melodies.

The composer of the universally popular WOODLAND SKETCHES, from which come *To a Wild Rose* and *To a Water Lily*, was born in New York City in 1861. After studying piano with Teresa Carreño, the famous Venezuelan pianist and teacher, he entered the Paris Conservatoire at the age of fifteen, remaining for three years. For five years after that he studied, played, and taught in the musical centers of Germany—Stuttgart, Wiesbaden, Darmstadt, and Frankfort—coming under the influence of the leading German Romanticists, notably his teacher, Raff, and Liszt. He found the artistic atmosphere of Germany so congenial to his nature and the German musical world so appreciative of his talents that for a time he considered the possibility of settling there permanently. In 1884, he married his pupil, Marian Nevins (1857–1956). He returned to America in 1887, settled in Boston, and appeared successfully as a concert pianist, introducing his two brilliant piano concertos, the second of which has remained a favorite both with virtuosi and their audiences. His piano works are idiomatic to the extreme. In 1896 he became the first professor of music at Columbia University. During his eight years there, he fought unceasingly to have music recognized as a full-fledged member of the curriculum, but despite his zeal, the university authorities did not accept his proposals, and in 1904 he resigned. His pioneer efforts in this direction later bore fruit and personal triumph, for his ideas became nationally accepted. For some of the remaining years of his life, he devoted himself to composing.

MacDowell remains America's greatest composer, truly original and romantically poetic. He was musically sensitive and most saliently individualistic. He possessed a thoroughly genuine lyric and rhythmic gift and personal style of a high order. His lyrical pieces, such as the two already mentioned, have found wide popularity in the nation at large; his more ambitious works, especially his brilliant SECOND PIANO CONCERTO IN D MINOR, Op. 23, have achieved a place in the world-wide repertory. We believe that the FIRST PIANO CONCERTO IN A MINOR, Op. 15, together with the second concerto remain, up to now, the greatest works of their genre in our native musical literature. He fought steadfastly for the cause of music in America, seeking to bring to it independence and self-expression; he was the first American to command respect from the musical circles of Europe. Like his contemporary, Henry James, he sought to combine the best in the old tradition with the new. In many of his works, such as the INDIAN SUITE and WOODLAND SKETCHES, he turned to Indian themes for inspiration, although, unlike Dvořák, who was active in this country in the same decade as he, MacDowell was not greatly influenced by Negro themes. In MacDowell, as in so many of the nineteenth-century composers, the Romantic impulse fused with the nationalistic. Like Dvořák and Grieg, he sought to adapt the German Romantic tradition to the needs of his native land. Like them, he is "folksy" at times; but there is a vein of rich, tender lyricism in his work, of real poetic imagination and deep feeling. His lyrical miniatures and "sets"

EDWARD MACDOWELL

for piano are unequalled natively and vie with the best of any European composer. The titles of some of his compositions are revealing: NEW ENGLAND IDYLS, Op. 62; SEA PIECES, Op. 55; FORGOTTEN FAIRY TALES, Op. 4; MOON PICTURES, Op. 21, after Hans Christian Andersen; HAMLET AND OPHELIA, Op. 22, Symphonic Poem; LAUNCELOT AND ELAINE, Op. 25, Symphonic Poem; FROM AN OLD GARDEN, Op. 26; SIX IDYLS AFTER GOETHE, Op. 28; SIX POEMS AFTER HEINE, Op. 31; THE SARACENS, Op. 30, after The Song of Roland; SONATA TRAGICA, Op. 45; SONATA EROICA, Op. 50; NORSE SONATA, Op. 57; KELTIC SONATA, Op. 59; FIRESIDE TALES, Op. 61; NEW ENGLAND IDYLS, Op. 62; INDIAN SUITE, Op. 48. To round out the picture of his romantic nationalism, it is interesting to note that he eventually made a practice of writing the tempo indications for his compositions in English instead of using the "allegros" and "adagios" of conventional musical usage—a sort of gesture of independence that some of his disciples have adhered to.

After his tragic death in 1908, his widow transferred his estate at Peterboro, New Hampshire, to the MacDowell Colony Association for use as an artists' colony. Here every summer, writers, painters, sculptors, and composers gather from all parts of the country to work. The name of MacDowell thus continues to be a symbol of the arts in America.

MacDowell's Suite No. 2 for Orchestra ("Indian") in E minor, Op. 48 [2]

This work is composed of five numbers: *Legend, Love Song, In War Time, Dirge,* and *Village Festival.* In the *Legend,* there is a melody of the Iroquois tribe and a Chippewa theme; the second number is built on a love song of the Iowa tribes; the third has a Dakota theme, as well as some features of an Iroquois scalp dance; the fourth is a Kiowa—a woman's song of mourning for her absent son; and the *Village Festival* includes a women's dance and a war song of the Iroquois tribe. The Suite, scored for piccolo, two flutes, two oboes, two clarinets, two bassoons, four horns, two trumpets, three trombones, bass tuba, a set of three kettledrums, a bass drum, cymbals, and strings, opens with a forceful though plaintive atmosphere created by an idealized Indian call in the horns only, followed immediately by the sombre low tones of the clarinet and strings—a mood and orchestral color creation of real poetic and musical genius. Note the subtle use of an *idée fixe,* or unifying motive, throughout all movements of the Suite which is derived from the first three tones of the Indian horn call at the onset of the work.

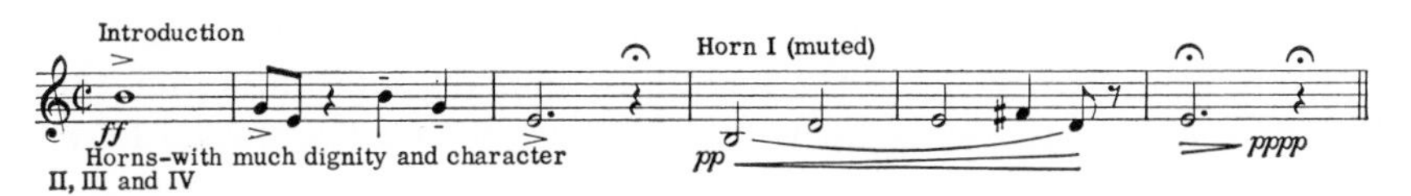

[2] MacDowell themes used with permission of Associated Publishers, Inc., N. Y.

I. *Legend:* Not fast, with much dignity and character. E minor, $\frac{2}{2}$. This number is reported to have been inspired by Thomas Bailey Aldrich's Indian legend, "Miantowona." The composer, however, made no attempt to relate the incidents of the poem, but suggested the general mood and atmosphere.

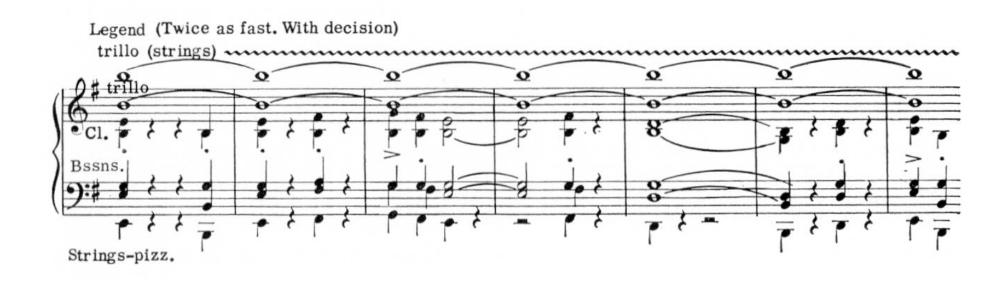

II. *Love Song:* Not fast, tenderly, A major, $\frac{6}{8}$. A lyrical melody introduced by the wood-winds is developed, with an answer from the strings that is followed by another melody, more determined in character, in the wood-winds.

III. *In War Time:* With rough vigor, almost savagely, D minor, $\frac{2}{4}$. Two flutes, unaccompanied, announce the chief theme in unison. A secondary theme is sung by two clarinets, also in unison and unaccompanied. The material is worked out in a well-knit musical form with frequent changes of rhythm toward the end from $\frac{2}{4}$ to $\frac{6}{8}$ and back again.

IV. *Dirge:* Dirgelike, mournfully, in G minor, $\frac{4}{4}$. The lamentation (two measures from the onset) is sung by muted violins in unison; these are then reinforced by violas, while wood-winds and two muted horns—one of which is played offstage as an echo—sustain the harmony of the tonic note G. Note the effective use of the pentatonic (five-tone) scale in the theme proper and the "falling" dirgelike motive; observe that the *Dirge* movement is derived from the first three horn tones at the onset of the first movement. This movement, along with the slow movement of the TRAGICA and EROICA Sonatas, is among the finest inspirations of this American genius.

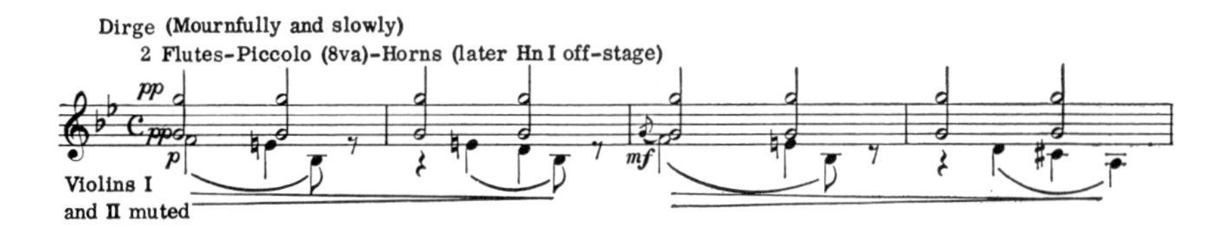

V. *Village Festival:* Swift and light, in E major, $\frac{2}{4}$. Several themes, all of them more or less related to those in the first movement, are developed in animated dance rhythms, capturing the general mood of a tribal festival. Note the use of the pentatonic scale, hints of modal feeling, and a suggestion of the opening theme especially at the tenth measure entry of the first violins, and recurring thereafter.

MacDowell was fond of using the pentatonic scales and mixing them with the tonal scales and medieval modes.[3] The pentatonic scales are perhaps the most universally used basic music structure; they are often found in the music of savage tribes. We meet them more commonly in Chinese, African, Scotch, American Indian, Old English, and in the music of some of the southeastern coastal states and the Appalachian Mountain region. The black keyes on your piano, played in succession, represent one of the several pentatonic scales. Many other familiar melodies and songs are based on these scales. *Peter Peter, Pumpkin Eater* is a good example.

[3] For a detailed discussion of the medieval (ecclesiastical) modes, see: Gustave Reese, *Music in the Middle Ages* (New York: Norton & Co., 1940); A. Madeley Richardson, *The Medieval Modes* (New York: H. W. Gray Co., 1933); and "Modes Ecclesiastical," *Grove's Dictionary of Music and Musicians,* 3rd ed., by H. C. Colles, (New York: Macmillan Co., 1947).

For the tonal and pentatonic scales, see: "Scales," *International Cyclopedia of Music and Musicians,* 6th ed. by O. Thompson (Toronto: Dodd, Mead & Co., 1952); C. Hubert Parry, *The Evolution of the Art of Music,* (London: Kegan Paul, 1893), Ch. 2; and Edward MacDowell, *Critical and Historical Essays* (Boston: Arthur P. Schmidt, 1912), Ch. 7.

ADDITIONAL SUGGESTIONS FOR LISTENING

Through the Looking Glass Suite, Op. 12, by Deems Taylor (1885–)

Typical of the cosmopolitan East is Deems Taylor, composer, music critic, and author of books on music. In composition he is known for his incidental music for the BEGGAR ON HORSEBACK; his opera THE KING'S HENCHMEN on a text by Edna St. Vincent Millay; PETER IBBETSON, based on a libretto adapted from a novel of du Maurier; and his ORCHESTRAL SUITE, based on and named after Lewis Carroll's *Alice in Wonderland.* This is our immediate concern. Originally written for chamber orchestra, Taylor later rewrote the score for full orchestra. His own program notes for the first performance of the suite (Brooklyn on March 10, 1923, and New York City the next day) offer the best introduction to the music.

The Suite needs no extended analysis. It is based on Lewis Carroll's immortal nonsense fairytale: *Through the Looking-Glass and What Alice Found There,* and the five pictures it presents will, if all goes well, be readily recognizable to lovers of the book. There are four movements, the first being subdivided into two connected parts.

Program Notes

I.

(a) Dedication

Carroll precedes the tale with a charming poetical foreword, the first stanza of which the music aims to express. It runs:

"Child of the pure unclouded brow
    And dreaming eyes of wonder!
Though the time be fleet, and I and thou
    Are half a mile asunder,
Thy loving smile will surely hail
    The love-gift of a fairy-tale."

A simple song theme, briefly developed, leads without pause to

(b) The Garden of Live Flowers

Shortly after Alice had entered the looking-glass country, she came to a lovely garden in which the flowers were talking:

"O Tiger-Lily," said Alice, addressing herself to one that was waving gracefully about in the wind, "I wish you could talk."

"We can talk," said the Tiger-Lily, "when there's anybody worth talking to."

"And can all the flowers talk?"

"As well as you can," said the Tiger-Lily, "and a great deal louder."

The music reflects the brisk chatter of the swaying, bright-colored denizens of the garden.

II.
Jabberwocky

This is the poem that so puzzled Alice, and which Humpty Dumpty finally explained to her:

" 'Twas brillig, and the slithy toves
Did gyre and gimble in the wabe;
All mimsy were the borogoves
And the mome raths outgrabe.

"Beware the Jabberwock, my son!
The jaws that bite, the claws that catch!
Beware the Jubjub bird, and shun
The fruminous Bandersnatch!

"He took his vorpal sword in hand;
Long time the manxome foe he sought—
So rested he by the Tumtum tree,
And stood awhile in thought.

"And, as in uffish thought he stood,
The Jabberwock, with eyes of flame,
Came whiffing through the tulgey wood,
And burbled as it came!

"One, two! One, two! and through and through
The vorpal blade went snicker-snack!
He left it dead, and with its head
He went galumphing back.

"And hast thou slain the Jabberwock?
Come to my arms, my beamish boy!
O frabjous day! Callooh! Callay!
He chortled in his joy.

" 'Twas brillig, and the slithy toves
Did gyre and gimble in the wabe;
All mimsy were the borogoves,
And the mome raths outgrabe."

The theme of that fruitful beast, the Jabberwock, is first announced (*lento*) by the full orchestra. The clarinet then begins the tale, recounting how, on a "brillig" afternoon, the "slithy toves did gyre and gimble in the wabe." Muttered imprecations by the bassoon warn us to "beware the Jabberwock, my son." A miniature march signalizes the approach of our hero, taking "his vorpal sword in hand." Trouble starts among the trombones—the Jabberwock is upon us! The battle with the monster is recounted in a short and rather repellent fugue, the double basses bringing up the subject and the hero fighting back in the interludes. Finally, his vorpal blade (really a xylophone) goes snicker-snack, and the monster impersonated by the solo bassoon, dies a lingering and convulsive death. The hero returns, to the victorious strain of his own theme—

"O frabjous day! Callooh! Callay!" The whole orchestra rejoices—the church bells are rung—alarms and excursions.

Conclusion. Once more the slithy toves perform their pleasing evolutions, undisturbed by the uneasy ghost of the late Jabberwock.

III.
Looking-Glass Insects

The score contains this extract:

This was anything but a regular bee; in fact, it was an elephant—as Alice soon found out, though the idea quite took her breath away at first. . . .

The gnat (for that was the insect she had been talking to) was balancing itself on a twig just over her head, and fanning her with its wings. It certainly was a very large gnat: "About the size of a chicken," Alice thought.

"—then don't you like all insects?" the gnat went on, as quietly as if nothing had happened.

"I like them when they can talk," Alice said. "None of them ever talk, where I come from. . . ."

"Half-way up that bush, you'll see a Rocking-horse-fly, if you look. Look on the branch above your head, . . . and there you'll find a snapdragon-fly. . . . Crawling at your feet, you may observe a Bread-and-butter-fly."

"And what does it live on?"

"Weak tea with cream in it."

"Supposing it couldn't find any?"

"Then it would die, of course."

"But that must happen very often," Alice remarked thoughtfully.

"It always happens," said the gnat.

Here we find the vociferous *diptera* that made such an impression upon Alice—the Bee-elephant, the Gnat, the Rocking-horse-fly, the Snapdragon-fly, and the Bread-and-butter-fly. There are several themes, but there is no use trying to decide which insect any one of them stands for.

IV.
The White Knight

He was a toy Don Quixote, mild, chivalrous, ridiculous, and rather touching. He carried a mouse-trap on his saddle-bow, "because, if they *do* come, I don't choose to have them running about." He couldn't ride very well, but he was a gentle soul, with good intentions. There are two themes: the first a sort of instrumental prance, being the Knight's own conception of himself as a slashing, dare-devil fellow. The second is bland, mellifluous, a little sentimental—much more like the Knight as he really was. The theme starts off bravely, but falls out of the saddle before long, and has to give way to the second. The two alternate, in various guises, until the end, when the Knight rides off, with Alice waving her handkerchief—he thought it would encourage him if she did.

We suggest selections from the following Suites (examples of Romantic, Classic, Impressionistic, or other tempers) as a beginning for your own compilation: ENGLISH SUITES, Nos. 2, 3, 4, 5, and 6 by J. S. Bach; MIKROKOSMOS SUITE, Bartók; L'ARLESIÉNNE SUITES, Nos. 1 and 2, Bizet; FOUR SEA INTERLUDES SUITE from *Peter Grimes,* Britten; SUITE FOR STRING ORCHESTRA, Corelli; LA MER, IMAGES, IBERIAN, and CHILDREN'S CORNER Suites by Debussy; SUITE IN F-SHARP MINOR Op. 19, Dohnanyi; EL AMOR BRUJO and NIGHTS IN THE GARDENS OF SPAIN, Falla; HOLBERG SUITE, Grieg; GRAND CANYON SUITE, Grofé; MATHIS DE MAHLER, Hindemith; THE PLANETS, Holst; MASQUERADE SUITE, Khachaturian; HÁRY JÁNOS, Kodály; HUNGARIAN SUITES, Nos. 2 and 10, Liszt; SERENADE (*Eine Kleine Nacht Musik*), K. 525, Mozart (see Chap. 26); PICTURES AT AN EXPOSITION, Mussorgsky, (arranged by Ravel); LIEUTENANT KIJÉ and SCYTHIAN SUITES by Prokofieff; ABDELAZER SUITE, Purcell; GASPARD DE LA NUIT and MA MÈRE L'OYE, Ravel; GLI UCCELLI, Respighi; ANTAR, SYMPHONIC SUITE, Op. 9 and COQ D'OR SUITE, Rimsky-Korsakoff (see also SCHEHERAZADE SUITE in Chap. 16); CARNIVAL OF ANIMALS, Saint-Saëns; CARNAVAL, Op. 9 for piano solo, Schumann; KARELIA SUITE, Op. 11 by Sibelius; MOLDAU, Smetana (see also Chap. 15); FIREBIRD SUITE, Stravinsky; FIVE PORTRAITS and PLOW THAT BROKE THE PLAINS, Virgil Thompson; BACHIANAS BRASILEIRAS SUITES, Nos. 1 and 2, Villa-Lobos; FAÇADE, Walton. Consult also the list of Ballet Suites at end of Chap. 11.

Courtesy New York City Ballet, Roger Wood, Photographer

SYMPHONIE CONCERTANTE

Wolfgang Mozart

11 Music and ballet

The spontaneous dances of the folk had their counterpart in the highly organized dance pageants that figured prominently in religious ceremonials and in the entertainment at the royal courts. In Greek tragedy, the chorus (from *choros,* a round dance) danced as it chanted. The ballet thus lent itself simultaneously to the needs of the theater, the temple, and the palace entertainment, absorbing elements from each.[1]

In our theater, the ballet figures in two ways; first, as a spectacular interlude in drama or opera; second, as an

[1] Those who are especially interested in the nature and history of the dance are directed to such references as: John Martin, *American Dancing: The Background and Personalities of the Modern Dance* (New York: Dodge Publishing Co., 1936), *Introduction to the Dance* (New York: Norton, 1939), and *The Dance* (New York: Tudor Press, 1946); Margaret Lloyd, *The Borzoi Book of Modern Dance* (New York: Knopf, 1949); Alma M. Hawkins, *Modern Dance in Higher Education* (New York: Columbia University Teachers College Press, 1954); and Margaret N. H'Doubler, *Dance: A Creative Art Experience* (New York: Crofts, 1940).

independent art form in which dramatic action and atmosphere are conveyed to the audience through dance pantomime. In either case, the music is of paramount importance both in furnishing an accompaniment for the actual dancing and in communicating and intensifying the mood. Ballet music as a rule combines the qualities of good dance music—melodious charm, strong rhythmic appeal, simplicity of form and content—with theatrical atmosphere, the dramatic *elan* of incidental music. It represents, in short, a fine fusion of the spirit of the dance with that of the theater.

Much of the outstanding ballet music of the nineteenth century was written as part of operas or as incidental music to dramatic performances, and might or might not be an integral part of the dramatic plot and action of the moment. For instance, in an opera like Gounod's FAUST, the plot and action cease for the moment, and out of the wings from either side of the stage flutter ballet dancers on the tips of their toes. They go through well-prepared, graceful movements, singly and in ensembles, presenting the eye with a pleasing sight of charm in rhythmic motion and design—all this to music of a comparable character. Degas, the French painter, has caught the various moods and life of such ballet dancers in many of his paintings. Similar ballets are to be found in many French operas from the time of Lully and before. A popular ballet of this type is Delibes' SYLVIA.[2]

As the ballet established itself as an independent art form, it employed music in conjunction with dance, pantomime, scenery, and costume to create a distinctive type of dramatic-musical entertainment. In some cases, ballets were arranged to music already in existence. Thus, Rimsky-Korsakoff's SCHEHEREZADE (Chapter 16) and Debussy's AFTERNOON OF A FAUN (Chapter 29) are two of the many famous orchestral compositions to which ballets were adapted. Often, however, the music was written specifically for the ballet. As with incidental music, the composers of these ballets frequently arranged the music into concert suites, some of which became popular as independent compositions, preserving as they did their excitement and rhythmic verve even when removed from the glamour of the ballet theater. Thus was established a continual interplay between music and ballet, with symphonic compositions moving into the ballet theater and ballet music becoming part of the symphonic repertory.

As to the relationship between the two arts, the reader may recall our discussion on musical architecture (in Chapter 6) where we pointed

[2] Essential listening for this chapter includes: PETROUCHKA by Stravinsky; SKYSCRAPERS by Carpenter or APPALACHIAN SPRING by Copland; and the MOTHER GOOSE BALLET by Ravel. All other ballets mentioned in the text and in the Additional Suggestions for Listening are to be considered supplementary and optional. If time does not allow complete performances of the required listening, select excerpts accordingly. Assigned listening outside of class may serve to cover the ground fairly well.

out that the qualities of symmetry and balance, which are space concepts in painting, sculpture, and architecture, become time concepts in music. The ballet affords a vivid example of the transformation from the one dimension to the other. The musical phrases that balance each other in time become in the music the basis for movements that balance each other in space in the dance, producing a synchronization of the two dimensions.

The new art form of the ballet, then, was built upon a story with a well-defined dramatic plot, and the action, or pantomime, served as the basis for telling the story and for providing a proper, desirable vehicle for the dancers themselves in the medium of their own art. Of course, the costumes, stage settings, and, what concerns us most for the moment, the music, combined to provide the complete performance, the result being a dramatic stage performance through dancing, pantomime, and music—*sans* words of the drama and *sans* singing of the opera. Naturally, to enjoy such ballets to the full, one must know the story and the plot, and the choreographic interpretation of these, and have an understanding of the other arts that fuse and amalgamate into this art form.

The familiar term modern dance in common with the companion terms modern music, modern art, modern architecture, and the like, is handicapped with the lack of general agreement in the precise meaning for the adjective "modern." How extensive in time does "modern" apply? When does it begin? When does it end? Does it embrace all artistic creations executed during that interval of time? Just what are its distinctive characteristics?

Nevertheless, when one contemplates some of the contemporary dances, even as a layman, it is obvious that there are many basic elements in common among the individual conceptions and expressions of the so-called modern dance, as exemplified by such leaders as Balanchine, Mary Wigman, Hanya Holm, Doris Humphrey, Charles Weidman, Martha Graham, and Helen Tamiris. Also, one can discern the same conditions in the writings of such experts and authorities as John Martin, Margaret H' Doubler, Alma Hawkins, and including Isadore Duncan in Curt Sachs' WORLD HISTORY OF THE DANCE. Fundamentally, the modern dance seeks to express through bodily movements certain emotions, feelings, moods, and suggestive meanings—or even relatively "pure" design of masses and forms in action. The dance may involve fantasies that are indigenous to patterns of movement, posturing, grouping and timing of the human figure, with or without a literary "program." The modern dance is striving to become an art which is unique among the fine arts, though, paradoxically, it is composed of elements and techniques common to the sister arts. The play of light, shadow, and color are very important in the modern dance. Then, too, the modern dance, viewed as a whole, borrows ideas and simulates action derived or even imaginatively reconstructed from ancient dances,

Courtesy The Metropolitan Museum of Art

BALLET REHEARSAL ON STAGE

Edgar Degas

Courtesy The Ballet Theatre, Presented by S. Hurok

A SCENE FROM THE BALLET "PETROUCHKA" — Igor Stravinsky

tion of the carnival mood. The music is taut and angular; this is the dance that the three stuffed puppets perform for the delectation of the unfeeling crowd. Notice the sharply contrasting timbres; the development of the theme by an interesting variety of instruments; the vivid, ever-shifting rhythms; above all, the overpowering gusto and virility of the music.

The second part centers about the appearance of the ballerina, accompanied by a dainty piano solo. Next, the music depicts the sufferings of the love-smitten clown, his rage at being rejected, his forlorn cries.

The third part is a brilliant carnival scene, one of the most colorful tone pictures from the composer's hand. A motley procession surges past our eyes—gay peasants, rollicking children, hawkers and fakirs and barkers, their cries intermingled with the tinny sounds of carrousels and hurdy-gurdies. There is much dancing and gaiety that is rapidly dissipated as the crowd scatters at the arrival of a peasant leading a trained bear.

The peasant pipes a tune; the bear walks on his hind legs to a ponderous accompaniment on the double basses. The spotlight soon switches to a rich merchant who amuses himself by throwing money to the crowd. Gypsies dance, snatching at the wind-tossed bank notes. Then coachmen and hostlers perform a vigorous dance marked by great stamping of boots to typical Russian rhythms.

The final scene depicts the masquerade at nightfall. Clowning motives in the bass herald the approach of the masquerade. Disguised as buffoons, devils, pigs, and goats, the merrymakers frolic together in a mad whirl. It is on this note that the concert ends, omitting the personal tragedy of the puppet who, from being put through the outer semblance of human emotions so unexpectedly, developed a soul—and a capacity for suffering—of his own.

Of course, the next step is to see the ballet as well as to hear it, if you can. Now for a more abstract and symbolic ballet by our own native composer, John Alden Carpenter.

Skyscrapers Ballet by John Alden Carpenter (1876–1951)

The ballet has been assiduously cultivated in America and several of our composers have produced highly successful scores. One of the outstanding among these, SKYSCRAPERS by John Alden Carpenter, not only is a fine example of modern tendencies in the art of ballet, but also presents to us in a racy, thoroughly alive idiom, the dynamic tempo, the vitality and surging rhythms of modern American life.

Carpenter, a descendant of John Alden, stands in the forefront of American composers. His music—delightful, intelligent, and witty—has attained wide popularity with the general public. SKYSCRAPERS is his best-known work; it was first performed at the Metropolitan Opera House in 1926 with scenery and costumes by the noted stage designer, Robert

Edmond Jones. Arranged as a concert suite, it has found a sure place for itself on symphonic programs.

The composer has built his music around the polarities of work and play, each, as he says, "with its own peculiar and distinctive rhythmic character." The fevered, restlessly pulsating rhythms of the work episodes alternate with the gay foxtrot and "blues" rhythms of the play episodes. The ballet is divided into six scenes: (1) Symbols of Restlessness (2) Abstraction of the Skyscraper; the Work that produces it; the Crowds passing it (3) The transition from Work to Play (4) An Amusement Park of the Coney Island type, and its varied, restless activities; a "flashback" to the idea of Work, and back again to Play (5) The return from Play to Work (6) Skyscrapers.

As in most ballet music, the rhythmic element predominates in the rhythms of jazz, of foxtrot, of subways and motors and machines, of carrousels and roller coasters—a brilliant and feverish conglomerate of the sounds and sights of the metropolis. The "symbols of restlessness" which permeate the first scenes; the blatant, hurdy-gurdy, "Coney Island" atmosphere of the fourth, with its hectic and synthetic gaiety; the *Dance of "Herself"* introduced by a muted trumpet; the *Dance of the Strutter,* the Negro scene which ushers in the *Blues; The Sandwich Man,* trudging along wearily between his gaudy placards; the factory whistle summoning the workers back to the shops; and the imposing chords at the end which drive relentlessly onward, symbolic of glittering skyscrapers thrusting against the sky—all these are interwoven in a score of compact brilliance that has humor, verve, and a topical pointedness.

Note particularly the colorfulness of the orchestration: the use of the brass and complex piano parts in the "Symbols of Restlessness" scene; the wood-wind and brass, in jagged rhythms, in the "Abstraction of the Skyscraper"; the happy-go-lucky dance tune on the banjo in the "Transition from Work to Play"; the muted trumpet and brass band effects in the "Amusement Park" episode; the crooning solo for English horn which introduces the "Negro scene"; the imaginative use of trumpets and horns in the "Sandwich Man" scene; and the fierce power and glitter of the finale. Here is a wealth of melodic ideas, striking harmonies that abound in pungent dissonances united with never-flagging rhythms in a composition of great excitement and forward drive.

Appalachian Spring (Ballet Suite) by Aaron Copland (1900–   )

This ballet and Paul Hindemith's HERODIADE (first called "Mirror Before Me") were commissioned in their musical and choreographic aspects by the Elizabeth Sprague Coolidge Foundation and first produced by Martha Graham at the Coolidge Music Festival held in the Library of Congress, Washington, D. C., on October 30, 1944. In the following year, Copland reworked most of the ballet music into a Concert Suite of the same name as the original ballet, and it is this version to which reference is made here. The title, "Appalachian Spring," was first chosen by Martha Graham from a Hart Crane poem, but the substance of the poem did not become a part of the ballet or suite.

The first few sections of the Suite, the setting of the Shaker melody, "The Gift to be Simple," [3] played in a rather mournful mood by a solo clarinet in a very appropriate orchestral setting, and the final three sections are among the most significant and moving pages of score Copland has so far produced. It should be observed by the listener that musical ideas from the first part reappear—either altered or not—throughout the work to serve as unifying factors in the composition. It is not difficult for the listener to perceive that the Suite is a decidedly Romantic work, employing some Classical tempers in the mid-section, and that it has a definite literary program. The middle section, in spite of its clever craftsmanship, is most open to criticism. It contains more than a few clichés of musical materials and the manner of using them, especially the too often repeated mannerisms of orchestration, and the influences of Shostakovich, Stravinsky, and even tin-pan alley.

The concert ballet suite, APPALACHIAN SPRING, apparently follows the ensuing brief of the scenario and musical sequence given out by the composer himself. Naturally, the sections, or scene sequences of the suite, are more apparent to the careful observer of ballet than they are to the average listener. Here is an abbreviated script:

1. *Very slowly,* a section in which the characters of the ballet and the pervading moods are introduced;
2. *Fast,* an agitated section signalized by a burst of tone from the strings, which settles down to a quiet, peaceful, and quasi-religious mood;
3. *Moderate,* a hymnlike version of the main theme is heard in the brass and wood-winds, ushering in a duet of alternate aggressiveness and tender sentiment apparently taking place between the prospective bride and groom;
4. *Quite fast,* a suggested folklike country square dance for the Evangelist and his followers, working up to a full-orchestra sonority;
5. *Still faster,* a ritualistic dance, reminding one very much of LE SACRE DU PRINTEMPS by Stravinsky, takes place for the bride alone as she contemplates motherhood;

[3] The "Shakers" was a branch of the Quakers (Society of Friends) which was organized in England about the middle of the eighteenth century. It was so-called because of the members' peculiar manner of "shaking" in religious fervor, when singing and marching during public worship. Settlements of Shakers came to New York City in 1774 and then settled in various places in the state of New York, New England, Ohio, Indiana, and Kentucky. The song, or hymn, used by Copland is *The Gift to be Simple* which came from a collection of Shaker songs collected by Edward D. Andrews.

6. *Very slowly,* this section recalls the religious atmosphere of the first part of the ballet;
7. *Calm and flowing,* a very effective and beautiful bucolic scene of the ordinary workaday life of the young couple in which the traditional Shaker tune, "Simple Gifts" is heard, followed by five variations, played by the solo clarinet, the oboe, the bassoon, the trumpet, and the trombones in a chorale-like version which sounds against a background of a discant-like effect in the strings, all of which works up to a *fortissimo* climax by the full orchestra;
8. *Moderate coda.* There is a return to the quiet, religious atmosphere of the beginning, which is ushered in by the muted (*con sordini*) strings, and the work ends in this tranquil mood.

The closing section also serves as a very successful compositional "binding" for the work as a whole—most artfully done—and it further provides a sort of cinema-like "fadeout" for the *dramatis personae,* thus satisfactorily completing the programmatic scenario as well as the musical and choreographic plots.

Ma Mère l'Oye Suite by Maurice Ravel (1875–1937)

Our last illustration is Maurice Ravel's ever popular MA MÈRE L'OYE (Mother Goose) SUITE. (More of this composer and his impressionistic suite, DAPHNIS AND CHLOÉ will be found in Chap. 29.) One reason for considering this particular work now is the value we can get in the way of appreciation of instrumental tone color or timbre if we listen carefully.

The MOTHER GOOSE SUITE music, originally composed for piano duet in 1908, was later orchestrated by Ravel and, like Debussy's AFTERNOON OF A FAUN, achieved popularity as a ballet. An interesting characteristic of Ravel is that although he transcribed for orchestra several compositions originally written for piano, his sense of style was so acute that the orchestral versions do not have that "made-over" feeling that so often attends transcriptions; they seem to have a personality of their own quite distinct from the original form of the piece.

The Suite, arranged from the ballet music, consists of five children's pieces. The *Pavane of the Sleeping Beauty* has a slow somnolent grace. A *pavane* is an old stately dance of Spanish origin; Ravel's other pavane, *For a Dead Princess,* widely popular in this country, has achieved the distinction (?) of inspiring a foxtrot. Note the effect of two solo flutes, later English horn and flute.

To the second number, *Hop o' My Thumb,* Ravel appended a quotation from Perrault, the great French writer of fairy tales: "He believed that he would easily find his path by means of his bread crumbs which he had scattered wherever he had passed; but he was very much surprised when he could not find a single crumb: the birds had come and eaten everything up." Note the effect of the oboe solo over the muted first and second violins. Can you notice also the frequent change of time?

Third is *Laideronnette, Empress of the Pagodas.* "Pagoda" once indicated not only the fanciful little tower but also the idol or image lodged in it. When the Princess Laideronnette, who had been cursed at birth with supreme ugliness, entered her bath, the pagodas and their ladies—grotesque little figures with movable heads—"began to sing and play on instruments: some had theorbos made of walnut shells, some had viols made of almond shells; for they were obliged to proportion the instruments to their figure." Note that the quick theme played by the solo flute resembles the nursery tune "Chop Sticks," or "Peter, Peter, Pumpkin Eater," which all of us have played in our youth on the black keys of the piano. Such a scale is called a *pentatonic* scale. Many Chinese melodies are in such a scale: thus Ravel was making a proper musical pun.

Next comes the *Conversations of Beauty and the Beast.* In the meter of a slow waltz, with a double bassoon representing the Beast, this number is one of the most popular of the Suite. Since Beauty was able to see through the ugly exterior of the Beast to the kind heart underneath, she was able to release him from his enchantment. "The Beast disappeared, and she saw at her feet only a prince more beautiful than Love. . . ."

The first of the following musical illustrations, for harp with clarinet solo, is used to depict the Beauty; the second, which is played by the contrabassoon and which sounds an octave lower than written, is a delightful characterization of the Beast.

The Fairy Garden, which closes the Suite, reveals to us the composer in an unusually poetic mood. In slow three-four time, the movement sums up the spirit of fairy-tale magic. Here Ravel weaves a spell no less potent than that of the fairies and magicians who people the tales on which his music is based. How the strings, played very softly, contribute just the right "atmosphere" for the fairy waltzlike theme!

ADDITIONAL SUGGESTIONS FOR LISTENING

Among the popular ballets, ballet-suites, and excerpts often heard on symphonic programs and which illustrate the nineteenth-century style in this genre, in addition to those already mentioned in the text, are: Alexander Glazounov's *Bacchanale* from the ballet SEASONS, and LES SYLPHIDES, Glazounov's orchestration and arrangement of selected works by Frédéric Chopin; the ballets COPPÉLIA and SYLVIA by Leo Delibes; the lively ballet, GAIETÉ PARISIENNE by Jacques Offenbach, composer of the TALES OF HOFFMANN; SWAN LAKE, SLEEPING BEAUTY, THE MONTHS BALLET SUITE (one number for each month of the year), NUTCRACKER SUITES (Nos. 1 and 2, available in full as ballets or as suites) by Peter Ilyitch Tchaikovsky.

Among the contemporary ballet-suites or ballets that might interest the listener are: (consult your latest record catalog for availability): MEDEA BALLET (also suite) by Samuel Barber; ADVENTURES IN A PERAMBULATOR by John Alden Carpenter; RODEO and BILLY THE KID by Aaron Copland; ERRAND INTO THE MAZE by Gian-Carlo Menotti; LA CRÉATION DU MONDE (The Creation of the World) by Darius Milhaud, an interesting and well composed concert piece constructed by a Frenchman out of American jazz idioms. It antedates and is superior in craftsmanship to the uneven and often unskillful RHAPSODY IN BLUE by George Gershwin, though the orchestration of this work by Ferde Grofé is by far the more fitting and effective of the two works under discussion; the gay, somewhat sardonic, and burlesquing THE INCREDIBLE FLUTIST, using a phonograph record *a la* Respighi by the American, Walter Piston; BUFFOON (*Chout*), Op. 21, LE PAS D'ACIER, Op. 41, L'ENFANT PRODIGUE, Op. 46, SUR LE BORYSTHÈNE, Op. 51, and ROMEO AND JULIET, Op. 64 (also in concert suite form), by Sergei Prokofieff; BOLÉRO by Maurice Ravel; *Yablochko* (or the *Russian Sailors' Dance*) from Reinhold Glière's ballet THE RED POPPY, which, by the way, is lustily satirized by Dmitri Shostakovitch in the latter's *Russian Dance* from the ballet THE GOLDEN AGE; selected ballets from LA FIAMMA, a melodrama by Ottorino Respighi; NEW DANCE (1934) and TROJAN INCIDENT (1938) by Wallingford Riegger; THE FIREBIRD and SACRE DU PRINTEMPS by Igor Stravinsky (the last-mentioned work is more fully discussed in the last chapter).

Courtesy The Metropolitan Museum of Art

DOODLE-SACK PLAYER Albrecht Dürer

This is a bagpipe, a favorite instrument of Scotland; its history is shrouded in unknown origins. Well known throughout the countries of the Middle and Far East, it later became familiar almost everywhere. The instrument is basically composed of a leather bag, or wind chest, a wind pipe for inflating the bag, a fingered single or double reed chanter pipe that plays the tune in a fixed key, and two, three, or more drone pipes with single or double reeds, that provide the bourdon of tonic and dominant (doh and sol) tones.

vibrating the left hand from the wrist as the finger presses against the string to produce a tremulous tone quality, *vibrato;* playing with the wooden part of the bow to create a strange hollow tone (*col legno*); rapidly repeating the same note with brusque up-and-down strokes of the bow to achieve the *tremolo,* the favorite for producing effects of suspense, danger, fear, and the like; sliding the left hand along the string while bowing with the right, the *glissando;* and pressing lightly at certain points of the string, which prevents the string from vibrating as a whole and brings into prominence the vibrations of its segments, thus producing those high-pitched, ethereal tones known as *harmonics.*

The four strings of the violin are tuned G_{-1}-D^1-A^1-E^2, ranging from the full-throated expressiveness of the G_{-1} string to the brilliance of the upper register of the E^2.

Its effective range is approximately three and a half octaves, beginning from G_{-1} below middle C^1. The modern symphony orchestra has two groups of violins, known as the first and second violins, with about sixteen players in each.

Our method of designating the octave pitches and all chromatic tones in between each octave is by the use of superior or inferior numbers placed after each pitch letter name. Thus starting with middle C^1 as the base, the small superior numbers are placed in the following manner—C^2, C^3, C^4—to indicate the octaves above middle C^1. To indicate octaves below middle C^1 small inferior numbers preceded by a minus sign are placed thus: C_{-1}, C_{-2}, C_{-3}. To illustrate, the pitch of the violin A string is designated A^1; the cello A string is designated A_{-1}.

The *Viola* is held and played like the violin, though it is larger in size. It may be called the "alto" or high "tenor" of the string choir. The four strings are tuned a fifth lower than the violin's, the top three strings being pitched the same as the A^1, D^1, and G_{-1} strings of the fiddle (the E^2 string is absent), and a C_{-1} string is added below the low G_{-1}. Although the viola does not produce the brilliant high tones of the violin, it compensates by going lower and sounding more sombre and mellow. Its tone may also be described as having a subdued and "veiled" charm and dignity unique among the strings. Passages on the lower range are often used by composers to suggest darkly brooding, nostalgic, or melancholy moods, such as Berlioz has done in HAROLD IN ITALY, Op. 16. The viola blends so well with the more brilliant violin or the richer-toned 'cello that for many years its own personality was subordinated to these two. But in the past century composers have grown more and more appreciative of its lyrical possibilities. Its subtle coloring, now gently mournful, now coldly penetrating, is an important part of the orchestral palette. Since most of its music lies between the bass and treble clefs, for convenience it uses the alto (movable C) clef (middle C is on the middle line):

It is capable of all the technical effects of the violin; its effective range is slightly less—about three octaves, from the C_{-1} below middle C^1. The symphony orchestra usually contains from ten to twelve viola players.

The *'cello* (a shortened, general name for *violoncello*) is much larger than the viola, so much so that it is held between the knees of the player, as were some *viols* that existed before perfection of the modern violin family between the late sixteenth and the early eighteenth centuries.[2] The 'cello may be considered the "low tenor" or the "barytone cantante." Often it is the real bass of the string choir when the double-basses are not used. Note the high-pitched, expressive melody of the 'cellos playing the second theme of the *Intermezzo* (the second movement) in the Schumann CONCERTO FOR PIANO IN A MINOR (Chap. 25). A good example of the 'cello acting as the bass may be observed in most of the Tchaikovsky excerpt at the close of this string section. The 'cello is fairly similar to an ancient bass instrument of the viol family called the *viola da gamba.* The 'cello has four strings, tuned an octave lower than those of the viola, C_{-2}, G_{-2}, D_{-1}, A_{-1} as follows:

It has a range of over three and one half octaves, from C_{-2}. There are usually eight to ten, sometimes twelve, 'cellos in the large modern symphony orchestra. Some composers have been successful in securing unusual effects from the 'cellos, such as Villa-Lobos in his brilliant BRASILEIRAS NO. 1 for eight divided 'cellos; the opening section of the SAKUNTALA OVERTURE by Karl Goldmark, where they are divided into six parts; the technically engaging CONCERTO FOR VIOLONCELLO IN B MINOR, Op. 104, by Dvořák; the facile CONCERTO FOR VIOLONCELLO IN A MINOR,

[2] This process of perfecting the modern stringed instruments of the violin family was due largely to the genius of such men, families, and workshop-schools as: Gasparo da Salo (c. 1542–1609); the Amati family, especially Niccolo (1596–1684); the Guarneri family, especially Giuseppe (1687–c. 1745), more generally known as "del Gesù" because of the Biblical symbol "IHS" (the Greek contraction of the name Jesus) which he used on his labels pasted on the inside of his instruments; the Stradivari family, especially the supreme master, Antonio (c. 1640–1737) who was a pupil of Niccolo Amati. All these were of Cremona, Italy. Also important was Jakob Stainer (1621–1683) of Absam, Tyrol (near Innsbruck, Austria).

Op. 33, by Saint-Saëns, and the technically difficult modern SONATA FOR UNACCOMPANIED 'CELLO by Kodály.

The *double-bass,* known also as the contra-bass, bass viol, or the string bass, is the lowest pitched and largest of the string family, and bears a kinship to the ancient double-bass viol, the *violone, consort viol,* and the *viola da gamba.* It is the "basso-profundo" voice of the string choir. The double-bass is greatly used to duplicate the 'cello parts, sounding an octave lower—hence the term double-bass. Its deep, heavy tone is equally effective in portraying placidity, force, fierce agitation, foreboding gloom, heavy-handed humor, or, when played *pizzicato,* softly and in unison, a somewhat ominous mood. It is seldom used as a solo instrument. A few notable exceptions are: the powerfully effective, sinister passage foretelling tragedy, for muted double-basses, in Verdi's opera OTELLO, Act IV, where Othello, who has been made madly suspicious of Desdemona by the machinations of Iago, peeks through a crack in the door at his sleeping wife. The scene is made even more poignant because Desdemona has just sung her beautiful and mournful *Willow Song* and the touching *Ave Maria.* As for solos for the double-bass, a virtuoso of the nineteenth century, Giovanni Bottesini (1821–1889), wrote a GRAND DUO CONCERTANTE FOR VIOLIN AND DOUBLE-BASS. In the prior century there lived the most amazing "Paganini of the contra-basso," Domenico Dragonetti (1763–1846). It is said that when he practiced his lightning fast scales, *arpeggi,* and other rumbling passages, the neighbors would rush into their homes as though a storm were threatening. More recently, Sergei Koussevitzky, late conductor of the Boston Symphony Orchestra, was a concert artist on the double-bass and gave infrequent solo recitals. He also wrote some *virtuoso studies* for the double-bass. Sergei Prokofieff (1891–1953) wrote an interesting passage for this instrument in his LIEUTENANT KIJÉ SUITE, Op. 60. Hear the spoofing of an Offenbach theme from ORPHEUS, in the sixth number, the *Turtles,* of Saint-Saëns' CARNIVAL OF THE ANIMALS, where the theme is played by the double-basses in unison. The average music lover is usually only slightly acquainted with this instrument as a solo medium, for the principal task of the double-bass is to supply a deep and firm bass for the harmonic structure above it, not unlike the lowest pitched pipes of the pipe organ.[3] Recently, this grand old instrument has been subjected to the indignities of the "jazzites," who force it

[3] This analogy between the double-bass and the pipe organ is more important than many listeners realize. Some organs have a very low 64-foot tonal register. There are not many who can actually hear the fundamentals of this register, but almost everyone is aware of the enriching effects of those unheard fundamentals when fused with the harmonies being played upon the manuals. Also, while one may not always be actually conscious of the lowest tones of the double-basses as such, their enrichment of the combined tonal quality (the *Klangfarbe*) is most salutary, as in Debussy's LA MER (especially at Nos. 1, 35, and 41 in the score), and Ravel's DAPHNIS ET CHLOÉ (at beginning, No. 40, 2 measures after No. 131, and a measure after No. 152), and in many other works.

to function as a percussion instrument by actually slapping the strings against the fingerboard.

For many years the double-bass had to be content with but three strings, but then a fourth and even a fifth were added. There are some five-stringed basses being used today. Here is the tuning of the four-stringed bass, though one should remember that the pitches sounded are actually an octave lower than written:

Its actual *sounding* range is slightly more than three octaves, from its low C_{-3} to about middle C^1. Harmonic tones sound still higher. The modern double-bass has either an additional (written) low C_{-2} string below the low E_{-2} shown above or a mechanism attached to the E string between the peg-box and the scroll which enables the player to descend to the low C_{-2} by half steps, *sounding* a pitch equal to the lowest C_{-3} on the piano.

For the first listening project hear either the INTRODUCTION AND ALLEGRO FOR STRINGS, Op. 47, by Elgar, or ADAGIO FOR STRINGS by Samuel Barber.

Between the brilliant, exciting tones of the violin, the "soft grays" and nostalgic quality of the viola, the rich and vibrant glow of the 'cello, and the deep pedal-tones of the double-bass, a capable and imaginative composer can run the gamut of tonal and expressive emotional range. The string choir is given the greater part of a score, for of all the instruments of the orchestra the listener tires least from sustained playing of the strings. These instruments can hold a firm, powerful tone or spin it out almost to nothingness with a smoothness unattainable by the other instruments.[4] When a soft, veiled effect is desired from the strings they are muted by slipping a split, three-pronged, comb-like contraption, usually of ebony, onto the top of the bridge of the instrument. The double-basses are not so treated, as a rule. Brass instruments use a mute of cone-shaped metal or papier-mache which is inserted in the bell, and jazz players sometimes use a derby hat for certain effects. Wood-wind instruments are rarely muted. Berlioz once tried it by putting the clarinets into a sack, but it was not satisfactory. Chamois or cloth are sometimes stuffed into

[4] Arturo Toscanini had a passion for securing an extremely subdued *decrescendo sin al pianissimo* (diminishing to the softest possible sound). Rehearsing a certain passage with the strings of the New York Philharmonic, he failed to obtain the very soft, spun-out tone he desired. He became utterly disgusted and rushed from the room. During the break, the concert-meister suggested to the players a strategy. Upon resumption of the rehearsal, the difficult passage was again reached. Amid the many "shushes" of the Maestro and his characteristic placing of the index finger of his left hand over his lips, the concert-meister gave a signal. The bows were lifted slightly *off* the strings, but the bow-arms slowly continued their downward motion as though actually sounding a tone. The Maestro stopped the orchestra, exclaimed, in effect, "That was exactly what I wanted all the time. *Bravo! Gratia!*"

the bell to mute a wood-wind instrument, as in PETROUCHKA by Stravinsky; but the intonation is apt to be adversely affected.

The *harp*, one of the oldest of musical instruments, is a stringed instrument sounded by plucking or gliding the fingers over the strings. The "double-action" harp, introduced by Érard about 1810, is tuned in C-flat, and the forty-seven strings are in a diatonic (scalewise) rather than a chromatic (half-step) sequence. The pitches of the strings are raised and lowered by foot pedals around either side of the bass. Those affecting the pitch tones (contra-clockwise) are: D-flat, C-flat, and B-flat for the left foot, a *forte* pedal, then an E-flat, F-flat, G-flat, and A-flat for the right. (The *forte* pedal is not too strong in resonating effect.) Each pedal affects only the strings of its own pitch name, but it does so throughout the *entire* harp. Thus, if the C-flat pedal is depressed to its first notch, all the C-flat strings of the harp are raised to C-natural; if pushed all the way down to the second notch, the C-natural strings then become C-sharps.

The tone quality of the harp has been variously described as "silvery," "ethereal," "like a gentle dripping waterfall or fountain," "like a lute or a guitar in the distance," and so forth; but it can also be brilliant and scintillating, and even percussive-like sounds may be produced. Modern harp techniques were developed in our country largely by Carlos Salzedo and Lucille Lawrence (see recordings, *Eight Dances for Harp* and *Transcriptions for Two Harps*), and by the foreign composers Ravel, Debussy, Respighi, Tournier, Noel Gallon, Stravinsky, and others. Beginners in the art of orchestration are usually fascinated by its tone and introduce the harp frequently in their scores (often confusing its dynamic power with that of the modern grand piano). Masters of the art, however, know its limitations as well as its values, and reserve its use for passages where it will be the most effective. One can hear it expertly used for its own solo effects and for its ensemble values in Rimsky-Korsakoff's SCHEHEREZADE SUITE (see Chap. 16). Debussy was one of the greatest masters in the use of the instrument; listen to its effectiveness in his AFTERNOON OF A FAUN. Also hear Ravel's SUITE NO. 2, DAPHNIS ET CHLOÉ; Respighi's FOUNTAINS OF ROME; the *Intermezzo* for flute and harp in Bizet's CARMEN, after Act II; and the beautiful and original American work, THE WHITE PEACOCK by Griffes.

The usual *written* range of the modern pedal harp is about six and one half octaves, from about the second C-flat below the bass staff (C-flat$_{-3}$), to G-sharp^4, or A-flat^4, above the treble staff. Harp music is written as it sounds, like that for the piano. The harp can play melodies, bell-like harmonics, simultaneously played intervals and chordal groups with either or both hands, many forms of dispersed or figurated chordal tones called *arpeggios*, (appropriately derived from the Italian word for harp, *arpa*), and *glissandi* made by sliding the finger, fingers or palm of the hand over the strings. The large modern symphony orchestra usually employs one or two harps.

The following is a brief excerpt from the harp part of this author's symphonic poem, THE ANCIENT MARINER, based upon Samuel Coleridge's romantic poem. The excerpt illustrates the playing of broken chords, an *arpeggio,* and a *glissandi.*

Here are the ranges of the various instruments of the string choir. We have given the usual four string, double-bass range, minus the low C. *Always bear in mind with all string, wood-wind, and brass instruments that while the lowest tones are determined by the acoustical build of the instrument itself, the uppermost limits depend largely upon the ability of the performer.*

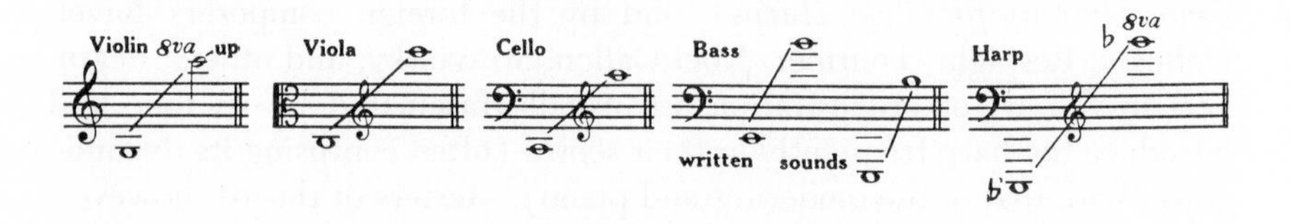

The following is a beautiful example of effective string writing from the final movement, *Adagio lamentoso* (slowly and mournfully), of the SIXTH SYMPHONY IN B MINOR the *"Pathetique"* by Tchaikovsky (measures 1-6). The composer has secured an unusually successful *slurred legato,* together with a natural emphasis upon the individual tones of the melodic lines and part-writing that cross between the first and second violins, and the violas and 'cellos. This crossing and alternating play among the parts, and the striking effect it secures when performed as the composer has written it, is the inspiration of a remarkable genius. The resulting melodic and bass lines and the interesting crossing of the parts are indicated by the use of broken lines between and among the notes. The crossing of the part lines is later omitted in the score at letter "G," where it is marked *Andante non tanto* (*ff*) (gracefully moving and flowing, but not too slowly). A comparison of the effects of the two versions by the acute listener should be interesting and revealing. Here is the principal theme in its first full appearance:

The Wood-wind Choir and the Acoustical Bases of Wind and Stringed Instruments

The wood-wind choir, with its great diversity and possibilities in tonal color, is one of the most fascinating sections of the symphony orchestra. It takes much training and experience on the part of the wood-wind performer to achieve perfection in fingering and cross-fingering, intonation, breath, lips and tongue control, phrasing, precision of ensemble, and tonal balance, and much on the part of the conductor to bring to life just what the composer desired. The various instruments of this choir have sharply differentiated "personalities," with the timbre changing throughout their ranges. Both the composer and the conductor have to bear in mind that the facial muscles of all wind players tire easily and that they must have frequent rests. All wind players phrase their music through adroit use of air and lips, and they constantly watch the condition of their reeds and moisture condensation in their instruments to prevent "bubbling," off-pitch, and "dead" tone quality.

Pitch and quality are not merely a matter of putting the correct fingers on the holes, keys, or valves. They are also dependent upon other factors, including the most basic—the perfection of the instrument itself. The serious listener will want to become acquainted with every musical instrument of the orchestra and band by sight, sound, design, function, and general manner of manipulation.[5]

[5] When a composer desires to use instruments acoustically built in differing key construction from the neutral key of C, so that they will all produce the same (or unison) pitch, or key (tonality), in this case C, he writes the playing parts of those instruments not in C but in a third key! This process is called *transposition*. Thus when the trumpet in a tonality of A, the clarinet in B-flat, and the French horns in F, are to play together to sound C, he writes the trumpet part in E-flat, the clarinets in D, and the horns in G. This is an expedient favoring the players rather than the conductors or score readers.

It might be well to enumerate for our general readers a few of the fundamental principles of sound pertaining to pitch and quality as they apply to musical instruments of the string and wind families.

In general, the longer the freely vibrating string, the greater its thickness and mass unit length weight, and the less the tension (tautness), the lower will be the pitch. Thus, the lowest strings of stringed instruments are weighted by winding them with a metal covering to compensate for lack of normal string weight and ideal proportional vibrating length; in addition, the tension is made comparatively less than in the higher pitched strings. The fingers of the left hand press down upon the bowed strings (called "stopping") to effect a shorter vibrating string length and, consequently, to produce a higher pitch. Of course, the manner in which the strings are set into vibration (by plucking, striking, bowing, etc.) plus the construction, design, and operation of the resonating chamber of a musical instrument will largely determine its tonal quality.

In the wind instruments, whether wood, silver, gold, brass, or other material, the *general* law of the fundamental pitch is that the longer the vibrating column of air within the pipe the lower the pitch will be. The pitch is affected if the bore enclosing the vibrating air column is cylindrical or conical, or is actually closed at the end or if the acoustical construction of the entire wind instrument and its operation causes the pipe to act as though it were closed at the end (such as the flute, clarinet, some organ pipes, etc.) The pitch is lower in a "closed" tube. Thus an open, 32 ft. long diapason flue-type pipe in the organ sounds an octave higher than a similar closed pipe of about the same length.

Both the pitch and the quality of a wind instrument are influenced by the following factors: (1), the manner in which the lips are used (loose or tense); (2), the variation of wind pressure; (3), the manner in which the air column is set into vibration and "speaks"; (4), the character, shape, dimensions, and general acoustical construction of the pipe or tube; (5), whether the mouthpiece and embouchure (ahm-boo-SHOOR) has one or two vibrating reeds; (6), whether the instrument has a "whistle" type mouthpiece construction, as in the recorder, or is as in the transverse (horizontal) flute with its blowing hole edge embouchure and resonating tube; (7), whether the vibrations in a "speaking" tube are set in motion by the lips, as in a cup mouthpiece used in most brass instruments such as the trumpet, French horn, trombone, tuba, etc.; (8), the size, shape, and design of the mouthpiece, bell and open end of the tube (compare the trumpet with the French horn); (9), temperature of the air outside and inside the instrument; (10), the natural key or scale and range produced by the tubes; (11), the fundamental or generating tone and its natural series of overtones; (12), the manner in which the fingers or pads cover the segmenting air column holes, the action of the valves, or the use of slides in certain musical instruments; (13), whether the diameter of the bore, in relation to the length, is irregular in shape (conical, cylindrical, or mixed) or uncommonly large or small, and (14), the use of various mutes. The quality of the human voice, which functions mainly as a wind instrument, is determined by the variable length, weight, and tension of the vibrating vocal chords, as in a stringed instrument, plus the acoustical character, shape, design, and use of the resonating or absorbing cavities above and below the vocal chords, the air flow, and so forth. The exact acoustical operation of the human voice is not yet well understood. There are other factors that enter into the determination of the pitch or quality that may be profitably and minutely pursued in other texts.[6]

[6] For those who desire to know more about the description, history, and detailed acoustical principles of musical instruments, we recommend: Wilmer Bartholomew,

The *transverse flute* is usually made of wood or silver; but it has also been constructed of gold, platinum, brass, tin, clay, glass, bone, ivory, and even *papier-mâché!* The modern transverse flute, as perfected by Theobald Boehm about 1847, with some minor improvements since then, is held horizontally to the right of the mouth.

The modern flute consists of a three-part, jointed, cylindrically bored tube, with the blowing end a bit parabolic in bore. It has an over-all length of about twenty-six inches, with the blowing end plugged and the opposite end open. Nevertheless, the flute *acts* as an open tube, due to the acoustical function of the lips. The stream of air blown across the edge of the embouchure hole, actually functioning as a sort of reed, sets the air in the tube in vibration. Thus, because of the open pipe operation, the flute easily overblows the octave with an increase of wind pressure and slight shift of the lips.

Along the length of the flute are scientifically spaced and sized holes bored through the top shell of the tube. Covering of these holes by the fingers, with or without the key mechanism, segments the vibrating air column (similar to touching or stopping a vibrating string) to produce the desired pitches. This is done according to the basic acoustical laws of pipes—the longer the tube the lower the pitch, and vice versa. Thus, the skillful player can produce tones ranging from the softest whisper to earsplitting shrillness, run up and down scales, arpeggi, and other such figures with agility, and skip around to produce trills, shakes, and graces that surpass all other instruments. Yet, the expert flutist (or "flautist") can "sing" a lyrical melody as warmly as the human voice.

The flute, though acoustically in D, is treated as though in C and sounds as written. The highest third of the flute's range, from C^3 to C^4, is brilliant, clear, and articulate, and even shrill when loud. The middle section, from about C^2 to E^3, is light, agile, and acute; and the lowest section, from C^1 to about E^2, is weaker, less brilliant and lyrical, and too often in the very lowest tones, somewhat fuzzy in quality and pitch. There is in use

---

Acoustics of Music (Englewood Cliffs, N. J.: Prentice-Hall, 1942), Ch. III, for general readers; Arthur Tabor Jones, *Sound* (New York: D. Van Nostrand, 1937), for music majors and those familiar with physics; E. G. Richardson, *The Acoustics of Orchestral Instruments and the Organ* (London: Edward Arnold, 1933); L. S. Lloyd, *Music and Sound* (New York: Oxford University Press, 1937), for music majors; Percy C. Buck, *Acoustics for Musicians* (New York: Oxford University Press, 1918); Sir James Jeans, *Science and Music* (New York: MacMillan, 1937), pp. 107-152; Charles A. Culver, *Musical Acoustics,* 4th ed. (New York: McGraw-Hill, 1956); Alexander Wood, *Physics of Music* (New York: Dover Publications, 1957), for advanced readers, Chs. 7, 8, and 9; and Floyd Rowe Watson, *Sound* (New York: John Wiley & Sons, 1935), for professionals.

For descriptive and historical data: Karl Geiringer, *Musical Instruments* (London: George Allen and Unwin Ltd., 1949 Ed.); and Curt Sachs, *The History of Musical Instruments* (New York: W. W. Norton and Co., 1940), a detailed and profusely illustrated text by one of the world's authorities on the subject for all readers.

today a *"bass flute"* in G, used effectively by Ravel in his ballet suite, DAPHNIS AND CHLOÉ. It sounds down a fourth from the written note, and is really an *alto flute.* There is also a real *bass flute* sounding down an octave. One also hears flutes in high D-flat, D, and E-flat in European bands.

Debussy makes great use of the flute in THE AFTERNOON OF A FAUN to suggest the syrinx or pipes of Pan. Ravel shows his fondness for the regular flute in his LA FLUTE ENCHANTÉE and DAPHNIS AND CHLOÉ BALLET SUITE; so does Tchaikovsky in the *Dance of the Toy Flutes* from the NUTCRACKER SUITE. Generally two or three flutes, one interchangeable with the piccolo, are used in a symphony orchestra. The following is a brief solo flute cadenza from the author's symphonic poem, NOCTURNE NO. I:

The *piccolo* (from *flauto piccolo,* the Italian term for "little flute") is about half as long as the flute with a range of about three octaves, from D^1 to B-flat^3, and sounds an octave higher than written. It is cylindrical in bore with no bell. In its lower register, it is rather weak and colorless, and is sometimes so used in popular music to imitate or simulate human whistling. (The human whistle is a transposing instrument, sounding up two octaves!) The upper register of the piccolo, especially when played loudly, is brilliant and facile like the flute; but it is shrill and piercing, and may be heard above a full orchestra. Its tone heightens and brightens the tonal colors of an orchestra, and it also serves to articulate rapid passages in the violins that would otherwise sound rather unclear. It is superb in rapid *staccato* passages, punctuating each tone to a sharp, crisp jot. No storm or wind effect would be complete without the piccolo. Who can forget the trombones and piccolos playing together in the *Stars and Stripes Forever* by Sousa? Pierné has used several piccolos in his humorous *March of the Little Fauns,* and Berlioz used the piccolo in his DAMNATION OF FAUST to suggest the bizarre, the fantastic, even the infernal. No wonder the piccolo has been nicknamed "the imp of the orchestra"! The following is a piccolo passage from the Pierné march:

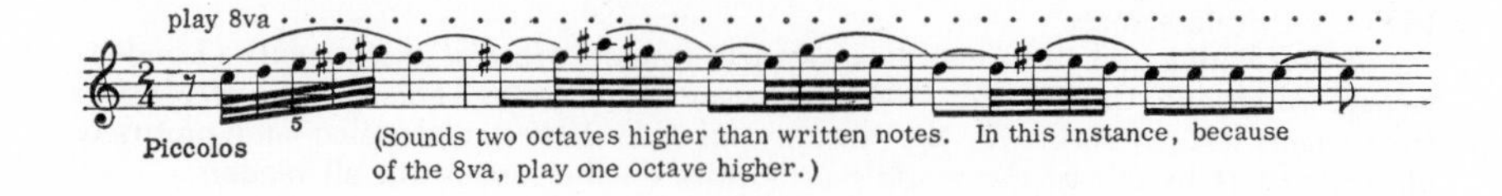

(Sounds two octaves higher than written notes. In this instance, because of the 8va, play one octave higher.)

The *oboe*, of ancient lineage, is a double-reed instrument with a conical bore and a small, gradually widening bell. The "lyric soprano" of the wood-winds, it is indispensable to tone painters of pastoral scenes. Its tone may be somewhat pungent, very reedy, and sometimes thin and strident, giving an oriental effect. It can have a startlingly human quality, similar to that produced by the *vox angelica* and *vox humana* stops on the older pipe organs, especially from D^1 to A^2 or C^3, the middle range.

The modern orchestral conservatory-type oboe is capable of performing agile running passages as well as skips and trills. The full range of the oboe is from B-flat$_{-1}$ to F^3 or G^3. There are usually two or three oboes (one doubling on the English horn) in a large symphony orchestra. Composers have also employed several variants of the oboe such as the *oboe d'amore, oboe da caccia, the baritone heckelphone,* and the more modern *alto English horn,* to say nothing about the large family of *sarrusophones.*[7]

The oboe was a favorite lyrical instrument of Haydn, Mozart, and others of that age, the late Romantic and Impressionist composers. Saint-Saëns secures an amusing effect by using the oboe to initiate the crowing of the cock in his DANSE MACABRE (see Chapter 14). Beethoven uses the oboe for the quail's call in the second movement of his *"Pastoral"* SYMPHONY and its more mournful sound in the *Funeral March* (second movement) of the *"Eroica"* SYMPHONY; and Berlioz uses it to represent a shepherd in the *Pastoral Scene* of his SYMPHONY FANTASTIQUE. Hear also Ravel's use of the oboe in the MOTHER GOOSE SUITE. The oboe's quality of tone does not always mix well with other wind instruments, and it is apt to be obtrusive if played too loudly and too long in a thin scoring.

Here is a beautiful passage for the first oboe from the *Prelude* to TRISTAN AND ISOLDE by Richard Wagner beginning with the thirty-third measure. This motif is called "Love's Longing" or "The Look."

The *English horn,* an old instrument of the oboe family, is strangely named, for it is neither English in origin nor, strictly speaking, a horn. Some historians trace its name from a corruption of the French *cor angle*

[7] Some orchestras prior to, and about the time of, Handel consisted of an unusually large number of wood-wind, brass, and sundry instruments in addition to the strings. *Grove's Dictionary* cites the orchestra of the Handel Commemoration held at Westminster Abbey in 1784, as consisting of 48 first violins, 47 seconds, 26 violas, 21 'cellos, 15 double-bases, 6 flutes, 26 oboes, 26 bassoons, 1 double bassoon, 12 trumpets, 12 horns, 6 trombones, 4 drums and 2 organs—a total of 157 strings and 93 winds, percussion, and 2 organs! The Handel Festival of 1856 at the Crystal Palace used an orchestra of 396, a chorus of 2,000 singers, and an organ.

(no doubt derived from the angular, double-reed crook, or mouthpiece). Later the pipe became straightened, but the reed has remained bent. The English horn is an alto oboe and has a conical bore with a swollen, gourd-like bell, and is about one and one half times as large as the oboe. It transposes down a fifth lower than written. It is really an instrument in F, with a sounding range from E_{-1} to about A^2. It substitutes a soft plaintiveness for the oboe's more penetrating reediness. Anyone who has heard the music drama TRISTAN AND ISOLDE by Richard Wagner will remember the mournful solo of the shepherd's pipe (played on stage by an English horn), beginning at measure 52 of Act III. Dvořák entrusts the beautiful and nostalgic melody in the *Largo* of his FIFTH, *"From the New World,"* SYMPHONY to the English horn. Here it is:

The *clarinet* is a wooden or metal cylindrically-bored instrument about two feet in length, with a narrow, slightly conical bell at one end and a gradual conical section at the other end into which the mouthpiece, containing a single reed, is inserted. This instrument is made acoustically in the keys of B-flat, sounding down two half tones, and A, sounding down three half tones from written C for the piano. A key mechanism enables the player to manipulate the opening and closing of the pads over the chromatic scale and trilling holes. The smooth, liquid tone of the clarinet is more varied in color than the oboe; it has something of the agility, coloratura effects, and brilliance of the flute. It has a great range of tonal volume, running the gamut from a soft whisper to a shrill sonority. Only the violin can equal the softly spun-out tones of the clarinet. Its lowest register, from about middle C^1 down, is called the *chalumeau register*—after an old prototype whose timbre it resembles—and is of a hauntingly rich quality of tone. One can never forget the ominous effect Von Weber produces in his *Overture* to DER FREISCHÜTZ (25 to 36 measures after the onset) with the *tremolos* of the first violins and violas, the soft off-beat of the timpani and pizzicati of the double-basses, together with the soft, sustained *chalumeau* tones of two clarinets. There are generally three clarinets in the modern symphony orchestra, one of which may double on the bass clarinet.

In the following musical example from Richard Strauss' tone poem, TILL EULENSPIEGEL, the clarinet in D is used to depict the moment when Till is hanged for his misdeeds. The incident is realistic enough, made even more so by the shrill, shuddering tones of the clarinet in D, which sounds up a whole step from a neutral written C. The following example is transposed to actual sounds. Note the extensive range and the rapid playing passage:

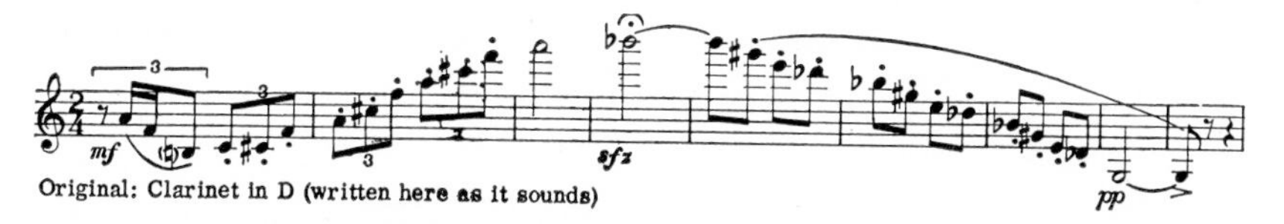

Original: Clarinet in D (written here as it sounds)

The sounding range for the ordinary B-flat or A clarinet is about three and one half octaves, from D_{-1} (or C-sharp$_{-1}$ for the A instrument) to high A-flat^3 (or C^4) two and one half to three octaves above middle C, depending upon the skill of the performer. Other good illustrations of clarinet passages may be heard in the *Scheherezade* theme in Rimsky-Korsakoff's suite by that name; in the wonderfully spirited *Overture* to TANNHAUSER by Wagner; in the G MINOR SYMPHONY by Mozart; and in Beethoven's SIXTH *"Pastoral"* SYMPHONY, where it simulates the call of the yellowhammer, and also gives the effect of the shepherd's call after the storm episode. Often heard in orchestras as well as in bands is a high E-flat clarinet which sounds up one and one half steps with a *sounding* range from G_{-1} to B-flat^3. Another type is the tenor clarinet in F, or Bassett-horn, which is infrequently heard, and *sounds* F_{-2} to C^3. It is used in SALOME by Richard Strauss.

The *bass clarinet* in B-flat sounds an octave lower than the regular B-flat soprano-like instrument. The music for the bass clarinet is written either in the treble clef (sounding down a ninth) or in the bass clef (sounding down a whole tone). Wagner sometimes writes for a bass clarinet in A, using the bass clef, and sounding down a step and a half. The bass clarinet has a single reed and, except for the bell and the segment next to the reed ligature, it is cylindrical in bore. It has a *sounding* range of E-flat$_{-2}$ or E_{-2} to F^2 or G^2, plus. The upper tones are rather thin, but the lower half of its range is extremely rich in timbre. It provides a good bass for the wood-winds, often much better, though more conspicuous, than the bassoons, and is an effective solo instrument. In the second act of LOHENGRIN, Wagner gives the sinister "warning" motive to the bass clarinet:

Bass Clarinet

In DIE WALKÜRE, Wagner gives the bass clarinet the "Wotan" motif of irritation and gloomy dejection. The first appearance of this theme in the music drama proper is in Act II, where it is marked "Ein wenig mehr belebend" (A little more animated). At this moment, the bass clarinet is accompanied by three bassoons in unison, and the double-basses are divided and played *tremolo*. The excerpt for the bass clarinet that follows is from DIE WALKÜRE. It is written as it sounds. Note the "growling" effect of the opening grace notes:

The *bassoon,* or *fagott,* is the usual bass of the wood-winds. It belongs to the oboe family, for it has a double reed and the pipe is a conical tube about eight feet in length which doubles back upon itself for handling and fingering convenience. (A famous make produced for generations by the Heckel family of Biebrich, Germany, may be distinguished by the ivory, doughnut-like ring that adorns the edge of the very small bell.) Since the bassoon's original form suggested a bundle of sticks, the Italians called this instrument *fagotto,* literally, a bundle of sticks. The modern instrument is capable of a thin, hollow, dry quality of tone in the highest pitches; a droll, blending quality in the middle register, plus an ability to skip about in rapid *staccato,* intervals, and smooth runs; and in the lowest tones can be gruff or richly full and reedy in quality. In truth, the bassoon is almost as agile as a flute! For proof of this statement, listen to Mozart's CONCERTO IN B-FLAT FOR BASSOON (K. 191). The bassoon can also play alluring lyric melodies of a sustained and expressive legato quality and in the next moment it can produce an unmistakable "Bronx cheer." It is often used to play the tenor rather than the bass part, as in the high pitched opening measures of LE SACRE DU PRINTEMPS by Stravinsky. Note the descriptive and comic effect of the hopping broom in THE SORCERER'S APPRENTICE by Dukas (Chapter 14); and the serene, lyrical theme in the second movement of Beethoven's FIFTH SYMPHONY (Chapter 21) shown here:

The whimsical nature of the bassoon is expressed in the happy-go-lucky theme of the *Narrative of the Kalendar Prince* in SCHEHEREZADE by Rimsky-Korsakoff (see Chapter 16). Note the effect of the "pinched" tones of the high register of the bassoon in the following excerpt:

The bassoon is a *nontransposing* instrument (sounds where written) and has a range of about three and a half octaves from B-flat$_{-3}$ to B-flat^1 or E-flat^2, or even higher, in actual sounds. There are two or three bassoonists in the modern symphony, one player doubling on the contra-bassoon when necessary.

The *contra-bassoon* is the equivalent in the wood-winds to the double-bass in the strings. It has the double reed and conical bore typical of the oboe family, and has a pipe sixteen feet long which is doubled back upon itself four times to end in a silvered, inverted, pipelike bell. It is pitched in C, an octave below the bassoon, and sounds an octave lower than written (B-flat$_{-4}$ to F^1, A-flat^1, or higher). It is so bulky that it rests upon the floor. Usually one instrument is enough for a symphony orchestra, for it is capable of providing a fair foundation for the entire ensemble. Its very lowest pitches, however, are not too well differentiated, one half step very closely resembling the "grunt" of an adjacent half step. The instrument serves well where a sepulchral or gloomy effect is desired, or for special effects like groans or growls. Yet it can produce a quiet and peaceful pedal point, like the pedals on a pipe organ. Here is the contra-bassoon "slithering" theme depicting "The Beast" in the MOTHER GOOSE SUITE by Ravel (see Chapter 11).

Other famous contra-bassoon parts are the Fafner reincarnation as the "Dragon" motif in Act II of Wagner's SIEGFRIED; one by Richard Strauss in SALOME, where its effect is a real stroke of genius; another, in his symphony, AUS ITALIEN; a superb virtuoso illustration by Deems Taylor in the *Fuga* section, beginning at figure [8] of the score of the *Jabberwocky*, the second movement in his *Suite for Orchestra,* THROUGH THE LOOKING GLASS, Op. 12.

Here are the practical, working ranges and transpositions of the usual wood-wind instruments heard in a symphony orchestra. It should be recalled that some lower extensions of ranges are secured by the introduction of extra fingering keys on the instrument, and that the highest tones may vary greatly according to the skills and adeptness of each individual artist.

PRACTICAL RANGES AND TRANSPOSITIONS OF WOOD-WIND INSTRUMENTS

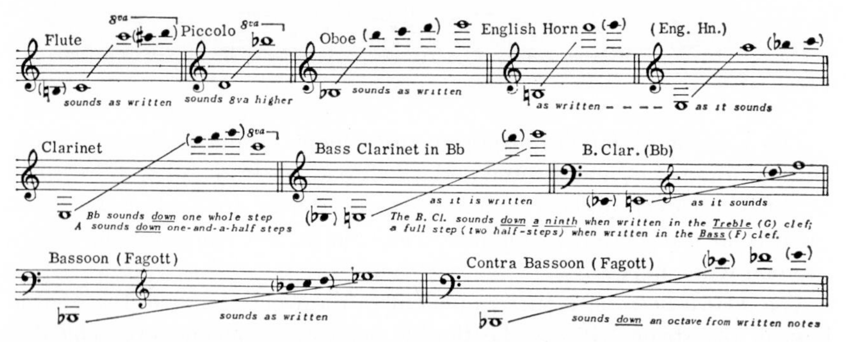

The hybrid *saxophone* family is related to the clarinet in that it is a single reed instrument; but it is conical like the oboe, and made of brass. The saxophone family of instruments consists mostly of the high *F-sopranino,* sounding up a fourth (five half steps)—there is also one in E-flat; the *B-flat soprano,* sounding down two half steps; the *E-flat alto,* sounding down a sixth (nine half steps); the *B-flat tenor* (there is also one in C) sounding down a ninth (an octave and two half steps); the *E-flat baritone,* sounding down an octave and a sixth; and the *bass saxophone* in either C or B-flat, sounding down, respectively, two octaves, and two octaves and a whole step. They all have, however, the same written range in the treble clef, from B-flat$_{-1}$ to F^{3}; quite a puzzle to unravel in reading the conductor's score.

John Alden Carpenter used the saxophone effectively in SKYSCRAPERS, and equally clever in its use were the Bostonians, Arthur Shepherd and Henry Gilbert. Bizet wrote an effective passage for the alto saxophone in the *Prelude* to L'ARLESIENNE SUITE, where the theme symbolizes "The Innocent!" Debussy wrote a RHAPSODY FOR SAXOPHONE AND ORCHESTRA and Massenet, Saint-Saëns, Delibes, d'Indy, and many others were also fond of this instrument. Stravinsky has made many effective uses of the "Sax." Ravel wrote a wonderful part for it in his superb transcription and orchestration of Mussorgsky's PICTURES AT AN EXHIBITION. Milhaud used it rightfully in his symphonic jazz work, CREATION DU MONDE, which may have spurred the Gershwin and Grofé team to produce the RHAPSODY IN BLUE a year or more later!

A double reed, conical bored brass instrument, called the *sarrusophone,* was invented by a French bandmaster, Sarrus, about 1863. It parallels most of the various instruments of the saxophone family, save the sopranino and contrabass, in pitch and range if not in quality of tone and ease of playing. In our country, only the double-bass instrument is heard now and then, usually in symphonic bands, and rarely in the symphony orchestra, where it clearly shows its superiority in tone quality and low pitch definition over the usual contrabassoon. Its range, as it sounds, is B-flat$_{-4}$ to B-flat$_{-1}$. Also, we usually write the sarrusophone parts, like the "Saxes," in the treble clef. Delius has made excellent use of the sarrusophone in his tone poem, EVENTYR; so has Ravel in his RHAPSODIE ESPAGNOLE, Florent Schmitt in his TRAGEDY OF SALOME and both Saint-Saëns and Massenet in some of their operas.

The Brass Choir

If the string choir usually provides the lyricism and the continuous harmonic blocks, figuration, and background for the symphonic tonal web, and the wood-winds that usually intertwine with the strings and supply the many changes of color and decorative solo effects, it is the brass choir that usually furnishes the patches and background of blazing color, the thunderous sonorities of conflict, the paeans of triumph, the solid, organ-like harmonies, and the firm bass foundation. There can be no inflexible rule, however, because many beautiful melodies and harmonic bases are supplied by instruments of all the choirs. The brass instruments, each with a cup-shaped mouthpiece, composing this group in the symphony orchestra include trumpets, cornets, French horns, trombones, tubas, and in rare cases the obsolete, keyed ophicleide, which Mendelssohn used in his ELIJAH and in the *Overture* to MIDSUMMER NIGHT'S DREAM.

Before the invention and perfection of valves for cup-shaped mouthpiece instruments, a player was confined to the production of the fundamental or generating tone which is not always producible, plus a few lower overtones, or "open tones." After the valves were perfected,[8] the player could, under favorable conditions, play the gamut of whole and half steps from the lowest to the highest practicable tones of each instrument, and in fair agreement with the pitches of the twelve-toned, equal-tempered scale, such as is standard on the modern piano and other instruments, and based upon "concert" C^1-261.63 cycles per second, or "concert" A^1-440 cps., often called "violin A."

It should be borne in mind that as in the case of a vibrating string, each division or complete cycle segmentation of a column of air [9] produces its own individual pitch in the form of a fundamental or open tone, overtone, or upper partial as the acoustician calls it, which may be selected and emphasized. These pitch segments may be heard separately or mixed into one tone. Thus, a vibrating column of air within a pipe or tube might have as its generating tone C_{-2} and the most prominent and useful open tones will be, in succession: C_{-1}, G_{-1}, C^1, E^1, G^1, B-flat^1 (out of tune), C^2, D^2, F^2 (a bit sharp), G^2, A^2 (out of tune), B-flat^2 (out of tune), B-natural^2 (a bit sharp), C^3 etc. An expert player of a valveless horn may select most of these open tones at will; but "chromatics" and "in between tones" of *some* of these open tones, as well as the fundamentals on natural as well as valve instruments, are either impossible, very evasive in "speaking," insecure in pitch, or impractical to play. ("Out of tune" is in reference to modern "equal temperament." See SOUND by Arthur T. Jones, p. 64.)

Usually, there are three valves on an instrument such as a trumpet, French horn, valve trombone, and so forth. The valve nearest the player lowers the fundamental and all its open tones and overtones a full step; the second valve

[8] The valves on brass instruments were due largely to the inventions of Blühmel (Silesia), Stölzel (Germany) in 1818; and later improved upon by Adolph Sax (1814–1894), (Belgium), Perinet (France), and by a Dr. J. P. Oates (London), c. 1851, whose inventions still serve brass instrument makers.

[9] "Complete cycle segmentation" means that such a sound wave in free air consists of regularly alternating density phases produced by a back and forth movement of a vibrating body; from a point of rest to its peak of pressure, then, reversing its direction, to its point of lowest pressure and back again to its starting point—two sequential and opposite phases thus form a complete "simple" sound wave. This concentric series of alternations moves outward in all directions, as spheres of greater and lesser pressure densities—as one observes when a stone is tossed into a quiet pool of water. When the series of phases reach the ears they may be sensed as sound and pitch within hearing range.

lowers them a half step; and the third and farthermost valve lowers them a step and one half. Each valve, in effect, transposes the instrument into another key with its own fundamental and series of open tones.

A general rule of transposition may be stated thus: the natural key of a wind instrument (wood-winds or brass instruments with cup-shaped mouth-piece) indicates the pitch that will result by playing a written C-natural. The results will sound *down* in pitch unless otherwise stated.

Sometimes there is a fourth valve on low tubas and low valve trombones which enables the performer to play all the half steps in the wide intervals between the lowest open tones that exceed the accommodation of the three valves. The fourth valve, or lever, may also change the basic key of an instrument, plus the fundamental tone and its open tones—such as in the new double combination F and high B-flat French horn. A sliding tube permits the trombones to do this, and a crook slide with a lever changes the B-flat trumpet, or cornet, to one in A. This last mechanism is being avoided because of faulty intonation.

The *trumpet* may be rightly called the "soprano" of the brass choir. It is approximately one-third conical and two-thirds cylindrical in bore, and the sounding range of the trumpet in B-flat is E_{-1} to C^3. The trumpet in A sounds a step and one half lower than written, or one half step lower than the B-flat trumpet. (There exist trumpets in C which are used today in many symphony orchestras and which sound where written. From the Edwin Franko Goldman collection, we recall the high D trumpet, sounding up a full step, from G-sharp$_{-1}$ or A_{-1} to C^3; a higher one in F, sounding up a perfect fourth, five half steps, from A_{-1} to C^3; a rare high one in A-flat, sounding up eight half steps; and another rare one, a *bass* trumpet in C, sounding *down* an octave from the written notes, from F-sharp$_{-2}$ up to C^2; and a foreign valveless instrument seldom heard in the U.S., the slide trumpet!) The hybrid cornet-trumpet model, usually in B-flat (and A), is the instrument most commonly heard. The larger professional symphony orchestras, however, seek to use the exact instrument called for in the composer's score, or the one which is truly traditional, as in the old Bach and Handel works. The trumpet's sharp, brilliant, and imperious tone is of great value in solo passages, in building up a *tutti* and heroic climaxes, as in the *Triumphal March* from AÏDA by Verdi. One of the most famous of trumpet calls is that announcing the arrival of the Governor near the onset of Act II of Beethoven's sole opera, FIDELIO, given here:

The trumpet is not confined to military-like calls and heroics, however, for it can play melodic and lyric passages, such as those in the SYMPHONY IN D MINOR by César Franck. Delius employs the trumpet in like manner throughout A SONG OF SUMMER and in his masterly APPALACHIA. Shostakovitch uses it in his CONCERTO FOR PIANO, TRUMPET AND STRINGS; Chausson in his SYMPHONY IN B-FLAT; Copland in APPALACHIAN SPRING. When the closed conical mute is used and the tone is forced, the player secures a snarling, defiant, and even a comic effect. There are dozens of different mutes available for the trumpeter, each producing its own peculiar effect. In DON QUIXOTE, Richard Strauss mutes the trumpets, as well as some other brasses, and has them "overblown" while at the same time directing the player to trill the tongue very rapidly (*flutter-tonguing*) in order to simulate the bleating of the sheep! When played softly with the mute, the trumpet's tone is sensitive and veiled—almost unreal—as in *The March of the Toys* from BABES IN TOYLAND by Victor Herbert. Wagner uses muted trumpets to personify the toylike trumpets of the *Guild of the Tailors* in the last act of DIE MEISTERSINGER. Here is Wagner's "Tailor Guild" theme:

The *cornet* is shorter and stubbier than the trumpet and is about two thirds conical and one third cylindrical—the reverse of the true trumpet. It has a flatter and larger bell than the trumpet and a more mellow tone and greater playing facility. The cornet is more often used abroad than in our own symphony orchestras. The same is true of another close cousin of the bugle and trumpet family, the B-flat *flügelhorn,* which Ottorino Respighi uses so effectively in the *Appian Way* section of his PINES OF ROME, and so does Vaughan Williams in his NINTH and last SYMPHONY.

The *French horn* was supposedly so named because of its once extensive use in the hunt by French kings. It was then a real hunting horn without valves, sounding only the natural overblown "open tones," or overtones, of the instrument. Now, with the improved conical tube, mouthpiece, and bell, and with the application of modern valves, the horn has become one of the most important and beautifully toned of brass instruments. It blends freely with either the wood-winds or the strings, as well as with the other brasses. The larger symphony orchestras use four French horns, two high (I, III), and two low (II, IV), and a relief first horn player. Experts call the horn the "noblest of the brass instruments," for its tonal quality can range from a sustained, soft pedal point to a lyrically expressive quality in medium voice. When played loudly it can express a really majestic, arresting quality. If the tone is forced to its full strength, it can be powerful, even menacing, especially if the tone is strongly overblown at the same time that an appropriate mute is stuffed well into the bell end. Such a passage is marked in various languages: *overblown and brassy, gedämpft, sons cuivres,* or *sordino e con sforza,* accompanied by such dynamic indications as *ff, fff,* or *sffz.* Usually a small mark (+) is placed above each note so affected—with a small "o" above normal tones. Following is an excerpt from this author's symphonic poem, THE ANCIENT MARINER, which illustrates the *gedämpft* effect we have just been discussing. We have transposed the four horns and three trumpets to their actual sounds.

Even with its modern refinements, the French horn has retained much of its original woodland associations, and no other instrument conveys nearly so well the sense of the spacious outdoors. The famous *Siegfried's Horn Call* from Act III of SIEGFRIED by Wagner follows:

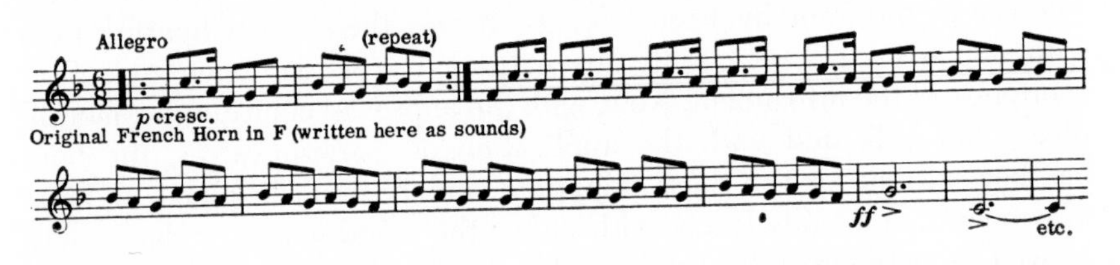

The horn can produce a soothing effect unsurpassed by any other instrument of the orchestra, save the soft strings. Recall the distant hunting horns in Wagner's TRISTAN AND ISOLDE and the restful magic of the four French horns as used in the *Nocturne* from Mendelssohn's MIDSUMMER NIGHT'S DREAM.

Carl Maria von Weber (1786–1826) has written a theme for four horns that has survived many generations, and still works its soothing magic, the *Faith motive* from his opera, DER FREISCHÜTZ. Here is a bit of it, transposed to the actual sounds. Note the freedom of movement in all the parts:

The practical *sounding* range of the modern (double) French horn in F and high B-flat is about three octaves, from (B_{-3} or C_{-2}) F_{-2} to about F^2 or G^2 plus. Formerly, by adding extra tubing through the use of crooks, there were some horns in the keys of B-flat alto, A, A-flat, G, F, E, E-flat, D, low C, B-flat basso, and others. With the introduction of the valves and other mechanical developments, however, the modern combined F and high B-flat instrument most nearly meets the demands of the contemporary composer. The F horn sounds a fifth lower than written, the high B-flat a full tone lower.

The *trombone*, a sliding tube affair related to the medieval *sackbut*, consists of a long cylindrical metal tube bent back upon itself twice and ending in a bell. The player can slide the moveable crook into any one of seven positions and thus with the tautness of the lips can produce the desired pitches by segmentation of the vibrating air column. The farther the slide is extended the lower will be the pitch of the fundamental and its overtones. Though the listener will more often hear and see the so called *tenor* (range E_{-2} to B-flat^2) and the *bass* (range C_{-2} to F^1) trombones, there also exist the more rare *alto* and *contra-bass* trombones, each with its individual tone quality and range. We have heard a tenor trombone with a special lever mechanism and extra pipe couplings which enables the player to go down by half steps from E_{-2} to B-flat$_{-3}$ and to go as high as B-flat^2 or even E-flat^2, as Tommy Dorsey often did. Unusual trombone ranges and speed sometimes heard are probably due to small instruments, "trick" mouthpieces, and special lip and slide techniques—usually with a sacrifice of tonal quality. There is also in use a valve trombone which can be played with greater facility and speed than the slide trombone.

The trombone is a stately, non-transposing instrument, though it is based acoustically upon B-flat as a fundamental tone. It is richer in quality and can be played in more accurate pitch than other brass instruments. It is effective in passages of solemn grandeur; and when loudly played, its tones are brilliant, powerful, and even threatening. When the three trombones, usually with the bass tuba, are played together in a soft, sustained passage, they sound like the blended intoning of men's voices, or the restful foundation (diapason) tones of a church pipe organ. Here follow several musical excerpts showing some of these qualities. The first one, imperious in quality and effect, is one of *Wotan's motifs* from DAS RHEINGOLD by Richard Wagner. The three trombones are played in unison (marked "A3"), and played crisply and loudly (*f*). Here is the *Compact* or *Agreement motive* of Wotan:

The next example, also for three trombones in unison, is rather "tricky" because of the speed and the somewhat ungainly, skipping intervals, which force a natural *ritardando.* It is a theme from this author's symphonic poem THE ANCIENT MARINER:

As an excellent and most exceptional example of the ability of the instrument to produce delicate shadings of dynamics and extreme softness of tone, we quote an excerpt that appears near the close of the SIXTH SYMPHONY, the *"Pathetique"* by Tchaikovsky. We have included the tuba part, which is indispensable in this passage. Note the harmonic distribution and pitches of the low lying harmonic tones, the dynamic marks and shading gradations (nuances) from *p* to *mp, mp* to *pp,* and so forth down to *ppppp*—which the musician pronounces pee-ahn-iss-iss-iss-ISS-ee-moh!!!

(Example of a Brass ensemble of 3 Trbn. & Tuba.)

The *tuba* belongs to a group of instruments equalling in number and variety the horn, clarinet or oboe families. The bass tubas in F, BB-flat, E-flat, or C are the most commonly used.

Nowadays the tuba most often has four valves (but there are also those with three to six valves). All are conical in bore, ending with a large bell. Although these tubas may be acoustically built in the keys of F, E-flat, C, B-flat or BB-flat, the parts for all of them are written as though they were non-transposing instruments in C. The tuba fulfills the same function in the brass section as the double-bass in the strings, or the contra-bassoon in the wood-winds, for it supplies the rock-bottom harmonic foundation. Usually one is sufficient for the orchestra, but a band may use four to eight. It is not frequently used as a solo instrument except to depict a sinister mood or character. Wagner uses it, together with the double-bassoon, to depict the dragon in SIEGFRIED:

It is used sometimes to evoke a comic or humorous response, as Stravinsky uses its high tones to portray the awkward antics of the dancing bear in PETROUCHKA. The late Vaughan Williams wrote a CONCERTO FOR TUBA!

Wagner helped to design a set of tubas in order to introduce a new tone color into the orchestra that would be different from the French horns, yet would combine with them to provide eight-part harmony. These "Wagnerian tubas" are usually tenor or bass, and are used in DAS RHEINGOLD, DIE WALKÜRE, GÖTTERDÄMMERUNG, and SIEGFRIED. There is also a whole family of seven (hybrid) *saxhorns*, invented about 1845 by Adolphe Sax; and such familiar brass band instruments as the *mellophone* alto in E-flat, the *euphonium*, or *baritone* in B-flat, and the *helicon* and *sousaphone* bass tubas in E-flat, or BB-flat; the last two wind themselves around the left shoulder, waist, and chest of the player. The *sousaphone*, named after the famous bandmaster, has its huge, highly polished, and widely flared bell facing the front. The range of the sousaphone and helicon are the same as that of the BB-flat tuba (from D_{-3} to F^1). And in the summer of 1955, there was a première performance of a double-tubed "tuba built for two" invented by William Bell of the New York Philharmonic. It is played by the two performers *vis-à-vis*.

In discussing the characteristics of the wood-wind and brass instruments, it should be interesting to show how one of the great masters combined the two choirs: the main theme of the *Finale* from the FOURTH SYMPHONY IN E MINOR by Johannes Brahms. This movement marked *Allegro energico e passionato*, is constructed in the form, tempo, and spirit of an old Spanish dance, variously called a *chaconne* or a *passacaglia*. Our preference here is "Chaconne" because of the evident harmonic rather than melodic nature of the theme (see Chapter 28).

The melody Brahms chose for his chaconne theme was probably borrowed from Bach's CANTATA NO. 150, *"Nach dir Herr, verlanget mich,"* but there is some doubt that the theme was original even with Bach! This theme is repeated thirty-one times by Brahms, ornamented with what are the most skillful contrapuntal variations since Bach. There is no extended *basic* change of tonality (key), and no protracted interludes between the reappearances of the theme! Yet there is no monotony or lack of driving force. Certainly this movement is one of the monumental achievements of its kind in all orchestral literature.

The melody, or theme, proper in the following excerpt, is in the two flutes, first oboe and, for the most part, in the first trombone. (We have transposed all the instruments, where expedient, to their actual sounds.) Watch the appearances of the variated theme—often cleverly concealed in the ornamentation—and try to follow at the same time the vital and skillful counterpoint. Meanwhile, enjoy the music *as such* to the utmost —an exciting challenge to the listener!

The practical working ranges and transpositions of the instruments of the brass choir follow. These ranges are, in many cases, approximate, especially in their lowest and highest tones:

RANGES AND TRANSPOSITIONS OF ORCHESTRAL BRASS INSTRUMENTS

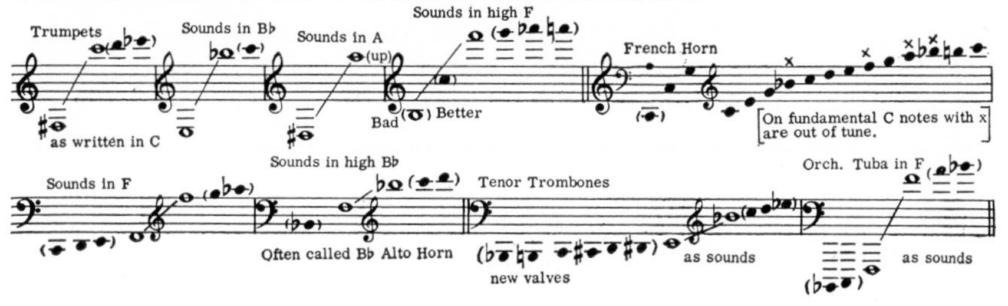

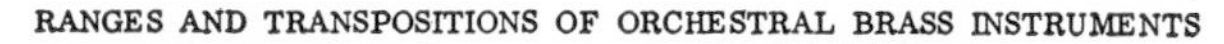

This is an opportune time for hearing the tone qualities of the instruments in a symphony orchestra. Listen to PETER AND THE WOLF by Prokofieff and YOUNG PERSON'S GUIDE TO THE ORCHESTRA by Britten.

The Percussion Group of Instruments

This group of instruments heard in the symphony orchestra is often called *the battery,* for reasons not difficult to guess. It is largely composed of many kinds of pitched or unpitched drums, bone and metal contraptions, and so forth. Many of these come from primitive peoples—and some are really children's toys, such as rattles, whistles, and bird calls. (Hear Haydn's jolly TOY SYMPHONY—as seasonable and joyant as the Christmas tree.) Many such instruments are merely rhythmic or noise making.[10] Others are more or less pitch producing, and still others have become standard orchestral instruments, such as the triangle, chromatic tubular bells or chimes, and the glockenspiel. Orchestras sometimes use electrical instruments of pitch producing value, as *carillons* (bells played individually or operated from a key board), *electric organs, vibrachords* and *keyboard glockenspiels.* Also heard are a wind machine (Strauss), a typewriter and sleigh bells (Anderson), and electric door bells (Antheil).

The *kettle-drums,* or *timpani,* are the most important instruments of the percussion group. They are made of large copper kettles, with a five or six inch air pressure compensating hole at the bottom and with the top covered with a tightly drawn sheep or calf skin. They sound fairly definite pitches (except the lowest tones), which are dependent upon the dampness of the membranes, their tautness, how the drumhead is struck, and the nature of the drumstick head. The older type of timpani was tuned through a series of screws around the perimeter of the drumhead, which were tightened or loosened by hand—the tighter the skin, the higher the pitch. Extended rests had to be given the drummer for

[10] Since there are no fixed agreements among makers of pitched percussion instruments concerning productive (sounding) ranges, and no established practices as to rules for written scores and parts, we have presented a composite of the most authoritative and up-to-date usage.

changing pitches. The newer drums have foot pedals that accomplish this mechanically, enabling the tympanist to perform a melodic passage or even a *glissando* in a comfortable tempo. An excellent example of the use of the pedal timpani is found in the beginning of Act II of DER ROSENKAVALIER by Strauss. The timpani are used to produce a rhythmic effect; to define the meter and tempo; to help build up the volume of sound rising to a climax; to create an atmosphere of suspense and mystery; to sustain a pitched pedal point; or to arouse a sense of impending doom. Even three or four tone chords performed by several players are possible, as heard in the SYMPHONIE FANTASTIQUE by Berlioz. Usually two to four timpani are used in a large orchestra—large drums capable of sounding from C_{-2} to A_{-2}, and from F_{-2} to C_{-1}, with a few tones added to either extreme, and smaller ones playing from C_{-1} to F_{-1}, and from D_{-1} to G_{-1}. At times, specially made higher or lower pitched drums are used. Sometimes a large number of timpani are called for, as in the *Tuba Mirum* portion of Berlioz's REQUIEM, which uses sixteen.[11]

The *snare, military,* and *side drums* are familiar. Their crisp, rattling tone is most frequently associated with martial effects and, when muffled with padded sticks or loosened snares, in formal funeral marches. These snares are either gut strings tightly stretched across and in contact with the bottom head or, in the case of single-headed drums, springy metal wires that may be turned off and on contact at will. The *bass drum* is prominent in any marching, symphonic, or dance band. It is used to accent the principal beats of a measure, or for desired effects and noise, with the cymbals separately played or attached to the drum's wooden shell. All the drums mentioned in this paragraph are of indefinite pitch.

The remainder of the percussion section may include a wide assortment of instruments—far too many to be completely catalogued here. The *tambourine* is usually associated with gypsy, Spanish, and oriental music and, in America, with the Salvation Army and the black-faced minstrels, as well as the symphony and dance orchestras. It consists of a stretched membrane over a small wooden hoop, with many pairs of metallic jingles wired in and around the hoop. It is either struck by the free hand or fist, or made to jingle by shaking or by rubbing a wet thumb around the edge of the membrane. There are many *oriental drums,* either long or short, barrel-like in shape, played by striking either or both ends at the same time. Some are drums with rope or gut runners

[11] In addition, at the section marked *Andante maestoso* of the *Tuba Mirum,* referred to above, the score of Berlioz (Peters Ed.) also demands the following: four flutes, two oboes, four clarinets, eight bassoons, twelve horns, four cornets, twelve trumpets, sixteen trombones, five ophiclides (some of the brass divided into four small bands placed in each of the four sides of the concert hall), eight extra bass drummers with sponge covered sticks, and four bass drums using timpani sticks, augmented strings and, to enter soon after, the full chorus!

More recent uses of unusual instruments are found in DYLAN by Holbrooke; BALLET MÉCANIQUE by Antheil; RHYTHMICANA by Cowell, and works by R. Strauss.

alternating between the two ends which, when squeezed with one hand while striking with the other, can alter the pitch.[12] This is much like the American Indian or oriental drum, the *tom-tom,* which is indefinite in pitch and dull in quality. Do not confuse this with the *tam-tam,* a large, metal, saucer-like gong of Far Eastern origin, used in every symphony orchestra. The tam-tam is of indefinite pitch, but it strangely partakes of the harmonic basis or "aura" of the music when struck. An expert can secure unbelievable effects on the tam-tam, from a mystical, eerie quality when softly played, to a terrifying crash when loudly struck with a hard tympany stick.

The *castanets*—pairs of small, shell-shaped wooden clappers held in the palm of each hand—are indispensable in gypsy and Spanish music. The orchestra percussion player of today usually employs a small stick to which are fixed on either side lead-weighted springs that slap the stick when shaken in the proper rhythmic pattern—a practical but unromantic transformation.

Cymbals are large, slightly cupped disks of brass which, when struck together loudly, produce a crashing, dramatic effect. They have no definite pitch. A single cymbal may be played with a hard or soft stick. The quality changes with the place and force of striking. They may also be "rolled" with snare or timpani sticks. When the cymbals are struck softly, they produce a bright, tinkling, metallic sound. In his AFTERNOON OF A FAUN, Debussy uses a pair of antique oriental bronze cymbals three or four inches in diameter that sound E^2 and B^2. The *triangle* is a metal bar bent into the shape of a triangle, with the ends free. When it is struck with a small metal rod, it produces a high pitched, tinkling sound of *indefinite pitch.* Liszt has written such a conspicuous part for the triangle in his PIANO CONCERTO NO. 1 IN E-FLAT that the work is often facetiously dubbed "The Concerto for Triangle."

The *xylophone* consists of a graduated series of tuned hardwood bars, without resonators. These bars are struck with two or four wooden, hard rubber, or metal ball-tipped mallets. It has a hollow, clanking sound and is used melodically to punctuate either the rhythm or tones of a rapidly played passage of the strings or wood-winds. Saint-Saëns used it effectively in his *Danse Macabre* (see Chapter 14). Its usual *written* range is from F_{-1} or C^1 to C^4, though the music sounds an octave higher. There are a number of variants of the xylophone: the *marimbaphone* (range approximately C_{-2} to F^3, sounds as written), with tuned resonators below each *wooden* bar; and the *vibraphone* (range from F_{-1} to F^3,

[12] Ravel, in his RHAPSODIE ESPAGNOLE, and elsewhere, uses a small, rather long Basque hand drum (a barrel type) that he calls a *tambour de basque.* The musician for a Basque dance usually slaps this drum with the fingers and palm of his left hand while he plays a *flageolet* (a whistle, flutelike instrument) with his right hand and mouth. The "tambour de Basque" should be called a *tambourin provençal,* according to Curt Sachs.

sounds as written), which has graded *metal* bars with resonators and an electrically powered revolving "tremolo" of disc-vibrators inside and near the lip of each resonating pipe.

The *glockenspiel,* or *orchestral bells,* consists of two parallel rows of graduated, tuned metal bars usually without resonators, and arranged like the black and white keys of the piano. The bars are struck with either wooden- or metal-headed mallets. Its written range is generally G_{-1} to C^3 but it sounds two octaves higher than written. Some recent models of the glockenspiel are operated with a piano keyboard mechanism with non-standardized ranges. There are also *tubular bells* with a usual, though not standardized, written range from G_{-1} to G^2 but sounding as written or as may be indicated in the score. The *celeste,* invented by Mustel (Paris–1886) uses tuned steel bars that are set in vibration by hammers operated from a small, piano-like keyboard. Tuned wooden resonators for each bar impart an ethereal quality of tone. The usual, though not standardized, written range (using both bass and treble clefs) is from C_{-1} to C^4, including all chromatics. It sounds an octave higher than written. The standard *piano,* with a range from A_{-4} to C^5 and sounding as written, may also be considered a stringed percussion instrument. There remain many additional percussion instruments for special effects—so many, in fact, that we refer the interested reader to the specialized references at the beginning of this chapter.

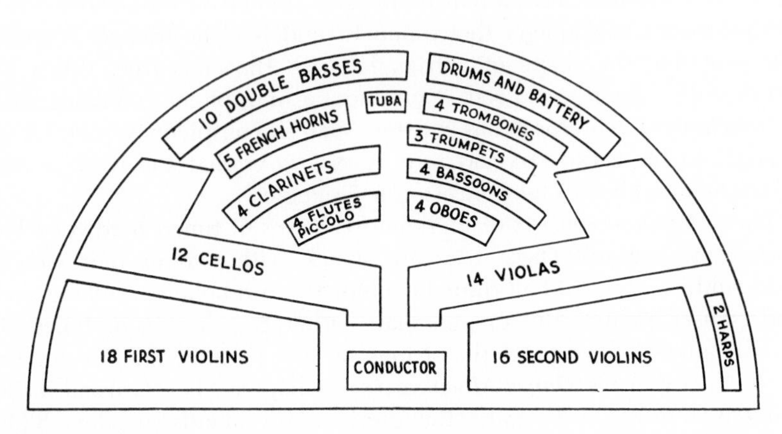

The conventional seating plan for players of a symphony orchestra. Soloists are placed between the conductor and the first violins toward the audience.

Seating Arrangement of a Symphony Orchestra

The adjoining diagram is a conventional seating plan of the symphony orchestra, in general use for more than a century. There are, of course, many variations in that plan. Among the major changes, the second violins may take the place of the 'cellos beside the first violins, and either the violas or the 'cellos may take the place formerly occupied by the second violins—usually the 'cellos. This arrangement is supposed to improve concert hall hearing and to give a better balance among the different choirs of the enlarged modern orchestra, as well as a more solid homogeneity of tone among the wood-winds, brasses, and violins, and better enunciation and saliency of the 'cellos and violas. The wood-winds, brasses, battery, and harps are also moved about. Naturally, the seating plans of an orchestra may require a number of changes in different environments.

Orchestration

Writing for a full symphony orchestra is an art in itself. The composer must not only create his themes, counter-themes, harmony, counterpoint, figuration, and so forth, but he must hear them from the onset of his creative process in their most effective timbres. Thus he must be very familiar not only with the "personality," detailed technical nature, and playing peculiarities of each kind of instrument but also with the different qualities within its entire range. The composer must anticipate the most effective use of solo instruments or combinations of them within a "choir," or in "mixtures" among the wood-winds, strings, brasses, battery and, if used, vocal or instrumental soloists, or chorus. In his orchestration, a composer must also secure proper tonal balance in the distribution of the counterpoint or harmonic figuration among the instruments as well as in the *tutti* in its various gradations of sound. All the foregoing factors change with the pitch ranges, speed, volume of sound, and combinations of instrumentation "colors."

The serious composers of symphonic music consider the orchestration of their works a highly personal, inseparable part of their expression in music.[13] Indeed, the experienced listener can often recognize a composer and his school or period by the style of his orchestration, which is sometimes as unique as his signature. Test this assertion by comparing, through listening alone, typical symphonic works.

The Full Composer's and Conductor's Orchestral Score

The actual writing of all the various parts involved in a musical work onto manuscript paper is called scoring, instrumentation, or orchestration. In this consolidation, the staves, or horizontal musical lines for the individual parts, are arranged one below the other from the topmost flute or piccolo to the lowest, the stringed double-bass. The sequence of staves

[13] For those interested in the art of orchestration we suggest the following excellent texts: Berlioz-Strauss, *Instrumentationslehre,* 2 vols., in German (Peters Edition); Cecil Forsyth, *Orchestration* (New York: MacMillan, 1936); Nicholas Rimsky-Korsakoff, *Principles of Orchestration* (Kalmus Edition, 1930); Gordon Jacob, *Orchestral Technique* (New York: Oxford Press, 1947) and Kent W. Kennan, *The Technique of Orchestration* (Englewood Cliffs, N. J.: Prentice-Hall, 1952).

follows a time-honored pattern, though there are variations. If the reader will glance a page or so ahead, he will see an excellent example of a composer-conductor score, the first page of the full orchestral score for the *Overture* to the opera, THE MASTERSINGERS FROM NUREMBERG, by Richard Wagner, a master of orchestration. Note the names of all the separate instruments on the left side, and how their parts are on musical staves proceeding to the right. A complete *measure* (a metrical unit) runs down the entire page vertically like a column rule on a newspaper, and the composer's instructions are all over the page, giving his intentions of performance as near as they can be made to exactness through musical symbols and words. The time signature is shown on each staff and it is understood that a printed meter continues until the composer changes it in his score. Zu.Z (zusammen, German) stands for zusammen, *a dúe* (ah-DOO-ee), or A², to indicate that the instruments involved should play together. Thus the musical score must be considered merely as an informative blueprint for the performers and the conductor. Many intangibles of musicianship—a thousand factors—may best be passed down from master to master and eventually be resolved by the orchestra through long, painstaking drilling and experience. (We have heard Toscanini rehearse the New York Philharmonic Symphony on an eight measure phrase in Beethoven's THIRD SYMPHONY for a full hour before he was satisfied. Only in this manner can perfection be achieved even with such an outstanding orchestra!) The "reading" of a score can only be taught as a specialized skill. It is very complicated but not forbidding to those who have the necessary talents, technical background, knowledge, and self-discipline.[14]

THE ORCHESTRA IN ACTION

The "Nutcracker" Suite by Tchaikovsky

For a first study of the entire orchestra in action, we have chosen the beautiful, very colorful, and thoroughly typical example of the Romantic temper, the NUTCRACKER SUITE, Op. 71 A, that the composer himself arranged from his NUTCRACKER BALLET, Op. 71 (1891–2), shortly before his death on December 6, 1893. The selected movements in their usual order are: *Miniature Overture, March, Dance of the Sugar-Plum Fairy, Trepak, Arabian Dance, Chinese Dance, Dance of the Mirlitons* (or the *Toy Flutes,*) and the finale, the *Waltz of the Flowers.* Tchaikovsky was

[14] As for the wisdom of using full orchestral scores in the *usual appreciation classes* by students who are deficient in the highly specialized skills of reading scores we have grave doubts born of long experience. There is a great deal of effort wasted in the average appreciation class by students who are not sufficiently trained in score reading. Thus they are unable to "hear" what they "see" on the score; or to "see" what they "hear" in relation to the full score. Without that ability, score reading is worse than a self-deluding myth.

THE MASTERSINGERS Richard Wagner

First page of the orchestral score.

then at the summit of his creative powers, and the score reveals an extraordinary master of instrumentation.[15]

The scenario for the ballet was taken from the elder Dumas' version of a fairy tale, "The Nutcracker and the Mouse King," in two acts, by E. T. A. Hoffmann, the writer of fantastic stories who exercised a powerful influence on many composers of the nineteenth century. He is known today chiefly through Offenbach's opera, the TALES OF HOFFMANN. The ballet centers about a little girl, Marie, and the wonderful dream that comes to her on Christmas Eve after everybody else has gone to sleep. The toys and sweetmeats around the Christmas tree come to life; the plain nutcracker she has received for her gift turns into a handsome young prince. Together they fly away to the court of the Sugar-Plum Fairy, where all the sweetmeats and the flowers come to dance for the happy young lovers.

1. *Miniature Overture.* Tchaikovsky omitted the bass instruments—'cellos, double-bass and lower brass—from his little overture, thus achieving a light and graceful effect.

The second theme, by contrast, is a flowing melody of simple quarter notes played *legato* by the violins. The music works up to a scintillating climax for full orchestra, after which both themes are repeated from the beginning with an even longer climax at the end.

Notice that in order to achieve the effect of intensification upon which the climax is built, the music grows increasingly louder and faster, the rhythmic figure more insistent, especially in the battery, and the instru-

[15] The listener who has the necessary skill to read scores is directed to the following pocket-sized orchestral scores, all of which are also available on record: Mendelssohn's SYMPHONY NO. 4, the "*Italian,*" Op. 90; Ravel's transcription and orchestration of Mussorgsky's PICTURES AT AN EXHIBITION; Debussy's PRELUDE A L'APRÈS MIDI D'UN FAUNE and LA MER SUITE; SYMPHONY NO. 5 by Tchaikovsky; SCHEHEREZADE SUITE by Rimsky-Korsakoff; DON QUIXOTE by Richard Strauss; CONCERTO FOR ORCHESTRA by Bartók; MATHIS DER MALER by Hindemith; SYMPHONIES NOS. 3 and 5 by Beethoven; SYMPHONY NO. 41 in C, the "*Jupiter*" K. 551 by Mozart; LES PRÉLUDES by Liszt; FANTASIA ON A THEME BY THOMAS TALLIS by Vaughan Williams; VARIATIONS ON A THEME BY PAGANINI by Brahms, also his VARIATIONS ON A THEME BY HAYDN; VARIATIONS ON A THEME BY PAGANINI by Rachmaninoff (the same theme as Brahms used); ENIGMA VARIATIONS by Elgar; *Prelude* and *Liebestod* from TRISTAN AND ISOLDE by Wagner; "*Prometheus,*" THE POEM OF FIRE, Op. 60 by Scriabin; Respighi's FOUNTAINS, PINES, AND FESTIVALS OF ROME; SYMPHONIE FANTASTIQUE by Berlioz. These and others provide the finest text books on orchestration in the world.

ments mount to the higher pitches. These are methods most frequently used to build an effective orchestral climax.

The shrill pitches in high register evoke a sharper response from our nervous systems than do the low, mellow tones. For this reason, a climb to the upper register together with greater intensity tends to produce an effect of intensification of emotion and increased brilliance of "color." Conversely, a descent gives the impression of fading color and easing of emotional tension.[16]

2. *March.* The march, with its brave opening flourish on trumpets, horns, and clarinets, is a gaily strutting affair. Here Tchaikovsky uses the rhythmic figure that occurs so frequently in trumpet and bugle calls, the triplet indicated by a small figure 3 over the eighth notes:

The dainty groups of notes that alternate with the flourish serve to remind us that this is a march for twirling ballerinas rather than for ordinary mortals.

The second theme is built on another of those pirouetting, *staccato* motives so dear to the heart of Tchaikovsky. Three flutes and a clarinet are echoed by violins and violas. Then the first theme returns in regular A-B-A form, with the strings and flutes providing new "sliding" effects in the accompaniment.

3. *Dance of the Sugar-Plum Fairy.* Nothing so well reveals Tchaikovsky's love of picturesque instrumental effects as his excitement at discovering the *celesta,* which he introduced into the orchestral family through this piece. He wrote enthusiastically to his publisher in June, 1891, after his return from America, that he planned to incorporate music for the new instrument—described as something between a piano and a glockenspiel, possessing a divinely beautiful tone—into his ballet. He instructed that it be ordered from Paris where he had discovered it and delivered in St. Petersburg in utmost secrecy, since he feared that Rimsky-Korsakoff or Glazounov might learn of it and, by using its effects before he could, thus detract from the sensation he expected to create.

[16] Tchaikovsky habitually uses very salient and differing tone colors of a chromatic or thematic nature as divergently moving foils to make the principal idea more outstanding and to effect his climaxes with emotional intensity. (Examples are manifold, but, to select two, we refer to the climaxes throughout the third and fourth movements of his SIXTH, the *"Pathetique,"* SYMPHONY, and the ROMEO AND JULIET FANTASY-OVERTURE, where, so often, the strings and wood-winds soar upward as the brasses explore the descending bass tones, chromatically or scalewise.)

After a short *pizzicato* introduction on the strings, the transparent celesta harmonics come floating gently downward:

This is interspersed with guttural comments by the bass clarinet that give a truly bizarre effect. The brief middle section ends with a brilliant cadenza on the celesta. (A *cadenza* is a flowery passage interpolated in a composition in order to show off the technical resources of the solo performer. Notice that the rest of the orchestra is silent during the cadenza, to focus attention upon the featured player.) The cadenza leads back to the opening phrase, now played an octave higher than before. We therefore have here another example of three-part or A-B-A form. Strings sound in the background; the silvery fairy floats aloft for a brief space—and fades away.

4. *Trepak* (Russian Dance). The *Trepak* brings us the full orchestra in an outburst of furious activity. One can see the figures bobbing up and down, arms akimbo, heels flying, in a folk dance of vigorous accents:

A contrasting theme appears, the first returns, in a clear-cut A-B-A pattern. The orchestration is brilliant throughout. Tambourines add gaiety to the proceedings. Ever faster and louder, the dance mounts to the brilliant upper register, and ends on a note of wild abandon.

5. *Arab Dance.* This number summons up the languor and allure of the East. Muted violas and 'cellos introduce a droning figure in the bass that is reiterated with a kind of hypnotic insistence, alternating between *piano* and *pianissimo.* A tom-tom throbs dully in the distance. Against this somber background two clarinets and an English horn intone the mysterious opening chords. The melody itself is sung by muted violins; there is but one theme, which rises and falls in a broad languid curve.

Presently an oboe lets out a long, piercing wail in that nasal manner associated with oriental song. The violas and 'cellos drone on and on; the tom-tom continues to weave its spell; the music fades away to the merest whisper, *ppppp*.

6. *Chinese Dance*. Flutes and piccolos running shrilly up the scale, *forte*, impart to the next dance its "Chinese" flavor. The strings answer, *pizzicato*, with a droll seriousness that reminds one of a Pooh-bah bobbing up and down. Throughout, the bassoons keep up a steady *staccato* beat deep in the bass.

If we compare the second theme with the first, we notice that it does almost everything Theme I does, but in the opposite direction. Where Theme I runs up the scale to a trill and then jumps down along the tones of the chord, Theme II runs down the scale to a trill and then jumps up along the scales of the chord; in other words, it is an inversion of Theme I:

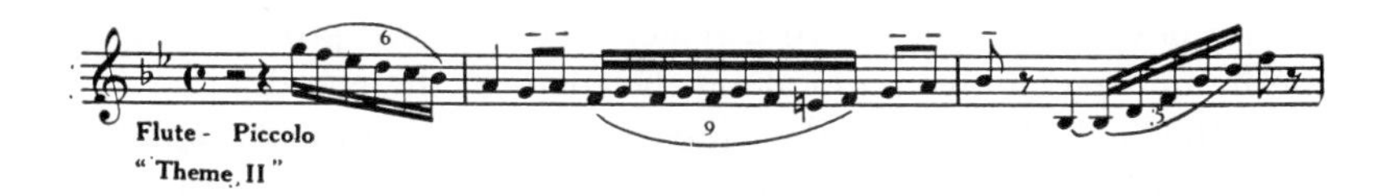

This device, rather difficult to handle, attests again to Tchaikovsky's mastery of the technical resources of his art.

After the inversion, the theme is heard in its original form, giving us an A-B-A pattern. The music works up in a steady crescendo to the climax, *fortissimo;* and comes to an abrupt end.

7. *Dance of the Toy Flutes*. Next comes one of Tchaikovsky's happiest inspirations. A brief introduction leads to the airy tune of *staccato* sixteenth notes played by three flutes, *piano*. This sparkling music captures the very spirit of the dance. After a fragment of *legato* melody sung by the English horn, the theme is repeated:

The middle section, in contrast to the opening, lies in a lower register and is given to the brass choir. Here we have a famous passage for muted trumpet, the theme of sixteenth notes rising and falling in a gentle swell. After this, we return to the melody of the flutes in a clear three-part, or ternary, form.

8. *Waltz of the Flowers.* This beautiful waltz has taken its place beside Johann Strauss' *Blue Danube* and *Tales From the Vienna Woods* as one of the world's beloved waltzes. Here we have Tchaikovsky's gifts as a ballet composer—a feeling for beautiful melody, rhythm, flowing line, and the sheer excitement of movement—at their best. The gracious opening theme of the horns, the gay second theme with its suggestion of swirling figures, the middle section, which veers to a tender melancholy—all breathe a gentle nostalgia. True, these flowers grew amidst red plush and crystal chandeliers, and the world out of which they stemmed really never was as we have pictured it. No matter—they bring us the gentle aroma of their period preserved for us by a master of sentiment and eloquent expression of it.

The introduction contains an elaborate cadenza for the harp, built of *arpeggios,* or broken chords. The reader should distinguish, incidentally, between an *arpeggio* and a scale. A *scale* is a series of neighboring key notes. But an *arpeggio* is built of the tones of a chord which do not necessarily lie next to each other. In a scale, therefore, we proceed stepwise, while in an *arpeggio* we jump along the tones of the chord.

After the final *arpeggios* of the cadenza fade into a gradual *diminuendo,* the horns announce the suave and rather jolly waltz theme, softly as from the distance. We shall call this Theme I, section "A." This is soon followed by a rippling figure for the solo clarinet which seems to wander about the score like a little boy at a fair, having lots of fun and "filling in" wherever possible. This clarinet melody we shall call section "B" of Theme I. Both themes are shown here:

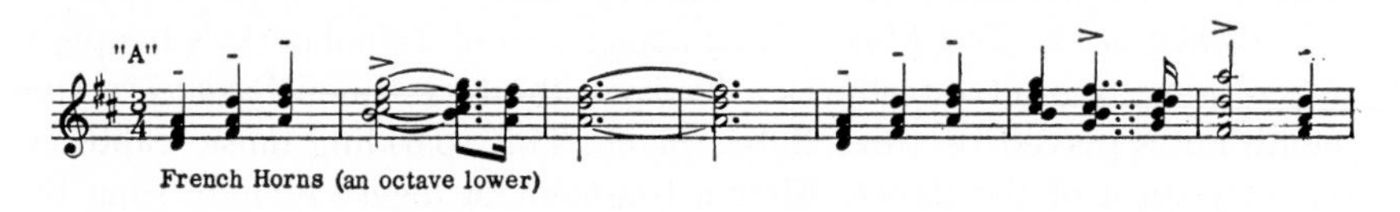

This wandering clarinet theme is followed by the gracefully swaying waltz theme, which we shall call Theme II. Notice how the string choir alternates with the wood-winds in a sort of jolly dialogue. Here is Theme II.

Presently Theme I returns, embroidered with a charming countermelody; therefore this section is a miniature ternary (A-B-A), or three part, form in itself.

The so-called "middle section" opens with a graceful theme first played by the flute and oboe as a contrast to the previous part of the movement, with the violins gliding downward as a countermelody. This theme, which we shall call Theme III, with its chromatically rising figure, seems to be in a pleading mood. Theme III follows:

Now there emerges a lyrical melody of a sombre nature in a low pitched range for the violas and 'cellos. Theme IV is given below:

Presently Theme III is heard but much transformed. Tchaikovsky cleverly reverses his orchestration, thus revivifying the composition. Now the violins carry the principal melody, while the flutes and oboes play the "downward gliding" countermelody. Thus, the middle section is also in a free A-B-A (ternary) pattern, as was the first section. Then the very first section is repeated as before, with a few changes in orchestration, tying the *Waltz of the Flowers* together firmly. The music rises to a brilliant climax; there is further acceleration, and the volume of sound is also increased; the brilliance and loudness of the orchestra rises irresistibly into a high pitched *fortississimo* (*fff*), overflowing with excitement and animation, and brilliant orchestral color, bringing the BALLET SUITE to a magnificent ending.

In its formal over-all and internal design, the Waltz, as a whole, with a well developed three-part, ternary, or A-B-A form, might be diagrammed as: A(aba′)–B(cdc′)–A′(a′b′a″)–Coda. Note, throughout, how all the commonly basic musical elements are used and often combined—(a), salient melodies; (b), rich, vivid harmonies; (c), compelling rhythms; (d), time and meter; (e), counterpoint; (f), clear-cut structures and designs that one can sense through listening powers alone; (g), imaginative and varied orchestral coloring; (h), emotional stimulants of widely differing effects—all these are artfully contrived and combined into a varied yet coherent and unified whole that is thoroughly satisfying.

ADDITIONAL SUGGESTIONS FOR LISTENING[17]

(*With but very few exceptions, the following are to be had on records, either domestic or foreign—78 or 33⅓ or 45 RPM.*)

(*Strings*): CONCERTO GROSSO, Op. 3, No. 3 by Geminiani; TWO ELEGIAC MELODIES, Op. 34 by Grieg; DIVERTIMENTO FOR STRING ORCHESTRA by Béla Bartók; SERENADE FOR STRINGS by Josef Suk; SYMPHONY FOR STRINGS by William Schumann; SERENADE FOR STRING ORCHESTRA by Wolf-Ferrari; SYMPHONY FOR STRINGS by Benjamin Britten; SERENADE FOR STRINGS by Dvořák; A PAGAN POEM for solo viola and orchestra, Op. 14, by Charles M. Loeffler; HAROLD IN ITALY, Op. 16, for viola solo and orchestra by Berlioz; CONCERTO FOR VIOLA by Bartók; NOTTURNO IN D, Op. 42, by Beethoven; CONCERTO FOR CELLO by Dvořák, Op. 104, another by Saint-Saëns, Op. 33, and still another by Robert Schumann, Op. 129. (*Flute*): CONCERTO FOR FLUTE AND ORCHESTRA by Jacques Ibert; NOCTURNE FOR FLUTE AND PIANO and (Virtuoso) ETUDES FOR FLUTE by George Barrère; INTERMEZZO FOR FLUTE AND HARP by Bizet; POEM FOR FLUTE SOLO AND ORCHESTRA by Charles Griffes; SONATA NO. 2 FOR FLUTE, VIOLA AND HARP by Debussy; NIGHT PIECE FOR FLUTE AND ORCHESTRA by Arthur Foote; NIGHT SOLILOQUY FOR FLUTE AND STRINGS by Kent Kennan; INDIAN SKETCHES for flute and strings by Lamar Stringfield. (*Oboe*): CONCERTO FOR OBOE, K. 293, by Mozart; CONCERTO FOR OBOE by Cimeroso; SONATA FOR OBOE AND PIANO by Charles Koechlin (I know of the work but of no present recording of it); FANTASY FOR OBOE AND STRINGS by Britten; CONCERTO FOR OBOE by Richard Strauss. (*Clarinet*): CONCERTO FOR CLARINET, K. 622, by Mozart; THREE PIECES FOR CLARINET SOLO by Stravinsky; FOUR PIECES FOR CLARINET AND PIANO by Alban Berg; SONATAS NO. 1 and 2, Op. 120, FOR CLARINET AND PIANO, and QUINTET FOR CLARINET AND STRINGS, Op. 115, by Brahms; QUINTET IN A (for String Quartet and Clarinet), K. 581, by Mozart. (*Saxophone*): Ensemble for Saxophone solo with flute, double bass and bassoon, "RACONTO," Op. 25, by Jorgen Bentzon, played by the saxophone virtuoso, Sigurd Rascher; CONCERTO FOR SAXOPHONE by Glazounoff; CONCERTINO FOR SAXOPHONE by Ibert. (*Bassoon*): CONCERTO FOR BASSOON, K. 191, by Mozart; DUET CONCERTINO FOR CLARINET AND BASSOON by R. Strauss; SONATA FOR BASSOON AND PIANO by Charles Koechlin. (*Wood-Wind Ensembles*): QUINTET A VENT by Jean Françaix; SUITE FOR WINDS (posthumous) and SERENADE FOR WIND INSTRUMENTS IN

[17] This list is not intended to be comprehensive. Instead, we have tried to present recordings of the various instruments of the orchestra in solo or salient parts, for "choirs" of their same types, or for mixed ensembles in order to aid the listener in acquainting himself with their various timbres. The reader should consult the latest record catalogs and Swann's "Long Playing Monthly Record Catalog"; annotated "Record Books" like those by Irving Kolodin, B. H. Haggin, J. M. Moses, David Hall, the Gramophone Shop Encyclopedia (N. Y.); the latest "Records" book put out by Knopf, and the like. Consult *The World's Encyclopedia of Recorded Music* by Clough and Cuming (London: Sidwick) the most comprehensive listing of phonograph records to be had.

E-FLAT by Richard Strauss; QUINTET IN E-FLAT (Piano and Winds), K. 452, by Mozart; CONCERT MUSIC FOR WIND ORCHESTRA, Op. 41, by Paul Hindemith. (*Trumpet*): IL CAMPO DI FIORI, for trumpet and orchestra by Kent Kennan (recorded?); CAPRICORN CONCERTO, FOR TRUMPET, FLUTE AND OBOE by Samuel Barber; TRIO FOR TRUMPET, TROMBONE AND HORN by Francis Poulenc; MUSIC FOR TRUMPET AND STRINGS by Armin Kaufmann. (*Horn*): POÈME FOR HORN AND ORCHESTRA by Ch. Koechlin (new French recording?); CONCERTO IN E-FLAT FOR HORN by Richard Strauss; KONZERTSTÜCK FOR FOUR HORNS AND ORCHESTRA, Op. 86, by Robert Schumann; SONATA FOR HORN AND PIANO, Op. 17, by Beethoven; TRIO FOR HORN, VIOLIN AND PIANO, Op. 40, by Brahms. (*Trombone*): SONATA FOR BASSOON, TROMBONE AND PIANO by Paul Hindemith; CONCERTO FOR TROMBONE by Rimsky-Korsakoff. This has been recorded by Symphony Artists Band, Circle, No. 51-103 (33⅓ rpm.). The final listing is a most pleasant surprise. (*Tuba*): CONCERTO FOR BASS TUBA in F minor by the great modern English composer, Ralph Vaughan Williams, première in London, 1954. For an unusual dessert we offer ROMANCE FOR SOLO HARMONICA with strings and piano (written especially for Larry Adler), also by Vaughan Williams. Its première took place in New York City in 1952.

Courtesy The Metropolitan Museum of Art

THE NIKE OF SAMOTHRAKE Ancient Greek, c. 306 B.C.

Nike, a goddess of victory, is now in the Louvre (Paris). It was created to commemorate a Greek naval victory over the Egyptians. This marble statue was reconstructed from many pieces and shows the goddess flying to the prow of a boat to blow the trumpet of victory. The figure, with its gracefully flowing gown and classically idealized lines, imparts a strong feeling of free forward movement. From such Grecian art, we have inherited the classical ideals and tempers.

13 Artistic tempers in music and other fine arts

There is no topic about the Fine Arts, especially music, that is more interesting and elusive, yet so ancient and worldwide, as the inquiry into why certain persons are able and moved to create, why their creations are so individual, and why the appreciators throughout the world, both civilized and primitive, react to the same work of art so differently. These questions have many explanations, but few agreements. It is not our purpose to try to solve what we believe will remain a mystery. We are among those who contend that, in its highest state and in the final analysis, a great work of art is its own explanation and reason for being. Thus our present task is to relate briefly some answers that professional inquirers have set forth and to offer some personal suggestions for thought on the subject.

It was not at all surprising that several philosophers of ancient Greece should have inquired systematically into the subject and offered what were to them proper and correct answers to the problems posed by the creative arts. These philosophers reached contrasting solutions which, nevertheless, continue to influence the thinking of aestheticians.

Plato (c. 427–347 B.C.), the "Father of Greek Philosophy," used the word *pathos* to connote those qualities which, when incorporated in a work of art, arouse in the appreciator such emotions as pity, compassion, sympathetic sadness, melancholy, and often a detached pleasure in their contemplation. Aristotle (384–322 B.C.), his principal pupil, believed the real essences in a work of art and the consequent reactions of the appreciator to be what he called *ethos*. This term implied those characteristic qualities in a work of art that invested and aroused in the appreciator the more universal ideals such as nobility of spirit, dignity, morality, ethics, the highest type of virtue in character, and intellectual ideas. These definitions seem to anticipate to some extent the connotations of the more modern term, *empathy*.[1] It is interesting to observe that the connotations of the Greek pathos and ethos persist in the consideration of the arts of our time, although the styles and techniques may differ greatly.[2] When ethos is deliberately flaunted or negated in the arts so that immoral suggestiveness and prurience are more obviously objective and predominant than purely aesthetic qualities, the works are considered inferior according to ageless tenets and traditions. A *cause célèbre*, recorded by the reactions of the general public and professional critics, concerned the prurient *nakedness* in Manet's (1833–83) painting DÉJEUNER SUR L'HERBE ("Luncheon on the grass").[3] Yet the use of the *nude* in Giorgione's (c. 1478–1511) masterpiece, CONCERT CHAMPÊTRE ("A Rustic Concert"), does not meet with similar criticism. (Some critics now consider Manet's work to a great extent, actually an inferior imitation of the compositional ideas of Giorgione's work.) Also compare for prurient traits, Manet's OLYMPIA, Ingres' ODALISQUE, Giorgione's SLEEPING VENUS.

[1] For a discussion of empathy see: Melvin M. Rader, ed., *A Modern Book of Esthetics* (New York: Henry Holt and Co., 1935), Chap. VIII; James Jarrett, *The Quest for Beauty* (Englewood Cliffs, N. J.: Prentice-Hall, 1957), pp. 132-141; Curt John Ducasse, *Philosophy of Art* (New York: Lincoln MacVeagh, 1929), Chaps. IX and X; Susanne K. Langer, *Philosophy in a New Key* (Boston: Harvard Press, 1942) or reprint (New York: Penguin Book Co., 1948); and John Dewey, *Art as an Experience* (New York: Minton, Balch and Co., 1934), pp. 101-102.

[2] For a critical analysis and comparison between the emotional, intellectual, and ideational bases of the philosophy and psychology of art read James L. Jarrett, *The Quest for Beauty* (Englewood Cliffs, N. J.: Prentice-Hall, 1957), pp. 135-150. Though somewhat biased toward rationalism and silent about some modern ideas and emotional movements in art, it is an interesting presentation of the subject.

[3] For those who would pursue the subject further we suggest: Bernard Berenson, *Aesthetics and History* (Garden City, N. Y.: Doubleday, 1954), pp. 94-95 and 147; John Dewey, *Art as an Experience* (New York: Minton, Balch, 1934), pp. 95-97; Theodore Meyer Greene, *The Arts and the Art of Criticism* (Princeton University Press, 1940), pp. 265-267; James L. Jarrett, *The Quest for Beauty* (Englewood Cliffs, N. J.: Prentice-Hall, 1957), Chap. XII; F. W. Ruckstall, *Great Works of Art and What Makes Them Great* (Garden City, N. Y. Publishing Co., 1925), pp. 427-431.

During the Middle or Dark Ages (c. 476–1000) and even into the Renaissance, the term *humors* was commonly used. At first, this referred to the four bodily fluids of blood, phlegm, choler (yellow bile), and melancholy (black bile). About the time of Shakespeare, the use of the terms and original functions in the humors fell into disuse. However, the spiritual, psychological, mental, physical, and emotional states they were supposed to affect replaced them—disposition, state of mind, temperament, mood, feeling, presentiment, individual habits, manner of thinking and acting, and other conditions.

THE ARTISTIC TEMPERS

In the previous edition of this book we called the reader's attention to some obvious, generally used categories of the artistic tempers. Now we shall delve further into these tempers as they pertain to the creative artist, the performing artist, and to the appreciator without whom all art would be futile.

The creative artistic tempers are essentially genetically endowed "gifts," aptitudes, urges, and special capacities which are psychological, intuitive, imaginative, and kinesthetic (overt or covert) in their source and nature. Yet there are a number of endowed "gifts," attributes, qualities, and mental-muscle combinations of genius that no one has yet fathomed or understood, least of all the creative artist, the true genius, the virtuoso performer—and also the psychologist. It is expected that the "ceiling" of development and perfection of some of these tempers and capacities varies in degree and intensity in the individual, from the merely talented to the genius.

These tempers are included in the general as well as the specific applications of the artist's intellect and knowledge, especially those that willfully or unconsciously direct his efforts in resolving and making decisions necessary to the general as well as detailed matters of his creative work. These may involve the choice of brush strokes, color, composition, words, the creation and scoring of music, or suggesting or guiding each chisel stroke of the sculpture, and many other matters.

Sometimes these attributes, skills and their applications may conflict; but here the artist's gifts, skills, including so-called "muscular memory" abilities, artistic "psyche," and experiences hold him in stead toward the attainment of his desired creative goals. Such mastery is gained only through great personal sacrifices, arduous training, and long and exacting experience coupled with unrelenting and rigorous self-criticism. Only in this manner can the creator attain the necessary facilities for the fulfillment of the facile expression of his artistic ideals. It will be seen that the artist must first become master of himself, his gifts, skills, and abilities. Then he is forced, to the degree that he approaches the genius classification, to become an obedient slave of his art—sometimes pathetically and tragically so. This the artist does in order to evoke the enjoyment, understanding, and spiritual elevation of the listener that only great art and consummate artistry can impart.

The foregoing detailed exposition which *in toto* we call the artistic tempers is a very complex subject, worthy of careful study. In order to make the tempers adaptable for ready use in general listening, we have consolidated them into six easily applied and fundamental aggregates as basic tempers that will henceforth be used throughout this book: (1) *Realism* or *Naturalism* (representational art); (2) *Classicism;* (3) *Romanticism;* (4) *Symbolism;* (5) *Impressionism*—often combined or confused with *Symbolism;* (6) *Expressionism.* Classicism and Romanticism will be expounded in the second half of this chapter—the remaining basic tempers in subsequent chapters. The surest and best means of getting to the spirit and meaning of a great work of art is through repeated, intimate, intelligent, and empathetic appreciation, plus the perception and response to the basic tempers and style (mostly outward aspects) inherent in the masterpiece itself.

A few years after writing the manuscript of the first edition of this book, we were delighted to come upon the anthology of poetry and prose, WRITERS OF THE WESTERN WORLD by the late Addison Hibbard, Dean of the English department of Northwestern University.[4] Although engaged in a similar scholarly venture but in a different art field, he reached basically similar conclusions to those expounded here concerning the nature, importance, techniques of use, and integration of the tempers within the Fine Arts. Dean Hibbard uses seven aggregates of tempers to suit his special field of application, *Classicism, Romanticism, Romanticism-Symbolism, Realism, Realism-Naturalism, Realism-Impressionism* and *Realism-Expressionism.* Robert Morse Lovett observes in his "General Editor's Notes," that Dean Hibbard "is careful to point out and illustrate the fact that *these tempers are not confined to the ages in which they are dominant, but are permanent elements in the human nature which seeks expression in literature.*" The author has stated his case for the use, nature, and value of the tempers in his Preface:

"If it is true that writing has taken on new attitudes and forms with different writers in varying periods, it is also true that attitudes and forms in different chronological periods have much in common. The mere matter of time does not explain enough. Instead, then, of thinking of literature as an expression changing with period and type, why not seek to understand the separate

[4] Addison Hibbard, *Writers of the Western World* (Boston: Houghton Mifflin Co., 1942). An anthology of outstanding prose and poetry from Homer to the present, together with critical, historical, and explanatory comments by the author. In addition the contents are classified according to various tempers. There are references appropriate to criticism, art, and music of each classification. Half-tone cuts of pertinent art works under discussion are included. This is a gem of a book for lovers of the Fine Arts.

tempers which prompt these changes?" He then goes on to show the constancy and permanency of the tempers by comparing the Romanticism of the poetry of Ovid in the first century B.C. with Keats of the nineteenth century, and the same temper in a story by Boccaccio compared with one by Robert Louis Stevenson. Further, he shows the same affinities of expressive tempers in the literature of different foreign languages, such as Chinese and English, Russian and French, Greek and Roman, etc. Continuing, he states: "If critics and academicians must classify—and it is evident that we must—why should we not seek to find a scheme which is applicable to any chronological period, to any geographical section and to any type of writing?"

Prof. Hibbard then proceeds with the specific, though succinct, explanation and differentiation of the seven categories of tempers as he has applied them to literature:

"The working basis for this simpler method of classification may be found, I think, in what we may call the *temper* of literature. I would suggest that when the writing is calm, restrained, when it subordinates content to form, it is likely that it is controlled by a temper essentially *classic* and that when it is exuberant, idealistic, when content dictates form, the temper is essentially *romantic*. When I come upon writing which, though romantic in spirit, is based essentially on symbols, which is systematically concerned with what it regards as "essences" and lays emphasis on musical effects, tones, and colors, in the manner of Rimbaud or Mallarmé, Poe or Baudelaire, I should think of it as by temper *symbolistic*. On the other hand, when the writer is determined to seek out truth, when he is dominated by a desire faithfully to portray character, when his whole manner is objective and he is more concerned with interpreting life through actuality than with telling a story of action, he is *realistic*. And I should accept as *naturalistic* that realism which goes beyond realism, which is deterministic and mechanistic in tone, and which tries to understand humanity by the methods of scientific analysis, particularly of man's environment and his heredity. And when I find a literary manner giving great emphasis to atmosphere, to the transcribing of the quality of an experience as it impresses itself on the emotions of the author under the spell of a momentary revelation, the manner of some of Conrad for instance, I should give it the name of *impressionism*. And then, when I find impressionism in reverse, the objective stated in terms of the subjective, the associated substituted for the actual, I think of it as *expressionistic*. Before this proposal is charged with being too complicated, I should indicate that the seven manners here suggested are essentially but three: *the classical, the romantic, and the realistic. Symbolism is essentially a phase of romanticism; naturalism, impressionism, and expressionism are but variations within the realistic temper*.

Style in Art

In contrast to the highly personal, inherently psychological, emotional qualities and spirit of self-expression usually connoted in the term tempers, *style* in art is more concerned with the manifestations of skills, the general and detailed use of compositional materials, elements of design, and the distinctive individual techniques and manner of employing them in the process of creation. The artistic characteristics of the individual or group, and the ways in which the artist uses all of these determine, shape, and identify the distinctive mode, appearance, type, and stylistic character of a work of art as it compares with other types of the same basic character. Of course, some personal tempers and the inescapable creative gifts of the individual artist may be used as "building blocks" in style. Sometimes the exact line of demarcation between temper and what is commonly or academically called style is a very fine one.

These elements and peculiarities of style may be observed in an unorganized "school," or group of artists, those who are in more or less sympathetic agreement concerning certain artistic characteristics or techniques, such as the "Hudson River School" of the early nineteenth century. Outstanding among this group were: Homer D. Martin, Alexander Wyant, and the early American Impressionist, George Inness (1825–1894). Or one may cite the so-called "Ash Can School," in and near New York and Philadelphia, so named because of their interest in "typical" American scenes—Greenwich Village back yards, alleys, prizefights, saloons, and other scenes. Among these artists were the leader and teacher, Robert Henri (1865–1929); Arthur B. Davies (1862–1928), an early American Impressionist and fantasist; George B. Luks; William Glackens; George Bellows (1882–1925), a painter of action, see his fight picture DEMPSEY AND FIRPO; and John Sloan (1871–1951), see his painting, BACKYARD.

Likewise certain stylistic characteristics may serve to distinguish between the artistic products of different generations, periods, epochs, ages, eras, and the like. One might point out the more or less contemporary and possibly ephemeral variations of Dadaism, Pointellism, or other styles in painting, or call attention to the popular musical styles of the Spanish gypsy or West Indian Negro dance music known as CALYPSO, the variations of the Schönbergian twelve-tone-row, serial system, etc. The interior decorator may consider equally important the styles in furniture such as Duncan Phyfe, Adam, or Empire, and so forth. And so one may go throughout history of art.[5]

THE CLASSICAL TEMPER APPLIED TO ART AND MUSIC

In this chapter we are primarily concerned with the Classic and the Romantic tempers and their artistic manifestations. First, let us discuss the Classic temper and the art works created in that spirit. An artist who

[5] The reader may be interested in reading the excellent article on "Forgeries in Paintings" in the *Encyclopedia of the Arts* (New York: Philosophical Library Pub. 1946), pp. 356-359.

is moved largely by this temper will react objectively (intellectually) rather than subjectively (emotionally) as much as possible toward his material, fashioning it into the most polished and enduring shape. He will be concerned not only with what he says—the content—but also with the perfection of the manner of saying it—the form. If he is a composer, he will be deeply involved with developing tonal design and metamorphosis of germinal musical ideas, as such, to the utmost of their potentialities. Fundamentally, this creator is the artist-philosopher, whose duty it is to present rather than to question, to affirm rather than to rebel. He will exercise restraint, present emotion "recollected in tranquillity"; he will aim for the conventional (in the best sense of the word) rather than for striking effects. He will work within established traditions, bringing them to a higher level of perfection rather than striking out into new paths. Chastity of style, harmony, or outline, simplicity, balance, and self-control—these will be foremost among his ideals. In short, such a creator will be a *Classicist.*

Let us ponder a bit over that term, "classical"; but first let us try to define it somewhat broadly and, if possible, so as to include as many of the Fine Arts as we can. The dictionary tells us that *classical* means "resembling, modeled after, or in the spirit of, the highest forms of ancient Roman or Greek art." Thus, one might deduce that any art created since that time which embraces or is influenced by a style or temper similar to that which prompted, or characterized, those ancient art works, may be said to be "Classical." (Be careful to distinguish between the words "classic" and "classical"—consult an unabridged dictionary.) But even this source leaves much to be desired for there are evidences of Symbolic, Realistic, and even Romantic tempers in the Ancient Egyptian, Assyrian, Grecian, and Roman arts.[6] Thus the word "classic" may have many definitions, especially in reference in music. W. Somerset Maugham put the case very well in a critique of Jane Austen's novel, PRIDE AND PREJUDICE, as follows: "What makes a classic is not that it is praised by critics, expounded by professors, and studied in college classes, but that readers have found pleasure and spiritual profit in reading it.[7] "

[6] An excellent example of classical symbolism in ancient Greek sculpture is THE NIKE OF SAMOTHRAKE. For Greek sculpture in the realistic temper, see OLD MARKET WOMAN 2nd cent. B.C. in *Art through the Ages* by Helen Gardner (New York: Harcourt, Brace and Co., 1948). A cut of the colorful and romanticized bust of Ikhnaton's wife, Nofretete (Egypt c. 1400 B.C.), may be seen in the 1936 ed. of *Art through the Ages.*

Alexander S. Murray in his book *History of Greek Sculpture* (London: J. Murray, rev. ed., 1890) tells of the traditions concerning sculpture as they were applied to the ancient Greek games. The typically stylistic, impersonal, and idealized type of portraiture was used for all winners save those who won the five separate contests of the *Penthathlon.* For these, busts were fashioned in a realistic, representational, and even romantic manner.

[7] *The Atlantic Monthly* for May, 1948, p. 103 seq. Used here with permission of the publishers.

Courtesy The University Prints, Newton, Mass.

THE PARTHENON FROM THE NORTHWEST

We refer you now to the picture of our National CAPITOL at Washington, D. C., in Chapter 6. You will see that there are unmistakable evidences of ancient Greek and Roman influences in this product of the Classical Revival during colonial times. Compare the CAPITOL with the PARTHENON, considered by many to be "the most complete example of the Doric style in temple architecture ever built.[8] This celebrated old temple was built by Iktinos and Kallikrates from the years 447 to 432 B.C.; it gives eloquent evidence to the highest degree of designing and building skill, and it is no wonder that it has been the marvel and inspiration of the entire Western world for the past 2400 years—so much so that the building, though a mere ruin, may be considered the very symbol of perfection. Here, in a

[8] For further readings about ancient and modern architecture see: David M. Robb and J. J. Garrison, *Art in the Western World* (New York: Harper & Brothers, 1942), Chaps. III and IV; Gilbert Highet, *The Classical Tradition* (New York: Oxford Press, 1953), about the influences of Greek and Roman art upon Western literature, esp. the Introduction and Chap. XIX; Frank Lloyd Wright, *In the Nature of Materials* (New York: Museum of Modern Art, 1941), about Romantic architecture; Upjohn, Wingert, and Mohler, *History of World Art* (New York: Oxford Press, 1958); and Oliver W. Larking, *Art and Life in America* (New York: Rinehart, 1949), Chap. XXII.

single edifice, are exemplified the perfect consonance of purpose and design and the attractive severity of line and surface. It is the epitome and triumph of mathematical and formal perfection, a monument to impersonal and epochal expression, and a model of quiet serenity and nobility without pomp or overindulgence of fancy. There are exemplified minutely calculated effects that never become ostentatious or conspicuous in themselves. Finally, one can see in the PARTHENON the ideal achievement in the relationship between the separate parts and the whole. Such richness of virtues was destined to fire the ideals of beauty in man in all the Fine Arts through twenty-five centuries, and to serve him as a perpetual model for those attributes he has chosen to call the spirit or temper of Classicism.

Now let us look at the reproduction of the classical painting, ORPHEUS AND EURYDICE by the French artist, Nicolas Poussin (1594–1665). The subject matter, or literary content, of this story has served as the basis for more operas than has any other. It is a classical tale, in the exact sense, and it is "told" in such a way that moral, intellectual, and emotional elements are set forth with utmost clarity of means. There is in this picture the positive spirit of the ideal perfection and the absence of excessive sensuality and flamboyance. Although the artist was not without influence from the spirit of the early *Baroque,* he steadfastly held to the traditional ideals of beauty. He strove to create paintings that evidenced harmony, concord, and masterly control, rather than turbulence, discord, and ecstatic emotional expression. His figures seem to be enlivened Greek statues—note the postures, as though they were arrested gestures during a dignified and graceful Greek dance. Poussin seeks to charm the appreciator, to mollify rather than to startle by novelty or shock by boldness of expression; all is polished perfection, as near as he could achieve the ideal.

In striving for such ideals, Poussin was not unlike Corneille and Racine in the theater, wherein man asserted his mastery over himself and his mundane fate through the control of his emotions and actions by the intellect within restrictions of time and place—really an ancient classical idea. The paintings of Poussin reflect that same kind of control and mastery of one's emotional expressions by means of a well-ordered and meticulously executed plan or design. Nothing was left to chance or to momentary extemporization. He was consciously concerned with making everything he painted exemplary of the characteristic rather than of the transient incident, exception, or personalized interpretation—a trait also marked in the aspects of conventionality that exist in "classical" music. We must observe, however, that though the emphasis is on the formal manner rather than free fancy, the latter is by no means absent; it remains a matter of *control and degree emphasis.* In ORPHEUS AND EURYDICE are observed those qualities which have provoked the term "heroic land-

Courtesy The Metropolitan Museum of Art

ORPHEUS AND EURYDICE Poussin

scape." It is unlike any scene one may have witnessed; rather, it is the ideal landscape for the setting of the picture according to tenets of the artist. Poussin may justly be called a typical Classicist.

THE ROMANTIC TEMPER AS APPLIED TO ART

An artist of a different temperament may seek to project his own personality into his art, to view the world about him through the lens of intense personal feeling. He will be proudly subjective, intuitive, and imaginative, and boldly proclaim his differentness. He will revolt against the established order, traditions, and fixed forms. He will stress personal emotion rather than logical cerebration, content rather than form (though he will not abandon the latter), and he will be attracted to what is strange, sensate, and picturesque rather than the conventional. He will *seem* to lean toward mysticism and expressive fervor rather than objectivity and the discipline of emotions and intellect; yet he will not be devoid of the latter, by any means. Technic and design will not be ends in themselves; instead, they will be the highly plastic vehicles for the projection of his individual, intensely immediate, as well as habitual and emotional, utterance. In short, such an individualistic creative artist would manifest the Romantic tempers in art; and he would be a Romanticist, regardless of when and where he lived.

Let us first consider the reproduction of the picture, THE ABDUCTION OF REBECCA by another French painter, Ferdinand V. Eugene Delacroix (1798–1863). Here is action, drama, force, conflict, imagination, novelty and highly individual and personal expression reminding one of the FANTASTIQUE Symphony of Berlioz! There is also what one might well call "controlled disorder" in the picture. Certainly it is typical of the Romantic temper. Delacroix has here painted a highly original work in which a certain deliberate indefiniteness of line, form, masses, composition, and action contrast strongly with the type of precise drawing and painting we ordinarily identify as typical of the Classical style and temper.

If we re-examine the Delacroix picture closely, we shall discern that the artist put into the picture very novel and highly imaginative contents of strong dynamic action, both graphic and literary. He has used color, as such, in a vivid and moving manner. Rather than trying to conform to an idea or a convention, the painter has projected a very individualized picture, and he has expressed it in a manner and with the means that best suited his fancy at the moment. He is not moralizing; yet he is telling a story, and with it he is giving one a psychological insight into the characters of the drama in a most uncanny manner. Over all, the picture involves an extra-plastic art—literature. The exciting moment of the tale that he desires to depict is evidently of greater importance to him than adherence to the traditional classical ideals. Finally, the onlooker is a

Courtesy The Metropolitan Museum of Art

ABDUCTION OF REBECCA Delacroix

much more active "participant" in the picture than is the case with the Poussin work. (*By all means study the picture in color.*) One is quite right in considering Delacroix a leader of the French Romantic "school" of the nineteenth century. By means of the high flights of his poetic imagination, one has a fleeting glimpse into the future, yet one might just as truthfully say the same of Poussin in regard to the Classical "school."

Nineteenth-century critics, sharing the love of their age for neat, watertight classifications, used the labels classic and romantic with much assiduity, with the result that there emerged two concepts, or styles, that were then considered diametrically opposed to each other. Yet it takes little reflection to discern that each "school" might often supplement, complement, and even include the other in varying degrees. Neither type exists in "pure" form. Further, the Classic and the Romantic styles, schools, and tempers may co-exist, in varying proportions, in the same age, in the same school, in the same person, and even in the same composition. The differences between them are due more to the combinations of tempers and the degree of emphases than in the complete opposition of kind. There are strong Romantic tempers manifest in some of the works of such Classicists as Virgil, Corneille, Michelangelo, Haydn and others. Conversely, there are salient Classical tempers evidenced in the works of Romanticists like Millet, Swinburne, Robinson, or Brahms. The composer who is most often considered the epitome of the classical spirit, Mozart, wrote measures that, for emotional expressiveness and imagination, have not their superior in all music; while such composers as Schumann or Chopin, who are represented as types of the romantic artist, display in some of their finest works, a finesse of form and a mastery of technique and design that bear comparison with the great figures of the Classical school. Conversely, how romantic Bach and Haydn could be when they so desired!

Equally misleading is the practice of labeling a selected number of years as a classical or romantic period or epoch almost exclusively, and then forcing everything created within those years to bear the stylistic character of its arbitrarily named period. So often has the eighteenth century been marked off as the special province of the classical spirit in art, and the nineteenth relegated to the romantic, that the student is likely to get the impression that between 1799 and 1800 Classicism died and Romanticism came into being. The error will be avoided if we consider the two tendencies as signposts revealing general trends, with generous overlapping and mixing of both characteristics. Actually the eighteenth century—the age that saw the culmination of classical form in music in the symphony—produced such utterly unclassical works as Rousseau's AUTOBIOGRAPHY, Hogarth's SHRIMP GIRL, Mozart's ABDUCTION FROM THE SERAGLIO, the lyrics of Robert Burns, and the poetry and drawings of William Blake. On the other hand, the qualities that we lump together under the general concept of Romanticism have flourished in one form or another throughout all periods, and may be found, now stronger, now weaker, from the Psalms, Homer, and Sophocles to Virgil and Catallus; from Dante and Petrarch to Michelangelo and Dürer; from Shakespeare and Rembrandt, Bach and Haydn, to Goethe, Schubert, Beethoven, and even the moderns.

It can readily be seen why the eighteenth century, dominated by an ultraconservative aristocracy, has come to be known in the history of human thought as the *Age of Reason,* and in the history of art, as the *Age of Classicism.* The nobility of the old regime had brought the business of living to the level of a fine art. The accent was on correct form rather than on deep feeling, on the manner rather than on the matter. Emotion was channeled within the confines of an exquisite art just as brooks were channeled within the balanced and symmetrically designed landscape of a formal garden. The artist, working under the system of patronage, had to satisfy the fastidious tastes of his noble benefactor. He did not lack either deep feeling or imaginative power. But within the prevailing social framework it was inevitable that he place enormous emphasis on the chiseled line, the exquisite finish, the restrained manner, the serene and objective vision that have come to be associated with classical art.

The nineteenth century, on the other hand, presented a completely different picture. The aristocracy of the eighteenth century was supplanted by the *bourgeoisie;* the cult of personal freedom, of aggressive individualism, had taken hold of the new industrial society. The world-shaking slogan of the Revolution—Liberty, Equality, Fraternity—released forces that had been pent up for centuries; the artificialities and restraints of the old order were swept aside.[9] Emancipated from his subservience to patrons, the artist now addressed a public audience. He could dare to be himself, to express his innermost feelings, to defy the stifling conventions. Intensity of feeling and picturesque effect were his natural idiom, as the classic style had been the natural idiom of his predecessor. The difference of expression did not mean that he was not as careful a craftsman, as great a master of technique, as the eighteenth-century artist. It meant simply that his interest in technique was subordinated, owing to the prevailing social pattern of the age, to the emotional and subjective, to the romantic elements of artistic self-expression.

We may get a good insight into the two idioms if we compare the didacticism, the impersonality, the objective "sweet reasonableness" of a passage such as the closing lines of Pope's *Essay on Man,* written in the 1730's and characteristic of the Age of Reason:

> Submit: in this or any other sphere,
> Secure to be as blessed as thou canst bear;
> Safe in the hand of one disposing Power,
> Or in the natal or the mortal hour.
> All Nature is but Art unknown to thee;
> All chance, direction, which thou canst not see;

[9] A scholarly political and cultural summary of the background of Romanticism and Nationalism may be read in: Carlton J. H. Hayes *A Political and Cultural History of Modern Europe* (2 vols.) (New York: Macmillan Co., 1937) Chap. XVII, pp. 151 to 280, Vol. 2; Egon Friedell *A Cultural History of the Modern Age* (New York: Knopf, 1931), Vol. 3, Chaps. I, II and Part III; Charles Gray Shaw, *Trends of Civilization and Culture* (New York: American Book Co., 1932), a study of culture and those who create it; Jacques Barzun, *Berlioz and the Romantic Century* (Boston: Little, Brown, 1950), 2 vols. Book I, Chap. 14.

All discord, harmony not understood;
All partial evil, universal good;
And spite of Pride, in erring Reason's spite,
One truth is clear, *Whatever is, is right.*

with the passionate lyricism, the subjectivity and intense feeling of a poem such as Shelley's *Ode to the West Wind,* which has so often been cited as the quintessence of the romantic attitude:

Oh! lift me as a wave, a leaf, a cloud!
I fall upon the thorns of life! I bleed!
A heavy weight of hours has chained and bowed
One too like thee—tameless, and swift, and proud. . . .

Or Heine's poignant:

Out of my great, great sorrow
I make my little songs. . . .

Or Byron's bitter:

I have thought
Too long and darkly, till my brain became,
In its own eddy boiling and o'erwrought,
A whirling gulf of phantasy and flame:
And thus, untaught in youth my heart to tame,
My springs of life were poisoned.

Or the no less significant hymn to the night in the love scene of Wagner's TRISTAN AND ISOLDE with its longing for oblivion:

O sink down upon us, night of love,
Let us now forget that we live,
Take us up within your arms,
Free us forever from the world!

Or Rousseau's defiant: "I am different from all the men I have ever seen; if I am not better, at least I am different!" Here we have the prevailing attitudes of the romantic artist. So, too, we might compare the delicate landscapes with their nymphs and shepherdesses of Watteau and Fragonard with the grand sweep and melodrama of the canvases of Delacroix and Géricault; or the exquisite finish of an early minuet by Haydn or Mozart with the surge and thunder of a composition by Wagner or Tchaikovsky.

THE ROMANTIC MOVEMENT IN MUSIC[10]

We have drawn a distinction between the spirit, or temper, of Classicism, and a contrasting spirit, or temper, of Romanticism as concepts in

[10] Essential listening for this chapter includes: *Minuet* from SYMPHONY IN E-FLAT by Mozart; *Liebestod* music from TRISTAN AND ISOLDE by Wagner; and the *Overture-Fantasy,* ROMEO AND JULIET, by Tchaikovsky.

art that are limited to no one century; and the Age of Classicism and the Romantic period as the epochs when the qualities associated with either one or the other tendency appeared to predominate. For the music lover, the Romantic movement of the nineteenth century is of particular interest, since practically nine-tenths of the music we hear today was either inspired by it or came under its influence. To begin with, the two masters who are most often held out as perfect examples of the classical style, Mozart and Haydn, sometimes showed strong romantic characteristics, especially in the works written in the latter part of their careers. Mozart died in 1791, two years after the beginning of the French Revolution; Haydn did some of his most important work in the following decade.

Beethoven, Weber, and Schubert encompassed the transition from the classical style to the spirit of the new century. Mendelssohn, Chopin, and Schumann saw the full unfolding of the Romantic Movement. Wagner, Liszt, Berlioz became the prophets of mid-nineteenth-century Romanticism. Brahms, Tchaikovsky, Grieg, Dvořák, Smetana, César Franck, Mussorgsky, Rimsky-Korsakoff, Saint-Saëns, Massenet, Gounod, Bizet, Verdi, Puccini, Elgar, MacDowell—these composers are of the Romantic Movement. One need not extend the list to make it apparent that, for all practical purposes, the general public of today still lives, musically speaking, in the Romanticism of the nineteenth century. And even after the twilight of Romanticism, when the interlude known as post-Romanticism bridged the gap between the nineteenth and twentieth century, the outstanding men—Sibelius, Richard Strauss, Debussy, Ravel, Falla, and their compeers—still preserved in new guise many of the influences of nineteenth-century Romanticism.[11]

In the following chapters, we shall study in detail a number of compositions that exemplify various characteristics of musical Romanticism. As an introduction, let us now listen to and compare an example of the Classical style and temper such as the *Minuet* from Mozart's SYMPHONY IN E-FLAT MAJOR, with a piece of Romantic music such as the *Liebestod* from Wagner's TRISTAN AND ISOLDE. The choice of such extreme examples of the two styles will the more clearly demonstrate the differences between them.

Perhaps the first thing that strikes us, as we listen to the two compositions, is the fact that Wagner's orchestra is much larger than Mozart's—a fact due to the tremendous increase in symphonic resources during the Romantic Period. From this increased size of orchestra there spring several other differences. Wagner's orchestral writing is generally much more involved than is Mozart's. Where Mozart's is a wonderful example of economy of means, Wagner piles on his effects with a lavish hand.

[11] Evidences of apparently Realistic and Romantic tempers in some of the ancient Greek and Roman music are mentioned by several historians of the first century A.D. and even long before that. Read Louis C. Elson, *Curiosities of Music* (Boston: Oliver Ditson Co., 1918) Chaps. II to XVII.

Mozart relies, in the main, on his string section with touches of color from the wood-winds and brasses. Wagner revels in the timbres of the clarinet, oboe, flute and bassoon families, and in the sonorities of the brass, and the sweep and power of the strings and battery. The dynamic range in Wagner's music, the contrast between soft and loud, and the intensity of the climaxes are naturally much more powerful in the Romantic master than in the Classical. The *Minuet* represents a simple and limpid texture; the *Liebestod,* on the other hand, is an elaborate tonal tapestry of great puissance, opulence, and splendor. It should not be assumed that the character of these two works mark all the works of Wagner and Mozart as being similarly differentiated.

In regard to form, the *Minuet* consists of regular phrases and periods and sections stemming from a clear, basic four-measure structure. In contrast, Wagner's music sweeps forward with either no segmentation at all, or with sections that run together in a continuous movement. In Mozart, the qualities of symmetry, balance, and contrast are presented in a graceful, easily perceived architecture. In Wagner, there is a mighty flow of sound, as of a current that threatens to surge over its banks. Mozart's writing stays securely within the key; that is to say, it is predominantly diatonic. Whatever modulations there may be are carefully prepared and negotiated. Wagner modulates continually in a restless chromaticism charged with emotion. Mozart's harmony is in the main consonant; the discords are placed at strategic points and resolved almost immediately; the prevailing mood is one of well-being and satisfaction. Wagner's harmony, on the other hand, abounds in dissonance, in active tones left palpitating in suspension, in all the accents of despair and longing. Mozart is suave and urbane, restrained and rationally objective; his melody is crystal clear, his harmony transparent. Wagner is tragic, sensuous, and passionate. Mozart's is a music of perfection, of pure beauty and delicate emotion, a song of sunlight and sensibility; Wagner's is a music of night, of ecstasy, of strange and hidden things, and emotional power!

Between these extremes are many shadings of the tempers where one may find the characteristics of one style imperceptibly blending with those of the other. It is the combination of the many factors involved that produces the total stylistic effect. Through the detailed analysis of the compositions we shall examine and hear in the succeeding chapters, it is hoped that the listener will gain increased enjoyment and a more intimate insight into the manner in which the composer manipulates and combines the various musical elements and determinants of style. Many listeners find that this is also a good way to become more sensitive to the subtle and distinctive qualities inherent in the various tempers and styles of all the Fine Arts.

PROGRAM VERSUS ABSOLUTE MUSIC

One of the most important characteristics of the Romantic movement of nineteenth century Europe was that music moved closer to its sister arts, especially poetry and painting—the reverse was sometimes also true, but with due respect for the other idioms and limits of each art. Composers chose "to tell stories," "to paint scenes," and "to convey general and rather indefinite poetic ideas, feelings, and moods." Such influences were, and are, usually aroused through the contemplation of nature, literature, painting, or some other objective stimulus, or simply conjured up by purely imaginative fantasy. These influences have proved to be enormously stimulating in the composition of music in general, and programmatic music in particular. But there are also extended types of program music, possessing some generally unifying ideas or purposes running throughout the single or several movements, each with its own individual program within the general programmatic idea as in a form of suite such as Debussy's LA MER or IBERIA, Rimsky-Korsakoff's SCHEHEREZADE SUITE, or a symphony as a whole, such as Berlioz's "Fantastique." It was in the nineteenth century that the descriptive and narrative tendencies emerged to a position of general dominance in European music. For this reason, even though program music in no sense originated in the nineteenth century, it has come to be considered one of the most characteristic developments of the Romantic movement in music.

The composer might also choose to express his ideas in a type of music which is supposed to be complete in and for itself without a program, as the so-called "abstract," "absolute" or "pure" music.[12] In this genre the composer seeks to occupy himself mainly with the "working out" of one or more musical ideas presented in formal designs.

Thus, Beethoven's FIRST SYMPHONY or Mozart's SONATA IN A MAJOR (K.331) are examples of absolute music; while Liszt's FAUST SYMPHONY, Beethoven's SIXTH SYMPHONY, Tchaikovsky's *Overture-Fantasy* ROMEO AND JULIET, etc. are examples of program music. The distinction between the two types is often a subtle one.

(In "absolute" music there are allegedly no extra-musical components or implications; but we shall presently see the self-delusion in such a thought.) To show how extremely objective and cerebral some aestheticians can become, here is a mathematical formula concerning the musical quality in poetry: [13]

$$M = \frac{O}{C} = \frac{aa + 2r + 2m - 2ae - 2ce}{C}$$

[12] See article "Absolute Music" in *Grove's Dictionary*.

[13] From a pamphlet entitled *A Mathematical Theory and its Application to Poetry and Music* by George D. Birkoff (Houston: Rice Institute, 1932).

Both the "programmatic" and the "absolute" types of music are equally valid. They are merely different in type and objective. There is no inferiority, as some critics would have us believe, in employing a program, provided the music itself is excellent and the investiture of the program is skillfully and artfully accomplished, with a heightening rather than lessening of the value of the music itself and its effects upon the listener. A first rate piece of program music stands upon just as high a plane as an equally first rate piece of "absolute" music. Donald Ferguson writes, in substance, that because of the very nature of the internal play of musical tones with the basic and inherent musical elements, and their consequent effects upon the listener, there is something of a "program" or an exciting and engaging "musical drama," or other extra-musical values, in all music, whether it is called "pure," "absolute," or "programmatic." [14] All sensitive musicians are aware of this. This is averred in face of an article in the HARVARD DICTIONARY OF MUSIC which states, "A good deal of the interest which composers have taken in program music is but the avowal of a lack of truly musical imagination and constructive ideas, a lack for which they hoped to make up by an interesting program." [15] One could list many composers to refute such a notion: Johann Kuhnau, Beethoven, Berlioz, Saint-Saëns, Richard Strauss, Wagner, Tchaikovsky, Stravinsky, Liszt, MacDowell, Rachmaninoff, Smetana, Respighi, Hindemith, Mussorgsky, Schönberg, Schumann, Handel, Bach, Loeffler, Hanson, Ravel, Debussy, Vaughan Williams, and thousands of others extending from Ancient Greek times to our own age. There are few musicians who would agree that these composers were so deficient in "musical imagination and constructive ideas" that they had to cover up those lacks by resorting to program music as a deceptive and protective ruse! Contumacious pedantry!

For our immediate purpose, the program has a definite and unique value. The person who has thought all his life in terms of verbal language in which each word has a concrete meaning inevitably feels bewildered when confronted with a language that consistently avoids all specific connotations. "But what does it mean?" is his first reaction. By tackling program music first, we can reduce this bewilderment to a minimum. The pictorial and literary associations will assist the listener while he is still learning the vocabulary and the meaning of so-called absolute musical expression. After that he will be free either to lean on the composer's story, or supply his own, or do without any at all.

If the enormously increased "programming" of music was the most

[14] See Donald N. Ferguson, *On the Elements of Expression in Music* (Minneapolis: University of Minnesota Press, 1944). Prof. Ferguson has a most unusual artistic understanding and the ability to communicate his ideas to others.

[15] Willi Apel, *Harvard Dictionary of Music* (Cambridge: Harvard University Press, 1944), p. 605. Quoted with permission.

striking characteristic of the art during the Romantic movement, it will be found that the program was generally of the kind that fitted in with the prevailing literary mood of the period. We shall discuss this problem at greater length in the chapter on Franz Liszt. At this point we may observe that the romantic composers were influenced by the same poets from whom the literary Romanticists drew their inspiration, chief among them such writers as Shakespeare, Goethe, Dante, Schiller, and Hoffman.

In the chapter on the orchestra we pointed out the enormous strides made in the art of orchestration during the nineteenth century. We can now see why these strides were made. In their search for new emotional effects, for picturesqueness and atmosphere, for brilliant execution and exotic coloring, the romantic composers turned in far greater degree than did their classical predecessors to the element of tone color as such. Certain general factors unquestionably helped: the mechanical improvements in instruments; the marked development of the orchestra in size and in the technical playing ability of its members.

In addition to these factors, there were several very important changes in the social conditions surrounding the making of music, such as the rise of a widespread middle class with an interest in the art, replacing the former patronage that had been limited to the nobility. With the rise of a music-hungry public, there came also the public concert as an important social institution, instead of the private musicales at the homes of the aristocracy that had characterized music-making in the eighteenth century. This public encouraged and was able to support orchestras much greater in size than those of the nobility; and the orchestra consequently forged ahead in importance.

Yet, despite all these external encouragements, the central stimulus to the growth of the orchestral art lay in the very nature of the romantic composer's attitude toward his art: in the exuberant emotionalism that demanded rich color effects and new expressive devices; in the unprecedented interest in the feelings evoked by the distinctive timbres of the different instruments and by strange combinations untried until then. We may therefore consider tone color—the reliance upon novel or picturesque orchestral effects—as the second outstanding characteristic of musical Romanticism; and we shall have frequent occasion to point out examples of it in the compositions we study.

PETER ILYITCH TCHAIKOVSKY (1840–1893)

We begin our study of the romantic style with a work by the composer who represents perhaps as fully as any other the spirit of late nineteenth-century Romanticism. Both in choice of subject and in spirit, the ROMEO AND JULIET OVERTURE fantasy exemplifies several important features of the program music of its time.

Peter Ilyitch Tchaikovsky was born at Kamsko-Votkinsk in 1840,[16] the son of a government official. He gave no early signs of his future eminence in music and did not, in fact, undertake serious musical study until after he had graduated from the School of Jurisprudence in St. Petersburg. For two years longer, while working in the Ministry of Justice, he vacillated between an official and musical career. At twenty-three, however, he made his decision, relinquished his post, and devoted himself rigorously to his studies in composition. In a letter to his sister he justified his choice, declaring that he must do the work for which he felt fitted. Whether he was to become a celebrated composer or merely a struggling teacher, his conscience would be clear and he would not grumble at his lot. In two years he completed his course at the Conservatoire of St. Petersburg.

For the next twelve years he occupied the post of Professor of Harmony at the newly founded Conservatoire at Moscow. The great pianist, conductor, and director of the Conservatoire, Nicholas Rubinstein, speedily recognized his pupil's gifts; he performed Tchaikovsky's works almost as soon as they were written. Slowly, doggedly, the young composer forged ahead. To this period of his life belongs the ROMEO AND JULIET OVERTURE, now one of the best beloved of his compositions, although it was hissed at Paris and Vienna when first performed; and the PIANO CONCERTO IN B-FLAT MINOR, which Rubinstein pronounced absolutely worthless and unplayable when he first saw it but which he later performed throughout Europe with the most brilliant success.

The Moscow period in Tchaikovsky's career came to an end in 1877 with his brief and unhappy marriage, followed by complete nervous collapse. The same year brought into his life Mme. Nadejda von Meck, the benefactress who for the next thirteen years supported him with a generous annuity, making it possible for him to give up his onerous duties at the Conservatoire and devote himself completely to composition. Their relationship forms one of the strangest chapters in musical biography. Although both lived in Moscow, they never met, carrying on their friendship through a series of intensely revealing letters. These, published in English by Mme. von Meck's grandniece and Catherine Drinker Bowen under the title of BELOVED FRIEND, furnish an interesting sidelight on the composer's character and music.

From 1877 until his death in 1893 Tchaikovsky produced, in a steady stream, the works upon which his fame rests. Success did not come easily; but he was sustained by the devotion and encouragement of a little band of trusted friends and by the inner conviction that his music would ultimately come into its own. In the last years of his life he overcame his

[16] According to the Gregorian calendar, established by Pope Gregory XII in 1582 and now in general use, the date was May 7. However, at the time of Tchaikovsky's birth, the Julian calendar was still used in Russia and hence the date would be about twelve days earlier. For this reason, dates pertaining to Russian artists are often confused.

Courtesy Theodore Presser Co.

PETER ILYITCH TCHAIKOVSKY

almost morbid fear of strangers sufficiently to undertake concert tours to popularize his works; he had the satisfaction of seeing himself become a European figure. In 1891 he was invited to come to America to conduct the opening concert at Carnegie Hall. Two years later, at the Jubilee celebration at Cambridge University, he was honored with the degree of Doctor of Music. He returned to Russia to finish his SIXTH SYMPHONY, the "*Pathétique*," considered by many his greatest work; went to St. Petersburg to conduct it; fell ill with cholera a few days after the first performance; and died on November 6, 1893, at the age of 53.

In his personal life Tchaikovsky was emotionally unstable, vacillating, hypersensitive, and subject to severe spells of depression; he could write "To regret the past, to hope in the future, and never to be satisfied with the present—this is my life." In everything pertaining to his art, however, he was the careful craftsman, the tireless and completely devoted worker for whom musical creation was the supreme function of living. A child of his age, only through music did he find the strength, the meaning, the sense of pattern that life itself denied to his overwrought temperament. The music written out of such circumstances is of necessity intensely subjective, sometimes to the point of morbidity; but it possesses a sincerity, an emotional exuberance, a richness of melody, and a brilliance of orchestral coloring that have endeared it to the broad masses of music lovers everywhere, and made Tchaikovsky, more than a century after his birth, one of the most popular and universally loved of composers. Nothing, surely, gives us so complete an insight into the intensely personal attitude of the man toward his art than the moving letter to Mme. von Meck in which he pays tribute to music:

> You see, my dear friend, I am made up of contradictions, and I have reached a very mature age without resting upon anything positive, without having calmed my restless spirit either by religion or philosophy. Undoubtedly I should have gone mad but for music. Music is indeed the most beautiful of all Heaven's gifts to humanity wandering in the darkness. Alone it calms, enlightens, and stills our souls. It is not the straw to which the drowning man clings; but a true friend, refuge, and comforter, for whose sake life is worth living. Perhaps there will be no music in heaven. Well then, let us give our mortal life to it as long as it lasts.[17]

Overture fantasy "Romeo and Juliet" (1869)

Tchaikovsky was twenty-nine years old when he wrote the ROMEO AND JULIET OVERTURE. This was, indeed, the first work in which his creative personality fully revealed itself. After three-quarters of a century, it still remains as one of the peaks of romantic program music—definitely conceived and built upon a literary story. The program was derived from Shakespeare's tragedy of the same title, but with certain basic changes or sequences from the play for purely musical reasons—so as to secure the maximum aesthetic and emotional effects. Thus, Friar Laurence is properly depicted in an introduction of a religious character; the *Allegro* suggests the enmity and consequent fighting between the Montagues and Capulets; the main themes suggest the persons and love of Romeo and Juliet; and the final scene consists of a dolorous and dirge-like mood established by a very artful transformation of Romeo's once ecstatic theme of love. These and other shiftings and omissions of scenes can be more easily seen comparing Shakespeare's play with the musical program.

The Overture was dedicated to the composer Balakirev, the leader of the Russian nationalist school, who suggested the literary basis of the

[17] Catherine Drinker Bowen and B. von Meck, *Beloved Friend* (New York: Random House, 1937). Used with permission.

subject. Tchaikovsky seems to have had some trouble in getting started. Balakirev wrote him to keep trying:

> First get enthusiastic over the scheme. Then arm yourself with galoshes and a walking-stick and go for a walk along the boulevards. Begin with the Nikitsky, let yourself be thoroughly saturated with your subject; and I am convinced that by the time you reach the Stretensky Boulevard some theme or episode will have come to you.[18]

The advice seems to have worked, for shortly afterward we find Balakirev writing:

> I am delighted that the child of your fancy has quickened. God grant that it come to a happy birth. . . . Do send me what you have done so far, and I promise not to make any remarks—good or bad—until the thing is finished.[19]

When Tchaikovsky complied with this request, Balakirev wrote back:

> As your overture is all but finished, and will soon be played, I will tell you what I think of it quite frankly. . . . The first subject does not please me at all . . . it has neither strength nor beauty, and does not sufficiently suggest the character of Friar Laurence. Here something like one of Liszt's chorales, in the old Catholic Church style, would be very appropriate. Your motive is of quite a different order, in the style of a quartet by Haydn, that genius of "burgher" music that induces a fierce thirst for beer.[20]

The famous Romeo theme—its lyrical attractiveness has survived even a modern popular dance version—Balakirev considered "very pretty, although rather colorless." The Juliet theme he called "simply fascinating."

> I often play it, and could hug you for it. It has the sweetness of love, its tenderness, its longing. . . . I have only one thing to say against this theme: It does not sufficiently express a mystic, inward spiritual love, but rather a fantastic passionate glow which has hardly any nuance of Italian sentiment. Romeo and Juliet were not Persian lovers, they were Europeans.[21]

The first performance took place in 1870 at a concert of the Moscow Musical Society. Unfortunately, Nicholas Rubinstein, who conducted, had just been involved in a lawsuit concerning his right to dismiss a student from the Conservatoire, and the entire musical world of Moscow was on hand to demonstrate its solidarity with him. A friend of Tchaikovsky's wrote:

> From the moment Rubinstein came on the platform until the end of the concert he received an extraordinary ovation. No one thought of the music; and I felt indignant that the first performance of "Romeo and Juliet" should have taken place under such conditions.[22]

[18] M. I. Tchaikovsky, *Life and Letters of Peter Ilyitch Tchaikovsky* (New York: Dodd, Mead and Company, 1924.) Used with the permission of the publisher.

[19] *Ibid.* [20] *Ibid.* [21] *Ibid.* [22] *Ibid.*

Tchaikovsky, too, was dispirited over the reception of his work:

> My overture "Romeo and Juliet" had hardly any success here, and has remained quite unnoticed. . . . After the concert a group of us went to a restaurant. During the whole evening no one said a word to me about the overture. And yet I longed so for appreciation and kindness.[23]

Considering that it is now one of the works upon which his fame most securely rests, the overture made its way into the European repertory with unbelievable slowness. In 1878 Tchaikovsky wrote to Mme. von Meck: "My overture . . . has been played in every capital, but always without success. In Vienna and Paris it was hissed; a short time ago it met with no better reception in Dresden!" At the end of the letter he affirmed his deep inner faith in the ultimate victory of his work:

> If fame is destined for me, it will come with slow but sure steps. History convinces us that the success which is long delayed is often more lasting than when it comes easily and at a bound. . . . An artist should not be troubled by the indifference of his contemporaries. He should go on working and say all that he has been predestined to say. He should know that posterity alone can deliver a true and just verdict. . . . Perhaps I can accept my modest share of success with so little complaint because my faith in the judgment of the future is unshakable. I have a foretaste during my lifetime of the fame which will be meted out to me when the history of Russian music comes to be written. For the present I am satisfied with what I have already acquired. I have no right to complain. I have met some people on my way through life whose warm sympathy for my music more than compensates me for the indifference, misunderstanding and ill-will of the others.[24]

The word *overture* (from the French *ouvrir*, "to open") originally referred to an orchestral composition played as an introduction to an opera, oratorio, ballet, or play, which generally prepared the audience for what was to follow by presenting the principal themes of the work. Being essentially a "curtain raiser," the conventional overture was spirited, swift-moving, and closed with a rousing finale. Many overtures became so popular that they began to be performed at concerts independently of the opera or play for which they had been written. Some of them survived long after the play itself had been forgotten. From this custom was derived the second meaning of the word: a concert piece for symphony orchestra built around a strongly dramatic or pictorial theme and lending itself to brilliant and theatrical treatment. Whether the overture is an introduction to an opera or an independent concert piece can generally be determined from the title. Thus, *Overture* to TANNHÄUSER indicates the existence of an opera by that name; while 1812 OVERTURE OF ROMEO AND JULIET OVERTURE FANTASY refers to an independent concert piece built

[23] *Ibid.*

[24] Catherine Drinker Bowen and B. von Meck, *Beloved Friend* (New York: Random House, 1937). Used with permission of the publisher.

around a respective theme. (The latter is styled an "Overture Fantasy" because Tchaikovsky treats the classical overture form with great freedom and individuality in the work to illuminate the literary program.)

The Overture opens in the pale twilight of a medieval chorale symbolizing the good Friar Laurence. (A *chorale* is a simple, hymnlike tune.) The churchly chords are played in simple, four-part harmony by two clarinets and two bassoons *andante quasi moderato* (fairly slow, almost in moderate tempo), in quadruple meter:

The mysterious effect in the foregoing illustration is enhanced by ethereal arpeggios played on the harp. Note the parallel perfect fifths and octaves as indicated in the third measure. They simulate antique musical usages, supposedly old *Gregorian Chants* with *Organum* (*q.v.*).

The chorale returns on the wood-winds with a running accompaniment in the strings. Gradually, with a *poco a poco accelerando* (faster little by little) and a steadily mounting *crescendo,* we are thrown into the fury and strife of the Feud theme, whose brusque, irregular accents aptly describe the ancient grudge and new mutiny of the Capulets and Montagues. The tempo is *allegro;* the theme is announced with the full orchestra in action, *forte,* and with those upward and downward scale-like sweeps on the violins that are so characteristic of Tchaikovsky's style:

A passage of mounting excitement through the running passages on the strings brings us the repetition of the Feud theme, this time *fortissimo.* Then the tumult dies; out of a tremulous background there emerges the love song of Romeo, with its broad lyric curve and poignant harmonies, sung by a solo English horn and muted violas, *mf, dolce* (sweetly), and *espressivo* (to sound expressively):

This song is answered immediately by the Juliet theme on muted violins playing in four-part harmony. The strings are therefore divided–

that is, they are playing in separate parts. Lawrence Gilman once remarked, "there are not many themes in modern music more justly and beautifully expressive, more richly poetic, than the mood of the enraptured pair as they watch the coming of the dawn in Juliet's chamber."

The two themes are now repeated in a somewhat more developed form that closes the first section of the work.

In the middle section, the violins again take up their broad sweeps. The Feud theme reappears in an exciting development, with echoes of the Friar Laurence motive in the horns, as though warning of impending disaster. The mood of strife is built up through a gradual intensification until the entire orchestra is alive and seething. A broadly sweeping passage on the strings leads us into the third section, which recapitulates the thematic material of the first with important changes. The Feud theme is heard *fortissimo,* substantially as before. Then comes the Juliet music, *dolce espressivo.* And then, following that, the Romeo theme is developed in one of those eloquent crescendos so dear to the heart of Tchaikovsky—wave upon wave of ingratiating sound, striving upward, accumulating, until the entire orchestra is surging forward in a mighty outpouring. The glow fades; stern outcroppings of the Feud theme carry us from the music of love to that which portends death. The epilogue is played at a moderate pace, marked by the somber chorale of the prologue, while arpeggios on the harp are heard above the muffled drum that beats a dirge for the dead and eternally faithful though tragically mistaken lovers. The spirit and mood of the Shakespearean play is thus told through the art of music by a great master, and prompted by the same temper as that of "The Bard," that of Romanticism.

The listener will, no doubt, be interested in comparing Tchaikovsky's ROMEO AND JULIET with Berlioz's dramatic symphony, ROMEO ET JULIETTE, for vocal soli, chorus and orchestra; with Gounod's opera of the same title, as well as with Bellini's opera on the same subject, THE CAPULETS AND THE MONTAGUES. Perhaps the persistently inquiring reader will want to pursue the same love story further as told in music by such forgotten composers as Barknorth, Dalayrac, Marchetti, Vaccai, Zandonai, Zingarelli, and the more modern and delightful operatic adaptation by Frederick Delius, A VILLAGE ROMEO AND JULIET (1900–1), which derived its story from PEOPLE OF SELDWYLA by Gottfried Keller, rather than from Shakespeare. Prokofieff composed a BALLET, Op. 64, on this theme, three Suites for Orchestra from it, and also a set of *Ten Piano Pieces,* Op. 76.

Courtesy The Metropolitan Museum of Art

ISLE OF THE DEAD — Böcklin

14 The symphonic poem: tone painting

We have just listened to an extended orchestral composition one purpose of which was to project through music the moods, emotions, and story suggested by a literary theme —the ROMEO AND JULIET OVERTURE by Tchaikovsky based on the play by Shakespeare.[1] In spite of the fact that this story served as the basis for the overture and prescribed the sequence of events to a great extent, the composer was careful to see that the musical work had a high musical value and a significant structure and organization of its own, aside from the dictates of the underlying drama; and, in several instances where the sequence of events in the story were in conflict with what the composer considered desirable musical structure, the musical signifi-

[1] Essential listening for this chapter includes: DANSE MACABRE by Saint-Saëns, NIGHT ON BALD MOUNTAIN by Mussorgsky, and the SORCERER'S APPRENTICE by Dukas—in that order. Rachmaninoff's symphonic poem, THE ISLE OF THE DEAD, may be considered as suggested supplementary listening.

cance determined the issue. Thus, certain musical themes appeared, were contrasted and developed, and reappeared within a broadly traditional musical framework; and the composer gave these themes and the process of musical development an interest and importance in themselves. One can see here the workings of the Classical as well as the Romantic tempers.[2]

The point becomes clear when we realize that in Shakespeare's play Friar Laurence appears in the middle of the play, while in the musical narrative the chorale symbolizing the Friar serves as prologue and epilogue. Similar evidences of compositional treatment exist in the *Overture* to the MIDSUMMER NIGHT'S DREAM, by Mendelssohn (Chap. 10), and in Beethoven's *Overture* to FIDELIO (Chap. 24).

There are many musicians and critics, both those who are responsible and those guilty of musical snobbery, who deprecate Romantic program music as inferior to the so-called abstract music of the Classical tempers. There has probably been as much inferior music written in the "abstract" genre as in Romantic program music—moreover, some of the greatest works in musical literature are of the programmatic type.

We now come to the most highly developed type of program music—the symphonic poem or tone poem—in which the form may be an existing one or it may be completely free, and determined to a great extent by the literary sequence of moods, poetic ideas, or underlying pictorial program. Just as the symphony represents the highest level of organization in absolute music, the symphonic poem or tone poem is the most ambitious type of program music. The symphony was perfected by the masters of late eighteenth-century Classicism. Similarly, nineteenth-century Romanticism, with its strong admixture of literary and pictorial influences, turned enthusiastically to the symphonic poem.

A symphonic poem does through music what a poem does through words: it tells a story, paints a scene, describes or projects a mood, or presents a general poetic idea in musical symbols. The time was when *symphonic poem* implied a story, and *tone poem* a scene or mood; but now the two terms have become practically interchangeable. The symphonic poem has no fixed form, this being shaped in each case by the inspiration of a particular program, with the transformation in the musical themes paralleling and reflecting changes in the poetic or literary idea. Naturally, the program in many cases clearly reveals the prevalent literary influences of the period. Thus, in the three tone poems that have been selected as an introduction to the form—Saint-Saëns' DANSE MACABRE, Mussorgsky's

[2] The listener will enjoy the six programmatic and realistic BIBLICAL SONATAS for harpsichord by Johann Kuhnau (1660–1722), based upon such Biblical stories as David and Goliath, David's Cure of Saul, Jacob's Wedding, etc. No doubt there were prior and more or less embryonic programmatic works in early Greece, the Middle East, and other countries. Consult a good music history, and "Program Music" in *International Cyclopedia of Music and Musicians.*

NIGHT ON BALD MOUNTAIN, and Paul Dukas' SORCERER'S APPRENTICE—we find in the music the same embodiment of the fantastic and the bizarre that played so prominent a part in the romantic literature of the time.

While we shall confine our immediate study of these three symphonic poems, and though future pages of this book will present additional examples of this form, it might be well to mention here a comparatively rare occurrence in music—a symphonic poem inspired by a painting.[3] This is Sergei Rachmaninoff's THE ISLE OF THE DEAD, after the painting of the same name by Arnold Böcklin (1827–1901). The symphonic work was written in Paris, in 1909, where the composer first saw the painting. Scored for a large orchestra, the work begins with a figure in the 'cellos suggestive of the quiet lapping of the water; then a softly intoned French horn theme is heard which serves well throughout the poem. A climax is reached, and the "Chant to the Dead," *Dies Irae,* comes forth from the brasses. Gradually the work calms down and a theme appears in the strings which is a development of the horn theme heard at the beginning. This theme is worked up to the real climax of the composition when the horn theme played in the beginning is loudly intoned by the brasses. Little by little the mood subsides; finally the symphonic poem closes with the material of the opening section being heard once more, and quiet reigns. (Rachmaninoff was born in Russia in 1873 and died in the United States in 1943. He is more generally known for his short piano pieces, songs, his four concerti for piano, and his four symphonies.)

CAMILLE SAINT-SAENS (1835–1921)

We pointed out earlier in this chapter that Romanticism was a middle-class art, as opposed to eighteenth-century Classicism, which was essentially aristocratic. The middle class, however, was too firmly rooted in practical affairs to float indefinitely in the mists of the supernatural and the bizarre. Thus there developed within the framework of literary Romanticism, and side by side with the emotional excesses of a Hugo, a Byron, or a Poe, a tradition of Realism which ran down the century, from Balzac and Flaubert to Dickens, George Eliot, and Thackeray, culminating at the end of the nineteenth century in the Naturalism of Zola, de Maupassant, Thomas Hardy, Ibsen, Chekhov, and the American school.

It need hardly be said that this tendency to capture all aspects of reality in literature made itself felt also in music. Liszt, Berlioz, and

[3] A more recent example of such an inspiration is Paul Hindemith's MATHIS DER MALER, originally an opera inspired by the Isenheim altarpiece by Matthias Grünewald. The music is usually heard as a symphonic suite. Max Reger also wrote a ROMANTISCHE (Böchlin) SUITE, Op. 127, after the same painting. It consists of four symphonic poems, the third being based on DIE TOTENINSEL (The Isle of the Dead). The suite is available on L.P. records.

their contemporaries of the middle of the century based their program music on highly symbolic and quite general literary or pictorial elements presented with a maximum of poetic suggestion. Throughout the last quarter of the century there was a steady movement in program music toward Realism, culminating in the 1890's in the tone poems of Richard Strauss (Chapter 19) which, substituting literalness and realistic representation for suggestion, may be considered the musical counterpart of the tendency represented by Zola. The beginnings of this tendency may already be traced in a work such as Saint-Saëns' (san-SAHN) DANSE MACABRE (Dance of Death), Op. 40, written in 1874. It combines the love of the macabre of nineteenth-century Romanticism with certain elements of satire and literalness of expression that were to dominate the program music of the end of the century. The symphonic poem of Saint-Saëns may therefore be considered as a kind of middle point between the tone-poem style of Liszt and that of Richard Strauss.

Camille Saint-Saëns is best known to the American music-loving public through the aria, *My Heart at Thy Sweet Voice* from the opera, SAMSON AND DELILAH; the ever-popular symphonic poem, DANCE MACABRE; and the *Swan* from the suite, THE CARNIVAL OF ANIMALS, which was transformed by the immortal Pavlowa into an unforgettable dance. He also wrote numerous concerti for piano, violin, and 'cello, the SYMPHONY IN C MINOR, and the brilliant violin work, INTRODUCTION AND RONDO CAPRICCIOSO. He composed at seven, gave his first piano recital at eleven, and won a prize in organ playing at the Paris Conservatoire at fourteen. His first symphony was performed when he was eighteen; at twenty-two he was appointed organist of the Madeleine, one of the most famous churches in Paris. He was thus spared much of the disappointment and bitterness that beset so many great musicians. Indeed, after the seventies, his career was an almost uninterrupted succession of triumphs. He composed ceaselessly in almost every branch of music and made brilliant concert tours as organist and pianist; his piano and violin concertos, his operas, symphonies, and tone poems were performed throughout Europe. He received the order of the Legion of Honor in 1868, was elected a member of the French Institute in 1881, and was given the honorary degree of Doctor of Music by Cambridge University in 1892. Witty, facile, and a tireless worker, he found time from his musical activity to dabble in literature, producing a volume of poetry, several farces, a number of essays on music and the theater, and, curiously enough, some papers on scientific subjects.

Saint-Saëns' music is brilliant and unerringly sure rather than emotionally moving, pleasant rather than profound. For this reason, a good part of his immense output is not bearing up well under the test of time. A very thorough craftsman and a master of orchestration, his melodies are facile, his ideas interestingly worked out. He is definitely a product of, and identified with, his period, rather than one of the chosen few who stand above all limitations of time and place. He appeared at a time when the French nation was completely apathetic to its own living composers. He devoted himself tirelessly to the cause of French music and, through the *Société Nationale de Musique,* which he helped found, fought for recognition for the young composers of the new French school. The wave of nationalism that swept France as an aftermath of the Franco-Prussian War helped bring the movement to its ultimate success. When the influence of Wagner came to dominate the musical life of the Continent, Saint-Saëns stood up for the particular qualities—clarity, measure, logical composition, poise—that his great contemporary, Anatole France, considered the essence of the Gallic spirit in art. He was, in effect, one of the most important influences in initiating and molding the modern French symphonic school. His was, however, the peculiar fate of all reformers who out-live their period: he began as a flaming radical in music, became more and more conservative as he went along, and ended completely out of sympathy with the very developments that he himself had been instrumental in getting under way. The last of the great nineteenth-century composers, he survived in a world completely alien to that which he had so ably represented; his death in 1921 at the age of eighty-six marked the end of an era.

Danse Macabre (*Dance of Death*)

Death had been a popular theme in art during the Middle Ages and the Renaissance. Holbein's famous DANCE OF DEATH shows the grim figure playing a *strohfiedel,* the medieval ancestor of the xylophone, which Saint-Saëns used so effectively in this work to imitate the rattling of skeleton bones. The Age of Classicism, of the Enlightenment, naturally discouraged the use of such obviously melodramatic themes. But when Romanticism turned for inspiration to the Middle Ages—just as Classicism had turned to antiquity—death became again a motif in art. In their reaction from the reason and light of the eighteenth century, the early Romantics swung so far toward the Gothic that an almost morbid preoccupation with horror and strangeness soon became one of the mannerisms of the movement.

DANSE MACABRE was written in 1874 and first performed the following year. Saint-Saëns originally wrote it as a song, but since the melody turned out to be somewhat hard to sing, he used it as the basis for his orchestral piece. The poem that served as his inspiration may seem rather crude and dated now. Cazlis' poem has been freely translated as follows:

> Zig, zag, zig, Death in cadence
> Striking a tomb with his heel,
> Death at midnight plays a dance-tune
> On his violin.

The winter wind blows, the night is sombre,
Moans are heard in the linden trees;
The white skeletons flit through the shadows,
Shrouded shapes moving strangely.

Zig, zag, zig, each one is frisking;
The bones of the dancers rattle . . .
But pst! suddenly the cock crows!
They quit the dance, they run, they fly.

Around this rather obvious program, the brilliantly ironic Saint-Saëns, with a kind of grim relish, constructed a composition that shocked and startled his contemporaries, although its devices have become familiar through incessant repetition. The twelve strokes of the clock sounded on the harp and the mysterious plucked strings of 'cellos and bass violins set the scene. Death tunes his fiddle, with the E string lowered out of tune; the dance opens with an appropriately cheerless theme on the flutes leading to the waltz tune proper. The xylophone imitates the clanking of skelton bones, while chill chromatic scales suggest the howling of the night wind. (*Chromatic scales* are scales that ascend or descend in half steps—that is, they include the sharps and flats. They belong to no particular key, and present twelve semitones, or half steps, within the octave. They are much used in "picture music" for storms, howling of the wind, and so forth.)

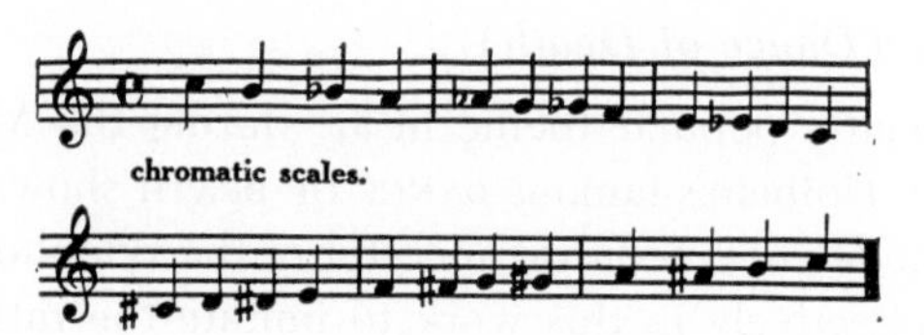

After a brief lyrical interlude in the violins, as though two spectres had met who remembered each other from happier days, the chromatic scales return, the dance grows ever faster, louder, more abandoned. Suddenly the horns announce the glimmer of dawn; the oboe imitates the crowing of the cock. Death packs his fiddle; the spectres unwillingly trudge back to their graves; the ghostly revel is over.

When DANSE MACABRE was first performed in London in 1879, the critic of the *Daily News* threw up his hands, calling it "horrible, hideous, and disgusting," and an example of the "intense and coarse realism that is entering into much of the musical composition (so-called) of the day." Saint-Saëns enjoyed the outcry; but his music aged more rapidly than either he or his critics suspected. What was so shocking to the 1870's has become fairly tame to the audiences of the twentieth century.[4]

[4] The work is one of a series—Berlioz' SYMPHONIE FANTASTIQUE, Liszt's DANCE OF DEATH and MEPHISTO WALTZ, Gounod's FAUST and Boito's MEPHISTOPHELES—in which the "diabolism" so dear to the Romantic poets and novelists found musical expression.

The two main themes out of which the composition is built offer an excellent contrast to each other. The first consists of rapid eighth notes, *staccato*, in brusque rhythmic patterns:

The second is a flowing, *legato*, waltz theme. The melody is presented with a kind of ironic warmth by all the strings in unison:

Besides the numerous variations in which the two principal themes are presented, we hear also, well on in the composition, a travesty of the *Dies Irae*, the medieval, impressive *Hymn to the Dead:* [5]

The orchestration is expertly done, making use of all the colors and contrasts of the various choirs and instrumental combinations. Notice how, when Saint-Saëns begins to build toward his climax, we hear the

---

From the horror stories of Mrs. Radcliffe to the fantastic tales of E. T. A. Hoffmann, from the ANCIENT MARINER and CHRISTABEL and KUBLA KHAN to the tales of Poe, the visions of De Quincey, and the novels of Victor Hugo, the love of the supernatural, the strange, and the picturesquely macabre constituted one of the strongest motifs in literary Romanticism.

[5] The traditional chant is as follows:

opening notes of Theme I bandied about in quick succession by trombones, horns, oboes, clarinets, and flutes, each imitating the other. As the music mounts in intensity in the final section, the brilliant voices of flute and piccolo are added to the ensemble. We hear a last fleet echo of the opening theme, and two chords plucked furtively on the strings (*pizzicato*) brings the piece to a close.

The form of DANSE MACABRE, like its orchestration, bespeaks the master craftsman. There are three sections: the first, in the nature of an introduction, includes the striking of the clock and Death tuning his violin; the second consists of the dance proper, in which the two main themes of the waltz are worked out; the third is a sort of *postlude,* or *coda,* which recalls some ideas of the first section. We shall meet this device—statement-contrast-restatement (A-B-A)—again and again in symphonic literature. The final measures remind the listener of the opening section and thus help unify the entire musical structure.

Rhythmically the music is compelling, particularly in the swaying triple meter of the waltz theme. The tempo is clear-cut. The piece begins in moderate waltz time—*mouvement modère de valse.* (Saint-Saëns used French musical indications instead of the conventional Italian.) As the dance gets under way and approaches the climax, there is a steady speeding up (*accelerando*). With the coming of dawn we return to *Tempo I,* known as *tempo primo,* or the first tempo. Thus, sections one and three are in somewhat identical tempo.

Equally simple is the dynamic design in DANSE MACABRE. The music opens *ppp* (*pianississimo*) the merest whisper; proceeds gradually to *pianissimo* and *piano.* The second theme enters *forte,* works up to *fortissimo,* and finally, at the climax, *fff* (*fortississimo*). With the return to *Tempo I,* the gradation of the opening is reversed: *p* leads to *pp,* and the music dies away *ppp.* We see here how both tempo and dynamics help to bring out the structural element and essential meaning—another instance of how the diverse elements of music supplement and complement one another in producing the total aesthetic effect.

MODEST MUSSORGSKY (1839–1881)

Modest Mussorgsky was born in Russia (Pskov) in 1839, of a family of landowners. Like many sons of the gentry he was prepared for a military career and became an officer in one of the fashionable Guards regiments. Like Tchaikovsky and Rimsky-Korsakoff, he began as a musical dilettante. Like them, too, he came under the influence of Mily Balakirev, the leader of the Russian national school. It was only then that he decided to devote himself to a musical career. He resigned his commission when he was nineteen and embarked upon a musical career rich in achievement yet darkened by the shadow of great hopes left unfulfilled. Mussorgsky aimed at naturalism in music, at uncompromising honesty as he himself felt, and at simplicity. He was profoundly interested in the nationalistic folk arts, especially folk songs. Technique as such was, for him, a species of artifice. Consequently, he never became as dextrous or as polished in musical composition as either Tchaikovsky or Rimsky-Korsakoff. On the other hand, he submitted much less than they to the traditional influences, Italian, German, and French; he stands today as one of the most indigenous of the Russian nationalist composers, his nationalism reaching its peak in his historical music drama, BORIS GODUNOFF.

Mussorgsky's life became a continual struggle against poverty and lack of appreciation on the part of the musical public of his time. He held an ill-paid government post; his personality, although most attractive and endowed with charm, was not strong enough to withstand the continual disappointments and strain to which he was subject. He sought refuge in drink and drugs, which ended by sapping his powers for sustained creative effort. He was able to finish small pieces—the wonderful songs, and the piano compositions of which the best known is the suite of sketches, PICTURES AT AN EXHIBITION. But most of his large works, operatic and orchestral, were either abandoned midway or left unfinished at his death. The manuscripts that he left were completed by his musical friends, chief among them Rimsky-Korsakoff. These include the comic opera THE FAIR AT SOROTCHINSK, the opera KHOVANTCHINA, the orchestral fantasy NIGHT ON BALD MOUNTAIN, and BORIS GODUNOFF, the historical opera.

Night on Bald Mountain

In 1860, when he was twenty-one, Mussorgsky wrote to Balakirev of "a most interesting work" he had been commissioned to do: music for the first act of THE BALD MOUNTAIN, to be based on Megden's drama, THE WITCH. It was to describe a gathering of the witches as they practiced some of their mysterious rites, a pageant of sorcerers, and in the finale, a dance in tribute to Satan. Mussorgsky was hopeful about the composition: he considered the libretto unusually good and announced that he had already conceived some of its themes.

As in the case of Tchaikovsky's ROMEO AND JULIET, Balakirev does not seem to have shared his protege's enthusiasm. Two years later Mussorgsky wrote to his mentor concerning the work that he was not to be shaken in his belief that his music was entirely satisfactory. He felt that the music was a genuine expression of the story it conveyed, "without tricks or pretensions." He remained adamant in his determination not to alter the plan or its development, but consented to change the percussion, which he admitted he had misused. He rewrote the fantasy in 1867, and intended on two occasions to introduce it into a dramatic work: once into a fairy opera MLADA of which he, Rimsky-Korsakoff, Alexander Borodin, and César Cui were each to write portions, and in which the symphonic poem was to serve as background for a fantastic scene, "The Sacrifice to the Black Goat on Bald Mountain." The scheme fell through because of financial reasons, and again in 1877, when he intended to introduce it as an interlude in his unfinished opera THE FAIR AT SOROTCHINSK.

The score was revised by Rimsky-Korsakoff, after Mussorgsky's death, and received its first performance in 1886 when Rimsky-Korsakoff conducted it with great success. It was the first work that earned for the composer the popular acclaim that had been denied him during his lifetime. Rimsky-Korsakoff appended Mussorgsky's program note to the score:

> Subterranean sounds of supernatural voices. Appearance of the spirits of darkness, followed by that of Satan himself. Glorification of Satan and celebration of the Black Mass. The Sabbath Revels. At the height of the orgies the bell of the village church, sounding in the distance, disperses the spirits of darkness. Daybreak.

The tone poem opens *allegro feroce* (fast and fierce), with a turbulent figure in the strings against which trombones, tuba, and bassoons thunder the Satanic theme:

The dance that ushers in the "glorification of Satan" is saturated with the Russian folk idiom and appears in strongly marked rhythms in the oboes and clarinets, presenting an effective contrast to the opening theme:

After the movement has somewhat slackened, the *allegro feroce* of the opening returns, the brass weaving its theme against rapid chromatic passages in wood-winds and strings. A new dance theme appears, at first in fairly slow tempo, but gradually working up to a frenzied climax.

At the height of the festivities the bell tolls mournfully six times. Strings and harp tranquilly announce the coming of dawn in a coda suffused with poetic feeling.

The music has verve and gusto, permeated by a supernatural aspect. Like the ROMEO AND JULIET OVERTURE, it is the work of a young and ardent imagination, projected with such sincerity of feeling and richness of fantasy that it needs no further intermediary between the composer and his listener.

PAUL DUKAS (1865–1935)

THE SORCERER'S APPRENTICE was written in 1897, almost a quarter century after DANSE MACABRE, in what has come to be generally known as the post-Romantic period. This was the transitional period from the nineteenth century to our own, when the great European Romantic traditions had begun to give way to a *fin de siècle* spirit—the "Mauve Decade," as Beer aptly called it, the period of Oscar Wilde and the *Yellow Book,* of Whistler, and Aubrey Beardsley. The rich emotionalism of the ROMEO AND JULIET OVERTURE, the demonic imaginativeness of A NIGHT ON BALD MOUNTAIN or DANSE MACABRE were retreating before the sophistication and the objectivity that characterized the then rising art-styles. This realistic and representational atmosphere made possible the Straussian tone poems. Gallic logic, and reason in full command of emotions, were the signs then appearing over the cultural horizon of Europe. From a purely technical standpoint, the experiments of Berlioz, Liszt, and Wagner had opened for their followers a new world of dazzling color effects in the orchestra and in daring compositional techniques of all kinds. It was out of this combination of influences that a number of exciting orchestral works, of which Dukas' joyous orchestral scherzo is typical, came into being.

Paul Dukas (dü-KĂHS) was one of the most distinguished French composers of his time. Born in Paris in 1865, he entered the Conservatoire at the age of seventeen and soon displayed a talent for composition. His first symphony was performed in 1896. The following year, when he was thirty-two, he wrote L'APPRENTI SORCIER (The Sorcerer's Apprentice), which has remained, with LA PERI, the most popular of his works. His operatic setting of Maeterlinck's ARIANE AND BLUEBEARD also won much acclaim. He was not only a versatile musician but also won distinction as teacher, editor, musical critic, and essayist. He was a member of the Legion of Honor, professor of orchestration at the Conservatoire, and holder of an official post in the ministry of fine arts.

The Sorcerer's Apprentice

The program upon which Dukas based his composition concerns the sorcerer's apprentice who could start a magic spell but could not stop it.

The theme had been popular for centuries—*The Golem* and *Frankenstein* are two famous variants—and may be traced to the Greek satirist Lucian. In Goethe's version the young apprentice has repeatedly watched his master utter a charm over a broomstick, whereupon the stick sprouted hands and feet and carried out the magician's bidding. One day, after his master goes out, the apprentice utters the charm and orders the broom-

Courtesy Walt Disney Productions

MICKEY MOUSE AS THE SORCERER'S APPRENTICE From "Fantasia"

stick to fetch water for his bath. When he tries to stop the stick, he realizes to his horror that he has forgotten the formula for removing the spell. The stick continues to haul the water; the apprentice falls into panic. He seizes an axe and splits the stick in half, whereupon two sticks proceed to fetch water. Just as the mounting flood threatens to engulf the luckless boy, the sorcerer returns, pronounces the formula, and with a brusque command sends the broom back to its corner. The apprentice has learned his lesson.

The introduction is in a *lento movement* (*lento* means slow, like *adagio*). The atmosphere of enchantment is established at the outset by the violas and 'cellos playing *harmonics.* These, the reader will recall, are the flutelike tones in the very highest register produced by touching the finger lightly to the string at certain points, causing it to vibrate in small segments, to produce an effect of delicacy and charm.

The theme of the magic spell is chanted *piano* by the muted violins, a plaintive melody in high register descending gradually in a series of little leaps:

The wood-winds and brass answer brilliantly with the choppy, *staccato* theme of the broom.

Notice the interesting contrast between the two themes out of which the composition is woven: the first in high register, languidly *legato*, played by the strings; the second in low register, brusque and *staccato*, given to wood-winds and brass.

Presently the apprentice utters the fatal formula. There is an ominous silence. Then the uncanny business begins, *allegro* and *piano*, with three bassoons and a contrabassoon keeping up a curiously hopping rhythm.

The music works steadily into a mood of feverish activity. The theme of the magic formula returns fleetingly, now plaintive, now with gleeful malice; the "broom" theme is tossed about among clarinets, bassoons, horns, and trumpets, while the rest of the orchestra weaves a shimmering background of chromatic scales. The mounting consternation of the would-be wizard is portrayed with brilliant drollery; horns and trumpets *fortissimo* blare out his frantic cries for help. The movement climbs steadily to the point where he splits the broom in two. There is a breathless pause—and then the cursed activity begins anew with bassoons and contrabassoon as at the beginning. The movement mounts in a steady *crescendo* to the final climax: the Sorcerer, announced by thunderous blasts in the brass, returns and puts an end to the spell. We hear again the magical chords of the introduction as the apprentice comes to, a sadder and wiser man. A final blast of the orchestra sends the broom back to its corner.

The work reveals Dukas as a composer of brilliant imagination and wit, a master of orchestration and color. From the moment when the broomstick begins its activity there is a rhythmic pulsation that sweeps the listener along with relentless energy. The meter, as the signature indicates, is $\frac{9}{8}$, a compound of triple meter; the student will have no difficulty in feeling the triple beat as soon as the movement gets under way. In general, the composition is more sophisticated and modern than DANSE MACABRE. The melodic line is jagged and brusque, the harmonies rich and complicated, the orchestration remarkably varied.

Dukas called his piece an "Orchestral Scherzo." Like Mendelssohn's "Scherzo" from the MIDSUMMER NIGHT'S DREAM music, Dukas' piece is strongly rhythmic; but where Mendelssohn's "Scherzo" is delicate and elfin, Dukas' is gaily boisterous. The structure is simple. There is the unifying prelude-postlude formation that we noticed in DANSE MACABRE in the Magic Spell theme. The movement itself falls into two parts: from the point where the broom begins until the moment when the apprentice splits it in two, and from then on until the return of the sorcerer. The dynamic scheme fits this structure: prelude and postlude generally *pianissimo* (interspered with outburst of furious energy when the broom theme is introduced); while in the two halves of the work itself there is a steady *crescendo* from the *pianissimo* of the three bassoons to the full orchestral outburst at each climax. The tempo outline fits this scheme. The introduction is *lento,* the action proper *allegro* with a steady *accelerando* to the climax, and the postlude is marked *Tempo I,* the same as the introduction. (Form and nuances resemble the *Bogenform.*)

The composition is largely built on the "broom" theme. The contrasting material includes the enchantment theme and a playful subsidiary theme that flits through the body of the work. But Dukas has relied for the necessary variety not so much on diverse thematic material as on the richness of his orchestral palette. Thematically, this piece is much less diversified than some of the others we have listened to; yet because of the brilliant handling of the orchestra, it sustains the interest of the listener throughout. Notice that Dukas, like Mussorgsky and Saint-Saëns, has used chromatic scales throughout the work to create a feeling of agitation and climax. It is evident that the chromatic-scale passage was a staple device in nineteenth-century program music. We shall encounter it again and again in symphonic climaxes.

(See also discussions about LA MER, a symphonic poem or suite, by Claude Debussy; also the same composer's AFTERNOON OF A FAUN; Ravel's DAPHNIS AND CHLOÉ; Respighi's FOUNTAINS OF ROME, and other works mentioned in Additional Suggestions for Listening—all in Chapter 29. Some of these works might well be studied in the present chapter if time permits. In fact, the careful reader will discover symphonic poems distributed throughout succeeding pages of this book. These directions are given in lieu of the usual end-of-the-chapter listings.)

Courtesy The Metropolitan Museum of Art

15 Music in national cultures

When one devotedly and religiously loves his home, his town, his country at large, there is unconsciously created in him a deep, all-pervading sense of loyalty and pride, a feeling of "oneness" with his land.

Constructively beneficent patriotism and benevolent nationalism are born and nurtured in such a milieu, and these loyalties transcend all artificial boundaries. There have thus arisen, along with the more tangible and material values, the many cultures of man, the artistic expressions of his ideals, devotions, and spiritual values. These irrepressible manifestations in countless romantic and traditional forms are included in what we call the Fine Arts and the minor arts. Nationalism in music may be basically defined as *the natural stylistic characteristics and essential spirit inherent in the use of compositional elements identified with the musical self-expression of a people or a nation.*

It is not inconsistent, however, to find in democratic

nations large social or religious groups of nationalities different from the majority, who continue to express their original native arts and cultures (such as the cities of Montreal and Quebec, in Canada). At the same time, these groups bear unquestioned loyalty to their adopted country, and adopt many of its cultural and artistic expressions.

These characteristics are most apt to be evident in those settlements of foreign origin that are fairly large, kept reasonably intact, and more-or-less self-sufficient in a linguistic, religious, or cultural sense, such as one finds in metropolitan cities. Certainly this is markedly true of those peoples who are somewhat physically isolated, such as the Basques in France and Spain, or the peoples of the Appalachian Mountains and certain regions along the seacoast of the southeastern states. (Some have preserved their original cultures for hundreds of years even more "undefiled" than have their native lands.) (See Chapter 5.) Of course younger generations, with more contacts with the outside world tend to shed their inherited customs and to adopt more general observances.

Similarly, the native idioms of our foreign-born citizens have been influenced by surrounding cultures, although certain native idioms of expression of these people have persisted, as anyone can see by motoring through parts of Pennsylvania, Louisiana, Arizona, or southern California. There is a persistent tendency, for good or ill, to level these divergent idioms to a lowest common denominator, and to amalgamate them into a fairly common, quasi-nationalistic expression of art. Of course, there are passing artistic fads that one should be careful not to interpret as permanent trends or true national idioms. Sometimes this is very difficult to discern at the time. It is probable that the catalyst most affecting this process of unification towards the ultimate realization of a nationalistic artistic expression in music is dual: (a) the tendency for uniformity engendered through the prevailing practices of music education in our nation-wide public schools; and (b) like it or not, the influence of the *essential spirit*—as opposed to the ephemeral mannerisms—of what may be generically called "jazz"! However, there are dangers in the extent and degree to which this artistic leveling takes place. Pure abstract art of all kinds, for instance, is antagonistic to nationalism.[1] However, Nationalism in the fine arts will cease to be only when man, his living conditions, his language, his heritage and ideals are reduced through force to a common manner of expression—which is the same as saying, "It will never happen!" The really great creators of music and the other arts have succeeded in being *nationalistic* and *individual* in their idioms, and *universal* in their appeal and acceptance. This is by no means a paradox; it is a great and oft *demonstrated truth*.

[1] This statement includes the "twelve-tone," "pan-tonal," "Schönbergian Row," and similar "systems" of musical techniques used as the basis of music.

Study and experience with the arts themselves is necessary to appreciate and evaluate the foregoing observations. This chapter is designed to aid in such a study. Let us first take a look at the conditions that cradled the so-called Romantic Period in Western Europe, roughly between the last half of the eighteenth and all of the nineteenth century, with several overlapping decades of the twentieth century.

Nationalism and Romantic tempers in the "Romantic period"

In literature, painting, and music we have the rise of strongly nationalist schools, embodying the Romantic tempers, out of which emerged some of the most memorable work of the period. The legends of the national hero furnished inspiration to such dissimilar works as the Arthurian poems of Tennyson, the historical novels of Walter Scott, the Finnish epic KALEVALA, used by Sibelius, the poetry of Pushkin in Russia, of Robert Burns in Scotland, of Mieczkewitz in Poland. David, in his epic canvases, aimed to perpetuate the glory of Napoleon; Constable and Turner celebrated the English landscape; the Barbizon painters did the same for France. National folklore inspired the FREISCHÜTZ of Weber, the fairy tales of Grimm, Andrew Lang, and Hans Christian Andersen. At a time when music was turning more and more to picturesque effects, to color and atmosphere, the folk tunes and dances of the various racial stocks became an inexhaustible treasure-house upon which composers could draw. Idiomatic melodies and characteristic rhythms united with the powerful emotional associations evoked by a patriotic program to open up a rich new field to music. Grieg became the musical voice of Norway; Tchaikovsky, Rimsky-Korsakoff, and Mussorgsky, of Russia; Weber and Wagner of Germany; Liszt, of Hungary; Chopin, of Poland; Dvořák and Smetana, of Bohemia; Villa-Lobos, of Brazil; Chavez, of Mexico; Bartók, of Hungary; Albeniz, of Spain; Elgar, of England; MacDowell, of our own country; Debussy and Ravel, of France; Sibelius, of Finland, and so on.

A composer could use his gifts to glorify the national heritage in various ways. He could utilize folk-song and folk-dance idioms of his people, as Dvořák did in the *Slavonic Dances,* Chopin in the *Polonaises* and *Mazurkas,* Liszt in the *Hungarian Rhapsodies.* He could weave his folk-like music around the life of a national hero or king, national myths, traditions and beliefs, as Wagner did in the music dramas based on the life of Siegfried, or Mussorgsky in his BORIS GODUNOFF. He could glorify the scenic beauties, the rivers and forests of his native land, as Johann Strauss did in his *Blue Danube* and *Tales from the Vienna Woods,* Smetana in THE MOLDAU, Respighi in THE PINES OF ROME, and our own Stephen Foster in *Swanee River* and *My Old Kentucky Home.* He could use an historic event that had great emotional significance to his countrymen, as Tchaikovsky did in the OVERTURE 1812. Or he could set his music to the work of a native writer, as Grieg did with Ibsen's PEER GYNT, Debussy with the poetry of Verlaine, Tchaikovsky with the dramas of Pushkin. Most nationalist composers used several of these methods to communicate to their audiences the essence of the spirit of their country.

Courtesy The Owner, Mrs. C. M. Gooch, Memphis, Tenn.

MIDNIGHT RIDE OF PAUL REVERE Grant Wood

Clarity and cleverness of design and composition; nationalistic realism with romanticism and some sentimentality; stylized mannerisms carried to a high degree of perfection; excellent brush technique; superb use of color; and clever programmatic storytelling all mark this as an exemplary painting by one of the foremost of contemporary American artists engrossed in the depiction of the local and national scenes. Paul Revere's ride is vivid and exciting.

As the century wore on, the struggle for freedom on the part of the oppressed nations became ever more bitter. Music, because of its intensely emotional appeal, became a weapon of first importance. Auber's MASANIELLO, with its stirring choruses in praise of liberty, became the rallying cry of an awakening Italy against the Austrian yoke. Later, when the operas of Verdi became popular, the frenzied shouts of "Viva Verdi" that greeted his works took on the nature of a political demonstration against the Austrians: the letters of Verdi's name happened to

Sultan announced *fortissimo* by most of the orchestra and pitched in a low register:

After some mysterious chords and a pause, a solo violin soars high above the *arpeggios* of the harp, *lento* and *espressivo* (slow and expressive)—the tender Oriental theme of the Sultana.

The introduction over, we are ready for the wonderful sea voyage. The entire movement is built out of two melodic figures, of which the first is repeated over and over but with ever-changing colors—now the reediness of the oboe fused with the warmer tints of the viola; now the distant fogginess of horns pitted against the shimmering clarinets and violins; and now the entire orchestra rising in a surge of storm and thunder while the gentle roll of the accompaniment persists throughout, weaving its hypnotic spell over the listener and painting in tones a magnificent picture of the sea. Above all, Rimsky-Korsakoff succeeded in capturing the wonder and unreality of the fairy tale, the feeling of "a painted ship upon a painted ocean." There never was such a ship, there never was such a sea—save in the dreams of poets, whether of words, or pigments, or tones.

The introduction is marked *largo e maestoso* (broad and majestic), the movement proper is *allegro non troppo* (not too fast), and is in six-four time, a fine example of the use of sextuple meter to achieve a sense of spaciousness and a gently rolling effect. The Ship theme is in reality the Sultan theme shifted into six-four time and provided with a rolling accompaniment, as though the Sultan listening to the tale were in fancy projecting himself onto Sinbad's ship:

It is a regular four-measure phrase, *legato,* noteworthy for the trill in the third measure. The two *staccato* notes in the last measure are repeated *pizzicato,* like an afterthought, by the rest of the orchestra, making a fifth measure—a charmingly irregular formation.

This theme, worked up in a *crescendo poco a poco* (gradually louder), alternates with the Calm-of-the-Sea theme, one of Rimsky-Korsakoff's happiest inspirations—a series of chords played by clarinets and bassoon, later by flutes and clarinet:

Notice that the phrase consists of a two-measure motive repeated an octave higher. Notice also the contrast between these two themes—the Ship theme in low register with irregular rhythm formations, the Calm theme ascending to the upper register in a perfectly regular rhythm. Such contrasts are most valuable in securing variety and balance. Equally noteworthy is the contrast between the two themes of the introduction: the Sultan theme in low register announced by full orchestra, grim and brusque, in a regular four-measure phrase of which the last two notes are repeated; the Sultana theme in high register played by solo violin in a highly ornamented arabesque, a cadenza-like passage that in its freedom of form and rhythm suggests an improvisation—a call for inspiration.

The movement as a whole is free in form. Unity is achieved through the constant reiteration of the Ship theme, a reiteration that assists materially in projecting the mood of the Oriental storyteller. Variety is achieved mainly through the wonderful interplay of the different instrumental colors. Now an oboe solo plays a countermelody to the Ship theme echoed by a clarinet, now the solo violin interposes with the Narrator (Scheherezade) theme, acting as a unifying thread to the movement. Now the Calm-of-the-Sea theme is given over to the violins, while clarinet and flute descend in broadly curving countermelody. The Ship theme is finally built up on a surging *crescendo* to a *fortissimo* climax, after which the whole movement is repeated with interesting changes in instrumentation and dies away *tranquillo* (tranquilly), *dolce* (sweetly), and *pianissimo.*

As for the other elements—the lyrical melodic line, the sensuous harmonies, the subtle modulations from one key to the next, the steady beat of the sextuple meter, and the brilliant interplay of instrumental timbres, all fuse in one composite and unified effect. The dynamic scheme is fairly simple: *forte* (Sultan) and *piano* (Sultana) in the introduction; thereafter a *piano* built up to a *fortissimo,* repeated, and dying away in a gentle *diminuendo.* Notice particularly the satisfying effect of the prolonged final cadence.

II. *The Tale of the Prince Kalender.* The second movement recounts the tale of the Prince Kalender. The Kalenders were a Persian sect of wandering beggar-dervishes. There are three who figure in the story of "The Porter and the Three Ladies of Bagdad," all by a coincidence disguised as princes. Rimsky-Korsakoff was careful not to specify which one he had in mind; nor, truth to tell, does it matter much. A whimsical folk tune on the bassoon hits off perfectly the happy-go-lucky quality of the wandering beggar. The melody is repeated, each time a little faster, as the Kalender gets off on his adventure. He plods along amiably until—has he come to one of those enchanted castles in which doors open mysteriously, luring the unwary wanderer from one room to the next? Perhaps he succumbs to temptation and slips an emerald into his pocket, or—worse still—catches a glimpse of something he should not have seen. Abruptly the mood changes: a trumpet call sounds closer; the violins shudder ominously; a grim march emerges. We do not know what sentence is decreed for the luckless beggar, but that it is one of those terrible punishments that abound in the ARABIAN NIGHTS there can be no doubt. But now we hear again the happy-go-lucky theme of the opening as he picks himself up and continues on his way.

The movement is introduced by the unifying Scheherezade theme on the solo violin, *lento* and *espressivo,* developed into a more elaborate cadenza than at the opening as though, having survived for the first night, the Sultana had greater confidence in her storytelling powers. Actually, Rimsky-Korsakoff is here following one of the fundamental laws of musical aesthetics: when a theme is frequently repeated, it should be varied or elaborated now and then to sustain interest.

After the introduction, the movement proper is *andantino* (somewhat slowly; faster than *andante*) and *capricioso* (capriciously). The bassoon announces the whimsical theme of the Kalender Prince, which opens with a grace note. (This term indicates a note of little value used before a note of measured value; thus an ornament or "grace" note.) The Kalender Prince theme contains grace notes in the second and third measures as well, providing a wonderful balance within the phrase—and simulating one of the characteristics of oriental music. The bassoon was a happy choice for this part.

The melody is marked *dolce ed espressivo* (sweet and expressively) is in $\frac{3}{8}$ meter, and in a plaintive minor mode.

The phrase is irregular, consisting of five measures. Notice the cadence effect obtained through the long note in the last measure. Throughout the movement Rimsky-Korsakoff eschews the regular four-measure structure. This irregularity, like the grace notes, contributes to the whimsical quality of the tale.

The theme is repeated several times in succession, each time in a higher register and *piu animato* (a little more animated) by the oboe, strings, and wood-winds. This continuous *accelerando* and climb in pitch is a wonderful buildup to the eventful middle section. The ominous trumpet call announced by trombones and tuba is echoed by muted trumpets. Notice the effective way in which the various brass instruments imitate each other. Tremolos on first and second violins complete the atmosphere of suspense. (A *tremolo,* the reader may recall, is a repetition of a note on a string instrument produced by moving the bow back and forth in a very rapid manner, thus creating a shuddering, scintillating, or agitated sound.)

The tempo changes to *allegro molto* (very fast). Just before the entire orchestra leaps into action, we hear the unifying theme of the Narrator spun out into an elaborate cadenza on the clarinet, as if the wily Sultana were tantalizing her audience before getting to the nub of the story. The grim march is played by full orchestra in a clear-cut quadruple meter. A somewhat sorrowful cadenza on the bassoon, derived from material of the Kalender theme, leads us back to the reappearance of the first theme where the luckless dervish proceeds on his journey.

The structure is a clear-cut basic ternary, or ABA, with the first and third sections balancing each other. The movement is unified within by the repetitions of the Kalender theme and united to the first movement by the reappearance of the Sultana theme. The clarion call and march of the middle section offer an effective contrast to the Kalender theme; particularly noteworthy is the use of special effects—*tremolo, harmonics,* and *pizzicato*—in the middle part.

The melodic line of the first section is notable for its plaintive, folk-tale flavor. In the middle section, by contrast, the melodies are brusque and vigorous. The harmonies support this contrast: in the first part, restful; in the middle section, pungent harmonic effects, abrupt contrasts, a sense of activity and suspense. The rhythmic pattern, too, contributes its part: in the opening, a flowing triple meter, gracefully nonchalant; in the middle, brusque irregular rhythms, frequent changes in tempo and meter, action and excitement. Timbre is used in the same way: in the beginning, mild strings and wood-wind colors blending imperceptibly; in the middle, the sharp colors of the brasses pitted against each other, shrill harmonics, and full tonal masses in the march. We see, therefore, that all four elements—melody, harmony, rhythm, and timbre—combine to bolster the structural contrast of the A-B-A form.

III. *The Young Prince and the Young Princess.* Again the composer has left no clue as to which prince and princess he had in mind; but there can be no doubt that they were young and beautiful and very much in love. We encounter here nothing of the narrative style that abounded in the Kalender movement. This is a mood of romantic sentiment with all the proper accoutrements. First, the young prince serenades his beloved in a lyrical melody. Then, the princess dances for her love to the muffled beat of the tambourine; and then we hear again the serenade of the prince.

First and second violins announce the melody of the Prince's serenade in a flowing sextuple meter, *piano:*

Here Rimsky-Korsakoff returns to the regular four-bar structure. Notice the longer notes that create the pause at the cadence. The tempo is *andantino quasi allegretto* (a subtle tempo somewhere between *andantino* and *allegretto*). When the theme is repeated, flutes and clarinets swoop up and down in broadly curving arabesques—, as if the eyebrows were opened wide in pleasant surprise!

The graceful dance of the princess, which begins *ppp grazioso* (gracefully) with a clarinet solo, is a regular two-phrase period (symmetry of structure is essential in a dance tune) accompanied throughout by the muffled beat of the tambourine:

After the symmetrical periods of the dance we return to the love song, *dolce ed cantabile* (sweet and in singing style). As it gets under way, the unifying Narrator theme (Scheherezade) breaks in *lento* and *espressivo* in the familiar violin solo with harp accompaniment, but this time still more elaborate than before. This continual adding of ornament to each repetition of the theme is in line with the aesthetic principle pointed out a few pages back and serves to keep the theme always fresh and interesting. Besides, it is a good trick of simulating native oriental music.

The cadenza is cleverly transformed into an accompaniment for the serenade of the prince. The flutes and clarinets now combine in languorous runs as the movement draws to a close. There is a last outburst of romantic fervor; then the music floats up in a delicate final cadence. This is the lyrical movement of the suite. The basic structure is a simple A-B-A; the $\frac{6}{8}$ meter makes for a broad flowing movement. The melody is smooth and gentle; the harmonies are consonant. Incidentally, notice the balance of movements: the first, pictorial; the second, an exciting narrative; the third, lyrical; and the fourth, the brilliant, vivacious, event-packed narrative of the Sultana.

IV. *Festival at Bagdad—The Sea—The Ship is Sunk on a Rock Surmounted by a Statue of a Bronze Warrior—Conclusion.* The final movement is a lively, colorful and exciting one, marked *Allegro molto e frenetico* (very lively and frenzied) and the dynamics *fortissimo* (*ff*, very loud), all of which portends a most exhilarating festival at Bagdad. The opening is a vivacious dance based upon a cleverly conceived variation of the Sultan theme, in which the wood-winds and stringed instruments of the orchestra (except the double basses) trill on the principal tones of the theme—simulating the playing of oriental instruments. The brasses and percussion instruments, (triangle, tamburo—a side drum—tambourine, and cymbals,) do their best to intensify the excitement of the passage; suddenly this comes to stop (a complete silence of the entire orchestra, for a full measure, which is known as a *pausa generale*, or grand pause, usually indicated in the score by a *fermata*, a hold.) This is followed by a very tricky triple and quadruple stopped cadenza for the solo violin and signifying the Narrator, or Sultana, theme—and, consequently, that another fantastic tale ensues. Then follows the dance proper, after an eight measure rhythmic introduction. This dance is a very fast one marked *Vivo*, the opening of which is played by the two flutes in unison (*a due*, *a*2), supported by rhythmic effects in the strings: and the rhythm is quite a complicated one, as will be observed in the musical excerpt below. Basically, the feeling is a vigorous, simple duple rhythm, and the phrases are in elementary four-measure dance phrases. However, see how the composer transforms these elemental means into a fascinating oriental dance which is anything but commonplace! Here is the theme of the dance at the onset of the fourth movement proper:

This dance takes on the general character of a *tarantella* as the strings take up the theme—and it is not difficult to conjure up the festive splendor in Bagdad at the time of Haroun-al-Raschid in the ARABIAN NIGHTS. Themes from previous movements of the work, such as those of the Sultan, the Kalender Prince, and the Young Princess, appear within the web of sound and as suddenly disappear in a sort of kaleidoscopic *montage,* or *collage*—a technique often used in contemporary paintings and the cinema. The music rushes on with insistence, developing the material of the movement and introducing the pertinent ideas of the moment. Suddenly, the listener is transported back to the ill-fated vessel of Sinbad. The ship draws closer to the "rock" during a violent storm, the waves rise higher and higher, the wind shrieks and howls, blowing the ship nearer to its destination. During the building of this climax, the Sultan theme from the first movement is thundered out by the trombones, the Young Princess theme from the second movement is blared out by the trumpets, clarinets, and 'cellos. (Note how the wave movements are depicted in the strings and harp when the trombones play the Sultan theme —as though the bronze warrior were not only pronouncing the doom of the ship, but also proclaiming its retribution. Also note the chromatic passages in the wood-winds when the trumpets and horns play the Sultan theme. How cleverly Rimsky-Korsakoff uses instrumental timbres and combinations of them, in addition to thematic material, for emotional and programmatical purposes!) The clarinets and trumpets loudly proclaim a variant of the Sultan's theme, over one bassoon, the 'cellos and basses, the loud pounding of the tympany, and the crashing of the cymbals. The tempo slows up after another "crash chord" in the brass, clarinets, one bassoon, and the low strings, indicating that the ship has struck the Rock and is sinking beneath the waves. The music tapers off in volume to a very soft degree (*pp*). The sea has become calm and the mysterious, rising wood-wind chords (Calm-of-the-Sea theme), previously heard near the beginning of the first movement, are most appropriately introduced at this time. The chordal figure rises higher and higher until the Sultana idea is played by the solo violin with sparse harp chords, terminating in very high harmonics on the E-string. The Sultan theme, now much less fierce and threatening than before, is played by the violins, with the "wave" figure reappearing, and the soft wood-winds sound the Calm-of-the-Sea theme with a background of soft horns (*pp*), a couple of rolled chords on the harp, a timpani roll *pianississimo* (*ppp*), *pizzicati* (plucked) strings and the solo violin soaring to a very high, sustained harmonic tone (E^4), bringing this masterly work to a musically satisfactory close. Programmatically, the lovely and fascinating Sultana has won her life and the Sultan's love! The climax of this last movement is one of the most masterfully contrived in orchestral literature and vies with those of Wagner's *Liebestod* from TRISTAN AND ISOLDE, Tchaikovsky's third movement of the SIXTH SYMPHONY, the "Pathetique," the *Finale* of Brahms' SYMPHONY NO. 1, and many others.

Throughout the nineteenth century, composers were concerned with attaining unity not only within the separate movements of their longer works but also between the movements. They began more and more to introduce in one movement themes and ideas already heard in a previous one, thus knitting their movements together more closely in a cycle. This type of compositional technique is known as *cyclical* and has become very popular with composers.[4] Thus far Rimsky-Korsakoff has unified his movements by the Narrator, or Scheherezade, theme running like a thread through all of them. In the final movement he further strengthens the bond by bringing back the themes of the Sultan, the Kalender Prince, and the young Princess. We have here an excellent example of the achievement of continuity in program music through the use of the cyclical structure and musical themes attached to definite characters.

[4] We pointed out in our discussion of form that the repetition of a theme solves the composer's problem of achieving unity in his work. As compositions grow more and more extended, there are likely to be quite a number of restatements of the original theme. To ward off the ever-present danger of monotony, composers have developed a fairly elaborate technique of varying their themes, thus achieving a kind of variety even within the unifying element. Episodical (new) material may be interlarded.

A theme may be varied, as in Tchaikovsky's NUTCRACKER SUITE, by changes in the orchestration. The rhythm may be changed: an example is the free, cadenzalike Scheherezade theme that is shifted into a sextuple meter when it reappears in the course of the first movement. The chords in the accompaniment may be different, as was the case when the Kalender Prince theme reappeared after the middle section. The melody itself may be elaborated or ornamented, as we saw in each reappearance of the Scheherezade theme. To sum up: the composer may keep the same melody with different timbre, rhythm, or harmony; or he may vary the melody itself; or he may use several of these changes in every possible combination.

ADDITIONAL SUGGESTIONS FOR LISTENING

From the works in the opening paragraph of this chapter, it will be easy and enjoyable for the listener to extend his listening according to his own wishes. Be sure to list the CAUCASIAN SKETCHES by Ippolitov-Ivanov. Remember to include some worthy moderns.

We might also suggest a few additional American Works employing orientalism, unfortunately not all available on commercial recordings: *Impressions of Chinatown* for piano, and several *Oriental Songs* by Leo Ornstein; STREETS OF PEKIN, and ORIENTAL SUITE (both for orchestra) by Henry Hadley; ORIENTAL IMPRESSIONS, CHINESE LEGEND BALLET, and BURMA by Henry Eichham, all for orchestra; *Bedouin Song* (for men's voices), *In the Gateway of Ispahan* (for women's voices), SUITE: OMAR KHAYYAM (for piano, and arr. also for horns and orchestra) by Arthur Foote; SUMIDIGAWAH (a chamber Japanese opera) by Horace E. Tureman; a four-act Chinese opera, LIFE IS BUT A DREAM by Charles M. Loeffler; *Songs of India* (voice), *Moroccan Mosaics, Egyptian Scenes, Himalayan Idyls* (piano) by Lily Strickland—and the list might be greatly extended by the listener.

Courtesy the Art Institute, Chicago

AMERICAN GOTHIC Grant Wood

Gothic is used here in a symbolic and typographical sense—a square cut, solid, and unadorned style. Observe the severity of mood, the austere facial expressions, and stiff attitudes of the couple. The artist employs the Romantic, Realistic, and Nationalistic tempers; but this picture also shows Classical tempers. This last may be observed in the working out of the three pronged pitchfork motive in the man's shirt stripes, overall bib, etc. These might be compared with the use of a musical "motto" or "idée fixe" in Beethoven's Fifth, *Liszt's* Les Preludes, *etc.*

17 Franz Liszt and the symphonic poem

Perhaps no single composer personifies so well the prevailing spirit, moods, and trends of the mid-nineteenth-century German Romanticism as does the colorful, controversial and ofttimes theatrical composer and piano virtuoso, Franz Liszt. He was born when the "new" trends had just got under way, and his career stretched clear across the century, almost until the nineties, by which time the "movement" had blended itself into newer modes of expression. For over half a century, his star shone with extraordinary brilliance over musical Europe and thence to the entire Western world as a composer, conductor, pianist, teacher, and benevolent friend of deserving "up-and-coming" musicians such as Wagner, Brahms, Schumann, Berlioz, Raff, MacDowell, Grieg and others. The effects of Liszt's genius and accomplishments have spanned the past century into our own time, and bid fair to remain as a fixed star of inspiration for the future.

FRANZ LISZT (1811-1886)

Franz Liszt was born in Hungary on October 22, 1811, the son of a steward on the estate of Prince Esterhazy. His father gave him his first lessons in piano playing. At the age of nine he performed in public with such success that some Hungarian noblemen granted him a subsidy. The great master Czerny was Liszt's piano teacher. At eleven he played in Vienna where Beethoven recognized his genius publicly; at twelve, in Paris where, ironically enough, the Conservatoire refused to admit the boy who was to become the greatest pianist of the age on the ground that he was a foreigner. Throughout the first phase of his career he made Paris his home and became the fashionable virtuoso. Here he drew close to the literary leaders of the French Romanticism—Victor Hugo, Lamartine, George Sand, Alfred de Musset—who exercised considerable influence on his artistic development. In 1834 he met the novelist Countess d'Agoult, known in the literary world as Daniel Stern. One of their daughters, Cosima, became the wife of Richard Wagner and, after Wagner's death, the organizing genius behind the Wagnerian festivals at Bayreuth.

Liszt concertized all over Europe for years and firmly established his reputation as a great, perhaps the greatest, pianist of all time. The emotional power and dazzling virtuosity of his playing have become a legend. Endowed with an electric personality, striking appearance, and a marvelous sensitivity to his audience, he captured the imagination of Europe much as Byron had done a generation earlier. Yet in 1847, at the height of his triumph, he gave up his public career as a pianist in order to develop himself as a composer and conductor. He was made the court conductor of the Grand Duke of Weimar, composed steadily, and became the champion of the "New Music," devoting himself to furthering the works of then unknown composers, especially Wagner, with an unselfishness and singleness of purpose which have few parallels in music. From the Weimar period, too, dates his friendship with the Princess Caroline Wittgenstein. Their home, the "Altenberg," became a center of artistic activity where the enormous musical and social influences of Liszt and the Princess were constantly exerted on behalf of all that was new and progressive in art. Some of the key events of the new movement—the production of Wagner's LOHENGRIN, TANNHÄUSER, and THE FLYING DUTCHMAN, of Berlioz' BENVENUTO CELLINI, of Schumann's GENOVEVA and music to Byron's MANFRED—took place under Liszt's direction at Weimar, the city where half a century before Goethe and Schiller had been instrumental in ushering in the reign of literary Romanticism in Germany.

In the last years of his life, Liszt divided his time between Weimar, Budapest, and Rome. In Budapest, his countrymen acclaimed the composer of the fiery HUNGARIAN RHAPSODIES in transports of patriotic fervor. At Weimar, aspiring young pianists came to him from all over the world to be instructed in the mysteries of his art, the majority of them unfortunately carrying away a style of piano-playing that retained all the acrobatics and bombast of the master but little of his poetry or fire. In Rome, the brilliant man of the world, the former radical, who in his youth had welcomed the Revolution of 1830 and indulged in atheistic tracts, fell more and more under the sway of the religious mysticism in his nature and ended by becoming an Abbé in the church. He joined the Order of St. Francis, wore priestly garb, and composed religious works—the GRANER MESSE for the Cathedral in Gran, the LEGEND OF ST. ELIZABETH, and the CHRISTUS—which contain some of his finest music. He died on July 31, 1886, appropriately enough at the Wagner festival in Bayreuth where the "music of the future" of his old comrade-in-arms, for which he had labored so well, was finally entering upon its hour of victory.

Liszt belongs to the most colorful era of the Romantic movement. His literary counterparts are Byron and Hugo; among painters, Delacroix, Géricault, and Turner stand closest to him in their theatricalism, colorfulness, and grand manner. If some of his music seems oversentimental to us, the tendency of his age must be remembered. Precisely because he so perfectly expressed the prevailing tastes and ideals of his own period he was bound to suffer an eclipse as soon as the pendulum had swung the other way. As is usual in such cases, the reaction against Liszt's ostentatious expression of emotionalism went a little too far. He was unquestionably one of the most gifted of the Romanticists, a pioneer in exploring new forms, a daring experimenter in compositional technique, harmonic invention, and creation of new orchestral effects. His ideas were borrowed not only by Wagner but to some degree by a large number of the composers in the second half of the century; and evidences of this borrowing are heard even today!

For a time, musical criticism was hostile to his music and everything he represented; but recent writers are evaluating his contribution more justly. The late historian, Paul Bekker, a discerning critic, said of him:

> Liszt was one of the great practical organizers of public musical activity. He thought of the artist as a sort of prophet—and he saw himself as one—who passes through the stage of virtuoso and champion of everything new and good, to become the high priest, the mediator between God and man. This was the course Liszt's own life took.[1]

Although program music received a great impetus fairly early in the Romantic Period—Beethoven wrote his *"Pastoral"* SIXTH SYMPHONY and

[1] Paul Bekker, THE STORY OF MUSIC (New York: W. W. Norton, Inc., 1927). No one so fully lived what he believed, at least in music, as did Abbé Liszt. Nevertheless, he has been called, at times, saint, wizard, devil and even charlatan!

his dramatic overtures in the first quarter of the nineteenth century—it was not until some decades later that there emerged the musical form that summed up most completely and remained most closely associated with the storytelling tendencies of German romantic music of the nineteenth century—the symphonic poem. It was Liszt who first used this somewhat romantic term to describe a musical composition, and he it was who played the decisive part in its development, with the result that he has come to be known in histories of music as the "father of the symphonic poem."

The characteristic most frequently associated with the Lisztian tone poem is the principle of *theme transformation,* which Liszt used to unify and integrate his work. Liszt transformed and varied his themes in rhythm, harmony, timbre, tempo, and general style to mirror the development or changes in the poetic thought. He applied the principle with great ingenuity and effectiveness and through its use secured a solidity of structure and unity of mood that the symphonic poem did not always achieve in the hands of his disciples. We shall have occasion to point out some interesting theme transformations in LES PRÉLUDES.[2]

The literary idols of the Romantic composers and painters, as we have seen, were Shakespeare, Goethe, Schiller, Dante, Petrarch. Their more immediate inspiration stemmed from Hugo, Byron, Walter Scott, Heine, and the imaginative E. T. A. Hoffmann (whose influence we noticed in the NUTCRACKER SUITE). The return to the spirit of the Middle Ages found expression in the Catholic revival of Lamartine and Chateaubriand (paralleled in England by Cardinal Newman and the Oxford movement). The pessimism of Schopenhauer and the all-embracing humanism that Goethe passed on to his disciples were no less important, while in the background stood the towering figure of Jean Jacques Rousseau with his doctrine of "the natural man" and the "return to nature."

We can see some of these influences at work in examining the titles of Liszt's symphonic poems: FUNERAL HYMN FOR A HERO, intended as the first movement of a revolutionary symphony, an intention never carried out as the young composer's radicalism subsided; TASSO, *Lament*

[2] Some authorities point to Berlioz as the rightful father of the symphonic poem. No doubt Liszt learned many things from the fiery French genius, not the least of which was what *not* to do with the formal elements. Berlioz adhered fairly well to the restrictions of the sonata-allegro form, or variations of it. Liszt, however, sensed that the strict form had to give way to the poetical and programmatic content, even if traditional forms had to be greatly altered or discarded altogether. So he depicted his story, moods, conditions, and scenes through music. In addition, he achieved the necessary structural unity and coherence through the *cyclical reappearance of the themes, and through the technique of representative themes and thematic metamorphosis,* rather than by classical means of development and evolvement. Our reasons for choosing LES PRÉLUDES for study in this chapter are that it remains an outstanding example among Liszt's symphonic poems in the use of these specialized techniques, and it is certainly one of the finest examples in the symphonic poem literature as a whole.

and Triumph, depicting the tragic career of the great poet, his hopeless love for Beatrice d'Este, and the triumph of his work after his death (both Byron and Goethe had treated the subject); LES PRÉLUDES, after the mystical Lamartine's POETIC MEDITATIONS; HUNGARIA, on a patriotic theme; WHAT ONE HEARS ON THE MOUNTAIN, dedicated to nature and solitude; MAZEPPA, dealing with the hero whose adventures had inspired Hugo, Byron, and Pushkin; PROMETHEUS, on the theme that had kindled the imagination of Shelley; FESTIVAL PIECE, to commemorate the fiftieth anniversary of the first production of Schiller's HULDIGUNG DER KÜNSTE; ORPHEUS, conceived during the rehearsals of Gluck's ORFÉO at Weimar; THE BATTLE OF THE HUNS, a return to the setting of the Dark Ages, inspired by Kaulbach's celebrated painting; THE IDEAL, after Schiller's poem; HAMLET, an attempt to unravel in music the riddle of Shakespeare's hero; FROM THE CRADLE TO THE GRAVE, consisting of three parts: *The Cradle, The Struggle for Life,* and *At the Grave, Cradle of a Future Life.* In addition, there are the two program symphonies, the first based on Dante's DIVINE COMEDY, containing an *Inferno, Purgatory,* and *Magnificat;* and the second his masterpiece, the FAUST SYMPHONY, after Goethe, giving three magnificent tone pictures of Faust, Marguerite, and Mephistopheles. We have in these titles a veritable catalog of the literary influences in music during the Romantic Period.[3]

Les Préludes (1854)

For Liszt, the program was merely a point of departure, a symbol to be translated into musical terms. The music suggested the symbol with all the pomp and grandeur of which tone was capable, but it seldom imitated or gave a too literal interpretation of the symbol. Nothing better illustrates this attitude than the fact that the program of LES PRÉLUDES was attached to the tone poem after the music was written. Almost a decade before he had written the music for a choral work, THE FOUR ELEMENTS (Earth, Winds, Waves, Stars), which he laid aside, discouraged by the stupidity of the words. He then made an orchestral version, but, still dissatisfied, discarded this also. In 1854, needing a new work for a benefit concert at Weimar, he recast the abandoned sketch in its present form and looked about for an appropriate poetic motto. Struck by one of Lamartine's poems, he lifted the title, wrote a program of his own that bears some resemblance to what Lamartine actually said, and attached this to his work with the subtitle "After One of Lamartine's Poetic Meditations." Thus, music that had begun by representing earth, winds, waves, and stars ended by symbolizing love, human aspirations, nature, and immortality. Liszt then, even though he was sufficiently a Romanticist to want literary associations for his music, at the same time

[3] Works of Liszt that we have mentioned, aside from LES PRÉLUDES, might well serve as supplementary listening for this chapter.

was musician enough to realize that these associations must of necessity be vague and that the music must present general emotional moods rather than the concrete details of a story.

The program that Liszt wrote for LES PRÉLUDES reads as follows:

> What is life but a series of preludes to that unknown song whose initial solemn note is tolled by Death? The enchanted dawn of every life is love; but where is the destiny on whose first delicious joys some storm does not break?—a storm whose deadly blast disperses youth's illusions, whose fatal bolt consumes its altar. And what soul thus cruelly bruised, when the tempest rolls away, seeks not to rest its memories in the pleasant calm of rural life? Yet man allows himself not long to taste the kindly quiet which first attracted him to Nature's lap; but when the trumpet gives the signal he hastens to danger's post, whatever be the fight which draws him to its lists; that in the struggle he may once more regain full knowledge of himself and all his strength.

We have here a number of elements characteristic of literary Romanticism: the religious mysticism and "intimations of immortality"; the idealization of love; the conception of life as a struggle against destiny, cruel and disillusioning; the longing for solitude and healing in nature's lap; and the glorious return to the battle. Liszt follows his program rather loosely, treating it as a motto rather than a restriction.

Although LES PRÉLUDES is written in a single continuous movement, close inspection will reveal that it is a work of a number of episodes (eight or nine) grouped into four contrasting sections which may be said to correspond roughly to the separate movements of a complete symphony—a sort of telescoping condensation. Then, too, most of the work is constructed out of the metamorphosis of a simple "germinal motive" which is heard in the third measure of the Introduction and which bears close observation throughout the entire symphonic poem.[4]

[4] This particular musical idea or germinal and cyclical motive seems to have some inherent universal significance, for one can find it in a number of works of widely separated periods, among which are: Bach's *C-sharp minor Fugue* (No. 4) of the WELL-TEMPERED CLAVICHORD, the *"Muss Es Sein"* STRING QUARTET, Op. 135, of Beethoven, the D MINOR SYMPHONY of César Franck, the FREISCHÜTZ OVERTURE of Weber, the Fate motif in Wagner's DIE WALKÜRE, and many other works. See also MacDowell's somewhat similar motive found in the Introduction of the first movement of his SECOND *"Indian"* SUITE (Chap. 10). While the various symphonic poems presented in this book may have certain common purposes in expressing a narrative poem, realistic story, poetic mood, or a dramatic content, their musical techniques in projecting these intents differ so greatly and present such individual listening problems as to necessitate separate treatment. Thus, they are presented where listening skills and interest are most germane and effective, with the listener's development given the prime consideration.

What we have chosen to call Part I opens with an introduction presenting the grave Questioning motive as part of the first theme, played by the strings. Note the ominous opening *pizzicato* tones and, in the third measure, the "germinal motive" marked with an "a"–, played with the bow (*arco*):

This phrase is repeated several times, with slight changes, until the movement proper begins *andante maestoso* (with majestic movement), with the theme sounded loudly in the trombones, 'cellos, and basses. As we have indicated, it is formed out of the "germinal motive" marked with an "a."

The strings frame this theme in an arpeggiated (broken-chord-wise) figure not unlike a wave.

Presently another theme is woven out of the germinal motive and played by the second violins, violas, and 'cellos, with a rippling figure in the first violins the while, and the basses *pizzicato:*

This idea is developed for some twenty measures, when the lyrical second theme proper appears in the French horns and muted violas, each divided into three parts. Though the theme is not without its trite sentimentality, it is, nevertheless, a clever development of the germinal motive as indicated:

Liszt builds this up to a passionate climax through the use of the full orchestra, only to calm it down suddenly into a brief dialogue between the strings and wood-winds (note the ethereal close with the sustained chord held by the wood-winds, delicately punctuated by harmonics on the harp—like tiny bells).

Immediately, Part II, not without its parallel to a scherzo movement, appears when the tempo suddenly hastens, *allegro ma non troppo* (fast, but not too much so). Here is a storm scene *par excellence*, with all the chromatic trappings and sound-effect tricks that often accompany such scenes in the cinema. It was a remarkable bit of writing when Liszt composed it—too frequent imitation has, however, deprived the idea of its freshness.

There should be little difficulty in visualizing tremendous wind and storm. In due time, quiet prevails and the idea set forth in Mus. Ill. 4 reappears in the wood-winds.

Part III, which follows the storm scene, might well be considered to parallel a usual romantic and lyrical slow movement of the symphony. Marked *allegretto pastorale* (fairly lively and in a rustic spirit), this main theme of the section is played, *in extensio*, by the first clarinet, but not until it has been anticipated in part by the solo French horn, and then the solo oboe.

It is a lovely theme that still brings with it the sprightliness and freshness of spring; and it still causes one to marvel at Liszt's compositional sensitiveness, for the theme is not beholden to the germinal motive. The theme is tossed about between the strings and wood-winds in a frolicsome manner. Eventually a climax evolves in which the theme of Mus. Ill. 5 is prominently set forth; the key changes markedly, the pulse quickens, and the brasses play bits of anticipatory fanfares.

Part IV, parallel to the finale in a symphony, is ushered in by scale passages, lively passes between the first and second violins, while the French horns and trumpets play the martial theme "A" and the trombones interrupt with the idea "B."—which was first heard in Mus. Ill. 3. The tempo is *allegro marziale animato* (in a lively and animated martial tempo).

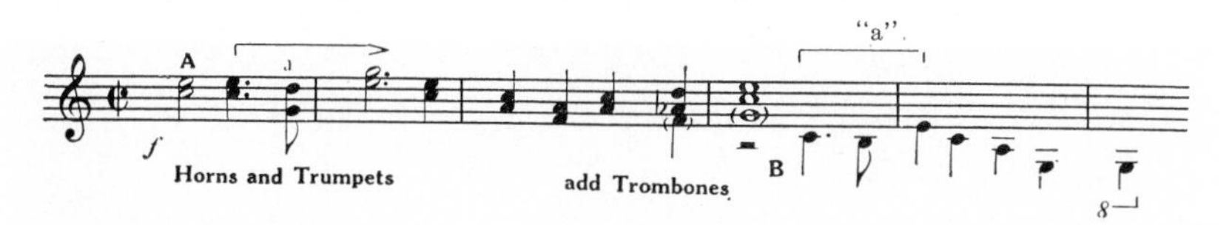

A complex tonal picture ensues, with the bass drums, snare drums, and cymbals adding to the volume of sound; the tempo broadens to a more majestic pace, with the trombones and strings returning to the ideas that came immediately after the introduction—serving to bring about a feeling of formal unity and coherence. Thus the symphonic poem, LES PRÉLUDES, closes in a lustily proclaimed victorious spirit.

SUGGESTED SUPPLEMENTARY LISTENING

Many additional works of Liszt have been mentioned throughout the earlier part of the chapter. For practical reasons, however, we have purposely omitted mention of the individual works for original piano, soli, transcriptions, concerti and other compositions involving the piano. The interested listener may consult an up-to-date long playing record catalogue. Be sure to include the CONCERTO NO. 1 IN E-FLAT, ETUDES AFTER PAGANINI, HUNGARIAN FANTASIA, HUNGARIAN RHAPSODY NO. 2, MEPHISTO WALTZ, and the SONATA IN B MINOR.

Courtesy Theodore Presser Co.

RICHARD WAGNER

18 Richard Wagner and the leit-motif technique

No picture of the orchestral idiom of the nineteenth century would be complete without a consideration of the career and achievement of Liszt's friend, Richard Wagner (1813–1883). Technically, Wagner was an opera composer, and his main reforms, as he thought of them, were carried out in the realm of dramatic music. Actually, he was one of the century's great masters of orchestral writing, whose innovations in harmony and instrumentation, as well as intensity of emotional pitch, exerted incalculable influence on the whole domain of romantic music. Indeed, it is not an exaggeration to say that Wagner's music influenced the course of orchestral writing thereafter; both through the composers who considered themselves his disciples, like Richard Strauss, Anton Bruckner, and Gustav Mahler, and those who, like Rimsky-Korsakoff and Debussy, sought to shake off his influence by seeking their own idioms. In any case, Wagnerism represents the very culmination of nineteenth-century Romanticism, a brilliant, impassioned style of overwhelming—sometimes almost brutal—power, of dazzling orchestral color and virtuosity, so distinctive that some historians of nineteenth-century art use it as a landmark. In our own time, too, although his music dramas still hold the center of the operatic stage, his greatest influence is in the literature of symphonic music. The excerpts from his operas are, to all practical intents and purposes, great tone poems, and everywhere considered among the staples of orchestral repertoire.

RICHARD WAGNER (1813–1883)

The career of this volcanic iconoclast makes one of the most colorful sagas in the story of music. His life, like Liszt's, stretches well across the nineteenth century. He was born in Leipzig in 1813, two years after his great friend, and died in 1883, three years before him. As a youth, Wagner was attracted principally to literature, particularly the Greek classics. At fourteen, having discovered Shakespeare, he wrote a grand tragedy in the course of the early acts of which forty-two characters died, a number of whom had to return as ghosts to keep the fifth act going. Hearing Beethoven's symphonies—the effect upon him was overwhelming—he forthwith decided that what his tragedy needed was precisely such music as this. In order to compose it, he borrowed a textbook on harmony and ploughed through it; but somehow the "system" described in the text could not be made to work. A few lessons from an organist named Müller disappointed him: he thought his teacher a dry pedant, and Müller considered his pupil pigheaded and eccentric. The boy's interest now turned back to literature. He fell under the spell of E. T. A. Hoffmann, the author who exercised extraordinary influence on Schumann, Weber, and other Romantic composers; and in Hoffmann's tales he came across some of the material that he later used in his operas. When he was seventeen, he managed to get an overture performed at a concert. It was, he admits in his autobiography, the high peak of his absurdities. The excesses of the drummer, who was directed to play a beat *fortissimo* every four bars, amazed the audience, which grew impatient and finally dismissed the work as a joke.

At the University of Leipzig, Wagner studied composition with Theodor Weinlig for about six months, this being practically all the formal musical training he ever had. Thereafter he buried himself in the scores of his idol, Beethoven. Leaving the university at twenty, he spent the next six years knocking about the third-rate opera houses that dotted provincial Germany, acquiring through practical experience as chorus master, stage director, and conductor that intimate knowledge of the stage that is one of the prime requisites for the successful opera composer. At Königsberg he married an actress of his company, Minna Planer —he was then twenty-three—and got an engagement as conductor at Riga. Growing dissatisfied with the rut into which he had drifted, he turned his eyes, as all ambitious young artists then did, toward Paris. He completed the first two acts of his grand opera RIENZI, *Last of the Tribunes,* based on the novel by Bulwer-Lytton, and set out with his wife to seek his fortune in the French capital. During the voyage through the North Sea, the legend of THE FLYING DUTCHMAN, which he had come across in a story by Heine, took possession of his mind. Thus the seed was planted for his first truly important work. It should be remembered that Wagner composed his own dramas and librettos as well as the music—an outstanding achievement in itself.

His life in Paris was a bitter disappointment, a grinding struggle with poverty, a futile knocking at doors that remained closed. Despite the letter of introduction given him by Meyerbeer—at that time the virtual ruler of grand opera—the young man was unable to gain a foothold anywhere. To support himself and his wife he was reduced to hack work, "arranging rubbish for various instruments—the cornet among them"; he wrote vaudeville airs, and at one time tried to get a job as a chorus man. "The conductor who tested my capabilities discovered that I could not sing at all, and pronounced me a hopeless case all around." Despite all obstacles, he finished RIENZI, which he dispatched to the Dresden Opera House, and set to work on the libretto of THE FLYING DUTCHMAN. In dire straits, he tried to write for a living and turned out some articles on music that were published in the Parisian journals. Just when the outlook was gloomiest, the news came that RIENZI had been accepted for performance at Dresden. He shook the dust of Paris from his feet and set out for his native land. With tears in his eyes, he tells us, he beheld the Rhine "and swore eternal fidelity to the German fatherland."

RIENZI scored a sensational success. Almost overnight the twenty-eight-year-old composer found himself lifted from obscurity to the position of *Kapellmeister* (conductor and general music director) to the King of Saxony. He now had everything a composer could wish for—security, a theater under his direction, an enthusiastic audience. He needed only to continue to turn out works in the conventional grand-opera manner. But his integrity as an artist would not permit him to do this. He had a vision of music drama more lofty than anything that had been done up till then and he was determined to force this vision upon the world. The audiences that had applauded the flamboyant RIENZI were totally unprepared for the stark simplicity and intensity of THE FLYING DUTCHMAN. They were repelled by the tragic ending of TANNHÄUSER and were puzzled by Wagner's new type of melody. When it came to LOHENGRIN, the second work that Wagner completed during his seven years at Dresden, the bureaucrats in charge of the Royal opera did not care to continue what they considered a dangerous experiment and refused to produce the work.

Wagner realized that he could not give the public what it wanted and that it would not accept what he could give it. It was borne in upon him that he would never be able to rescue operatic music from the triviality and vulgarity into which it had fallen. His projected reform for the theaters of Saxony fell on the deaf ears of the conservative ministers who expected him to supply the court with conventional pleasantries. His restless intellect led him further in his search for the original evil. He saw that in order to reform the theater he would have to reform the social scene itself and its basic determinant, the state. This line of reasoning led Wagner straight into the revolutionary camp, and he had to flee the country.

With the years of political exile which he spent in Switzerland began the mature period of his creative career. He decided that the only way to create an audience for the "art work of the future" was to take up his pen to propagandize and explain his theories. For five years he wrote no music, turning out his chief literary works—ART AND REVOLUTION (1849), THE ART WORK OF THE FUTURE (1850), and OPERA AND DRAMA (1851)—besides a host of shorter essays on related subjects. Having thus cleared his mind for action, he attempted to put his principle into practice in the fully developed music dramas—he coined this term to distinguish his works from the conventional opera—of his maturity. How widely his practices veered from his theories is, by now, common knowledge.

The remaining three decades of his life he devoted, with a singleness of aim that has few parallels in the story of art, to imposing his will and his vision upon the world. How he forged ahead in a Europe that at the onset understood neither his music nor his ideas, and how he finally got the world to listen, to understand, and to worship, is one of the most incredible success stories of the nineteenth century. We get an insight into the lack of understanding he had to face at this period from the following description by Gasperini of Wagner's interview with the director of the Théâtre Lyrique in Paris, where he had gone in the hope of getting TANNHÄUSER performed:

> One evening, arriving at Carvalho's house, I heard an extraordinary noise! Wagner was at the piano, struggling with the finale of the second act of TANNHÄUSER. He sang, he shouted, he performed all kinds of contortions; he played with his hands, his wrists, his elbows. M. Carvalho remained impassive, waiting with a patience worthy of antiquity for the bedlam to subside. The score finished, Carvalho stammered a few polite words, turned and fled.

Fortunately, Wagner did not have to conduct the struggle completely alone. Liszt was a staunch friend who did more perhaps than any other to launch the "music of the future." Other disciples included Hans von Bülow, the great pianist and conductor, and the fiery young Nietzsche, for whom the master's music was—for a time—the revelation of a new world. Liszt produced LOHENGRIN at Weimar; other productions of THE FLYING DUTCHMAN and TANNHÄUSER followed throughout Germany. Wagner was unable to hear these, for he was still forbidden to enter his homeland. Gradually the movement for Wagner's pardon gained strength. Through the intercession of Princess Metternich, the ban of exile was finally withdrawn and Wagner returned to Germany after an absence of eleven years. He plunged at once into the composition of his one comic masterpiece, THE MASTER SINGERS OF NUREMBERG. Despite all this, the darkest period of his life now approached. Having completed the first two dramas of the RING OF THE NIBELUNG, he faced the realization that Europe contained neither a theater nor singers capable of presenting them. His efforts to get TRISTAN AND ISOLDE produced fell through. He was estranged from his wife; his romantic friendship with Mathilde Wesendonck, who had played an important part in the inspiration of TRISTAN, ended in an unhappy separation. At last his power of resistance was broken. He thought of suicide, and finally decided to give up his public career.

And then the miracle happened. The throne of Bavaria fell to the eighteen-year-old Ludwig II, who had been an enthusiastic devotee of Wagner ever since he had heard LOHENGRIN. One of the first acts of the young King was to invite Wagner to come to Bavaria to finish his work. Thus opened the final and triumphant chapter in Wagner's life. He closes his autobiography at this point: "I was never again to feel the weight of everyday hardships of existence under the protection of my exalted friend."

He settled at the capital, Munich, where in 1865 TRISTAN was produced under his supervision, von Bülow conducting. He now completed DIE MEISTERSINGER (*The Master Singers of Nuremberg*), twenty-two years after his first sketch of the poem. After an interruption of nine years, he returned to the RING and finished the poem and music of the fourth and final drama, GÖTTERDÄMMERUNG (The Twilight of the Gods). "THE RING OF THE NIBELUNG, as a whole, is certainly one of the greatest achievements of the mind of man," writes H. L. Mencken. Yet in addition to the RING, Wagner wrote TRISTAN, DIE MEISTERSINGER, LOHENGRIN, PARSIFAL, and other music dramas. He was truly one of the few giants among geniuses in all fields of endeavor. Wagner was soon joined by Liszt's daughter, Cosima, one of the most extraordinary women of her time, who brought him the personal understanding and sympathy he needed, together with an unflagging will and energy equal to his own in building the Wagnerian Festival Theatre at Bayreuth. The lifelong friendship between Liszt and Wagner received its first wrench at this domestic drama, for Cosima was the wife of Wagner's disciple von Bülow, and her decision occasioned a scandal that Wagner's enemies were only too eager to exploit. In 1870, after all legal obstacles had been swept away, they were married. There followed the crowning act of Wagner's life—the building of the theater at Bayreuth, made possible by the contributions of Wagner societies throughout the world. In 1876 the first Bayreuth Festival was given, with the four dramas of the RING OF THE NIBELUNG (DAS RHEINGOLD, DIE WALKÜRE, SIEGFRIED, and GÖTTERDÄMMERUNG) performed in their entirety for the first time twenty-eight years after Wagner had begun to work on the librettos. Bayreuth now became the mecca of all the adherents of the "music of the future"; the festivals, given every four years, later annually, became the focal point from which Wagner's music and ideas emanated all over the world. Every technical detail, from the seating plan of the theater to the singing and coaching of the performers, was superintended by Wagner himself and represented the final realization of his notions of musical-dramatic art. Here his last work, PARSIFAL, was first produced (1882). A year later he died in Venice, at seventy, and was laid to rest in Bayreuth. Ernest Newman sums up his life well:

> He lived, indeed, to see himself victor everywhere, in possession of everything for which he had struggled his whole feverish life through. He completed and saw upon the stage every one of the great works he had planned. He found the one woman in the world who was fitted to share his throne with him when alive and to govern his kingdom after his death with something of his own overbearing, inconsiderate strength. He achieved the miracle of building in a tiny Bavarian town a theatre to which, for more than a generation after his death, musicians would still flock from all the ends of the earth.[1]

In his attempt to make the orchestra express all the emotional experience of his characters—love, passion, hate, despair, revenge—as well as the pictorial and scenic aspects of the myths upon which he built his dramas—storm, flame, the magic of the forest, the wonder of the rainbow, the shimmering of the Rhine—Wagner made his richest contribution to the symphonic idiom of expression. The orchestra comments upon the drama itself, and the emotional values implied in it. It carries the function of the Greek chorus of ancient Attic drama to a logical, aesthetic conclusion. Wagner, through his unique genius, created a magic tapestry

[1] Ernest Newman, *Wagner as Man and Artist.* (New York: Alfred A. Knopf, Inc., 1924.)

of kaleidoscopic wizardry, interweaving poetry, philosophy, drama, and music, depicting a world of color, beauty, and imagination unrivaled in all music history, and which remained unchallenged until the flowering of French Impressionism and Symbolism in the late nineteenth and early twentieth centuries. Through the use of new orchestral techniques, thematic ideas, and color combinations, particularly in the brass and woodwinds, through new harmonic progressions and the use of a restlessly chromatic and contrapuntal idiom that modulated ceaselessly from one key to the next, he immeasurably extended the capacities of the art for emotional expression and tone painting. His daring chordal combinations and their uses paved the way for a new concept of harmony, which, inspired by TRISTAN AND ISOLDE, no doubt gave birth to the modern Viennese or Schönbergian school. His writing became the basis of most subsequent developments in the final decades of the nineteenth century, and his influence has carried over even to this day. It is possible that Wagner wrote more original musical ideas per page than any composer who ever lived; it is equally possible that he wrote more pages of boresome music than anyone else.

Another contribution that Wagner made to music was the tremendous technical and poetical development of the use of leading motives, *leit-motifs.* He is not here credited with the invention of this technique, for it was known long before his own time; but he did gradually perfect its use. It was not until the composition of TRISTAN AND ISOLDE that Wagner's own slow mastery and conception of the leit-motif evolved from a brief, characteristic, and identifying figure to the point where the leit-motif assumed a real, environmental, even transcendental significance which required extensive restatement of long passages, such as the repetition of entire sections from the duet in the second act of TRISTAN AND ISOLDE to the Love Death of the last act. Not until then did Wagner's "system of leit-motifs" really mature to equal the genius of the master himself. Since this technique is such a characteristic part of Wagner's style, it is well to inquire into it, and we shall use the TANNHÄUSER OVERTURE as a typical example; but, first, we should acquire a better concept of the *leit-motif* itself. Such a motif is a characteristic theme or musical figure that the composer attaches and associates to a person such as Venus or the Sirens, to a thing such as a Sword or Holy Grail, to a condition such as Love or Hate, or even to an abstract idea or emotion such as Glorification of Venus, Love's Spell or, if you prefer, Delusive Enticement. Thus, whenever these ideas are pertinent to the moment in the storytelling, the appropriate motif or motifs will be heard.

Obviously, if the listener is in possession of the composer's intentions and connotations pertaining to the motifs, a running communication and narration are quite feasible. The extent to which Wagner made this communication intelligible without loss of musicality is one of the wonders of this many-sided genius.[2]

Overture to "Tannhäuser"

The Overture to TANNHÄUSER, when heard in the opera house, provides an appropriate introduction to the drama. When heard—as is much more often the case—apart from the opera, it is an exciting symphonic poem built around the inner conflict within the hero of the drama. As with much program music, knowledge of the drama is an aid to the fullest appreciation of the score. The *Overture* is really a condensed preview of the essence of the opera itself.

The knight Tannhäuser is torn between his love for Elisabeth, who represents all that is best in his nature, and the pagan goddess Venus. Surfeited with the goddess' sensuous rites and revels, he tears himself away from her and returns to the world of mortals. The second act centers about the Tournament of Song in Wartburg, the Thuringian castle of Elisabeth's uncle, in which each of the knightly minstrels sings in praise of love. When his turn comes, Tannhäuser, under the spell of the goddess, mocks the spiritual conception of love and sings the *Hymn to Venus,* a passionate dithyramb on the pleasures of voluptuous love. Finally realizing the depravity of his soul, he undertakes a pilgrimage to Rome to do penance. But the Pope, shocked at the enormity of his sins, tells him there is as much chance for his soul to win salvation as for the Holy See's official staff to sprout leaves. Tannhäuser, returning home in deepest despair, is on the verge of giving himself over to Venus and eternal perdition; but the faith of Elisabeth, who dies with a prayer for him on her lips, recalls him to his better self and saves him. As he falls dead on her bier, the pilgrims returning from Rome bring news of a miracle: the Pope's staff has sprouted leaves, and the sinner has won salvation through the steadfast love and sacrifice of Elisabeth.

The Overture to the opera delineates, in condensed form, the central conflicts of the action that is to follow, and we shall name the leit-motifs as they appear in the Overture so that their narrative function can be

[2] While it must be admitted that a *knowledge* of the leit-motifs, together with the recognition of their dramatic and emotional associations as they appear in the performance, enhances the enjoyment, it is to Wagner's everlasting credit that the music, when performed as concert music, is fully capable of standing on its own feet; and often the difference of enjoyment resulting from intimate knowledge of the motifs is in kind rather than degree. However, "The Perfect Wagnerite" (read G. B. Shaw's book by that name) will know all the leit-motifs as well as the perfect baseball fan knows the rules of the game and the men who play it. It is interesting to differentiate between the leit-motif of Wagner and the germinal motive as used in Liszt's LES PRÉLUDES, in the SONATA IN A MAJOR for violin and piano by César Franck (Chap. 27), the FOURTH SYMPHONY of Sibelius, and Schönberg's PIERROT LUNAIRE (see last chapter).

more clearly apprehended. First we hear the stately hymn, the *Pilgrims' Chorus,* called the Salvation by Grace motive in the old Breitkopf and Härtel edition that is serving as a source book. This hymn is played softly at the beginning, as though heard from afar, and it increases in volume as it approaches, in a slow and majestic pace (*andante maestoso*). It is played, at the onset, by two clarinets, two horns, and two bassoons.

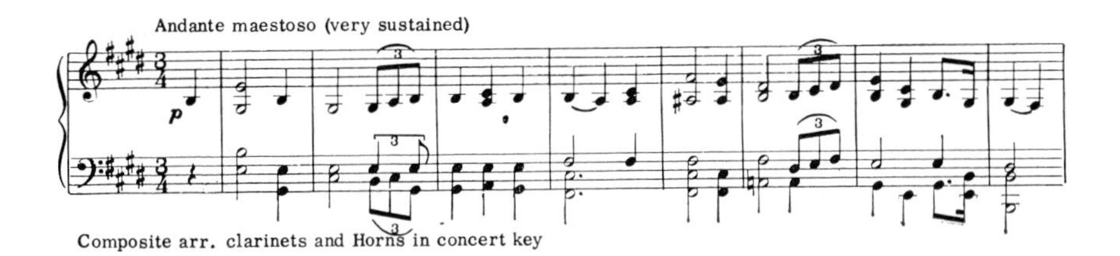

Gradually more instruments are added until the full orchestra bursts forth with a new motif called The Pulse of Life, or Unfettered Passions. This is a descending sixteenth note figure that appears in the first and second violins, while the trombones and tuba blare out the melody, Salvation by Grace, just heard. The descending figure in the violins should be noted carefully as it assumes a most important part in the composition of the Overture.

This motif goes on for some time, working itself up to a *fortissimo* climax which eventally dies down to a small volume of tone, when the Pilgrims' Chorus theme of penitence (*Gnadenheil-motif*) is heard as though it were far in the distance. Observe how Wagner has thus provided a well-balanced section. Notice that for the hymnlike effect Wagner has adhered to the regular, square-cut, four-measure phrase so common in actual hymns.

Suddenly, and in complete contrast, a theme appears like a whisper in the violas, amidst the *tremolo* figure in the violins; all is hushed, and still, and quietly subdued, suggesting the enchanted background against which the nymphs and bacchantes of Venus' train disport themselves. In fact, this theme is known as the Venusberg motif, or one of the nine (*sic*) Bacchanale motifs.

No sooner has this wisp of a suggestion passed by when another Bacchanale motif is heard, very softly in the strings and wood-winds, only to give way to the seductive Sirens motif heard in the flutes, oboes, and clarinets, with the strings playing a harplike *arpeggio.*

Soon the Venusberg theme is heard again, this time played at first by the clarinet and then tossed to the bassoons and violas, to be joined at last by the oboes. The dance becomes louder and more impassioned, and presently a new motif is heard in the first and second violins, with a rumbling and most exciting chromatic figure in the 'cellos. The new theme, in the violins, is merely another Bacchanale motif as follows:

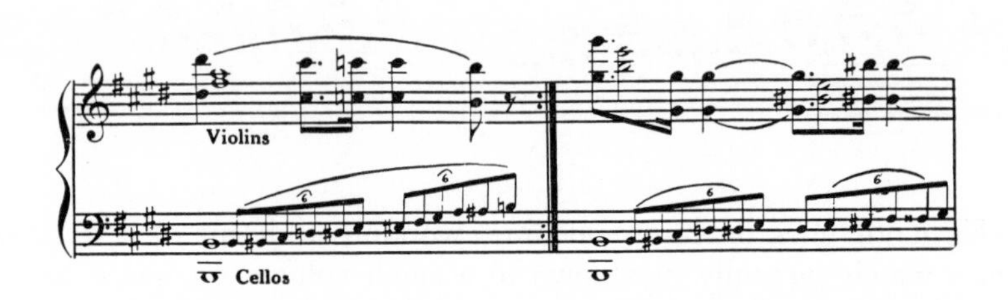

This last motif is worked up to a loud, *fortissimo* climax, where still another motif bursts forth. This time it is in the strings and wood-winds, and it is called the Glorification of Venus motif:

It is obviously a theme of mock majesty, of pomp and circumstance, and it is worked up to a mighty volume of tone by the full orchestra whereupon, with a sudden drop of dynamics to a mere *piano*, the Venusberg theme appears in the violas with the Siren motif in the wood-winds. The music becomes softer and softer, and almost ethereal, as the strings put on their mutes (*sordini*) and softly trill as though the scene were in an enchanted forest. A note of melancholy, of nostalgia, now is injected into the carefree orgy of the Bacchanale by a somber melody played by the solo clarinet.

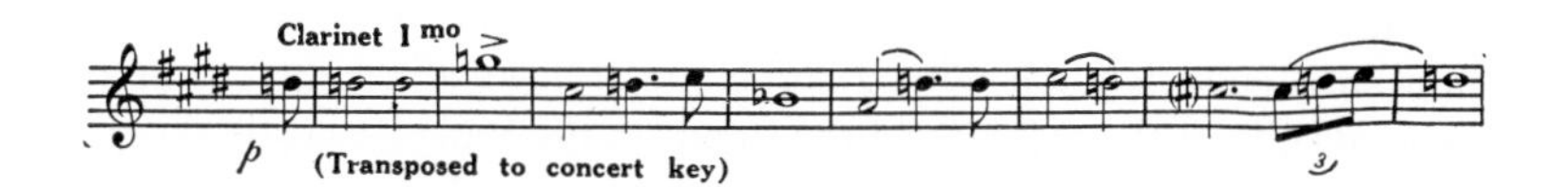

This melody is called by some the Love's Spell motif; Ernest Newman calls it Venus's Cajoling Invocation or Enticement; and the Wagnerian expert, Windsperger, calls it Liebesbann. It is promptly dispelled by the intrusion of the Venusberg motif; and still another Bacchanale motif is heard, until the full orchestra awakens into new life. All is alive with renewed vigor and agitation, as the Glorification of Venus motif blares forth with all its pomp and power. Without lessening, the Siren motif returns, this time played by the full orchestra, and one realizes that, finally, here is the real climax of the Overture.[3] The Venusberg and Unfettered Passions motifs assume prime importance in the scheme of the composition. Gradually the volume of tone subsides, the strings continue with the Unfettered Passions motif, while beneath is heard the *Pilgrims' Hymn*. An appropriate and brilliant coda is appended for the close in the concert version, providing a subject for much debate among musicians. Perhaps you would like to discuss the appropriateness of the close provided for the concert version. Have you noticed the counterpoint in this work?

[3] In the so-called "Paris Edition," which Wagner reluctantly made in 1861 to meet the demands of the Paris Opera authorities, he changed the opera in many places, among the most dramatic being the closing of the opera itself, the Introduction to the Third Act, and, most important, in the Overture and the Bacchanale in Act I. It is at this last point in the program that the curtain rises, revealing the Venusberg scene with the ballet in progress; of course the music continues without interruption. Read Ernest Newman's book *The Wagner Operas* (New York: Alfred Knopf, 1949), especially pp. 100-104, for more details of the changes made for the so-called Paris edition and the further alterations he made in the opera as late as 1871 or 72.

ADDITIONAL SUGGESTIONS FOR LISTENING

We have previously mentioned, among ot er works in the chapter on religious music, the *Preludes* to LOHENGRIN and PARSIFAL. For other examples of Wagner's symphonic style, listen to the *Prelude* to DIE MEISTERSINGER and to the famous excerpts from the four dramas that constitute the RING OF THE NIBELUNG. From DAS RHEINGOLD (the first of the cycle), hear the *Prelude* describing the River Rhine, and the final scene, the *Entrance of the Gods into Valhalla.*

From DIE WALKÜRE (The Valkyrie) listen to the stirring *Ride of the Valkyries* and the *Farewell of Wotan,* culminating in the *Magic Fire* scene. The Ride is built upon a clarion figure repeated over and over with a kind of brutal insistence, while headlong chromatic scales and a luminous orchestral background suggest the neighing of the steeds as the Valkyrie hurtle through the storm. In the Magic Fire scene that closes the opera, Wotan takes leave of his favorite daughter Brünnhilde. Because she has disobeyed him, Brünnhilde must lose her power as goddess and know all the sorrows of a mortal woman. But Wotan consents to ring her about with a wall of fire so that only the hero may pass through and claim her as his bride. The warrior maiden lies down on the magic rock, clad in her armor, and falls asleep as Wotan summons the god of fire, Loki, to wrap the rock in flame. Lifting his spear, Wotan proclaims that only he who knows no fear may pass through the fire. As he does so he sings the theme of Siegfried, who will claim the sleeping goddess in the next opera. The curtain falls upon one of the most poetic scenes on the lyric stage.

The magic of the forest is captured in the *Forest Murmurs* from SIEGFRIED when, as the hero lies dreaming in the woods after having killed the dragon, the forest whispers to him of his godlike ancestry and a bird tells him of the sleeping beauty who awaits him on the burning height.

From GÖTTERDÄMMERUNG listen to *Siegfried's Rhine Journey* which proclaims the joyously defiant clarion call of young Siegfried; and from the final act of the opera, Siegfried's *Funeral March,* which has been called the "greatest threnody in all music" (Gilman), and rightly so for, with the aid of leit-motifs borrowed from all the dramas of which Siegfried was a part, the life story of Wagner's hero is told out in symbolic detail.

To round out the suggestions for additional Wagner works, be sure to include that delightful chamber orchestra work written as a serenade for Cosima, SIEGFRIED IDYL. Though this work does not come within the strictest meaning of a symphonic poem, largely because of a lack of a fixed program, literary basis, or the like, it is among the most cherished individual smaller works in all orchestral literature. It is a masterpiece in the expressive musical feeling, craftsmanship, the eloquent use of symbolical and narrative implications of the leitmotifs (derived from the music drama, *Siegfried*) plus the addition of a traditional lullaby, *Schlaf' mein Kind, schlaf' ein,* which is wonderfully woven into the masterful and transparent contrapuntal texture. It should be observed that the score is also notable in its frugality of instrumentation: 1 flute, 1 oboe, 2 clarinets, 1 bassoon, 1 trumpet, 2 horns and strings. Originally the strings consisted of 2 first violins, 2 second violins, 2 violas, 1 'cello and 1 double-bass. Nowadays, the strings are usually increased. From here on it should not be difficult for the music lover to make up his own list of Wagner favorites.

Courtesy the owner, Edward B. Benjamin, New Orleans. Photo by Caldwell, Greensboro, N. C.

BETTER TIMES Martha Van Elliott

The title is the owner's. This contemporary, Romantic portrait is executed with swift and firm brush strokes. The face is strong and hopeful in spite of the "better times" the character might once have enjoyed—as suggested by the lines, form, and sensitive character in the face, versus the cold background and the candid implication in the armful of papers yet to sell. The portrait is deeply affecting and without maudlin sentimentality.

19 Richard Strauss and the temper of realism

It was inevitable, once a musical form had been evolved that was expressly designed to project the message of poetry or painting by means of music, that composers should begin to experiment to achieve an even more graphic style in the depiction of programmatic values. During the decades after Liszt, the symphonic poem moved steadily closer to realism. This shift was undoubtedly accelerated by the tendency toward realism that made itself so strongly felt in the sister arts, especially in literature and painting, throughout the second half of the century. One need but mention the Naturalism of Zola, who dominated the literary scene in France, of Hardy in England, of Howells and Crane in this country, and the romantic Realism of such painters as Courbet, Manet, and Millet.[1] All these artists were deeply con-

[1] We wish to mention here one of a number of American realistic artists, Elizabeth O'Neill Verner of Charleston, S. C. Most of the reproductions of her work are found in her published books: *Prints*

cerned with drawing their art closer to life, with transplanting the elements of reality with the closest possible fidelity into the art work.

As to composers, those who came after Liszt fell into two camps as far as their handling of the tone poem was concerned. On the one hand were composers like Tchaikovsky and Dukas, who continued in their essentially Romantic attitude toward the program, making the music suggest the symbol rather than attempting to give a literal tonal imitation of it. On the other hand were realists like Saint-Saëns who, in his DANCE OF DEATH, gave a graphic representation of the rattle of the skeletons' bones, the howling of the winter wind over the cemetery, and similar details. This tendency was brought to its high state of development by Richard Strauss, the great naturalist in tone, who adapted Liszt's romantic conception to the more sophisticated temper of our own time and brought the symphonic poem to a stage of Realism that Liszt had never foreseen.

RICHARD STRAUSS (1864–1949)

Born in 1864, a year before Sibelius, Strauss blazed a cometlike path across the musical sky of the 1890's. By this time Liszt and Wagner, the high priests of Romanticism, were dead. Their successors—Saint-Saëns, Tchaikovsky, Rimsky-Korsakoff, Dvořák, Grieg—were middle-aged men entering on the final phase of their careers. They had brought the movement to its final stage; the time was ripe for a new departure. It was in this *fin de siècle* atmosphere that the young Richard Strauss wrote his witty, brilliantly original tone poems, startling and scandalizing his contemporaries, in effect ushering in the "Modern Period."

Strauss was born in Munich amidst a combination of circumstances well-nigh ideal for a future composer. His father was the leading horn player of the Munich Opera orchestra, a thorough musician who saw to it that Richard's musical training was in the strictest classical tradition. His mother came from a wealthy brewing family, so that the budding composer was spared the searing effects of poverty. He showed his talent early: at the age of six he composed a polka and a Christmas song. By the time he entered the University of Munich at eighteen, he already had had a number of compositions published and performed. Unlike Tchaikovsky and Sibelius, Strauss did not wait until his gradua-

---

and Impressions of Charleston, Other Places, and *Mellowed by Time.* Many of the originals are in the Gibbs Art Museum of Charleston, S. C., and elsewhere. Her works are faithful to realities, show excellent draftsmanship, and are pleasing artistic expressions of scenes and places here and abroad, interpreted by a very gifted and thoroughly capable American artist. These pictures are in the media of painting, etching, and the fast disappearing art of working with the pencil. Other examples of Realism are mentioned elsewhere.

Courtesy The University Prints

PORTRAIT OF GEORG GISZE Holbein

Here we have an excellent example of Realism, wherein the hand of the artist tries faithfully to set forth what the eye beholds. Before the advent of photography the sole means of simulating objectivity was through man's skill in art. One cannot but admire the truth and uncanny facility of Holbein's perception and draftsmanship.

tion to decide on a musical career. He left the university at the end of his first year and thenceforth devoted himself to composition.

His early works—a symphony, sonatas, concertos, and quartets in the conventional style—gave no hint of the future *enfant terrible* of program music. When he was nineteen he met Alexander Ritter, nephew of Wagner and one of the most fervent apostles of the "music of the future," as the new style of Wagner and Liszt was called. The young man was forthwith converted to the programmatic approach—and found his medium. To Ritter he attributed his understanding of Liszt and Wagner and the molding of his style into the poetic and expressive qualities characteristic of the "music of the future."

Strauss soon became the leader of a group of composers whose motto was: music for expression; their goal: to make music express life. Their use of the temper of Realism went far beyond the tentative, often naïve efforts of Saint-Saëns and his generation. They believed that there was no facet of human experience, whether abstract philosophical speculation, psychological analysis, biting satire, or raw comedy, that music could not be made to express. If the result was sometimes harshly dissonant, that too was an expression of reality: since life was at times discordant and ugly, why shouldn't art be?

From his twenty-third year when he wrote DON JUAN, considered by many his masterpiece, Strauss turned out a series of tone poems and operas that made him the most important composer of the early 1900's. He seemed to herald the dawn of a new era in music, one that captured the mood of Europe before the First World War—the fevered restlessness, the hectic gaiety, the romantic nostalgia, the wit, the disillusion, the weariness, the need of strong stimulants—as few other composers succeeded in doing. Using a gigantic orchestra, which he handled in masterly fashion—his scores are of a complexity far beyond anything Wagner or Liszt had dreamed of—the young iconoclast set out to express things in music that no one had ever before attempted. Whether it was the jabbering of the market women in TILL EULENSPIEGEL, the bleating sheep and whirring windmills in DON QUIXOTE, the battle music in A HERO'S LIFE, or the inner turmoil in Don Juan's soul, there was no situation, no subtlety of characterization or quirk of plot, that Strauss did not feel supremely able to depict in tones. On the one hand, he aimed to develop the descriptive powers of his art to such an extent that it would be possible "to describe a teaspoon in music." On the other hand, he was able to say of his THUS SPAKE ZARATHUSTRA, with a courage that would have abashed a more hardened philosopher, that he intended it as a musical expression of the development of the human race from its origin to Nietzsche's Superman.

We may well understand the bewilderment of the musicians of the old school. After hearing THUS SPAKE ZARATHUSTRA, Sir George Grove, the venerable author of the great musical dictionary, wrote:

> What can have happened to drag down music from the high level of beauty, interest, sense, force, grace, coherence, and any other good quality which it rises to in Beethoven . . . down to the low level of ugliness and want of interest that we had in Strauss' absurd farrago? *Noise* and *effect* seem to be so much the aim now.[2]

Nothing so well illustrates the forward march of history as the fact that Grove held up as the high representative of "beauty, interest, sense" and all the other good qualities Beethoven, who less than a century before had shocked his contemporaries with a new conception of beauty in music. (What would these musicians say of the music of our time?)

As for Strauss himself, he was not crushed by the opposition, he seemed positively to thrive on it. His early works breathed an amazing vitality and zest, scorching humor, buoyancy, and exuberance—the lusty defiance of a young giant with supreme confidence in his power. To the tone poems we have already mentioned may be added MACBETH and DEATH AND TRANSFIGURATION, the latter somewhat more in the poetic tradition of Liszt, and his three principal operas—SALOME (1905), an extraordinarily effective setting of Oscar Wilde's one-act play; ELEKTRA (1909), a powerful one-act music drama centering about the heroine of Greek tragedy; and DER ROSENKAVALIER, or CAVALIER OF THE ROSE (1911), a comedy in the eighteenth-century manner combining Mozartian grace, the Viennese waltz, and the piquant harmonies of the late romantic idiom.

In all these works Strauss managed in an astonishing way to fuse his romantic heritage with the idiom of a more modern age. He will go down in the history of music as one of the first great composers of the post-Romantic era. For, although he stemmed from Romanticism—his use of strikingly dramatic plots, his reliance upon theatrical effects of orchestration, and his luscious melodies are all in the great romantic tradition —there is an element of intellectuality in his work, of sophistication and objectivity that stamps him as a post-Romantic, a child of the twentieth century. Strauss has been called the prose artist of music, the one who substituted the tone of the modern realistic novel, with its psychological probings, its devotion to detail, its objectivity, for the poetic drama of the earlier epoch. In short, Strauss achieved in music what the "naturalist" writers of the end of the century—Zola, de Maupassant, Chekhov —achieved in literature. Through his wonderful sense of musical characterization, his bold imagination, the sweep and power of his style, he was able to describe, to analyze, to satirize, to conjure up the details

[2] Sir George Grove, *Dictionary of Music and Musicians.* (New York: The Macmillan Company.)

Courtesy Metropolitan Museum of Art

MLLE. CHARLOTTE DU VAL-D'OGNES Constance Marie Charpentier

Because of the style of drawing, great care and detail of draftsmanship, and realistic pose, this work was, until recent years, attributed to Jacques L. David, the master of realistic draftsmanship. Note the graceful lines and interplay of the rhythmic folds of the dress, the hair, and the shawl on the chair, the "Empire" gown, window scene, even the crack in the window pane which actually is an integral part of the composition!

of a scene with a vividness never before achieved. DON JUAN, TILL EULENSPIEGEL, DON QUIXOTE—these are no mere symbols for generalized poetic moods as the protagonists of the earlier tone poems had been. These are fully realized, distinctive individuals hit off with deep insight and psychological acumen, projected with merciless clarity, with an incisiveness and completeness little short of the phenomenal.

The Merry Pranks of Till Eulenspiegel (*1895*)

Of all Strauss' works, the brilliant portrayal of the medieval rogue, Till Eulenspiegel, has attained the widest popularity. Strauss was thirty-one when he wrote it. He had already written MACBETH, DON JUAN, DEATH AND TRANSFIGURATION, and the opera GUNTRAM. Whether because he was smarting from the reluctance of his fellow musicians to respond to his art or because his genius for comedy was coming to maturity, Strauss now turned his gifts to sarcasm and impudent waywardness. In more than one spot the mocking laughter of the vagabond-rogue seems but to echo his own. As we listen to the startling leaps of flutes and oboes, the bold curve of the melodic line, the novel harmonies and orchestral effects, it is difficult to believe that this music was written but four years after the NUTCRACKER SUITE and two years before FINLANDIA.

The young composer chose a fit symbol, for Till is one of the eternal rebels who fail to fit into the accepted social patterns. He is related to François Villon and Gil Blas, to Puck and Robin Hood, to Rabelais' lusty Pantagruel and Anatole France's equally lusty Tournebroche. In German folklore he occupies a position analogous to that of our own Huckleberry Finn and Katzenjammer Kids. (The "Till" theme crops up impishly now and then in Strauss' later works.)

Historically, Till Eulenspiegel—the name, literally translated Till Owl-Glass, is derived from an old German proverb to the effect that "Man sees his own faults as little as an owl recognizes his ugliness in looking into a mirror"—came into German literature through a collection of folk tales and anecdotes about his doings written by Thomas Mürner (1475–1530). It was a period of vast social change. The feudal system was breaking up under the rise of the guilds and burgesses; the semi-independent barons were being subdued by the centralized monarchy of the modern European state; the new humanism was raising its head against medieval scholasticism; the scene was being laid for the deepest upheaval of all—the revolt against the Church of Rome, the Reformation. In English literature we have a stirring expression of the period in PIERS PLOWMAN, in Malory's DEATH OF ARTHUR, and in the works of Chaucer. Mürner, in open revolt against the clergy, told the life of Till as a satire against the smug monks, the domineering lords, and the grasping bourgeoisie. He pictured Till as continually outsmarting the victims of his wit, dying peacefully in bed after a long and eventful career, and at the very last playing a joke on his heirs by refusing to lie still in his grave. By the end of the nineteenth century, as Strauss knew, society was much more effectively organized to deal with such spirits. His "Till" accordingly pays on the gallows for his daring.

Unlike LES PRÉLUDES and FINLANDIA, in which the music gives a vague suggestion of a vague program, the music of TILL EULENSPIEGEL depicts the adventures of the rogue in the most literal, realistic terms. Consequently, a knowledge of the program is much more important for a proper appreciation of this music than is the case with Liszt's or Sibelius' tone poems. Here the listener cannot substitute for the program of the composer whatever image happens to strike his fancy, for the music at any given moment is depicting a concrete detail of the story. If less leeway is given to the imagination of the hearer, there is compensation in following the cleverness and rich fancy with which the composer has transcribed the images of the everyday world into the world of tone. The program was derived by Strauss' closest friends from the markings of the principal themes in Strauss' own copy of the score; the music falls into several distinct episodes.

"Once upon a time there lived a wag." Violins announce a tender "dipping" theme, *piano,* setting a mood of long ago and projecting the essential lovableness of the rogue:

"Named Till Eulenspiegel." The *staccato* Mischief theme symbolizing the wayward side of Till's nature is announced by the horn, *piano,* in $\frac{6}{8}$ time. Notice the subtle shift of accent in the melody whereby the little figure marked "A" begins each time on a different beat or part of the beat, in the measure.

Like all truly great orchestrators, Strauss hears his themes not as abstract melodic patterns but always in the tone color of a particular instrument. This theme is fundamentally a horn theme; it is literally molded to the personality and technical peculiarities of the instrument that announced it. It reveals the secrets of Strauss' brilliance in orchestration—he always makes the instruments do what is specially fitted for them. These two themes and their ingenious transformations will reappear throughout the work. In his use of theme transformation Strauss, a faithful disciple of Liszt, carried the device to even greater lengths than the master.

"Off for new pranks." Repeated in quick succession by various instruments in a rapid *crescendo,* the Mischief theme is built up into a brilliant climax in which it is proclaimed by the entire orchestra, *fortissimo.* The scene is set for Till's first escapade. The tender Till theme with its characteristic dip is now transformed into roguishness on the clarinet, speeded up into a most flippant rhythm:

"Till in the market place." We hear the click of hoof-beats as Till approaches the market place. The two themes leap about maliciously. He catches sight of the women who sit gossiping in front of their stalls. Till's fertile brain hatches a plan. He sidles closer on his horse; looks about him innocently; suddenly jumps his horse right into the middle of the crowd. There is a terrific din and confusion: fishwives scream, pots and pans clatter, geese cackle—all of which gives Strauss an opportunity to indulge in one of those orgies of orchestral noise of which, as a realist, he was so fond.

"Till and the priests." The scene shifts. We hear a sort of swaggering, untroubled marching theme. This two-part tune is played by the first clarinet, both bassoons, and violas divided into two parts, with the bass-clarinet, third bassoon, two horns, second violins, 'cellos, and basses, *pizzicato,* supporting. The upper part of the melody is given here *concert* (as it actually sounds):

Coming as he did at the end of the century, Strauss completely emancipated himself from the regular four-measure-phrase structure. Yet, notice that here when he wishes to give the effect of a hymn he reverts to the regular phrase pattern.

"Disguised as a pastor, he drips with unction and morals." Till seems to be taking part in one of those theological disputations that formed one of the favorite pastimes of the Middle Ages. But a clarinet sliding precariously down the dip of the Till theme reminds us that despite his clerical garb "out of his big toe there peeps the rogue." The priests suddenly realize that Till is mocking them. Little shuddering triplets seem

Courtesy Metropolitan Museum of Art

to warn that the scoffer will come to no good end. The first Till theme returns, insouciantly: he isn't afraid—as yet.

"Till in love." A long *glissando* on the violin tells us that Till is now deep "down in the dumps," a victim of the tender passion. (A *glissando* is a wailing, gliding sound made by passing the fingers in a smooth, unbroken manner over the keys or strings—a common humorous effect used in the cinema.) The *glissando* goes from the topmost E-flat to the G below middle C—the lowest string on the violin.[3] In this romantic episode, Strauss has his opportunity of poking fun at the emotional extravagances of the Romantic composers. The Till themes languish, grow sick with longing, now light up with ardor. A lovely *romanza* (built, as it should be, on the regular four-measure-phrase pattern) emerges as the impassioned swain serenades his beloved. But the lady says *no,* which only whets the suitor's ardor. The Till theme, on brass and strings, becomes agitated. He storms and fumes and threatens to depart, but the fair one remains adamant.

At this point Strauss transforms the whimsical dip theme into one of anger by augmenting the time values of the notes—that is, playing them as dotted quarters instead of eighth notes. This kind of transformation is called *rhythmic augmentation.* Compare this version with the first Mus. Ill.[4]

The opposite of augmenting a theme would be to diminish the note values; speed it up, as it were. This process is known as *diminution.* We had an example of this when the Till theme reappeared in sixteenth notes on the flutes before the market episode.

Having been rejected in love, his theme is flung out angrily by the entire orchestra as poor Till storms away. A moment later, we hear again the mischievous, carefree undulation on the clarinets, and we are aware that Till is off on his next adventure.

"Till and the Philistines." A persistent, plodding rhythm in the darkest register of the winds announces the advent of the professors and pedants, the pompous mediocrities and "stuffed shirts"—in short, the pillars of society against whom the artist, especially when he is still young and unsuccessful, is in perpetual revolt. A brilliant orchestral colloquy follows, with the sparkling Till theme hurled in defiance against the plodding, nagging chords of the Philistines. The opposing tonal masses seem to represent personalities and viewpoints that can never come together.

[3] For those who can read the score, the glissando is twelve measures before Figure 15.

[4] One measure after Figure 19 in the orchestra score.

"Till's self-questioning: should he reform?" A delightful street song, with something very naïve and childlike about it (quite like a polka), ushers in the next episode:

(Note that this is at Figure 26 in the printed score—Aibl Edition.) Notice that here, too, in order to give the effect of verisimilitude, Strauss uses a folk-songlike regularity in the four-measure phrase structure. As Till watches the contented folk about him, there steals into his heart that sense of loneliness which comes sooner or later to all who refuse to submit to the accepted order of things. A wave of tenderness passes over the orchestra as Till catches a glimpse of what life might really be if he would only mend his ways. The wood-winds utter a searching question (not unlike the questioning theme in LES PRÉLUDES, with an appropriate rising inflection): should he not try to reform? Just as he is about to succumb, we hear the ascending horn theme of Mischief followed by the whimsical dip motive, both slowly gathering strength, becoming louder and louder as the realization sweeps over Till that he can never change, that he must remain true to the fundamental character of his nature. Till he is and Till he must remain, come what may!—the orchestra bursts forth in triumph; the Mischief theme, originally played in *staccato* eighth notes, is now heard in a rhythmic augmentation played by the four French horns and two trombones (at Figure 31 in the printed score and here transposed into the concert key for convenience):

The music breaks forth presently with a joyous, furious dance. The above theme and the roguish Till theme are developed in intricate orchestral tone patterns and tossed about cleverly from one instrument to another. Now, thinks Till, I can really be myself.

"The judgment of Till: his sad end." But those who dare to defy society must pay the price. At the height of the festive mood, the brasses proclaim the opening measures of the chorale—the warning of the priests is about to come true. A long drum-roll announces the convening of the court of justice: the culprit has been arrested and brought to trial. Menacing and ponderous chords, *ff*, in the low, dark registers of the brasses, low wood-winds and strings over a roll in the drums, announce the ministers of the law. Unabashed, the irrepressible Till greets them with his defiant

theme on the clarinet as though he were mocking them: he is confident that he will wriggle out of this fix as he has out of so many others. The drums roll again; but Till is still cocky. As the court proceeds he loses his composure; the judge obviously means business. The clarinets indicate that Till has become panicky; we hear again the shuddering little triplets from the episode with the priests. Lower strings and brasses pronounce sentence: Till is to be hanged by the neck until dead. There is a savage snarl in tubas and contra-bassoons as the trap door is sprung. Clarinets and flutes whine piteously. "There he swings; he gasps for air . . . the mortal part of Till is no more." The hanging of Till is an outstanding example of stark and brutal realism.

Epilogue. A long pause. And then we hear again the opening measures of the tone poem. "Once upon a time there was a wag named Till—and now you have heard his story." It is a gallant farewell to Till, a passage drenched in nostalgia and dreams. Perhaps he wasn't so bad after all. . . . There is a final outburst of roguery just at the end. Till is dead—but his spirit lives on!

Strauss called his work "a rondo in the old roguish manner." He had a somewhat mischievous intent in labeling his completely programmatic and realistic tone poem with a term reserved for one of the most abstract forms of so-called pure music. Increasingly the charge was leveled at the program composers that their music possessed no inherent musical structure, that it derived all its organization from the literary program. Strauss took up the challenge by showing his critics that his piece had a musical form, and a quite intricate one at that, at the same time that it told a highly complicated story. Strauss proved his point in brilliant fashion. Yet it must be remembered that any tone poem that tells the adventures of a central character can often be adapted to rondo form, if for no other reason than that the theme of the central character will reappear quite naturally after each of the episodes. If this be a rondo, it is certainly one such as the eighteenth-century masters of that form never conceived.

So firmly has the work established itself in the affections of present-day audiences that it is difficult to understand the reactions it aroused only a generation ago.

ADDITIONAL SUGGESTIONS FOR LISTENING

Among the works of Richard Strauss mentioned in the text of this chapter, we suggest that the reader listen to any or all of these Symphonic Poems: DON JUAN, DON QUIXOTE, DEATH AND TRANSFIGURATION, HELDENLEBEN (A Hero's Life) and THUS SPAKE ZARATHUSTRA. It will not be difficult to add to this list, if the reader is eager to hear more of this composer's works.

It will be a splendid challenge to the listener, at this point, to review and compare the character and use of the "germinal motive" of Liszt, the "leitmotif" of Wagner, and the realistic "descriptive theme" of Richard Strauss.

Courtesy National Broadcasting Co.

THE NBC SYMPHONY ORCHESTRA (Arturo Toscanini, conductor)

20 The sonata and the symphony

We have, up to this point, occupied ourselves largely with various kinds of programmatic music, or music that had extra-musical values—the symphonic poem, opera and music drama, oratorio, suite, ballet, the different kinds of songs, and so forth.[1] We now come to the domain of so-called *absolute* music in which the composer does not necessarily rely on extra-musical associations, either literary or pictorial; in other words, where the story of the music is the music itself, and the action consists of the working out of musical themes to their fullest possibilities, as the composer sees them.

Since in *absolute* music, as we here use the word, there is no external literary plot to hold the music together,

[1] Essential listening study for this Chapter: SYMPHONY NO. 5 IN E MINOR, *"From the New World"* by Dvořák. Suggested parallel works are: SYMPHONY NO. 1 IN C MINOR by Brahms; SYMPHONY IN D MINOR by César Franck; SYMPHONY NO. 2 IN E MINOR by Rachmaninoff; and SYMPHONY IN B MINOR, the *"Pathétique,"* by Tchaikovsky.

the form naturally plays a most important part in supplying cohesion and clarity. We may therefore expect to find that the flowering of absolute music is bound up with the emergence of extensive musical forms. Of these, unquestionably the most important is the *sonata* (from *sonare,* to sound, indicating a piece to be sounded, as distinct from *cantata,* a piece to be sung). The sonata is an extended musical composition in several contrasting movements, generally three or four, of which the first usually is designed in the sonata-allegro form. It is well to emphasize the word "usually." For just as every novel presents another version of the basic formula of development, climax, and denouement, so here there are so many variations of the form of the sonata as a whole, so many exceptions to the rule, that only the most generalized picture of the entire structure can be drawn. Actually, in our study of the sonata we shall aim principally at understanding the basic aesthetic principles that underlie it rather than the resulting technical details.

THE SONATA

The sonata, as signifying a work of several movements, is a form used for all the instruments. There are solo sonatas for piano, for violin, 'cello, organ, and the like, or for any two instruments. If three instruments are involved, we may speak of it as a trio sonata; if four, as a quartet. Quintets, sextets, septets, octets—all refer to the same form, the difference in title merely indicating the number of instruments used. Naturally, the more instruments the greater the opportunity for interplay and contrast among them and the more extended and elaborate the basic form becomes. If the form as a whole is used for solo instrument and orchestra, we have a concerto: thus, we speak of a Beethoven *Piano Concerto,* or a Mendelssohn *Violin Concerto.* And if the form is written for full orchestra, we have one of the noblest and most ambitious types of composition in music, the symphony.[2]

The rise of the sonata was intimately bound up with two of the most important developments in the history of Western European music: the shift in emphasis from vocal to instrumental forms, and the establishment of our major-minor system of keys. We have had occasion to touch on both. As a result composers faced other aesthetic problems. As long as

[2] When we speak of a *sonata,* we refer to an entire work of several movements; but when we use the term *sonata form,* we refer to a specific first-movement, or *sonata-allegro,* structure consisting of three sections: exposition, development, and reprise. For a fuller description and history of the sonata than we can give here, see articles "Sonata" and "Symphony" in Grove's *Dictionary,* Thompson's *International Cyclopedia of Music,* Hadow's *Sonata Form* or any standard reference in music. The sonata-allegro structure may be used in other movements than the first in extended musical works.

they set their music to a text, whether religious, dramatic, or poetic, the meaning of the words furnished a skeleton upon which they could drape their musical inspiration. But in attempting to write for instruments alone they had to organize their musical thinking without any assistance from verbal association or dramatic plot. They had, in other words, to learn to think along purely musical lines. At first they clung for support to the popular dance rhythms of the day and developed the *suite*, a group of fairly short movements based on popular dances in various rhythms and tempos but all in the same key. As they grew more confident of their ability to think along purely musical lines, they branched off into the more extensive form of the *sonata*.

At the same time that instrumental modes of thought were shaking the supremacy of the vocal style, the new major and minor system of keys was supplanting the modes of scales that had been the foundation of medieval church music. The two tendencies amalgamated in the sonata. Not only did this form represent a more highly organized attempt than had ever been made before to think in terms of pure music by presenting and developing themes that had a distinct personality of their own, but in an even deeper sense the sonata became a drama of contrasting tonalities in which the action shifted from the home-key center, the tonic, to surrounding tonalities, mainly the dominant, and then triumphantly fought its way back to the original key. The plan and form of the sonata came to be based upon the new awareness of thematic character, keys and their relationships, and upon what were then daring experiments in modulation, transpositon, and development. Throughout the eighteenth century composers experimented with this new "drama" of keys and themes. Their experiments bore fruit, in the second half of the century, in a magnificent flowering of the classic sonata form, which reached its peak in the art of the masters, Haydn, Mozart, and Beethoven. Within two centuries music had evolved a new language and a new technique, the sheer perfection of which still dazzles us.

The first movement of a typical nineteenth-century sonata is generally *allegro*. This is, as a rule, the most important of the movements as regards structure, wealth of thematic material, and ingenuity of development. The second movement, for contrast, is *andante* or *adagio* in tempo, and *cantabile;* this is the most lyrical and melodic movement of the set. The third movement, often a *minuet*, or *scherzo vivace* in character, is the dance movement, strongly rhythmical and sprightly. The fourth movement, like the first, is elaborate and structurally of impressive dimensions. In the classical symphony it is generally a *rondo*—an *allegro molto* or a *vivace* built on a dance pattern. In the nineteenth century, the fourth movement more often became a triumphal climax in which the struggle and aspiration of earlier movements were brought to their resolution. Sometimes composers reviewed in the final movement the themes of the previous movements, thus unifying their work most effectively. (Of course it is to be understood that the foregoing is intended only as suggestive generalities, for there are actually no hard and fixed rules.)

We have, then, in the typical sonata, a sequence of four movements, of which the first and fourth are fast and intricate; the second slow and lyrical; the third lively, strongly rhythmic, and dancelike. Sometimes composers switch the second and third movements about. In his *"Pathétique"* Symphony, Tchaikovsky deliberately transposes the slow movement to serve as the Finale.[3] In the celebrated MOONLIGHT SONATA, Beethoven begins with an *adagio* and follows it with a *minuet* and a *presto;* but this is a compositional, essential, and self-evident Romantic inspiration necessitating its unusual order.

We may at this point differentiate between the sonata and the suite of the eighteenth century, which also had several movements. The suite movements were each based on the persistence of a uniform dance rhythm. The different movements were all in the same key. They therefore exhibited none of the dramatic contrast of key and theme, of theme development and organization, which was the very basis of the sonata. In short, the movements of the suite did not aim at that impression of organic unity, of architectural organization, of diversity of mood and material, which distinguished the sonata.

THE SYMPHONY

We have, so far, referred to the sonata as being played by a solo instrument, or by several such instruments grouped into a small chamber ensemble; but we now come to the use of the form in a composition to be played by the large number of instruments comprising the modern symphony orchestra—and we appropriately refer to the form thus used also as a *symphony*. Therefore, in a general way, we may think of a symphony as a sonata performed by an orchestra. Of course we realize that countless qualifications and exceptions might be made to such a generality, and we shall soon experience some of the conformities as well as exceptions as we go along in our study. For the present, the general definition is adequate and provocative.

Of course it is to be expected that this larger playing organization, the orchestra, should enrich the structure of the sonata, and that the form, in turn, bind together the many different instruments and players that might otherwise seem to be antagonistic to each other or even to fall

[3] The author has always considered this a mechanical rather than a compositional transposition; and that the third movement is, in reality the Finale proper. Witness audience reaction after the third movement. We have become so accustomed to hearing the transposition, however, that it would seem strange, indeed, to re-transpose the movements.

apart—the form unifies the performing medium. The inherent musical possibilities of the different instruments making up the orchestra gave a new life and value to the sonata form. Composers were not slow in realizing these possibilities, and their imaginations were awakened; they gave free rein to their inventiveness and experimented with new ideas and effects. Out of this has emerged the modern symphony—both the form and the performing medium. Composers dreamed of new vistas and made them come true; and they are still dreaming and experimenting with this seemingly inexhaustible combination of idea and reality—the sonata form and the symphony orchestra.

We thus have an extraordinary growth in the power and sweep of the nineteenth-century symphony that spread like wildfire over the entire musical world. The symphony became the most important form in music —the equivalent in the tonal art of the fully developed novel of Tolstoy, Thackeray, or Balzac. Just as in the great novel, we have in the symphony the sense of an intensely concentrated emotional experience; the satisfaction of realizing the perfection of the minute parts in their relationship to the nobility and sweeping power of the grand structure; and, withal, the feeling of having actually lived with the varicolored and vitalized themes for a space of time, and of having watched them grow, develop, and pass on, as we do with the leading characters in a great novel.

And all these desiderata can be accomplished with or without extra-musical implications. Truly a great and noble instrument had come into the hands of the composer, and the rich symphonic literature that is our heritage stands as eloquent evidence to the justification of the efforts and circumstances that brought both the large symphonic form and the large symphonic orchestra to their present high state of perfection.[4] The years have shown the adaptability of both form and medium to the highly diversified individual needs of our great composers, not the least among these being the symphonic poet of the common folk—Antonin Dvořák (DVÔR zhäk).

ANTONIN DVOŘÁK (1841–1904)

We begin our listening study with the perennially popular SYMPHONY IN E MINOR, *"From the New World,"* Op. 95, of Antonin Dvořák. This has a special interest for Americans, since it was written while the composer was living in this country and it presents some of his impressions of the New World. By far the most generally accepted of his works in this form, the vigorous rhythms and lovely melodies of this symphony have won for it a high place in the affections of the public, and it is today, more

[4] It would be traditional to stop here for an inquiry into the factual and technical details of the sonata–symphony form; but, we shall do so only after we have enjoyed the listening experience itself.

than half a century after it was written, one of the most widely played compositions in symphonic literature.

The composer of the universally beloved *Humoresque* and *Songs My Mother Taught Me* was born in 1841, a year after Tchaikovsky, near Prague. His father, a poor village butcher and innkeeper, could do little for the boy, whose musical gifts were evident from childhood. Local musicians who believed in Antonin's talents helped him through the period when poverty threatened to put an end to his musical aspirations. But when he reached the age of sixteen, he was able to get to Prague, where he pursued his musical education in earnest.

For more than ten years, during which he supported himself by playing viola in the orchestra of the Czech National Theatre in Prague and by giving private lessons, only a few of his intimate friends knew anything about his attempts at composition. Gradually, though, his works made headway and began to attract the attention of the musical world. His first great success came in 1873, when he was thirty-two, with his HYMNUS, a work for voices and orchestra infused with intense devotion to his fatherland, which was under Hapsburg dominion. From then on he espoused the cause of Czech nationalism. He turned to the folk songs, dances, and legends of his beloved Bohemia and, under the influence of his older contemporary, Smetana, became one of the leading figures of the Czech nationalist school. The songs and dances of the gypsy fiddlers who had passed through his father's tavern, the songs and dances of the village folk among whom he had grown up, formed the chief source of his inspiration.

Enabled by his success to devote himself exclusively to composition, he produced a series of works that spread his fame and the cause of Czech music throughout the world. Among the works directly inspired by his nationalism may be mentioned the MORAVIAN DUETS, the popular SLAVONIC DANCES, the three SLAVONIC RHAPSODIES for orchestra, the dramatic overture HUSITSKA, dedicated to the national ideal of religious freedom as symbolized by the martyr Jan Huss and the Hussite movement, the oratorio LUDMILLA, and the folk operas, RUSALKA, KING AND COLLIER, THE CUNNING PEASANT, and THE PIGHEADED PEASANT, all set to the works of Czech nationalist poets and suffused with the folklore of Bohemia.

Like Tchaikovsky and Sibelius, Dvořák was not solely a nationalist. Besides the program works directly inspired by his love of country, he wrote much in the "absolute" forms, carrying on the great tradition of Beethoven and Schubert, Schumann and Mendelssohn. His symphonies, trios, quartets, and quintets, while adapting the hallowed classical forms to his needs as a Romantic and a Nationalist, nevertheless show an impressive command of musical structure and an ability to think in the classical spirit, or temper. In this domain he was influenced and encouraged by Brahms, who became his staunch friend.

Toward the end of the century, Dvořák was recognized as one of the ranking composers of his time. In 1891, at the tercentenary celebration of Cambridge University, he was among the musicians—Tchaikovsky was another—who were given the honorary degree of Doctor of Music. He was made professor of composition at the Prague Conservatoire, elected to the Czech Academy of Art and Science, and decorated by the Austrian government. In 1892—a year after Tchaikovsky's visit to America—he was invited to come to New York to direct the National Conservatory of Music. He was enthusiastically welcomed here and remained for three years, achieving great success as teacher, conductor of his own works, and composer. He traveled through the country, responding to its vastness, its great cities, its sense of power and promise. His summers he spent in the simple, intimate atmosphere of the Czech colony at Spillville, Iowa, where the homesick composer had gone to be as close as possible to the language and customs of his native land.

Despite his great success in this country, his homesickness grew apace. In 1895 he returned to Europe. His joy at the prospect of homecoming found expression in a series of short piano pieces, the *Humoresques*, of which the seventh has become a most popular gem. After his return he took up his post at the Prague Conservatoire, becoming director of the school in 1901. In the final period of his career, he devoted himself exclusively to symphonic poems and operas based on legendary material. His best work along these lines, the poetic opera RUSALKA, belongs to these years. His death in 1904 at the age of sixty-three was mourned by the entire Czech nation as well as by music lovers all over the world.

He was a master of warm, spontaneous melody, of poetic and lyrical moods. His peasant stock and his love for the folk came out in his vigorous rhythms and his strongly accented musical speech. He was one of the masters of orchestration, achieving magical effects with the subtlest of means, especially in his works for smaller instrumental combinations. A poet of nature, he was steeped in the music of the rivers and plains of his fatherland. There is a warmth and freshness of feeling about his music, a verve and manliness, a tenderness and humanity that have endeared him to the multitude.

Symphony in E Minor ("From the New World"), Op. 95

The most famous of Dvořák's orchestral works was completed in 1893 at Spillville, where he could almost fancy himself back in his native land. It aroused a violent controversy when it was first performed: did it really capture the spirit of the New World, or was it, despite the Negro and Indian flavor of some of its themes, a work fundamentally Czech in character and outlook? The issue no longer seems as crucial as it once did. There can be no question that Dvořák, a great nationalist composer acting as teacher and guide to the younger generation of American musicians, gave much thought to the establishment of an American school and the development of a musical idiom that would express the spirit and strivings of the new continent. Music in America at that time was largely in the hands of men who had been trained abroad in the traditions of German Romanticism and who had simply transplanted those traditions to another soil. Edward MacDowell, the first American composer to make an impression on the world scene, was still a young man. Stephen Foster's songs, in the true folk style, had been thus far the only real attempt to discover a distinctively American vein. Dvořák naturally felt that his students ought to do the same thing that he and Smetana had done in Bohemia, that Tchaikovsky and Rimsky-Korsakoff had done in Russia: they should turn to the indigenous rhythms and melodies of the folk. In attempting to portray in music his impressions of the New World and the emotions that it aroused in him, Dvořák is said to have turned, in parts of the symphony, to the inspiration of the Negro and Indian musical idiom, though the composer himself denied the contention. At the same time he was a European writing in the musical language that was natural for him. It would therefore be erroneous to regard the symphony as American music. Rather it presents the impressions of a gifted and sensitive visitor to a foreign land, just as does the *Italian Caprice* of Tchaikovsky or the *Spanish Caprice* of Rimsky-Korsakoff.

In any case, the *"New World"* SYMPHONY reveals Dvořák's gifts—spontaneous melody, vigorous rhythms, colorful orchestration, firm grasp of form, and a natural flow of ideas—at their best. Note how Dvořák obtains a feeling of unity and coherence between the several movements of the symphony by restating themes that had appeared in previous movements —a species of cyclical treatment. See if you can discover the reappearances of such themes. The structure and form of the symphony is very orthodox and classical.

FIRST MOVEMENT: Adagio—allegro molto. E minor. $\frac{2}{4}$ time. The slow introduction gives a sense of mystery and spaciousness, beginning *pianissimo* and bearing traces of Indian song. The opening phrase of the 'cellos is answered by flutes and oboes. The music seems to draw nearer and nearer in a great swell and plunges us into the brusqueness and vigor of the movement proper, *allegro molto.*

The principal theme is announced by the horns in E minor, *mf* (*mezzo forte*), a bold *arpeggio* ascending and descending along the tones of the chord in the syncopated rhythm that already had impressed Dvořák as characteristic of the American musical idiom. (*Syncopation* means that the accent falls not on the strong beat of the measure, where we normally expect it, but on the weak beat, the "offbeat," producing an effect of waywardness and irregularity that adds a pleasant snap to the rhythmic effect.) Thus, in the theme below we have in the second and fourth measures an unaccented eighth note falling on the principal beat of the measure, the "one," while the accented quarter note is shifted to the offbeat. This effect, characteristic of the shuffling dance steps of the Negroes of the South, became one of the most distinctive features of American dance music.

The vigorous syncopation is retained as the theme is unfolded, first *ff* by the strings in unison, then *fff* by the entire orchestra. A short bridge, which modulates to G minor, leads to the first part of the second theme, announced by flutes and oboes, *pianissimo,* that has all the poignance of a Bohemian folk tune.

The naïve character of this melody is accentuated by the regular phrase structure. Shifted into the major mode, it is ingeniously transformed into a typical frontier song and has been used as accompaniment for countless western scenes in the movies. Notice the engaging syncopation of the rhythm and the F-natural in the last measure.

The second part (or real second theme) follows and, for reasons of comparison, the original *Swing Low* melody is shown below it.

Notice the regularity of phrase structure, the effect of the syncopation in the second and sixth measures, and the major mode. With the *fortissimo* repetition of this theme we come to the double bar, whereupon the entire section is repeated. Compare the second theme with *Swing Low.* This strikes one as more of intent of similarities than pure accident or coincidence. Also compare the first two measures of example "A" with measure two of example "B."

In the next section the themes are developed, or worked out. Fragments of the *Swing Low* melody are tossed about among the various choirs. The ascending-descending *arpeggio* figure of the first theme is hurled forth intermittently by the bass instruments. The themes take on new life from these startling juxtapositions; the music modulates frequently, shifting us from one tonality to another. After a *fortissimo* climax, a gradual retransition leads us back to the home tonality of E minor, where we hear the first theme as we heard it originally.

From then on we hear the three themes substantially as they appeared in the first section. For reasons that we shall soon consider, they are not in the same key as they were in the first section of the movement; they have been shifted bodily, or transposed, to other keys. But the melodies themselves are unchanged.

The third theme is followed by a coda (a tailpiece) marked by impetuously descending chromatic scale passages. The first theme, boomed forth triumphantly at the end by strings and trombones, leads into the stirring final cadence.

We therefore see that the *first-movement form* consists of three sections. In the first the themes are presented, or exposed; hence this section is known as the *exposition*. In the second, the *development*, the themes are developed or worked out. In the third, the *recapitulation*, or *reprise*, the themes are repeated or reviewed as at first. An introduction may often open the movement and a coda usually brings it to a close.

At this point the reader will quite naturally see a resemblance between the *sonata-allegro (first movement) form* and *ternary (A-B-A) form.*[5] While the first-movement form contains three sections, of which the first and third are similar, the structural principle is not quite the same as in A-B-A form. In the latter we have unity in the two "A" sections and contrast in the "B." In first-movement form, the exposition ("A") contains a contrast within itself, since two or more themes and keys are presented. The development ("B"), although it contains contrast and variety, nevertheless uses the same basic thematic material as the first section presented in a new guise. The third section, the recapitulation, restores the themes in their original form to the "home" key. We have here the same basic effect of unity, contrast, and variety as in the simple A-B-A form, but this is achieved in a far more intricate design. These two forms satisfy a similar fundamental human desire for balance and symmetry. If the first-movement form had for its object merely the presentation of a succession of pleasant melodies, it would not differ substantially from the suite, or any of the lighter forms, such as *salon music*. But because it

[5] The terms *first-movement form* and *sonata-allegro form* are here used interchangeably.

presents these melodies of a more serious vein in an intricate, highly co-ordinated key organization, the first-movement form takes its place as one of the most ingenious and significant homophonic structural forms in music. Here key and modulation become the very determinants of form, and they do this, as we shall see, efficiently and subtly.

SECOND MOVEMENT: Largo, D-flat major. $\frac{4}{4}$ *time. Three-part, or song, form.* Mysterious chords, *ppp,* on bassoons and brass instruments usher in a solo on the English horn—one of the most famous melodies in symphonic literature.

The reedy, yearning quality of the instrument brings out to the full its poignant wistfulness. Here the son of a Bohemian village merchant has caught a world-wide feeling and has expressed it eloquently. It has been said that Dvořák was thinking of "Hiawatha's Wooing," but there is little substantiation for this. Set to the words of "Going Home," the melody has become widely popular with singing groups.

After the unfolding of the melody, which is based on a three-phrase pattern, we are shifted from the serene major mode into a dark, somber minor, *pianissimo,* in a passage of brooding tenderness. It argues well for the universal quality of music that while for some this part has the flavor of a Bohemian lullaby, for others it might have the awesome beauty of a night on the prairie or a connotation closer to the individual listener's fancy.

Note that after the main theme of the *largo* is fully announced, there comes a short transition passage played by two French horns, muted, fashioned in a typically horn-call style and played over the sustained strings. There follows a contrasting section that is in a slightly faster tempo (*Un poco più mosso*), and in a new key (a mode-like C-sharp minor, compared with the previous D-flat major). This new section is really a development of a bit of the main "Largo" theme, and it is ushered in by the flute and oboe playing the melodic matter, supported by the second violins and violas played *tremolo* and softly. This section continues to unfold, first over a *pizzicato* bass, which gives way to a lovely sustained melody in the first violins on their G strings, over a *tremolo* accompaniment in the lower strings.

Now the oboes, joined in rapid sequence by the clarinets and later the violins, begin a swiftly flowing triplet figure, while many trills are heard from the other instruments. The onset of this section is shown in the following excerpt:

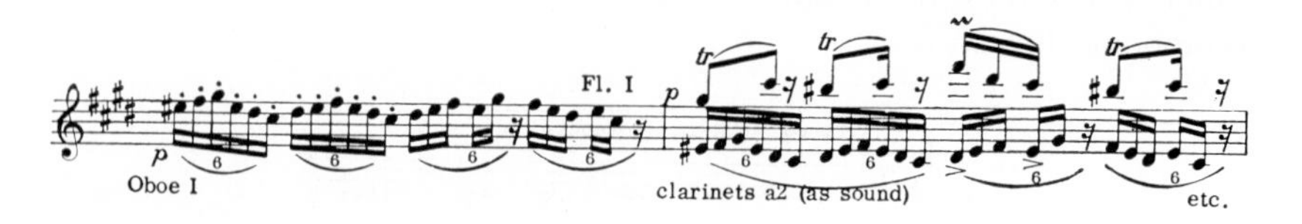

Violins follow suit; the tempo quickens; the whole orchestra becomes tremulous with excitement. When it subsides we return to *Tempo I;* the *Going Home* melody is sung by the English horn; the movement flows on for a little while and then dissolves in a *pianissimo* chord for double basses.

THIRD MOVEMENT: Scherzo. Molto Vivace. $\frac{3}{4}$ *time. E minor. Minuet and trio (A-B-A) form.*[6] In the "scherzo" Dvořák forgets all about the New World and lets himself be swept away in a wave of nostalgia for the folk dances of his native land. A strumming accompaniment on violins and 'cellos introduces the first theme, its gaiety subtly overcast by the minor mode, as so often happens in Slav dances. (The student may have noticed from the heading that we are now back in the E minor tonality of the first movement.) An abrupt, twitching rhythm imparts a curious zest to the theme, which is piped *staccato* in high register by flutes and oboes:

As in many folk dances, the structure here is based on the regular four-measure phrase. The melodic imitation in this passage is interesting to follow.

[6] According to the eminent American theorist, Percy Goetschius, this is a song-form with *Two* Trios; according to an equally eminent English theorist and program annotator, Donald Tovey, the Scherzo is a simple song-form with *One* Trio and an interpolated interlude. Others describe the form as a Minuet and Trio with *Two* themes each.

After a repetition of this section we are brought into a suave major mode, *poco sostenuto* (a little sustained), where a gracefully swaying, almost languid dance is intoned by flutes and oboes against a string accompaniment. The asymmetrical formation—a three-measure phrase answered by one of five measures—lends an elusive charm to the movement (Goetschius calls this the first Trio):

The melody is brought back in the bass, sung in mellow tones by bassoons and 'cellos, while the chords of the accompaniment soar high above. Then, *a tempo* (in the prevailing time), we return to the brittle staccato of the opening theme. Presently, in what Goetschius calls the *second* Trio and what many others call the *one* Trio proper, the strings play a bell-like reiteration over which the wood-winds play a motive not unlike a trumpet call.

The *Da Capo Scherzo* (repeat the scherzo from the beginning) rounds off the contrast with the Trio. In the coda the reminiscence of the first movement suddenly returns, but this time it materializes into a full-fledged appearance, *fff*, of the ascending-and-descending arpeggio theme. As it fades, the rhythm of the opening of the scherzo flits past, *ppp*, and a *fortissimo* final chord brings the movement to an abrupt close.

FOURTH MOVEMENT: Allegro con fuoco (fast, with fire), *E minor.* $\frac{4}{4}$ *time. First-movement, or Sonata-Allegro form.* Out of a tempestuous introduction emerges a marching song given out *fortissimo* by horns and trombones. Even the minor mode cannot dim the sense of power and promise, the high determination, and courage that breathe through this music.[7]

[7] Dr. Sigmund Spaeth, in his book *A Guide to Great Orchestral Music* (New York: Random House, 1943), suggests that the opening theme of the final movement might have been influenced by an American folk song, "Peter Gray," and, further, that the final gay theme resembles "Yankee Doodle."

(Note that the D-natural at the mark N.B. shows the underlying scale structure to be the Aeolian Mode, an old Church "scale.") The theme is repeated with heightened color by violins and wood-winds in high register. The music broadens into a torrent of triplets that courses onward, sweeping everything before it. There is a lot of energy and exultancy about this transitional passage that leads to the second theme.

The mood changes to one of reverie. The second theme, given to the solo clarinet, unfolds in broad curves of melody to a climax on the strings (note the frequent interruptions by the 'cellos):

We are plunged into a popular *fortissimo* melody, each of whose phrases ends with three detached descending notes. This third (or closing) theme is sung by flutes and violins:

Expansive and joyous, it is a song for vast multitudes. The three descending notes at the end are repeated in the bass by 'cellos and basses and then blossom out as the opening of the familiar tune "Three Blind Mice" bandied about by the orchestra with humor and imagination. Now deep down amidst the bass strings, now high up on the wood-winds, this distinctive descending motive persists in imitative style against an intricate countermelody and finally disappears, imitated by a number of instruments at various registers in a continuous downward curve.

The development section is a rich mosaic of the three themes, the connective material, plus reminiscences of previously heard themes. The

March theme on the horns, sounding mysteriously as from a distance, is pitted against fragments of the "Three Blind Mice" theme. Familiar melodies heard in new rhythmic patterns are interspersed among the energetic triplets that lent such verve to the exposition. Echoes of the "Going Home" theme from the *Largo* wreathe about the March theme like a pale memory. The syncopated *arpeggio* of the opening theme of the symphony suddenly spurts upward in a surge of excitement, ever more pressing, until the March theme appears *fortissimo* against downward chromatic scales. The music veers toward the home key of E minor.

In the recapitulation, Dvořák touches upon the thematic material of the exposition. The March theme appears in E minor, strangely subdued. The dreamy second theme rises to a sonorous curve as before, but its orchestral coloring is altered. The popular song (third theme) has a plaintiveness about it. The recapitulation is in the nature of a brief review, preparing the way for the electrifying coda. The ascending-and-descending *arpeggio* of the opening movement gives way to a *fortissimo* entrance of the March theme. From a headlong climax we are thrust into the opening chords of the *Largo,* while the strings produce an upward thrust of great billows of sound. An abrupt *diminuendo* and a fragment of the "Going Home" theme sweep past in startling juxtaposition to the twitching opening rhythm of the *scherzo.* It is as though all the themes we watched grow and expand in the earlier movements were hurrying past for a brief summation before the close. A last solemn announcement of the March theme, and we are swept into the final board cadence on an E major—instead of minor—chord, an ending called, *Tierce de Picardie.*

SCHEMATIC OUTLINE OF A SYMPHONY AS A WHOLE

The first-movement, or sonata-allegro, form

The first movement is often the most important of the entire work. It carries, in the sonata-allegro form, the fundamental principles of musical structure—unity and variety—to their utmost realization. Just as in the novel the action consists of the psychological and emotional interaction between several clearly defined personalities and the working out of their destiny in relation to one another, so here we are presented with two well-defined themes or groups of themes in contrasting character and tonalities, the action consisting in exploring their possibilities as independent entities and in working out their relationship—their struggle—with each other.

Since the first movement of the sonata is generally *allegro,* the first-movement form has come to be known as *sonata-allegro form.* The term is not entirely satisfactory, since it is easy to confuse *sonata-allegro,* which refers specifically to the first movement, with *sonata,* which covers the three or four movements of the entire work. For this reason, many theorists in this country prefer to use *first-movement form,* which is not a good term either, since the form is sometimes used also for other movements, notably the fourth; but it is the best nomenclature we have.

We have seen that the first-movement form consists of an exposition, a development, and a recapitulation, which work out the contrast or conflict between two groups of themes in contrasting keys. Let us now see how this theme and key organization is worked out.

The exposition. The function of the exposition is to present the two themes or groups of themes out of which the movement is to be constructed. The first theme or group of themes is placed in the home, or tonic, key; the second theme or group of themes is in a foreign key. (In the typical classical symphony, the second theme was generally in the key of the dominant—the key whose "tonic," "keynote" or "doh" is a fifth (five scale steps) above the tonic proper—when the first theme is in the major. If the first theme is in a minor key, the second theme is in the relative major, the major key whose key-signature is the same as that of the minor key. For instance, if the first theme is in C major, the second theme is in G major; if the first theme is in A minor, the second theme is in C major.)

Listen intently to the themes as they are presented in the exposition. Hear them repeatedly until they are memorized, so that you can enjoy them in their original states as well as in their transformations when developed. Also note the varied instrumental colors, or timbres, in which the themes are presented in their many appearances.

In the first-movement form, the contrast in character between first and second theme may be reinforced by a contrast in dynamics (such as first theme *f*, second *p*); in register (first theme high, second low); in tempo (first theme fast, second slow); in rhythm (first theme vigorous, second languid); in phrase structure (first theme regular, second irregular); in tone quality (first theme *legato,* second *staccato*); in timbre (first theme given to strings, second to wood-winds or brass); and above all in mode, by far the most effective contrast of all (first theme major, second minor). It is apparent that a striking combination of these contrasting elements will produce a complete emotional and psychological opposition between the two themes. Thus, in Beethoven's FIFTH SYMPHONY the first theme is brusque, passionate, choppy, in a somber, assertive and commanding spirit (in C minor):

The second is serenely lyrical, tender, *legato,* in major—yielding (in E-flat major, the relative major key):

Similarly, in Tchaikovsky's FIFTH SYMPHONY, the first theme is rhythmically abrupt, in minor mode, intoned by the wood-winds (in E minor):

The second is *legato,* flowing, sung by the strings (in B minor—here an unusual relative key) and is derived from the bridge passage:

In musical texts the first theme is generally referred to as the principal theme; the second as the subordinate. This terminology is somewhat misleading, since it implies that the first is more important than the other, whereas what is meant is simply that the first is in the tonic, or home, key, and the second in the foreign key. Many theorists are therefore abandoning these terms and speaking of the first, second, and third themes.

Between the first and second themes or groups of themes comes a transition to lead us from the home key to the foreign key. This bridge plays an important part in the design, since its function is to carry us through the modulation from the tonality of the first theme to that of the second theme. Besides the first theme, bridge, and second theme, the exposition may contain an introduction, generally slow, before the composer plunges into the *allegro* of the movement proper, and a coda or codetta to round out the exposition of the themes. The introduction, which precedes the first theme, will be in the home key. The *coda* or *codetta,* which follows the second theme, will be in the foreign key, the same as the second theme. The composer sometimes employs a third, or closing, theme in the exposition, often in the home key.

The development. In the exposition, the composer makes use of his ability to create memorable themes; in the development, he exhibits his ingenuity in working them out—he displays his mastery over the technical resources of his art. He may take a snatch of his principal theme and combine it with a few bars of the subordinate theme, exhibiting both in an altogether new light. Or, strains of his slow introduction may be used with various combinations of either of his themes. The development explores the latent possibilities of thematic material, and reveals it in an altogether new light. The development is the most strictly intellectual part of the first movement. It is easy to understand how intellectual composers like Beethoven and Brahms brought this section to the highest level of importance and achieved some amazing effects in the manipulation of their thematic material.

The exposition, as we have seen, is built around two tonalities, or key centers, the tonic of the principal theme and the foreign key of the subordinate theme. But the development, which must give the listener the sense of leading him on to ever-fresh vistas, avoids the stabilizing effect of a definitely established tonality. In other words, just as it shifts constantly from scraps of one theme to another, so it shifts from one tonality to the next, this freedom of modulation contributing to the continual piquancy and interest of its progressions. It does, however, avoid the home key, which is saved for the return in the next section.

When the composer has had his say in the working out of his themes, he gets ready for the return to the tonality and mood of his principal theme. Here he makes use of a rather elaborate transition that brings us to the threshold of the home key.

The recapitulation, or reprise. The main point about the recapitulation is that it must resemble rather closely the exposition, with all the principal themes back *in the original key,* so that, after all the complexity of the development, we get here the definite impression of a return home, a feeling of satisfactory balance and unity. The recapitulation therefore re-exposes the first theme in the tonic key. When we come to the bridge, however, the composer abandons the plan of the exposition for a very good reason. In the exposition, the bridge and second theme modulated to a foreign key because the whole movement was ahead. Now, however, we are too close to the end of the movement to be able to leave the home tonality with impunity. The composer therefore presents the melody of the second theme as formerly—but he shifts it from the former foreign tonality into the home tonality; in other words, he transposes it to the key of the first theme. After this comes the closing theme and then the coda, which affirms as emphatically as possible the cadence chords of the home key in what is often a most stirring finale to the movement. The recapitulation is therefore either entirely in the tonic key or as close to it as possible.

We say "or as close to it as possible" because when the first theme is in the major and the second theme in the minor, or vice versa, the second theme often cannot be exactly transposed in the recapitulation to the key of the first. What the composer then does is to shift the second theme, if it is in minor mode, to that minor key that is closest in relationship to the major key of the first theme, though composers often do change the modes to conform to the first theme. Usually a coda brings the movement to a close.

The following diagram will aid the student in visualizing the entire first-movement structure—bear in mind that this is merely a practical, general classical pattern, and that variants and exceptions abound in the past and the present.

FIRST-MOVEMENT, OR SONATA-ALLEGRO, FORM

Slow Introduction (optional)

Exposition	*Development*	*Recapitulation*
1. Principal theme Tonic key	modulates freely	1. Principal theme Tonic key
Bridge, or transition, modulating to	avoids home key	Bridge remains in or close to home key, or is curtailed
2. Subordinate theme foreign key (dominant) or relative major (usually) (Possible third, or closing theme) *often* in tonic key *Codetta*, ending in foreign key, usually the dominant ("double bar and repeat" here in classical form)	presents the thematic material of exposition in new combinations and transformations. Leads back, via transition to—	2. Subordinate theme transposed to tonic key (all other themes in tonic key) or closely related keys *Coda* reaffirming tonic key but they deviate *Finale* and closing cadence.

The second movement

If the first movement is a highly involved part of the symphony, exhibiting a deep intellectual grasp of the material, the second movement, by contrast, is the more simple, lyrical, songlike section. Here the composer abandons the complexities of formal structure for melody pure and simple, of a pensive, serene, or often melancholy character. This is the usual slow movement of the symphony, marked *andante, adagio,* or if very broad, as in Dvořák's NEW WORLD SYMPHONY, *largo.* The form frequently used is the simple, two-part (binary) or three-part (ternary) song—that is, either an A-B or A-B-A structure. The theme-and-variation form is also favored by composers; examples are to be found in the second movements of Haydn's SURPRISE SYMPHONY and Beethoven's FIFTH SYMPHONY. The mood of the slow movement is intensely lyrical, intimate, personal, in contrast to the loftiness and more abstract character of the first movement. If the latter were stormy and agitated, in the *andante* all is tenderness and serenity. Schubert, Schumann, Beethoven, Brahms—all have revealed their deep humanity in the *andantes* and *adagios* of their symphonies and sonatas. Sometimes sonata-form, *sonatina* (an abbreviated sonata), and other forms are used in the slow movement.

It must be emphasized again that in this description only the typical outline, one might even say the stereotyped outline, of the form of the sonata is being presented. The reader must guard against the notion that there is anything rigid about musical form. Actually, the form springs out of what the composer has to say and the materials with which he says it. At the beginning of his career the composer will tend to shape his material on the accepted molds of the masters before him. But as he grows in maturity he grows also in freedom and changes the accepted forms or alters them to suit his own needs. Form, in this sense, is a fluid, ever-shifting essential in art, and any attempt to regard it as fixed or inflexible must lead to a basic misconception of its real value and function. So here the composer is free to do in the second movement, or the third, what he feels necessary in order to express his conception. What the technical analyst of form can state is merely that at a certain period a number of composers seem to have preferred some forms to others.

The third movement

The third movement, in contrast to the lyrical slow movement, is the dance-like movement; of the sonata; in it one or more marked rhythmic patterns predominate. The mood is often *vivace;* the tempo is usually a lively *allegro.* In the classical sonata or symphony, the minuet was the dance preferred for this movement, capturing the courtly grace of the eighteenth century. Beethoven substituted the *scherzo* (from the Italian word meaning a "jest")—a rapid, lilting movement in triple meter like the minuet, but faster, jollier, more vivacious. Sometimes it even had an overtone of grimness, as at some cosmic jest that only an ironic destiny would have conceived. Actually, even some of the Haydn minuets at the end of the eighteenth century absorbed an extraordinary folk flavor. With the Beethoven scherzo, however, the third movement was emancipated from the formal elegance of the minuet form and became in the hands of the Romantic composers a remarkably flexible medium for the most varied moods of the dance.

In form, the classical third movement consists of a minuet and trio (so called because in the early eighteenth century the trio section was generally played by three instruments. As often happens in music, the name has persisted long after the practice has become obsolete). After the trio, the minuet is repeated. Instead of writing it out again, composers would generally indicate the repetition by putting down *minuet da capo* (the minuet to be played from the beginning). The minuet-and-trio form is therefore a species of A-B-A structure. The minuet and/or the trio sometimes contain two tunes each, arranged in a simple pattern so that each section is like a small three-part form. In meter, the minuet, as our modern waltz, is in triple time. In mood, the trio is somewhat less sprightly than the minuet itself—more *legato* and sustained.

The *scherzo* keeps the general outline as well as the meter of its predecessor, but it goes at a much faster pace. Sometimes it is in duple meter. Its outstanding contribution to the entire work is a mood of boisterous, headlong gaiety communicated through clever, compelling rhythms. Of course, composers are free to use other basic forms for this movement. For example, Tchaikovsky in his FIFTH SYMPHONY uses a waltz for the third movement; in his SIXTH SYMPHONY, a melody in $\frac{5}{4}$ time!

The fourth movement

Since the second and third movements are comparatively simple in form, the composer often uses an ambitious structural form for the final movement. In the classical symphony, the *rondo,* gay, light, and good-humored, was preferred. This form, we saw, came from an old French dance form, the *rondeau,* in which the opening tune comes back again and again; as in A-B-A-C-A, or A-B-A-C-A-D-A. The rondo leaves the audience in a good humor; it reached its greatest popularity in an epoch when optimism was a prevailing mood in art. Sometimes a theme and variation form was used, and also the sonatina, a miniature variant of the sonata-allegro form, in which the development section was either absent or present only in a rudimentary state. Less often the sonata-allegro form was used.

As the romantic composers began to experiment with the sonata, good humor at the end gave way more and more to a mood of exaltation, of triumph, of dramatic achievement. Thus, the complex sonata-allegro form came to be frequently used in the finale, balancing the first movement; in the symphony, the final movement often became an impassioned hymn of victory. Beethoven's FIFTH and NINTH, Tchaikovsky's FIFTH, Dvořák's NEW WORLD, the symphonies of Brahms, César Franck, and Sibelius all exhibit this quality of a sort of victory at the end. As often as not, the final movement contains references to themes heard in earlier movements—a kind of farewell review, in which case we speak of the work as *cyclical* in treatment. In any case the fourth movement generally ends with an imposing finale that does double duty in providing *a fitting ending not only for this particular movement but for the work as a whole.* We may now diagram the entire symphony as follows, but we offer it merely as a schematic guide. It is not intended to be comprehensive of all existing and potential future variations.

In all probability the rule of this scheme is more often observed in the breach than in conformity, simply because the form must always reflect and accommodate the musical, poetic, and emotional contents. Inasmuch as these basic elements differ with each new work, with each individual composer, and with each differing age or style, so the various details of the form shall also change. If it were not so, form would be an inhibiting and overbearing tyrant rather than a willing servant of good art.

First Movement:

Sonata-allegro form.
Tempo: *allegro*—usually though not always.
Intricate structure. Seriousness of mood. Absolute style.
Presents principal themes of the movement or the entire work.
Intellectual manipulation and organic development of materials.
Thematic development and architectonic treatment predominant features.

Second Movement:

Simple binary or ternary song form.
Theme and variation, sonatina or other forms used at times.
Tempo: *andante, adagio, largo, andante cantabile,* and so forth.
Emotional, lyrical, personal, melodic. Songlike character of themes predominates.
Intimacy of mood.
Emotional content predominant. Simplicity of structure.
Sonatina or one of several rondo forms sometimes used.

Third Movement:

Minuet and trio form (Minuet repeated after trio, *da capo,* A-B-A). Other dance forms used.
Tempo: *vivace, allegro vivace,* and so forth.
Rhythmic, lively, graceful. Dance character predominant.
After Beethoven, the minuet was supplanted by the scherzo, or other forms.
Vigorous, very fast. Simple structure, relatively.
Both minuet and scherzo were usually in triple meter.
Novel dance forms sometimes used.

Fourth Movement:

Rondo form (one of the several variants) most popular in the classical sonata.
Theme and variation; sonatina form sometimes used.
Sonata-allegro form favored by Romantic and Contemporary composers.

Tempo: *allegro molto, allegro con brio, allegro con fuoco,* and so forth.
Triumphal in mood. Imposing coda or finale; *or often a quiet mood.*
Sometimes contains references to themes heard in previous movements—cyclical form; an effective device for unifying the work.
Climactic drive and cumulative aspects predominant. *Provides fitting climax for work as a whole.*

ADDITIONAL SUGGESTIONS FOR LISTENING

Since symphonic literature is distributed throughout this book in more than adequate amounts, the listener should go on to the succeeding chapter without diversion.

Courtesy Theodore Presser Co.

LUDWIG VAN BEETHOVEN

21 Beethoven: classic and romantic tempers in ideal balance

Between the Classical spirit of the late eighteenth century and the Romantic upheaval of the early nineteenth stands Ludwig van Beethoven, heir of the old and harbinger of the new, one of the most arresting figures in the whole realm of art. He was in his early twenties when the slogan "Liberty, Equality, Fraternity" lit a flame in the heart of modern man.[1] He was barely thirty when the armies of Napoleon Bonaparte, who was then still the symbol of the new order, swept over Europe. Beethoven, therefore, as Edward Carpenter has well said, stands as the prophet of a new era launched by the nineteenth century—a forerunner of Shelley and Whitman in poetry, Turner and Millet in painting. He it was who became the spokesman of the new Romanticism, who brought into music the pathos, the sense of man's struggle with destiny and of his ultimate triumph, the passion, and

[1] See Romantic and Classic tempers, Chapter 13.

the surging emotion of the new era. Like Bach and Wagner, Shakespeare and Goethe, he towers above his age, giving expression to its profoundest stirrings and leading it into new paths of self-realization.

LUDWIG VAN BEETHOVEN (1770–1827)

Ludwig van Beethoven was born in Bonn, the famous university town near Cologne, December 16, 1770. Both his father and grandfather were musicians in the court band of the Elector of Cologne. He learned to play the violin and clavier from his father, and the organ from the court organist. His gifts revealed themselves early in his childhood. At eight he appeared in concert; at ten he began to compose. He was organist of the chapel at eleven and conducted the opera band at rehearsals when he was twelve. The first important event in his life was his first visit to Vienna when he was seventeen. Mozart, hearing him improvise on a theme, remarked, "Pay attention to him; he will make a noise in the world some day."

He continued in the Elector's service until he was twenty-two, playing viola in the opera band and, like Wagner after him, acquiring the technical foundation of his art through practical experience. In 1792, when Haydn passed through Bonn on his way back from London, Beethoven submitted a cantata to him that won the master's warm praise. The Elector now decided to send the young genius to Vienna to study at his expense. In November Beethoven left his birthplace, never to return to it.

He took lessons in strict counterpoint from Haydn, but the two men were too different temperamentally ever to achieve a truly cordial relationship. Becoming dissatisfied with the progress he was making—Haydn was probably much too occupied with his own affairs to pay more than perfunctory attention to his pupil—Beethoven transferred his study to the celebrated theoretician Albrechtsberger. The old master, Haydn, does not seem to have been impressed by his pupil. He told an inquirer, "He has learnt nothing, and will never do anything in decent style."

His playing, especially his improvising, which has become something of a legend, rapidly spread his fame among the music-loving aristocracy of Vienna. Prince Lichnowsky, Prince Lobkowitz, and Count Fries were among the circle of noblemen who soon became his fervent admirers. From the innumerable anecdotes that have come down to us, there is no question that they had to put up with quite a bit from the temperament of the young genius. For Beethoven, in his dealings with his noble patrons, was the very opposite of the easy-going, at times even subservient Haydn. Morbidly sensitive, abrupt of manner, of a proud and fiery nature, he was the symbol of that new republicanism. Indeed, he was the first great composer to fit into the nineteenth-century romantic pattern of the "temperamental genius." In a previous age his defiance

Courtesy New York Public Library

BIRTHPLACE OF LUDWIG VAN BEETHOVEN AT BONN

(*In the uppermost, or mansard, story*)

would have been unthinkable; now the courts and princes not only did not resent what they considered his eccentricities but accepted them, in nineteenth-century fashion, as a concomitant of his genius. Once when he was playing a duet with Ries at the home of Count Browne, and a young nobleman at the other end of the room persisted in talking to a lady, Beethoven suddenly lifted Ries's fingers from the keys and announced loudly, "I play no longer for such swine!" He once fancied himself slighted at a party at Prince Lichnowsky's. Leaving in a huff, he wrote the Prince a note: "There have been princes before you and there will be after—but there is only one Beethoven!" With Beethoven the artist unquestionably comes into a new social status. Whereas Mozart's revolt, as we shall see, turned out to be premature and was crushed; Beethoven, aided both by a stronger personality and the new spirit of the times, was able to sweep all before him.

This "natural man," in a Rousseauesque sense, in revolt emotionally and intellectually against all that was conventional and artificial, was manifestly the one best fitted to become the voice of the new Romanticism and to lead the art of music away from its eighteenth-century heritage. He could not improve greatly the formal elegance or the exquisiteness of design to which Haydn and Mozart had brought it; but he could widen its boundaries, deepen its emotional capacities to a degree undreamt of until then, smash the rules, and bring music into tune with the needs and emotions of the new age. This he probably would have done in any case, since the time was ready for it. But the intensity with which he did it, the specifically Beethovenian pathos that he introduced into his art, were indubitably heightened by one of those soul-shattering experiences that, if they do not break a man, leave him changed for the rest of his days. On the threshold of a brilliant career, just as he was beginning to try his wings in music, he found himself going deaf. The disaster seemed to portend the certain end of his career as a composer: he had no way of knowing that he would create his greatest works by hearing them only in imagination. Even more, the deafness was threatening to cut away all normal contact with his fellows. The victim of a physical defect always tends to magnify its effect out of all correct proportion. Given Beethoven's morbid sensitivity, his emotional insecurity, his social self-consciousness, we may well understand why he reacted as he did.

In a profoundly touching letter to his brothers, written from Heiligenstadt, the suburb of Vienna where he spent the summer of 1802, he lamented the loneliness that his deafness imposed upon him. He shrank from any normal social relations, dreading to admit an infirmity in the one sense in which he felt he should be more perfect than others. He had gone to Heiligenstadt still hoping that the malady might be arrested. Now he gave up all hope; his thoughts dwelt on escape through death. Throughout the long lonely walks of that summer there raged within the thirty-two-year-old artist the crucial battle between what Carlyle so well described as the nay-saying and the yea-saying. And when he emerged, the will to live, to struggle, and to create had triumphed over the will to die. In the valley of shadow he had come to realize that life could not be for him as for other men—that only through his art could he hope to make up for all that reality itself would forever deny him—that out of the very renunciation he must build a new universe for himself. By a stupendous effort of will he lifted himself above despair, above illness, above frustration, into the Olympian sunlight of immortal beings. For the twenty-five years of life that remained to him—a period of supreme achievement—there was to ring through his music the strength, the courage, the heart-warming affirmation of life possible only to one who had known the worst and conquered it. From bitter knowledge, he extracted that sense of man struggling with fate that so inflamed the imagination of the nineteenth century; that wonderful awareness of the pathetic element in life; that intensity of emotion and high ethos that set his music apart from the music of other men. "He who truly understands my music," he remarked to Bettina von Arnim, "must thereby go free of all the misery which others bear about with them."

More and more as he withdrew into himself he left his generation behind. His final piano sonatas and quartets were a century ahead of their time. When the violinist Radicati, puzzled by the "RASOUMOWSKY" QUARTETS of the "middle" period, said to him, "But surely you do not consider these works to be music," Beethoven retorted, "Oh, they are not for you—but for a later age." The familiar picture has come down to us of the short, stocky man striding hatless through the fields, his shaggy hair tossing in the wind, crying out and waving his arms as he stopped now and then to make a notation in his sketch book. In the fields and woods on the outskirts of Vienna, alone with nature, his great works were sketched and resketched, erased and rewritten, and by an incredibly slow process advanced toward their ultimate shape. In his personal life Beethoven might have been slovenly, absent-minded, impatient; in all matters pertaining to his work he was supremely meticulous, infinitely patient, one of the most hard-working and fastidious artists who ever lived. His method of composition was the very opposite of Mozart's spontaneous flow. After months, sometimes years of pondering, the work took shape, emerged in its final perfection. The opening chords of the "*Eroica*" were rewritten literally scores of times; the themes of the FIFTH SYMPHONY appear in his sketch books seven years before it was finished. If Mozart's music gives us the impression of having "leaped into being full-formed like Athena from the brain of Jove," Beethoven's music is of the slow "growth of the soil."

Because of the lack of adequate documentation, it is difficult to gauge the exact cause and nature of Beethoven's deafness. The malady seems to have appeared in its incipient stages as early as his twenty-eighth year. By the time he was thirty-two, as we know from the Heiligenstadt Testament, he could no longer hear the songs of the birds. In 1815 he was still able to take an active part in the rehearsals of his opera FIDELIO. For a few years afterward he still insisted on conducting his own works, but the musicians would only pretend to follow him. As affecting as the aged Haydn's farewell public appearance at the performance of the CREATION was Beethoven's at the first performance of his last and greatest symphony, the NINTH, in 1824. Although the choir and orchestra were instructed to watch his direction, they paid no attention to his beating of the time. At the close of the scherzo there was a burst of tremendous applause. Beethoven fumbled with his score, deaf to the acclaim, until one of the singers pointed to the audience. Then he turned and bowed, and there was not a dry eye in the theater.

The three years that were still left him witnessed the production of the final string quartets, those magnificent works in which he completely transcended the limits of the early nineteenth century and struck out on new paths for the later age. Yet, having reached the most mature and exalted period of his life, the master was strangely humble. "It seems to me as though I had just begun to write!"

We have a last vivid glimpse of the composer visiting his brother and the latter's wife in the autumn of 1826, just before his final illness, deaf, untidy, unpresentable, ignoring every household rule. After a quarrel with his relatives, Beethoven abruptly decided to return to Vienna. Refusing to wait until a suitable carriage could be procured, he made the trip back in an open chaise. The cold, damp weather caused a "cold in his stomach"; an inflammation of the lungs supervened, soon complicated by dropsy. He was in bed for several months, without any inkling that death was near. Toward the end of March, 1827, his condition took a sudden turn for the worse; the truth dawned upon him. *"Plaudite amici, comoedia finita est!"* (Applaud friends, the comedy is over) he muttered to his companions. It had been something even more than a divine comedy—a deeply human one. His last gesture was typically Beethovenian. A sudden storm and clap of thunder roused the dying man. He shook his clenched fist and fell back dead.

Unlike his predecessor Mozart, he had made a deep impression on the Viennese; his funeral was his most triumphant public appearance. The schools were closed, the crowd was enormous. Soldiers cleared the way for the cortège; it took an hour and a half for the short trip from his house to the church. Mozart's REQUIEM was performed, as it had been at Haydn's funeral. One of the chief mourners was Franz Schubert, who died the next year at the age of 31. He was laid to rest near Beethoven. Their paths crossed—Mozart, Haydn, Beethoven, Schubert—the four great names of the Viennese school that conferred upon the City of Music a luster that cannot fade.

Of the four, Beethoven has come to be looked upon as the greatest in actual achievement. Like Wagner in the following generation, he left the imprint of his mighty personality upon his age. He seemed single-handedly to have changed the course of music and to have opened up new vistas for the musicians who were to follow. He ushered in the era of distinctive personalities—Wagner, Liszt, Chopin, Schumann, Brahms, Tchaikovsky—each of whom was to add an intensely personal accent to a universal language, to pour the innermost griefs and longings of the soul into what had hitherto been a somewhat impersonal art.

THE ACHIEVEMENT OF BEETHOVEN

Like Haydn and Mozart, Beethoven was a versatile composer who was at home in every form: his songs and cantatas, his oratorio THE MOUNT OF OLIVES, his SOLEMN MASS, his solitary opera FIDELIO, his incidental music to Goethe's EGMONT, and his concert overtures are all landmarks in their respective fields. But his gift was pre-eminently in the realm of absolute instrumental music, and his contribution was greatest to the development of the sonata form—the solo piano sonata, the duo for violin and piano, the chamber music combinations, trio, quartet, quintet, sextet, septet, octet, with special emphasis on the string quartet, the piano as well as the violin concerto, and, last and greatest, the symphony. Before turning to a detailed examination of the most famous and popular of all symphonies, his FIFTH, it may be well to summarize, however briefly, the achievements that are specifically associated with his name.

The first-movement, or sonata-allegro, form Beethoven immeasurably enlarged and enriched both from the standpoint of structure and of emotional content. He increased the size and complexity of the development until it became perhaps the single most important section of the movement, a truly intellectual working out of all the implications of the thematic material of the exposition, as well as of new material specially introduced here in a mood of free fantasy. So, too, he introduced a new freedom in the key relationships between principal and subordinate themes and a new daring in modulation, as well as a greater flexibility in the employment of subsidiary themes. As for the coda, which had previously been mainly a rounding off of the movement, he transformed it almost into an independent chapter as rich in emotional content and imaginative fire as the movement itself. Above all, he created in his greatest first movements—such as those of the THIRD, FIFTH, and NINTH SYMPHONIES, the APPASSIONATA SONATA, the SERIOSO QUARTET, Op. 135—the mood of titanic struggle, of tragic grandeur, of the Hero pitted against Fate that is the essence of the Romantic symphony.

In Beethoven's hands, the slow movement was deepened from an atmosphere of gently reflective lyricism to one of intense pathos and deeply personal utterance. The Beethovenian *adagio* in the sonatas, the quartets, and the symphonies, is a passionate outpouring of the soul, the first expression of the exalted lyricism of the great slow movements of nineteenth-century music. Indeed, Beethoven's slow movements are unsurpassed, perhaps unequaled, in all music.

The third movement of the Classical symphony had been the dainty, aristocratic minuet; but this dance was hardly congenial to the mood and spirit of the new age. Although Haydn had sought a dance more lively and gay than the minuet for the traditional third movement, it was Beethoven who actually achieved the spirited movement called the *scherzo*—that vivacious and often boisterous outburst of Homeric laughter. As Schauffler points out in his biography of the composer, Beethoven did not really invent the *scherzo;* rather, after Haydn gave the minuet a new tempo, Beethoven broadened, deepened, and quickened it, and transformed the spirit and character of the movement into one of his most idiomatic and "pungent" formal creations. He sometimes invested the scherzo with a mysterious, sardonic, or menacing mood—as in the FIFTH SYMPHONY.

As a necessary adjunct of his dramatic power, Beethoven used nuance to a far greater degree than had his predecessors—*pianissimo* whispers gradually swelling to shattering *crescendos,* these further dramatized by sudden *pianissimos* again. His scores abound in these violent, dramatic contrasts to a far greater degree than do those of Haydn or Mozart. What is most important, they were *an integral part of his composition,* and he was much more careful than they in writing down the symbols indicating the exact effects he desired. Building on the experiments of both Haydn and Mozart, Beethoven made great advances in the techniques of handling the orchestra. His tonal effects—notably in the use of the different choirs for color and contrasts, in the achievement of orchestral sonorities, in the freer and more effective writing for the horns, the wood-winds, the violas, the double basses, the kettledrums—were definite steps forward. In his effort to knit the various movements of his works into a more cohesive whole, he developed the procedure of quoting in one movement a theme, or themes, that had been employed in a previous movement—the cyclical treatment that became one of the most popular devices of the nineteenth-century composers. (The word "cyclical" is also used to mean that form of melodic treatment in which the material unwinds and evolves out of its very self. See César Franck, Chapter 27.) In Beethoven we find the ideal balance of Romantic and Classical tempers.

The Fifth Symphony in C minor, Op. 67

The most popular of all symphonies affords us a good insight into the master's style. We know from the sketchbooks that some of the motives of this symphony germinated in Beethoven's mind as early as 1800. It was finished in the summer of 1807, together with the *"Pastoral,"* the SIXTH. At the first performance the following year, the two symphonies were numbered the other way around. The announcement of the concert throws an interesting sidelight on the musical conditions of the time:

This second theme is promptly answered by the brass and *tutti* orchestra (*ff*), only to give way again to a subdued (*pp*) passage. The slow triple meter gives an effect of great dignity and breadth. The regularity of the phrases, the care with which the cadences are marked, above all the beautiful curve of the melodic line in both themes, add to the sense of spaciousness and freedom.

The variations serve not so much to show off the composer's ingenuity as to explore to the full the emotional possibilities of the thematic material. The first theme is presented again in a steadily flowing succession of sixteenth notes that retain the contours of the original. The second melody then returns, borne aloft by oboes and brass against a more elaborate accompaniment in thirty-second notes. The first theme is further elaborated into a running succession of thirty-second notes on the violas and 'cellos, repeated *pianissimo* by the violins against a *pizzicato* accompaniment on the lower string instruments, and then as a running bass melody on 'cellos and double-basses against loud chords in the rest of the orchestra. Now the upward-sweeping second theme is sounded forth by the full orchestra, reaching a triumphal climax and leading to the *fortissimo* statement of the first theme by first and second violins. The *coda* has an interestingly rhythmic accompaniment and works up to a powerful final cadence.

THIRD MOVEMENT: Scherzo. Allegro. C minor. $\frac{3}{4}$ *time. Minuet and Trio form.*[3] The third movement begins *pianissimo* in the somber tonality of the first. A mysterious phrase emerges from the deep register of the 'cellos and double-basses, answered by the violins:

[3] This movement is sometimes described as a "Song-form with Trio."

Suddenly the horns announce a theme bearing a striking resemblance in rhythm to the Fate motif of the opening:

The two themes alternate, the Fate rhythm this time proclaimed triumphantly by wood-winds and brass. A new melody, a tender dance, sounds awhile before giving way to the ineluctable Fate rhythm.

The middle portion of the *scherzo,* corresponding to the Trio of the minuet, opens with 'cellos and double-basses scampering through a rapidly running figure that reminded Berlioz of the "gambols of a frolicsome elephant."

The figure is ingeniously imitated, each time in a higher register, by violas and bassoons, second violins, finally first violins assisted by flutes and oboes. Note the frolicsome humor in the second part of the Trio section, where three starts have to be made by the 'cellos and basses ere they are on their way—as though they had made mistakes in this difficult, fast music.

The Trio subsides into the mysterious *pianissimo* of the opening; the first part is repeated. We hear as from afar the mysterious tapping of the Fate motive rhythm. Then begins the unforgettable transitional string passage connecting the third and the fourth movements, with the kettle-drums keeping up a steady beat, first *ppp,* then *pp* and, in the last eight measures, a gradual *crescendo,* until, like a sudden blaze of light, the full orchestra fairly leaps, without a break, into the exultant and triumphant C major first principal theme of the last movement, *fortissimo (ff).*

FOURTH MOVEMENT: Allegro. C major. $\frac{4}{4}$ *time. Sonata-Allegro form.* Nowhere do we see more clearly the contrasting emotional coloring of major and minor than in the C major chord that introduces the marchlike first theme of the final movement:

This is music of triumph, of irresistible power, of exultation and of glory! One is reminded of the observation of the biographer, Theodore Baker, when he said, in part, "Beethoven's loftiest originality, and that whence the differences in formal construction naturally flowed, is the intensity and fervor of subjective emotion which pervades his works. It is this mood of profound subjectivity, of individual, powerful soul-expression which, most of all, differentiates Beethoven's music from that of Bach, or Haydn, or Mozart, and which opens the era of 'romantic' composition." [4]

A subsidiary idea to the first principal theme is heard in the wood-winds and horns. It is fashioned largely on the tones of the C major chord, C-E-G—the tonic chord of the established key, as the musicians identify it. It is called "subsidiary" because it is very closely related, musically speaking, to the principal theme. However, it is more subdued, flows more smoothly, and is more reflective in mood than its "superior" theme. Be careful to distinguish between "primary" and "secondary" themes. Here is the subsidiary theme as played by the wood-winds and horns:

The foregoing idea is worked up to a *fortissimo* which leads, through a transitional linking theme, to the second principal theme proper. The link is played by the violins; and the second theme first by the violins and then by the wood-winds. Here are the transitional idea and the second principal theme:

[4] Theodore Baker, *Biographical Dictionary of Musicians.* (New York: G. Schirmer Inc., 1940.)

The tripping triplet theme, the second principal theme proper, is worked over, tossed from the strings to the wood-winds and back again, and soon turns into a *fortissimo* (*ff*) sixteenth-note scale passage which culminates in two loud, crisp, *tutti* climactic chords. Immediately following these *staccato* chords, there is heard a new theme which is subsidiary to the second principal theme of the movement. It is a descending motif, or theme, characterized by the entry tone sharply accented and quickly softened *forte-piano, sfp* (or simply *fp*). This device becomes fascinating as the clarinet, the bassoon, and the violas enter with the theme, to be followed by additional entries, the 'cellos coming in among the last, each entry being made clearly evident by this *fp* attack. Here is the subsidiary theme to the second principal theme:

The orchestra as a whole works up to a loud declaration of this subsidiary theme, and with a few cadential chords in the key of C, there comes the familiar, classical use of the repeat sign when the entire exposition should be repeated. This traditionally marks the end of the *exposition,* the repetition of which is nowadays more honored in the breach than in the observance; also, the double-bar-and-repeat sign indicates the beginning of what is, in the sonata-allegro form, called the *development,* or *"working-out"* section. In this division, the composer takes the themes he has presented in the exposition (sometimes adding one or two new ones), and transforms them in orchestral color, rhythm, harmony, and melody. The listener will enjoy observing the many manifestations of the themes he has heard in the previous section, and to see how much enjoyable musical material can be extracted from what seems, at first, to be simple thematic statements. Incidentally, Beethoven and Brahms are much alike in making a great deal of interesting, beautiful, and ofttimes complicated music out of these simple, almost folk-like principal themes.

If in the sonata-allegro structure of the first movement Beethoven pared to the bone, he allowed himself ample room in this movement. The development is one of those highly intricate and extended working-out sections so closely associated with Beethoven. The ascending triplet figure is inverted, and the thematic material of the exposition is intertwined in a rich mosaic of imitations from one choir to another. New material springs out of the old with the "germinating" inevitability of the first movement. The *crescendos* are spacious, the climaxes sustained and cumulative, the modulations swift and bold. At the very summit of development, Beethoven, by a daring stroke of imagination, plunges us into the insistent Fate rhythm of the opening of the *scherzo,* a final reminiscence before the close. The introduction of the Fate motive at this particular place in the work is a great stroke of Romantic imagination. From a formal consideration, this theme marks the close of the development section and the onset of the reprise. Here is the music of the Fate motive as it appears at this point—note the first violins playing softly with the bow (*arco* as it is called), very soft (*pp*) supporting chords by the second violins, violas, and the 'cellos plucking the strings (*pizzicato*). Observe also the orchestral coloring effected by the entry of the march-like tune in the clarinets as indicated:

This motive grows into a cleverly contrived *compositional crescendo* as opposed to the more usual dynamic (mere increase of loudness) *crescendo.* Suddenly, as though inspired by overcoming the impending doom, the full orchestra bursts forth loudly (*ff*) with the first principal theme of this movement (*allegro:* $\frac{4}{4}$). A forceful paean of victory, made all the more effective in its reappearance by a dramatic foil, the Fate motive appearing immediately before. From a formal or structural aspect, the entry of this "*Paean of Victory*" first principal theme marks the onset of the *recapitulation,* or *reprise* section. In this division, the principal themes and their important subsidiary themes—first heard in the *exposition* section—are again reviewed pretty much as at first. There are these chief possible differences, however, in the practical reprise: (1), the keys or the tonalities of *all* the themes are usually now in the key of the movement, or the work as a whole; (2), the modulatory links which were necessary in the exposition because of the diversity of tonalities, are now recomposed to suit the conditions; (3), sometimes not all the principal themes are reviewed, and not always in the exact sequence; (4), sometimes entirely new material is interwoven in the compositional warp and woof. This is to be expected when the composer wishes to curtail the reprise and to put special emphasis upon the ensuing closing section—the *coda.* Ever since the middle period and later works of Beethoven, the coda has assumed more importance than the conventional "hurry-up-and-finish" ending.

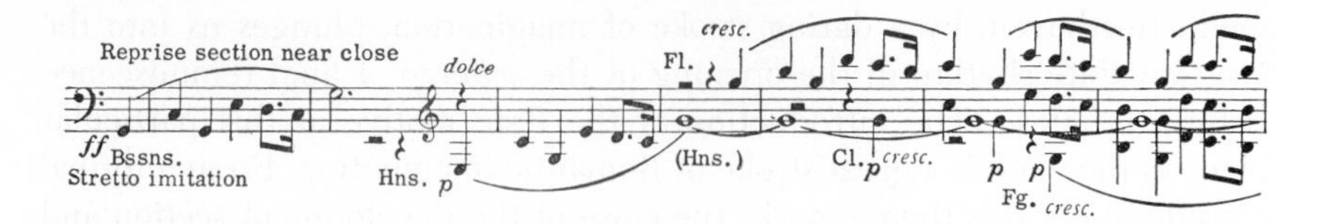

Note the interesting *stretto* (close imitation) that Beethoven fashions out of the subsidiary to the second theme of the closing section just after the sixth "crash" chords of the *coda* and not far from the ensuing and final section of the movement, *Sempre Più Allegro* and the final *Presto* section with its "cut-time," ending not only the final movement but also the symphony as a whole. Note also Beethoven's characteristic dynamic contrast succeeding the last illustration.

Thus Beethoven's FIFTH SYMPHONY, one of the greatest musical masterpieces of all time, closes in a powerfully moving, triumphant, and exalting mood.

In contemplating the musical design of the Finale just heard, the listener will have observed, no doubt, that this movement, like the first, is fashioned in the sonata-allegro form. This form might well be boiled down and schematized simply as: (A), the exposition, (B), the contrasting development or working-out section and (A′), the reprise, or recapitulation, of the main ideas of the work, the aesthetically balancing section to achieve unity and coherence after so much variety. Finally, there is the *coda.* As for the typical symphony or sonata as a whole, a time-honored, humorous description says: the first movement shows how clever, resourceful, and knowing the composer is; the second, how deeply and lyrically he can feel; the third, how humorous and gay he can become; and the fourth movement shows how anxious and thankful he is to be through with the thing!

If, as some still maintain, there is no truth to the story about the "Destiny knocking on the door" program of the symphony, the very nature of the symphony—a paean of victory of Faith over Fate—warrants the interpretation. Polling records show that this symphony is probably more frequently performed than any other, by a wide margin. Never has so great a masterpiece been created out of so meagre and so unpromising a basic material. The best way to know this work adequately is to hear it again and again—intently and *empathically.* The sympathetic and eager listener will find something new and beautiful in it at every hearing, even if he knows the work perfectly from the first note to the last—for that is the way with genuinely great masterpieces. Man sorely needs this kind of beauty for his welfare, his happiness, his spirituality, and his whole emotional health and well-being.

ADDITIONAL SUGGESTIONS FOR LISTENING

Besides the FIFTH SYMPHONY of Beethoven, we suggest that the listener hear his other symphonies in the following order, determined by polling many classes plus polls of public concert audiences in the larger cities: the THIRD (the "Eroica"), the SEVENTH, FOURTH, EIGHTH, SIXTH (the "Pastoral"), NINTH (the "Choral"), the FIRST and then the SECOND. As for the other works of Beethoven, we suggest that reference be made to the chapters in this text discussing the concerto, the overture, the string quartet, and other ensembles. Opera lovers will want to hear an actual performance, or to listen to good recordings of Beethoven's only opera (and a very troublesome one it was to him!)—FIDELIO. Listen to selections from: the ten SONATAS for VIOLIN AND PIANO, the five SONATAS for 'CELLO AND PIANO; the many concerti for solo instrument(s) and orchestra; the thirty-two SONATAS FOR PIANO SOLO (excellent new 33⅓ RPM recordings of these are available). Listen to the choral works, MISSA SOLEMNIS, Op. 123, the MOUNT OF OLIVES, Op. 85 and the MASS IN C, Op. 86.

For reference readings about Beethoven and his works, we suggest the following: the definitive biography by Alexander Wheelock Thayer, *The Life of Beethoven,* 3 Vols. translated and edited by Henry E. Krehbiel (New York: The Beethoven Assn. 1921), original ms. was written in English but first published in Germany; Paul Bekker, *Beethoven,* translated from the German by Bozman (London: Dent and Sons, 1925); Robert H. Schauffler, *Beethoven: The Man Who Freed Music* (New York: Tudor reprint, 1947), a popularized viewpoint; Vincent d'Indy, *Beethoven: A Critical Biography,* translated from the French by Theodore Baker (New York: G. Schirmer, 1940), an excellent standard study of his works; J. W. N. Sullivan, *Beethoven: His Spiritual Development* (New York: Knopf, 1927); W. J. Turner, *Beethoven: The Search for Reality* (London: Dent, 1927) excellent; Edwin Evans, Sr., *Beethoven's Nine Symphonies* (London: Reeves, 1923-24) 2 Vol., one of the most detailed analyses of his symphonies; Daniel Gregory Mason, *The Quartets of Beethoven* (London: Oxford, 1947), a fine detailed critical study; Donald Francis Tovey, *Beethoven* (London: Oxford, 1945), up to his usual excellence; Donald Ferguson, *History of Musical Thought* (New York: Crofts & Co., 1948), Chap. 32, pp. 289-324; Theodore Thomas and Frederick Stock, *Talks About Beethoven's Symphonies* (Boston: Ditson, 1930); Donald Tovey, *Essays in Musical Analysis* (London: Oxford, 1945) Vol. I, pp. 21-67 and Vol. II, pp. 1-45. Of course, consult Grove's *Dictionary of Music and Musicians* (New York: Macmillan, 1946); *International Cyclopedia of Musicians* (New York: Dodd, Mead and Co., 1949); *Analytic Symphony Series No. 3* (Boston: Ditson, 1927), edited and arranged for piano, 2 hands, by Percy Goetschius—and other similar sources. Those who can read French should see Vincent d'Indy, *Cours de Composition Musicale* (Paris: Durand, 1899-1900), Vol. II, "Nine Symphonies by Beethoven," Chap. II, pp. 121-147, a brief, but superb insight!

Courtesy the owner, Professor Jan Philip Schinhan

JOHANNES BRAHMS

After an original drawing
by Anton Forster.

22 Brahms: the classical romanticist

It was not without justification that von Bülow made his now famous epigram, "The three B's—Bach, Beethoven, and Brahms."[1] Schumann, in an article which created quite a disturbance at the time, called Brahms the true successor to Beethoven. Whether such comparisons are fully justified or not, they do indicate that Brahms occupies a lofty position among the great musical geniuses of all time. His works are found in the field of song, chorus, chamber music, concertos for various instruments, solo and duo sonatas, trios, and a number of orchestral

[1] This chapter may be transposed to a position at the end of the symphony unit (after Haydn), or immediately after Mozart, if achievement levels indicate the advisability of such a postponement. The author suggests the following priority order as an aid in reducing the unit further to meet time allowance: 1-Dvořák and Beethoven, 2-Mozart, 3-Brahms, and 4-Haydn. Eliminate in reverse order. Obviously the number and sequence of symphonies in this unit have been carefully determined and verified in practice by the author; thus the unit is to be preserved and studied as indicated in the text, if possible.

works, including four symphonies; but he wrote no opera. We have mentioned Beethoven as being the link between the Classical and Romantic periods in Germany; and we can consider Brahms, coming at the peak of the period, as still another span to the same bridge between the two great stylistic tempers that pervade the music of history—Classicism and Romanticism. Brahms, like Beethoven, was great enough to embrace both to a superior degree. In this, the music of Brahms and the poetry of Browning have much in common.

JOHANNES BRAHMS (1833–1897)

We stated in the discussion of the Romantic and Classic tempers in art that the two may exist side by side, not only within the same period, but even in the works of the same composer. Nowhere is this point better exemplified than in the music of Johannes Brahms. In the fervor of his emotion, in brooding introspection and passionate lyricism, he is one of the foremost romantics. Yet, in an age dominated by the theatricalism of the Wagnerian music drama, by the flamboyant program idiom of Liszt and Berlioz, Brahms adhered steadfastly to the great symphonic tradition of the past, a serene Olympian figure, the last in the long line of great German masters whose supreme achievement was the perfection of organic structure, the development of germinal forms in so-called "absolute" music. Yet, we reiterate, Brahms was an ardent and sincere Romanticist at heart.

Brahms was born in Hamburg in 1833, the son of a double-bass player in the theater orchestra there. His mother had a profound influence on his development. Both in his youth and manhood, Brahms remained extremely attached to her, and her death in 1865, when the composer was thirty-two, is said to have inspired one of the most touching elegies in all music, the GERMAN REQUIEM.[2]

Brahms displayed his musical gifts from early childhood. He received a sound musical education, both in piano and theory, and made a public appearance as a pianist at the age of fifteen. The following year he appeared as a composer, playing a *Fantasy on a Favorite Waltz*. After a few years of diligent study, mostly with the teacher Marxsen, he became, at the age of twenty, the accompanist to the gypsy violinist, Eduard Reményi. On their tour through North Germany, he met the great violinist Joseph Joachim, who became a lifelong friend and played a notable part in Brahms' career. (The superb VIOLIN CONCERTO IN D, Op. 77, was dedicated to Joachim.) Joachim, who soon realized that Brahms' true gift lay in creative writing rather than in performance, gave him a letter of introduction to Schumann, who was living at Düsseldorf.

[2] There are good reasons for doubting the accuracy of this statement, but the spirit underlying it is worthy of preservation.

His meeting with Schumann was a key event in the young composer's career. The older man, in a famous article in the *Neue Zeitschrift für Musik* entitled "*Neue Bahnen*" (New Paths), hailed the twenty-year-old Brahms as a genius, focusing on him the attention of all musical Europe—and history has proved how right Schumann was.

From then on, the history of Brahms' life is the history of his works. His personal existence was uneventful, compared with the story careers of Wagner and Liszt, for example. With external difficulties mitigated to a large extent, he was free to devote himself to the creation of the works that soon stamped him as one of the foremost composers of his time. From 1854 to 1858 he was concert director at the court of the Prince of Lippe-Detmold, a post that he resigned in order to give all his time to composing. He lived for a time in Hamburg and in Switzerland; but after 1862 he settled in Vienna, which remained the center of his activities until his death. Here he was for a year the conductor of the Singakademie, producing the choral works of Bach, Beethoven, Schumann, and others, after which he held no post that entailed regular duties. Save for occasional concert appearances and holiday tours, the last three decades of his life were devoted to composing. He remained a bachelor, a burly, jovial figure in the musical life of Vienna, surrounded by a wide circle of admirers and friends. He was inclined to be forbidding and caustic with strangers and had very little patience with sham and social airs; but underneath the gruff exterior was a nature bubbling over with kindliness and affection. Among the most cherished of his friends was Schumann's widow, Clara (nee Wieck), one of the leading pianists of her time, who became a most sensitive interpreter of his works and played an important role in the criticism of them before they were offered to the world. (The F MINOR PIANO SONATA was dedicated to her.) It was at Mme. Schumann's funeral that he caught a chill that is believed to have hastened his end. He died at the age of sixty-four and was buried not far from Beethoven and Schubert.

It was inevitable, in an age when music had turned toward such strong literary and pictorial influences, when all the riches of orchestral coloring, all the fascination of the bizarre and the picturesque had engaged the adherents of the "new music," that the music of a composer like Brahms should become a rallying point for all who desired the art to maintain its great traditions. The divergence between the two schools of thought was dramatized by the acrimonious debates between the "Brahmins" and the "Wagnerites" that lent so much excitement to the artistic scene of the late nineteenth century. Seen from the perspective of over half a century, the conflict does not seem to matter so much today, since we have accepted both masters into our musical heritage, taking from each what he alone has to offer. Yet the reader should note that it is not altogether correct to regard the issue between the two factions merely as a difference between classic and romantic ideals. Brahms is fundamentally one of the most romantic among composers. But he represents a different type of Romanticism from that of the extreme Romantics such as Wagner and Liszt who would have less to do with the spirit of Classicism than Brahms. Because he poured the impassioned content of his speech into the hallowed molds of the great Classicists, because his imagination perceived the particular, the personal in its most universal and general aspect, because for him texture was often more important than color, workmanship more vital than bizarreness, because of the serenity of his vision, the loftiness of his utterance, his unfailing mastery of his material in the most absolute sense, his unflagging devotion to what he considered eternal in art, Brahms may be considered—like Beethoven—a classical Romanticist. Wagner was convinced that the music drama was the logical continuation of the choral *Finale* of Beethoven's NINTH SYMPHONY. On their side, the conductor von Bülow and other adherents of Brahms called his FIRST SYMPHONY the "TENTH." It is curious and illuminating that the two diametrically opposed tendencies within the late Romantic movement should both have claimed a common source. Posterity, the ultimate judge, seems now to favor Brahms rather than Wagner as the true inheritor of the mantle of Beethoven.

Except for opera and the symphonic poem, which he never attempted —he once remarked to the critic Hanslick that it would be as difficult for him to write an opera as to marry, but that after the first experience he would probably try a second—Brahms essayed and enriched all the forms of music. He ranks with Schubert and Schumann as one of the masters of the German lied, infusing his songs with a wealth of poetic suggestion and tragic intensity. (See Chapter 7.) We have seen that, where melody was concerned, Brahms could be extraordinarily close to the spirit of the folk. In his choral works, as Fuller-Maitland points out in his excellent article in Grove's *Dictionary of Music,* Brahms "touched a point of sublimity that had not been reached since Beethoven." Most famous among these are the GERMAN REQUIEM, the TRIUMPHLIED, written in 1871 to celebrate the German victory over France, the beautiful SCHICKSALSLIED (Song of Fate), and the RHAPSODIE for alto solo and male chorus and orchestra. His chamber music and his piano music are among the finest in the literature of their respective forms. But his supreme achievements, as far as the musical public at large is concerned, are the orchestral works: four symphonies, two overtures, the SERENADE, two piano concertos, the violin concerto, the double concerto for violin and cello, and the brilliant and masterful VARIATIONS ON A THEME BY HAYDN, for symphony orchestra.

Brahms was past forty when he approached the composition of his first symphony, but he was already the master of a distinctive style and in the full maturity of his gifts. Consequently, he had no apprenticeship period in the symphonic form: his FIRST SYMPHONY IN C MINOR is one of the greatest "firsts" ever written. The symphonic idiom of Brahms is noteworthy for its simple diatonic melodies that achieve a quality of the highest lyricism, together with that sense of inevitability that characterizes only the greatest art. Brahms' symphonic works are also distinguished by spacious harmonies, rich and intricate rhythmic changes and combinations—in which he follows in the footsteps of Schumann—strange, subtle chord progressions so individual that they can be instantly recognized by the experienced music lover as being from the pen of Brahms, and for a remarkably complex interweaving of the inner voices in a splendid polyphonic texture—he was an unquestioned master of counterpoint. The slow movements have an atmosphere of brooding, of tenderness and ardent lyricism breaking through the reserve of a deeply introspective spirit, of nobility and strength that is in the Beethovenian tradition, yet is completely Brahmsian. But what truly distinguishes him from the romantic symphonists of his time is the spacious, plastic architecture in which this music is made manifest, the epic dimensions of the form, the technical mastery of the material. Here we find incisive themes germinating, developing with the inexorable power that is the hallmark of true symphonic style. The symphonic movement evolves out of the themes, the simple motives reveal undreamt-of-possibilities, all explored and unified within the logic of a well-wrought and inevitably correct structure —a splendid illustration of the working of the classical temper in a romantic spirit and mood.

One technical device of Brahms is especially noticeable in the FIRST and SECOND SYMPHONIES, where he introduces a germ motive quite distinct from the themes proper and which he develops individually; sometimes, as often happens in the FIRST SYMPHONY, he does so with greater attention to the germ motive than to the organic themes themselves. Then, too, he uses this germ motive in several movements or even throughout the entire work, not unlike the Fate motive in Beethoven's FIFTH SYMPHONY, as a cyclical or unifying factor—and sometimes as a compositional foil for the organic theme sounding at the time. This technique is clearly seen in Brahms' SECOND SYMPHONY. Thus the listener has a more involved problem than heretofore in that he is to be concerned consciously with the observation of the development of the regular themes of the movement *plus* the appearances and development of the germ motive—though we hasten to add that this is not as difficult as it appears in print. (After hearing Brahms' symphony, compare the character and function of this germ motive with the germinal motive of Liszt, the leit-motif of Wagner, the descriptive motive-theme of Strauss, and the Fate motif of Beethoven. An interesting and enlightening discussion may be made on this point; try to introduce the concepts of Romanticism and Classicism into the discussion.)

Symphony No. 2 in D major (1877)

For an introduction to the symphonic style of Brahms, consider the SECOND SYMPHONY. The FIRST has tragic and Olympian grandeur. The THIRD, abounding in wonderful melody, is one of the most poetic of symphonic works. The FOURTH is more melancholy, with luminous flights of fancy and a final movement based on one of the forms of the Baroque Period, the *passacaglia* or *chaconne* (see Chap. 28), is one of the most extraordinary feats of musical architecture in the literature. But for warmth and geniality and simple songfulness, for surging rhythms and brilliant climaxes, the SECOND takes precedence. (We are here reminded of a Toscanini story. Brahms was one of his favorite composers, and when asked which of the four symphonies was his favorite, Toscanini replied, "The one upon which I am working at the moment.") Here, in the SECOND SYMPHONY, Brahms is in a most personal mood; and thus this work affords a fine beginning for anyone to become acquainted with the Brahms symphonies. Its complexity will also prove to be a real challenge to listening skills accumulated at this point in our study.

FIRST MOVEMENT: Allegro non troppo. $\frac{3}{4}$ time. Sonata-Allegro form. The first part of the first theme is announced in a mood of reverie by the horns against a somber background of 'cellos and double-basses. Observe how the motive marked "A" appears throughout the movement, both in its original form and in many changes, plus the generative idea.

A broadly curving melody in the violins, in the nature of an interlude, is the second part of the principal theme, and leads to the lyrical second

theme on the 'cellos—a fine example of Brahmsian song that serves as main contrast to the first theme:

Two subsidiary themes are added to the basic material, strongly irregular in rhythm; the first, *ben marcato* (well marked), with broad leaps and vigorous accents, presented by the strings:

The second, played by bassoons and double-basses, answered by flutes and oboes, has the sprawling, ungainly contours of which Brahms was so fond in his transitional material and drives forward with great propulsion:

The different melodic strands are intertwined in a complex tonal fabric with the two basic themes reappearing in all sorts of ingenious variations. The movement reaches its peak in the resurgence of the first theme and gradually subsides into a mood of joyous placidity.

SECOND MOVEMENT: Adagio non troppo: A-B-A (or first Rondo) form. In this slow movement, we glimpse the restrained feeling, the tenderness and shy sensitivity that, for the admirers of Brahms, are among his greatest charms. Not all the reserve of the intricate polyphonic texture can hide the passion of this outpouring; yet the prevailing quality is one of manly feeling, the sensitivity that is filled with compassion. There are a number of simple, though very beautiful, themes. The opening song of the 'cellos is intertwined with a contrasting countermelody in the bassoons:

The main theme is presented with oboes imitating the horns against a plaintive countermelody:

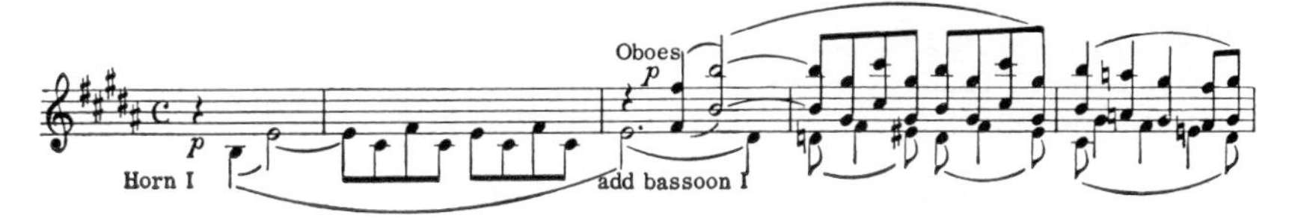

The second melodic idea presents the wood-winds in a syncopated melody, *dolce,* against the *pizzicato* of the 'cellos:

Like the slow movements of the other three symphonies, this is one of the intensely human and ingratiating songs of Brahms.

THIRD MOVEMENT: Allegretto grazioso: Minuet and Trio form.[3] Instead of the Beethovenian *scherzo,* Brahms gives us, in the third movement, a mood whimsical and tender. Oboes announce a simple theme, *allegretto grazioso* (*quasi andantino*)—lightly and gracefully, in a place somewhat faster than *andante*—the grace note on the third beat giving just a hint of waywardness that is almost wistful:

How charmingly this theme savors of the graceful, classical minuet, of the time of powdered wigs, even to the frequently accented third beat!

The meter changes suddenly to $\frac{2}{4}$; the tempo becomes *presto.* One scarcely recognizes the wistful tune of the opening measures in this bubbling, *staccato* variation with brusque accents off the beat. But if you compare the two melodies, you will discover how artfully the second is derived from the first. (This is an excellent example of rhythmic diminution. An interesting observation might be made here in respect to style and form. These two paces, one slow and graceful, the other lively and vivacious, alternate with each other throughout the movement, as though Brahms had telescoped a regular minuet movement with that of a *scherzo.* Watch for this effect.) This mastery of formal structure along with the mastery of thematic development is characteristic of Brahms. The lively (B) theme follows:

[3] According to Goetschius there are two trios in this movement.

Strings, wood-winds *et al* announce a new theme, strongly accented and impetuous:

Presently this theme, too, is altered in tempo and meter, retaining only its general contour as it is played by the wood-winds:

The movement returns in the end to the wistfulness of the opening theme, as though the *presto* interlude had been like something glimpsed but not fully realized until it had passed by.

FOURTH MOVEMENT: Allegro con spirito: Sonata-Allegro form. This movement, to be played lively and spirited, is a joyous, headlong finale that has in it something of the *rondos* of the Classical era, although in a more full-bodied, earthier form. The first theme is a proud and vigorous statement, even though the strings announce it *sotto voce* (almost whisperlike):

The second theme out of which the movement is built is one of those diatonic tunes that seem quite simple when we first hear them; but that, containing within themselves the miraculous life-giving element, achieve, when they reveal themselves in their full splendor, an effect that is quite magnificent:

Two subsidiary themes now follow: the first a pleasant interlude with descending bass:

the second one marked by the brusque rhythmic figure that we met in another context—the Scotch Snap:

This completes the principal organic material.

The development section reveals not a few instances of the genius of Brahms in transforming a theme, and his mastery of contrapuntal technique. It would lead us too far afield and into too deep waters for the present to attempt to discover all such points of interest; but repeated hearings will eventually reveal these virtues to those with sufficient interest.

The reprise is regular save for a few additional contrapuntal evidences of Brahms' craft, and we draw the attention of the listener to an interesting version of the second subject as it appears in the trombones, which, though quite solemn, blossoms forth presently into a glorious triumph. The mood brightens and sweeps forward in a resistless torrent, growing in power and abandon until it achieves a momentum of triumphant energy with vigorous chords hurling forth syncopated accents with all their power, and the sonorous brasses joining in a climax of frenzied acclamation at the end.

ADDITIONAL SUGGESTIONS FOR LISTENING

In this chapter, most of the principal larger works of Brahms, excepting some choral compositions, piano solos and songs (see pertinent chapters) were mentioned, and thus there is no point in reviewing them here. On the other hand, it might be advantageous to the listener to enumerate some of the orchestral works of other composers that also illustrate the balancing of the Romantic and Classic tempers. This is especially valuable when such works involve the expression of highly personalized feelings, flights of imagination, and freedom of individual artistic liberties, while at the same time combining the composer's regard for the conformities of the more formal and traditional conventions of the so-called classical compositional elements.

These composers, like Brahms, evidence some sort of combination of the Romantic and Classic tempers. The listener is pleasantly challenged to discover for himself the presence and degree of these tempers.

Barber, SYMPHONY NO. 2, a skillfully wrought contemporary work of a Romantic thinking in Classic tempers; Borodin, SYMPHONY NO. 2, in B minor; Bruckner, SYMPHONY NO. 4, the *"Romantic";* Chausson, SYMPHONY IN B-FLAT, Op. 20; Copland, SYMPHONY NO. 3, showing his habitual use of some Classical tempers in the thematic development and conventional forms, together with certain Romantic tempers of expression; Diamond, SYMPHONY IN D MAJOR, an American contemporary composer who, to some degree, favors the Classical tempers; Franck, SYMPHONY IN D MINOR, a superb work which is developed cyclically out of a few brief germinal motives—a sort of colophon of the Franck school. Listen for the cleverly contrived climax idea (really a "peak-chord idea" within a recurrent, accumulative, and syncopated melodic and harmonic figure which is evolved from a motive on the very first page of the score, and which continues almost to the very last page). Note also the cleverly telescoped *scherzo* and slow-movements into one single movement. Glazounoff, either the FOURTH or SEVENTH SYMPHONY; Goldmark, SYMPHONY IN E FLAT, the *Rustic Wedding;* Hanson, SYMPHONY NO. 4, Romantic tempers of feeling with Classical tempers of technique; Harris, SYMPHONY NO. 3, evident use of Romantic tempers of expression plus Classical techniques; d'Indy, SYMPHONY ON A FRENCH MOUNTAIN AIR, Op. 25. Note Romantic tempers plus "Franckish" idioms; Liszt, FAUST SYMPHONY, excellent example of very strong Romantic tempers and the use of individualized Classic tempers in thematic metamorphosis; Mahler, SYMPHONY NO. 10, or, better, DAS LIED VON DER ERDE for solo voices and orchestra; Mendelssohn, either the *"Italian"* or the *"Scotch"* SYMPHONY or both, Classic and Romantic tempers in quite disciplined use, but favoring the former; Miaskovsky, SYMPHONY NO. 21 IN F-SHARP MINOR, Op. 51—he wrote some thirty symphonies almost all strongly indicative of the emphasis of contemporary use of the Classic tempers; Oldberg, SYMPHONY NO. 3 IN F MINOR, a serious, skillful American composer who evidences more Classic than Romantic tempers; Prokofiev, CLASSICAL SYMPHONY IN D MAJOR, a whimsically sardonic and satirical musical spoofing of some of the idioms and styles of the German (Haydn-Mozart) Classical Period; Rachmaninoff, SYMPHONY NO. 2 IN E MINOR, Op. 27, deep Romantic feelings together with consummate mastery of Classical compositional techniques—an unusually long (fifty measures) *crescendo* approach to the climax in the slow movement is a marvel of composing skills; Schumann, SYMPHONY NO. 4, the best of the four symphonies by this leader of German Romanticism, who, in many instances, anticipates quite pointedly the Sibelius' technique of using germinal motives; Sessions, SYMPHONY NO. 2, built upon contemporary tenets of adapted or modified Schönbergian pan-tonal, or atonal neo-Classical systems, with little of his natural Romantic tempers; Sibelius, SYMPHONY NO. 4 and NO. 8 (See last chapter for discussion and analysis of the FOURTH SYMPHONY); Stringham, SYMPHONY NO. 1 IN B-FLAT MINOR, an extended work with second and third movements telescoped into one, an example of Romantic and Classical tempers in conflict—score is in the Free Library, Fleischer Collection, Philadelphia, and the Library of Congress, D.C.; Sowerby, SYMPHONY NO. 1, an American contemporary who leans heavily upon Classical tempers; Vaughan Williams, the *"London,"* the *"Pastoral,"* the FOURTH and the SIXTH SYMPHONY—superb works by an outstanding contemporary master—Romantic and Classic tempers in well controlled and effective balance, mixed with some Impressionism and a facile and frequent use of modal melodies and harmonies; SYMPHONIES NOS. 3, 4, or 6 by an American, Piston—these are neo-Classical and influenced by Schönberg.

THE PURSUIT Fragonard

23 The classical symphony: two Viennese masters—Mozart and Haydn

Just as we viewed the symphonic poem and the program overture against the background of nineteenth-century Romanticism, so must we approach the first great masters of the symphony against the background of eighteenth-century Classicism. In the case of Romanticism the general social and cultural upheaval following the French Revolution had the most direct repercussions in the arts. Likewise, the social background of the feudal-aristocratic *ancien régime* exercised no less powerful an influence upon the artist. The preponderance of this influence, as was pointed out in an earlier chapter, tended in the direction of the Classical spirit.[1]

The fact that eighteenth-century art functioned in great measure under the system of patronage meant that the artist of the time was in much closer contact with his audience and much more susceptible to its immediate

[1] See Chapter 13.

demands and influence than was the nineteenth-century artist, who worked for the open market. In this sense, art in the eighteenth century may be said to have reflected its social milieu much more faithfully than that of the nineteenth. To begin with, classical art had before it the ideal of aristocratic formalism that animated the society out of which it sprang. It took over the sane objectivity upon which the Age of Reason prided itself; it looked upon unrestrained or too ostentatious expression of feeling as being not quite in good taste. It expressed deep feeling, but always with exquisite sensibility and restraint rather than outspoken torrential passion. Emotion here was sane and refined, contained within beauty of line and perfection of form. This was a healthy, optimistic art, molded and balanced, impregnated with the ideal of moderation of the antique world, good-humored and lovable, and achieving, at its greatest, a serene loveliness, an exquisite finish, such as have never been equaled.

Within this eighteenth-century style, we have to distinguish between the ROCOCO and the CLASSICAL. The Rococo was the overdainty, overelaborate, and overprecious manner in architecture, painting, furniture, decoration, sculpture, and music that summed up the main trends in art at the middle of the century, especially in France. The word "rococo" comes from the French *rocaille,* a term used to describe the fantastic rock arrangements of the gardens at Versailles during the reign of Louis XV (1715–1774). Later, the rococo style was carried to rather absurd extremes in Italy and Germany. The original French idiom was not deeply emotional; rather, it was characterized by relief forms derived from the artificial rock-work and pierced shell-work, water-worn rocks, fanciful scrolls, and other highly conventionalized forms of ornamentation. Further, the graphic and plastic arts were marked by curved spatial forms, light and fantastically curved lines, often excessively flowing lines of draperies, and reversed or unsymmetrical forms. Hence, the word has generally come to mean almost any extravagant curvature and ornamentation. In the plastic and graphic arts this spirit expressed itself in the fragile grace of Dresden china, in the nymphs and shepherdesses of Boucher and Fragonard, the delicate fountains and groves of Watteau. In architecture, we have the elegant palaces of the rococo style, surrounded by formal gardens and furnished with all the ornaments—from crystal chandeliers to smiling cupids and dainty screens—that gave a proper background for powdered wig and crinoline. The musical counterpart of the popular idea of the rococo is to be found not in the major works of Haydn and Mozart—as is all too often stated—but in the cheerful, highly ornate *rondos* and *allegros* of a host of composers who came before them, such as Domenico Scarlatti (1685–1757), François Couperin (1668–1733), Johann Stamitz (1717–1757), Luigi Boccherini (1743–1805), Claude Daquin (1694–1772), and Karl Phillipp Emanuel Bach (1714–1788).

An appropriate reproduction of a painting by Jean Honoré Fragonard

(1732–1806), THE PURSUIT, may be seen at the beginning of this chapter. Here we have an example of the daintiness, the graceful and fanciful style that was so characteristic of this painter. There is in this work a "prettiness" and exquisiteness that could have found expression only at that time; a style that has been called "opera scenery." However, Fragonard was a master of his craft, and, according to the authors of ART IN THE WESTERN WORLD, his work is marked with "cosmopolitan wit and sophistication" and carefully wrought frivolity of unquestioned beauty and charm. It will not be difficult to compare this type of painting with analogous musical styles.

The classical spirit, on the other hand, reached great heights in the art of music during the latter half of the century. This spirit had set the prevailing tone in literature for a century—from the drama of Racine and Corneille to the poetry of Pope and Thomson, Goldsmith and Gray, and the stately prose of Dr. Johnson, Edmund Burke, Gibbon, and Voltaire. In painting, the spirit that had animated the masters of the Renaissance of such widely separated men as Raphael, Michelangelo, Verocchio, and da Vinci was due for a revival in the second half of the century through the neo-Classicism of Reynolds, Gainsborough, David, and Ingres. In music, the Classical spirit reached its peak for this epoch in the works of Mozart and Haydn. Although these men, as we shall soon see, inherited the traditions of the rococo and shared some of its characteristics, they deepened the content and emotional scope of music far beyond its former confines. They brought to music the sustained line, the vaulting patterns, of the great classical painters of the Renaissance. They did some of their most significant work in the final decade of the century, on the very threshold of Romanticism. To see Mozart and Haydn as the musical embodiment of the rococo is to miss the essence of their genius and their achievement. True, they worked within the conventions of their time, just as Shakespeare or Raphael worked within the conventions of theirs. And there is unquestionably a side of both Haydn and Mozart that fits well into the notion of the courtier in silk breeches amidst the Venetian lace of the rococo palaces. But they are, above all else, the two masters who brought the truly great classical style of the late eighteenth century to its perfection and left for the nineteenth century, and for all time, an ever-inspiring revelation of absolute beauty in music.

WOLFGANG AMADEUS MOZART (1756–1791)

In discussion of the artistic tempers we warned against the danger of drawing too rigid distinctions in art, of compartmentalizing periods and styles and individual creators. We tried especially to show how closely interrelated and universal in time and place were the Classical, Romantic and other tempers, and how erroneous it was to draw a rigid and inflexible

Courtesy Theodore Presser Co.

WOLFGANG MOZART

boundary between them. Nowhere is this warning more in order than in regard to the composer we now approach. One of the supreme figures in the history of the art of music, Mozart is also one of the most consistently misrepresented. If he had been no more than the polished master of the "Gallant style" of the late eighteenth century, he would have gone the way of dozens of his forgotten contemporaries. It is precisely because what he produced is so distinctive, so completely above the limitations of any one time and place, that he occupies a special niche in the story of music. Mozart expressed the spirit of his age, but in a far greater degree he transcended it. Into the conventional molds of his time, he poured the quintessence of eternal art. One has but to look beneath the outward grace and mannerisms of the period to see revealed in his full stature the luminous inner spirit, the creator of unfading beauty, the artistic companion of Raphael and Keats in many ways.

Like Beethoven, Mozart came between the close of one great epoch and the beginning of another. His works are not only the culmination of what had gone before, but also a harbinger of a new era. There is indeed something strangely prophetic in the music of Mozart. The opening theme of the G MINOR SYMPHONY is in some respects, as romantic as Shelley's poem, *Ode to the West Wind;* the serenity and exquisite formalism of the old intermingles with the passionate lyricism of the new. It is this that constitutes the fascinating duality of the Mozartian style. In him, the two elements meet in perfect fusion, strengthening and balancing each other. The classic serenity is humanized by heart-piercing emotion, and this, in turn, is purified by classic repose and restraint. Nothing better illustrates this duality in Mozart than the fascination which this so-called arch-Classicist had for the most romantic artists. Chopin is reported to have murmured on his death-bed, "Play Mozart in memory of me—and I will hear you." Marié Henri Beyle (Stendhal), who carried the banner of literary Romanticism in CHARTREUSE DE PARME and ROUGE ET NOIR, as well as in a number of works on musical subjects, wrote for the epitaph on his tombstone: "This soul adored Cimarosa, Mozart, and Shakespeare." Tchaikovsky, one of the most romantic of the Romantics, wrote to Mme. von Meck: "I not only like Mozart, I idolize him. To me the most beautiful opera ever written is DON GIOVANNI. No one else has ever known how to interpret so exquisitely in music the sense of resigned and inconsolable sorrow (*sic!*)....It is thanks to Mozart that I have devoted my life to music."[2] If one were to choose the five greatest works in almost any form—opera, symphony, string quartet, and so on—a work by Mozart would most certainly be included in each of the forms.

Wolfgang Amadeus Mozart was born in Salzburg, January 27, 1756, the son of Leopold Mozart, a musician who gained more than local fame

[2] Catherine Drinker Bowen and B. von Meck, *Beloved Friend.*

Courtesy Metropolitan Museum of Art

PIETÀ Michelangelo

This early sculpture, produced when Michelangelo was but twenty-four, now is in St. Peter's, Rome. It is an excellent example of somewhat modified classical Renaissance art, showing influences of the Greek masters. However, because of the foreshortening of the figure of Jesus, the graceful and rhythmical lines of the flowing garments, the pyramidal mass, and the symbolic but restrained expressions of both Mary and Jesus, this piece shows Michelangelo's projection into future art. The highly polished marble serves to heighten the feeling of classical perfectionism.

as a composer, teacher, and vice-Kapellmeister to the Archbishop of Salzburg. Wolfgang's genius manifested itself from earliest childhood: indeed, he is the most extraordinary example of musical precocity in all history. He picked out tunes on the harpsichord at the age of three; he composed at four. At six he appeared in concerts with his sister, who was some years his senior. Their father took the two prodigies on a tour over Europe; they played at the Austrian, French, English, and Dutch courts, arousing the greatest enthusiasm everywhere. Thus, Mozart's career opened under brilliant auspices. By the time he was twelve he had already written his first cantata, ten symphonies, an Italian opera, and the charming German operetta BASTIEN AND BASTIENNE (1786). The following year, a tour spread his name through Italy, then the world center of music, where he amazed his audiences with his organ playing and his powers of improvisation. At Rome the boy caused a sensation when, after one hearing of Allegri's fairly long and involved MISERERE at the Sistine Chapel, he wrote down the entire work, note for note, from memory—an almost incredible feat!

The remainder of his brief career presents a fantastic pattern of ups and downs, of disappointments dotted with flashes of success. Through it all he carried on with lightning speed and fluency the creation of his great works. The system of patronage was still all-powerful: a composer, painter, or poet depended for his livelihood not on his earnings but on the whims and vagaries of princely patrons—public concerts and public support through purchase of publications had not yet come into practice. Ironically enough, Mozart, who so often has been held up as the very incarnation of the classical spirit, was the first composer to revolt against the system of patronage; just as, some decades earlier, Dr. Johnson had been the first man of letters to defy it. Mozart refused to put up with the indignities that his patron, the Archbishop of Salzburg, heaped upon him as a matter of course.

Unfortunately, while the old system of patronage was beginning to crack, it was still too powerful to be defied. Haydn gracefully submitted and got through life peacefully. Beethoven brushed it aside—but that was two decades later. Mozart came a generation too soon—and was crushed.

Having broken with his patron, he decided to try his fortune in Vienna. Everything depended on his obtaining a permanent appointment at the court. Had he been able to find a patron as appreciative of his genius as Prince Esterhazy was of Haydn's, there is no doubt that his life would have taken an altogether different turn. But despite the fact that both the Empress Maria Theresa and her son, Joseph II, were aware of his gifts, they never gave him more than passing recognition. Why the greatest musician of his time should have had to go begging for a permanent post when all about him mediocrities were established in comfortable sinecures is one of those mysteries that leave one aghast at the caprices of chance.

Actually, Mozart had none of the suavity of the courtier when his artistic integrity was at stake. When the Emperor Joseph II remarked to him that his opera THE ABDUCTION FROM THE SERAGLIO (1782) seemed to have "much too many notes," the composer replied frankly: "Exactly as many notes as are necessary, Your Majesty." So too, when the King of Prussia, who was very proud of his orchestra, asked him what he thought of it, Mozart answered, "It contains great virtuosi, but if the gentlemen would play together they would make a better effect."

Lacking the mainstay of economic security, Mozart was doubly exposed to all the emotional instabilities of his temperament; one moment he was in high spirits, the next in deepest dejection. Amidst all the worries and distractions of a hectic life, the divine music continued to pour forth, but at an ever greater cost to its creator. His marriage with Constanze Weber, a pretty, thoughtless girl who seemed to combine in herself all the qualities necessary to make for him the least suitable wife, only added to his difficulties. Extravagance, debts, and illness followed in a constant cycle, aggravating the lack of a deep emotional relationship which might have given him the balance and strength he so desperately needed. Most tragic of all was the lack of understanding and appreciation he so often had to face as an artist from those who played the most decisive parts in his life. Against this dismal background was produced some of the most consistently pleasant music the world has known.

The last years of his life were brightened by the enormous success of his comic opera THE MARRIAGE OF FIGARO (1786) and of his dramatic masterpiece DON GIOVANNI (1787). In both of these he at last had a librettist worthy of him—the Italian poet-adventurer, Lorenzo da Ponte, a colorful character who ended his checkered career in the United States. DON GIOVANNI was written for Prague, where Mozart had his greatest triumph and where he spent the happiest weeks of his life. He composed it while sitting among his friends, enjoying the friendly chatter about him, taking his turn at a game of bowls, and then returning to put down another few lines of the matchless score. Like so many of his works, it was written in its finished form at the first attempt without revision or correction, for it had been thoroughly worked out, down to the last detail, in his head.

Within little more than six weeks in 1788, Mozart produced his three last and greatest symphonies, those in E FLAT, in G MINOR (the one we shall study presently), and the one in C (the "Jupiter"). During the three years that were left him there flowed from his pen a steady output of great works. But the struggle against discouragement was becoming ever more unequal; he was, as he put it, "always hovering between hope and anxiety." In the final year of his life, despite a continual turn for the worst in his physical and mental condition, he produced a number of his finest concertos, chamber music of all kinds, his greatest choral work, the REQUIEM MASS, and the opera THE MAGIC FLUTE (1791). This wonderfully gay fairy opera was written in the spell of dejection when he returned home, empty-handed, from the coronation of the Emperor Leopold II in Prague. The opera was written for Schikaneder, the impresario of a little theater on the outskirts of Vienna, who told Mozart that he could, "to a certain point, consult the taste of connoisseurs and your own glory," but must have "a particular regard to that class of persons who are not judges of good music. . . ." In this manner was born one of the first, if not the first, German romantic operas that paved the way for Weber and Wagner.

Mozart survived the première of THE MAGIC FLUTE by only two months, working feverishly all the while on his REQUIEM MASS. The writing of this work forms the final and strangest chapter of his career. He had received a visit from a stranger who had commissioned him to write a "Mass for the Dead" for his master who desired to remain unknown. Mozart accepted the order; but the mystery surrounding the whole matter made a strange impression on him. Actually, it was nothing more than a"ghosting" job for a Count Walsegg, who wished to pass himself off as a composer and needed a Mass in memory of his wife. As Mozart was starting out for the coronation in Prague, the mysterious stranger reappeared, asking what had become of the REQUIEM MASS. Profoundly disturbed, Mozart promised to have it ready as soon as he returned. In his highly unsettled state of mind, the summons of the stranger gave him the notion, which grew into a fixed idea as he proceeded, that he was writing his own requiem—and that he might not live to finish it. He redoubled his efforts, working against time on what was to remain his choral masterpiece and one of the greatest of all requiems. He did leave it slightly incomplete; it was finished by his pupil, Franz Süssmayer, who also completed the opera, THE CLEMENCY OF TITUS.

Now, when it was too late, bright prospects opened before him. He learned that a number of Hungarian nobles had formed a fund to provide him with an annuity and that in Amsterdam a subscription fund had been started to commission new works from him. Night after night, in the illness of the final month, he would follow in his imagination the performance of his MAGIC FLUTE at Schikaneder's theater, looking at his watch and going over the arias as the time for them arrived. He died of what is commonly held to have been a malignant typhus fever,[3] on December 5, 1791, a month before his thirty-sixth birthday.

He was given a pauper's funeral. A violent storm was raging; the half dozen friends who had come to the service followed to the city gates and then forsook him and turned back. No memorial marked his last

[3] Some authorities considered his death due to a general collapse from overwork and irregular living. According to Dr. J. Barrant, and quoted by W. J. Turner in his authoritative biography (Knopf, 1938), Mozart died of Bright's disease.

resting place; the site was soon forgotten and has not since been discovered. But his monument is truly "more lasting than bronze": an art which for sheer refinement of feeling, exquisiteness of line, and transparency of texture has never been equaled. It is a music of pure song, of fresh and sunlit things, of early morning and never-fading youth—a song dedicated to the eternal ideal of pure and perfect beauty in art.

Symphony in G minor, No. 40 (K. 550)

The SYMPHONY IN G MINOR about which Schubert said, "You can hear the angels singing through it!"—is one of the three last symphonies written with incredible speed in the summer of 1788. Finished on July 25, it seems to have taken little over ten days to compose. It is, for many music lovers, Mozart's most personal utterance: one of the few works in which the serenity of the artist has been pierced through by the torment and despair of the man; and it is one of the best examples of Mozart's deliberate dramatic expressions in instrumental music.

FIRST MOVEMENT: Allegro molto. G minor. Alla breve tempo. Sonata-Allegro form. The symphony opens, after a brief, restless pulsation, with a clearly romantic theme; a song of tenderness and grief purified in the flame of a proud and luminous spirit. (*Alla breve tempo* means that the pace is doubled up—twice as fast as usual.) The first theme is announced by the first and second violins, *piano*, and the theme successfully establishes the somber coloring of the minor mood:

Notice the graceful regularity of the structure, built in four-measure phrases. The Classical period is, understandably enough, the period of maximum observance of the four-measure phrase and the careful layout of related tonalities.

A bridge of formal design modulates to the key of the second theme (B-flat). Gentle, sustained, and *legato,* this theme offers a striking contrast to the opening melody. It is in major where the first was in minor; in a high register where the first was not; it is "pleading-like" whereas the first was most assertive; it is shared by strings and wood-winds, quite different in rhythmical outline from, and in a more lyrical mood than, the first theme. It is also characteristically Mozartian in its chromatic composition. Like the first theme, it is in regular four-measure structure. The second theme follows:

The *codetta* (a brief closing section) is composed of a figure in which an active, suspended tone descends in a poignant downward resolution, "as a sigh," intertwined with the principal figure from the first theme. Vigorous scale passages complete the exposition, which ends in a double-bar and a sign that the entire exposition section should be repeated.

The development section is fashioned out of the opening figure of the first theme, bandied about amongst the various instruments, and then presented in ever-new combinations of instrumental color, with intricate countermelody woven about it, and the harmony, the while, modulating from key to key. Having exploited its possibilities to the full, the composer launches on a long passage of coming back to the original tonality, which gives a certain sense of satisfactory balance. At the end, the liquid tones of the clarinets complete the retransition and return us to the G minor tonality of the first theme in its original state.

The recapitulation (the restatement of the material of the exposition) pursues the same course as the exposition up to the bridge passage to the second theme. Now Mozart does something extremely interesting. If he were to keep the melody of the second theme *exactly* as he presented it in the exposition, he would have to lead the music into the major mode. That would be out of the question, so he not only transposes the second theme into the tonic, but he actually shifts it from the major into the minor mode, thus maintaining the G minor tonality and modality. The *codetta,* with its poignant, sighing resolutions of the active tones to the more inactive ones (the tones of the tonic chord are the ultimate "rest" tones, and of these, the tonic, or key-tone, is of absolute "rest"), is shifted to G minor; and the scale and chordal passages leading to the final cadence make a vigorous affirmation of the "home tonality."

SECOND MOVEMENT: Andante. E-flat major. $\frac{6}{8}$ *time. Sonata-Allegro form.* As though fearful of having been too self-revealing in his first movement, Mozart retreats in the second to the bejeweled graces of the rococo style. Tender, sparkling, and graceful, the music withal avoids the tone of deep personal feeling that the nineteenth-century composers infused into their slow movements. The use of the first-movement form for the slow movement is not usual.

The first theme, announced *piano,* is taken up and fugually imitated in turn by viola, second violin, and first violin. Here follows the principal theme:

The much more graceful second theme, played by the strings, is as follows:

There is something ineffably Viennese in the graceful intervallic dip of the violins at the beginning of the second phrase of the first theme. In the delicate little clusters of thirty-second notes with which the principal theme is ornamented upon its return, and in the lacy lines of the movement as a whole, one glimpses the gallantry and formality of the eighteenth-century style and manner. The structure is based on regular eight-measure periods with courtly cadences at the close of each. Noteworthy are the wonderful interweaving of melodies with constant imitations of the theme on the part of different instruments and the subdued coloring in which the movement as a whole is pitched. There is no *coda.*

THIRD MOVEMENT: Minuetto. Allegretto G minor. $\frac{3}{4}$ time. Minuet and Trio form. The third movement brings us back to the somber G minor tonality of the first movement. We hear a proud, stately dance that is more staid and serious than light and carefree. The vigorous, assertive theme, sprinkled with syncopations, is announced by the strings and wood-winds. Its structural irregularity—a six-measure phrase answered by one of eight measures—lends it something of a wayward quality.

The trio section is in a contrasting G major, and it is much more suave and serene than the first theme—notice how the question of the strings is answered by the wood-winds:

The peculiar six- and eight-measure formation that was observed in the minuet proper is retained. After brief colloquy between the lower strings —'cellos and double-basses—and upper wood-winds, the trio works up to a subtle climax. Then comes the direction, *menuetto da capo,* which means that the minuet proper is repeated from the beginning and the final close comes just before the trio.

FOURTH MOVEMENT: Allegro assai. G minor. Alla breve. Sonata-Allegro form. In the last movement, we have one of those remarkable coincidences in music. The principal theme, with its upward sweep of the outline along a chordal formation, is similar to the main theme of the *scherzo* movement of Beethoven's FIFTH SYMPHONY (see Chapter 21). Likewise, the movement illustrates the subtle effect of the minor mode upon themes and rhythms that might well be considered to embody the spirit of the dance. There is to be found throughout the movement quite a play between the wood-winds and the strings, as though in dialogue, and frequent alternate moments of exquisiteness and compelling power —contrasted in a most dramatic manner, and, of course revealing the expression of *both* the heart and the intellect of the composer. The tempo is very lively (*allegro assai*) and in double-quick time (*alla breve*).

The first theme is given to the strings and played softly and crisply (*piano* and *staccato*). It is regular in formation, with the cadences holding forth at the appointed places.

The second theme is a perfect foil for the first. The principal theme ascends in a chord line while the second opens with sustained tones and moves in a much less vigorous manner—in a lyrical way, in fact. Then, too, the second theme is quite chromatic, as we have, by now, come to expect in Mozart's subsidiary themes. Again, to point out essential differences between the two themes, the first is in a minor mode while the second is in a major; the first is restless and impetuous, while the second is suave and smooth; the first is to be played *staccato,* crisply and detached, while the second is to be played in a *legato* manner with the tones slurred, well joined together. The second theme is played by the first violins:

The development section opens with a curiously whimsical and even humorous version of the principal motive—the *arpeggio* up the tones of the chord. This is worked out into ingenious imitations amongst the different instruments. (Try to follow it closely in its development.)

In the recapitulation, Mozart repeats his device of the first movement and shifts the second theme into G minor, thus not only transposing it (putting it into another key) but also changing its mode. The entire section is predominantly G minor, leading straight into the brief but vigorous affirmation of the home tonality by the final cadence. There is no *coda.*

FRANZ JOSEPH HAYDN (1732–1809)

The career of Franz Joseph Haydn presents a strong contrast to that of Mozart. He adapted himself to the system of patronage and was fortunate enough to find in the Esterházy princes understanding, generous, and magnanimous patrons who, throughout the thirty years of his supremely successful career, gave him every opportunity to develop his powers. Largely because of their wealth and generosity, and the way in which these were dispensed, Haydn was able to exercise and develop his genius to its utmost.

Haydn was born in 1732 at Rohrau, in Lower Austria, the son of a master wheelwright, and showed his musical gifts in early childhood. "Almighty God, to whom I render thanks for all his unnumbered mercies, gave me such facility in music that by the time I was six I stood up like a man and sang masses in the church choir, and could play a little on the clavier and the violin." He was given a chance to become chorister at the celebrated St. Stephen's Church in Vienna, where he sang until his voice began to break. Thrown then upon his own resources, he took whatever pupils he could find, and devoted himself to the study of composition. At twenty he wrote the music for a comic opera, THE NEW CROOKED DEVIL, which attained a certain popularity. The next few years he spent in teaching, accompanying, above all in learning the essentials of the musician's craft. He had no regular training; but through his own industry he acquired an independent style that marked all his works with originality.

A serious impetus to his composition dates from 1755 when he was invited to Weinzerl, the country home of a nobleman who was a patron of music. Adapting himself to the musical resources at hand—a few string and wind players—he turned out his first symphony and his first string quartet, the two forms in the development of which he was to play so important a role. But the turning point in his career came in 1761 when, at the age of twenty-nine, he was appointed Kapellmeister to Prince Paul Esterházy at Eisenstadt. Thus began one of the most notable relationships between prince and artist in the history of music, an example of the patronage system at its best. For almost thirty years Haydn lived on the magnificent Esterházy estate, freed from all care and devoting himself wholeheartedly to his art. He had a complete orchestra and a body of singers at his disposal, and turned out a steady stream of symphonies, operas for the court theater, cantatas, choral works for the chapel, and chamber music, constantly experimenting and refining his work until he became one of the two great masters of the Classical period.

During the lifetime of Prince Nicholas Esterházy, designated "the Magnificent"—his establishment at Esterháza rivaled Versailles—Haydn steadfastly refused all invitations elsewhere. In 1791, however, after the Prince's death, he took up the proposal of the impresario Salomon and went to England, composing the *Salomon Symphonies*—twelve in all—especially for the occasion and conducting them himself at the pianoforte. The visit was a sensational success; as a result, he made another three years later. He was feted by the Royal family and the nobility and received the degree of Doctor of Music from Oxford.[4] He was often at the house of the Prince of Wales, where the King's three sons took the 'cello, viola, and violin parts in the orchestra. The London concerts not only assured him additional financial reserves but also spread his name

[4] The so-called OXFORD SYMPHONY, written for Paris in 1788, and first performed in London in 1791, was so named in recognition of the honor that had been accorded him by Oxford University (1791).

more than ever throughout Europe. He himself often said that not until he had been in England did he become really famous in Germany. (How similar to the case of our own Edward MacDowell!)

Of special interest to students of English literature are his two oratorios, THE CREATION, based upon Milton's PARADISE LOST, and THE SEASONS from James Thomson's celebrated poem of that name. The oratorio, as we saw in Chapter 9, had become enormously popular in England during the lifetime of Handel, who dominated English music throughout the first half of the eighteenth century—and for much later, as a matter of fact, along certain lines of composition and instruction. During his visit to England, Haydn became thoroughly acquainted with Handel's music and, upon the suggestion of his manager, Salomon, essayed the form in which the great German had so distinguished himself. The nobility of Milton's subject found a ready response in the deeply religious Haydn. "Never was I so pious as when composing THE CREATION. I knelt down every day and prayed God to strengthen me for my work." The oratorio made an extraordinary impression; the audience at the first performance was deeply moved. As for Haydn himself, he wrote, "One moment I was as cold as ice, the next I seemed on fire. More than once I was afraid I should have a stroke." THE CREATION spread rapidly all over Europe, equaled in popularity only by Handel's masterpiece, THE MESSIAH. From the final years of the century, too, dates Haydn's most famous song, *God Save the Emperor*, which became the national anthem of Hapsburg Austria, as well as in a later setting, *Deutschland über Alles*. The hymn was a favorite of Haydn's; he introduced a set of masterly variations on it in the slow movement of his "EMPEROR" STRING QUARTET.

The last years of his life were spent in seclusion; his long, arduous career had sapped his strength. An intimate circle of friends and distinguished visitors lightened his struggle with the infirmities of old age. He appeared for the last time in public at a performance of THE CREATION at the University of Vienna in 1808 when he was seventy-six. He was carried into the hall in his armchair. Salieri conducted. As the words "And there was light" rang out, Haydn, greatly moved, lifted his arm and exclaimed, "It came from there!" As the work proceeded, his excitement rose and it was thought wiser to take him from the hall. The audience flocked to do him honor; Beethoven kissed his hand and forehead. At the door, he raised his hands as if in blessing. The occasion recalls the triumphal entry of the aged Voltaire into Paris.

His final illness came while the armies of Napoleon were bombarding Vienna. Five days before the end, he called his servants around him and, having been carried to the piano, played the *Emperor's Hymn* three times. He died on May 31, 1809, and was buried in a suburban churchyard outside the battle lines. The French invaders joined with his own countrymen in paying tribute to his greatness. When Mozart's REQUIEM

MASS was performed in his honor, French officers of high rank joined the mourners and ordered a French guard of honor around his catafalque. In 1820, his remains were transferred to the parish church at Eisenstadt on the Esterházy estates, where he had spent the greater part of his creative life.

In the matter of compositional style, Haydn was the last of the eighteenth-century masters. Both by temperament and achievement, he was part and parcel of the so-called Classical age. "Papa Haydn" he was called affectionately. Nothing could better sum up the geniality that characterized the man and the artist. His is a solid, forthright kind of music that has all the beauty of health and lucidity, of perfect balance and measure; in his *rondos* and *allegros*, he transports us to a sunny world where we smile in spite of ourselves—there is nothing in all music quite like the final movements of his symphonies, with their outspoken life, vitality, and thoroughgoing good humor. Haydn was a most methodical and painstaking worker, in spite of the seeming spontaneity of his works. He was utterly unlike the romantic concept of the artist that came to be popularly accepted in the nineteenth century. He composed slowly, mulling over the themes deliberately before he wrote them down. His melodies were simple and flowing; his taste was impeccable; his imagination of inexhaustible fecundity. He was completely devoted to his art; indeed, he had toward it the almost religious attitude of Bach, Handel, and the older masters. He inscribed his scores "*In Nomine Domini*" (In God's Name) at the beginning and "*Laus Deo*" (Praise Be to God) at the close. His genius he regarded as a gift from on high, to be put only to the loftiest uses.

Haydn has been called the father of the symphony and of the string quartet, and the composer who determined the make-up of the modern symphony orchestra. While these assertions are not exactly true, there can be no question that he, like Mozart, played a decisive part in the history of instrumental forms and in establishing the basic character of our modern orchestra; and we owe them both more than can be told in the matters of compositional and instrumentation techniques. It was Haydn who helped to perfect the sonata-allegro form.[5] It was he, too,

[5] The reader who is interested in pursuing the historical and formal aspects of the subjects just mentioned should note the contributions to the sonata-allegro form made by G. Sammartini (1701–1775), B. Galluppi (1706–1785), F. Gossec (1734–1829), and especially K. P. E. Bach (1714–1788) and Johann Stamitz (1717–1757). Both Haydn and Mozart owed a great deal to Stamitz in the perfection of the form as well as the performing medium of the symphony. See also: Vincent d'Indy, *Cours de Composition Musicale* (Paris: A. Durand et Fils, 1909), in French, Book II, Ch. V, p. 375; Percy Goetschius, *The Larger Forms of Musical Composition* (New York: G. Schirmer, 1915), pp. 150-231; W. H. Hadow, *Sonata Form* (London: Novello, 1896); Karl Eschman, *Changing Forms in Modern Music* (Boston: E. C. Schirmer); p. 140 *et seq.;* and Stewart Macpherson, *Form in Music* (London: Joseph Williams), pp. 115-253.

who laid down many of the basic principles of writing for string quartet as well as for the orchestra.

Every composer is indebted to the preliminary work done by a number of pioneers who precede him, many of whom may be forgotten later. In this sense, Haydn built upon the work of those who had come before him, bringing their work to a still higher level of artistic expression and passing that on to those who succeeded him. At the same time, he was unquestionably original and daring and had the type of mind that was congenial to large, clearly evolved structures. He laid much stress on the architectural values of his art. In his string quartets, which contain some of his most significant music, he transcended the gaiety and impersonality that have been held up as the two main characteristics of the rococo age; the slow movements are exquisitely felt, personal songs projecting all the moods of wistful tenderness associated with a later age —and one must say that Haydn exhibited many traits of the Romantic temper, as well as not a few of the Realistic temper. His long life summarized his heritage and his time. Other masters may stir us more poignantly, but no one else gives us such a sense of well-being, of placidity, kindliness, and solid contentment. All these are excellently set forth in the symphony we are about to study.

Symphony in D Major, No. 104 (Salomon No. 2), the "London"

Of the twelve symphonies especially composed for his English trips in 1791–2 and 1794–5, this D MAJOR SYMPHONY, catalogue No. 104 (Salomon No. 2) is Haydn's last symphony and is generally regarded by Haydn authorities as the foremost among this composer's instrumental works.[6] It is usually listed as SYMPHONY NO. 2 IN D MAJOR (the "*London*") for it is the second of the Salomon "London" series. Sir Francis Tovey puts the case of Symphony No. 104 in this way: "This SYMPHONY IN D MAJOR is, arguably, the greatest of Haydn's instrumental works, together with QUARTET FOR STRINGS IN F MAJOR, Op. 77, No. 2, as its compeer." Among the more popular "Salomon" symphonies besides the one now being discussed, we might name those dubbed "*Surprise*" IN G MAJOR No. 94, the "*Military*" No. 100 IN G MAJOR, the "*Clock*" No. 101 IN D MAJOR and the "*Drum Roll*" No. 103 IN E-FLAT MAJOR. The so-called "*Paris*" SYMPHONIES, Nos. 82-87, are also generally familiar.

There is much use of the tempers of Romanticism and Realism, as well as Classicism, in Haydn's works, especially in those he composed in maturity. Thus it is not difficult to see how Haydn, the "teacher"

[6] The *Cyclopedia of Music and Musicians*, Oscar Thompson, editor, (first edition) designated this Symphony as Cat. No. 104, Salomon No. 7. Still other authorities dispute both listings we have cited.

Recently several heretofore-unknown symphonies have been discovered and attributed to Haydn. However, general approval of this conclusion is yet to come.

of both Mozart and Beethoven, became the "student" of them both; and how the two young pupils, in turn, publicly acknowledged their admiration and indebtedness in dedications—Mozart in six of his STRING QUARTETS, K. 387, 421, 428, 458, 464, 465; [7] and Beethoven in the first few of his thirty-two SONATAS FOR PIANO.

This D MAJOR SYMPHONY opens with an arresting *Introduction, Adagio*, based upon a simple four toned figure (*ff*) that somehow, in spirit and vigor at least, forecasts some of the openings used by Beethoven, and a few of Mozart's later works. Even the sudden appearance of the soft passage (*p*) after the two-measure opening reminds this writer of Beethoven's FIFTH SYMPHONY, though Haydn does not make the opening figure an organic part of the tonal tapestry of the first movement, to say nothing of the symphony as a whole, as is the habit of Beethoven.

Here is the first part of the *Introduction, Adagio*—note the dynamics and be sure to observe that it is in the remote key of D minor:

FIRST MOVEMENT: Allegro. D Major. $\frac{4}{4}$ time. Alla breve. Sonata-Allegro form. After a rather commonplace *fermata* (hold) over the last quarter rest of the introduction (a frequent device during Haydn's time), the first movement proper begins. Here in the first section, the exposition, the principal themes of the movement are disclosed. The following is the first theme, part one, played softly by the first violins, in "cut time," *alla breve.*

A contrasting and loud (*ff*) theme, with its second beat, slow trill follows; and eventually (at "B" of the score) it makes a definite *cadence* in the key of A.

The student of academic theory will probably receive a shock to note that Haydn often ignored the academic rules of his time concerning portions of the sonata-allegro design. Here in the second theme proper he makes the first theme, with little change, do double duty by serving also as the second theme, part one, though he does show obeisance to

[7] The letter "K" following the opus number of Mozart's works refers to the generally accepted cataloguing of his works by the Viennese editor, Ludwig von Köchel, more recently revised by Alfred Einstein.

the rules of proper key relationship. (The first theme being in D major, and the second theme in A major—the key is the dominant—on the fifth tone of the scale.) This second theme, part one, is a soft (*p*) passage that is quite interesting in orchestral color, as it is tossed about between the strings and wood-winds. It, too, ends in a *tutti* (*ff*) passage, interesting from a rhythmic and dynamic standpoint—note the off-beat accents. Here is the second theme, part one proper. (Recall the third and fourth measures of the first theme, part one):

This is another evidence of the cleverness of Haydn in his expression of the Classical temper through the manipulation and development of germinal figures and themes, in the use of contrapuntal imitation, and in his making effective use of solo orchestral colors and combinations of the orchestral sections or choirs of his time. Mozart and Beethoven learned much from Haydn in all these aspects plus many of the diverse possibilities in the expression and treatment of formal design and structure, and sudden surprises of key, harmony, rhythm, etc.

Soon there appears another new bit of a theme—a germinal figure would be closer to the truth—for its brief derivations are more important than repetitions of the theme as is. (One might possibly call this whole statement as theme two, part two.) Here is that jolly, wooden shoe-like dance, with figure "a" being a sort of "vamping," followed by a new theme resembling the first and second themes, but inverted—another bit of Haydn cleverness. This motive is in the first violins and the *staccato*, choppy accompaniment is played by the second violins and the violas, with an occasional thump from the 'cellos. This is all played *piano* (*p*) until the imminent approach to the classical repeat sign of the entire exposition, when it becomes really boisterous and *forte*. Here is the second theme, part two. Note parts marked "a" and "b":

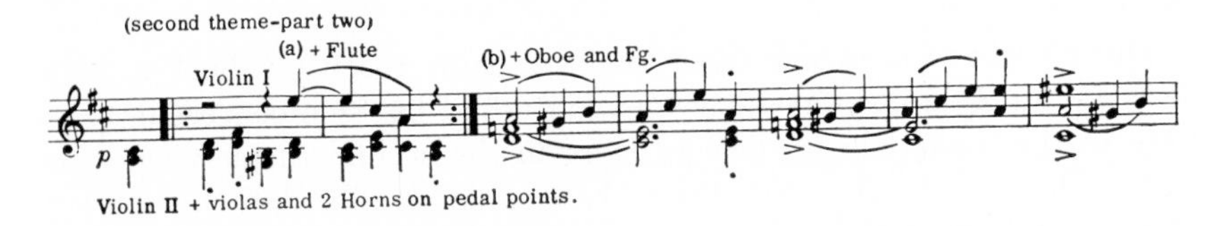

You will observe that the off-beat rhythm of section "a" is somewhat new, but that the beginning of section "b" resembles both the first and second themes. Some theorists call "b" an integral part of theme two.

At the climax of the exposition, about twenty-four measures after the onset of the theme just cited, there appears a conspicuous sign of the sonata-allegro form of the Classical school of Haydn and Mozart (even to and beyond Beethoven's time)—a repetition bar line consisting of two or more pre-bar line dots to each separate part, then a fine bar line down the entire score, followed by a heavy bar line, also down the full score, *which signifies that the entire exposition should be repeated.* Nowadays this is seldom followed.

Immediately following this repeat sign the "development" or "working-out" section begins, and it is primarily concerned with figure "y" of the second theme, part one, and development of other portions. This particular section of the first movement is about 69 measures, and is terminated by another unmistakable sign of the time—a *fermata* or hold (which jazz musicians call a "bird's eye" because of its semblance) over the last half of the measure, just before letter "F" in the score. This is the sign that the reprise is on its way. (Note the excellent climax Haydn has built up to the *fermata!*) The listener will gain more enjoyment in discovering for himself the themes, or figures, that are developed, and the gross outline of the structure than he will in being told too much about it. The reprise recalls the themes of the exposition, *except that the connecting "joints" differ and the themes are now in the basic key of the main theme* of the first movement as a whole (D major). Following the reprise comes the *coda,* that Beethoven and Brahms later expanded so much,—and which marks the close of the first movement of this beautiful symphony. We also hope you noticed the skill with which Haydn tones down the loud *tutti* to a *piano,* then to *pianissimo,* before resuming the final *fortissimo* (*ff*) *coda.*

SECOND MOVEMENT: Andante, in Rondo form, $\frac{2}{4}$ *time.* This gracefully moving theme was daring even for its time! We shall refrain from showing excerpts of the *episodes* heard between the recurrences of the principal theme, for they are rather obvious. Instead, we shall show only the main themes. Following is the *principal theme* of the *andante*—quite typical of its time. Note here, and in the *menuetto* as well as the *finale* to follow later, the clever use Haydn makes of the *off-beat* and unexpected rhythms and accents. We have marked some of these with an "N.B." in the musical illustrations. Observe, also, the superb orchestration, the sudden and Beethoven-like contrasts of dynamics, the repeats, the unusually frequent and florid flute and wind parts, the cadenza-like

passages, and sometimes abrupt melodic changes and stops. Note the G.P. (*Grand pausa,* meaning one or more full measures of silence for the entire orchestra) immediately before the letter "K"; the three *fermate* just before the letter "N" (35 measures before the end); and the *remote keys* just before the *coda!*

THIRD MOVEMENT: Menuetto, Allegro in D major. $\frac{3}{4}$ *time.* Haydn seems more at home in this movement than in the previous one. He has set forth the overall pattern of the movement in the familiar classical *Minuet and Trio* design and follows it fairly closely. However, he invested the music with his own inimitable spirit, humor, and ebullient personality. Note its bustling character, sparkling good nature, surprising off-beat accents, sudden changes of dynamics, and overall freedom of orchestration, changes of keys (in the trio especially), and marked thematic contrasts. Haydn was the master of his musical ideas, and he willingly "jumped the fence" of conventionalities when and if he believed his music was better for so doing—such individual freedom is one of the facets of the Romantic temper.

The classical minuet design is an adaptation of the "minuet and trio" design of the old courtly dance itself. However, Haydn often plays tricks with it, and the result is a refreshingly original and jolly movement. Here is the principal theme of the minuet movement:

The minuet of the classical style should have the accent on the *third,* not the *first,* beat of each measure as in the waltz. Observe how faithfully, even humorously, Haydn accentuates this rhythm. The main section of the minuet proper is in two sections, the second of which is repeated. Both these sections are in the key of D, the key of the symphony as a whole, instead of offering diversity. Notice the two measures of *tutti* silence [8] in the last of the second part, preceded by the high-D "hiccough tone," and followed by the trill on the "dominant seventh" chord in A, which, of course, leads directly to the key-tone (tonic) chord on D for the repeat.

The trio section which follows the minuet proper has a running and quite playful theme. Refreshingly, it begins in the key of B-flat major, instead of the then more usual key based upon the *fourth tone of the*

[8] We are reminded of Ruskin's remark, "While there is no music in a rest, there is the making of music in it."

scale of the minuet (known by musicians as the key of the *sub-dominant,* which, in this case would be the key of G). After the first repeat, the trio explores several keys other than D major, the key of the symphony, such as G major, C minor, F major, B-flat major, E-flat major—passages of sleight-of-hand deceptions. The passage eventually hovers about, then lands firmly upon the *da capo senza ripetizióne* (back to the very beginning of the minuet without repeats) chord—A major. This is called the dominant-seventh chord of D major which serves as the expected modulating and joining chord back to the beginning of the minuet proper. The ending of the entire movement is usually indicated by the Italian word, *fine*—at the last chord of the minuet, just before the trio.

Here is the principal idea of the *trio,* a smoothly running theme with an ingratiating lilt:

FINALE: Allegro spiritoso $\frac{4}{4}$ *time. Alla breve.* This movement also departs from the academically expected *rondo* form of the time. Instead, Haydn again anticipates Mozart and Beethoven in the use of the sonata-allegro design; probably for the very good reason that in the latter he had more opportunities for thematic development within a form that is inherently more solid.

The *exposition* opens with an octave pedal-point on a low D in the two horns and the 'cellos. Two measures later, the first theme proper is heard in the first violins. The first theme, part one, is a merrily and softly sung theme, such as one might hum to himself when in a contented mood: [9]

Not more than nine measures after the onset of the first theme, part one, Haydn begins to do tricks with the theme. Here, the oboe and first violins play the theme proper, while the second violins have an in-

[9] This technique of first presenting portions of a theme, or apparently casual and vagrant short musical ideas, and then realizing their full consummation later on, anticipates the later and more intricate development of this method and style by Brahms, Schumann, and still later by Sibelius.

teresting counter-theme to it, the violas and the 'cellos still another (though much more simple and less lyric), while the basses and the two horns—in unison hold the low D pedal-point. Over it all is a calm sort of hush, *piano*. Here is theme one, part two, reduced to the first and second violins. Note the musical ideas marked "a," "b," "c," and "d" for they will become quite important later, being significant developments of the principal theme:

As it appears in the full score, this is an excellent example of the Classical temper in the objective use of techniques, yet romantic in mood. The eminent English authority, Tovey, calls this the second theme proper.

The contrasting and lively part of the first theme is a gay, hopping-like theme in the first violins. It is replete with *joie de vivre:* It conceivably might suggest a lively dance scene in the town square, where the peasants' wooden shoes stomp a lively rhythm upon the cobble-stone pavement. This is, surprisingly enough, a motive from the first theme, measure 3, as developed and played by the first violins. Theme one, part three, follows:

The rest of the orchestra emphasizes the dance rhythm. All this is at letter "O" of the score.

As one would expect, the second theme, part one, is a beautiful and contrasting theme to those previously heard. It is more sustained (played by the first violins, in part with the first oboe), woven in a contrapuntal texture of the full orchestra, and in the proper key of the dominant, A major. Haydn presently offers a couple of pages of score that are puzzling in tonality and direction to all save the initiated. In fact the orchestra indulges in a sort of tonal legerdemain.[10] (Mozart also indulged

[10] We are also here reminded of a technique of many present-day composers. When they wish to make a tonality sound fresh, they sometimes indulge in devious vagaries or deliberate foreign and remote keys, with the result that the "new" and desired

in such tricks. See the Introduction to the String Quartet in C.K. 465 with its strange key implications. The great theorist Fetis presumptuously tried to correct the "wrong" notes in Mozart.) Here is the second theme, part one. The figure marked "a" later serves Haydn well for some "crack-the-whip" playfulness. Note well the counterpoint of this passage, especially theme two, part one, in the violin I and theme one, part one, against it in the flutes, bassoons and violin II:

A scale figure in the strings and bassoons is theme two, part two. This reminds one somewhat of a similar but more intricate passage in Beethoven's FIFTH SYMPHONY, *Andante con moto* movement, beginning at the eighth measure after the *fermata* on a tutti E-flat. First, let us hear the Haydn theme—note the somewhat dissonant crossing of first and second violins:

Now, compare this with the once radical passage in Beethoven's FIFTH SYMPHONY played by the wood-winds. The reader may be surprised to learn that this passage for flute I and oboe I on the two upper parts, and two clarinets on the two lower parts was considered "very daring" and too discordant in its first rehearsals! Now, of course, the average listener takes both Haydn's and Beethoven's passages in their stride, with no aesthetic or playing technic difficulty. Listen to the Beethoven's passage from the slow movement of the "Fifth": [11]

---

tonality will be very acceptable by the listener. The "traditional" composers, who are also in command of the twelve-tone technique, might write a bridge passage of deliberately indefinite *non-* or *pan-tonality*, so that *any* key chosen as the objective will sound fresh—*even though it is the same key previously used.* Likewise, thoroughgoing twelve-tone row users find it necessary, in extended works, to change their basic *Schönbergian Rows* now and then to achieve contrast and variety before the final settling down, or making a desired emphasis.

[11] To some listeners, this passage might also recall the rapid, antiphonal scale passage, played loudly and fiercely between the strings and wood-winds, in the so-called third movement, *Allegro molto vivace,* of the SIXTH *"Pathetique"* SYMPHONY by Tchaikovsky.

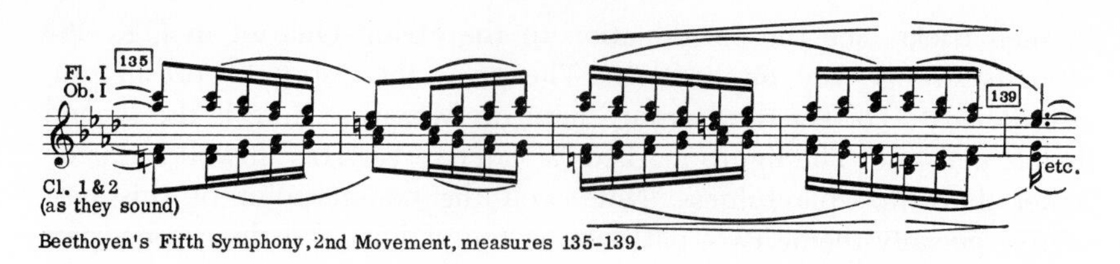

Beethoven's Fifth Symphony, 2nd Movement, measures 135-139.

A beautiful, softly played closing theme follows all the rush and hurry, as though it were a moment of meditation and soulful introspection. The theme is first played by the first violins over a string quartet-like moving support by the remainder of the strings. Then, in the third measure of this theme, the two bassoons in unison make their entry in a canon-like manner (see footnote 26, Chap. 27). This all takes place at and after the letter "Q" in the score, and the whole passage is marked *piano* (*p*). A few measures of "amens" follow in *pianissimo* (*pp*). Here is the beautiful closing theme of the exposition of the fourth movement:

Following this section the entire orchestra bursts forth playing a variant of theme one, part one, of this movement, another example of a characteristic personal idiom of Haydn. This theme one, part one, runs smack into the classical "double-bar-and-repeat" with its first and second endings, signifying the end of the exposition section. One cannot help wondering at the many themes Haydn has presented thus far in the movement, for such a number and variety might destroy unity and coherence. But Haydn was too great a master to lose either these essentials or the formal design. He accomplished this by giving the various themes a semblance and feeling of subtle "family relationship."

In the "second ending," and thus entering the "development" section, Haydn shows some hidden aspects of the themes he has already presented in the exposition, beginning with the first theme, part one, then a sort of "hiccoughing" motive, and so forth as you will enjoy discovering through listening. Suddenly (before letter "S" in the score) comes a silent *gran pausa* measure. This is followed by the beautiful closing theme of the exposition, which leads through a clever and unsuspected modulation back to the tonic, the basic key of D major which is the signal that the very compressed and original *reprise* is on. The rhythmically gay wooden shoe theme (theme one, part three) is played by the full orchestra (*f*). After this, there is a *coda* consisting of a veritable parade of clever transformations of themes closely knit together. Note the use of the figure we have called the "hiccough motive," which is blown up so that it reminds one of the "Donkey's Bray" motive in Mendelssohn's OVERTURE, *The Midsummer Night's Dream!* Even the meditative, closing theme of the exposition undergoes some magical treatment—but look for these yourself. The symphony comes to an impressive and powerful (*ff*) ending with a very simple dominant-seventh to tonic cadence (a chord built upon the fifth tone of the scale, A, followed by another chord built upon the first tone, D, of the key of D major).

FREISCHÜTZ

(*Overture*)

Carl Maria von Weber

Weber

"DER FREISCHÜTZ" OVERTURE

First page of score.

24 Classical form and romantic content in the overture

Before we turn to the classical sonata forms as used in the concerto and in chamber music, it will be well to examine a common genre in which the sonata-allegro design is wedded to a programmatic content—the overture. This is usually an extended symphonic composition, frequently in sonata-allegro form in which both the first and the second themes take on programmatic significance, either from the drama or opera for which the overture might serve as a curtain raiser or, if the overture is an independent concert piece, from the implications of the literary associations. We have here, then, an interesting fusion of what might seem at first glance to be the irreconcilable elements of "absolute" and "program" music.[1]

[1] It should be recalled at this time that we have already presented similar works in previous chapters, though for quite different purposes. Among such works are Tchaikovsky's *Fantasy Overture*, ROMEO AND JULIET; Mendelssohn's MIDSUMMER NIGHT'S DREAM

HISTORICAL BACKGROUND OF THE OVERTURE

The overture goes back to the early Italian operas of the opening years of the seventeenth century. Many of the first operas, including those of Monteverde, were preceded by short instrumental preludes, sometimes little more than a preliminary flourish of trumpets. These were expanded throughout the century, somewhat haphazardly, until the period of Jean Baptiste Lully, the "father of the French opera," who established the dramatic prelude that served as a model for his contemporaries and successors.

In Lully's pattern, the "French Overture," there was first a stately introduction, followed by an *allegro* in fugal style; a slow section, or minuet, closed the work. Frequently one of the popular dance forms of the time was included. Since these were generally of solemn character, they fitted in well with the lofty style of Lully's overture.

The "Italian Overture" form, due largely to A. Scarlatti, began with a quick movement, followed by a slow, melodic interlude, then returned to a fast, lively tempo. (One can see here a foreshadowing of the movements of the symphony of a century later.) Since opera in Italy was dependent on popular patronage, while in France it was bound up with the Bourbon court, it was natural that the Italian overture was much less elevated than was the French overture.

Until the time of Christoph Willibald Gluck, the overture had no special relevance to the work it introduced. An overture intended for one opera was often used for another. The early eighteenth century represented a degeneration of taste and style in the form. The frivolous audiences of the day did not pay attention to the proceedings on the stage until the entrance of their favorite star. The composer had little incentive to take pains with the overture, knowing that it would hardly be listened to.

GLUCK AND THE CLASSICAL OVERTURE

It was the Italian, Lully, working for Louis XIV who had given the overture its start as an art form. It was a German who met his greatest triumph in the Paris of Marie Antoinette a century later who restored it to a lofty place in the art. With Gluck, the overture took an important step toward becoming an integral part of the drama. In the preface to ALCESTE he says: "My idea was that the overture ought to indicate the subject and prepare the spectators for the character of the piece they are about to see." While

---

Overture; and Wagner's TANNHÄUSER *Overture.* These might be profitably and pleasurably reviewed along with the contents of this chapter.

he had not yet hit on the idea of incorporating in the overture themes from the work itself—the simplest way of uniting it with the drama—he ran his overtures continuously into the first scene of the opera. In his IPHIGENIA IN TAURIS, the orchestral introduction foreshadows the storm with which the opera opens and is the most advanced example of unity between overture and opera that had been achieved; the introduction to IPHIGENIA IN AULIS is one of the finest examples of the dramatic overture of the period.

Mozart's *Overture* to DON GIOVANNI marked the next forward step. Here the overture was identified with the opera thematically: the introductory *andante* of the overture presages the music that accompanies the entrance of the statue in the final scene. Similarly, the solemn opening chords of the *Overture* to THE MAGIC FLUTE suggest the mystical elements of the libretto. With Mozart, the overture also took over the sonata-allegro, or first-movement, form that had emerged as one of the most flexible structures for extended musical works. Mozart also "adapted" the form; in his *Overture* to THE MARRIAGE OF FIGARO, he used an abridged version commonly known as the *sonatina form*—that is without the usual development section.

Beethoven, in FIDELIO, continued the process by incorporating themes from the opera in the three LEONORA overtures. Through the two overtures that he wrote for famous plays—Collin's CORIOLANUS and Goethe's EGMONT—he also opened up the path for the development of the overture into an independent concert piece in strongly dramatic style. What is most interesting here, however, is that in the works of Beethoven the sonata-allegro form came to be freely adapted to the moods and purposes of a programmatic content.

ABSOLUTE FORM VERSUS PROGRAMMATIC CONTENT

In a certain sense, this blending represented a union of fundamentally different elements. The sonata-allegro form is based on the presentation of musical themes, their working out, and their restatement more or less in their original shape. The underlying principle of drama, on the other hand, is a combination and working out of the events to create a situation different from that which existed in the beginning. In a sense, the two ideas are in opposition. It is possible to reconcile them because the overture does not *have* to tell the story—the opera or drama does that—but it can use the dramatic material symbolically, or selectively; that is, it can lift themes and work them out along purely musical lines—or nearly so. Since, from an early time, the program was treated suggestively rather than literally, composers were able to evolve a form that projected the mood of the drama and at the same time lent itself to effective treatment from the musical point of view, structurally speaking.

THE OVERTURE OF THE ROMANTIC PERIOD

Despite his contributions to the development of the overture, Beethoven's genius was symphonic rather than dramatic. It remained for his gifted younger contemporary, Carl Maria von Weber (1786–1826), to open the overture to the diverse influences of the new Romantic style. Weber has often been acclaimed as the "father of the German romantic opera," the precursor of the Wagner of FLYING DUTCHMAN, TANNHÄUSER, and LOHENGRIN. He turned to the legends of the folk, the magic of woodland and mountains. In his operas the overture is part and parcel of the play, in musical themes *and* mood and color, a subtle tone painting projecting the audience into the emotional atmosphere of the play. His overtures to DER FREISCHÜTZ, OBERON, and EURYANTHE are justly ranked among the masterpieces in the form.

From Beethoven and Weber the path led directly to the overture of Schubert, Schumann, and Mendelssohn, culminating in the romantic overture of Berlioz and Wagner, of which we have studied a notable example from TANNHÄUSER. The golden period of the romantic overture fell within the first half of the nineteenth century. With the rise of the Lisztian symphonic poem, the influence of the overture as an independent concert piece waned, for the symphonic poem, with its greater freedom of form, was better adapted to the emotional requirements of the age than a programmatic type of music that still held on to the classical sonata-allegro form. Within the opera house the overture witnessed something of a decline for another reason. Wagner, in his later works, realized that there was no point in telling the story in the overture if the opera itself was going to do that. In his music dramas he therefore substituted the prelude, a pure mood piece, to establish the emotional atmosphere. The composers at the end of the century steadily reduced the dimensions of the introductory piece. Then, too, the new type of audience in the lyric theater, coming with a true eagerness, made a protracted curtain raiser psychologically unnecessary. Such a typical end-of-the-century work as LA BOHÈME, for example, has but a few measures of introduction.

Weber's Overture to "Der Freischütz" (1821)

A decade and a half after the dubious success of FIDELIO, an opera swept Germany as few operas have done before—Carl Maria von Weber's romantic folk tale DER FREISCHÜTZ (The Free Archer). To a Germany torn by internal dissension, discouraged in the wake of the Napoleonic conquests, and somewhat under foreign domination, Weber's opera came as a wonderful awakening, the first victory of a new national art. Based on a

Courtesy The Biltmore Co., Asheville, N. C.

VANDERBILT'S "BILTMORE HOUSE" Richard Hunt, Architect

This is an architectural gem of the past epoch. The principal architect was Richard Hunt (1828-95), who synthesized some of the salient features of French Renaissance chateaux, particularly those of Blois and Chambord. This fabulous display of wealth was five years in building and cost about four and one half million dollars. The Biltmore House, surrounded by formal French gardens, still contains many of the old paintings, furniture, tapestries, oriental rugs, Chinese porcelains, and a magnificent library. In many ways, this mixture of styles and structure forceably reminds one of the potpourri overture *still in use.*

legend of the Black Forest, steeped in the very essence of German Romanticism—a love of the mystical and the supernatural—the work completely captured the German imagination. Three generations in Germany have been brought up on its hunting and bridal songs; many of its melodies have passed into the domain of folk song, and one, the horn theme heard in the first part, is a popular hymn tune!

This gifted, richly imaginative composer died from consumption at the age of forty at the very height of a brilliant career. Death came to him while he was composing and conducting in London, and so the first of German nationalists in music was buried in foreign soil. The REQUIEM of

Mozart was performed at the funeral service, as it had been at that of Haydn, Beethoven, and Schubert. When Wagner became director of music at the Saxon court, he took an active part in the movement that brought back to Germany the remains of his idol. He arranged the music for the ceremony that accompanied the second interment, and read the oration, an interesting prose work.

By the world at large, Weber is remembered chiefly for the overtures to his three romantic operas—DER FREISCHÜTZ, OBERON, and EURYANTHE—each a masterpiece in its genre, and for the perennially popular *Invitation to the Dance*. The operas themselves have not retained their place in the usual repertory outside Germany, but the overtures are among the popular orchestral pieces of all lands. The *Overture* to DER FREISCHÜTZ was successful from its opening night. In his diary, Weber writes that the opera was received with enthusiasm, the overture and folk song were encored, and fourteen out of the seventeen music pieces were stormily applauded. It spread over the Continent and to England at once and was performed in New York as early as 1825, only four years after its first performance. The story of the opera is built around one of those tales of magic and the Evil One of the vintage of "Ondine," "Giselle," and the fantasies of E. T. A. Hoffmann. The action concerns a young hunter, Max, who almost falls into the toils of the Evil One by selling his soul in return for a magic bullet, but is saved in the end by the love and faith of Agatha, his betrothed. The opera ends in the triumph of young love and the defeat of the forces of evil.

In the quarter century after Mozart's death, composers came to realize how effective it would be if they incorporated the principal themes of their operas in the overtures. In a short time, this *potpourri* type came to popularity. Our light opera, operetta and musical comedy type of overture is very likely to be a potpourri. Weber's *Overture* to DER FREISCHÜTZ, although organized on the solid foundations of the Classical sonata-allegro form, exhibits some characteristics of the new type of potpourri, for the subsidiary themes, instead of serving merely as transitional material between the main themes out of which the overture is constructed, are actual tunes from the opera, attractive in their own right.

Weber's overture is a crystallization of the atmosphere of his drama. The magic of his orchestration projects in masterly fashion the delicate colors of woodland life, the sinister fascination of the evil powers, and the emotional conflicts of his characters. Weber was perhaps more completely the writer for the stage than Beethoven. His imaginative use of instrumental color to create picturesque effects was developed to a greater degree than any of his contemporaries. He blazed the trail for the Romantic symphonic colorists, Wagner, Berlioz, and Liszt; for the overture as a new genre; for the birth of the symphonic poem as a distinct form; and for the development of modern instrumentation. So many of his innovations have, by now, lost their novelty because of continual imitation, so much so that we fail to realize the fertile imagination that brought them into significant being. But, standing as he did on the threshold of the new age, there can be no question that Weber enriched and influenced the course of music, especially operatic and symphonic music.

The *Overture* to DER FREISCHÜTZ, opens with a slow section, *adagio,* in C major, with the opening measures on the tone C sustained in unison by the strings and wood-winds creating at once a feeling of expectancy. This is followed in measure two by a questioning motif, *forte,* with a rising inflection, only to be succeeded in the third and fourth measures by a descending phrase, played softly. These first four measures are then repeated at an interval of a fourth lower, immediately after which there is a pause for the entire orchestra indicated by a *fermata.* Note how magically he depicts a mood of wonder, foreboding, and mystery from the very onset. How successful Weber is in the music that follows in establishing moods that end ultimately in one of overflowing joy! This is real Romantic music.[2] Here is the opening theme of the introduction:

Presently, after the hold, a quartet of French horns, above the strings played *pianissimo,* intones a Chorale of Faith of great loveliness and serenity—a symbol of constancy. The tune has been adapted to the words of a popular hymn. The horn theme follows:

Suddenly the mood darkens: ominous *tremolos* in the lower strings, the plucking *pizzicato* tones of the double-basses, and the sinister beating of the muffled drum usher in a 'cello passage, creating an atmosphere of foreboding. The *tremolos* swell to a *fortissimo,* then die away. We are now ready for the main body of the overture, *molto vivace* (very lively), in a somber C minor mode, and played in a brisk, double-time, *alla breve,* tempo.

[2] Compare the opening motive of this work with similar ideas used in the compositions listed in footnote #4 in Chapter 17.

The first theme emerges from the deepest gloom of the low tones of the 'cellos in an agitated *pianissimo*, delineating Max's fear that he may have fallen into the clutches of the Evil One:

The music becomes louder, little by little (*crescendo poco a poco*), and leads to a tumultuous transition in which a striking *arpeggio* (chordwise) theme and a brusque chordal passage sweep along with almost demoniac energy:

Notice what a perfect contrast this theme presents to the fearful Max theme, and how effectively Weber has utilized differences in pitch register, change of mode, instrumental tone color, rhythm, and general melodic contour to project the differences between the two.

After a warning outcry on the horns, repeated thrice, there emerges, *con molto passione* (with much passion), a theme on the solo clarinet, sustained high above the shuddering *tremolos* of the strings: it is the cry of Max when, on his way to meet the emissary of Satan at midnight to cast the magic bullets, he catches sight of the dread abysses of the Wolf's Glen.

Now the second theme proper appears in the more happy major mode (in the key of E-flat major); it is a broadly flowing melody, expressive of Agatha's love and faith. First given to clarinets and first violins, it is repeated *dolce* by flutes, clarinets, and the bassoons, and its square-cut, regular, four-measure phrase structure and the definite cadence at the end lend a great deal to the feeling of determination and solidity:

The development section that follows combines, in a most skillful manner, fragments of the two subsidiary themes—the *arpeggio* and chord figures—and the Agatha theme. The brilliant modulations of the music and its headlong pace are irresistible. The recapitulation returns to the home tonality of C minor with the somber Max theme deep in the bass as before. This section follows the course of the exposition, except that where we formerly heard the troubled clarinet solo before the appearance of the Agatha theme, we now hear a brief reminder of the foreboding that preceded the *molto vivace*. Then all sadness and fear are swept away by the proclamation of the Agatha theme on the violins and flutes against a jubilant orchestral background leading to the brilliant *coda*. It is not difficult to understand the programmatic implications of this musical speech, and the divergence from the strict form of the reprise is condoned, especially when one hears the second theme proper in the coda—a very clever manipulation of musical materials, thematic as well as design. Almost all the brilliant coda comes from the *Finale* of the opera itself; again, a stroke of imagination on the part of Weber. A vigorous repetition of the "sunny" chord of C major, as contrast to the more prevalent, "somber" C minor chord, brings the overture to a most satisfying close.

Beethoven's "Leonora" Overture No. 3 (1806)

Beethoven's solitary venture into the operatic form, FIDELIO, cost him no end of trouble. He did not have that flair for the stage that came to Mozart naturally. Then again, Beethoven's high concept of the ethical nature of music rendered him out of sympathy with the type of story that opera composers of the day customarily chose; he was shocked that Mozart should have set plays like DON JUAN and the MARRIAGE OF FIGARO—a view that throws much light on his qualifications as a dramatist. His choice finally fell on a highly edifying story, *Leonora, or Conjugal Love,* based on a novel by Bouilly. The action deals with the self-sacrificing devotion of Leonora, whose husband Florestan is imprisoned in a dungeon through the machinations of the unscrupulous Pizarro, governor of the prison. Leonora disguises herself as a man and under the name of Fidelio—symbol of her wifely fidelity—braves every danger to rescue her husband. The villain is foiled in his plot to kill Florestan by the resourcefulness of Leonora and by the timely arrival of the Minister of Justice, who metes out punishment to Pizarro as Leonora removes the fetters from her husband.

The opera was beset with difficulties from the start. The singers insisted that the music was unsingable—the same complaint that faced Wagner a generation later. Beethoven had introduced a concept of vocal line in advance of his age—and the singers clamored for what they were accustomed to. The rehearsals were exasperating to everyone concerned. The first performance, November 20, 1805, found Vienna in the hands of the French army, Bonaparte at the Imperial Palace at Schönbrunn, and the capital deserted by the Emperor, the nobility, and the wealthy patrons of music. The work was a failure, which could not be blamed entirely on the political situation. Beethoven's friends urged him to revise the book and the score. He was adamant at first, but finally consented. The new version, produced in 1806, made a somewhat more favorable impression; but this time, Beethoven quarreled with the manager of the theater and the opera was withdrawn. He was prevailed upon (in 1814) to make still another revision for a new production of the work and the opera was finally launched, with a measure of success, in the form in which we have it today.

The opera has caused much division of opinion. Some insist that the nature of Beethoven's genius was fundamentally unsuited to the stage and that FIDELIO is weak in dramatic power. Others maintain that it is one of the most powerful of operas and that not only was Beethoven not lacking in dramatic talent, but he succeeded in fusing the symphonic and dramatic elements with a mastery equaled by few. The opera has never become a really popular work, yet it has never disappeared altogether from the boards. Of late there appears to have arisen a new interest in it; but it is not unlikely that the opera will eventually be known largely through the overtures Beethoven composed for it.

Beethoven actually wrote four overtures for FIDELIO, three known as LEONORA NOS. 1, 2 and 3, and one known as FIDELIO—one each for the productions in 1805, 1806, and 1814, and one that did not see the light until after his death. Of these, the LEONORA NO. 3, which he prepared for the revised version of 1806, has become the most popular, having established itself in the symphonic repertory as a work of great dramatic power. The so-called FIDELIO overture to this opera has often been termed a symphonic poem. Whatever differences of opinion may exist as to the opera itself, in the LEONORA NO. 3 Beethoven projected the very essence of his opera, creating a symphonic drama of fiery eloquence and intensity. Here he was able to think in purely musical terms, undisturbed by the machinery of the stage.

The overture opens *adagio,* in the key of C major. A *fortissimo* chord fades into a sorrowful downward-moving figure on wood-winds and strings, suggestive of Florestan's despair as he descends to his dungeon.

The music modulates from C major down to B minor, then again to A flat, where wood-winds, accompanied by strings, sing the poignant opening measures of Florestan's famous aria in the prison scene in the second act, "In life's springtide, happiness has flown from me."

A transitional passage of great emotional power, rising from a *pianissimo* mood of foreboding to a *fortississimo* (*fff*) outburst by the full orchestra and then subsiding to a mysterious *pianissimo,* launches one into the *allegro* of the movement proper, in C major, *alla breve.* The principal theme is played by the violins and 'cellos—a melody of great nobility and courage. Notice the striking syncopated rhythm in the first and fifth measures of the illustration.

After an impetuous unfolding of the first theme and a transitional passage of modulation, the second theme emerges, played by flute and violin (*piano* and *dolce*), in a tenderly appealing, upward inflection in E major:

This theme is unfolded with care and skill. The development section is carried out with Beethoven's rich sense of the possibilities implicit in his thematic material. Fragments from the "pleading" second theme are interspersed with hints of the first theme against a seething orchestral background. This culminates in the thrilling trumpet call in the last act of the opera, which signalizes the arrival of the Minister of Justice just as Pizarro is about to carry out his plot against Florestan.

This famous trumpet fanfare is played on the stage during the opera and, usually, behind the scenes during a concert performance. Inasmuch as this theme has nothing to do with the musical material of the rest of the overture, Beethoven was severely censured by his contemporaries; he felt fully justified, however, since the theme comes from the opera itself and serves, in the overture, to maintain the underlying story or program—one of the compromises between slavish following of the classical form and the freedom of romantic program music.

The orchestra quivers with excitement; the trumpet call is repeated; then the music surges ahead into the recapitulation. The themes of the exposition are rehearsed, with the second theme transposed to the home key of C major, and then the music enters the dramatic *coda*. Here the main themes again come into play and the work comes to a brilliant close with many reaffirmations of the tonic, C major chord, sounding in the full orchestra. Truly, this is a marvelous synthesis of the classical sonata-allegro form, a real overture for an opera and, over all, a fine example of all these factors used together to provide ideal concert programmatic music.

ADDITIONAL SUGGESTIONS FOR LISTENING

It is hoped that the listener will add to his list Mozart's *Overtures* to THE MARRIAGE OF FIGARO, THE MAGIC FLUTE, and DON GIOVANNI; Beethoven's EGMONT and CORIOLANUS *Overtures* (especially the last mentioned for study in structure and form); Weber's OBERON and EURYANTHE *Overtures;* Mendelssohn's *Overture* FINGAL'S CAVE. Listen also to Sir Edward Elgar's very jolly salute to London, "COCKAIGNE" *Overture,* Op. 40, subtitle "In London Town"—in a well-nigh perfect classical sonata-allegro form which can easily be recognized. The orchestration is masterfully executed. Some listeners may enjoy the programmatic *Overture* to the opera WILLIAM TELL by Rossini; also the *Overtures* to BENVENUTO CELLINI, to KING LEAR, and the popular ROMAN CARNIVAL OVERTURE—all by Berlioz, that eccentric and brilliant genius in the use of the

Romantic tempers, and one of the great innovators and masters of orchestration. By all means listen to the delightful ACADEMIC FESTIVAL OVERTURE, Op. 80, by Brahms with its brilliant orchestration and skillful weaving of themes from student songs, which Brahms wrote as his "thesis" of appreciation upon receiving the degree of Doctor of Philosophy at the University of Breslau in 1881.

Courtesy Metropolitan Museum of Art

Ludovicus Grovvelus

DOUBLE VIRGINAL (FLEMISH, ABOUT 1600)

25 The concerto for solo instrument and orchestra

In the modern sense, the word *concerto* indicates a composition for solo instrument and symphony orchestra that affords the soloist ample opportunity to display his virtuosity. The word derives from the Latin *concentus,* a species of church compositions probably first used by Ludovico Viadana, in 1602, to describe his motets for voices and organ, which he published as *Concerti Ecclesiastici.*[1] In another, wider sense, the word *concerto* was used in older musical writings to describe a performance in which musicians joined forces in a united, concerted effort.

The form of the late seventeenth- and early eighteenth-century concerto was established largely by the composers of the Italian school, such as Corelli, Tartini, and Vivaldi. In this form there was not one soloist, but a group of soloists—strings, winds, keyboard, or any combination of

[1] See Grove's *Dictionary of Music and Musicians.*

these desired by the composer—who were used singly or together as a contrasting element to the orchestra as a whole. This small group of soloists was called the *concertino;* the remainder of the orchestral players, the *ripieno;* and together, the *concerto grosso.* The form itself came to be known as the *concerto grosso,* and, as such, flourished throughout the eighteenth century. It consisted of a sequence, or collection, of movements in diverse spirits and tempi somewhat analogous to the suite, but depending for its effect on the interplay and contrast of the two groups—the *concertino* and the *ripieno.* (For more extended treatment of the *concerto grosso,* see Chapter 28.)

With the rise of the sonata in the period of Haydn and Mozart, the concerto grosso gradually receded in popularity and was supplanted by the solo concerto, which better served to focus the attention on the solo instrument, its interplay with the orchestra, and permitted the latter to indulge in purely symphonic development of the musical ideas in the orchestra as a whole. This interplay as a dramatic element was heightened when, instead of two groups pitted against each other, a single instrument became the protagonist of the action against the background of the orchestra, just as in Greek tragedy the single character is pitted against the chorus. One might say then, that the concerto drew inspiration not only from the concerto-grosso traditions but also from the opera, in which the solo singer alternated with the *ritornellos,* or interludes, of the orchestra. These influences, combined with the new virtuosity on the solo instruments that came to the fore in the late eighteenth and early nineteenth century, produced a flexible, varied, and highly imaginative form. During the period of Mozart and Haydn, when the solo instruments had not yet become important enough to warrant a full concert of piano or violin music, the combination of piano and orchestra, or violin and orchestra, became the medium through which composer-virtuosi displayed their powers. A typical program might include—this was a period of gargantuan programs—a new symphony or two by the composer, a new piano sonata, several vocal excerpts from a mass or opera, and, to top off the list, the latest concerto!

Mozart played a decisive role in the rise of the solo concerto, developing it as an enormously effective dialogue between soloist and orchestra. He left the form basically as it has come to be known in modern times: in three movements, a fast, a slow, and a fast, with a brilliant *cadenza,* usually in the first, and sometimes in the last, while the orchestra maintains silence to focus attention on the soloist. In the days of Mozart and Beethoven, when the artist was also the composer, the cadenza was a free improvisation on the themes of the movement. As the art of improvisation waned, the cadenza was written out by the composer, by some soloist who had a flair for improvisation, or by some other composer.

Mozart wrote between forty and fifty concertos for various instruments. They became the foundation upon which later composers constructed their works. In the piano and violin concertos of his mature period, we find revealed in full his mastery of the style of each instrument and his sensitivity to the possibilities of each.

The emergence of the concerto was intimately connected with mechanical improvements in the solo instruments themselves, and in the technical mastery of playing throughout the eighteenth century. This is particularly true of the piano during Beethoven's career. Just as Beethoven expanded the emotional domain of the solo piano in his thirty-two sonatas for that instrument, so he broadened the form of the concerto. In his five piano concertos and one violin concerto, the solo instrument is treated more orchestrally than in the Mozart works; the conflict between the opposing tonal colors and masses is dramatized to the highest degree. (Especially the Beethoven CONCERTO FOR PIANO IN G MAJOR, Op. 58, or the more popular one in E-FLAT MAJOR, Op. 73, called the "*Emperor*" by someone other than the composer.)

In many of the concertos written under romantic influence, one can find evidences of highly personalized expression. One may discover experiments in the form as a whole and in matters of internal structures. There are also brilliant and colorful orchestration and bravura solo playing, as well as submergence of the solo part into the orchestra itself—sometimes the solo part is, in reality, just another orchestral instrument. The *tutti* of the romantic concerto is often of the greatest importance as a symphonic entity, as a means of development of thematic material, or as a vehicle for the introduction of new themes that are of more immediate attraction than they are for future organic development. One often discovers both the romantic and classic tendencies in the same work!

Then, too, this Romantic type of music makes frequent use of nationalistic characteristics of melody, rhythm, and instrumental color. Ofttimes there is an adaptation of actual native folk tunes and native peculiarities, even in the use of indigenous harmony and sound effects. Thus one might continue; but these works and their special effects are much better heard than described.

In view of such a complex situation and limitations of space, our immediate task is best accomplished by selecting one or two outstanding and broadly representative works in the concerto form. While the concertos chosen should readily ingratiate themselves into the listener's favor, they should also afford basic tuition for experiences which will come in the future.

We have chosen the PIANO CONCERTO IN A MINOR, Op. 54, by Robert Schumann, and the VIOLIN CONCERTO IN E MINOR, Op. 64, by Felix Mendelssohn-Bartholdy for detailed analysis.

Courtesy Theodore Presser Co.

ROBERT SCHUMANN

ROBERT SCHUMANN (1810–1856)[2]

Surely no one was more to the fore in the Romantic movement in Germany than Robert Alexander Schumann, not only for his own compositions, but also through his critical writings, personal encouragement, and active aid to worthy young composers (among them Brahms and Chopin). Born in Zwickau on June 8, 1810, he came to a tragic end near Bonn, the birthplace of Beethoven, on July 29, 1856. He did not come from a musical family. yet his talent expressed itself in original composition as early as the age of six. His more formalized education began in 1820, first at the Zwickau Gymnasium, then at Leipzig University where he took a law course. Later, in 1829, he pursued law and philosophy at the University of Heidelberg and studied music on the side—practicing as much as seven hours a day at his "hobby."

Schumann lived at the home of Friedrich Wieck, his piano teacher, and continued with his training in composition with H. Dorn at the same time. It was during his strenuous period of piano study that Schumann hit on a mechanical idea designed to strengthen the fourth finger of his right hand—he was determined on a career as a concert pianist; but this contraption only resulted in the crippling of the finger so that his ambition as a piano virtuoso came to an abrupt end. His career as a composer now became his chief concern.

The composer was in love with Clara Wieck, the daughter of his piano teacher, which met with the great displeasure of the father. The affair was finally brought to a court of law, with a verdict in favor of the young lovers. Their marriage became one of the most ideal romances to be found in art—paralleled in many respects by that of Marion and Edward MacDowell. Clara proved to be a great source of inspiration to Schumann, and a flood of songs and piano works flowed from the pen of the happy composer.

Schumann founded and edited the *Neue Zeitschrift für Musik,* for which he wrote many significant essays and criticisms from 1834 to 1844. In 1840, the University of Jena conferred upon him the degree of Doctor of Philosophy for his literary as well as musical achievements. That year he was mainly concerned with the composition of his greatest songs, 1841 with his symphonic works, and 1842 with his chamber music.

Schumann lived in Dresden, teaching and composing, until 1850, when he unwisely accepted a post as town musical director at Düsseldorf. Evidences of impending mental trouble began to be manifest, culminating in his attempted suicide by jumping into the Rhine. This forced his incarceration in an asylum near Bonn, and his death followed, mercifully,

[2] Some may prefer to reverse the order of the Schumann and the Mendelssohn concertos in this chapter.

a few years later, in 1856. Brahms, long a friend of the Schumanns, now became a great source of consolation and friendly aid. Clara resumed her professional public career as a concert pianist, and carried forward the reputation of Schumann and his music, much as Marion carried forward Edward MacDowell's music in our own country.

Schumann's Concerto in A minor, Op. 54, for Piano and Orchestra

Out of the many critiques written about this concerto, we have selected one from THE ART OF MUSIC, a fourteen-volume work edited by Dr. Daniel Gregory Mason, one of America's foremost composers and scholars.[3]

> The concerto stands as a flawless masterpiece. The themes are inspired. There is no trace of sentimentality or morbidness. The form is ruled by an unerring and fine sense of proportion and line. It is neither too long nor too short. There is no awkwardness, no tentativeness, no striving for effect. No note is unwisely placed. The treatment of both pianoforte and orchestra leaves nothing to be desired, either when the one is set against the other or when both are intimately blended. Though it in no way suggests the virtuoso, it is perfectly suited to the piano, bringing out unfailingly the very best the instrument is capable of.

High praise indeed from a great authority!

FIRST MOVEMENT: It was originally composed as a *Fantasie* for piano solo and orchestra in 1841. Later, in 1845, the second movement, *Intermezzo,* and the *Finale,* the third and last movement, were composed, and the three movements joined together into the concerto as we now know it. The first movement, marked *allegro affettuoso* (lively and tenderly), opens with a *forte* chord for full orchestra, immediately followed by the impetuous descending cadenza-like introduction of the solo instrument. Here is the introduction to the movement proper:

The first theme appears in the wood-winds and horns, played softly (*p*), and with the theme itself in the solo oboe part. Note well the germinal figures, or motives, marked "A" and "B," for these are developed

[3] Leland Hall (Ed. in charge), *The Art of Music,* 14 Vols. (New York: National Society of Music, 1915). Vol. 7, page 237. Quoted by permission.

throughout the three movements; even the principal themes are derived or related to them, as we shall observe. Here is the first theme:

There is much working over the motive "A" of the first theme between the piano and the orchestra; a rapid octave passage leads to a *tutti* which, in turn, leads into a charming duet, *andante espressivo* (fairly slow and with expression), between the piano and the solo clarinet, based on the motive "A." This quiet mood is abruptly dispelled by a reappearance of the opening idea which is bandied about between the solo instrument and the orchestra; the first theme is heard again, this time as a duet between the solo flute and the piano, with the remainder of the orchestra filling in, and finally in the wood-winds and horns.

The transition theme, sometimes erroneously called the second theme, is played by the violins on the G string with the piano affording an accompaniment in true piano style. It is interesting to see how the composer used the solo instrument as an accompanimental background for solo orchestral instruments, as a solo instrument itself, and as an additional orchestral instrument in the more sonorous *tutti.* Note well the eventual development of the motive marked "A" and the one marked "B" (in the transitional theme proper). The latter assumes such importance in later development (in the piano part particularly) that it might almost be dubbed a major second transitional theme. Here is the transition theme, *in extenso,* as played by the first violins—solely on the G string, as indicated:

The wind theme is now played by the piano, at the termination of which the solo clarinet plays with animation (*animato*), the ensuing theme, which grows out of motive "A"; the strings provide the necessary support.

This theme is developed, and bandied about most cleverly along with previously announced themes.

Presently the entire orchestra joins in to make a stirring climax, at the peak of which the piano comes to its *cadenza,* made largely out of motives "B" and "A," in that order, of the first theme. The movement then quickly comes to a close. This, a beautiful, almost perfect movement, is a model of compositional craftmanship and orchestration, and it caters to no mere technical virtuosity. It is composed of lovely lyrical music, with a wonderful wedding of the solo instrument and the orchestra.

SECOND MOVEMENT: Intermezzo. Andantino grazioso (rather slowly and gracefully). An interesting development of the "B" motive of the first theme in the first movement, it sets off the piano with a happy, naïve theme and playful musical dialogue with the orchestra. Note the interplay of instrumental color of the following first theme; the development and evolvement of the succeeding part of the movement. Here is the first theme:

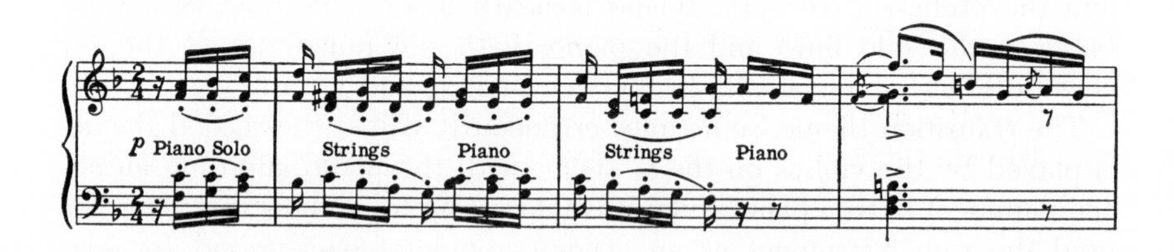

The *staccato,* four-note figure in the first theme persistenly recurs, relieved now and then by contrasting material of a flowing, lyrical character. The second theme, played so expressively high upon the A string of the 'cellos, is taken up by the clarinet and a fagott an octave apart, to be resumed by the 'cellos and violas twenty-one measures later. The first violins, soaring high on their E strings, with the second violins doubling an octave lower, assist the 'cellos to the achievement of a vibrant, emotional climax which the attentive listener cannot fail to observe and delight in. The following illustration shows the beginning of the 'cello theme, the second theme proper:

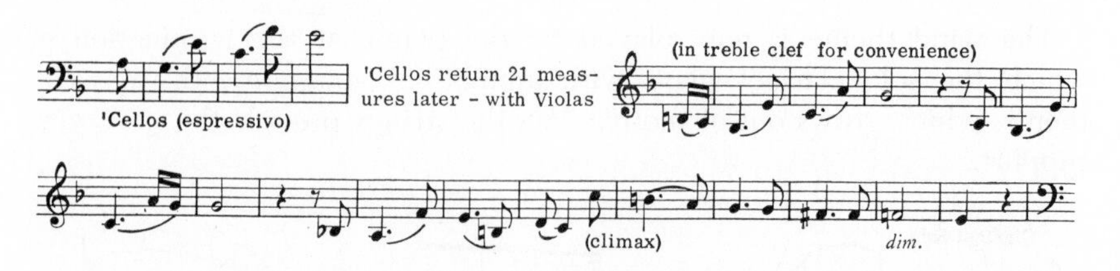

The hard working, four-note figure of the first theme of this movement (derived from the first theme "A" of the first movement) reappears and is tossed about between the orchestra and the solo instrument, until a distant clarion call is heard in the wood-winds while the piano indulges in rapidly descending chordal figures. Suddenly, with a loud upward sweep of the strings (in octaves), the quiet, lyrical Intermezzo rushes without a break (save for a loud crash-chord) into the finale. Here is the essence of the music for this wonderful link between the two movements:

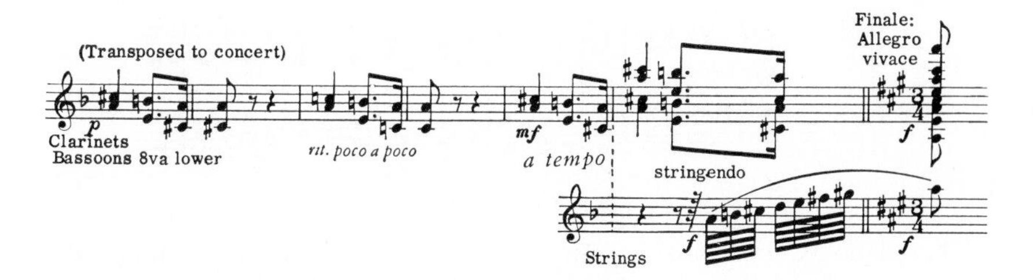

FINALE: Allegro vivace (fast and sprightly). The first theme proper appears about nine measures after the crash chord just mentioned. The first theme of this movement is derived from the "B" motive of the first theme of the first movement—another example of Schumann's command of the technical side of his craft, as well as the purely musical elements. Here is the first theme of the finale, played by the solo instrument over a soft string accompaniment:

Soon a rapidly flowing episodical, subsidiary theme appears in the piano solo, gently supported by more or less scantily-sustained tones in the strings. Here is the new piano theme:

The piano runs on its way, still supported by the strings, until the real second theme appears in the strings (*pp*), echoed by the solo instrument.

This second theme is marchlike; but with a very cleverly conceived, syncopated-like rhythm which seems to the listener to confound the duple and triple meters in a delightfully deceptive manner. (Some theorists would call this marchlike theme the second part of the principal theme because of its later importance in the development of the movement.) Here is this strange triple meter march theme for the strings:

The piano is soon busy again with a running, episodical figure that breaks into a *tutti* based upon the opening theme. There appears a new theme in the development, however, at the sudden and abrupt change of key. It is a lyrical theme played by the solo oboe over the strings. This idea soon becomes the subject for "conversation" between the piano and successively the oboe, the flute, the violins, and eventually the violas. We see how well Schumann understands the effective idiomatic use of the orchestra and with what delight he presents the unexpected in original manner! Here is the oboe theme already pointed out:

The finale is a warmly glowing movement, full of overflowing vigor and healthfulness. The world can be eternally grateful for this masterpiece.

FELIX MENDELSSOHN-BARTHOLDY (1809–1847)

The second illustration of the solo instrument type of concerto is the CONCERTO IN E MINOR, Op. 64, for violin and orchestra, by Jakob Ludwig Mendelssohn-Bartholdy, more familiarly known as Felix Mendelssohn. It was completed on September 16, 1844, only three years before his untimely death in 1847. This precocious and prolific composer, who reached extraordinary maturity in his compositional art before he was twenty, had the singular good fortune among musical geniuses of enjoying a comfortable life, although he was always extremely busy and hard working, and occupied posts of great responsibility.

He was born in Hamburg, February 3, 1809, of Jewish ancestry, though for a generation past the family had embraced the Christian faith. At the age of ten he entered the Singakademie, though he had studied violin, piano, and composition before that. The very year he entered the Academy, his original setting of the NINETEENTH PSALM received its first public performance! His home life was not only free of monetary woes, but it was a musical one, for his father saw to it that a small orchestra or an ensemble performed at home every Sunday. Felix thus had an excellent opportunity to hear his own works and to receive training in conducting, which later enabled him to become director of the famous Gewandhaus Symphony Orchestra of Leipzig.

At the age of seventeen, Mendelssohn composed what many consider his greatest work, the overture to A MIDSUMMER NIGHT'S DREAM (see Chap. 10) and the superb OCTET FOR STRINGS, Op. 20. The same year he entered the University of Berlin, offering as his evidence of ability a translation of Terence. The next year he composed the opera DIE HOCHZEIT DES CAMACHO. But an amazing experience awaited him at the age of twenty: he produced, for the first time since the composer's death, J. S. Bach's PASSION ACCORDING TO ST. MATTHEW! What a world of inferences might be drawn from that event and the circumstances involved! In 1829 a series of nine musical travels to England were undertaken, and again one might ponder over the influence that Handel and Mendelssohn had over English music. His appearances throughout England and the Continent were in the manifold capacities of conductor, composer, pianist, and organist, and he had remarkable success in all. In 1833 he conducted the Düsseldorf Music Festival and accepted the position of Town Music Director. In 1835 he became conductor of the Gewandhaus Orchestra in Leipzig, which for so many years stood out as one of the finest symphony orchestras in all Europe. Later he organized and directed the Conservatory of Music at Leipzig (since 1876 it has been known as the Royal Conservatory of Music). On hearing of the death of his beloved and idolized sister, Fanny Hensel, he suffered a stroke and died six months later. His compositions include almost all types of musical forms. His style embraced contrapuntal, classical, and romantic types; and although some of his compositions have undergone a temporary eclipse, many authorities maintain that not a few of his best works in each of these types will achieve immortality. Certainly Mendelssohn had a vital and tremendous influence on music.

Mendelssohn's Concerto in E minor, Op. 64, for Violin and Orchestra

Few musical works have enjoyed such world-wide popularity and consistent favor among the musical elect as has this concerto. Only a few years ago Donald Francis Tovey, the great English musicologist and critic, said of this work that it is "the most remarkable stroke of genius in this most popular of violin concertos." [4] Here classical purity of style and perfection of formal aspects unite with spontaneous melody, fertility of romantic imagination, marked personal expression, and also the elfin lightness of touch that was, perhaps, Mendelssohn's most salient and charming gift. (Ferdinand David, a violin master and close friend, aided Mendelssohn frequently during the composition of this concerto.)

It was the custom in the more strictly classical tradition of performing solo concertos to have the orchestra play all the way through the exposition and then, at the repetition (signified by the usual double-bar-and-repeat sign), to have the solo instrument join in. Some contemporary conductors ignore this procedure, even in the works of the masters.

FIRST MOVEMENT: Allegro molto appassionato. The solo violin is heard in the first theme after an introduction of only a measure and a half. There will be no difficulty in noting its appearance.

This material is worked up into a climactic *tutti.* Then the orchestration thins out considerably, the ensuing theme serving as the basis of a transition to the second theme.

The solo violin soars, plays alternately up and down the strings, poises for a moment upon a high G and then B above it, and then down again to the lowest string of the violin (G below middle C), above which the wood-winds (flutes and clarinets) play the second theme proper, softly (*pp*) and peacefully (*tranquillo*). Presently the same theme is picked up by the solo violin.

The development section begins with the transition melody, and modulates freely in a brilliant dialogue between the solo violin and the orchestra. Then portions of the first theme are developed by both in turn

[4] Sir Donald Francis Tovey, *Essays in Musical Analysis,* Vol. 3 (Oxford University Press, 1936). Quoted by permission.

and, with a sustained, *fortissimo* chord, the orchestra becomes silent while the solo violin performs a fanciful *cadenza.*

Mendelssohn's cadenza joins the reprise in clever manner; the soloist continues with his final arpeggiated figure of the cadenza, while the orchestra brings back the opening first theme in E minor. The reprise is somewhat shortened in comparison with the exposition. The *coda* achieves exhilarating momentum and ends with a brilliant outburst by the solo violin with the orchestra.

SECOND MOVEMENT: Mendelssohn joined the two movements with a holding tone in the first bassoon; but one most often hears the work with a distinct interruption, due more to wrongfully placed applause than to anything else. At any rate, the second, the slow movement, marked *andante* (in a slow, walking pace) is very lyrical, filled with breadth and dignity of expression, and quite moving in its simple melodic line. The form is that of an ordinary ternary, or three-part, A-B-A structure. The quiet opening theme is played by the solo violin after eight measures of introduction:

This theme leads to an agitated middle section, which carries with it not a little feeling of anxiety; but this passes, and the serene and peaceful opening theme reappears. True, Mendelssohn does not sound the depths of human emotions, nor does he attempt to move mountains; it is not that kind of a slow movement. Let us appreciate what the composer does project with such a sure hand—tranquility and peace and beauty!

THIRD MOVEMENT: Like the first and second movements, it is not detached in the original score. Mendelssohn placed a hold over the last chord with the solo violin, supported by the strings, entering on the up-beat in what one might call an adjoining interlude marked *allegretto non troppo* (with movement but not too fast). This interlude lasts for only fourteen measures and leads, without interruption, into the movement proper, marked *allegro molto vivace* (fast and with much spirit). A courtly flourish of horns, bassoons, and drums, interrupted four times by a swishlike figure in the solo violin, then the first theme proper appears in the solo violin, embellished with *staccato* passages in the wood-winds. The first theme follows:

This sort of exchange of conversation between the solo violin and the wood-winds, with the strings plucking the tones here and there, continues until, with an upward sweep of the violin, the entire orchestra sounds forth the second theme which vies with the first in sprightliness and vivacity. (Tovey calls this a "cheeky" theme.) Four measures from its entry after the *tutti* the solo violin plays the second theme proper, as follows:

Second Theme (solo violin)

A closing theme is heard after a bit of solo display as follows:

Closing theme (solo violin)

But this soon passes and the first and second themes again become the object of attention and thematic development throughout the remainder of the movement. A brilliant, almost pyrotechnical coda based largely on the second theme brings this work to a most satisfying close.

ADDITIONAL SUGGESTIONS FOR LISTENING

The following list is offered as a solid foundation for further individual study. All the numbers are available on commercial records.

Before going on to the more or less familiar concertos for orchestra with one or several solo instruments, the serious listener may wish to become thoroughly acquainted with the following Concerti Grossi: Bach's BRANDENBURG CONCERTI. First listen to No. 2 in F major, for trumpet, flute, oboe, and violin as the *Concertino* and the string orchestra as the *tutti.* Then go on as you wish with the remainder, Nos. 3, 1, 5, 4 and 6 in that suggested order. (See also Chapter 28.) Listen to the superb CONCERTO GROSSO for piano and strings by Ernest Bloch, the outstanding contemporary contribution, and the "CHRISTMAS CONCERTO" by Corelli, Op. 6, No. 8 in G minor. Try these by Handel: NO. 2 IN F MAJOR before studying NO. 1 IN G MINOR, NO. 3 IN E MINOR, NO. 5 IN D MAJOR, and NO. 6 IN A MINOR. A pair of beautiful examples of this form are: Locatelli Op. 1, No. 2, and Vivaldi Op. 3, NO. 11 IN D MINOR.

Now, for the Concerti for orchestra and one or several solo instruments, we suggest selected numbers from: Bartók, CONCERTO FOR VIOLIN, CONCERTO FOR ORCHESTRA; Beethoven, CONCERTO NO. 4 IN G MAJOR, Op. 58, and the so-called *"Emperor"* CONCERTO IN E-FLAT MAJOR, No. 5, Op. 73 (both for piano), CONCERTO IN D MAJOR, Op. 61 (violin); Brahms, CONCERTO IN D MINOR, No. 1, Op. 15, and NO. 2 IN B-FLAT MAJOR (both for piano), CONCERTO IN D MAJOR, Op. 77 (violin) and the DOUBLE CONCERTO IN A MINOR, Op. 102 (violin and 'cello); Bruch, CONCERTO NO. 1 IN G MINOR (violin); Chausson, POÈME FOR VIOLIN AND ORCHESTRA, Op. 25 (not a real concerto); Chopin, CONCERTO NO. 1 IN E MINOR, Op. 11 (piano); Dvořák, CONCERTO IN B MINOR, Op. 104 ('cello)—

he also wrote a CONCERTO FOR VIOLIN, Op. 53; Franck, VARIATIONS SYMPHONIQUES (for piano); Glazounov, CONCERTO IN A MINOR, Op. 82 (violin); Grieg, CONCERTO IN A MINOR, Op. 16 (piano); Liszt, CONCERTO IN E-FLAT MAJOR, No. 1 (piano); Lalo, SYMPHONIE ESPAGNOLE, Op. 21 (violin); MacDowell, CONCERTO NO. 2 IN D MINOR, Op. 23 (piano) also NO. 1 IN A MINOR, Op. 15, for piano. Mendelssohn, CONCERTOS NOS. 1 AND 2 (for piano) and the CONCERTO IN E MAJOR (for two pianos); Mozart, CONCERTO IN A MAJOR, K. 488 (for piano), CONCERTO IN C MINOR, K. 491 (for piano), CONCERTO IN D MAJOR, K. 218 (for violin) and CONCERTO IN A MAJOR, K. 219 (for violin). See list of Mozart's work in *Mozart: The Man and His Works,* by W. J. Turner (New York: Alfred Knopf, 1938). Paganini, CONCERTO NO. 1 IN D MAJOR, Op. 6 (violin); Prokofieff, CONCERTO NO. 3 IN C MAJOR, Op. 26 (piano); CONCERTO NO. 1 IN G MINOR, Op. 63 (violin); Rachmaninoff, CONCERTO NO. 2 IN C MINOR, Op. 18 (piano). Some listeners may later enjoy CONCERTO NO. 3 IN D MINOR, Op. 20 and NO. 4 IN G MINOR, Op. 40, both for piano. Ravel, CONCERTO FOR THE LEFT HAND (piano). The listener might also like his pyrotechnical display for the violin, TZIGANE. Respighi, CONCERTO GREGORIANO (violin) in which that great Italian composer bases his work upon the Gregorian Chants, *Victimae Paschali* (in the pure Dorian Mode) and the *Alleluia: Beatus vir qui timet Dominum (Dorian and Aeolian modes)*; Schumann, CONCERTO IN A MINOR, Op. 129 ('cello); Saint-Saëns, CONCERTO NO. 1 IN A MINOR, Op. 33 ('cello); Sibelius, CONCERTO IN D MINOR, Op. 47 (violin); Tartini, CONCERTO IN D MINOR (violin); Tchaikovsky, CONCERTO NO. 1 IN B-FLAT MINOR, Op. 23 (piano), CONCERTO IN D MAJOR, Op. 35 (violin); Vieuxtemps, CONCERTO NO. 4 IN D MINOR, Op. 31 (violin); Viotti, CONCERTO NO. 22 IN A MINOR (violin)—one of the real foundational works in the literature. He wrote 28 other Concerti for violin. Walton, CONCERTO FOR VIOLA IN A MINOR—a brilliant work by a contemporary British composer who has also written an excellent CONCERTO FOR VIOLIN; Wieniawski, CONCERTO NO. 2 IN D MINOR, Op. 22 (violin).

The listener who is really interested in following up the literature of the concerto, can easily do so, and according to his own personal liking, by consulting an up-to-date record catalog.

Courtesy Freer Gallery, Smithsonian Institution

26 Chamber music: the string quartet

The term "chamber music" once meant that type of music which was played to best advantage in the drawing room, or private chamber, in contrast to the church or theater.

Later definitions broadened this early meaning of the term to embrace types of music of a more or less intimate nature, capable of being performed in a comparatively small hall by a group of solo instrumentalists such as comprise a string or wind duo, trio, quartet, quintet, sextet, septet, octet, nonet, with or without the piano, and having no duplicate, or *ripieno,* parts, as is the case with the symphony orchestra. Mixed groups (wind and string) are frequent, and though vocal parts may be sometimes found (such as Arnold Schönberg's "Pierrot Lunaire" with its *sprechstimme* vocal part), the term "chamber music" usually is restricted to instrumental ensembles of solo parts, and seldom does the number of performers exceed nine or ten.[1]

[1] See the Introduction to *Cobbett's Cyclopedic Survey of Chamber Music,* by Walter Willson Cobbett. (Oxford University

Being of an intimate character, chamber music has been naturally selective in its audience, and its comprehension and appreciation is more limited than the type of music heard in the opera, the church, or in our major symphony orchestra programs. A great deal of chamber music is likely to be esoteric and to present a real challenge to the abilities of the listener; though we hasten to vouch for its ultimate enjoyment if one will make an effort to listen to it empathically, again and again.

It might be well, at this point, to compare some of the more salient characteristics of the symphony orchestra of the usual proportions (about one hundred players) with that of the string quartet consisting of one first violin, one second violin, one viola, and one violoncello (see Chap. 12 for description of these instruments). The following description of contrasting characteristics of the two is not intended to be exhaustive or inviolable; it is, however, sufficiently general and provocative to warrant inclusion here.

String quartet music is written for, and played by, four performers, and, thus, instead of the infinite variety of tonal colors that can be secured from an orchestra, it possesses the pure, concentrated tone qualities of a family of bowed stringed instruments. There are, however, great possibilities for flexibility of performance in the string quartet because of the nature and smallness of the ensemble. The sonorities of the quartet are naturally less than those of the orchestra, and so the quartet is well suited to intimate recital hall performance. However, the listener loses less of the actual intention of the composer. The quartet affords more delicate nuances than the orchestra, and thus the listener can delight in an endless variety of shades of expression and sensitiveness of adjustment in intonation and musical details that are naturally more limited in the orchestra. In place of the compelling masses of tone in the orchestra, the quartet affords greater purity of tone and near-perfect blending of tone and ensemble. The rhythmic effects of the large symphony orchestra, with its use of exotic, realistic, and often ostentatious percussion instruments, are replaced in the quartet by more subtle means, for the rhythmic effects must, perforce, be an inherent part of the music itself.

The orchestra blares forth themes and makes them more obvious by means of "doubling" or sharply contrasting tone color. But in the string quartet, the listener has often to discover the themes, figures, and other musical ideas amidst a closely woven tonal design, a type of writing that might well produce tonal chaos in the *full* orchestra. Finally, the listener has the opportunity of "the enjoyment of the ultimate" in the purity of instrumental part-writing in the quartet and in shifting the attention from part to part, to several instruments at once, or to the

---

Press, 1929.) We have quoted freely from this monumental and invaluable work, with permission from the publishers.

entire ensemble. This is something that must be experienced to enjoy; and this type of enjoyment, though common both to the orchestra and the quartet, is likely to be more frequent and more intense in the latter. Chamber music demands more active, more creative, and more intensely sustained interest than do most other types of music. Even the most capable listener finds it necessary to hear a worthwhile quartet over and over in order to appreciate it properly and to "possess" it permanently. Nothing in the way of formalized and detailed study can ever take the place of the listening process. Most experts agree that in some of the later quartets of Beethoven there remain depths yet to be plumbed, even after some 125 years.

Collection of Museum of Modern Art, New York

GIRL IN FEATHERED HAT, AN INK DRAWING Matisse

Note economy of line.

A few observations on how we listen to many parts played simultaneously might well be in order. When more than three independent, contrapuntal parts are played at once, one does not hear all the parts individually and horizontally. (Only a very few trained musicians can hear three independent parts, and it is believed by psychologists that no one can hear four distinctly separate parts.) What actually happens in such listening is that the attention shifts, very rapidly and almost unconsciously from one, or perhaps two, parts to another. Usually the outside voices (comparable to the soprano and bass voices) first attract the attention, or, as is often the case, the composer writes parts that shift in saliency. These the listener notices, while the others remain in the margin of consciousness. When all the parts play a single, vertical (harmonic) entity, they are most likely to be heard as a "klang"-like composite, separated only by analysis on the part of trained musicians or laymen. But this shifting of attention is done so quickly and effortlessly that the listener gets the effect of *all* the parts. A moving picture presents about 16 static pictures a second, but the proper speed of run-off gives the impression of uninterrupted motion. Something similar goes on in the music listener's mind. He should anticipate, shifting the attention automatically to the salient ideas in the different instruments, while still maintaining the basic line and conception of the whole, in addition to feeling the emotional and spiritual qualities of the composition—a formidable but worthwhile challenge.

These comparisons have been between two musical types; now let us contrast them with other art media. A large symphony orchestra may be likened to a fresco or oil painting of large proportions where the painter deals with gross forms in his composition, large masses of forms and colors, and where he indulges in striking contrasts of content, means, and dynamic action—as though he were painting with a large brush and were concerned with salient rather than minute and subtle effects. A good example is Michelangelo's JUDGMENT DAY on the front wall of the Sistine Chapel (and to a less extent, Raphael's THE SCHOOL OF ATHENS); an excellent instance of the small-brush, realistically detailed painting may be seen in the Holbein PORTRAIT OF GEORG GISZE; and a striking illustration of economy of means is seen in the etching, THE PALACES, by the American artist, James McNeill Whistler at the beginning of this chapter. An extreme economy of line is shown in the ink drawing, GIRL IN FEATHERED HAT by Henri Matisse, and in a middling degree, the Dürer etching of the DOODLE-SACK PLAYER. Each type of art serves its own peculiar purpose in its own medium. Anyone who would appreciate them properly should adjust his receptive attitude and judgment of values accordingly. A sculptor, executing such a lofty and spacious work as the STATUE OF LIBERTY in New York Harbor,[2] had a different purpose in mind than Michelangelo had in creating smaller and more detailed pieces such as his MOSES, DAVID, and PIETÀ; and the beholder should consider both their similarities and dissimilarities along with the other concomitants of appreciation. When poetry is under inquiry, one does not demand identical appreciator reactions from such divergent forms as a sonnet, a narrative poem, a lyric poem, a folk ballad, an epic poem, and so forth. Quite the contrary, one enjoys the peculiarities of each. So should it be in considering musical types. Since we believe that the reader would be interested in making his own comparisons between the various types of music we have presented thus far, we leave that matter for his own accomplishment and consequently greater enjoyment.

Most of the instrumental music presented in the text up to this point has involved the use of the large symphony orchestra. To effect a smooth and gradual transition to the small, comparatively restrained, and more intimate ensemble exemplified by the string quartet, let us first hear Mozart's serenade, EINE KLEINE NACHTMUSIK, in G major, K. 525.[3] This was written as a *divertimento* "for soloists or a body of players," but it is usually heard as a work for string orchestra—where the original parts are duplicated by having additional instruments of similar kind

[2] By Frédéric Auguste Bartholdi, French sculptor, 1834–1904. The Statue of Liberty was dedicated in New York harbor on Oct. 28, 1886.

[3] Originally written for 2 violins, viola, 'cello, and double basses *ad libitum*. W. J. Turner, Mozart's biographer, gives Aug. 19, 1787, for the composition of this serenade.

including the double-basses join in the performance. The serenade was written especially for a gala festivity in Vienna, when the composer was in his thirty-first year.

***Eine Kleine Nachtmusik* (*A Little Night Music*),**
A serenade for strings, K. 525.

The over-all form of the serenade, constructed with four separate and contrasting movements, is not unlike the complete symphony form, on a much smaller scale. The first movement, instead of being in the usual sonata-allegro form, is without a real development section and thus is generally styled a *sonatina* form.[4]

FIRST MOVEMENT: Allegro. G major. $\frac{4}{4}$ *time. Sonatina form.* This movement is of a brisk, gay, marchlike character. There is a definite feeling of the gaiety of social festivity, as noted by Cobbett. The principal theme is played by all the instruments in unison, in a loud (*forte*) and spirited manner. Try to follow the use of this and the other themes as they course through the movement, whole or in part, or altered.

The second theme is *piano,* contrasting its daintiness with the burly good humor of the first.

There is also a third theme, often called a "closing theme" by the theorists, light and gay and altogether charming. Notice how much the trill contributes to this effect.

A brief *codetta* brings us to the double bar at the end of the exposition; the whole section is then repeated.

The development section of the sonatina is so brief as to be practically nonexistent. The recapitulation follows the thematic sequence of the exposition save that all the themes are now in the home key of G major.

SECOND MOVEMENT: Romanze. Andante. C major. Alla breve. Second Rondo form. The second movement, the slow one, is a *romanze,*

[4] Some theorists call this general sort of structure a species of rondo.

or *romance,* and, as its name implies, is tenderly lyrical and melodic in character. Here the personal note of the serenade is most in evidence, although the sentiment never becomes deeper than is appropriate for a charming summer evening. Note the inimitable grace of the opening measures, the finish and elegance of the style throughout. Like the themes of the first movement, this one is built on the regular four-measure phrase, two-period formation. There is something well-bred and stately in the bare outlines of such structural regularity.

The theme is varied, and, after a bit of adventure, returns to a suggestion of the main, or first theme.

THIRD MOVEMENT: Menuetto. Allegretto. G major. $\frac{3}{4}$ *time. Minuet and Trio form.* The minuet is bright and airy in the best eighteenth-century manner.

The trio contains a soaring bit of melody that only Mozart could have written.

After this comes the inevitable *menuetto da capo,* a return to the first section of the minuet proper, without repeats this time and ending at the word *fine* at the close of this section, just before the trio.

FOURTH MOVEMENT: Rondo. Allegro. G major. $\frac{4}{4}$ *time.* This movement is concerned largely with two themes, "A" and "B." The first and principal idea of the rondo is a jolly theme introduced by a group of three ascending *staccato* chord tones. Note the graceful and typical turn in the second full measure—Mozart was fond of this embellishment. The second, "B," is more flowing and *legato,* but note the syncopations in the third measure of the illustration. What a gay and debonair dance, summery and colorful, the composer has set forth!

The principal idea returns again and again, its reappearances separated by lively episodical material—the rondo form as we have come to know it by this time. Note how smoothly and inevitably Mozart returns to the main theme, after wandering through related keys and transient moods. The writing is wonderfully clear and perfectly suited to the style and character of the strings. There is a vigorous *coda* at the close, terminating with a good-humored cadence passage built on the simple lines of the G major chord.

It was noted in the foregoing comments about Mozart's work that the five instruments (first and second violins, violas, 'cellos, and double-basses) were usually duplicated by having additional players on each part. Now let us listen to a very romantic movement from a well-known work for the string quartet alone—just the solo instruments (without the double-basses), the slow movement, *Andante Cantabile* from Tchaikovsky's Quartet, Op. 11.

Andante Cantabile, in B-flat (*from The String Quartet Op. 11, in D major*)

This is a most beautiful and exquisite movement, of great melodic charm and simplicity. The structural design is that of a ternary (A-B-A) main body of three periods of about sixteen measures each (instead of the more usual binary form of the average minuet), plus a trio section. The principal theme, played at the onset by the first violin, is a working out of a Russian folk song that the composer heard his carpenter singing one day. Note its shifting between $\frac{2}{4}$ and $\frac{3}{4}$ meters. The instruments are muted (*con sordini*), giving the impression of a veiled, mystical tone of tenderness and nostalgic remoteness.

This theme is answered by another sixteen-measure period, which is developed out of the main idea; then the first period is repeated, with four measures added to it to effect a desirable close.

The trio section proper appears after an introductory pair of measures, with the first violin again taking the melodic burden and the 'cello plucking (*pizzicato*) a reiterated bass part, technically known as a *basso ostinato.* (Is there here a suggestion of the Russo-Tartar-Gypsy instrument, the balalaika?)

After the trio, there is, as in the traditional minuet and trio form, a return to the main section, after which a *coda,* reminiscent both of the trio and the first theme, brings the movement to a conclusion.[5]

No doubt by this time the listener is eager to hear a complete string quartet, and is capable of giving it the intense interest it must receive. One could hardly choose a more fortunate example to begin with than Dvořák's STRING QUARTET IN F MAJOR, OP. 96, with its lilting melodies, lively and contagious rhythms, excellent instrumental writing, unexpected and fascinating harmonies, and divergent and highly stimulating emotional content—in turn happy, carefree, and gay, sadly sweet and not without sentiment, and often downright poignant.

String Quartet in F major. Op. 96. Antonin Dvořák

This deeply personal and highly romantic work is more often known by its soubriquet "American," so dubbed because it seems to reflect something of the spirit of the New World in which the composer found himself in 1892. (See also Chap. 20.) He had come to the United States to accept the directorship of the National Conservatory of Music in New York City. However, he yearned for closer contact with folk of his own nationality, and spent his summers in the Bohemian colony at Spillville, Iowa. No doubt it was here rather than in New York that the "American" spirit affected him.

At any rate, the composer did seem to catch enough of the spirit of some of our folk songs to justify a belief on the part of many writers and critics that there was some actual native influence; although one must add that these themes were certainly greatly transformed by the composer's individual manner of expression.

Speculating on the influence that this little American-Bohemian village had on Dvořák in general and on the creation of this work in particular, Professor Ottakar Sourek says in Cobbett's work, "Here, then, is the origin of the fundamental mood which inspired this charming, quickly written (in three days) but detailed work, touched in places with painful yearning, yet with a smiling, idyllic sentiment prevailing throughout.

[5] Those who enjoy working out puzzles in musical form will be interested in discovering Tchaikovsky's use of "a ternary form within a ternary form" in this movement. We have merely hinted at it in passing.

Courtesy Metropolitan Museum of Art

STRING QUARTET Levine

Note that the painting draws the eye from one player to another: similar to the shifting attention in listening to a String Quartet.

Here, too, is the reason why so many of the ideas in the quartet are simple in substance, and why the themes are frequently exposed in a kaleidoscopic fashion. The quartet is interesting harmonically on account of its swift and unexpected modulations through related and remote keys, in which there is a surprising charm of artifice that only serves to strengthen the fundamental—as if it were improvised—style of the whole work." [6]

FIRST MOVEMENT: Allegro ma non troppo. F major. $\frac{4}{4}$ *time. Sonata-Allegro form.* Most of this movement is in the spirit of the tempo marking—"lively but not too much so." The first theme, appearing in the viola after two measures of sixteenth note *trillo* introduction by the first and second violins, is a happy-go-lucky melody of a simple four-measure duration. Most of the development throughout the movement is concerned with either the syncopated figure of the first measure ("A") or the arpeggiated figure in the fourth measure ("B") of the ensuing illustration of the principal subject. Try to follow these two melodic figures

[6] Walter Willson Cobbett, *Cyclopedic Survey of Chamber Music,* 2 Vols. (London: Oxford University Press, 1929). Used with permission. See article on Dvořák.

in their development as they are altered or tossed about. Here is the principal theme, first movement:

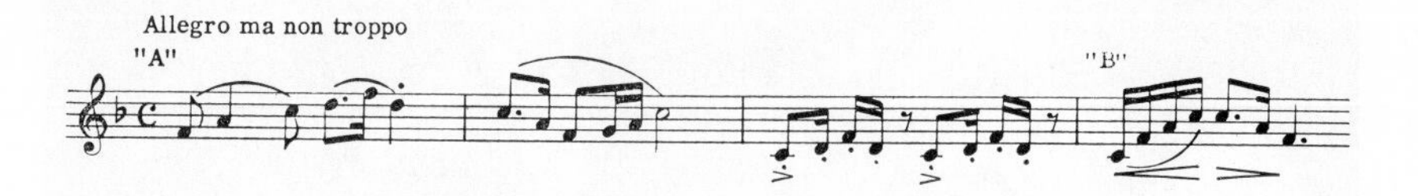

A subsidiary theme appears in the second violin part in the twenty-sixth measure. Being more *legato* in character, it is somewhat of a foil for the vigorous, dancelike first theme, and it also serves as a subtle anticipation of the second theme.

Presently the music subsides in volume and becomes an almost plaintive whisper, and when it vanishes to a *pianissimo* (*ppp*), the first violin plays the second theme proper (in A major), which is, no doubt, derived from the first subject.

Soon the development sets in, the viola again dealing with the happy, syncopated idea of the first theme.

The reprise can easily be identified, for the viola announces the first theme as it was when heard in the exposition. Note how Dvořák accomplishes a virtual repetition of material that has appeared in the exposition, yet with artfully different treatment. The second theme appears in due season and as it was in the beginning—though it is now in the home key of F major. A brief *coda* follows in which the 'cello sings a melody woven out of the second theme and played high up on its A string; but almost as soon as the arpeggiated figure "B" makes its re-entry, the movement comes to a boisterous and abrupt close.

SECOND MOVEMENT: Lento. D minor. $\frac{6}{8}$ *time. Modified binary form.* What a highly personalized and melancholy song this is, as though the singer's heart were breaking. "It is a genuine pearl among Dvořák's lyrical movements, captivating in its lovely, singing melodic line, its depth of sentiment, and the special charm of its pure harmony." [7]

[7] *Ibid.*

One has only to listen sympathetically to get the real import of the movement; little elucidation is necessary. The design, interesting in its almost naïve simplicity, consists of four balanced periods (a-b::c-a), each section repeated more or less exactly, excepting the curtailed and modified final period. Note how the insistent accompanimental figure continues in the viola or the second violin (mostly the former) throughout the movement up to the return of the main idea (high on the 'cello), where it is replaced by an alternating *arco* (bowed) and *pizzicato* (plucked) chordal accompaniment. The principal melodic idea of the movement follows:

THIRD MOVEMENT: Molto vivace. F major. $\frac{3}{4}$ *time.* This sprightly movement is evolved out of a single theme in three-four time and has a strong off-beat accent on the second count. It is announced at the onset by the second violin and 'cello in octaves.

From here on, Dvořák has shown what genius can do with simple ideas to produce a most ingenious design and telling effect. The structure consists of a series of miniature variations on the single theme; but these are arranged and contrasted in such a manner, and with the retention of a fundamental $\frac{3}{4}$ meter, that the traditional minuet-and-trio design is more than merely implied. In reality, also, the movement is basically in two sections appearing three times in alternation. Note the *rhythmic augmentation* of the theme in the second section—in the second violin, then the 'cello, and finally in the first violin. After the "variations," as one might expect, there is a return to the main section, quite like the *da capo* treatment in the traditional minuet-and-trio design. Here is what is meant by rhythmic augmentation: a drawing out, or elongation, of the time value of the notes.[8] The theme originally appears as "A"; the same theme augmented as at "B."

[8] Composers also use intervallic augmentation, where the original intervals of the melody are increased. The reverse is rhythmic and melodic diminution, where the original time values and tonal intervals are made smaller as a means of "development."

See if you can recognize this compositional technique whenever it is used in this movement. Also note the exotic flavor throughout, the brusque rhythms, the disposition of the purely accompanimental parts whenever there is a new "variation," and the characteristic and frequent use of the bare fifths here and there in the accompaniment.

FINALE: Vivace ma non troppo. F major. $\frac{2}{4}$ time. Rondo form. There is, at first, a lengthy yet interesting introduction of thirty-two measures, characterized by a gaily rhythmic and percussive drumlike accompaniment over which there is more than a sly preview of the dancelike main theme. This last makes its appearance eventually in the first violin.

This theme is developed, and presently, with no forewarning, the key of A-flat major is jumped into and a subsidiary theme of a lyrical nature appears in the first violin over the drumming accompaniment heard in the introduction.

In the midst of this peaceful, sustained second section, a chorale, organlike passage appears, which Sourek maintains "is undoubtedly a reminiscence of the church at Spillville," where Dvořák was wont to play the organ during services.

A lively episode ensues, followed by a reappearance of the main theme, which is interrupted, in turn, by a section that plunges into a series of colorful harmonies.[9]

[9] For those interested in such technicalities, these chords are "borrowed," one might say, from the keys of (F major), D-flat major, G-flat major, E-flat minor, D minor, C major, A minor, and eventually back to the home key of F major.

Thematically, the passage is concerned with bits of the main theme. Soon, however, the subsidiary theme appears; but the persistent and not-to-be-ignored main theme intervenes once more and carries the movement forward through the *coda* and on to the vigorous and boisterous close.

ADDITIONAL SUGGESTIONS FOR LISTENING

The literature of chamber music is voluminous, and since individual tastes are likely to differ widely, it is difficult to be selective. However, the listener might select from the following firm basis for subsequent building: Haydn's *"Emperor"* QUARTET IN C MAJOR, Op. 76, No. 3; Mozart's QUARTET IN D MINOR, K. 421, and the one in C MAJOR, K. 465 (the quartet with the startling dissonances); Beethoven's QUARTET IN F, Op. 18, No. 1, of the early period, Op. 59, No. 1 in F, of the middle period, and, for the bold, the quartets from his third period, Op. 127, Op. 130, Op. 131, and Op. 133, the one with the *Grand Fugue;* Brahms' QUARTET IN A MINOR, Op. 51, No. 2; Schubert's *"Death and the Maiden"* QUARTET; Debussy's STRING QUARTET IN G MINOR, Op. 10; Ravel's QUARTET FOR STRINGS IN F MAJOR; and Béla Bartók's SIX QUARTETS, especially Nos. 5 and 6. Advanced listeners might be intrigued more by Nos. 3 and 4, as far as form and compositional techniques are concerned. From there on into the other contemporary works, the listener may choose as he desires. It is interesting to learn that Benjamin Franklin is reputed to have composed a QUARTET FOR THREE VIOLINS AND VIOLONCELLO, the manuscript of which was discovered in the Bibliothèque Nationale (France) in 1941 by G. E. Van. Also listen to the string quartets by Quincy Porter, Darius Milhaud, Shostakovitch; and for "novelties" (both recorded), try the one in E MINOR by Verdi, and one in A MINOR by Fritz Kreisler!

Before leaving this chapter, we should like to direct the reader's attention to the quintet—the usual string quartet with an added instrument, either another string or a basically different type, such as the piano, horn, or a clarinet. We urge the reader to become acquainted with Schumann's QUINTET FOR PIANO AND STRINGS IN E-FLAT; Brahms' QUINTET IN B MINOR FOR CLARINET AND STRINGS, Op. 115; César Franck's QUINTET IN F MINOR FOR PIANO AND STRINGS; and Ernest Bloch's QUINTET FOR PIANO AND STRINGS, which we believe compares favorably with the best in the literature of all time.

Courtesy Theodore Presser Co.

FRÉDÉRIC FRANÇOIS CHOPIN

27 The piano solo and the violin and piano sonata

The rise of the solo instruments is intimately bound up with one of the most interesting developments in the art during the past two centuries—the emergence of the solo performer. From Mozart to Liszt to Josef Hofmann and Vladimir Horowitz, and from Paganini to Fritz Kreisler and Jascha Heifetz, there stretches a long line of great artists. There are times even in our own age when the virtuoso overshadows the composer and many persons attend a concert just to hear (or to see) the noted performer rather than listen to Bach or Beethoven. This is understandable, for these great performers have often exerted a profound influence on music itself: on the steadily rising level of technical skill in performance; on the mechanical improvement of the instruments themselves; on the type of music that composers write; and, most important of all, on the general taste and standards of the musical public.

In tracing the rise of the solo performer, it is important

to bear in mind that the Middle Ages and the Renaissance regarded the playing of music primarily as a group activity. One has but to look at the many paintings and sculptures of the period to realize that generally there were three, four, or more persons playing and singing together. (See the paintings of the MUSICAL ANGELS by Fra Angelico and one of the SINGING CHOIR sculptures by della Robbia.)[1] In the magnificently developed choral bodies of the sixteenth century and in the smaller chamber music groups of the succeeding period, the individual was first a part of the group; and a great deal of the instrumental playing was in connection with the singing groups—a quite faithful duplication of the vocal parts.

The rise of Italian opera at the beginning of the seventeenth century of necessity turned the attention of composers to the advantage, from the point of view of dramatic effectiveness, of concentrating attention on the individual singer. Meanwhile, interest shifted from an almost exclusively vocal art to a more comprehensive one which included the keyboard instruments, such as the virginal, harpsichord, clavichord (precursors of the modern piano), and the organ. Here the foundation was laid not only for the development of new instrumental styles but also for the gradual emergence of a new type of solo performer. Naturally, it took composers some time to adapt themselves to this new outlook and to evolve an effective solo performing style. As with all historical processes, this one advanced through trial and error, through daring experiments and cautious withdrawals, for upward of a century and a half before there finally came into being the general conception of the soloist as we know him today.

Until the end of the eighteenth century the great solo performers were primarily composers. When one went to hear the famous organists —Buxtehude, Reinken, or Bach—it was to hear them play their latest works. When Mozart or Beethoven gave a concert, interest centered on their newest sonata or concerto rather than on their performance of it. Only with the coming of the nineteenth century did there come into acceptance the artist-musician whose function was almost exclusively the performance and interpretation of the works of other men. The separation of the two roles was most fruitful for the art. On the one hand, the performer could devote himself completely to acquiring great technical skill and to solving the performance problems of the music; on the other, the audience, listening to an artist who was exclusively a performer, became ever more critical of the performance and demanded the highest standards. This new attitude toward performance was bound to have a stimulating effect on all branches of the art, including the mechanical perfection of the musical instruments themselves.

Significant advances in musical technique are likely to involve the complex relationship of composer, performer, listener, and instrument-maker

[1] See frontispiece.

—each of whom influences the others. The great composer is often ahead of the other three in his technical demands. His advanced compositions often require a more advanced style of playing, a finer type of instrument, and a somewhat different attitude on the part of the audience than those that obtained previously. Once the new types of instrument, performer, and listener have come into being, the composer who follows is ready to forge still farther ahead. Sometimes the composer, working in close harmony with a gifted performer or instrumentmaker, follows their lead (*vide* Paganini and Liszt as instances of the former, and Theobald Böhm and Adolphe Sax as instances of the latter). Such was the case at the end of the seventeenth century when the achievements of the great Italian violinmakers paved the way for the compositions of Vivaldi and Tartini. The process is usually a reciprocal one. When we listen, for instance, to a great artist, playing upon a sonorous, modern concert grand piano, accompanied by a symphony orchestra under the baton of a Maestro, broadcasting a Brahms concerto to millions of listeners, we witness an end result of long development, with diverse musical and scientific factors functioning in their most advanced historical context.

THE PIANO[2]

For a century and a half, the piano has been one of our most popular solo instruments. Unlike the string and wind instruments, the piano is completely self-sufficient, for it is able to play both the melody and its accompanimental harmony at the same time. For this reason, it became the favorite household instrument of the nineteenth century. The ancestry of the piano may be traced to the early keyboard instruments of the fifteenth and sixteenth centuries—the spinet, the dulcimer, and the virginal—that were popular in Elizabethan England. In the seventeenth century, the organ, the clavichord, and the harpsichord became the chief instruments of the keyboard group; a supremacy they maintained until the piano supplanted them at the end of the eighteenth century. In the clavichord, the tone was produced by a tangent, generally made of brass, that was driven against the string and held there. Its tone was metallic and never powerful. Because of the variety of tone possible to it, many composers found the clavichord a sympathetic instrument for intimate music. In the harpsichord, the string was plucked by a quill, giving a bright, vigorous tone, though somewhat tinkling in quality. The power and character of the tone could not be varied save by mechanical or structural devices. The harpsichord was the favorite instrument for supporting the bass of the small orchestra of the period and for concert use. Since its tone had no staying powers, composers developed a highly

[2] More exactly the *pianoforte,* commonly shortened to *piano.*

ornamented style of writing, full of trills and flourishes and silvery cascades of scale and *arpeggio* passages that seem to typify the grace and delicacy of the rococo style.

The piano was perfected in the first decade of the eighteenth century by Bartolomeo Cristofori, a harpsichord maker of Padua (though musicologists point out several previous instances of the instrument). This instrument was called a *Piano e Forte* (soft and loud), to indicate its dynamic versatility, and its strings were struck by a recoiling hammer with a felt-padded head. The wires were much heavier than in the earlier instruments. A series of mechanical improvements continuing well into the nineteenth century, including the introduction of pedals to sustain or dampen the tone, the perfection of a metal frame, and steel wire of the finest quality, finally produced the instrument we now know, capable of myriad tonal effects from the most diaphanous harmonies to an almost orchestral sonority, from a liquid, singing tone to a sharp, percussive brilliance.

FRÉDÉRIC FRANÇOIS CHOPIN (1810–1849)

The composer who has come to be regarded as the culmination of the piano style, the "Poet of the Piano," was Frédéric François Chopin, who lived for the greater part of his creative career in Paris and who created what still remains the chief ornament of the pianist's repertoire. He was born in Warsaw, Poland, February 22, 1810, and died in Paris, October 17, 1849. The family name was Szopen, but this had been dropped for the more common Gallic and phonetically translated Chopin.[3] His early education was received at the Warsaw Gymnasium together with private musical training from Zywny and Elsner; so rapidly did he become proficient in playing the piano that he appeared in public at the age of eight. His first essay in composition was published when he was a lad of fifteen. In 1830, after several concerts in Warsaw, he left for Paris—with concert engagements in the large musical centers on his way—and arrived at the French capital a year later. He did not have to wait long to become a social and artistic favorite, and his reputation spread throughout the Continent. Robert Schumann, in his critical articles, hailed him with the now famous "Hats off, gentlemen, a genius!" and Mendelssohn, Berlioz, Liszt, and many other leading musicians, saw in him the divine spark of genius. His appearances as a soloist were frequent, and his days were filled with teaching, so much so that he wrote only a few compositions. His strange friendship with George Sand (Mme. Dudevant) extended from 1837 to 1847, during which period his health failed rapidly because of tuberculosis. In spite of a delicate constitution, he

[3] See James G. Huneker, *Chopin, the Man and His Music* (New York: Charles Scribner's Sons, 1914).

visited England for a concert tour. He returned to Paris a year later only to succumb to his malady a few months after his arrival. His funeral at the Madeleine was a long and impressive one, during which the celebrated REQUIEM of Mozart was performed.

Unlike the other great composers we have studied up to this point, who usually composed for several media of performance, Chopin's genius was almost exclusively devoted to the piano.[4] For him the keyboard comprised the whole magic realm of music—and most experts are agreed that within that realm he was master. Even the shortcomings of the piano—its inability to sustain the tone as do the voice and the wind and string instruments—were transformed by Chopin, with an intuition bordering on the miraculous, into advantages, by surrounding his poetic and flowing melodies with floating columns of wonderfully figurated harmonies and with the most delicate of traceries and arabesques intertwined. He discovered what the piano could do best, and he applied his inexhaustible inventiveness to achieve that best. Although he wrote four sonatas and two concertos, his imagination gravitated naturally to the shorter forms, many of which he himself created, and all of which he brought to new levels of development and beauty—the waltzes, nocturnes, preludes, mazurkas, etudes, scherzos, polonaises, impromptus, and ballades that have come to constitute the quintessence of pianism.

In Chopin, the ultraromantic fused with the ultranationalist; he was greatly affected by the sufferings of his native Poland, and in his proud polonaises and mazurkas, he voiced his dream of ultimate liberation. His works reveal him as one of the most daring of the experimental harmonists of his time, one of the most original masters of tonal color and chromaticism, and a supreme master of the intricacies of the classical as well as romantic internal designs of form and structure (as we shall show presently in the BALLADE). Schumann called Chopin "the boldest and proudest poetic spirit of our time," and we of today have yet to appreciate him to the full. His hold upon the public of our time is enormous and world-wide. Artists like Paderewski, de Pachmann, Lhevinne, Godowsky, Brailowsky, and Hofmann have built special reputations as Chopin interpreters. At their greatest, Chopin's works have a refinement, an aristocratic distinction, that reminds us of the composer he worshiped—Mozart. He successfully achieved what he called in his early twenties a "perhaps daring but noble resolve—to create a new era in art." As long as the piano endures, its golden age will be synonymous with the noontide of Romanticism—and Chopin.

In spite of Chopin's preoccupation with the piano, he left a comparatively small output for that instrument—some two hundred compositions

[4] Chopin's divergences included a Trio for piano, violin and 'cello, Op. 8; a SONATA IN G MINOR, Op. 65, for piano, 'cello (or violin); an INTRODUCTION AND POLONAISE IN C MAJOR for piano and 'cello, Op. 3; and *Seventeen Polish Songs*, Op. 74.

in all. Yet so constant was he in expressing the noble and the beautiful, that Sir George Grove would have him ranked among the greatest—"because of his breadth of content and the variety of mood, as well as the manner of expression." [5] His superlative musicianship and unerring command of the many and intricate techniques of the craft of composition, especially those pertaining to melodic, harmonic, and structural elements, as well as idiomatic pianistic effects, are unexcelled in the annals of music history. He had a high standard of excellence. There are very few moments of digression in his works that fall to a low quality.

It would be difficult to select a more appropriate work for the moment than Chopin's beautiful BALLADE (No. 3) IN A-FLAT MAJOR, Op. 47. This composition illustrates in an eloquent manner the character of piano music in general, and, in particular, Chopin's individual style.[6] At the same time, it offers the listener a masterpiece of romantic expression.

Ballade, No. 3, in A-flat major, Op. 47

The word "ballad" (*ballade* or *ballata*) once meant a song to accompany a dance or a dancing-song; more usual, however, was the meaning of a folk-like song that told a story of a descriptive nature. Later, when the word was used in connection with the lied, the term designated a narrative song of dramatic character. It was natural that the poet in Chopin should adopt words of poetical connotation for music inspired by a lyrical mood.[7] We have Chopin's own words to the effect that he had a program in mind when writing the four Ballades, for he confessed to Robert Schumann that he had been moved to their creation by the Lithuanian poems of Mickiewicz, the Polish poet; [8] but the composer wisely left the matter indefinite. However, Huneker goes so far as to identify the third Ballade as the "Undine" of this set of poems.

Another writer (Louis Ehlert) said that this work gave forth the voice of the people, and ventured his belief that the basic program was a love story. One can cite authority after authority, only to end with the conviction that any story the listener wishes to concoct—or no story at all—will be defensible.

The moods of the work are variously described as: aristocratic, gay, graceful, piquant, playful yet ironical in spots, filled with deep passionate emotions, coquettish grace, irresistible charm, sweet contentment (Ehlert), "the composer shows himself in a fundamentally caressing

[5] Sir George Grove, *Dictionary of Music and Musicians.*

[6] It is not to be inferred that we assume it to be the greatest of the four ballades. We have chosen it, rather, because it best serves our immediate purpose.

[7] The word *ballad* also has the meaning of a simple song, narrative in content and strophic in form, using the same melody for the several verses and, sometimes, having a chorus, or refrain. (The Christmas carol was originally a ballad.)

[8] See also *Chopin, the Man and His Music,* by James Huneker (New York: Charles Scribner's Sons, 1900.)

mood" (Niecks),[9] "there is moonlight in this music and some sunlight too" (Huneker).[10] The listener will be interested in comparing his reactions with these.

As to the compositional techniques of the work, wonderful things are concealed underneath the surface—as in all good art. The basic structure of the third Ballade may be said to be a freely and marvelously adapted sonata-allegro form, although not precisely according to the strict rules of Classicism in the appearances of the main themes, their keys, and their more obvious spirit. But who would have it thus prescribed? The eminent American composer, scholar, and teacher, Dr. Edgar Stillman-Kelley, was one of the first to observe that the larger and greater works of Chopin adapted the spirit and basic structure of the sonata-allegro form—"sonatified," as he used to say to those of us who were his students.[11] The critic Huneker observed a great deal of contrapuntal skill displayed in the development section of this work. Chopin was sufficiently a master of the classical form to bend it to the best advantage of the expression of his musical and poetic ideas. He adapted the traditional structure of the romantic spirit to his material, rather than the material to the mold, as was often the tendency of the classical spirit. The student of harmony as well as the student of form will find in this work much for exploration—and wonder. The ingenuity and skill shown in the working-out section alone are worthy of the best of thematic "manipulators," and the consummate subtlety shown in many modulatory, or transitional, passages—actual or often feinted—is astounding! Of course Chopin does not accomplish these in the same way as the more classically minded, for he was a Romanticist. It is enough that he uses all forms, harmonic structures, sequences, and key relationships to the best advantage of his poetical moods. He demonstrated how flexible the sonata-allegro form could be, and not a few contemporary composers owe a great debt to him for freeing the form. "Nowhere marred by a formal flaw, quite free of sentimentality (except as sentimentality is applied to it by wrong-headed performance), and airly solid, the A-FLAT MAJOR BALLADE is one of Chopin's masterpieces."[12] Let us examine some of these evidences.

The section that would traditionally be the exposition is announced at the onset by the first theme, which is in two sections—"A" as though a woman's soprano voice were singing, and "B" as though a man's bass voice were answering in this imaginary tête-à-tête.

[9] Friedrich Niecks, *Frederic Chopin as a Man and a Musician.* (1888.)
[10] James Huneker, *op. cit.*
[11] See *Chopin the Composer,* by Edgar Stillman-Kelley. (New York: G. Schirmer, 1913.) This is an erudite and valuable work, not only on the compositional techniques of Chopin, but also on the craft of composition in general.
[12] Quoted from *Chopin* by Herbert Weinstock (New York: Knopf, 1949) by permission of the publisher.

After the conclusion of this rather square-cut, eight-measure first theme (though poetic and peaceful in spite of its formality!), there follow seventeen measures of development based upon germinal ideas derived from various portions of the theme itself. Then appears a motive that seems to "bow itself gracefully into our pleasure"!

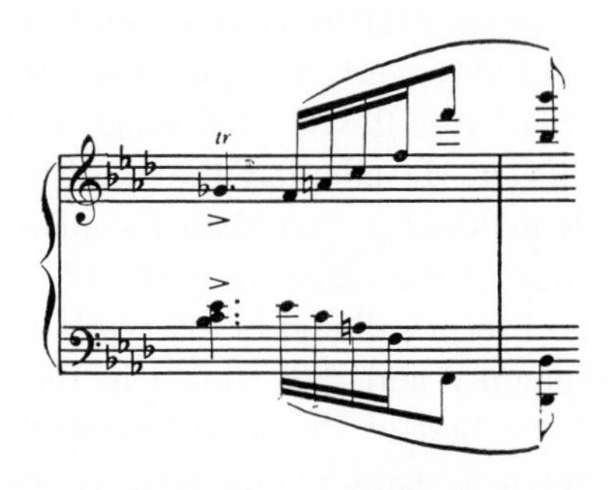

After eleven measures of this interpolation, the main theme is re-stated much as at first, but ends, finally, with a long sustained *tonic chord.*

The second subject soon follows, though not in the strict classic tradition concerning key and character. It is a coquettish theme, achieved largely by use of the "hoppinglike," eighth-note rhythmic figure. Note the quaintly nodding octave skip that introduces this theme and that later becomes an integral part of the second subject.

Note also the constant shifting of key feeling throughout this section, so that the harmonies seem to float unhampered by mundane realities.

From here on Chopin displays some facile developmental writing as he toys with the first and then with the second subject in dazzling manner, in which rhythms, melodies, and harmonies join in a dancing whirl of scintillating colors and ever-changing forms. It is difficult to know just where the second theme proper ends and where its development begins; but any chance of chaos is averted by a sudden appearance of the second subject, note for note for ten measures as it was first heard. A welcome feeling of having one's feet on the ground; but this feeling is only temporary, for a clever development of the "bowing" figure previously illustrated interposes; it is suggestive of the reversal of the former figure, as though seen through a mirror.

Again the development resumes—note the sinister and highly contrasting effect of the change of key (into C-sharp minor) with a low, fast-running figure appearing in the bass part.

It is in the next section, which corresponds to the traditional reprise, or recapitulation, that Chopin shows his artistic intuition as well as his rational process, for he brings back the main theme, first in an anticipatory glimpse, then in full bloom with a greatly altered accompaniment. This is worked up to an impressive climax, only to be interrupted at the close by the reappearance of the fourth musical figure shown above. The second theme is absent in this section, for it has been heard often enough in the working-out. An affirmative cadence closes this poetic love story.

We suggest you now try the more formidable, involved, and less obvious BALLADE IN F MINOR (the fourth). James Huneker compares this work favorably with Bach's CHROMATIC FANTASIA, the first movement of Beethoven's piano SONATA IN C-SHARP MINOR, and the opening of Schumann's C MAJOR FANTASIA!

THE VIOLIN; THE VIOLIN AND PIANO SONATA; THE TRIO

For many music lovers, the vibrant, soulful tones of the violin are second only to those of the human voice for sheer sensual beauty and capability of stirring one's emotions to their depths. Because its tone can be controlled in its dynamics while being sustained, the violin can achieve melodic effects impossible for the piano; though, of course, it cannot produce the chordal structures and volume of tone of the latter instrument. For these, as well as for other reasons, the violin is not often heard solo—though there are exceptions as far as actual compositions are concerned. Most notable are the SIX SONATAS FOR SOLO VIOLIN by Bach; but these are difficult, virtuoso pieces, esoteric in appeal, not likely to be heard in popular concerts or radio programs.[13] However, one can often hear both the piano and the violin, for in this duo the singing tone of the one is happily combined and contrasted with the sonority and harmonic possibilities of the other. It is an ideal combination, and composers of European and American countries have written some of their best works for it; among them, few, indeed, have excelled the French composer, César Franck.

CÉSAR (AUGUSTE) FRANCK (1822–1890)

In his biography of this master, Vincent d'Indy (Franck's outstanding pupil) gives several unforgettable pictures of him: one, as he rushes about with his coattails flying, giving private lessons—for his fame was not such as to assure him a professorship at the Conservatoire until after the age of fifty; another, probably the most faithful, is of the master seated at the console of the organ at Sainte Clothilde, improvising as no one had done so well since the time of Bach (a comparison made by the Abbé Liszt). His religious spirituality and modesty of character were so marked that he was looked upon as a father by his pupils, who invariably called him "Pater Seraphicus." (It is interesting to note some of those pupils—d'Indy, Chausson, Duparc, Fauré, Pierné, Ropartz, Lekeu, and Vidal.) It was during his music lessons at the organ that Franck imparted his compositional ideas, and thereby virtually created the first modern French school, especially noteworthy for its contributions to the large symphonic forms and chamber music. (The opera, the ballet, and salon music had been the chief concern of French composers before this time.) Still another aspect of wonder concerning this master, again brought out by d'Indy, is that the bulk of his compositions came *after* he was fifty, and that most of his greatest works (especially orchestral and instrumental) were produced *after* he was sixty: the SYMPHONY at sixty-seven, the STRING QUARTET at sixty-seven, and the SONATA FOR VIOLIN AND PIANO at sixty-four! One thinks of Michelangelo, Titian, Tolstoy, and Verdi.

During his early years, however, Franck wrote most of his short works, operas, and choral and church compositions. Especially noteworthy is his immortal oratorio, LES BÉATITUDES, written when he was fifty-seven.

Franck was born a Belgian, but he came to France at an early age as a student at the Conservatoire and lived so long in Paris that his genius

[13] See Chapter 28 for description and illustration of a *chaconne* (or *ciacona*) taken from *Sonata for Violin Alone, No. 4.* There are new orchestral versions of the Chaconne, and many recent recordings of Bach's entire six original *Partitas* (or Sonatas) *for Unaccompanied Violin.*

enabled him to become a spokesman for his adopted country.[14] His style in composition is marked by a fortuitous combination of the Gallic preoccupation with ratiocination and the Belgian heritage of deep human feeling. His music is vigorous, with a driving force and dramatic power that is sensed by the untrained and learned alike. Always the mystic whenever mysticism could inject itself into such an abstract art as music, he was, nonetheless, keenly alive and sensuous in his own way. He was a master of his craft, especially in two seemingly divergent aspects, harmony and counterpoint, and he had an unusual command of, and respect for, traditional forms and design. He used the arts of Bach and the Classicists for his deep romantic feelings, and put his musical ideas into the strictest of contrapuntal species when he chose (as we shall see in the Finale of the Sonata); but, on the other hand, he did not hesitate to burst the bonds of chromaticism when that procedure best served his purpose.[15] These altered chords add a colorful novelty to the music, even in our day of ultrasophistication in matters concerning harmony, in their individual structures and unexpectedness and resolutions.

Sonata in A major for violin and piano

We have chosen this work for a number of good reasons, of which only a few need be stated. First, the work is a masterpiece of its type and style, and one that should be eagerly added to every listener's repertory.[16] The sonata is replete with beautiful melodies that ingratiate themselves at first hearing. Then, too, the work is emotionally gripping, at turns lyrical, dramatic, moody, and compelling; and, at times, it rises to the heights of nobility and spirituality. The composer is successful in balancing and contrasting the two instruments, with the utmost respect for the peculiarities of each instrument. The violin and the piano seem to vie with each other in bringing to the fore salient musical ideas.

Another reason for this choice is that the work presents a large number of opportunities for discovery of subtly concealed beauties, and the lover of good music—fairly well prepared through experience by this

[14] We are aware of the belief held by many of the "moderns" of France. "Franck is not even considered a Frenchman by us," one of the famous group *Les Six* told the author.

[15] Here is a simple example of a chromatically altered chord: if one were to change any one or several of the tones of the simple tonic (first) triad in C major, C-E-G, so as to appear as C sharp-E-G, C-E-G flat, C flat-E-G, C-E-G sharp, C sharp-E flat-G flat, and so forth, while the tonality was still maintained as that of C major, the changed chord might be said to have undergone chromatic alteration. Watch for these chords as they make their appearance in the sonata; they will be salient enough, even for the novice—or should be!

[16] An eminent authority on appreciation, Walter A. Spalding of Harvard University, ventures the belief in his excellent book, *Music: an Art and a Language* (Boston: Arthur P. Schmidt Company, 1920), that this sonata ranks, with those of Brahms, among the finest of its kind. He further opines that it might be declared by some as without an equal!

time—will be handsomely rewarded for his close application. Some of these challenges are likely to be elusive, but we believe that with a little guidance they can be successfully sought out and assimilated at this stage of the listener's development.

Chopin's BALLADE involved some nicety of discernment pertaining to compositional features, not apparent on the surface, that necessitated an advanced accumulation of listening skills to perceive and comprehend properly. So it is with this sonata, to a still greater degree.

We have previously mentioned a compositional device known by the term "cyclical," whereby the composer brings about a closer unity among the several movements of a large work, such as a symphony or a suite, by recalling themes, or other musical ideas, that had appeared in previous movements.[17] Now we wish to present another connotation of the word: the evolvement of melodic, or thematic, lines brought about through the development, or extension, of one or more basic, germinal motives—where "the melody seems to grow right out of itself," or where different themes seem to bear the resemblances one might expect in a close, blood relationship. Perhaps this meaning can be made clearer by reference to an observation made by d'Indy in one of his great books on the techniques of composition to the effect that the whole structure of this sonata is based upon these three generative motives:

It might be of interest to discover the use of these generative motives in the constitution of the principal themes that are used in the different movements, as well as to observe them in the process of "working out" as each movement itself progresses. Such detailed discernment is not at all to be considered a *sine qua non* in the appreciative process. It is in the aesthetic *effect* of such technical devices, rather than in their *identities,* and the recognition of the same, that the composer achieves his purposes in music as such.

FIRST MOVEMENT: Allegretto ben moderato.[18] *A major,* $\frac{9}{8}$ *time. Sonatina form.* After a wistful four measures of introduction, a mood of elation and freedom is conveyed in this flowing and lilting first theme of triple measure, which is a direct outgrowth of the generative motive "A":

[17] See especially Beethoven's FIFTH SYMPHONY, Chap. 21; Dvořák's NEW WORLD SYMPHONY, Chap. 20; and Rimsky-Korsakoff's SCHEHERAZADE SUITE, Chap. 16.

[18] *Allegretto ben moderato:* in a well modulated, or moderate, rate of speed that is slower than *allegro.*

The lyrical and limpid second theme, in the traditional key of the dominant (in this case, the key of E major), makes its appearance in the piano part as an extended section of some sixteen measures. Note that when the violin does enter, it refuses to take up the second theme just presented by the piano—as is the usual practice at this juncture.[19] Instead, the violin persists in the reiteration of the first theme and will have none of the second, leaving that theme exclusively to the piano. Here is the second theme, delightful in melodic flow and lilt, in its harmonic content and its rhythmic design: [20]

There is no working-out, or development, section (thus the form of the movement is styled a *sonatina*), and the reprise brings back the first theme in the violin, quite like the exposition; but the piano now has a massive, chordal accompanimental figure. The second theme, as in its first appearance in the exposition, is played only by the piano. The two

[19] In the slow movement of the PIANO CONCERTO IN G MAJOR, Op. 58, by Beethoven, there is a somewhat similar condition between the orchestra and the solo instrument. There is this difference, however, that there is no "reconciliation" and "adoption" in the Franck sonata.

[20] Note that the first two measures of the theme ("X") are repeated in the next two measures ("Y"), but that the "Y" is sounded up three scale steps (comparing the melodies of both sections, note with note, we have a B in the "X" answered by a D in the "Y" section, A by a C natural, a G sharp by a B, etc.); this device is called a *transposition* or *sequence*. Wagner was especially fond of using it.

instruments join, with the violin clinging to the first theme, soaring and broadening, while the piano brings forth a suggestion of the wistful figure it had in the four introductory measures. Note the dramatic suddenness of the *pianissimo* (*pp*) in the two last notes—a compact, unified, and delightfully free flowing movement.

SECOND MOVEMENT: Allegro; D minor. $\frac{4}{4}$ *time. Sonata-Allegro form.* The first theme is heard after the three measures of piano introduction. It is an animated and exciting theme, cleverly concealed in the warp and woof of an arpeggiated figure in the piano part. (A development of the generative motive "A".)

The violin picks up this theme, vigorously, along with the piano, and a minor climax appears, which suddenly ends in a very soft (*pp*) passage with a new idea that might be dubbed a secondary theme; but it, too, is soon dispelled by the reappearance of the noisy and bustling first theme. Note, presently, a bridge passage in the violin, which is based on the first theme of the first movement. This is the transition passage to the second theme, now in the classically proper tonality of F major, and it is heard in the violin—a lyrical theme with a harplike accompaniment in the piano.

Both the first and the second themes are developed, mostly the former. Note the reference to the main theme of the first movement just before the reprise sets in, and also note the somewhat slow (*quasi lento*), contemplative episode that interrupts and delays—quite teasingly—the reappearance of the principal subject in the reprise. The reprise section will be unmistakable, for the first and second themes (the last now in the key of D major) enter quite regularly. Note again the reappearance of the main theme of the first movement—proclaiming itself as the *idée fixe* of the entire work. But see how irresistibly forceful and insistent Franck now makes it! A rather extended *coda* ensues, based largely on a rising four-note scale figure (with the violin playing *tremolo*—a quivering of the bow), reflecting once more the spirit of the principal theme of the movement.

THIRD MOVEMENT: Recitativo-fantasia. Ben moderato. The word *recitativo* was met when the opera was discussed in Chapter 8. It is applied to a kind of musical declamation in which the inflections, accent, and emphasis are closely related to dramatic speech, free of the formal rhythm or regular phrase structure usually observed in song. The *fantasia* usually denotes a fanciful piece, irregular in form, and of an improvisatory character in spirit and style, yet Franck seems to have combined orderliness of construction with the spirit of freedom, with no sense of restraint. Cobbett ventures an explanation of this seeming contradiction in terms and practice: he states that Franck had a greatly developed and almost inordinate respect for the classical traditions concerning form, and thus would be disinclined to give this movement a classical title in view of the formal deviations (evidences of the romantic spirit) within the movement.[21]

Along with many other virtues, this movement is distinguished for its long violin solo, intermittently accompanied, which is in the spirit of a recitative improvisation. Again, the violin delays its appearance until after an introduction of four measures on the piano. The tonality eludes fixity in the first theme, for it wanders from D minor to F-sharp minor. The mood is pensive, gloomy, and sad in the accompaniment, which is based upon generative motive "A," while the violin is capriciously wistful, soaring about in running, arpeggiated figures.

A second theme, based on the generative motive "B," now is heard in the violin (in F-sharp minor), and with it a harplike accompaniment in the piano. Note how suddenly and dramatically Franck introduces this theme *pianissimo* in the midst of a very loud, *fortississimo* (*fff*) passage. (Franck is not unlike Beethoven in the dramatic use of nuances.)

[21] Walter Willson Cobbett, *Cyclopedic Survey of Chamber Music.* (London: Oxford University Press, 1929.)

Also observe the first occurrence of the generative motive "B" at the end of this lyrical phrase in the violin:

This lovely *cantabile* (singinglike) melody is extended until there appears a quickening and broadening of the mood with a theme in the violin derived from a portion of the second theme of the second movement. Watch for its future use in two of the episodes of the Finale—a wonderful glimpse into the secret workings of Franck's compositional style, well worth the listener's effort. We show, first, the source from the second movement: [22]

Here is the theme as it appears now in the third movement—not only pleasing in itself but also another excellent example of the compositional device known as melodic–rhythmic augmentation.[23]

[22] We are aware that many of these details, here and throughout the text, are likely to be more *immediately* meaningful if one can read the printed score as the music progresses; and the author confesses to conspiratorial intent. However, with careful and repeated listenings, one who is not so trained may attain a comparable understanding. For those who can read musical notation, we refer to page 18, fourth line, third measure of the piano score for the source indicated (G. Schirmer edition).

[23] See Chapter 19 for detailed explanation of these terms.

The movement is brought to a close with a *coda* employing a transformation of the *idée fixe*, and the theme last mentioned above. These are worked up to a forceful climax, *fortississimo* (*fff*). The final cadence (in F-sharp minor) is of exalted beauty, with its aura of mysticism and spirituality, as the soft, organlike chords intone on the piano high above the earnestly pleading song of the violin. The whole passage contrasts with what has gone on only a moment before, as the violin again plays the melancholy and entreating figure it had sounded in the early measures of the movement. Although no words are found in the score, many listeners contend that the close of this movement, though wordless, is nonetheless articulate with heartfelt eloquence, a veritable *Miserere mei, Deus!*:

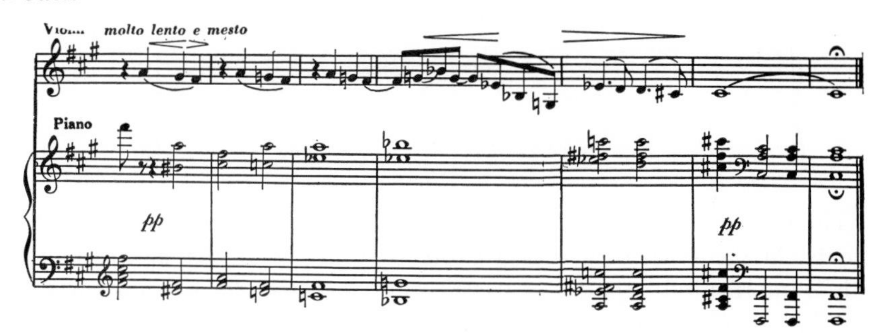

FINALE: Allegretto poco mosso: A major. $\frac{4}{4}$ *alla breve. Rondo form.*[24] A number of fascinating musical features may be observed throughout this movement. First, it is as joyful and gay as the previous movement was melancholy and introspective. It flows along with themes that are filled with gentle—never boisterous—cheerfulness. The gross form of the movement is that of the traditional rondo, composed of three main sections [25] setting forth and recalling the principal theme (four appearances if one counts the repetition just before the *coda*), with intervening free and contrasting episodes and, finally, a *coda*.

[24] *Allegretto poco mosso:* lively and gaily but slower than *Allegro.* $\frac{4}{4}$ *Alla breve:* a broad, fast duple measure, to be played as though it were $\frac{2}{2}$ time—"double quick" or "cut" time as it is often called in modern terminology.

[25] The sections bringing back the main theme are also known as "refrains."

But perhaps this movement is best known for what is generally regarded as the most spontaneous and flowing *canon* in all the literature.[26] The principal theme, used as a canon, is proclaimed at the beginning of the work, without the usual introduction, by the piano, and the violin follows a measure behind.

The first episode is another interesting example of counterpoint, with the generative motive "C" in the piano, while the violin plays an embroidery overhead. (It will be recalled that the first appearance of the "C" motive was in the third movement, the Fantasia.)

Then follows a sort of banter, or sparring, between the two instruments, in the form of a canon evolved from the principal theme; but this is interrupted by a clever passage in which the "C" germinal motive, just heard in the piano, is played by the violin and the "embroidery" counterpoint is played by the piano—this is known as invertible, or double, counterpoint. Note the figure in the bass, a variant of generative motive "B" of the first movement:

[26] The *canon* is a form of contrapuntal technique in which a lead-off part (called the *antecedent*) is imitated and repeated, note for note, by another part (called the *consequent* or *answer*), or above or below antecedent, such entries continuing until all the parts have joined in; then all of them proceed together, still imitating each other. The popular songs *Three Blind Mice* and *Row, Row, Row Your Boat* are good examples of canons, which, for obvious reasons, are more particularly called "rounds." The word *canon* comes from the Italian, *canone,* meaning law or rule—for the imitating voice must repeat the lead-off voice note for note. The oldest recorded six voiced round-canon with the two lowest voices as an *ostinato* or *pes* is the lovely *Sumer Is Icumen In,* which is usually supposed to have been composed in England about 1240 by a monk, John of Fornsete. See *Sumer Is Icumen In:* a revision by Manfred F. Bukofzer (University of California Press, 1944, Vol. 2, No. 2). He places the date of origin about 1300 to 1325. Even this date is now in dispute.

The refrain, or reappearance of the main theme, is in the form of a canon, but with the harmonic figuration in the piano greatly changed —another indication of the compositional skill of Franck.

(Canon between Bass part and Violin).

The ensuing brilliant climax is a canon of the first four notes of the principal theme, which sounds forth as though it were simulating loud, clanging bells. The dynamic level is suddenly lowered to *piano* (*p*), and a theme emerges that had previously appeared in the second movement, constructed out of the germinal motive "A."

A second episode is presently heard. It, too, is based upon the principal subject, but now in the key of B-flat minor, with the violin playing the main theme, and the generating motive "B" is a "mirrored" canon (inverted and reversed) in the bass part of the piano.

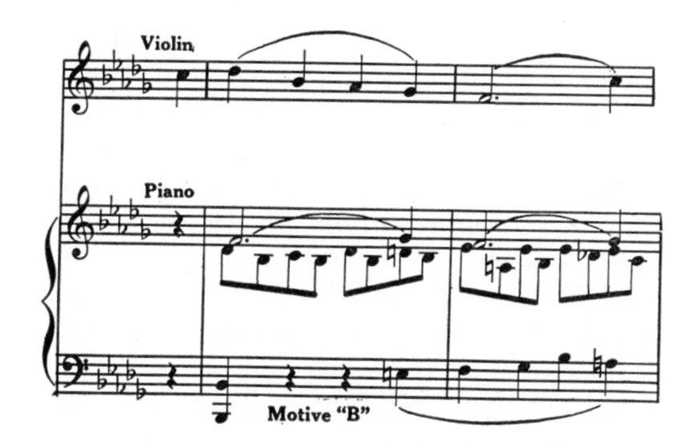

After a resounding interlude on the piano, based upon a portion of the main theme, there is a dramatic entry of the majestic melody from the Fantasia which is almost immediately repeated in a still more *grandioso* manner. Franck is now building up the climactic section, not only for this movement, but for the entire sonata. He goes about it in a skillful manner, piling up intensified and agitated emotion, sweeping one irresistibly along with the music, and firmly tying together the work as a whole. This is a work of great significance in craftsmanship, musicality, and spirituality. The third refrain is heard, again in canon, and the emotions are further aroused as the principal theme is repeated (the fourth refrain, it might be called) with no let-up in the onward sweep. Then one is plunged directly into the *coda* proper, which is based upon the main theme, in canon, but sounding once more as though the music were coming from giant cathedral bells, proclaiming their joyful message of triumph to the world. The violin trills vibrantly above the clanging and dissonant chords in the accompaniment, which latter eventually turn into what composers call "horn tones," or "horn fifths," [27] so commonly used in trumpet fanfares.

It is not difficult to conjure up a triumphant mood picture as these tones rise higher and higher to the end punctuated, finally, by a decisive open octave tone on the key note, A.

One is *richer* for having listened to such a beautifully moving and inspiring work as this, and *better* for adding it to the treasury of memory.

ADDITIONAL SUGGESTIONS FOR LISTENING

Piano: The literature for piano solo is exceeded in volume only by that of song, and it is therefore impossible to select a list of suggested supplementary listening that will be comprehensive and universal in approval. After a few suggestions as to what to listen to immediately after the Chopin Ballade just presented, we leave the listener to his own initiative. Try to hear representative works of Chopin in the various forms styled waltzes, nocturnes, preludes, mazurkas, etudes, scherzos, polonaises, impromptus, barcarolles, fantasies, sonatas, and, of course, the remaining three Ballades. No doubt you will also enjoy Schumann's CARNAVAL; Liszt's HUNGARIAN RHAPSODIES, especially number two; Mendelssohn's SONGS WITHOUT WORDS; Schubert's IMPROMPTU or MOMENTS MUSICAUX; Beethoven's PIANO SONATAS, especially Op. 13 ("PATHETIQUE"), Op. 53 ("WALDSTEIN"), Op. 57 (the "APPASSIONATA") or Op. 27 ("MOONLIGHT"); Mozart's PIANO SONATAS IN A MINOR and A MAJOR; Rachmaninoff's PRELUDES IN G MINOR and C-SHARP MINOR; MacDowell's WOODLAND SKETCHES, SEA PIECES, NEW ENGLAND IDYLS, ETUDES and the TRAGICA SONATA (we hope these works by MacDowell will soon be recorded); Grieg's LYRIC PIECES, HOLBERGS ZEIT, and SONATA IN E MINOR; Debussy's ARABESQUES, SUITE BERGAMASQUE, ESTAMPES, IMAGES, PETITE SUITE and so forth; Ravel's JEUX D'EAU, PAVANE POUR UNE ENFANT DEFUNTE, GASPARD DE LA NUIT, or SONATINE; César Franck's PRELUDE, CHORALE, and FUGUE; PRELUDES by Scriabin; and the more contemporary composers according to taste and availability in recordings—yes, try Schönberg's THREE KLAVIERSTÜCKE, Op. 11, and also the CONCORD SONATA, for piano, by Charles Ives. However, there will be more fun in compiling your own list.

Violin: The listener might begin to enlarge his repertory with such violin and piano sonatas as the following; a choice of Bach's SIX SONATAS FOR VIOLIN

27 

ALONE; Beethoven's Op. 24, in F major, C minor, Op. 30, No. 2 in A minor, Op. 47 (the "Kreutzer"), or the one in G major, Op. 96; Brahms' in A major, Op. 100, or the one in D minor, Op. 108; Corelli's in D major; Dvořák's SONATINA, Op. 100; Grieg's SONATA IN C MINOR, Op. 45; Handel's in A major; Mozart's in C major (K. 296), in G major (K. 301), in E-flat major (K. 302), in C major (K. 303), A-flat major (K. 304), in E minor (K. 305), in G major (K. 379), or the one in A major (K. 526); Schubert's in A major, Op. 162.

The Trio: It is to the *trio* that we wish at the moment to direct the listener's attention, especially to trios for piano and strings. Inasmuch as good recordings of such works are none too plentiful, we can only suggest a few titles for a start, hoping that manufacturing conditions will continue to improve along with the increase of listeners' interest. Try the trios by Mendelssohn, especially the one in D minor, Op. 49; Mozart's in E major (K. 542), in C major (K. 548), and in G major (K. 564), and the one for piano, clarinet, and viola (K. 498) if recorded; Beethoven's Trio in B-flat, Op. 97 and the one in D major, Op. 70; Schubert's Op. 100 in E-flat major; Tchaikovsky's in A minor; Dvořák's in A major, Op. 81; Brahms' in C minor, Op. 101, the Horn Trio, Op. 40, and the one for clarinet, 'cello, and piano, Op. 114—but we are already transgressing upon the pleasures and prerogatives of the listener.

Courtesy University Prints, Newton, Mass.

ECSTASY OF ST. THERESA — Bernini

28 Bach and the polyphonic style: the reformation and the baroque

Throughout the Middle Ages, music found its highest function in the service of the Church. In the colorful ritual of the Roman Catholic Church, almost all the arts played an important part. The lofty vaults of the cathedral, the paintings in the chapels, the sculpture and carving and tapestry around the altar, the appeal of the incense, the pageantry of the processions—all these provided the setting for impressive ceremonials. But a central place in this confluence of the arts was reserved for music. From about the thirteenth century on, a long line of brilliant composers created the contrapuntal Masses and Motets that have remained one of the chief glories of sacred art, culminating in the second half of the sixteenth century in the works of Palestrina (1525?–1594), Orlando Lassus (1530?–1594), and Tomas Luis Victoria (1549–1611).[1]

[1] In matters concerning biographical data, dates, etc., throughout this text, we have freely consulted a number of authoritative references, such as *Grove's Dictionary*, the *Oxford History*, Nef's

In writing the early type of music for the voices of the choir, composers matched one "point," as notes were previously called, of the soprano against the corresponding point of the alto, tenor, or bass; in other words, *punctus contra punctum,* or *point counter point.* (This phrase is the title of a novel by Aldous Huxley, in which he matches the decisive points in the lives of a group of characters in an essentially polyphonic manner.) *Counterpoint,* therefore, may be said to be the art, or science, of combining several melodies, or parts, simultaneously. As a science, it was carried to great lengths by the medieval masters who were able to combine, with dazzling facility, twenty, thirty, forty, and even more than fifty parts, all flowing on at the same time. *Polyphonic* music is based upon counterpoint and is said to be *contrapuntal. Homophonic* music, on the other hand, with a background of chords, is based upon harmony—the art, or science, of the construction and sequence of chords—in which the voices move along in blocks of combined parts. The composers of the nineteenth century, accordingly, thought along harmonic lines as naturally as those of the sixteenth thought in contrapuntal, or horizontal, lines.

Comparing further, the point-counterpoint type of music was conceived as a series of lines flowing along horizontally, and the harmonic type consisted of vertical blocks of sound chords in which one combination of several tones, produced simultaneously, proceeded to another such combination. The old music, therefore, was polyphonic, contrapuntal, horizontal, primarily vocal, and choral, and was largely religious. The later Protestant music was more likely to be homophonic, harmonic, conceived with a horizontal melody against, or along with, a vertical foundation of chordal tones, secular, with the emphasis on the solo voice (as in opera), and ere long became instrumental. The new conception of melody demanded one clear-cut tune impinging upon the hearer at one time, to which everything else was subordinate. The old conception had presented a melodic confluence of many voices in which the texture as a whole was melodious, even when no one tune dominated.

For purposes of simplifying and highlighting the contrast, we speak of the two styles as though they were diametrically opposed to each other. One needs only to reflect upon the point, however, to realize that often one style imperceptibly shades into, or mixes with, the other. For, in a Mass or Motet by Palestrina, with every voice flowing along its own line, if you stopped the music at any one point, a chordlike block of tone would best represent the cross-sectioning. Similarly, even though chords are vertical blocks of tone, as they move along from one point to another, the individual tones are likely to trace horizontal paths, not unlike the voices of

---

(Pfatteicher) *Outline of History of Music;* but we have leaned most of all upon Baker's *Biographical Dictionary of Musicians* (New York: G. Schirmer, 4th Ed., 1940).

counterpoint; and, of course, there are countless instances where the two styles of composition are deliberately compounded, as in Handel's MESSIAH. (See Chap. 9.)[2] No doubt the reader has heard two tunes sung together such as *Swanee River* with either *Solomon Levi* or Dvořák's *Humoresque*, or some other combination. In this way one tune became a foil for the other, yet both blended well together and formed counterpoint.

The following examples attempt to contrast the basic differences in the two styles of music discussed in the foregoing. Note in the *Doxology* that though the voices other than the melody move along in blocks, or chords, the bass part is melodic and interesting in a horizontal direction; and also note that at any juncture of three or four voices in the *Sanctus*, a chord, or harmony, results.

[2] It will be recalled that the *Finale* of the César Franck SONATA FOR VIOLIN AND PIANO employed the contrapuntal device of the *canon* very frequently. We shall see presently, in Bach's works, another application of this basic device, polyphonic imitation, in the form known as the *fugue*.

The concept of *countermelody* that plays such an important part in the orchestral music of the nineteenth century (and our own time) is essentially contrapuntal. So, too, when the composers of symphonies toss a theme from one choir to another, from one combination of instruments to another, or from one solo instrument to another, interweaving it the while the other thematic, or figurated, material, they are thinking in terms of "voices" and interweaving, contrapuntal lines. Beethoven, Wagner, Tchaikovsky, and their compeers developed a high degree of skill in this modern kind of orchestral polyphony.

In the early stages of the development of instrumental music, the composers treated the instruments as though they were voices. In fact, the old music was likely to have a notation "For Voices or Instruments." Thus, a great deal of the early music for the organ, the keyboard instruments, and the small chamber-music groups during the seventeenth century was polyphonic in style, taking its character from the vocal music. Gradually, as the more pure and individual instrumental style developed, and keyboard instruments were perfected, the music also began to take part in the transition to a homophonic type of thought. This transition was accelerated by the fact that instrumental music lent itself excellently to the homophonic style. The organ was ideal for the great blocks of chords that were the foundation of the new style. The violin, accompanied by harpsichord, could be treated like a solo voice with a background of harmony. The harpsichord itself was much better at tracing a melody with one hand and an accompaniment with the other than at tracing several horizontal lines simultaneously. The shifting of the spotlight from vocal to instrumental music meant, in effect, that music had passed from the polyphonic era to the homophonic. By the time of Mozart and Haydn, the shift had been pretty well accomplished.

Bach, coming at the beginning of the eighteenth century, was the composer who best summed up in himself both modes of thought. He was the last and greatest of the polyphonic masters, the culmination of centuries of music history and one of the first great artists in the new instrumental-homophonic style. (But note Schönberg, Chap. 30.)

BACH AND THE REFORMATION

If the style and texture of Bach's music were determined by the historical transition of polyphony into homophony, its content, its emotional wealth and coloring, and its prevailing mood stemmed directly out of the far-reaching religious and social upheaval that Martin Luther set in motion at the beginning of the sixteenth century. We pointed out in the chapter on the oratorio that Bach expressed the spirit of the Reformation in music in the same sense that Milton expressed it in poetry and Rembrandt in painting—in the passionate humanism, the intensity of inner vision, and the almost mystical devotion that transformed art into a purifying experience.

Bach felt deeply about the most significant problems of his life and times—and projected that feeling through his work. Since music was the upwelling of the profoundest convictions and intuitions of the composer, there could be no room for bombast, for mere showiness, for exhibitionism, for cheap sentimentality, as objective ends in themselves. It it a mistake to think of Bach as a pedantic or unemotional composer. He is, on the contrary, among the most passionate, the most rhapsodical of artists; but his passion and his rhapsodizing happen to be religious rather than theatrical. They are nonetheless intense. As skepticism spread through the world and the spirit of scientific research brought in a new intellectual current, the artist turned to other sources for the emotional impact of his inspiration. But Bach's age was still aglow with the memory of men who had died on battlefields to uphold their religious convictions; and this spirit found expression in the art of the time. Thus, Bach's magnificent works for the organ, his monumental Masses (especially the B-MINOR MASS), his five PASSIONS, CHURCH CANTATAS, and other works are generally considered the peak of Protestant Church music, the loftiest and most enduring monument of all that the Reformation contributed to the aesthetic-spiritual development of modern European culture.

If the music of Bach differed from that of the great Roman Catholic masters, it was a difference not so much between individuals as between two world views. The gentle loveliness of Italian music had culminated in the golden art of Palestrina. Here was mysticism, too, the smooth mellifluous harmonies that transported the hearer to the realm of saints and miracles, a naïveté and tenderness that fitted in with the atmosphere of sacred processions and pilgrimages, of the adoration of relics, of all the exuberance that the Latin temperament brought to religion. The mysticism and the coloring were Italian; the love of sweet melodic effect was Italian; above all, the sensitivity to the powers of the human voice was Italian. The Reformation, with its quest for spiritual values, its slow, dogged search for what it conceived to be the truth, stemmed from the more sturdy temperament of the North. Its music was above all a music of inwardness and intensity, of great concentration of purpose; a music of titanic conflict and sublimity. The tenderness here is of the shaken and storm-tossed man rather than that of the child. A shaggy strength infuses the great dissident harmonies of Bach's fantasies, as different from the progressions of Palestrina as the fog of the North Sea is different from the blue of the Mediterranean, or as the Rome of the Sistine Chapel was different from Luther's Wartburg. Bach knew and loved the Italian influence; but he was as German as Beethoven, or Wagner, or Brahms. With every breath he drew, with every note he wrote, he affirmed the deepest convictions, the innermost thoughts and feelings, of the folk that had bequeathed to him his most important heritage.

BACH AND THE BAROQUE

The art of the *Baroque,* with its roots firmly planted in the classical traditions of the Renaissance, and with its topmost branches reaching into the Romanticism of the future, is difficult to define with an over-all, pigeon-hole characterization. However, the term *baroque* has come to designate the general tendencies of European art during part of the sixteenth, the seventeenth, and the first half of the eighteenth century.[3] The Greek sculpture, LAOCOÖN (lay-OCK-oh-on), though probably carved c. 25 B.C., embraces the Realistic (even Romantic) as well as the Classical tempers—and, surprisingly, definite Baroque tendencies.[4] It was a breaking away from the restraint of the Renaissance, and the movement underwent a number of different influences and stylistic manifestations as the rising-, high-, and ebb-tide of the spirit of the Baroque materialized in several countries, especially Italy, Spain, France, and Germany. Thus, it is difficult to encompass all the aspects in a paragraph or two, and we shall have to confine ourselves to the more general and salient characteristics, hoping that an enticing glimpse will generate a desire for further study.

The essential spirit of the Baroque arose out of a world given over to extremes of self-indulgence: religious asceticism, and extravagant ritualistic ceremonials; deep scientific and philosophical thought, and silly superstitions; noble benevolence, and wholesale crime; dire misery, and ostentatious display of wealth. Side by side with leaders of superstitions (astrology, demonology, witchcraft) were such men as Harvey, Kepler, Leibnitz, Locke, Newton, and Spinoza.

Naturally, the art expression of the times showed these influences and became more spectacular and dramatic, even seeking to burst the bounds of the medium in which it was conceived and to take on attributes that a different medium might more fully satisfy. Sculpture often

[3] For more detailed analyses of the Baroque than we can possibly give space to here read: Sacheverell Sitwell, *Southern Baroque Art* and *German Baroque Art* (New York: Doran, 1928); David M. Robb and J. J. Garrison, *Art in the Western World* (New York: Harper & Brothers, 1942), Chaps. VIII, X, XI, XXI, XXVIII, and XXIX; Helen Gardner, *Art Through the Ages* (New York: Harcourt, Brace, 1936); Paul H. Lang, *Music in Western Civilization* (New York: Norton, 1941), Chaps. IX-XIII; Egon Friedell, *Cultural History of the Modern Age,* 3 vols., trans. Charles F. Atkinson (New York: Alfred A. Knopf, 1931), Vol. II; and Elie Faure, *History of Art,* 5 vols., trans. Walter Pach (New York: Harper & Brothers, 1924), Vols. III and IV; Manfred F. Bukofzer, *Music in the Baroque Era* (New York: W. W. Norton, 1947).

[4] See Gilbert Highet, *The Classical Tradition* (New York: Oxford University Press, 1949), pp. 372-374, a scholarly presentation, with copious notes, showing Greek and Roman influences upon Western literature and other arts.

strove for effects that better suited painting, for example, and painting sometimes sought to achieve effects that were inherently the province of the stage. Architecture sought to achieve the plastic forms and spatial illusions that are usually associated with painting and sculpture.

At its best, baroque art was a vigorous art, having exuberant imagination, elaborate detail, and great emotional fervor. It was intense and dramatic, and, more than the art of any period before, it strove to incorporate the beholder, identifying him as a vital participative part of the creative process—*empathy*. The effects of light and shade, of color and form, of curves contrasted with straight lines and angles, and horizontal lines cutting off or modifying the vertical—all these, along with the subject matter of sensual splendor, display of wealth, free expression of "high living," and the ecstasy of sacred as well as profane emotions, shaped the baroque style. Though one should add that these same attributes do not belong exclusively to the Baroque and are to be found in the art of other periods, it should be remembered that it is in their combination and emphases that the period achieves its individuality.

At its worst, the Baroque was likely to be bombastic and inflated, filled with cheap and maudlin sentimentality, vulgar, often quite degenerate, overlavish and overornate, madly confused and reckless in divergencies and contrasts in the basic content as well as in its manner of execution. However, one should consider both the virtues and the vices of the style when contemplating the Baroque, for the presence of both extremes is a significant characteristic in itself.

At the beginning of this chapter is a reproduction of a sculptural work, SAINT THERESA IN ECSTASY, by one who has been called "the father of the Baroque," Gian Lorenzo Bernini (1598–1680). This work reposes in the Sta. Maria della Vittoria Church in Rome and depicts a dream which St. Theresa herself has described.[5] In this sculpture of her dream, the Angel appears before the Saint, with a dart in his hand—a symbol of divine love—and Bernini has caught the moment when the Angel is about to pierce the heart of the sleeping dreamer. The sculptor has taken a dramatic moment and intensified the emotion through his means of execution. Note the flamboyant decorations and background of clouds and gilded streamers of light from a heavenly source, the decorative and compositional functions of the folds of the draperies, and the impression that the group belongs to the space surrounding it—heightened by the extended foot and head of the Saint. Note also the play of light and shade, almost as though the medium were painting, and how Bernini has succeeded in communicating a poetic religious expression through their means.

In painting, the baroque spirit may be seen in the works of such artists as Peter Paul Rubens (Flemish, 1577–1640), with his show of action,

[5] Readers who are interested in the biographies of the two saints of like name, though centuries apart, might enjoy *The Eagle and the Dove* by Sackville-West.

Courtesy Metropolitan Museum of Art

TOLEDO El Greco

movement, excitement, and great areas of healthy pink flesh, and in the realism of Michelangelo Caravaggio (Italian, 1569–1609).

A sense of showmanship is often indicated with an almost theatrical play of highlights and bold use of colors and shadows; and now and then there is likely to be outright sensationalism of topic as well as means of expression—encouraged by the Church itself, it might be said, as an effective and legitimate instrument of proselyting. With El Greco (born Domenico Theotocopuli, a Greek, 1541?–1614), the bridge between the High Renaissance and the Baroque was accomplished. Along with some of the characteristics already noted, El Greco was much fascinated by nature, man, and God, and he sought an emphasis of his imaginative and creative ideas through willful distortion of forms and the use of certain colors. These become powerfully effective when the sympathetic imagination of the appreciator functions creatively in contemplation. A reproduction of El Greco's VIEW OF TOLEDO is shown here. This was painted late in his life and represents the height of his powers. Note the play between the line formed by the crests of the buildings, the contour of the hills, and the winding roads; also note the counterpoint between the forms in the clouds themselves and the patches of ground—and the ominous mood that grips one as does a tense moment at the theater: these are intensified in the original painting through El Greco's use of color. See other works of his in art museums, or, if this is not possible, in color reproductions.

In music, one can feel the spirit of the Baroque, sometimes to a greater extent than in the sister arts, due to the preponderance of religious feelings of the time and the adequacy of music to express them. Religion sought for vastness of proportions in its expressive forms, along with a tendency toward a display of splendor. The music was replete with tonal color, frequent and intricate ornamentation, and, often, glorious bursts of harmonic as well as contrapuntal means. It was often of the theater, both literally and figuratively speaking, and the homophonic and polyphonic styles vied with each other to produce original effects and overpowering climaxes. Witness the motets of G. Gabrieli (Italy, 1557–1612), with their colorful chromatic harmonies (and the same, even to a greater degree, in the Masses and Madrigals of Gesualdo—1560–1613, Naples). Witness the pompous, brilliant, and elephantine scores of Arazio Benevoli (Italy, 1605–1672), with as many as fifty-three separate parts in a score—bringing to mind the romantic Berlioz who came two hundred years later; and witness the works of Heinrich Schütz (Saxony, 1585–1672), with their continuation of the Italian grand style of choral music, religiously serious and powerfully moving. Then, too, there was the music of George Frideric Handel (Germany, 1685–1759), with its simplicity of melodic line, fresh harmonic backgrounds, lively and rhythmic counterpoint, and, over-all, a vigorous and dramatic spirit that is enthralling as it is so often "a loud and glorious sound." But it is with the incomparable Johann Sebastian Bach that we are most concerned here.

JOHANN SEBASTIAN BACH (1685–1750)

The life of Bach offers less material for romantic legend than does that of almost any other composer. His personal experience was identified in the most immediate way with his art. We have but the scantiest biographical data of an intimate and personal nature. He taught, he played, he wrote the record of his emotional and spiritual growth into his works, and when he had about finished his task, he died.

Courtesy Theodore Presser Co.

JOHANN SEBASTIAN BACH

Bach was born in 1685, in Eisenach, Thuringia, of a family that had produced, from the time of his great-grandfather, upwards of fifty composers and performers; some of them were among the most illustrious musicians of their time, so much so, that "Bach" and "musician" were almost synonymous. He grew up in Eisenach, in the shadow of the stately Wartburg where Luther's translation of the Bible saw the light of day, and where, in the legendary age of the Minnesinger, the gracious Elizabeth had listened to the songs of the noble minstrels and awaited the return of Tannhäuser. Johann Sebastian's father, who was court musician at Eisenach, died when the boy was ten. Brought up by an elder brother who was the organist in a neighboring town, Ohrdurf, the future composer displayed his gifts early in life. He possessed a beautiful soprano voice, sang in the church and school choirs, and received his first regular instruction on the clavichord from his brother.

At fifteen, Johann Sebastian became a chorister at Lüneburg. Here he was able to listen to Georg Böhm, the organist at St. John's Church, whose playing made a profound impression upon the young musician. This was the golden age of the organ in Germany. For, as long as music revolved around the Church, the organ occupied a central place in the scheme of things. Out of the simple chorale melodies that the congregation sang, the organists of North Germany had evolved a wonderful art of improvising and elaborating upon a theme, the art of the *chorale prelude* and the *chorale fantasy*. It was during his stay at Lüneburg that Bach undertook the famous pilgrimages on foot—he was too poor to go otherwise—to Hamburg, thirty miles distant, to hear Reinken, an outstanding organist of the time. At the age of eighteen, Bach became the organist at Arnstadt; and in 1705, when he was twenty, he went to Lübeck to hear and meet the great Danish composer and organist, Buxtehude, from whom he learned so much.

The first important period of Bach's career as a composer coincides with the nine years from 1708 to 1717 that he spent at Weimar as court organist and chamber musician to Duke Wilhelm Ernst. The Duke was passionately fond of the organ and of religious music. This, accordingly, was the period of Bach's great organ works and the early church cantatas.[6] The organ works marked a new epoch in the literature for the instrument. For complexity, grandeur of effect, and richness of texture they surpassed anything that had been accomplished in the field. In the organ works, the rhapsodical quality of Bach's emotion and his amazing mastery of polyphony combined with all the splendor of the Baroque style to produce works that, in their kind, have never been even remotely approached. To hear a fine organist perform the FANTASIA AND FUGUE IN G MINOR, or the great PASSACAGLIA IN C MINOR is one of the deepest of musical experiences.

The close of his stay at Weimar—later the city of Goethe and Schiller, and still later of Liszt—was marred by friction with the Duke. Bach seems

[6] A *cantata* is a work for chorus, soloists, and accompaniment, on a sacred or secular subject, in which the lyric drama or story is adapted to music but is not intended to be acted. Bach wrote some 200 of these for the complete Lutheran church-year—about five entire yearly cycles.

to have resented the fact that his master had neglected to offer him the post of *Kapellmeister* when it fell vacant. A man of independent spirit, he asked for permission to leave the ducal service. The Duke, displeased with the manner in which Bach had asked for his release, placed him under arrest and kept him in confinement for a month. On regaining his liberty, the composer joined his next patron, Prince Leopold of Anhalt-Cöthen.

The Prince of Cöthen was as fond of chamber music as the Duke of Weimar had been of the organ. The Cöthen period in Bach's life (1717–1723) is, therefore, the outstanding period of his chamber music composition. He experimented with the secular instrumental style, adapting himself to the combinations of instruments that he happened to have at hand. It was still too early in the development of instrumental style for Bach to apply his inventive faculty to the solution of problems of instrumentation and tone color; he simply used the instruments at hand in his parish to accentuate the contrapuntal lines of his musical texture. His works were, however, a contribution of first importance to the evolvement of a distinctive instrumental style. The Cöthen period saw the production of the BRANDENBURG CONCERTOS, the SUITES FOR ORCHESTRA, the VIOLIN CONCERTOS, and the INSTRUMENTAL SUITES. During this period, too, Bach turned to the clavier—we use the term, as he did, to include both the harpsichord and the clavichord—and enriched its literature with such works as the CHROMATIC FANTASY AND FUGUE, the ENGLISH and FRENCH SUITES, and the LITTLE PRELUDES and INVENTIONS that have remained indispensable training material for the young pianist.

At Cöthen, also, he produced, primarily for the education of his older children, the first part of what is to this day one of the most significant works in music, the WELL-TEMPERED CLAVIER (*Das Wohltemperierte Klavier*). The importance of this work is bound up with one of the most pressing problems in the period of transition from the church modes of medieval choral music, through the experiments in the so-called *mean-tone temperament* (or scale tuning), to the major-minor system of scale tuning of our present-day music.[7] The organization of intervals within the major scale depended on the fact that there was only one pattern of whole and half steps, which had to sound the same (and in tune) no matter at what point on the keyboard one might choose to begin. This, in turn, meant that the octave had to be divided into twelve half-steps,

[7] Consult appropriate articles on "Acoustics," "Modes," "Mean-tone," "Equal-temperament," "Temperament," etc., in Grove's *Dictionary of Music and Musicians,* and articles by the present author in Thompson's *International Cyclopedia of Music and Musicians.*

N.B. Albert Schweitzer's authoritative work *J. S. Bach,* translated by Ernest Newman, uses the term WELL-TEMPERED CLAVICHORD, throughout save for one exception. Spitta, in his definitive three-volume work on Bach, uses both "clavier" and "clavichord."

each of which was equal in intervallic (ratio) size to all the others. In order to accommodate the harpsichord and clavichord to the needs of the new musical theory, the sharps and flats could no longer be tuned according to the strict natural laws of musical intervals derived from the ratios of the intervals of the overtone series; rather, they had to be shifted or "tempered" so that enharmonics were exactly alike. (Thus D-sharp should be the same as E-flat, F-sharp the same as G-flat, B-sharp the same as C, A-flat the same as G-sharp, and so forth, on our piano.) The WELL-TEMPERED CLAVIER was the result of this accommodation to the new system of equal tuning in which it was possible to have a major and minor key starting from each of the twelve tones of the octave, with the preservation and interchange of enharmonics. To illustrate the possibilities of this new relationship between the keys, Bach wrote a prelude and a fugue in each major and minor key, producing the twenty-four preludes and fugues of Book I of the WELL-TEMPERED CLAVIER, to which he later added the twenty-four of Book II. These *Forty-Eight Preludes and Fugues* have become the foundation work for piano and organ the world over.

The death of his beloved wife, Maria Barbara, in 1720 and the desire to provide better educational facilities for his children than Cöthen offered, led Bach to look for a new post. In 1722 he became cantor of the celebrated St. Thomas' school of Leipzig, where the musicians who furnished the music for the city's churches were trained. The post, one of the most important in Germany, was first offered to two other composers, neither of whom was available, and was then given to Bach, one of the members of the Council remarking that as the best musicians were not free to take it, it was necessary to accept one "of second rank." Bach pledged himself to lead a modest life, to teach the scholars with devotion, to show the Council all due respect and obedience, to provide music neither too diffuse nor too operatic, and not to leave the town without the burgomaster's permission. He remained in Leipzig for twenty-eight years until his death in 1750. It was here that the third and greatest period of his creative career unfolded.

As at Weimar and Cöthen, Bach's versatile genius adapted itself to the requirements of his employers and to the resources at his disposal. It was his duty, besides teaching the scholars of the Thomasschule their singing and their Latin, to compose music for the church service. It was here that all the influences that had molded his art—the splendor of the Baroque, the mastery of vocal polyphony that was his heritage from the past, and the spirit of Lutheranism as objectified in music through the chorale—converged to produce his great religious music. The Leipzig period saw the production of the later church cantatas, of which almost two hundred have come down to us, including ST. JOHN and ST. MATTHEW PASSIONS, the CHRISTMAS, EASTER and ASCENSION ORATORIOS, the MOTETS,

Courtesy New York Public Library

ORIGINAL MANUSCRIPT OF AN "ORGAN PRELUDE" J. S. Bach

the four LUTHERAN MASSES and the great MASS IN B MINOR. There were also the secular cantatas to celebrate important occasions at the University of Leipzig and celebrations at the court of his royal patron, the Elector of Saxony. Despite his preoccupation with choral music throughout the Leipzig period, he did not entirely cease writing instrumental works. The ITALIAN CONCERTO, the second book of the WELL-TEMPERED CLAVIER, the concertos for one, two, three, and four claviers, as well as numerous partitas for harpsichord and clavichord, and chorales, sonatas, preludes, and fugues for organ, and DIE KUNST DER FUGE, all belong to the final years of his life.

Bach's contemporaries did not have any idea of his true stature as a composer; his life and activity were too circumscribed for his fame to spread as did that of his contemporary, Handel. In a list that Mattheson, the foremost critic of the day, drew up arranging composers in order of their rank, Bach made seventh place, Handel fourth. The works of the more favored men have been all but forgotten. If Bach impressed his contemporaries at all, it was as an organ virtuoso. In the final decade of his life, he achieved even more than local fame in this respect. There is the famous visit he made in 1747 to the court of Frederick the Great. The King, an ardent flute player, was practicing when the arrival of the composer was announced. "Gentlemen, old Bach has arrived!" he exclaimed in some excitement. Bach extemporized on the new pianofortes that were then coming into fashion, astonishing the King with his powers. Frederick played him a subject on which to improvise; Bach forthwith created a fugue in six parts upon it. On his return home, he developed Frederick's theme into a "Musical Offering" that he dedicated to "a sovereign admired in music as in all other sciences of war and peace."

Bach's was a life of continual labor; his complete works represent a colossal creative output. A simple, steady man, there were in his life none of the emotional upsets so frequently associated with genius. He found his happiness within the family circle and in the companionship of his second wife, Anna Magdalena—famous because of the notebooks of simple pieces he wrote for her instruction that are now excellent practice material for begining pianists.

Of his twenty children, several followed in his footsteps. Karl Philipp Emanuel was perhaps the most important composer in the period between the death of Bach and the rise of Haydn and Mozart, both of whom he profoundly influenced. Bach's other sons, Wilhelm Friedemann, Johann Christoph, and Johann Christian, were among the most illustrious composers of their time. In teaching them, as well as a distinguished group of pupils, in discharging his duties as Cantor of the Thomasschule, and in rearing the monumental edifice of his compositions, his life ran its course. As with Milton and Handel, his labors affected his eyesight and he was blind toward the end of his life. He died in 1750, at the age of sixty-five, the last and greatest of the old masters, and, in the opinion of many, of the new as well.

His art was too much rooted in the past to please his contemporaries. The following age turned so completely to the fascinating ramifications of the new sonata form and homophonic styles of music that the greatest composer of the age was all but forgotten. For the better part of a century his masterpieces lay neglected, until the young Mendelssohn, stirred to highest enthusiasm by an appreciation of their worth, led the way to a true appraisal of the master by his revival of the ST. MATTHEW PASSION. The Classical period had been too dazzled by the "new music" to be able to take the true measure of Bach. It remained for the Romantics, strangely enough, to rehabilitate his works. To an age that is increasingly rejecting the emotional extravagances of the Romantics and the formal elegance of the Classicists, it is to be expected that the music of Bach would offer something enduring and substantial, rich and deeply significant to those of our own time. Relegated to what might have been oblivion until a century ago, the music of Bach has finally taken its place as one of the most potent forces in all modern music.

The chorale preludes

For generations, the organists in the Lutheran Church announced to the congregation the chorale that was to be sung. Seated at the organ, their fingers "preluding" seemingly at random over the keys, their musical imagination took wing as they wreathed the simple hymn tune that was to ensue in a new harmonic and contrapuntal setting—purely instrumental in character, but retaining the original melody of the chorale. Thus arose the art of the *chorale prelude.* The chorale preludes of Bach constitute the credo of the inner man, an outpouring of his creative personality. And what Bach had then to say was so deeply felt that even now the chorale preludes remain by common consent among the most noble rhapsodies of music. We can present only a few out of the many that Bach wrote.

"Christ Lag in Todesbanden"
(Christ Lay in the Bonds of Death) [8]

This is an organ prelude on a melody that Bach wrote and used in his EASTER CANTATA of the same title, having derived the melody from a popular Lutheran hymn. Grief breathes from the melody, a sense of desolation that in the end gives way to a simple, deep faith that the Lord has, indeed, risen from the dead. There is inner conviction in the music,

[8] The author advises the use of both the original (organ) version of the chorale preludes and the more modern orchestral transcription, so that a proper comparison of values may be made. Also be sure to listen to the original vocal recording of the chorale which inspired the chorale prelude—or better, sing it.

with its beautiful melody and its somber, rich harmonies. (Note how much more freely and melodically the individual voice-parts move about in the chorale than they do in an average present-day hymn tune.)

Externally, Bach presents a picture of a simple, earthy man. Yet deep at the core of his nature was the mysticism that, as the years went by, turned his thoughts increasingly to the subject of death and the hereafter. Some of his most moving melodies are built around the thought of his reunion with God, a motif that takes on increasing prominence in his later works. *Komm Süsser Tod* (Come Sweet Death) is truly a song of faith in which the otherworldliness of Bach finds its purest and most serene expression.

In the effective orchestral transcription by Leopold Stokowski, the melody is played by the 'cellos after an introduction by the double basses. Muted violins wreathe a delicate countermelody high above. The tune is repeated in the wood-winds, finally in the strings, while slowly ascending *arpeggios* on the harp create a properly celestial atmosphere. Those listeners who are attracted to this form will want to listen to two suggested supplementary preludes, *Sleepers Awake! A Voice Is Calling,* in the beautiful orchestral setting by the Italian Impressionist, Ottorino Respighi; and *Jesu, Joy of Man's Desiring,* in the Stokowski orchestral version; note the significant and flowing countermelody given to the oboe.

Transcriptions of organ works

Since the orchestra has become the principal instrument of our time, just as the organ was in the time of Bach, many great organ works are heard today in modern orchestral transcriptions. Also, throughout the long period of the ascendancy of the piano, a number of Bach's organ masterpieces, most of them dating from the first great period of his creativeness during his stay at Weimar, were arranged for piano by Liszt, Busoni, and other master pianists. The listener should be aware of what is Bach and what is the work of the transcriber, by hearing both versions. In the original manuscript, Bach wrote few, if any, performance directions; perhaps because he wrote the music largely for himself or for those whom he knew. The instructions we do find in Bach's published works have been added by subsequent editors.

The fugue

The following is a humorous description of a five-voiced fugue from Robert Browning's "Master of Fugues of Sax-Gotha":

> First you deliver your phrase,
> Nothing profound that I see
> Fit for itself for much blame or much praise
> Answered no less where no answer need be;
> Off start the two on their ways.
> Straight must a third interpose
> Volunteer needlessly help,
> In strides a fourth, a fifth thrusts in his nose,
> So the cry's open, the kennel's a-yelp,
> Arguments hot to the close.

Little Fugue in C Minor [9]

This famous composition remains as one of the most popular of Bach's fugues. Written for the organ, it has achieved new popularity in the orchestral transcriptions.

[9] The word *fugue* is derived from the Latin *fuga,* meaning "flight," and the application is warranted because a fugue is actually concerned with the musical exploration (or flight) of a single theme. This theme is treated in imitation, or canonical, style, and is alternately called the "subject" or the "answer" as it enters, part by part (usually in a tonic-dominant, or *doh* and *sol,* key relationship), until all the parts have joined in. Of course, those voices, or instruments, not actually producing the subject or the answer, continue on their way the while, with counterpoint that is appropriate for the moment.

Now after all the voices are in, thus completing that portion of the fugue known as the *exposition,* or *enunciation,* a free and contrasting episodical section appears. This may involve new material or it may develop musical figures taken from the exposition. Such a section is called an *episode.*

Presently the main theme (the subject) reappears in an order different from that which obtained in the exposition. This kind of a section is called a *middle entry,* and the composer may indulge in as many alternations of episodes and middle entries as he thinks his material indicates—or time and length permit.

Then, at the close, the composer might indulge in a fugal device—most common in textbooks about music—known as a *stretto,* which consists of a piling up of the theme at a closer interval of time than that which separated the subject and answer in the exposition. Thus, if the answer came three measures after the start of the subject in the exposition, the composer might reduce, or overlap, this succession to a measure or even less. This device is often used to build up a climax or to intensify the emotional effect in general. Then the composer might sound forth the theme in a glorious final presentation, which is often heightened by having a drone, or *pedal-point,* on the tonic, or the dominant, or both. A punctuating cadence brings the work to a close, and often, if the work is in a minor key, this closing cadence will dramatically put forth the major instead.

Those who enjoy the compositional aspect of the fugue should follow closely the course of the theme. It is a very good practice, and a lot of fun in itself, to sing the theme every time it appears in the composition while the work is being performed. If there is a group listening, all might join in the singing, later discriminating more faithfully with the allocation of "parts."

In the orchestral version of this fugue, the theme is announced by the oboe and is handed about to all the choirs in a series of climaxes that drives forward to the final pronouncement of the subject by the full orchestra. In the course of this development, the theme is shifted from minor to major, then returned to minor, as the orchestra summons up its most brilliant sonorities for the ultimate crescendo and final cadence in the major; note also the pedal point on the dominant (fifth tone of the scale), three measures before the last. Surely everyone will enjoy the thrilling experience of listening to this fugue, and it is hoped that other fugues of Bach also will be heard.

Although the fugue form is rigid in certain aspects and circumscribes the composer to some degree (especially a composer who is motivated by an emotional, romantic spirit), there are many opportunities within the structure for individual expressions of skill. No two fugues are exactly alike. The search for the substantiation or refutation of this statement is bound to be as exciting as it is pleasant.

Bach was in the habit of preceding the more or less strict form of the fugue with a free or improvisatory piece called, at various times, a *prelude,* a *toccata,* or a *fantasia.* The prelude and the fantasia emphasized the element of emotional outpouring; the toccata (literally, a "touch" or display piece) leaned toward brilliance and virtuosity. Bach's TOCCATA AND FUGUE IN D MINOR should be among the supplementary listening numbers. We illustrate only the exposition section of the LITTLE G MINOR FUGUE:

(Counterpoint I and II above)
Tenor Voice. The "Subject"
Bass Voice
The "Answer"

The author suggests a listening "game" which he has used successfully for many years. Follow the theme and indicate in some way every entry until it is easy to do. Then try to identify and follow the counter-subjects and various contrapuntal parts, shifting the attention rapidly from one to the other. Now forget the "game" and enjoy the music to the full.

Theme and variation forms: the passacaglia and the chaconne

For composers who thought so largely in terms of line, as did Bach and those who preceded him, the *theme-and-variation* form offered rich possibilities for musical invention and display of compositional skill as well as emotional expression. Where Haydn, Mozart, and their successors thought of the variation as an ornamentation or elaboration of the melody, the earlier composers more often retained the melody in its original simplicity and obtained the desired variety in the possibilities of the counterpoint. They thus achieved, in its completest form, the ideal of unity and, at the same time, variety. The *variations on a ground,* or *on a ground bass* (sometimes called a *basso ostinato*), so popular during the seventeenth century, and consisting of a short, distinctive tune of a few measures repeated over and over in the bass, over which the contrapuntal variations became increasingly intricate, culminated in the *passacaglia* and the *chaconne.* The passacaglia, an old and stately Spanish-Moorish dance whose name, according to some, was derived from a phrase, "Passo Gallo," meaning "rooster step," consisted of a solemn melody in triple (some say duple) meter and in the minor mode. Others think the word comes from the Spanish verb *pasar,* to walk, and the noun *calle,* meaning street. The latter seems closer to the truth. However, the theme of the passacaglia as a contrapuntal musical form was often reiterated in the bass, as was once the rule of the *chaconne* against ever-varying counterpoint in the upper parts. In later days, the reiterated passacaglia theme might be found in any of the four or more parts. Scholars have never quite agreed as to how the chaconne differs from the passacaglia. Some maintain that the distinguishing feature of the chaconne is in the emphasis on the harmonic character of the theme, while the passacaglia subject is more likely to stress the purely melodic aspect. Until a better definition is agreed upon, the foregoing might well be accepted. In any case, when we use the terms today, we generally have reference to the monumental example of each form that Bach left in the PASSACAGLIA AND FUGUE IN C MINOR FOR ORGAN and the CHACONNE IN D MINOR FOR UNACCOMPANIED VIOLIN. Both are heard today in the orchestral versions.

Passacaglia in C minor

By the time the passacaglia reached the hands of Bach, it had lost its original dance character. The theme on which he built his C MINOR PASSACAGLIA is a solemn and dignified eight-measure phrase (see the first line of the ensuing musical illustration) adapted from a work by the seventeenth century French composer, Andre Raison, TRIO EN PASSACAILLE (1688). Upon this simple theme Bach built a series of twenty "variations," rising steadily in power and intensity, in a structure that for sheer imagination and mastery of technique has never had an equal. (We are able to show only seven of these variations in the illustrations.) At first the theme is kept in the bass, while the parts above it change in ever-more intricate contrapuntal patterns. Then we hear it in the uppermost part, while the lower accompaniment shifts about. Then the theme is heard in an inner part, while the counterpoint is woven above and below it. Finally, the work builds up to a triumphant pronouncement of the theme, against massive chords and lively, running passages. When the composer seems to have extracted every possible variation, he takes the first half of the theme, combines it with another genial melody, and proceeds to construct a *double fugue* (a fugue on two subjects instead of the usual single theme) that is as exciting as all that has already transpired. Never has the artistic imagination functioned on such a high, noble, and unsurpassable plane in a similar form. Centuries of discipline and experience were necessary before the PASSACAGLIA IN C MINOR could come into existence; and, through the ardors of this aesthetic experience and discipline, finally came that freedom which is reserved only for the anointed.

A few pointers for listening: Note the theme, first of all; memorize it by singing it *along with the performance.* Then observe how it repeats itself throughout the piece—hum the theme as it is reiterated, in whatever part it may appear. You may have to try a few times before you overcome the tendency to go astray. After you perceive this aspect of the work clearly, go through the composition again and again, noting the more involved tonal patterns and designs that the composer has woven into the richly inventive contrapuntal fabric. Try to notice what is going on in the other "voices" while the theme is being sounded. With sufficient time and practice, you will be able to hear several principal features going on at any moment as a composite whole, or in such rapid shifts of interest that the effect will be almost the same. However, do not lose sight of the aesthetic values of this as well as *all* other compositions.

The following illustrations show the theme, together with initial portions, of seven selected "variations."

f
N.B. Theme in soprano
ff
sf
ff
sf
f

Chaconne in D minor

Though the *chaconne* is more often heard nowadays in the orchestral version than in its original medium, it will be well to hear the work as Bach conceived and wrote it *along* with the more modern orchestral transcription. The original of the *chaconne* is a movement from one of the set of SIX SONATAS that Bach wrote for the unaccompanied violin, and, as such, is one of the show pieces for virtuosi. When one is fortunate enough to hear a great violinist perform this work, he will be moved by that rare blend of pathos, of lyrical intimacy, of nobility and power and complexity all upreared on the tenuous foundation of four violin strings! By all means, listen to Bach's original solo violin version. If that is not possible, the orchestral or organ transcriptions will prove acceptable to all save the purists, because of the work's Gothic spaciousness, its impressive power, and its architectonic massiveness. Bach's limitless fecundity of invention, his originality of thought, his flowing linear construction—above all, his power to say great things in the greatest way—are apparent in both the *passacaglia* and the *chaconne.*

The CHACONNE (*Ciaccona* in the original MS.) consists of more than sixty variations for violin alone on the following theme, which is copied from the original:

ADDITIONAL SUGGESTIONS FOR LISTENING

The complete works of Bach have been published by the *Bach-Gesellschaft* in forty-seven volumes; surely the most diverse tastes should find gratification amidst this monumental output. Other types and forms of Bach's works have been presented in previous chapters—we have reserved the present one for some of the larger instrumental works. Thus a review of these references may be in order. As has been our custom in suggesting supplementary listening, we shall present only a few that seem opportune immediately after the compositions just studied in this chapter.

The listener should become acquainted with more of the preludes and fugues of the WOHLTEMPERIERTE KLAVIER, in two volumes of twenty-four pairs each. First try selections from the two-part and then the three-part *Inventions;* then choose Preludes and Fugues among numbers 1, 2, 4, 5, 8, 9, 16, 21 of Part I and numbers 5 and 9 from Part II of the WELL-TEMPERED CLAVICHORD to begin with; follow along with the BIG G MINOR, BIG A MINOR, and D MAJOR FUGUES from the more than forty organ fugues. The more daring and advanced will want to make selections from DIE KUNST DER FUGE [10] now obtainable on records. Then the reader, after hearing a few selected works in the original or transcribed versions, will have made a good beginning in the literature of Bach with one notable exception—the *concerto grosso*.

The Concerto Grosso

Bach wrote six of these works, which have become known as the BRANDENBURG CONCERTI [11] (for they were written in 1721 for the Margrave of Brandenburg); in them the composer employs a different instrumentation for each concerto. We shall give only a brief description of each:

Number 1, in F major, is for 2 violins (with a *piccolo violino* tuned, according to Grove, a minor third higher than the usual violin), viola, 'cello, bass, 2 horns, 3 oboes, bassoon, and harpsichord. The *Adagio* movement is regarded by many as "one of the most impassioned expressions in music of poignant grief." Note the deviation from the strict form of the concerto by the addition of a minuet, a polacca, and two trios.

Number 2, in F major, is for trumpet, flute, oboe, and violin, with a string band as *tutti;* it is probably the most popular of the six at the moment, no doubt because of the beautiful *Andante* and the very vigorous first and last movements. It is recommended as the listener's introduction to these concerti.

Number 3, in G major, is for 3 violins, 3 violas, and 3 'cellos to form the *concertino,* with the accompaniment of double-bass and harpsichords; the solo instruments play in three groups, and the work, according to the Bach authority, Spitta, contains some of the finest music in German instrumental literature.

Number 4, in G major, is for violin, 2 flutes, with the strings as the *tutti;* note the alternating concerti and *tutti* in the *Adagio,* and the wonderful *accompanied fugue* in the last movement.

Number 5, in D major, is for flute, violin, and harpsichord, with the usual string *tutti;* note the prominent place Bach gives to the harpsichord in this work, especially the many brilliant cadenzas.

Number 6, in B-flat major, is for 2 violas, 2 *viole da gamba* (an obsolete instrument slightly smaller than the 'cello, having 6 strings with frets on the fingerboard; it is held between the legs, hence its nickname, "leg viol") and the 'cello, with the double-bass and harpsichord accompaniment. This number requires virtuoso viola players, and the 'cello usually replaces the *viole da gamba.*

It is obvious from the foregoing descriptions that Bach's *concerto grosso* is not to be confused with the *solo concerto* as we know it today. (See Chapter 25.) His works are more like *suites* with a group, or groups, of solo performers, plus contrasting or supporting, or "filling-up" (*ripieno*) instruments. The group of solo performers pitted against the *tutti* is called the *concertino.*

[10] DIE KUNST DER FUGE (The Art of Fugue) is a collection of fifteen fugues for solo instrument, two for two claviers, and four canons, presenting almost every conceivable kind of contrapuntal device and variants on a single theme; it is a monumental treatise on the art of fugal writing that was left unfinished at the time of Bach's death. The serious student will find this work an inexhaustible mine of instruction.

[11] The reader is directed to the music volume *Chamber Suites and Concerti Grossi,* edited by Albert E. Wier. (New York: Longmans, Green and Company.) The actual conductor's scores are used.

Courtesy Carolina Art Association, Gibbes Art Gallery

PINELANDS (*Watercolor*) Alice Huger Smith

An excellent example of Impressionism by a contemporary American artist of the South. Note how the artist has introduced novel effects of light and shadow, vague forms of the pinetree forest, and suggestions of flowers and underbrush. The picture projects a mood of peaceful quietness similar to that experienced in a large Gothic cathedral, with the sunlit colors streaming from the stained glass windows and slanting across the nave, seeking out and dispelling the shadows. The pines stand like tall pillars, spreading out and forming intricate fan-vaulting in the overgrowth and hanging moss.

29 Tempers of impressionism and symbolism in music and allied arts

After Bach had reached the apex in the types of polyphonic and religious music that were current during his creative life, and through which he marked a distinct epoch in music history, there was little more of equal significance to be said in those particular idioms.[1] Moreover, more recent intriguing influences had arisen in the world of music, such as: the general acceptance of metrical (poetic and dance) patterns and their consequent forms; harmonic inventions and their homophonic functions; the inventions and perfections of the piano-forte with its superior, full-toned sonority and effective hammer and

[1] Essential listening for this chapter includes: symphonic poem, L'APRÈS-MIDI D'UN FAUNE ("The Afternoon of a Faun") and, if possible, LA MER ("The Sea") by Debussy; DAPHNIS ET CHLOÉ Ballet Suite No. 2, by Ravel; THE FOUNTAINS OF ROME by Respighi; and, when time allows, *The White Peacock*, an orchestral sketch arranged from the ROMAN SKETCHES for piano by Griffes; and *On Hearing the First Cuckoo in Spring*, a symphonic sketch from TWO PIECES FOR SMALL ORCHESTRA by Delius.

damper action; and the practical and general adoption of the twelve-toned, equal-tempered tuning. Another potent factor in the changing styles of music at the time was the waning of *Pietism,* which so deeply affected Bach,[2] and the rising of the "Age of Enlightenment." This "new" movement, embodying some of the spirit of the Renaissance, proclaimed the supremacy of reason over emotion, and faith and devotion as experiential facts of religion. One can appreciate the tremendous impact of these new forces by recalling that Bach's music suffered an almost total eclipse after his death in 1750. The outstanding sons of Bach, Johann Christoph Friedrich, Wilhelm Friedmann, Karl Philipp Emanuel, and Johann Christian, espoused generally the newer homophonic styles of music rather than the polyphonic. (As a matter of fact, Bach himself had anticipated the change and experimented with its idioms successfully! Witness the many jolly homophonic dance suites, the first *Prelude* in the WELL-TEMPERED CLAVICHORD, the endless number of *chorales,* and so forth!)

Then followed Mozart, Haydn, Beethoven (and later Brahms) who carried on the torch of the homophonic style, although these composers were able to express themselves in masterly polyphonic music. Not long after Beethoven had brought the sonata, the symphony, the string quartet, trio, and other works based upon the *sonata-allegro* design to Olympian heights of expression, the Romanticists Wagner and Liszt joined together the arts of music and literature to give birth to still newer forms, the music drama and the symphonic poem. In the final decade of nineteenth century in Europe, the last of the Romantic Movement—Wagner, Liszt, Brahms, Tchaikovsky, Dvořák, Rimsky-Korsakoff, Mussorgsky, César Franck, Grieg and others—had *seemingly* exhausted the possibilities of the so-called "grand style." Thus, the young composers in the post-Romantic era, as happens to the rising creators of any age, had to seek new means and forms of expression—regardless of the cost and indifference to comparative evaluations. (This ever-changing spirit is the eternal song of creative youth. The alternative to this regenerative spirit is artistic decadence.)

Let us see what a few young composers actually did. Richard Strauss adapted the brilliant and virtuoso orchestral techniques of Wagner and Liszt and others to the more sophisticated and realistic trends of his time. Sibelius added to the emotional exuberance of a Tchaikovsky the power, intense concentration, and nationalistic spirit of his own introspective personality. Across the borders of the west to France, Claude Debussy, through his intense interest in the poetry of Verlaine, Mallarmé, and Baudelaire and the paintings of Manet, Monet, Whistler, Pissarro,

[2] The red ink inscriptions to be seen at the onset and the close of the original manuscripts of the major sacred works by J. S. Bach leave no doubt that their very composition was an act of deep religious devotion.

Cézanne, and others, became identified with the current revival of the Impressionistic and Symbolistic tempers. He sought, little by little, to accomplish in music what had been done in poetry and painting. Thus he firmly established the so-called French School of Impressionism in Music of the last half of the nineteenth and early decades of the twentieth century. The influence of this "school" has since become of world-wide importance. This is so not only because of the peculiar characteristics of the French school of Impressionistic Art, but, more importantly, because the "new art" shows a relationship, in many respects, with the temper of Romanticism.

However, the immediate incitation of the movement in France was a revolt against the emotional extravagance and theatricalism of the German Romantics, especially Liszt and Wagner, and those in France, such as Berlioz, and the spectacular opulence of the operas and ballets by Gounod and Verdi. The name of the movement sprang from the derisive use of a title of a picture by Manet, SUNRISE—AN IMPRESSION. In a way, this open revolt gave definition to the aims and ideals of the painters who rebelled against the traditionalism and academicism of the previous "schools." The first exhibition of the Impressionists in 1870 ushered in one of the most exciting periods of French painting.[3] The "movement" that ensued was dominated by such artists as Edouard Manet (1832–1883), Camille Pissarro (1830–1903), Edgar Degas (1834–1917), Alfred Sisley (1840–1899), Claude Monet (1840–1926), Pierre Renoir (1841–1919), and one who has since been acclaimed as among the greatest painters of all time, Paul Cézanne (1839–1906), although Cézanne was more of a Classicist at heart and spoke the passing impressionistic "language" with a strong "foreign" accent. Subsequently Cézanne wrote a letter to Pablo Picasso (1881–), the Spanish-French virtuoso painter, outlining the basic principles of the Cubistic and Abstract arts that were yet to be born—"Everything in nature adheres to [the geometric forms of] the cone, the cylinder, and the cube." (The sphere was added later.)

IMPRESSIONISM IN PAINTING

The Impressionists, working in *plein air* instead of piecing together their recollections in the studio, abandoned the structural and plastic values, the literary or history-telling aims, the intellectual and emotional attitudes of the great Romantic painters. They attempted to capture the fleeting loveliness of the external world, the impression of the moment,

[3] The author has some personal knowledge and understanding of what such an artistic shock can be, for he saw the effects a similar occasion had upon those who attended the *First International Exhibit of Cubistic Art* at the Art Institute of Chicago, Mar. 24–Apr. 16, 1913. Being a young composer and ripe for artistic revolt at that time, we sympathized heartily with the "new art." See footnote 2, Chapter 30.

the ever-shifting colors, the vibrating atmosphere and elusive contours of a setting where all objects were delicately shaded into one another. *They abandoned the fixed attitudes and rigid lines of the academic style for the fascinating interplay of light and color, the dynamic qualities, and*

Courtesy Metropolitan Museum of Art

ROUEN CATHEDRAL Monet

the transparence of a delicate dream world always in flux. They reduced color to its subtlest gradations; they created a color technique of shimmering iridescence, a style of subtlety and finesse. In their canvases, all was bathed in light; colors and surfaces swam together in a richly imaginative interplay. Theirs was a sensate, "surface art," in many aspects, compared with the emotional richness and depth of the older masters—an art held together by an overall effect of brilliance and animation rather than by the deeper values of emotion, intellect, and structures; but within its limited sphere, it was an altogether revelatory art, opening the way for the refinement and sensitivity that have come to be considered the hallmark of French painting.

For the Impressionists, the momentary excitement of the eye was the criterion of emotional reaction to reality. No other group of artists ever succeeded so well in catching this peculiar expression of spontaneity, freshness, wonder, and delicate nuance. From their canvases innumerable separated points of color strike the eye, caught as it were in a state of suspended animation—infinitely deft little strokes that are combined and blended in the eye of the beholder (especially in the technique known as *pointillism*). Subject matter, composition, detail, structure—everything is subordinated to the momentary impression. It has been said that the Impressionists looked at nature through a keyhole. They were careful not to pick subjects that required profundity or vigor. Country scenes, river scenes, still lifes, delicate glimpses of Parisian life—the cafés, the ballet rehearsal, the picnic near the Seine, the Latin Quarter, Montmartre and Montparnasse—these fascinated the painters of this school. Thus one may say that the Impressionists were a direct *outgrowth* of Realism and Romanticism. Other influences were felt, such as oriental art, the physics of light and color, the psychology of seeing, and the particularized influences of the other fine arts, especially poetry and music.[4]

IMPRESSIONISM AND SYMBOLISM IN LITERATURE[5]

In literature, the reaction against the pompousness of Hugo and Lamartine, the exuberance of de Musset and George Sand and de Vigny, was no less marked. Charles Baudelaire, strongly influenced by our own Edgar Allan Poe, led the way toward an employment of poetic moods and symbols to create a twilight world in which language took on the qualities of music and painting, of perfumes and visions and dreams. Just as the Impressionist painters rebelled against the structural rigidity of academic painting, the Impressionist poets, the Symbolists and Imagists, rebelled against the restrictions of rhyme, verse, and strophe of Classical poetry. The painters abandoned literary moods and intellectual meaning; the poets rebelled against the fixed associations of words. They began to

[4] See Degas' REHEARSAL ON STAGE, Chap. 11. Observe NOCTURNE by Whistler, with its vagueness, PINELANDS by Alice Huger Smith, and ROUEN CATHEDRAL by Monet, all in this chapter. Note their realistic basis, made more apparent when the photograph of the Cathedral is compared with Monet's painting.

[5] Bear in mind that while Impressionism may have a basis of Romantic feelings and sensations, Symbolism is more apt to be associative and fanciful, bearing traditional references or meanings, or psychological and mental, rather than sensual impressions "based upon a foundational reality"—standing for something other than its apparent self. The lines of demarcation are not always clear, however, especially when the two terms are compared in the art of music. It is even difficult to put the discussion into words! The differences should be experienced.

use words for their musical properties, rather than for their thought content. Words to them were symbols for the hidden meanings beneath, keys to unlock a world of subterranean associations and dream patterns. Words were tones that started a stream of overtones in the brain, all kinds of subconscious implications that stood to everday language in the same relation as dreams do to waking life. The Romantics depicted; the Symbolist Impressionists suggested. The Romantic painted in brilliant color; the Imagist worked his ideas out in delicate pastel tints. Where the Romantic was dramatic, the Impressionist moved in a pale dream of things half said and half seen. Stéphane Mallarmé, Paul Verlaine, Arthur Rimbaud, Maurice Maeterlinck—these were the men who created in the final decades of the century a new lyric poety made up of subtle suggestion and pale colors, of floating images and luminous symbols. One has but to read a few lines from Baudelaire, Verlaine, or Rimbaud to get the richly evocative nature of this poetry.

Like Impressionism in painting, poetic Impressionism was mainly French—one might almost say Parisian—in character and inspiration, combining mysticism, sensuality, Bohemianism, the transparence and purity of the French language, the music of words, the subconscious emotional associations of images and symbols, and above all the somewhat exaggerated preciousness of *fin de siècle* sophistication. If there was about this poetry something of the "utterly utter" quality that Gilbert and Sullivan lampooned in PATIENCE, it opened up a new realm of delicate perception and insight, of fleeting impressions and moods, that crossed the borderline between poetry and the other arts, conferring upon words the magic of color and music.

IMPRESSIONISM IN MUSIC: CLAUDE DEBUSSY (1862–1918)

Musical Impressionism in nineteenth century France came to such perfect flowering in the art of Claude Debussy that the man and movement have become indissolubly associated—though there were parallel movements in England, Spain, Italy, Russia, and the United States. He was the first of the great "modern" Impressionists in music; and, despite a host of disciples and imitators, he still remains the greatest.

Born in 1862, Debussy entered the Paris Conservatoire when he was eleven, and studied there until his twenty-second year, winning honors in piano and composition. During his student years he spent several summers as pianist to Mme. Nadejda von Meck, Tchaikovsky's patroness.

In 1884 Debussy won the highest honor of the Conservatoire, the Grand Prix de Rome, with his cantata THE PRODIGAL SON. Even in his undergraduate days at the Conservatoire he had constantly chafed at the restrictions of the conventional style of composition. The works he pro-

Courtesy University Prints

ROUEN CATHEDRAL (Photograph)

Compare this photograph with the oil painting of the cathedral by Monet on another page. Both are from approximately the same angle, and at the same hour of the day. Note that Monet has subordinated the details almost to the point of elimination. See a first class color reproduction of the painting to note how marvelously Monet uses colors to create form and further the emphasis of highlights and the contrasting shadows. After looking at both views for some time, you will note how much more satisfying from an aesthetic standpoint is the impressionistic painting.

duced during his stay in Rome aroused the anger of the academicians and sounded the note of revolt against accepted usage that was to make him the foremost iconoclast of his time. If in the first phase of his career he vacillated between the influence of his teacher Massenet and the dominating figure of Wagner, after his return from Rome he set himself resolutely on the path to the evolution of a purely French style that would break both with the sugary lyricism of the French Romanticists and the turgid extravagance of the Bayreuth music drama. A frequent visitor to Stéphane Mallarmé's salon, he came into contact with the poets and painters who were the mainstay of the Impressionist movement. Strongly influenced by them, he endeavored to transplant their aestheticism into the art of music. In 1892 he wrote his PRELUDE to Mallarmé's ecologue, THE AFTERNOON OF A FAUN—the first triumph of musical Impressionism. There then began two decades of creative effort during which he produced the works that won for him the ranking place among the Impressionists—the song settings of poems by Baudelaire, Verlaine, Mallarmé, and Pierre Louÿs; the three NOCTURNES for orchestra; the piano pieces, especially the sets, IMAGES (of 1905 and 1907), the two sets of PRÉLUDES (in 1910, and in 1915, in two books); the unique STRING QUARTET IN G MINOR; the suite, or symphonic poem, LA MER, which we believe to be his greatest orchestral work; the exotic IBERIA reflecting so sympathetically the idioms, color, languor, and pulsating active life of Spain—though we believe he (like Bizet) never travelled in that land; and his superbly beautiful setting of Maeterlinck's PELLÉAS ET MÉLISANDE, which many critics consider the most perfect opera ever written (others would pair it with DON GIOVANNI by Mozart).

In these, as well as in a host of lesser works, Debussy gave eloquent expression to the dominant artistic currents of the turn of the century. Coming at the waning of the dominance of German Romanticism as a distinct "period," Debussy—to greater degree than either Richard Strauss or Sibelius—became the prophet of the "new" musical epoch. He revolted not only against the "overblown" passions of Wagnerism but also against what seemed to him the outlived and restricting molds of the classic and romantic structural patterns, especially the sonata-allegro forms. Debussy was thoroughly Gallic, and though he naturally worshiped originality, logical clarity and order, limpidity, restraint, balance, and measure in music, he could not completely escape general formal traditions—as indicated by his single STRING QUARTET IN G MINOR (influenced greatly in structural character by Franck's cyclical treatment and Borodin's lyricism); and the THREE SONATAS, No. 1 for 'cello and piano (1915), No. 2 for flute, viola and harp (1915), and especially No. 3 for violin and piano (1917). This last sonata comes closest of the three to the orthodox sonata-allegro form. Just as the poets and painters of that epoch sought original means of expression, so Debussy sought to compose music that was subtly elusive rather than monumental; suggestive, sensual, and evocative rather than burdened with very conscious, cerebral development of thematic material. (It is said by good authority that Debussy would walk out of a concert performance of a piano sonata—even one by Beethoven or Brahms —when the development section of a movement was to begin!) Rather, blurred or fused outlines and forms, "twilight" colors, subtle nuances, appeals to the senses—these became the trade-mark, or colophon, of the new music. But Debussy was sometimes *très précieux*—a bit affected and "fussy." Through strangely exotic, almost unearthly, scintillating, and crepuscular harmonies and tonal effects, Debussy succeeded in conjuring up opalescent visions, vague impressions, and moods that were the musical counterpart of the misty impressions of Monet or Pissarro, the countless hues of basic colors of Cézanne, the pearly softness of Renoir's pastels, or the coalescent, pointillistic subtleties of Seurat. Within their own framework and purposes, these delicate melodies and harmonies were fully as sensuous, as emotional and tremulous as the blatant sonorities of the Germanic School of High Romanticism.[6] Yet Debussy could be forceful and powerfully dynamic when such was the essence of his musical thoughts and expression! *Debussy is the poet-painter-musician supreme!*

The great orchestra of Wagner was not reduced in size by Debussy; but it was handled with a new delicacy, the brass often muted, the wood-winds used with uncanny effectiveness in low registers, the strings divided; the percussion assumed a new importance, supplying glockenspiel, celesta, triangle, and harp, wreathing the tonal mass in a soft luminosity. The melody is shaded, the harmonies dissolve into each other and float away in an evanescence that lends a special charm. To a generation brought up on the robustness of Wagner, the homely strength of Dvořák, the rich coloring of Rimsky-Korsakoff, the tempestuous climaxes of Tchaikovsky, this music seemed strange and esoteric.

Many influences besides those of the poets and painters of the Mallarmé circle played upon Debussy. Turning back for inspiration to the glories of French music—he styled himself *musicien français*—he fell under the aristocratic charm of the eighteenth-century masters, Couperin and Rameau. In the Paris Exposition at the end of the century, he heard the exotic effects of Balinese music, the weird gongs and shifting harmonies of Java and the Far East, and incorporated their strange tones in his

[6] It is often difficult to discern accurately in a few hearings whether Debussy's harmonies, and melodic ideas growing out of them, are really harmonic entities in the traditional structural logic; or whether they are, in fact, scalelike passages, or dispersed chordal-like structures derived from real or quasi modes, or pentatonic, tonal, exotic, or mixed scales. Debussy is concerned, of course, only with the expression of the resultant effects regardless of any analysis. Even the whole-tone scale and its derived harmonies, with which this composer is so generally identified, are vague. Impressionism is not concerned with thematic "working-out" or "development" as such; and the "formal" structures are consequents of musical, poetic, purely aesthetic, or sensate musical content.

Courtesy Art Institute of Chicago

color palette. During his stay with Mme. von Meck, he came in contact with Russian music and fell under the sway of the then unknown Mussorgsky. Upon all these, he managed to lay the imprint of his own personality, all those qualities that his great contemporary, Anatole France, considered the essence of *l'ésprit gaulois.* Although he relied on titles—often fanciful and poetic ones—to *suggest* the atmosphere of his creations, he *achieved* this atmosphere through purely musical means.

This music did not seek to imitate nature; it suggested nature in subtle musical terms. The title was merely the starting point for musical vision and was forthwith left behind. As in the case of Liszt, we get a good insight into the creative horizons of Debussy by examining the titles of his works. Among them we find THE BLESSED DAMOZEL, a lyric poem for female voices and orchestra, after Rossetti's poem; THREE NOCTURNES FOR ORCHESTRA—*Clouds, Festivals, Sirens;* THREE PRINTS FOR PIANO —*Pagodas, An Evening in Granada, Gardens in the Rain;* THREE IMAGES FOR PIANO—*Reflections in the Water, Homage to Rameau, Movement;* a SECOND SET OF IMAGES—*Bells Across the Leaves, And the Moon Descends on the Temple That Was, Gold Fish;* and the orchestral suite, LA MER. Some of the titles of the two sets of PRELUDES FOR PIANO are no less indicative of the Impressionistic tempers, i.e., *Veils, What the West Wind Saw, The Girl With the Flaxen Hair, Interrupted Serenade, The Submerged Cathedral, Dead Leaves, The Fairies Are Exquisite Dancers,* the *Terrace of Audiences of Moonlight.* There is a kind of Romanticism in this atmospheric music; but it is a Romanticism so different in spirit from that of Wagner's TRISTAN AND ISOLDE or Tchaikovsky's ROMEO AND JULIET or Rimsky-Korsakoff's SCHEHERAZADE, so much more sophisticated and objective, so intellectualized and distilled, so purged, indeed, of many of the elements that we associate with the Romantic temper, that we can almost consider it the very inversion of Romanticism.

We should also point out Debussy's special contribution to the literature of the piano. Trained as a pianist, he found a particularly sympathetic medium in the instrument of Chopin; he became the greatest composer for that instrument after the Polish "Poet of the Piano," and one of the foremost piano composers of all time. The piano, with its ability to trace evanescent melodies against floating masses of tone, was indeed an appropriate instrument for the Impressionistic style. Where Chopin and the Romantics had exploited its power to sing a melody against a fluid accompaniment, as well as its harmonic figuration and its flashing sonority, Debussy transformed it into an instrument of shifting harmonies and twilight colors, of continually fluctuating moods, now dry and brittle, now soft and mysterious. He virtually inaugurated a new type of piano technique (both manual and pedal) and gave a new lease of life to an instrument whose golden age had seemed to be over with the first half of the century.

Frequently associated with Debussy, although he was by no means the first composer to exploit its possibilities, is the whole-tone scale. The student will recall that our ordinary major scale consists of a pattern of eight tones, spaced a whole-step apart except between the third and fourth, and seventh and eighth tones which are only a half-step apart. Debussy found much more congenial for his art a scale composed exclusively of whole-steps—a pattern produced on the piano if we play in succession C, D, E, F-sharp, G-sharp, A-sharp and C. One has but to

Courtesy Theodore Presser Co.

CLAUDE DEBUSSY

Courtesy Freer Gallery, Smithsonian Institution

NOCTURNE, A CANAL IN HOLLAND Whistler

Whistler spent many years of his creative life in Paris. His penchant for poetic and musical titles, along with his peculiarly decorative use of color, tone, and indefinite masses, aligns him with early French Impressionism. "Nocturne" successfully conveys the fleeting and vagrant moods aroused by a Holland Canal scene in the misty evening hours.

hear this scale to become aware of its potentialities for bizarre or picturesque effect. In fact, this scale is an old oriental one, found in the music of other peoples, including the American Indian. Classicism and Romanticism had risen to their peaks within the system of the major-minor scales. Wagner and Liszt had loosened the boundaries of key, passing from one tonality to the next in an ever-shifting chromaticism. Debussy took the next step by frequently abandoning the major scale. This ambiguity of tonality in Debussy's work, which passed freely to and from the conventional major-minor system to the more piquant whole-tone scale system, added to the elusive coloring and the harmonic strangeness that characterized musical Impressionism.

We have then, in this poet of *fin de siècle* music, an artist of the utmost sensibility, a dreamer of visions. He created no mighty architecture as Bach and Beethoven did, no system capable of development or organic growth (it can almost be said that Debussy *created and exhausted* an entire "school" of music thought); he treated no vast spiritual issues; he did not plumb the depths of the human soul, nor did he touch its highest moods of exaltation and triumph. But within his style, he wrought patterns of loveliness and brought back the ideals of refinement and beauty to an age that had been dazzled by the bombastic and the grandiloquent. For this, he must be ranked as a worthy disciple of the great eighteenth-century masters whom he worshiped.

Prelude to "The Afternoon of a Faun"

This first triumph of musical Impressionism—it has remained Debussy's most popular work—was composed in 1892 when the composer was thirty. Inspired by a prose poem of Mallarmé that has been termed a "miracle of unintelligibility," it is, nevertheless, a miracle of clarity, uniting in almost uncanny fashion the simple, sensuous tonal beauty of Impressionism, the chastity of style of the antique, and the richness of Debussy's imagination functioning at its most poetic level. Here is the primitive creature, half man, half goat, transported from the sculptures of classical antiquity to the aesthetic subtleties of Parisian life. The result is a thing of sheer loveliness and utmost sophistication; a miracle of blending poetic, musical, and sensorial creative imagination into a well-nigh perfect compositional form, vaguely suggesting one of the delicately balanced three-part structural designs.

Debussy himself explained that his music was intended as free illustration of Mallarmé's poem, to evoke "the successive scenes in which the longings and desire of the Faun pass in the heat of the afternoon." The poem, published in 1876 with illustrations by Manet, has become known to English readers through the famous paraphrase of Edmund Gosse describing the awakening of a faun in the forest and his attempt to recall his experiences of the previous afternoon. Dreamily he wonders whether it were in dream or in reality that he was visited by nymphs; he seems to see a vision of whiteness among the brown reeds at the side of the lake. The impression fades; he settles in the warm grasses again to seek the dream once more.[7]

The flutes, used in their most unusual lower register, "sultry" oboes, mysterious horns, and antique cymbals mingle in an atmosphere of enchantment. Strangely gliding themes conjure up the dusky land that lies between waking and sleep, between "then" and "sometime." The music is steeped in pagan beauty, in glimmering visions of the childhood of man, in the magic of strange forests and forms and visions. Even today, the score retains its delicacy and charm. What it must have sounded like to those of the 1890's, one can well imagine.

The work, which is free and rhapsodical in form, opens with a sensuous melody announced by the flute in $\frac{9}{8}$ time:

The theme is played *piano, doux et expressif* (sweet and expressively), and *très modéré* (very moderately). Nationalist that he was, Debussy made a point of writing his directions in French instead of the usual Italian.

Silvery *glissandos* on the harp are heard as the music gets under way. The theme is repeated by a solo flute against a background of tremulous strings. Oboes, clarinets, and French horns weave a limpid tapestry of sound; strange chords emerge and momentarily dissolve; the rhythm shifts back and forth among $\frac{9}{8}$, $\frac{6}{8}$, $\frac{12}{8}$, $\frac{3}{4}$, and $\frac{4}{4}$ time. The music quickens to the beginnings of a *crescendo,* but it dies away forthwith and the languorous flute theme returns, now decorated with fanciful arabesques. Presently there emerges a new theme on the oboe, plaintive and rapturous (the first four notes being the "germinal motive" of the whole work):

In a steady heightening of intensity, *toujours en animant* (getting steadily livelier), we reach the third theme announced by the wood-winds,

[7] Get the translation of Mallarmé's poem, L'APRÈS-MIDI D'UN FAUNE by Aldous Huxley quoted in Addison Hibbard's *Writers of the Western World,* p. 877. Read the poem *aloud* a number of times to get the feel of the sound effects, the changing moods, the fleeting images, the delicate nuances and its distinctive over-all "bouquet." Our emotional, imaginative, and sensorial (and intellectual) reactions can best come into active creative play only when this type of poetry is read aloud. *In fact, all poetry is best read in this manner.*

Courtesy Museum of Fine Arts, Boston

THE WAVE, WITH FUJI IN BACKGROUND Hokusai

Katsushika Hokusai (1760-1849) was a prolific and internationally famous Japanese master of painting and print making. His best work was in landscape painting, as well as in idyllic prints of flowers, birds, etc., and some thirty-six views of Fujiyama. His work is marked by great imagination, vigorous dramatic action, powerful brush strokes, and symbolic implications. In this picture, note the strong, determined sweep of the single lines, the asymmetrical composition, and the dramatic strife between nature and man. The principal tempers involved are Symbolism and Romanticism.

expressif et très soutenu (expressive and very sustained), a theme that, according to the French musicologist, Louis Laloy, "speaks of desire satisfied." (Note the "germinal motive"):

Now the music rises to its rapturous climax in a measure of *fortissimo* that immediately subsides—a departure indeed from the sustained ecstasies of the Wagnerian trumpets and trombones. The first theme returns, *avec plus de langueur* (more languorously). Everything is wreathed in a soft haze; muted horns weave darkly tinted patterns;

oboes and flutes scamper about in light, staccato tones. The vision fades; a solo 'cello lingers a while with the flute; the music dissolves into a dream-like *pianissimo;* the enchantment vanishes with the tones of two antique symbols.

The world moves rapidly. Only a generation ago the name of Debussy was synonymous with aestheticism; his music supposedly appealed only to a select few, the "advance guard." Today his harmonies and melodies reappear as foxtrots or as the theme songs of popular radio pragrams. (Even in Gershwin's "*Rhapsody in Blue!*") And the supreme citadel of the aesthetes, the AFTERNOON OF A FAUN, has become one of the most frequently played numbers in the symphonic repertoire.

La Mer: Three Symphonic Sketches

In order to show clearly the maturity and perfection of the expressive techniques of musical Symbolism and Impressionism that had gestated in Debussy's art since the composition of THE AFTERNOON OF A FAUN, we suggest that LA MER: *Three Symphonic Sketches* be studied at this point. It was written between 1903 and 1905, ten years after "the Faun." It consists of a sequence of three separated yet closely knit movements. In fact the three movements are unified and seem to have been woven out of a single over-all conception, so that the work is often called a symphonic poem—"of moods and impressions." In its broadness of scope and relationship of the movements, LA MER is like a symphony! The first movement is in a slow tempo marked *Très lent* (very slow), and entitled, *De l'aube à midi sur la mer* (From dawn to noon at sea); the second is *Jeux de vagues* (Play of the waves) and marked *Allegro: dans un rythme très souple* (Lively: with a very flexible rhythm); and the third movement, *Dialogue du vent et de la mer* (Dialogue of the wind and the sea), marked by the composer *Animé et tumultueux* (Animated and tumultuously.)

Outwardly, this work has certain aspects of a modern or contemporary orchestral suite; but internally, Debussy has pretty well shunned conventional forms and mechanics, permitting the musical substance to express itself to the full according to its own inherent architectonic character, balance and ultimate aesthetic satisfaction. (We point to certain evidences of the unifying effect of cyclical technique, however, especially in the first and third movements.) In regard to the musical portrayal of the poetic content, there is use of the tempers of Realism (even outright representational values) as well as Symbolism and Impressionism throughout the work, though they are subtly used. There is no underlying "literary program" as far as can be ascertained from Debussy's letters or the score itself. Rather, the entire work is a musical expression of the many mysteries, moods, memories, and impressions that were aroused in Debussy by the contemplation of the sea, which "held him with inescapable fascination." *The orchestration helps to create the form.*

The Impressionist movement at the end of the century represented a drawing together of the arts of literature, music, and painting to a far greater degree than before. For, once the elements of art were used primarily to suggest or symbolize, the processes of suggestion and symbolism tended to break down the barriers between the arts themselves so that they might coalesce more perfectly.

This synthesis of aesthetic effect has come to be known as *synesthesia*, which may be defined as the use in one art of effects and qualities properly belonging to another. In a narrower sense, synesthesia implies the transference of a sense impression of one kind to a sense impression of another kind. The most familiar example would be the vivid color associations produced in many people by music. The doctrine played an important part in aesthetic discussion at the turn of the century. Actually, the synesthesia of the Impressionists was the logical culmination of that drawing together of music, literature, and painting that characterized the early Romantic period. It carried the alliance of the arts to its farthest extreme—to the point where each not only was influenced by the others, but actually usurped the others' images and symbols.

Aesthetic synesthesia gave rise to much heated discussion among the aestheticians and aesthetes. The problem continually presented itself: to what extent should one art attempt to function in terms of another? Could it do so at all successfully? Did it enrich music to try to suggest the color richness of painting, the descriptive qualities of poetry, the "sounds and perfumes of the evening air"? This type of discussion was popular in a period of bold experimentation when the "art-for-art's-sake" tendency focused attention on the "how"—the manner and technique of art—rather than on the "what"—the content.

In listening to typical Impressionistic music, the sensuous appeal of instrumental colors, the effects of masses of tone and their contrasting values, and the perception of fragmentary and fleeting themes, or melodic figures, are infinitely more important than the discernment of thematic development. This is music for the senses and imagination rather than for the intellect, and it should make its appeal in the same manner. Thus we have not indulged in minute directions and analyses. Impressionism, above all else, requires a sympathetic attitude in listening. The listener is, more than ever before, "on his own."

MAURICE RAVEL (1875-1937)

The one contemporary of Debussy in France who shared something of his eminence was Maurice (Joseph) Ravel, who was born in Ciboure, Basses-Pyrenees, on March 7, 1875, and died in Paris on Dec. 28, 1937, following a brain operation. His formal musical education began at the early age of seven, but his major training began with his advanced classes at the Paris Conservatoire in 1891 when he was admitted to the classes of Charles de Bériot, the great violin virtuoso and teacher. In due time he advanced to the classes of Pessard, Gabriel Fauré (composition) and André Gédalge (counterpoint and fugue). He won the coveted *Prix de Rome* in 1901 with his cantata MYRRHA. The phenomenal popularity of his ballet BOLERO [8] has overshadowed his better works such as the ballets DAPHNIS ET CHLOÉ (1909–11 for Diaghilev the director of the famous Russian Ballet), and MA MÈRE L' OYE (Mother Goose Ballet-Suite, 1912). From then on his position in France was secure. Ravel composed works for piano, orchestra, opera, chamber music of various combinations, songs, and a number of orchestrations of other composers' works, such as Mussorgsky's PICTURES AT AN EXHIBITION, Chabrier's MENUET POMPEUX, and Debussy's L'APRÈS-MIDI D'UN FAUNE (for two pianos). It is erroneous to consider Ravel a mere imitator of Debussy. Although he was at home in the idiom of Impressionism, the perspective of time reveals increasingly an independent personality, witty and urbane, who, unlike the other French musicians of the period, was able to resist the overwhelming influence of Debussy and strike out on paths of his own. In him, the Impressionistic tendency was united with a stringent Classicism—he was completely sympathetic to the eighteenth-century forms—and to a kind of intellectual detachment that seemed to have descended to him from the classical masters. The poetic mistiness of Debussy gave place in Ravel to an incisive wit, a tongue-in-cheek sophistication. The twilight moodiness of the master of Impressionism was replaced in Ravel by a clarity and epigrammatic lightness: where Debussy worked in blending pastels, Ravel turned to the clear outline of the etcher. If Debussy leans to the mystical overtones, the hidden meanings that make him akin to Proust—was not Vinteuil in "Swann's Way" fashioned after him?—Ravel reveals another side of the French genius, the lightness and grace, the irony and sharp, clear thinking that we find in the writings of Anatole France, for example.

We have already presented Ravel's MOTHER GOOSE SUITE (see Chap. 11) as a splendid example of his feeling for instrumental color in the symphony orchestra, his charming melodic gift, and his ability of realistic musical description.

As an example of Ravel's ability to use these techniques to depict the atmosphere of ancient Greek scenes, while providing actual dance music for a ballet on the subject, we present:

[8] The BOLERO was written especially for Mlle. Rubinstein of the "Rubinstein Ballets" and received its première at the Paris Opera on Nov. 22, 1928. It is really a "stunt" in composition and orchestral techniques and skills. A trivial, wearisome theme, having a complex Spanish bolero rhythm, is constantly repeated in the same tonality until just before the climax. At each repetition of the theme, there is a building up of richer instrumentation and louder dynamic sonority until the perfectly timed climax arrives, and the noisy, discordant close follows soon afterward.

Courtesy of Art Institute of Chicago

BATHING NYMPHS AND CHILD Camille Corot

In several aspects, Corot is a Barbizon painter, one of those original painters who took the easel out-of-doors to paint nature as actually seen by the artist! In other ways, Corot may be considered a Romantic precursor of the French Impressionists. He was fond of restricting his range of colors from hazy grays to soft and diffused yellows—as though the scene were half concealed in a misty haze. The composition is often asymmetrical so as to emphasize its more significant parts and mood projections. His use of strong lighting effects with the contrasting darkness of the deep woods is striking.

"Daphnis and Chloé," Suite No. 2, for Orchestra

The score itself is the source for the following descriptive action of the three divisions of the suite, and if it is identified anew with the music as it passes by, the pleasure of listening will be greatly increased. The Ballet was first produced by the Ballet Russe in Paris in 1912, with the great artists Nijinsky and Karsavina taking the leading roles.

1. *Daybreak.* Daphnis lies stretched before the grotto of the nymphs. Little by little the day dawns. The songs of birds are heard. . . . Herdsmen enter, seeking Daphnis and Chloé. They find Daphnis and awaken him; in anguish he looks about for Chloé. She at last appears encircled by shepherdesses. The two rush into each other's arms. . . . The old shepherd Lammon explains that Pan saved Chloé (from the pirates) in remembrance of the nymph Syrinx, whom the god loved.
2. *Pantomime.* Daphnis and Chloé mime the story of Pan and Syrinx. Chloé impersonates the young nymph wandering over the meadow. Daphnis, as Pan, appears and declares his love for her. The nymph repulses him; the god becomes more insistent. She disappears among the rocks. In desperation he plucks some stalks, fashions a flute, and on it plays a melancholy tune. Chloé comes out and imitates by her steps the accents of the flute.
3. *General Dance.* The dance grows more and more animated. In mad whirlings, Chloé falls into the arms of Daphnis. Before the altar of the nymphs he swears his fidelity. Young girls appear; they are dressed as Bacchantes and shake their tambourines as they dance. Daphnis and Chloé embrace tenderly. A group of young men come on the stage. There is a joyous tumult, and a final, general dance.

OTTORINO RESPIGHI (1879–1936) AND HIS "FOUNTAINS OF ROME"

There is no question that the Impressionistic movement was closely identified with France, not only as the place of its inception but also as the country in which it reached its peak and practically exhausted itself as a movement. However, the French influences were felt in other European (as well as American and a few oriental) countries, not the least among which was Italy.

French Impressionism was skillfully combined with Italian tendencies toward lyricism, modality, fervent nationalism, and Romantic dramaturgical exposition in the genius of Ottorino Respighi (ress-PEÉ-ghēē). He was born in Bologna, July 9, 1879 and died in Rome, April 18, 1936. The Liceo Musicale at Bologna admitted Respighi at the age of twelve as a violinist. Later in 1898, he studied composition with Torchi and Martucci, and subsequently became a composition pupil of Rimsky-Korsakoff in St. Petersburg (1900) and with Max Bruch in Berlin (1902). Meanwhile, he had become a virtuoso concert violinist, and almost as capable on the piano, in addition to his career as a composer. In 1913, he became a professor of composition at the Liceo di Santa Cecilia in

Rome, a post he held until his death. Respighi's compositions include works for opera, ballet, piano, orchestra, songs, chamber music, etc.

Respighi is widely known for the fervent expressions of love for his country underlying the remarkable "Roman Cycle" of symphonic poems, or "essays," THE FOUNTAINS OF ROME (1917); THE PINES OF ROME (1924); THE FESTIVALS OF ROME (1928); plus the suite, VETRATE DI CHIESA ("The Church Windows," 1927, four impressions of famous stained glass church windows of Rome for orchestra, three of which were originally *Melodic Gregorian Preludes* for piano—the fourth, S. *Gregorio Magno,* "Saint Gregory the Great," according to the composer himself, was composed for orchestra especially for this suite.) In these works, Respighi succeeded in combining the medieval ecclesiastical modes and skillful counterpoint with modern tonalities and harmonic devices, romantic lyricism, and outstanding contemporary virtuoso skills in orchestration. (Note the use of a phonograph recording of a nightingale's song in the "Pines," and the exceptionally large orchestra, ear-splitting noises, and dynamic intensities in the "Festivals.") Above all, Respighi was immensely successful in creating poetic and idyllic moods to contrast with the intense dramatic climaxes and vividly convincing realism. He was one of the greatest masters in orchestration of all time.

In THE FOUNTAINS OF ROME, observe the slowly awakening *pastorale* of dawn with its suggestive sounds and moods. (Each section of this work depicts a certain Roman fountain at the hour of the day when it appeared to be most effective to the composer, as he disclosed to this writer, and he spent untold hours in discovering "just the right hour and moment of the day.") Observe the realistic depiction of the gushing waterfall that introduces section two (figure 14 in the score)—a real *tour de force* of orchestration, and one of the best of its nature to be found in music. Then also note—still in section two beginning at the onset, marked *Vivo*—the monotonously repeated French horn pedal-point on middle-C which continues unchanged throughout section two (the "Triton" fountain). Section three is a rather noisy, Wagner-like bedlam of sound, not all of which is good. In section four, ("The Fountain of Villa Medici at Sunset," marked *Andante* at figure 18 in the score), listen to the exquisite orchestral effects that Respighi has conjured up to suggest the dripping water of the slender spouting streams as they reach the summit of their arcs and lazily fall as individual drops into the fountain pool. The orange-red light of the setting sun shines through each drop, transforming it into a burst of sparkling colors, as though every stream of droplets were a diamond necklace suspended in the air. The impression of the fountain as a whole is indescribably beautiful—and so is the musical score! (Try to analyze the orchestral effects through hearing alone.) Another bit of musical magic in the score takes place five measures from the close and continuing to the end. As one rightly expects in Rome, the air of the early evening hour is filled with the sound of church bells, large and small, of all pitches. Respighi has given us a wonderful impression of this time of day; and especially an orchestral effect of the difference between the "ding" and the "dong" sounds as a large nearby bell swings to and fro. This is superb musical imagination and realism.

The composer himself wrote and attached the following program of THE FOUNTAINS OF ROME to the score:

PART I. *The Fountain of Valle Giulia at Dawn:* The first part of the poem, inspired by the Fountain of Valle Giulia, depicts a pastoral landscape; droves of cattle pass and disappear in the fresh damp mists of a Roman dawn. [Muted strings, oboes, and clarinets serve—just as they did in the days of Liszt—to suggest the diaphanous mists, the murmur of water, the pastoral scene.]

PART II. *The Triton Fountain at Dawn:* A sudden loud and insistent blast of horns above the trills of the whole orchestra introduces the second part, the Triton Fountain. It is like a joyous call, summoning troops of naiads and tritons, who come running up, pursuing each other and mingling in a frenzied dance between the jets of water.

PART III. *The Fountain of Trevi at Mid-Day:* Next there appears a solemn theme, borne on the undulations of the orchestra. It is the Fountain of Trevi at mid-day. The solemn theme, passing from the wood to the brass instruments, assumes a triumphal character. Trumpets peal; across the radiant surface of the water, there passes Neptune's chariot, drawn by sea-horses and followed by a train of sirens and tritons. The procession then vanishes, while faint trumpet blasts resound in the distance.

PART IV. *The Villa Medici Fountain at Sunset:* The fourth part, the Villa Medici Fountain, is announced by a sad theme, which rises above a subdued warbling. It is the nostalgic hour of sunset. The air is full of the sound of tolling bells, birds twittering, leaves rustling. Then all fades peacefully into the silence of the night.

ADDITIONAL SUGGESTIONS FOR LISTENING

Throughout this chapter we have named a number of works by Debussy, Ravel, and Respighi that might well serve as supplementary listening, and prompt the listener to discover other works through his own initiative. In addition to the works by Ravel already mentioned, the listener might be interested in: RHAPSODIE ESPAGNOLE, LA VALSE (a virtuoso orchestral work—"an apotheosis of the dance"); the chamber opera, L'HEURE ESPAGNOLE; STRING QUARTETTE IN F; and TZIGANE (a virtuoso violin piece). We offer the further suggestion and ardent hope that the vocal, piano, and chamber music of Alexander Tansman, the mature works of Duparc, Fauré, Franck, and others will be numbered among the listener's "finds." In Spain, Manuel de Falla (FAH-yah) has been most apt in adapting the technique of Impressionism to his native idioms. Try listening to his *Suite for Piano and Orchestra,* NOCHES EN LOS JARDINS DE ESPAÑA ("Nights in the Gardens of Spain"), in three parts.

A few of the outstanding Russian examples of Impressionism are: THE ENCHANTED LAKE by Anatol Liadov; certain sections of the *Symphonies,* the *Preludes* for the piano and some parts of the first five *Piano Sonatas* of Alexander

Scriabin; portions of Part II of Stravinsky's LE SACRE DU PRINTEMPS; DIE TOTENINSEL ("The Isle of the Dead") by Sergei Rachmaninoff; certain portions of works by Modest Mussorgsky that are not obviously realistic, especially those in A NIGHT ON BALD MOUNTAIN and PICTURES AT AN EXHIBITION (use the Ravel orchestration); and, of course, pertinent selections from the SCHEHERAZADE or ANTAR SUITES, SKAZKA, ("An orchestral fairy tale") or selections from the operas MAY NIGHT or COQ D'OR by Rimsky-Korsakoff. Then there are scattered bits in other works, such as ON THE STEPPES OF CENTRAL ASIA by Alexander Borodin.

In Great Britain, there are a number of Impressionists, outstanding among whom is Cyril Scott with his once popular LOTUS LAND, DANSE NÈGRE, JUNGLE BOOK IMPRESSIONS, and the *Overture* to PELLÉAS ET MÉLISANDE (which preceded Debussy's opera of the same title). Frederick Delius (1862–1934) is perhaps most closely identified with Impressionism, with such works as: ON HEARING THE FIRST CUCKOO IN SPRING, which is built around a Norwegian folk-tune "*I Ola Dalom*" ("In Ola Valley," a theme that Grieg also used in his Op. 66, No. 14), BRIGG FAIR, IN A SUMMER GARDEN, SEA DRIFT, on a Walt Whitman poem; *The Walk to the Paradise Garden,* from the opera A VILLAGE ROMEO AND JULIET; and the tone-poem, PARIS. The melodic, chromatic, and harmonic counterpoint, subtle compositional uses of the theme-and-variations technique, the vague, ever-changing moods, melodic lyricism, fascinatingly blended orchestral colors—these are most salient in his works. Ralph Vaughan Williams has also written many pages employing the Impressionistic temper—along with other tempers. Such expressions may be found in A LONDON SYMPHONY (1914 revised 1920), the PASTORAL SYMPHONY (1922) and the SYMPHONY NO. 6 IN E MINOR, especially in the extraordinarily impressionistic, meditative, and mystical final movement which the composer has titled *Epilogue.*

The United States was influenced by the spirit of French Impressionism. THROUGH THE LOOKING GLASS SUITE FOR ORCHESTRA, Op. 12, a successful work by Deems Taylor, contains many pages of romantic Impressionism and Realism —and marked influences of Richard Strauss; better, are parts of the "Dreaming True" scenes in his opera, PETER IBBETSON. Before him, Arthur Foote (1853–1937) of the "Boston School" wrote some effective examples of this temper, joined with Romantic lyricism, especially in his NIGHT PIECE FOR FLUTE AND STRING QUARTET, and his undeservedly neglected OMAR KHAYYÁM SUITE for piano. Henry Hadley (1871–1937), also of the "Boston School" wrote some realistic and impressionistic pages, especially in the orchestral suites ORIENTAL, SILHOUETTES, SAN FRANCISCO, and STREETS OF PEKIN, and other works including selected passages from his operas AZORA and CLEOPATRA'S NIGHT. Among the more outspoken disciples of Impressionism is Charles Martin Loeffler (1861–1935); of his works, we suggest A PAGAN POEM (after Virgil), Op. 14, for orchestra, and LA MORT DE TINTAGILES (after Maeterlinck), Op. 6, for full orchestra and *viola d'amore,* and other works. It is believed by many that Loeffler, Griffes, and Debussy discovered many Impressionistic techniques quite independently of one another—"it was in the artistic air of the time." Edward MacDowell is usually spoken of as a thorough-going Romanticist with strong nationalistic traits; quite right as far as it goes, but he was also one of the earliest if not the *first* American Impressionist. In fact, many of MacDowell's shorter piano works are perfect gems of the use of the temper of lyrical

Impressionism. In his larger works, one finds the use of the Impressionistic temper here and there, but we point out especially the *Slow Movement* of the SONATA EROICA, Op. 50 for piano, marked *"Tenderly, longingly, yet with passion,"* which, according to the composer, is woven around the thoughts, feelings and "impressions" aroused by the "imagined picture" of Guinevere in the Arthurian legend. We should certainly include parts of the SUITE NO. 1 FOR ORCHESTRA, Op. 42, with the movement (No. 3) *"October."* Charles Tomlinson Griffes (1884–1920), was one of America's most gifted and promising composers, and one of our early Impressionists, whose career was so prematurely ended. Listen to his symphonic poem, THE PLEASURE DOME OF KUBLA KHAN, which is generally believed to be his most important work; *The White Peacock*, re-composed from the ROMAN SKETCHES for piano, 1917, should be a "must"; THREE TONE PICTURES, Op. 5; and for sterner stuff, the wonderful, prophetic, and neglected SONATA IN F (1921) for piano. (Here, in this composer's better works, is to be found excellent craftsmanship, poetic feeling for form and content, a highly original idiom of harmonic color, oriental idioms and thematic invention, together with vigor, strength, and varied rhythmic expression, which are all too rare at any stage in our nation's musical history.) John Alden Carpenter (1875–1951) was one of our best equipped and most able craftsmen: hear his SEA DRIFT, a beautiful, Impressionistic tone poem; the Lake Scene from his ballet suite, ADVENTURES IN A PERAMBULATOR (see also Chap. 11 for his SKYSCRAPERS BALLET.)

Courtesy Art Institute of Chicago

TRINITY (OIL ON CANVAS) Charles Howard

Howard, an American, was one of the English surrealist group, but there are suggestions of realism in this painting which may be variously interpreted. As with most abstract art, the observer should not read into the work representation or any semblance of realism. Rather, take the work in and for itself as design, pattern, lines, masses, composition, etc. View it repeatedly with a will for understanding.

30 Expressionism and other contemporary trends: four modern composers

The average listener, as we have previously observed, usually feels more "at home" with the music and other Fine Arts that have been created during the century past than with the arts of the present.[1] As a rule it is also difficult to enjoy and understand the music of the distant past or from unfamiliar peoples. The art of the "*avant-garde*" is generally bewildering and often distasteful, enigmatic and even repellent. Neither amateur nor professional should be berated for these natural reactions for they are commonplace, world-wide, and varied in degree even in the metropolitan cities, where there are more frequent opportunities for contact with esoteric and radical works. Perhaps no other period in art history has more pointedly

[1] Essential listening for this chapter includes: the orchestral suite, LE SACRE DU PRINTEMPS by Igor Stravinsky; the melodramatic chamber music setting of PIERROT LUNAIRE by Arnold Schönberg; the orchestral suite MATHIS DER MALER by Paul Hindemith; and the FOURTH SYMPHONY IN A-MINOR, Op. 63, by Jean Sibelius.

and eloquently exemplified the principal of cause and effect in the artistic expression of the cultural and social ideals of the various ethnic and social groups than the present century. This has come about, we believe, because the creative artists have, save for several exceptions, enjoyed greater facilities and freedom of expression and exhibition. The exceptions have been in Germany under Hitler, in Italy under Mussolini, behind the "Iron Curtain," and in a number of countries and religious sects which are restricted by traditions. Recent years have provided a more fertile soil and climate for experimentation; an opportunity to break away from what some creative artists felt were restraining circumstances for the fullest freedom in individual expression. With such sudden opportunities it was not unexpected that the experimental creative artist would mount his horse and rapidly race in all directions at once. These confused artists suddenly found themselves in an equally confused world.

The very mention of the term "contemporary art" reminds one of its vagueness and ambiguity. Our present use of the term "modern art" is said by many critical writers to apply more precisely to the various radical styles that began to appear in France and Germany, and some in England and America, around 1850. These styles of art expression came to fruition before and immediately following the First World War.[2] The "ultra-modern" movements, with their increased strangeness and still wider breach from artistic traditions, may be said to have come forth slightly prior to and immediately after the Second World War. The reader should use these dates merely as rough guide posts rather than fixed points in history, for the vital changes in art forms and styles are singularly indifferent to the calendar as such. Prof. Pitirim A. Sorokin points out that there are and always have been variable time-lags between social and cultural conditions and sundry causations, and their manifestations in the various media of the Fine Arts.[3] This analysis may be applied to the present discussion of social and other causes and their artistic effects. It is well to bear in mind that the two World Wars were to a great degree symptoms and consequences of the then existing social, political, and spiritual conditions. However, these wars, as with most major conflicts, became generating causations of turbulent conditions.

[2] The first International Art Exhibition of "modern" art from France, Germany, Austria, and other countries was given in 1913 in the New York City Armory and at the Art Institute of Chicago. It consisted of typical examples of Impressionism, Cubism, Expressionism, Futurism, *"Les Fauves,"* Vorticism, Dynamism, etc. Among the exhibits were the paintings, THE BLUE NUDE by Matisse (later burned in effigy by Chicago art students), the cubistic DANCE AT THE SPRING by Picabia, the popular NUDE DESCENDING A STAIRCASE by Duchamp, and a number of canvases by Picasso. Also there were the sculptures, KNEELING WOMAN by Lehmbruck, THE KISS and MLLE. POGANY by Brancusi (see elsewhere in this chapter).

[3] Pitirim A. Sorokin, *Social and Cultural Dynamics* (New York: American Book Co., 1937) Vol. I, Chap. V.

As a result of these upheavals, mankind often became bewildered, skeptical, and protesting, thus losing contemplative calm and inspirational spirituality.

The world of creative art has naturally been deeply affected and distorted, both as a symptom of the times and as a consequence and source of artistic influence. Many creative artists became so disturbed by the wars that they, too, lost their direction. Consequently, communication between the creator and appreciator has often been obscured, confused, or entirely absent. Artistic criteria were lost or confused.

Some creative artists have substituted mere technical skill, novelty, and even unintelligibility for those artistic qualities that appreciators have always looked for and enjoyed. Others have deliberately cast to the winds the traditions of many centuries, flinging tones, paints, and words hither and thither. Still others substituted mere novelty for genuine artistic expression. We do not wish to imply that this century has not produced some excellent, serious artists, nor that sincere artistic experimentation and exploration should be curtailed by any force save the creator's own artistic conscience and the ultimate verdict of the public which no artist can escape. In the long-run, it is the art-loving public which determines, by means of its support, indifference, or condemnation of what the artists produce, the very conditions that affect creators. The public provides the soil of fertility or sterility for artistic expression in all media. During the course of many years, the likes and dislikes of the public operate automatically, the experts and professionals notwithstanding. Of course, the worthy, sincere, and dedicated artist, be he a novelist, poet, composer, painter, sculptor, architect, or whatever, is rarely so insincere after reaching personal and artistic maturity as not to have unquestioned artistic integrity and a firm expressive personality. Transient fads and innovations affect him little, though subtle influences are ever at work.

The average appreciator, as well as the critic, is bewildered and often disturbed upon seeing the supposedly serious art works of the post-war periods: the kindergarten-like pastings or montages, twisted hay-wire, wrought iron puzzlements, or "what are they"? Amidst these have appeared paintings of astonishing photographic realism, with a technique reminiscent of Holbein—such as a weather-beaten barn door covered with sundry articles, implements, musical instruments, newsclippings, programs, and whatnot. These painters often have an abundance of technic but little of what that technic should be for.[4] Some painters lean to the use of a fence painter's air brush. Others, in order to catch the artist's

[4] As an example of this sort of photographic realism, see painting, OLD MODELS by William Harnett in *Art and Life in America* by Oliver W. Larkin (New York: Rinehart and Co., 1949), p. 266.

Courtesy the Artist

EDGE OF DARKNESS (COLORED ETCHING) Ernest Freed

This is an unusual, highly original, and artistically significant tinted etching by an American artist. It is 24 by 18 inches, yet the artist has succeeded in tying together this large space and bringing about interesting internal designs, rhythms, masses, contrasts, and delightful round-about eye movements; while, at the same time, indulging in free extemporization (more vivid in the original color). The outstretched arm and upturned hand are of symbolic and allegorical significance—and a gesture to romantic realism.

most fleeting expressions, squeeze paint tubes or pour the paint directly onto the canvas.[5]

In one amusing incident, a group of Parisian artists, in protest against the atrocious art being exhibited by the "Salon des Indépendants," tied a paint brush to a donkey's wagging tail, brought the canvas close up

[5] Photographs of some of these types may be seen in the interesting book, *Abstract Painting and Sculpture in America* by Andrew C. Ritchie (New York: Museum of Modern Art, 1951).

to it, dipped the brush in different colors, and stimulated the "artistic feelings" of the donkey by feeding it sugar cubes. The resulting smear "painting" was subsequently submitted, under a fictitious name, to the show. It was accepted and gained enthusiastic encomiums from the Parisian "radicals" and the critical press.[6]

One of the most striking and widespread movements in art to come out of the turmoil of the present century is Expressionism. However, there is such a wide variety of techniques and styles employed, to say nothing of "states of mind" of the creators, that the movement has not yet jelled. The course that the movement has taken in various countries leaves confusion as to its basic techniques and philosophy. Elie Faure says that Expressionism is perhaps nothing but the temper of Impressionism "passing from the French objectivism to German subjectivism, from the plastic plane to the musical plane."[7] The devotees of Expressionism nowadays generally insist upon self-expression at any cost and by any means, as long as it is deeply personal.

Sheldon Cheney believes that Cézanne was the inspirational "high priest" of early expressionistic techniques and principles.[8] However, traces of the expressionistic temper were exhibited long before Cézanne by such painters as Matthias Grünewald (1500–1530), El Greco (1548–1625), and others. In the opinion of this author, Cézanne was the leader of the post-impressionistic style, originator of the fundamental principles of cubistic abstraction, and the unquestioned prophet of Expressionism. He is one of the great painters of all time. His work reveals extraordinary technique, great originality, keen insight, intellectuality, and highly controlled emotional expression. He took nature as he visualized it and resolved it into a fundamental aesthetic of mobile color, related and contrasting masses of "cone, cylinder and cube abstractionism" without losing contact with reality.

The French school of Expressionism, with its traditional Gallic love for logic and order and brilliant artistic techniques, was for a time content to leave the "emotional sprees" to the Germans. Thus the French artists stressed intellectuality and sensual and emotional effects in the uses of color within the bounds of rationality (*ethos*) and the then newly discovered techniques of painting. These attributes may be observed in Matisse, with his planar, Oriental-like decorative pattern (see THE GIRL IN THE PURPLE ROBE in Chap. 16); Paul Gauguin in his exotic, colorful, basically primitive paintings of the Tahitian natives; the tragic Vincent van Gogh with his excessive emotionalism, striking, contrasting, mobile color and forms, and great stress upon compositional

[6] See F. W. Ruckstull, *Great Works of Art* (Garden City, N.Y.: Garden City Pub. Co., 1925), pp. 449-459.

[7] Elie Faure, *History of Art*, trans. Walter Pach (New York: Harper, 1924), Vol. V, p. 473.

[8] Sheldon Cheney, *Expressionism in Art* (New York: Tudor Pub. Co., 1948 ed.).

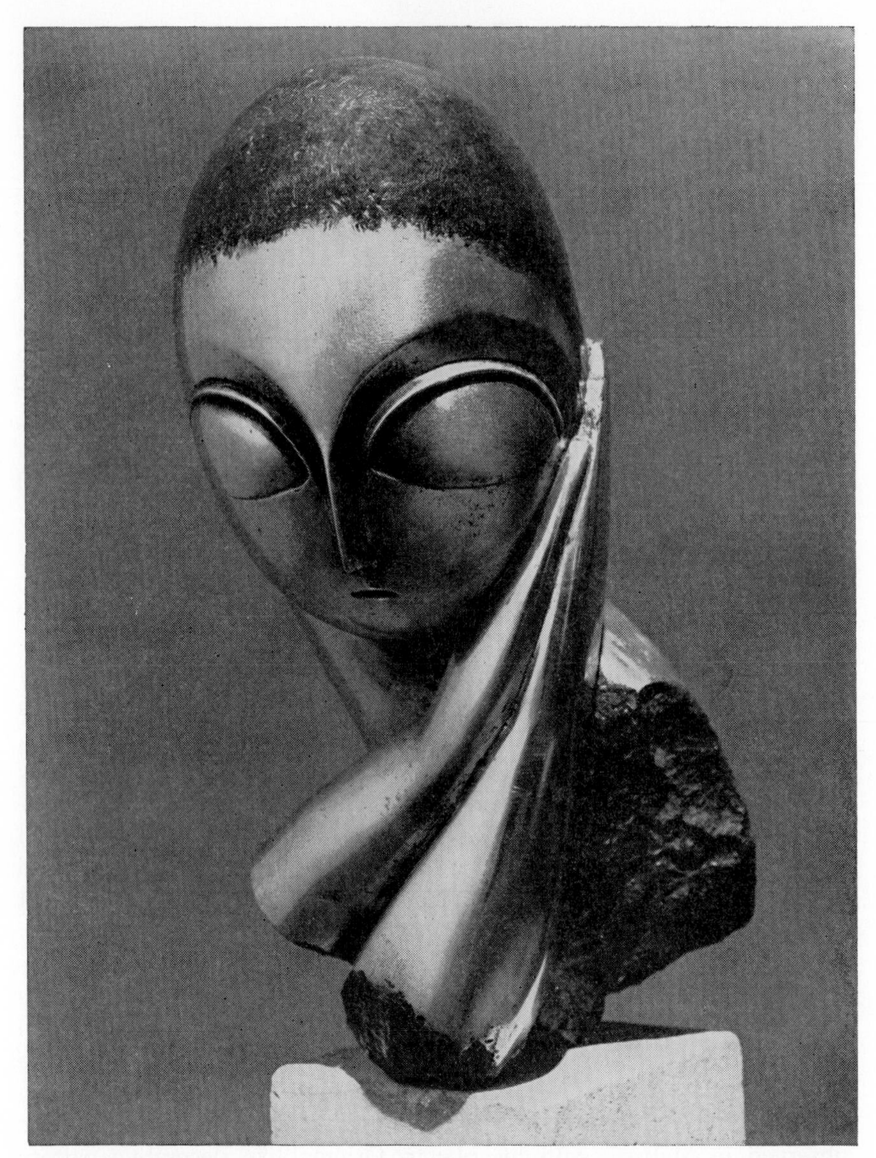

Collection of the Museum of Modern Art, New York

MLLE. POGANY Constantin Brancusi

An example of a quasi-abstract art. Original of polished silver. A number of versions were subsequently made by Brancusi. The bust above has a suggestion of a close cut coiffure. Note the exaggerated eyes, nose and mouth, used presumably to avoid realism. The flirtatious or pensive pose of the head nestled against the palmed hands conveys an emotional as well as a compositional value.

lines and masses; Georges Rouault's heavy dark outlines suggesting stained glass cathedral windows; and, of course, in many works of the Spanish experimenter and master painter, Pablo Picasso.

Expressionism in Germany manifested itself in a daring and distinctive manner. It soon became divided into two rather separate groups. The first appeared about 1903 with such painters as Max Pechstein, Ludwig Kirchner, George Grosz, and Emil Nolde, whose emphases were upon emotional impulses (pathos) and their unhampered expression. Another of this group was the Austro-Czech, Oscar Kokoschka, who sought to depict the subjective feelings aroused by realities in an art which he called "soul-expression." Their paintings were often marked by dark outlines and thick, palette-knife application of striking colors for psychological effect. The second group emerged about 1911 and includes the Swiss dadaist-expressionist, Paul Klee with his witty implications and whimsical fantasy, Marc Chagall, Franz Marc with his horses, and the Russian, Vasily Kandinsky. One should also include such sculptors as Ernst Barlach, and William von Lehmbruck, whose KNEELING WOMAN is familiar. THE ENCYCLOPEDIA OF THE ARTS gives four categories of Expressionism: (1) *Subjective,* based upon untrammeled expression of emotion; (2) *Objective,* where the artist paints the expressive character of natural objects rather than a true likeness; (3) *Abstractionism,* consisting of non-real designs, geometric forms, and lines; (4) *Magic, Realism,* and *Surrealism,* which do not entirely lose their contact with representation and nature.

Among the American artists who were contemporary with, or variously influenced by the German Expressionists of the first group are such painters as Albert Ryder, Robert Henri, Morgan Russell, Charles Howard, Charles Burchfield, William Gropper, Ben Shahn, and Philip Evergood; and the sculptors include the early works of William Zorach (he is now really a neo-classical expressionist) and the expatriate Sir Jacob Epstein. Occasional touches of the expressionistic temper are found in the works of Gutzon Borglum, George Gray Bernard, and Robert Garrison whose work can be seen at New York's Rockefeller Center and the Riverside Church. Among European sculptors were the expressionistic-abstractionists, such as Brancusi, Meštrovič, Lipchitz, and others of similar trends.

In literature the expressionistic influence is evident in such works as: EIMI by e. e. cummings; the experimental poems of Arthur Rimbaud; the novel, FINNEGAN'S WAKE by James Joyce, THE WASTE LAND of T. S. Eliot, and THE HAIRY APE by Eugene O'Neill.

The complexity of music has likewise increased greatly since about 1850, and this complexity has made greater demands upon the listener. The basic elements of music have undergone more or less radical changes since Wagner first startled the world with TRISTAN AND ISOLDE in 1865. Wagner's work was not solely responsible for the many changes and innovations; rather, his music and ideas served as a source of technique and influence in the general movement towards newer and more fertile fields of exploration which has continued to the present.

According to the many polls and tests made by this author over the years, some of the factors in contemporary music that often disturb a great percentage of listeners and tend to isolate them from the composer and his music are: the predominant and generally considered excessive use of noise, harmonic discord, or dissonance; the lack of fairly obvious underlying metrical and rhythmic designs; and the absence of lyrical melody, the comfortable feeling of tonality, and readily felt emotional content. The complicated structural forms that are generally used do not help the average listener very much, either.

Let us consider melody, which, along with harmony and counterpoint, has undergone radical changes. The melodies of today are not often of the long lyrical line which once was standard. Some can hardly be called melodies at all, certainly not in the same sense that characterized the "singing," "voice-like" melodies of the past. It is not the prevailing practice of the *avant-garde* among contemporary composers to write such extended lyrical melodies as Bach's *Air* from the THIRD ORCHESTRAL SUITE IN D MAJOR, Beethoven's *Andante cantabile* from his SONATA FOR PIANO, Op. 13, or the arias, *I Know that My Redeemer Liveth* from Handel's MESSIAH, *If With All Your Hearts* from Mendelssohn's ELIJAH, or those found in the lieder of Schubert and Brahms. Modern composers are often more concerned with the technical intricacies in the intellectual compositional development of fragmentary tonal figures. Naturally, there are many contemporary composers who still respect traditional ideas of melody, but their works are modified by individual characteristics and contemporary trends. Among these are Bernard Rogers, SOLILOQUY FOR FLUTE AND STRINGS and Samuel Barber, ADAGIO FOR STRINGS.

Ever since the "golden age of singing" of the seventeenth century, the Italian school of composers and its initiators in other lands have sought novel means of using the solo voice, especially in the frequent *fioriture* and *cadenzas*. An outgrowth of these effects has been the songs, entitled *Vocalise,* such as those by Rachmaninoff and Respighi. Later, comparable novelties were also sought in many choral works, among which is this author's *Ave Maria* for mixed chorus. In these songs neutral syllables are used, rather than poetic verse, in order to achieve certain vocal or atmospheric, instrumental-like effects. Beautiful examples of these mystic and atmospheric impressionistic techniques are to be heard in Debussy's Nocturne, *Sirènes,* and Ravel's ballet, DAPHNIS AND CHLOÉ. Because of the trend of a number of contemporary composers to treat the voice instrumentally and compositionally as a member of the ensemble, brief and fragmentary ideas have been used to develop a distinct technique, as may be heard in some works by Schönberg, von Webern,

Courtesy Paul Rosenberg and Co. Loaned to Museum of Modern Art

THE THREE MUSICIANS Picasso

Around 1920, Picasso became interested in painting figures of Greek and Roman mythology—his "Neo-Classical" period. In 1921, he returned to cubism, and in the summer painted two pictures, both called THREE MUSICIANS. *The cut above is the first of the two. Here the artist is concerned with a synthetic cubism, its "rectilinear phase." The picture shows, left to right, a clarinet-playing Pierrot, a Harlequin guitarist, and an organ-playing Monk, judged by their gay, colorful and festive costumes and masks. There is a strange, mixed mood of incongruity, humor, gaiety of coloring, and overhanging somberness evident in this picture. The three-dimensional planes of the human figure are reduced to simple mass and structural planes of two dimensions, but realities are not completely abandoned.*

and others. Following are two typical examples of the quasi-instrumental treatment of the voice. The first (Example "A") is from "*Das Augenlicht*" (literally, "The Eye-light"; idiomatically, "The Bright Side") by Anton von Webern, from Op. 26. The second (Example "B") is from "*Der Mondfleck*" (The Patch of Moonlight) from PIERROT LUNAIRE, Op. 21, by Arnold Schönberg. Note that these examples have a deliberate non-tonality, and observe the non-lyrical nature of the voice parts and the constantly varying rhythmic patterns. The small cross marks on the stems of the Schönberg illustration indicate that the voice is to use a sort of half-sung and half-spoken *sprechstimme* technique which sounds very odd and disturbing to many.

Although musical rhythm and the poetic patterns of the metrical foot were discussed in an earlier chapter, we have hardly touched upon the term meter as it applies to music. Meter, as used in music, may be broadly defined as an arrangement of groups of beats or sounds in regulated patterns of accented and unaccented pulses, to form, regulate, and maintain a freely flowing rhythmic movement. The metrical design of sounds or beats is a stolid *cantus firmus,* or "complementary foil," upon which the varied and free rhythmic designs in the melody, harmony, counterpoint, tempo, and even a number of successive rests may be most effectively written and perceived.[9] There are countless instances when the metrical patterns of beats or pulses may themselves be primarily due to time duration, differences, or even interspersed rests. At other times, after the pulse-accent pattern has been more or less fixed, the effect of the repeated metrical pattern may be affected through memory, imagination, or compounded stresses in simultaneously played metrical patterns of differing designs, as happens in combining $\frac{3}{4}$ meter with $\frac{2}{4}$, where the strong stresses of each coincide and reinforce each other every third measure of the $\frac{3}{4}$ meter, as follows:

2/4 UM-ti/	UM-ti/	UM-ti/	[UM]-ti/	UM etc.
3/4 UM-ti-ti/	UM-ti-ti/	UM-ti-ti/	[UM]-ti-ti/	etc.

The metrical pattern may also be propelled by residual kinesthetic impulses. In addition, the metrical foot-pattern may, under certain circumstances, have both primary and secondary accents, as in some $\frac{6}{8}$ meter patterns.

Now let us observe how one of the modernists, Igor Stravinsky, handles metrical and rhythmic variety and sequence in the *Mock-Abduction,*

[9] Apropos of the propulsive and dramatic effects of the onrush of the tempo plus the meter against the rhythmic flow and the rests, it would be difficult to find better examples than the stunning effects to be found in the climax just before the coda (*Più allegro,* faster, "cut-time," four-four time or meter, with but two beats to the measure) in the finale of SYMPHONY NO. 1 IN C MINOR by Brahms, Op. 68 (at one measure before letter "M" in the score, and later six measures before the letter "N" in the score.)

section four of Part I, of LE SACRE DU PRINTEMPS, concert version. From the score number [39], there appear in passing (with some repetitions) to number [48] the following metrical and time signatures that the listener should *feel* rather than *analyze:*

4/8, 5/8, 9/8, 12/8, 9/8 (4/8 plus 5/8), (5/8 plus 4/8), 6/8, 7/8, 3/4, 6/8, 2/4, 6/8, 3/4, 9/8, 3/8, 5/8, 3/8, 4/8, 5/8, 6/8, 5/8, 2/8, 6/8, (3/4), (6/8), 2/8, 6/8, 4/8 (2/4), 6/8, 3/4, 4/8 (2/4), 3/4 and 4/4!

Little wonder that there is confusion on the part of the listener as well as the performers!

Dissonance in harmony is no longer considered a novelty and, in certain compositional techniques, seems to have reached its saturation point for musical effectiveness. Thus, there is already to be observed a definite return to more traditional harmonic systems, "spiced up" here and there with well-placed dissonances and rejuvenated contrapuntal devices in which novel harmonic inventions are "toned-down." The techniques of most composers have undergone great, fundamental changes in music, as they have in painting, sculpture, and other Fine Arts. No one knows for certain in what direction the arts will go, but we venture a guess that the untrammeled uses of the Classical-Expressionistic and Realistic tempers which now dominate music and the other arts will be replaced by increased uses of Romantic (guided emotionalism) and Symbolic tempers.

Now let us examine and analyze several of the harmonic "idioms" that may befuddle the average listener. It might be well first to review the familiar "common chord" or "chord of nature," the triad. This is a chord of three tones, or four if one of them is doubled. This *major triad* is a smooth, consonant chord which has been the very foundation of traditional Occidental music. The series of natural overtones, or partials, was figured out from a vibrating string by Pythagoras, an ancient Greek philosopher and mathematician. Below we show the harmonic series, or overtones upon a fundamental tone—in this case C_{-2}—as this series is analyzed up to and including the sixteenth *partial.* We have placed crossmarks above the notes that are somewhat out of pitch with the same tones of our modern equal tempered tuning system. Notice the *minor triad* consists of partials six, seven and nine. It is less stable, defined, and consonant than the *major triad*—the fourth, fifth, and sixth partials.

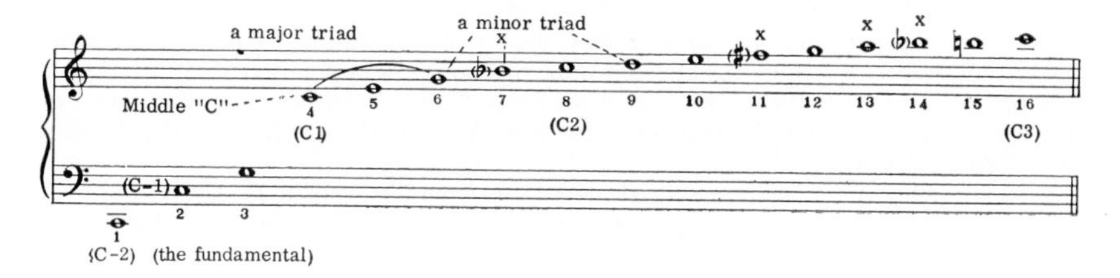

It is likely that one of the earliest users of the simultaneous sounding triad-chord construction was Guillaume Dufay (Netherlands, c. 1400–1474). However that may be, composers after Dufay soon began to use other chords, consisting of still more added thirds to a root-tone. They eventually constructed these chords upon all degrees, or steps, of the key-scale and chromatic scale. Besides, they raised or lowered any of these tones a half or a whole step by placing an *accidental* before the desired note.[10] In the following illustration, we show a triad, "A," a chord of the seventh, "B," a chord of the ninth, "C," a chord of the eleventh, "D," a chord of the thirteenth, "E," and, with the addition of another third, at "F," we show how the series of superimposed-thirds construction begins all over again on the same root but in a different octave. All these chords are shown as being built upon the root-tone "C."

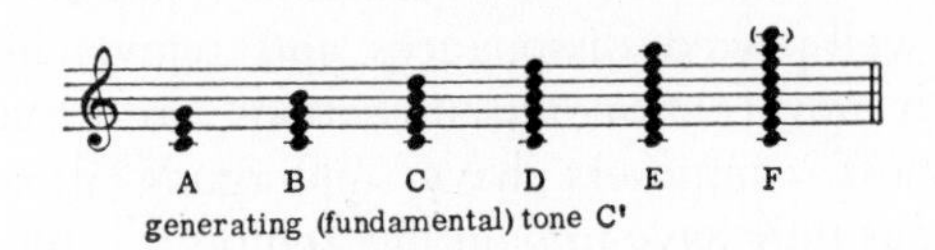

These methods reached their climax in the chromaticism of Richard Wagner, especially in TRISTAN AND ISOLDE and in the tone poem, EIN HELDENLEBEN, "A Hero's Life," by Richard Strauss. Since then there has appeared a long line of experimenters and iconoclasts who strongly felt a need for more varied and promising sources of compositional techniques. These included Erik Satie (1866–1925),[11] a forerunner of French impressionism, with his many musical eccentricities and free uses of the dominant chords (those constructed upon the fifth step of a key); Claude Debussy (1862–1918) with his impressionistic techniques and exhaustive uses of the whole-tone scale and, at that time, strange harmonic and orchestral effects; Frederick Delius (1862–1934) with his chromatic harmonies and harmonic counterpoint; Ferruccio Busoni (1866–1924) with his invented scales and harmonies; Arnold Schönberg (1874–1951) with his realization and perfection of the equal-tempered, "twelve-tone row" techniques and his great structural skills; the Moravian, Aloïs Haba; and the Americans, Hans Barth and Joseph Schillinger (1895–1943), with their preoccupation with microtones, especially one-third, one-quarter, one-eighth, and even one-sixteenth of a tone!

We have previously discussed the traditional system of harmony by

[10] Thus a flat lowered the pitch a half step, a double-flat a whole step; a sharp raised the pitch of the note a half step, and the double-sharp raised it a whole step. A natural sign cancelled the effect of a previous sharp or flat on a specific note. See also *Music Notation and Terminology* by Karl W. Gehrkens (New York: Ludlow Bros., 1942), Chap. III.

[11] Along with Satie were included devotees generally known as the *Groupe de Six* ("Group of Six"), including Honegger, Milhaud, Auric, Germaine Tailleferre, Durey, and Poulenc.

superimposing one or more thirds upon a root-tone. Here follow four musical illustrations which show erstwhile radical constructions of chords by means other than that of added thirds. "A" is a chord made by capriciously or orderly superimposing fourths; "B," in fifths; "C" in seconds; and "D" in sevenths. The twelve-tone, equal-tempered scale (half-steps) is preserved, however, though any of the tones of the various chords may be altered by the use of accidentals, or freely transposed. These chords are often used for their novel harmonic color, voice leading con-

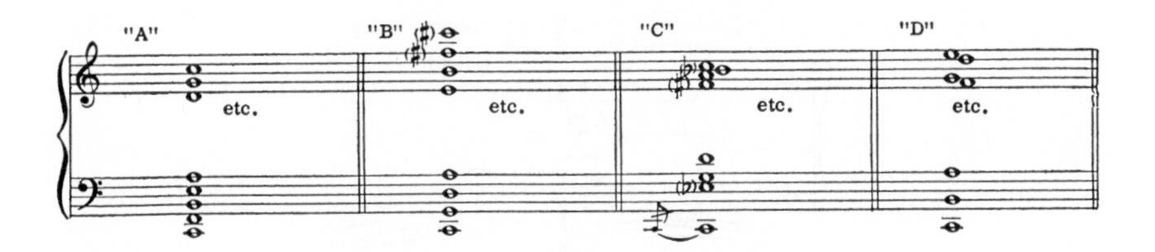

sequents, or for deliberate biting, klang, or shock effects. Other novel harmonic effects, where the obviously percussive "tonklang" and rhythmic use of the chords are stressed, are shown in the following musical illustrations from two early American expressionists, Leo Ornstein (1905–) and Charles Ives (1875–1954). From the latter, we show a "tone cluster," or "tonklang," from the *Hawthorne* movement of his SECOND PIANO SONATA, the "Concord" (1920), as Mus. Ill. "E"; and from Ornstein, reductions from IMPRESSIONS DE LA TAMISE, Op. 13, No. 1, as Mus. Ill. "F," and another Mus. Ill. "G," *Dance of the Dead,* from the POEMS OF 1917. We have also included an excerpt from the second number of THREE PASTELS FOR ORCHESTRA (1912),[12] by Edwin John Stringham, as Mus. Ill. "H." This last excerpt is used here to illustrate the employment of polytonality, the writing of parts or chords in two or more different keys, sounding simultaneously. Stravinsky uses this technique frequently in LE SACRE DU PRINTEMPS, Milhaud in most of his early works for chamber music or orchestra, and Cyril Scott in SONATA FOR VIOLIN AND PIANOFORTE, Op. 59.

(*To be played with a board 14¾ inches long and heavy enough to hold down piano keys)

[12] A piano solo version of the THREE PASTELS by Stringham is also available. (New York: Edward Marks, 1942.)

There were other novel methods of harmonic construction. One of these was that originated by the Russian, Alexander Scriabin (1872–1915). While he based his "system" within the conventional, equal-tempered, diatonic, and chromatic tonal traditions, he contrived to incorporate into his harmonic structures the higher portions of the overtone series, plus certain aspects of chords built upon superimposed fourths (perfect or altered) together with some thirds, as in Mus. Ill. "K" given below. These chords were dubbed "mystic chords" by Scriabin's biographer, A. Englefield Hull, and an arbitrary, harmonic-like formation served as the thematic as well as harmonic bases for a definite work. Scriabin drew freely upon the tempers of Classicism, Romanticism, and Expressionism in his emotional as well as rationalized techniques. The following musical illustrations are "mystic chords" reduced respectively from Scriabin's SONATAS FOR PIANO—the *Sixth,* Op. 62, "J," the *Seventh,* Op. 64, "K," the *Eighth,* Op. 66, "L"; and "M" is from *Two Piano Pieces,* Op. 57. These should give the reader a clear and general idea of the basic harmonic techniques used by this mystic and theosophical composer.

"J" "K" "L" "M"

Another group of innovators, who can best be described as a "noise-making, ultra-realistic, charivari cult," is exemplified by George Antheil (1900–) and his BALLET MÉCHANIQUE, and THE IRON FOUNDRY and other works by Alexander Mossoloff (1900–). Some may recall the early realistic works by Arthur Honegger (1892–), RUGBY and PACIFIC 231 (an imitation of the noises of a heavy freight locomotive); or, one might choose the emotionally descriptive WILD MAN'S DANCE by Leo Ornstein, and Henry Cowell's (1897–) BATH OF TONE played on the piano by hands, fists, and forearms.

The real flowering of a radically different system of musical techniques concerning tonality, scales, melody, harmony, counterpoint, and even internal structural designs was due to Josef Hauer (1893–), who anticipated Schönberg and his "School" in the use of the "tone-row," especially after his THREE KLAVIERSTÜCKE, Op. 11. There followed a host of "tone-row" users, among whom were Anton von Webern, Egon Wellesz, Alban Berg, Louis Krasner, and Ernst Křenek. All these, to a greater or less degree, use the "tone-row" system or some variant. The influence of these foreign composers spread to the United States through their music, their pupils, and their actual teaching in this country. An American, Roger Sessions, has adopted a somewhat modified "tone-row" system and has written a text to expound his ideas.

Following are a couple of examples of Schönberg's rows: the first, "N," is reduced from the *Valse*, one of his FIVE PIANO PIECES, Op. 23; and the second, "O," from his STRING QUARTET NO. 3, Op. 30. Note that these "rows" consist of twelve tones such as may be found in a portion of a chromatic-like series of tones. The "row" is not to be considered a scale. Unlike the chromatic series, however, all semblances to, and dependence upon, a tonal center, or key-tone, are absent in the *arbitrary* arrangement of the "row" and its compositional functions.

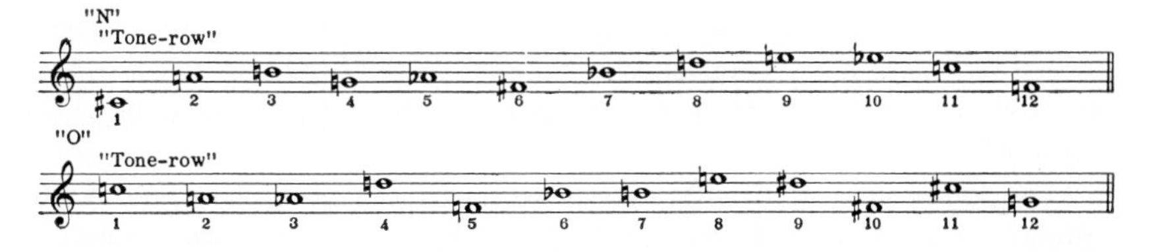

The aesthetic and technical functions of the chromatic scale and "tone-rows" are basically unlike. There are prescribed rules for the strict observances of "tone-row" techniques. Some of these, according to Egon Wellesz, one of Schönberg's pupils, are: (1) the tones of the "row" are to appear in a piece of music as in the sequences of the row itself; (2) no tone is to be repeated until the entire row has been used; (3) the tones of the row are to serve vertically (harmonically) as well as horizontally (as in generating motives, or counterpoint without "foreign tones" being interposed); (4) chromatic half-steps, or even whole-steps, in contiguous sequences are to be avoided along with the slightest likelihood of establishing a tonal, or key, center; (5) notes that are contiguous in the basic-tone row may jump an octave or more at will, but must avoid establishment of tonality; (6) discords are not considered as dissonants and thus should prevail—consonants are comparatively rare; (7) all forms of imitation, canon, fugal treatment, etc., should be used instead of the usual homophonic forms; (8) transposition, inversions along with retrogressions of the "row" may be freely made; (9) the internal and overall structures are dependent upon the course of the compositional construction.

There are more rules in the strict usage of the "row" technique, but the foregoing gives a fair picture of the basic conditions that the composer is supposed to follow. These restrictions have become more and more modified by recent users of the tone-row system.[13] It is amazing to observe such outright arbitrary and purely rationalized and "worked out on paper" music couched in the traditional forms. Such music is usually devoid of lyrical melody or highly personalized emotional expression. It is possessed with ceaseless and restless cacophony, and replete with forms and structures that cannot possibly be determined or even perceived through listening alone. There is little tranquility, surcease, or aesthetic appeal in this music, as far as the general listener is concerned.

FOUR MODERN COMPOSERS

We have selected the following four composers for study in this chapter not only because their works contain typical tempers and contemporary stylistic tendencies, but because it has been demonstrated over the years that the average listener can apply these directly to the works of most other contemporary composers. Others such as Bartók or Shostakovitch might have been chosen for study, but these which we have selected are familiar to most readers and they have greatly influenced the music of our time.

Few composers of recent times have had more immediate and widespread influence upon other composers than has *Igor Stravinsky* (1882–).

[13] See *Studies in Counterpoint* by Ernst Křenek (New York: G. Schirmer, 1940). The author suggests "a knowledge of strict Palestrina counterpoint as a prerequisite" for his book.

He is more generally known as a composer of music for the *Ballet Russe* that was organized and directed by Sergei Diaghilev (1872–1929). We have already mentioned THE FIREBIRD and discussed PETROUCHKA in detail (see Chap. 11). However, our present concern is with a ballet suite which many consider one of the great musical works of the twentieth century. Regardless of the form, LE SACRE DU PRINTEMPS ("The Rites of Spring") is a masterpiece of orchestration, rhythmic variety and effects, and polytonality.

Ballet Suite, "Sacre du Printemps" (1912–1913) by Igor Stravinsky

LE SACRE DU PRINTEMPS by Stravinsky was first produced in Paris in 1913. Its premiere provoked a riotous demonstration; not only for certain actions in the ballet itself, but also because of the then very unusual, cacophonous music. The story of the ballet is concerned with the choreographic representation of the ritualistic ceremonies of springtime in the pagan and primitive Russian tribes—a nationalistic expression of realistic, primitivistic, romantic, and expressionistic tempers in the emotional rather than rationalistic direction.[14] The following programmatic outline of the ballet-suite was prepared by the composer himself, essentially as follows:

PART I. THE ADORATION OF THE EARTH: Introduction—Harbingers of Spring—Dance of the Adolescents—Mock Abduction—Spring Rounds—Games of the Rival Tribes—The Procession of the Wise Men—The Adoration of the Earth—The Dance of the Earth.

PART II. THE SACRIFICE: Introduction—Mysterious Circle of the Adolescents—Glorification of the Chosen One—Evocation and Ritual of the Ancestors—The Sacrificial Dance of the Chosen One.

The music is often brutal and powerfully moving in its elemental force, its strange, almost infinite variety of complicated, unusual rhythmic and metrical patterns, tempo, orchestration, and the deliberate, strongly accented "on and off" beats. It is not at all difficult to sympathize with poor Nijinsky, one of the greatest among Russian ballet dancers, when he first futilely tried to dance this ballet "under Stravinsky's exacting and merciless directions." Yet, in contrast to the brutal force of the music most of the time, it is sometimes quite lyrical and tender, and even impressionistic. The orchestration is conceived and executed on a huge scale of color and sonority, and is almost overpowering—especially when the music is being expressed by the full orchestra in harsh, biting, and unrelenting dissonants, discords, and plain noise. In the music one will find frequent use of polytonality.

The brasses, for instance, may be in one key, the wood-winds in another, and the strings in a third; or, again, the brasses themselves

[14] See also Sheldon Cheney, *A Primer of Modern Art* (New York: Horace Liveright, 1924), pp. 206-369; E. H. Gombrich, *The Story of Art* (New York: Phaidon Press, 1951), pp. 419-440; Sheldon Cheney, *The Story of Modern Art* (New York: Viking Press, 1941), consult the Index; and Andrew Ritchie, *Abstract Painting and Sculpture in America* (New York: Museum of Modern Art, 1951).

might be playing in three different keys. The metrical and rhythmic devices are manifold and often startling. The climaxes are especially noteworthy, such as those in the *Sacrificial Dance of the Chosen One,* where they are vivid, powerful in intensity and in relentless movement, and are sometimes actually physically exhausting to the listener. This work has had a profound influence upon compositional techniques and especially the art of orchestration throughout the Western World. By all means, LE SACRE should be a "must" on everyone's list.

LE SACRE DU PRINTEMPS is a good example of the rather free emotional type of Expressionism in music, although it was not couched without strong discipline and order. Now let us examine a work of a composer whose compositions since Op. 11 well represent the rationalized, highly intellectualized branch of Expressionism: the acknowledged leader of this type, Arnold Schönberg. From his works we have chosen No. 18, *Der Mondfleck* (*The Patch of Moonlight*) from PIERROT LUNAIRE, Op. 21, based on a series of romantic poems by Albert Giraud. We have chosen this particular number because it is one of the outstanding masterpieces in its form, style, and in the "tone-row" technique.

ARNOLD SCHÖNBERG (1874–1951)

Arnold Schönberg, born in Vienna, was originally self-taught in music, but later studied with Zemlinsky. Upon the recommendation of Richard Strauss, Schönberg entered the Stern Conservatory in Berlin (1901–3), after which he returned to Vienna. His compositions were influenced by Mahler, Liszt, Wagner, and R. Strauss. In 1910 he became an instructor of composition at the Royal and Imperial Academy. Later he taught privately in Berlin. In 1907 Schönberg became interested in oil painting and was greatly influenced by his expressionist friends, Kokoschka, Kandinsky, Loos, Kraus, and others. It was somewhere around 1910 and 1911 that Schönberg became an exponent of the "twelve-tone-row system" as is revealed in its early stages in the KLAVIERSTÜCKE, Op. 11. Before that time, this composer was a Wagnerian Romanticist, as may be observed in his VERKLÄRTE NACHT (Transfigured Night), which was first written for a string sextet (1889). It was with the composition of his GURRE-LIEDER, and especially the FIVE PIECES FOR ORCHESTRA, Op. 16, that Schönberg emerged as a full fledged advocate of the "twelve-tone-row." From then on he was blessed with many devotees, rewards, and honors. In 1933 he came to America, and eventually was appointed a professor of music at the University of California at Los Angeles (1936–44). He became an American citizen in 1940. His TREATISE ON HARMONY (1911), and his works for some time before he died, were less restricted to the severe discipline of the original "tone-row" rules; and at the last, he was "rediscovering" the works of Beethoven, and editing and arranging many works in the conventional tonal system. He wrote this author that he felt he had reached a cul-de-sac in the use of the "tone-row." As a composer, Schönberg may not survive for long; but as an innovator in music, his influence will probably become widespread and continue for many years.

Schönberg's Der Mondfleck from the Melodrama Pierre Lunaire, Op. 21

Der Mondfleck which the critic James Huneker called *Sick Moon,* is a wonderfully conceived and executed composition, at least from a formal and structural standpoint. We know of no other work, old or new, that can compare with its compactness, ultimate use of limited musical material, unbelievably skillful contrapuntal technique whether in the tonal or "tone-row" systems, and its adroit manipulation of five instruments and voice. This particular number, No. 18 of the set, is written for solo piccolo, solo B-flat clarinet, solo viola, solo violoncello, piano, and a voice declaiming in *sprechstimme* style. The notes for the voice, with crosses on the note-stems, indicate the approximate pitches and intervals, and exact time or duration. The result is a very strange one for the listener, for the first few times at least.

We have, in the first musical example of this Schönberg work, shown the first two measures in full. Note that one canon is taking place between the piccolo and the clarinet, and another between the viola and the 'cello. If the piano part is examined carefully, one will discover that it is a three-voiced fugue, the theme of which is a rhythmic augmentation of the theme between the piccolo and clarinet! The voice part is free. (Note that the fugue theme in the piano is the actual sounding tones of the B-flat clarinet raised an octave.) Here is the first musical illustration from *Der Mondfleck:*

Now compare the notes of the above Mus. Ill. with the closing measures of the Mus. Ill. which follows. (The voice and piano parts are omitted in the latter for reasons of limited space.) Compare the notes of this first measure of *Der Mondfleck* with the last measure by reading the notes of measure one from *left to right,* and the notes of the last measure from *right to left.* They are identical. (A jump of an octave or two, or more, even between half-steps, is always considered "legal" in the twelve-tone row system. This aids in the avoidance of tonality or any momentary tonal center). Here is the closing measure of *Der Mondfleck:*

Voice and piano omitted

Thus, one suspects that the canon is the same going and coming—musicians call this a *canon cancrizans* ("crab" canon), *canon per recte et retro, canon rectus et inversus,* or a *retrograde canon;* in English, *palindrome canon.*[15] A "palindrome" is a word, sentence, or phrase which reads the same backward as forward, as in "Able was I ere I saw Elba."

Schönberg has even provided a second palindrome canon between the viola and the 'cello, and it proceeds simultaneously with the palindrome canon in the piccolo and clarinet parts! Then, as if this were not sufficient, he writes a three-part fugue, the theme of which is a rhythmic augmentation of the palindrome canon theme between the piccolo and clarinet! The fugue goes along simultaneously with the two canons, though it is not written in the palindrome form. The voice part, likewise, goes its separate way, busy with the words and sentiments of the poem. Although Schönberg pulls out many of the classical temper "stops" in fashioning this extremely *rationale* type of Expressionism, he remains, in the depths of his artistic soul, a Romanticist!

[15] A fairly good musical and literary parallel of a *canon ordinaire* may be found in the discussion of a "Fugue," in *Music and Literature: A Comparison of the Arts,* by Calvin S. Brown. (Athens, Georgia: Univ. of Georgia Press, 1948.)

When the forward moving ends of the canons meet with the oncoming beginning at the midpoint of *Der Mondfleck* (halfway through measure [10]), it is much like a rolling wave from one direction meeting and "passing through" another wave from the opposite direction without altering either wave. This peculiar effect is clearly seen in the next musical illustration where we have inserted a vertical broken line at the exact midpoint of this piece. Compare every note in each of the four parts, note-by-note to the right, then to the left, of this dotted line. Observe the nuances also. (In the piccolo part we have taken the liberty of splitting the original engraving time value of the high A-flat and using a tie in order to divide the measure exactly in the middle—it does not alter the music, however.)

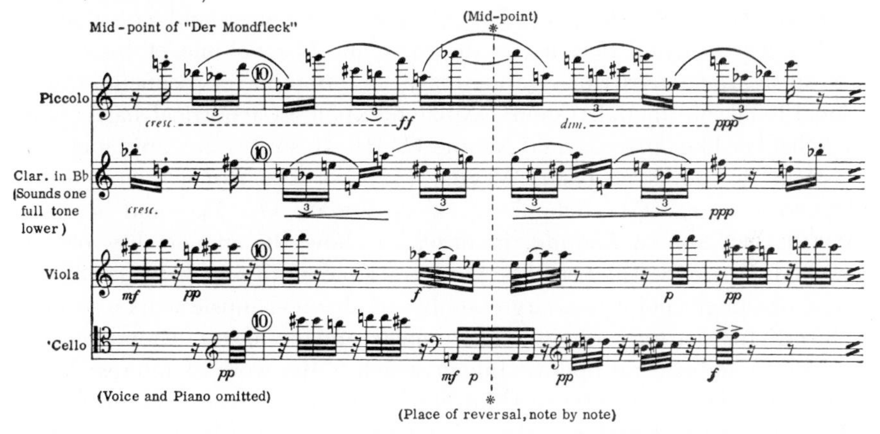

Yet all these contrapuntal wonders take place in only nineteen full measures! Listen to this work frequently and study it intently. It is not easy to understand. In fact, most of the contrapuntal wonders cannot possibly be discerned through hearing alone. A study of the score itself is essential. The real beauty is above and beyond mere technics of form and contrapuntal structures—the essential spirit of the *tout ensemble*—and it is well worth discovering. You might also like Schönberg's romantic work, VERKLÄRTE NACHT (*Transfigured Night*), Op. 4, revised for full orchestra. Try it!

PAUL HINDEMITH (1895-)

Paul Hindemith, born in Germany in 1895, is a composer, musical theorist, viola soloist, and string quartet player. He was early recognized as one of the most erudite, original, and prolific composers among the then younger German "school." At the early age of twenty, Hindemith became the concertmaster at the Frankfort Opera, a position he held for eight years, after which he formed his own string quartet and toured the musical centers of Europe. He became a teacher of composition at the Berlin Hochschule für Musik in 1935; subsequently, he became a leader of the *Gebrauchsmusik* movement which was concerned with the composition and performance of "practical, work-a-day music," as contrasted with the more esoteric and highly artistic variety. (There were some repercussions and influences of this movement in America, mostly concerned with educational music in our schools.) Hindemith toured and taught in America in 1937, and returned in 1940 to become Professor of Music at Yale. He became a U.S. citizen in 1946. He was elected to the National Institute of Arts and Letters. The compositions of Hindemith may be loosely divided into three period types: (a) rather free, polyphonic writing on the borderline of the atonal "twelve-tone-row" system; (b) around 1924 he returned to classical tonal styles and frequent use of modality strongly influenced by German folk music; and (c) a more or less experimental period (as shown in the first volume of his CRAFT OF MUSICAL COMPOSITION), apparently an attempt to reconcile traditional tonal and modal systems, explained upon an acoustical basis, plus a Schenker-like analysis and synthesis. He illustrates by applying his "system" to works of Bach, Wagner (TRISTAN AND ISOLDE), Stravinsky (PIANO SONATA, 1924), Schönberg (KLAVIERSTÜCK, Op. 33a) and his own MATHIS DER MALER *Prelude,* in order to show the universality of his methods.[16] Among the principal works of Hindemith which are pertinent here, one might point to a large number of chamber music works, several concerti for one or more soli instruments and orchestra, choral works, art-songs, and several operas, among which is the work of interest here, the opera, MATHIS DER MALER (Matthias the Painter). Selected music from the opera was first performed as an orchestral suite in 1934 by the Boston Symphony Orchestra. Hindemith has also written a number of theoretical works pertaining to music, such as TRADITIONAL HARMONY and CRAFT OF MUSICAL COMPOSITION.

Hindemith's Orchestral Suite, Mathis Der Maler

The three panels of the Isenheimer Altarpiece at Colmar in Alsace, painted by the German master, Matthias Grünewald, in a realistic and expressionistic style, served as the inspiration for Hindemith's Opera and

[16] It might be well to recapitulate briefly the salient bases of the various systems pertaining to tonality. (1) *Tonality* exists where there is established a definite key center, around which the other tones of a scale gyrate, or are attracted as by a magnetic center, or where there are definite *primary* and *secondary dual tonal centers* or points of repose, as in some exotic or antique scales or modes (including many pentatonic scales); (2) *Atonality* may be said, broadly, to exist where there is no well defined tonal or key center to which all the other tones are attracted, where a key or tonal center is avoided or deliberately destroyed; (3) *Pantonality* ("Pan" is from the Greek meaning "ALL"), according to writers on Schönberg, is where there is *no fixed* and inflexible *tonal center,* or *singular tonal* feeling, but where there might be an implication or *vague feeling of one or more passing* or aggregate impressions of tonal centers, purposely made vague, unestablished, shifting or undefinable. (Schönberg himself is not clear on this.)

Suite, MATHIS DER MALER (1934). The orchestral suite is written in three movements, following the spirit, moods, and thematic plan of Grünewald's altarpiece, and are titled: I. *Angelic Concert;* II. *Entombment;* III. *Temptation of Saint Anthony.* The suite has unmistakable evidences of predominant romantic tempers along with not a few classical tempers, a great deal of superb counterpoint, and free use of old ecclesiastical modes, especially in numbers I and III. Hindemith was fond of using the old modes and pentatonic scales, and disdained deliberate programmatic or descriptive use of his musical materials. But one can, by close analysis, find programmatic functions in the broadest use of the term now and then in his music, especially in his middle and late periods.[17] His later works show a more contemporary universality and include a five act opera, THE HARMONY OF THE WORLD (premiere in Munich, 1957), and ASPEN SERENADE for small orchestra, written for the 1957 Music Festival at Aspen, Colo.

JEAN JULIUS CHRISTIAN SIBELIUS (1865–1957)

Inasmuch as a brief biographical sketch of Sibelius was given in Chapter 15, we may immediately proceed with a study of his FOURTH SYMPHONY.

Symphony No. 4 in A-Minor, Op. 63, by Sibelius[18]

Although this was first heard in Finland in 1911 and premiered in New York in 1913 by the New York Symphony under Walter Damrosch,[19] this great symphony is included with the works of three outstanding contemporary "modernists," Stravinsky, Hindemith, and Schönberg. After a thorough listening study of this composition, we suspect that there will be no feeling of incongruity regarding its inclusion here. Sibelius himself said that the FOURTH was his favorite, rivaled only by the SEVENTH, Op. 105—his last symphony. Further, critics and musicians are in fair agree-

[17] It will be noted that the music of Hindemith has passed through almost as many stylistic phases as that of Stravinsky who, of late, in his CANTICUM SACRUM, has seemed to venture very close if not actually into the camp of the "twelve-tone-row."

[18] The music illustrations used for the works of Schönberg and Sibelius are presented here with the permission of the Associated Music Publishers, Inc., New York City.

[19] It is very difficult to reconcile the reactions today to the FOURTH SYMPHONY with the comments of Dr. Damrosch and the almost unanimous "panning" by the music critics at its premiere. Damrosch made a vindicating speech before the performance, the substance of which was that the work of Sibelius did not necessarily express his personal judgment or approval, rather it was on the program "out of a sense of duty"! Some of the critics condemned the symphony for being too "cubistic," or "as inconsequential as the ravings of a drunken man,"—or that Sibelius had "parted company with himself" and spewed up a mess of distasteful musical ideas and techniques.

ment that the FOURTH is the most peculiarly individual, self-revealing of his symphonies.[20]

Let us try to discover the most salient musical qualities and individual characteristics that evoke such world-wide acclaim. First, it is unquestionably great music that affords much aesthetic listening pleasure. The work is ostensibly, though not precisely, in the traditional, four-movement layout, and the separate movements often deviate widely from the traditional and classical internal designs. Here and there, this symphony combines, in a masterly way, several of the basic tempers.

Sibelius causes form, both internal and over-all, to be subject to, and the result of, the musical and expressive content of the moment as well as of the movement and work as a whole. In this trait Sibelius follows Beethoven. There are no startling innovations of either harmonic, melodic, or thematic nature, as one knows them in previous compositions of Sibelius. Rather, he is highly individual and original in the *manner* in which he uses these basic musical elements, and in the personal musical idioms and their peculiar treatment that are evident to the listener from the first note to the last. In his deviations from traditional practices, and in his use of fugitive bits of thematic ideas, we now realize that Sibelius was far in advance of his time; a leader in the development of compositional techniques rather than an ephemeral rebel. Yet these highly individual stylistic idioms never become mere mannerisms, as they have with some of his followers. Above all, he has something of import to say, and he has the genius to express himself in a unique and forceful manner.

Sibelius is one of a small number of composers of our time who have employed instrumentation in a highly effective and individualistic manner. This technique is apparent right from the opening of the FOURTH SYMPHONY. Sibelius adroitly creates and maintains a puissant, relentless mood of gloom which, despite its length and infrequent relief, does not become fatiguing. Further—through the use of fragmentary figures, compositional contrasts, and orchestral interplay—climaxes and salient sonorities of varying degrees are constructed and the generating motives undergo metamorphosis during the pulsating momentum of pitch, intensity, orchestral color, and tempo.

One is filled with admiration for the skillful manner in which Sibelius uses the instrumental tone colors, not only to express emotion, but also—and this is a rare accomplishment—*to serve in defining, building, and sustaining the passing internal formal structures and over-all compositional designs.* (We do not refer to Impressionism.) Schumann anticipated a similar technique but never fully developed it. This functional compositional technique of Sibelius is possessed by very few creative

[20] For an interesting and non-technical account of this symphony (and many others), see Donald Ferguson, *Masterworks of the Orchestra Repertoire* (Minneapolis: Univ. of Minnesota Press, 1954).

artists in any medium. A few such creators and their works are: Berlioz, SYMPHONY FANTASTIQUE; Debussy, APRÈS-MIDI D'UN FAUNE and LA MER; Ravel, DAPHNIS ET CHLOÉ ballet; Rimsky-Korsakoff, SCHEHERAZADE SUITE; Koechlin, SYMPHONIE; MONT STE.-VICTOIRE, Cézanne; SUNDAY ON THE ISLAND OF LA GRANDE JATTE, Seurat; "NOCTURNES" and "ARRANGEMENTS," Whistler; BOULEVARD DES ITALIENS, Camille Pissarro; or, to go back many years, the paintings of Tung Yüan of the Chinese Sung dynasty (960–1280 A.D.) and, to a less perfect degree, the Japanese print, THE WAVE. There are others, including some by Tintoretto and El Greco. These painters, with color and brush, succeeded in evoking comparable mood responses and suggestive effects of form and design that Sibelius and other composers accomplished through sound. Because of the peculiar character of their medium of draftsmanship, brush strokes, color and design, these painters also projected three-dimensional perspective, the nature of the material or substance, and even movement. Poets have also achieved many of these effects by a variety of technics.

This achievement of Sibelius is all the more significant when it is realized that he has accomplished his purposes through the unique and typically Sibelius' employment of a few fragmentary musical ideas, which cannot be called themes in the usual sense. Prior to the FOURTH, Sibelius usually tied together or coalesced these separate germinal fragments of a section or a movement into a unified lyrical theme, or melody. In this symphony, however, the musical and thematic fragments are, more often than not, left vaguely suspended in the air, and are not coalesced *save through the instrumentality of the creative listener himself as the necessary means for consummation.*

The listener to the SYMPHONY NO. 4 IN A MINOR can readily perceive that Sibelius was masterful in the use of non-story-telling, programmatic suggestions, in the use of Romanticism and, here and there, some Classicism, especially in the manner of using musical materials to gain certain basic objectives of formal development. He also employed the spirit of nationalism and the tempers of Realism, which sometimes becomes quite representational. He used all these as they best expressed his musical and poetic desires. All nonessential material is pared to the bone, and musical ideas are presented without superfluous adornment.

FIRST MOVEMENT: Tempo molto moderato, quasi adagio (somewhat slower than moderate speed), $\frac{4}{4}$ *time.*[21] The first movement opens with a gloomy motive, played by the first bassoon, first 'cello section, and the first string bass section. The second sections of these divided instruments persistently hold a low C_{-2}. This undulating and moaning

[21] We present a rather detailed "running" description of the thematic, orchestral, and other features of this symphony to facilitate its study and enjoyment. Read these analytical notes as the music unfolds for the first few hearings; for the complexity and fragmentary nature of the thematic material and orchestration indicate this treatment.

motive sets the mood of the first movement as well as the entire symphony, as though it were a "motto" theme or *idée fixe.* Even the separate portions, "X" and "Y," in the following musical illustration become of increasing importance throughout the four movements of the symphony. Note their appearances. Here are these initial ideas:

The first movement differs markedly from the traditional *sonata-allegro* form most frequently used for the initial portion of a symphony. Instead of being in the usual *allegro tempo,* it is in a slow, unhurried pace, and of a singular, persistent mood established by fragmentary, mood-evoking motives. It is more in the form and spirit of a symphonic poem.[22]

Almost two full measures after the end of the first subject, a 'cello solo plays a theme, or a fragment of one, that might for our purposes be called a "second theme."

Much is made of this 'cello figure as it works up in pitch and intensity through the muted strings supported by the divided double-basses, with their *basso-ostinato* derived from the initial figure, four muted French horns, and the low wood-winds. The music becomes louder and comes to a typically Sibelius idiom, *sfp-cres-sffz* (an accented *forte-piano, crescendo* or swell to *fortissimo,* with a briefly accented sharp *cut-off* of the tones). All this happens at letter "B" *adagio,* measure 29 of the score. The immediately overlapping passage, sounding angrily and forcefully, is for four horns, two trumpets, two trombones, two bassoons, with the double-basses still maintaining the "bourdon drone" like the low groan of the sea. The thematic content is a rising chromatic one in thirds. Another equally startling idea interrupts and overlaps this forceful passage, further piling up the emotional state and "scene." This new figure is mainly for loud, high-pitched strings, *senza sordini* (without mutes). In this new figure there is an abrupt change of key at the double-bar (measure 32), from a previously prevailing tonality of C-major to the remote key of F-sharp minor. There is also a change of meter from $\frac{4}{4}$ to $\frac{3}{2}$, together with a fluctuation of the dynamics in the violins and violas, and horns and trumpets from a moderate loudness (*mf, mezzo-forte*) to a sudden swell (*ff, fortissimo*), save for the bassoons, 'cellos,

[22] An excellent thematic analysis of this symphony can be found in the booklet *Sibelius, The Symphonies* by Cecil Gray (London: Oxford University Press, 1935).

emotion and *seeming* indifference to the perfection of form and design *per se*. The Classic tempers are most evident in the deliberate and objectified derivations, manipulations, and development of musical ideas.

FOURTH MOVEMENT: Allegro (quickly and lively). *A major.* $\frac{4}{4}$ *time, Alla Bréve.* If the previous movement strikes the listener as being fanciful and rhapsodic, this movement is in sharp contrast. The finale is much more extended than the third movement and wonderfully well designed as far as symmetry, contrast, and balance are concerned. The initial theme of the *finale* is really "thrown in for good measure," for it is not used again—save for a vague resemblance some ten measures before letter "H." Here is the initial theme, played by the first violins:

This initial theme *may* have been derived from a combination of the musical ideas expressed in the second theme and figure "A," of the third musical idea, both of the first movement. The themes of this symphony seem to have such a common family relationship that it is often difficult to discover distinct differences. Yet these family similarities do not lessen fresh interest and continued response on the part of the listener. Note the use of the glocken-bells,—not the glockenspiel—appearing almost immediately after the conclusion of the initial theme. Sometimes this glocken, or bell-like motive is simulated by other instruments of the orchestra, such as the following for two clarinets answered by two flutes, along with a new motive in the violas of which much is made later on, the 'cellos playing a brief, three-note octave figure, *pizzicato,* and the timpani softly tapping out the rhythm of the theme in the violas.

This is immediately followed by a rapid running violin scale passage in thirds—the first of many such scale flourishes to be played by various instruments as the score progresses. Here is that first string passage:

It is followed immediately by a brief but important and subsequently much used fragment, or motive. This unintrusive fragment (note the augmented fourth motive marked "X") is here shown played by the violas:

A sort of impassioned (*affettuoso*) passage is soon played by the solo 'cello in a broad-stroked manner; the solo violin then takes up this theme, followed in *stretto* fashion by the second violins and violas. Here is the 'cello theme:

This seems to be a fresh idea, and is a sort of declamatory flourish that has no immediate source.

The second subject seems to consist of several musical ideas, interlarded with new and secondary fragments of themes that pop up most unexpectedly and which, in turn, give way to still other ideas. An anticipatory part of the second subject is played by the solo clarinet, right after the glocken motive, in a flourishing and cadenza-like manner, thus: (It is written in concert pitch—as it actually sounds!)

The string section then sets up a nineteen measure quasi-development section beginning with a slow, trill-like figure that recalls the initial idea of the first movement. An harmonic background is provided by flutes, oboe, and timpani rolls, with the glocken motive creeping in. Presently, (at letter "D" in the score) out of this slow, murmuring string background, one hears again the motive first heard in the violas, but now it is played by the flutes and bassoons two octaves apart (in a section that has the appearance of a *reprise* though it can hardly be that). Later, this same theme is even more plaintively played by the solo oboe over a rhythmic figure in the timpani, an appearance of the glocken idea, a syncopated and well-punctuated descending bass figure in the 'cellos, and a unison sustaining tone (on E^1) sounded (*p*) on the horns, muted.

For good measure, still more of this scene is to be heard immediately. It comes with the violas softly playing the clarinet theme, plus a running and shimmering figure in the strings over a descending scale passage and syncopated bass.

Suddenly, out of the foregoing quiet scene (at the second measure after letter "E" (in the score) the solo horn blasts out the motive previously heard as the fourth Mus. Ill. of the finale, when it was rather unobtrusively played by the violas. A number of brilliant ascending scale passages in thirds or in single-toned flourishes on the flutes and solo clarinet flash across the score like roman candles on a festive night. Eventually the full orchestra sounds forth in an alternating chordal (on beat, off beat) effect between the strings, basses, and timpani, and the wood-winds over a reiterated syncopated pedal point in the 'cellos and double-basses. This is the orchestral preparation and poetic stage setting for the appearance of the first portion of the second theme proper —a fantasia-like passage that ostensibly has only the earmarks of a traditional *sonata-allegro form,* which Sibelius rightly treats with indifference.

After this sort of rhythmical, antiphonal, chordal effect (at letter "F" of the score) the first part of the second theme, "A," is played by the wood-winds with the melody in the first flute and oboes (note the effect at "X"). This same idea, without the bassoons, is repeated after a sort of "pumping-like" passage, but it is a half-step higher in pitch. Here is the wood-wind passage with the clarinets transposed to concert (sounding) pitch:

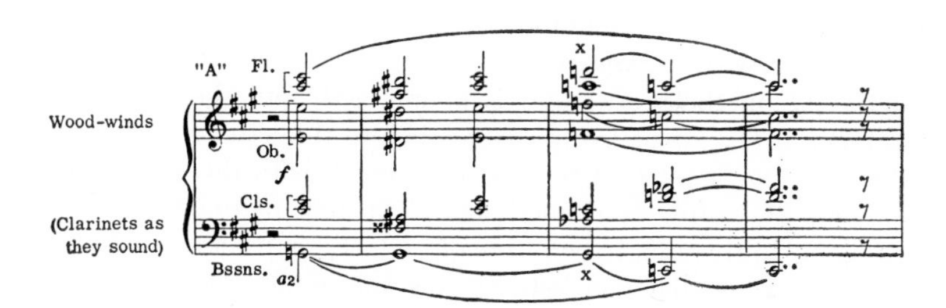

Presently (twelve measures after the letter "G" in the score), the second part, "B," of the second theme proper is played by the strings, with a chromatic and syncopated descending motive in the violins while the "pumping" bass figure continues in the 'cellos:

The violins pick up an important first part of the second theme as a reminder, as shown here:

The so-called development section is unconventional, brief, and lacking in significant thematic "working out" of previous ideas. It consists of a repeated, undulating, and wave-like scale figure in fourths or fifths between the first and second violins on one part, and the violas and 'cellos on the other. Surely this is a seascape.

The reprise section follows (at letter "I" in the score) but it does not get down to serious business until twenty-two measures later, when the oboes recall, in greatly changed rhythmic values, the initial "motto" of the first movement! And from here on to the longish coda, Sibelius recalls thematic or fragmentary ideas that have previously appeared, not merely in the last movement, but from other movements. However, these ideas are presented in new effects and new instrumentation rather than in direct quotation.

The *Coda,* which begins eight and one half measures before "R" in the score, is linked with the close of the reprise by one of the individual "signatures" of Sibelius—a fluttering effect in the string section. This passage begins with a *pianissississimo,* and gradually works up to a *forte* (at letter "O" in the score) and is maintained until the full orchestra bursts forth (*fff*) (about five measures before the letter S) on a motive like the principal "motto" of the first movement, with the glocken loudly pealing out its joyful, four-toned figure. Shortly before the close, the strings again softly sound their *tremolo* effect (*ppp*) as a *codetta,* followed by a sort of dialogue between the solo flute and solo oboe. The work closes with the strings playing broadly the repeated A minor chord and the gloominess is intensified by the *tessiture* of the chord with its third (C below middle-C) just above the double-basses in the 'celli and sounding clearly.

As a footnote to the last movement, we cannot do better than paraphrase what Gerald Abraham has said about the form of the *finale.*[23] He reminds one that the gross structure is one long used by a number of German composers and called by them a "*Bogenform*" (formed like

[23] *The Music of Sibelius,* edited by Gerald Abraham (New York: W. W. Norton Co., 1947).

an arch) with the various sections lettered and designated as follows: "A′," the first subject and its allied group of themes; "B′," the second subject and its group of "satellites"; "C," a brief development; "B²," a return of the second subject; "A²," a return of the first subject and a few fragments or motives from the last and other movements (especially the first); the coda, made of previously heard motives; and the short codetta which brings the last movement and the entire symphony to a fitting, aesthetically satisfying close.

Schumann was well acquainted with this form. What we have been hearing in this symphony, and especially in the last movement, has been an almost miraculous use of the technic of germinal thematic construction, together with superb orchestration, in and for its own timbre values, with its peculiarly Sibelius technique of employing it for basically structural and compositional values.

The music, throughout, has been most enjoyable, understandable, and clearly communicative of Sibelius' meanings and purposes.

Postlude

We have attempted, in the preceding pages, to introduce the reader-listener to a broad world of music from many lands, and over many centuries. This music was composed by numberless minstrels and folk musicians as well as by acknowledged, world-wide masters of the art and skills of music composition. We have tried to break down and explain the more formidable technical and listening difficulties by means of readily understood expository methods that are presented in a running commentary style. The methods used here also seek to present the musical masterpieces in an ingratiating and pleasurable manner.

Further, we have sought to integrate music with the other Fine Arts—painting, drawing, sculpture, poetry, the dance, architecture, and the drama. This has been accomplished through a real integration rather than merely by resorting to the more usual, very questionable coincidences of parallelism. However, integration is employed only when it can enlighten and make more enjoyable and meaningful the music under discussion at the moment. Of course, in so doing, the reader-listener is also subtly introduced to the other Fine Arts with the hope that they will entice further exploration and experience in their respective fields, on the listener's own initiative. In the end, the reader will have made the acquaintance and actual perceptive and appreciative experience with many types and styles of music and the other arts. Thus the process of true integration becomes a more broadening, meaningful, and enjoyable method of fruitful learning.

This process of artistic integration is made more helpful and significant through the technique and employment of the so-called *tempers*. These tempers are introduced in an early chapter, and their characteristics and purposes made understandable in their various combinations and applications. Their use should be most helpful in clarifying the perception and appreciation of music and the other arts, once the understanding of their separate categorical meanings is acquired and proper applications become habitual through actual practice during listening.

Then, too, the function, importance, and participative contributions of the listener and observer in the ultimate realization, consummation, and fulfillment of an artistic masterpiece are fully explained throughout the book. This new appraisal of the status and function of the appreciator should shed more light upon the art works themselves, indicate new responsibilities and privileges of the appreciators, and show added pleasures and aesthetic rewards that may accrue to the mentor, composer, interpreter, listener, and observer. It gives the average, nontechnically equipped listener as well as the professional and student musician potentially greater and more equitable appreciative status, in individual responsibility and importance.

Throughout this book we have tried to show the appreciator a worthy pathway, a practical and amply proved method and practice toward artistic enrichment and self-fulfillment—all of which we hope will serve as a firm foundation for future listening.

In other words, we are happy in the thought that we have been privileged to acquaint the reader with still another "art"—*The Art of Creative Listening.* So we wish "good listening" to all our readers, and may you be the happier, better, and richer for your artistic experiences.

Appendix

Reference list of selected readings on the subject of "Aesthetics" and allied topics especially pertinent to Chapter 1.

Additional references are suggested throughout the book, wherever they may be useful. Altogether, these lists offer a wide variety of choices for the reader. The books offered were selected for their bearing upon the immediate subject of inquiry, whether or not they are in agreement with the views of the present author. The subject of aesthetics is controversial and many-sided, so it is well for the reader to inquire into a number of differing viewpoints.

Many of the books cited contain excellent biographies so that the reader, whether he is primarily interested in music or whether he is pursuing the subject under the general classification of the HUMANITIES, will have available a large number of additional readings with a still greater opportunity for satisfying special individual needs and desires. The books are listed alphabetically by author, with no evaluation implied in the order of sequence:

Berenson, Bernard, *The Italian Painters of the Renaissance.* New York: Phaidon Press, 1954. One of the outstanding art critics of our time.

———, *Aesthetics and History.* Garden City, N.Y.: Doubleday & Co., 1954.

Birkhoff, George D., *Aesthetic Measure.* Cambridge, Mass.: Harvard University Press, 1933. A mathematical method for advanced students.

———, "Mathematical Theory of Aesthetics and Its Application to Poetry and Music," Rice Institute Pamphlets, Vol. XIX, No. 3, 1932. For advanced students only.

Chandler, Albert R., *Beauty and Human Nature.* New York: Appleton-Century, 1934. A study of the elements of psychological aesthetics pertaining to "aesthetic appreciation and artistic production." One of the best books on the subject.

Darrell, R. D., *Guide to Books on Music and Musicians.* New York: G. Schirmer, 1951, pp. 4-5.

Davidson, Morris, *Understanding Modern Art.* New York: Tudor Publishing Co., 1934.

Dewey, John, *Art as Experience.* New York: Minton, Blade and Co., 1934. An authoritative and inspiring work by one of the great philosophers and teachers of our time. Difficult reading.

Diserens, Charles, *Influence of Music on Behavior.* New York: D. Appleton Co., 1926. Not up-to-date, but a good starting point.

Ducasse, Curt John, *Art, the Critics and You.* New York: The Liberal Arts Press, 1944. A delightful and enjoyable book for the average reader. It contains a most unique chapter on "The Art of Personal Beauty."

———, *Philosophy of Art.* New York: Lincoln MacVeagh, 1929. An excellent, advanced philosophical study of aesthetics and criticism.

Gombrich, E. H., *The Story of Art.* New York: Phaidon Press, 1951.

Greene, Theodore Meyer, *The Arts and the Art of Criticism.* Princeton: Princeton University Press, 1940. For advanced students, this is a thorough, comprehensive, and monumental work on philosophy, aesthetics, and criticism. However, many of the sections on music may seem arbitrary and academic.

Edouard Hanslick, *The Beautiful in Music,* tr. Gustav Cohen. London: Novello and Co., 1891. An old, but still interesting, exposition.

Highet, Gilbert, *The Classical Tradition.* New York: Oxford University Press, 1953. A very scholarly presentation, with copious notes, for all interested readers, but especially for those in the HUMANITIES.

Jarrett, James L., *The Quest for Beauty.* Englewood Cliffs, N.J.: Prentice-Hall, Inc., 1957.

Jeans, Sir James, *Science and Music.* New York: The Macmillan Co., 1937. On acoustics.

Kant, Immanuel, *Critique of Aesthetic Judgment,* tr. J. C. Meredith. New York: Oxford University Press. For advanced study.

Langer, Susanne K., *Philosophy in a New Key.* Cambridge, Mass.: Harvard University Press, 1942, Mentor edition, 1948. A study in the symbolism of Reason, Rite, and Art. See Chap. VIII on music.

Lee, Vernon, pseud. Violet Paget, *The Beautiful.* New York: Cambridge University Press, 1913. An empirical case study of emotional and imaginative responses to music. Excellent for students of music appreciation methods.

———. *Music and Its Lovers.* London: George Allen & Unwin, 1932.

MacColl, D. S., *What is Art?* London: Penguin Books, 1940.

Malraux, André, *The Voices of Silence: Man and His Art,* tr. Stuart Gilbert. New York: Doubleday & Co., 1953.

Mason, Daniel Gregory, *Artistic Ideals.* New York: W. W. Norton & Co., 1927. A book that should appeal to all potential and professional artists.

———, *Music as a Humanity.* New York: H. W. Gray, 1921.

Mursell, James L., *Psychology of Music.* New York: W. W. Norton & Co., 1937. See especially Chap. VI.

Parker, D. H., *Principles of Aesthetics.* Boston: Silver Burdett Co., 1920.

Prall, D. W., *Aesthetic Judgment.* New York: The Macmillan Co., 1931.

Rader, Melvin M., *Modern Book of Esthetics.* New York: Henry Holt & Co., 1949. A good, readable, and brief survey-anthology of writers on aesthetics since about 1890. A fine bibliography is included.

Santayana, George, *The Sense of Beauty.* New York: Charles Scribner's Sons, 1896.

Schoen, Max, *Art and Beauty.* New York: The Macmillan Co., 1932.

———, *Effects of Music.* New York: Harcourt, Brace & Co., 1927.

———, *The Understanding of Music.* New York: Harper & Brothers, 1945.

Sorokin, Pitrim A., *Social and Cultural Dynamics.* New York: American Book Co., 1937. Vol. I.

The *Modern Book of Esthetics* by Rader might well be one of the first on the reader's list; *Art, the Critics and You* is another splendid "kick-off" book for those interested in a general, over-all view of the subject of aesthetics. Then, too, one can always investigate such standard authorities as Bergson, Croce, Kant, Edman, Pater, Schiller. Schopenhauer, *et al.*

Pictorial illustrations

Index

A

D

G

H

Q

S

T

THIS book, which has charmed and informed thousands of "armchair musicians" as well as countless students in hundreds of colleges and universities since 1946, has been extensively revised and rewritten so that it proves even more conclusively than before the three main points of its thesis:

—Music is a vital part of living, an indispensable means of arousing a desired emotional state, as well as a means of expressing or enhancing the emotions which are bursting for outward expression;

—Music is an art closely related to the other Fine Arts not only in such basic elements as rhythm and harmony, structure and design, but in the more elusive qualities of temper and style;

—Music, like her sister Arts, is essentially *communication* and is only fully consummated when it reaches perceptive and empathetic listeners who contribute something aesthetically vital and pertinent in their individual response.

Everything Stringham does in this book is designed to effect such close "communication" between the composer and his listener as to make music an increasingly vital part of the listener's life. Beginning with familiar experiences